Computational Principles of Mobile Robotics

Mobile robotics is a multidisciplinary field involving both computer science and engineering. Addressing the design of automated systems, it lies at the intersection of artificial intelligence, computational vision, and traditional robotics. Now in its third edition, this textbook for advanced undergraduates and graduate students covers algorithms for a range of strategies for locomotion, sensing, and reasoning.

The new edition includes recent advances in robotics and intelligent machines, including coverage of human–robot interaction, robot ethics, and the application of advanced AI techniques to end-to-end robot control and specific computational tasks. This book also provides support for a number of algorithms using ROS 2, and includes a review of critical mathematical material and an extensive list of sample problems. Researchers as well as students in the field of mobile robotics will appreciate this comprehensive treatment of state-of-the-art methods and key technologies.

Gregory Dudek is Distinguished James McGill Professor of Computer Science at McGill University. He is also a member of the Center for Intelligent Machines, and associate member of Mila, and has been co-author of over 300 refereed publications on robotics, machine learning, and computer vision. He has also served as a Vice President with Samsung Electronics and founding Lab Head for the Samsung AI Center in Montreal, Canada. With Michael Jenkin, he has played many roles in the field including co-founding Independent Robotics Inc. and establishing the Canadian Robotics Research Network.

Michael Jenkin is Professor of Electrical Engineering and Computer Science at York University. Working with intelligent autonomous machines for over thirty years, he has helped develop autonomous systems that have operated on and below the water's surface, and has worked on robot systems that were designed to operate in environments ranging from nuclear power plants to contaminated crime scenes.

'This book is an indispensable tool for any – both pre-university and university – course on mobile robotics. In relation to the first edition, this current one has been sufficiently updated. I recommend this book to researchers – particularly those who study localization or mapping – and doctoral students who are interested in investigating the latest approaches and techniques in the mobile robotics field.'

Ramon Gonzalez Sanchez, *Computing Reviews*

'... a great resource for an intermediate or advanced course on mobile robotics.'

R.S. Stanbury, *Embry Riddle University, Choice*

Computational Principles of Mobile Robotics

Third Edition

Gregory Dudek
McGill University, Montréal

Michael Jenkin
York University, Toronto

CAMBRIDGE
UNIVERSITY PRESS

Shaftesbury Road, Cambridge CB2 8EA, United Kingdom

One Liberty Plaza, 20th Floor, New York, NY 10006, USA

477 Williamstown Road, Port Melbourne, VIC 3207, Australia

314–321, 3rd Floor, Plot 3, Splendor Forum, Jasola District Centre, New Delhi - 110025, India

103 Penang Road, #05-06/07, Visioncrest Commercial, Singapore 238467

Cambridge University Press is part of Cambridge University Press & Assessment, a department of the University of Cambridge.

We share the University's mission to contribute to society through the pursuit of education, learning and research at the highest international levels of excellence.

www.cambridge.org
Information on this title: www.cambridge.org/highereducation/isbn/9781108498470

DOI: 10.1017/9781108682404

© Gregory Dudek and Michael Jenkin 2024

First published 1997
Second edition 2010

A catalogue record for this publication is available from the British Library

Library of Congress Cataloging-in-Publication Data
Names: Dudek, Gregory, 1958- author. | Jenkin, Michael, 1959- author.
Title: Computational principles of mobile robotics / Gregory Dudek and
    Michael Jenkin.
Description: Third edition. | New York : Cambridge University Press, 2023. |
    Includes bibliographical references and index.
Identifiers: LCCN 2023033779 (print) | LCCN 2023033780 (ebook) |
    ISBN 9781108498470 (hardback) | ISBN 9781108736381 (paperback) |
    ISBN 9781108682404 (epub)
Subjects: LCSH: Mobile robots. | Robotics–Mathematics.
Classification: LCC TJ211.415 .D83 2023 (print) | LCC TJ211.415 (ebook) |
    DDC 629.8/932–dc23/eng/20230812
LC record available at https://lccn.loc.gov/2023033779
LC ebook record available at https://lccn.loc.gov/2023033780

ISBN 978-1-108-49847-0 Hardback
ISBN 978-1-108-73638-1 Paperback

Additional resources for this publication at www.cambridge.org/dudek-jenkin3e.

For Krys and Heather

Contents

Preface

The authors surrounded by a collection of some of their robots and sensors.

A great deal has changed in mobile robotics since the second edition of this book. A revolution in neural networks has had significant impact on sensor processing and algorithms for a range of robotics tasks. The need for effective human–robot interaction has been driven by the deployment of autonomous systems in a range of different domains, and the cost of autonomous systems has dropped to the point that drones are ubiquitous and many houses have robot vacuum cleaners operating within them.

As the field of robotics has expanded and matured, so has the material that is presented in this volume. The third edition of this text includes new chapters related to human–robot interaction, the application of deep learning to robotics, and roboethics. When teaching robotics in a single semester course, it becomes more and more difficult to cover the entire field, and it is common in an introductory course to focus on certain aspects of robotics and to only touch lightly on other topics. For example, in a computer science program it might be prudent to only lightly review chapters related to robot hardware (e.g., Chapters 3, 4, and 5), and to concentrate more heavily on deep learning (Chapter 6), algorithms related to planning (Chapter 7), system control (Chapter 8), pose maintenance (Chapter 9), and mapping (Chapter 10). Students from an engineering background, on the other hand, might find Chapters 3 through 5 particularly relevant and might instead prefer to only touch lightly on robot collectives (Chapter 11) and human–robot interaction (Chapter 12). Robot Ethics (Chapter 13), Robots in Practice (Chapter 14), and the Future of Mobile Robotics (Chapter 15) are relevant for most courses in robotics and provide a conclusion to the material.

In teaching robotics, a common question involves how close to the hardware does one need to go. Advances in the development of a common robot middleware has made dealing with real robots more practical in an introductory course. This book is supported by an online repository at www.cambridge.org/dudek-jenkin3e, which includes ROS 2 code that supports many of the examples given in this text and an introduction to ROS 2 as well.

Acknowledgments

This book would not have been possible without the active support of our students and colleagues who suffered through early drafts, provided imagery and papers, and put up with us while this volume was being put together. The list of people who helped is much too long to include here, but some require special mention: the International Joint Conferences on Artificial Intelligence (IJCAI), for letting us do a tutorial on mobile robotics that started us on the journey; students at McGill and York, including Eric Bourque, Andrew Hogue, and Yiannis Rekleitis, who suffered with photocopies of early drafts; Prof. Evangelos Milios for his helpful comments and Prof. Evangelos Papadopoulos for his help on space robots; Rob Sim for his figures; and Louis Dudek for his proofreading and helpful comments.

Finally, we thank Lauren Cowles and Cambridge University Press for encouraging us do this in the first place.

1

Overview and Motivation

"... let's start with the three fundamental Rules of Robotics – the three rules that are built most deeply into a robot's positronic brain." In the darkness, his gloved fingers ticked off each point.

"We have: one, a robot may not injure a human being, or through inaction, allow a human being to come to harm."

"Right!"

"Two," continued Powell, "a robot must obey the orders given it by human beings except where such orders would conflict with the First Law."

"Right!"

"And three, a robot must protect its own existence as long as such protection does not conflict with the First or Second Laws."[1]

Powell and Donovan discuss the laws of robotics. This text first appears in the
March, 1942 issue of *Astounding Science Fiction Magazine.*

The ability to navigate purposefully through its environment is fundamental to most animals and to every intelligent organism. In this book we examine the computational issues specific to the creation of machines that move intelligently in their environment. From the earliest modern speculation regarding the creation of autonomous robots, it was recognized that regardless of the mechanisms used to move the robot around or the methods used to sense the environment, the computational principles that govern the robot are of paramount importance. As Powell and Donovan discovered in Isaac Asimov's story "Runaround," subtle definitions within the programs that control a robot can lead to significant changes in the robot's overall behavior or action. Moreover, interactions among multiple complex components can lead to large-scale emergent behaviors that may be hard to predict.

Mobile robotics is a research area that deals with the control of autonomous and semi-autonomous vehicles. What sets **mobile robotics** apart from other research areas such as conventional manipulator robotics, artificial intelligence, and computer vision is the emphasis on problems related to the understanding of **large-scale space** – that is, regions of space substantially larger than those that can be observed from a single vantage point. While at first blush the distinction between sensing in large-scale space, with its requirement for mobility, and local sensing may appear obscure, it has far-reaching implications. To behave intelligently in a large-scale environment not only implies dealing with the incremental acquisition of knowledge, the estimation of positional error, the

[1] Asimov, I. [47], Reprinted by permission of the Estate of Isaac Asimov c/o Ralph M. Vicinanza, Ltd.

ability to recognize important or familiar objects or places, and real-time response, but it also requires that all these functionalities be exhibited in concert. This issue of extended space influences all of mobile robotics: (i) the tasks of moving through space, (ii) sensing about space, and (iii) reasoning about space are fundamental problems within the study of mobile robotics. The study of mobile robots in general, and this volume in particular, can be decomposed into the study of these three subproblems.

Mobile robots are not only a collection of algorithms for sensing, reasoning, and moving about space, they are also the physical embodiment of these algorithms and ideas that must cope with all of the vagaries of the real world. As such, mobile robots provide a reality check for theoretical concepts and algorithms. They are the point where literally the "rubber meets the road" for many algorithms in AI, path planning, knowledge representation, sensing, and reasoning.

In the context of humanity's ongoing quest to construct more capable machines – machines that match or even surpass human capabilities – the development of systems that exhibit mobility is a key hurdle. The importance of spatial mobility can be appreciated by observing that there are very few sophisticated biological organisms that cannot move or accomplish spatially distributed tasks in their environment. Just as the development of the wheel, and hence wheeled vehicles, marked a turning point in the evolution of manually operated tools, the development of mobile robots is an important stepping stone in the development of sophisticated machines.

Many different terms have come to be applied to the field of autonomous systems or mobile robotics. The words **autonomous**, as in autonomous system, and **automaton** have their roots in the Greek for *self-willed* (*auto+matos*: $\alpha \upsilon \tau o \ \mu \alpha \tau o \varsigma$). The term **robot** itself was introduced by Karel Čapek in his 1923 play *R.U.R.* (R.U.R. stands for Rossum's Universal Robots). The word "robot" is derived from the Czech or Polish words "robota," meaning "labour," and "robotnik," meaning "workman." It is interesting to note that the word *automaton* implies a degree of self-will that is not conveyed by the term "robot" and that **autonomous robot** might be construed as self-contradictory.

Robots that are manufactured following the same general structure as humans are known as **anthropomorphic robots** or **humanoid robots**, and in fiction, robots that are indistinguishable from humans are sometimes known as **androids**.

Although at the time of writing this book androids are beyond today's technology, anthropomorphic robots and robots with anthropomorphic features exist today. There are many reasons why researchers develop robots in an anthropomorphic mold. In addition to a desire to develop an agent in "one's own image," there are practical reasons for developing systems with anthropomorphic features. The operating environment for many mobile robots is the same environment that humans inhabit, and we have adapted our environment to suit our performance specifications. By mimicking human structures, at least at an operational or functional level, a robot may be better suited to operate in our environment. Human physiology, perception, and cognitive processes have been studied extensively. Thus by using locomotive, sensing, and reasoning systems based on biological models, roboticists can leverage the extensive literature that already exists in these fields. In addition, people seem to have a fascination with human-looking robots that goes beyond the pragmatic. That being said, mobile robots are not limited to mimicking existing biological systems, and there exist many other mechanisms, from infrared sensors to alternative drive mechanisms, that are leveraged in the design of mobile robots.

(a) Eddy2

(b) KROY

(c) Milton

(d) DragonBall

Figure 1.1. Some sample autonomous vehicle designs that are not wheeled mobile robots. (a) Eddy2 [172], an autonomous surface vessel. (b) KROY [233], a swimming legged robot, (c) Milton [171], a thruster-based unmanned underwater vehicle, and (d) DragonBall [222], a spherical (rolling) robot. Many more robots exist. For a more complete gallery of robot designs see robots.ieee.org.

Mobile robots come in a wide range of different forms and to meet a wide range of different applications. Wheeled mobile robots are very common, but only scratch the surface of the various kinds of robots that can be constructed. Space does not permit including imagery of even a representative sample, although online one can find websites that attempt to archive a representative selection of basic robot designs. That being said, Figure 1.1 highlights some robots to suggest the breadth of the design space.

The study of mobile robots is an intrinsically interdisciplinary research area that involves:

- **Mechanical engineering**: vehicle design and in particular locomotive mechanisms.
- **Computer science and engineering**: representations, and sensing and planning algorithms.
- **Electrical engineering**: system integration, sensors, and communications.
- **Cognitive psychology, perception, and neuroscience**: insights into how biological organisms solve similar problems.
- **Mechatronics**: the combination of mechanical engineering with computer science, computer engineering, and/or electrical engineering.

Although many mobile robot systems currently in operation are fundamentally research vehicles and are thus experimental in nature, a substantial number of mobile robot systems are deployed outside of the lab. Real applications in which current mobile robots have been deployed successfully are characterized by one or more of the following attributes: the absence of an on-site human operator (often due to inaccessibility), a potentially high cost, long duty cycles, and the need to tolerate environmental conditions that might not be acceptable to a human. As such, mobile robots are especially well suited for tasks that exhibit one or more of the following characteristics:

- An environment that is inhospitable, so that deploying a human being is either very costly or very dangerous.
- An environment that is remote, so that sending a human operator is too difficult or takes too long. Extreme instances are domains that are completely inaccessible to humans, such as microscopic environments.
- A task with a very demanding duty cycle or a very high fatigue factor.
- A task that is highly disagreeable to a human.

Successful industrial applications for mobile robots typically involve more than one of these characteristics. Consider the application of mobile robotics to underground mining as an example. The environment is dangerous, in that the possibility of rock fall or environmental contamination due to the release of hazardous gas or dust is quite real. The environment is remote, in that humans operating in underground mines must travel considerable distances, typically many kilometers, in order to reach the rockface being worked. At the rockface, the miner is confronted with an operational environment that can be cramped, poorly illuminated, hot, and dangerous. Other "ideal" robotic operational environments include contaminated, nuclear, extraterrestrial, and underwater environments.

Mobile robots are feats of engineering. The actuators, processors, user interfaces, sensors, and communication mechanisms that permit a mobile robot to operate must be integrated so as to permit the entire system to function as a complete whole. The physical structure of a mobile robot is complex, requiring a considerable investment of both human and financial resources in order to keep it operating. "Robot wranglers"[2] are an essential component for the successful operation of any robotic system. Thus, one of the goals of this book, in addition to provoking new research, is to act as a reference of mobile robot tools and techniques for those who would develop, maintain, or work with a mobile robot. Rather than concentrate strictly on the sensors required for a mobile robot [258], or on the physical design of small autonomous robots [396], presenting standard robot operating software, for example, ROS [645], or collecting together the seminal papers of the field [192], this volume considers the computational processes involved in making a robot sense, reason, and move through its environment.

1.1   From Mechanisms to Computation

Robots can be considered from several different perspectives. At a physical, hardware, or mechanistic level, robots can be decomposed into the following:

---

[2] Graduate students and research technicians.

- A power source, typically based on batteries.
- A mechanism for making the robot move through its environment – the physical organization of motors, belts, and gears that is necessary to make the robot move.
- A computer or collection of computers that controls the robot.
- A collection of sensors with which the robot gathers information concerning its environment.
- Communications infrastructure to enable the robot to communicate to an off-board operator and any externally based computers.

At the device level, the hardware details can be abstracted, and a robot can be considered as:

- A software-level abstraction of the motors, encoders, and motor driver boards that allow the robot to move. Most mobile robot hardware manufacturers provide support for the underlying hardware at this level rather than force the user to deal with the details of actually turning motors.
- Software-level mechanisms or libraries to provide access to the robot's sensors, for example, the current image obtained by a video camera as an array of intensities.
- A standard communications mechanism, such as wired or wireless network access to an operator or the outside world.

From a still more abstract perspective, we can consider mobile robots at a purely computational level such that the sensors, communications, and locomotive systems are seen simply as software modules that enable the robot to interact with its environment. Typical components in a software architecture include:

- A motion control subsystem,
- A sensor control subsystem,
- A sensor interpretation subsystem.
- A mission control subsystem.

Even higher levels of abstraction exist. The term **cognitive robotics** is used to refer to the use of artificial intelligence (AI) techniques within a mobile robot and often assumes the existence of an idealized computational abstraction of the robot. Although this volume touches on a number of aspects of mobile robots, here we concentrate on the computational underpinnings of these devices.

1.2   Historical Context

Autonomous Robots in Fiction

Thou shalt not make a machine in the likeness of a human mind.[3]

Autonomous devices have a long and checkered past in legend and literature. From ancient legends to modern films and literature, many different robots and robot-like devices have been constructed to extend the will of their creator or owner. Much of the

---

[3] F. Herbert, *Dune* [346].

fictional literature on autonomous systems is cautionary in nature: the "robot" may follow its instructions too literally, or it may grow to have a will of its own and not follow its instructions at all. For example, in Isaac Asimov's story "Runaway" a robot is told to "get lost," which of course it does, while "Robots of Empire" and "Robots of Dawn," also by Asimov, describe the process of robots evolving their own rules of operation. Given their supposed infallibility, fictional robots have also been proposed as final arbitrators of judgment. For example, in the 1951 film *The Day the Earth Stood Still*, Gort is a universal police officer who enforces the law without being influenced by sentiment.

Perhaps the earliest reference to a "robot" in literature can be found in Greek mythology. According to ancient Greek or Cretan mythology, Talos was an "animated" giant man made of bronze who guarded the island of Crete and enforced the law. One of Talos' flaws was that he was too literal minded in the interpretation of his directives, so that he became a burden. Even in this legend, problem specification and representation was an issue! This notion of the robot as protector also appears in Jewish folklore. According to legend, in sixteenth-century Prague, the Jewish population turned to a golem to protect them from the gentiles who wanted to kill them. A rabbi fashioned the golem out of clay and breathed life into it.

Clay and bronze are not the only potential building materials for fictional "robots." In works of fiction, autonomous agents are also constructed out of biological components. In 1818, Mary Shelley wrote *Frankenstein*, which tells the story of Dr. Frankenstein and his efforts to animate dead tissue. As one inspired job advertisement put it, "Dr. Frankenstein was more than just a scientist – he was an electrical engineer with the creative capability for bringing extraordinary ideas to life." Nor are all fictional accounts of robots based on anthropomorphic designs. In his 1880 *The Demon of Cawnpore*, Jules Verne describes a steam powered elephant[4] whereas the film *Blade Runner*, based on Philip K. Dick's novel *Do Androids Dream of Electric Sheep?* [223], describes a world in which animals are almost extinct and robotic pets are popular.

Isaac Asimov is often regarded as a key contributor to the genesis of robotics due to his copious science fiction writings on the topic and, most notably, his "three laws of robotics." Introduced in 1942 in "Runaround" and reprinted at the beginning of this chapter, they are as follows:

1. A robot may not injure a human being, or, through inaction, allow a human being to come to harm.
2. A robot must obey the orders given it by human beings except when such orders would conflict with the First Law.
3. A robot must protect its own existence as long as such protection does not conflict with the First or Second Laws.

In later works, Asimov added a zeroth law that required a robot not to injure humanity. Many of Asimov's stories revolve around robot (and human) attempts to find new definitions or loopholes in these laws. Although the relevance of these laws to real robotics research is questionable, they nevertheless have proven to be both inspirational and provocative.

---

[4] The *Demon of Cawnpore* was also published as *The End of Nana Sahib*.

Figure 1.2. A Dalek, a half-robot/half-biological creature from the BBC TV series *Doctor Who*. Copyright Barry Angel. Used with permission.

Since the 1940s, mobile robots have become a common feature of science fiction literature and film. Famous fictional robots include Robbie (*Forbidden Planet*), Gort (*The Day the Earth Stood Still*), Rosie (*The Jetsons*), Robot (*Lost in Space*), Floyd (*Stationfall* and *Planetfall*), R2D2 and C3PO (*Star Wars*), Data and the partly biological Borg (*Star Trek*), HAL (*2001* and *2010*), Bender (*Futurama*), the Terminator (*Terminator*), and of course Marvin, the paranoid android (*The Hitchhiker's Guide to the Galaxy*). More details on the evolution of robots in literature can be found in [44]. See also Appendix A and [334]. It is interesting to note that fictional robots usually do not suffer from the computational, sensing, power, or locomotive problems that plague real robots. How the Daleks (see Figure 1.2) from the long-running BBC television series *Doctor Who* managed to conquer most of the galaxy without having to navigate a set of stairs was only finally addressed when modern CGI enabled them to fly. On the other hand, fiction serves not only to predict the future, but also to inspire those who might create it. Stork [742] provides some insights into the differences between a specific fictional autonomous system – HAL from *2001* – and the state of the art in terms of real systems.

Early Autonomous Robots

Various robotic or robotic-like systems can be found scattered throughout history. Mechanical robotic systems can be traced back to Greek and Roman times. The Roman historian Appian reported a mechanical simulation of Julius Caesar. In the fifteenth century Leonardo da Vinci developed a number of robotic systems, perhaps the most famous of which was an anthropomorphic device with controllable arms and legs [676]. Less well known perhaps is Leonardo's robotic car or automata. This device resembled a differential drive robot and used springs and cams to program the robot to follow different trajectories as it moved. (See [676] for an indepth review of the design of this vehicle.) The late eighteenth-century autonomous Japanese tea carrier Karakuri is described in [675].

Autonomous vehicles built by Nikola Tesla in the 1890s are probably the earliest electrical mobile robots. In the 1890s Tesla built wireless, radio-controlled vehicles [159]. One of his remote-controlled aquatic vehicles is shown in Figure 1.3a. The first steps toward modern electronic robotic systems were made during the early to mid-1940s.

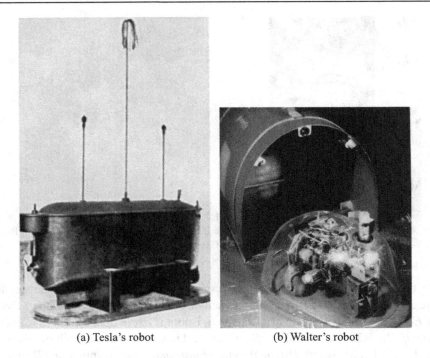

(a) Tesla's robot   (b) Walter's robot

Figure 1.3. Analog robots. (b) Copyright Owen Holland. Used with permission.

Norbert Wiener is considered the inventor of **cybernetics** and hence modern robotics. A mathematician, Wiener studied regulatory systems and their application to control. During World War II, he was involved in a project to develop a controlling device for an anti-aircraft gun. The development of such a device, which integrates sensory information (radar) via processing (simple control laws executing on an analog computer) into action (directing and firing the anti-aircraft gun), resulted in one of the first robotic systems. As Wiener mused in his January, 1949 article in *Electronics*,

> It has long been clear to me that the modern ultra-rapid computing machine was in principle an ideal central nervous system to an apparatus for automatic control; and its input and output need not be in the form of numbers or diagrams, but might very well be, respectively, the readings of artificial sensors such as photoelectric cells or thermometers, and the performance of motors or solenoids.[5]

At the same time that Wiener was developing an automatic anti-aircraft gun, work in Germany on the V1 and V2 – autonomous aircraft and self-guided rocketry – was establishing the basis for autonomous vehicle design (see Figure 1.4). The V1 and V2 were known as **Vergeltungswaffen** (reprisal weapons). The V1 was equipped with simple sensors to measure distance traveled (a propeller in the nose), altitude, and heading. This was sufficient to permit the device to be launched from France and Holland and to strike at population centers in England. Roughly 8000 were launched [656].

---

[5] *Electronics*, January 1949. Reprinted in [505].

Figure 1.4. V1 flying bomb. Shown hanging in the Imperial War Museum, London.

William Grey Walter built one of the earliest fully autonomous vehicles. Described in a series of articles published in 1950 and 1951 in *Scientific American*, and in his book *The Living Brain* [815], Walter's electronic robot (see Figure 1.3b) had phototube eyes, microphone ears, contact-switch feelers, and capacitors used as memory devices to perform associations. Walter named the robot Tortoise after the creature in *Alice in Wonderland*. The Tortoise performed tasks such as heading toward well-lit regions, locating the recharging hutch, and wandering without mishap.

With the development of digital computers came the potential for more complex mobile robots. Between 1966 and 1972, Nils Nilssen, Charles Rosen, and other researchers at the Stanford Research Institute developed Shakey, the first mobile robot to be operated using artificial intelligence techniques [578]. The five-foot-tall robot used two stepper motors in a differential drive arrangement to provide locomotion and was equipped with touch-sensitive bumpers. An optical rangefinder and vidicon television camera with controllable focus and iris were mounted on a tilt platform for sensing. Off-board communication was provided via two radio channels – one for video and the other providing command and control. Shakey is shown in Figure 1.5a.

Work on Shakey concentrated on automated reasoning and planning, which used logic-based problem solving based on **STRIPS** – the STanford Research Institute Problem Solver. The control of movement and the interpretation of sensory data were secondary to this logic-based component. Simple video processing was used to obtain local information about empty floor space, and Shakey constructed a global map of its environment based on this information. A typical mission for Shakey was to find a box of a given size, shape, and color in one of a specified number of rooms and then to move it to a designated position. Being able to accomplish these tasks depended on a simplified environment containing simple wooden blocks in carefully constrained shapes. Shakey had to cope with obstacles and plan actions using a total of 192 K of memory (eventually upgraded to 1.35 MB).

The **Stanford Cart** [539, 540, 541] (see Figure 1.5b) was developed at SAIL (the Stanford Artificial Intelligence Laboratory) between 1973 and 1979 and moved to CMU (Carnegie Mellon University) in 1980. Throughout this period it underwent major modifications and served as the initial test device upon which solutions to a number of classic robot problems were developed. The Stanford Cart relied on stereo vision in order to locate objects and planned paths to avoid sensed obstacles using a world model based on stereo data. The stereo vision algorithm was based on a single camera that was mounted

(a) Shakey   (b) Stanford Cart   (c) CMU Rover

Figure 1.5. Early wheeled digital robots. (a) Image by Carlo Nardone, and licensed under Creative Commons Attribution-Share Alike 2.0 Generic License. (b) and (c) ©1983 IEEE. Used with permission.

on a sliding track that was perpendicular to the camera's optical axis. A single "view" of the environment was based on nine images taken at different positions along this track. A comparison of the images over time was used to determine the motion of the cart, whereas comparisons of the images from a single position were used to build an environmental model. The robot was controlled by an off-board computer program that drove the cart through cluttered spaces. The cart moved roughly 1 m every 10 to 15 minutes.

The kinematic structure of the Stanford Cart introduced a number of limitations in the robot. Recognizing these limitations, the CMU Rover project (started in 1980) developed a robot (Figure 1.5c) that relied on a synchronous drive–like assembly rather than the car-like steering of the Stanford Cart. The Rover added infrared and sonar proximity sensors to the robot, and modified the camera mount for the video sensor so that it could pan and tilt as well as slide, which were not possible with the Stanford Cart.

Another early robot system, the **Hilare** project and robot family developed at Laboratoire d'Analysis et d'Architecture des Systeèmes (LAAS) in France [122, 313]; also represented a milesone in performance. Hilare I, developed in 1977, was an indoor mobile robot based on a differential drive system (two powered wheels and one free wheel for balance) and included a laser rangefinder. Hilare's perceptual system relied on sonar units, a video camera, and a laser rangefinder. The laser and camera were mounted on a pan-and-tilt station in order to direct the sensor in different directions.

In parallel with these early wheeled mobile robots, legged robotic systems began to appear in the 1960s. The first legged or walking robots appeared in a patent for a mechanical horse in 1893, but it was not until the early 1960s that an operational walking vehicle was constructed. Perhaps the most famous of the early legged vehicles is the General Electric Quadruped (see Figure 1.6) [474, 547]. Each of the four legs of this vehicle had three simple joints; the knee joint was composed of a single joint, and the

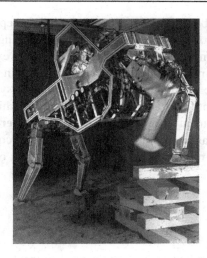

Figure 1.6. The GE Quadruped. Museum of Innovation and Science. Used with permission.

hip joint used two. As can be seen in Figure 1.6, the GE Quadruped was controlled by an on-board operator. In practice it was a very difficult device to control, although the vehicle did exhibit considerable mobility.

From the mid-1980s on, there was an explosion in mobile robot design. A number of companies began to manufacture and market mobile robot platforms. With the availability of standard platforms, many different robotic projects emerged, but almost all could trace their underlying design to one of these early robot designs. A survey of mobile robot systems prior to 1986 can be found in [121].

1.3   Biological Inspiration

As in many AI-related fields, the designers of autonomous robots often find motivations and inspiration from biological systems. These inspirations may influence the physical design or the sensory mechanisms or even the underlying model of computational control. Perhaps the most often-cited reason for examining biological systems for inspiration in autonomous robots is that biology provides an existence proof that the problem can indeed be solved. Even very simple biological systems – such as ants or bees – are capable of locomotion, sensing, and reasoning tasks under a wide variety of environmental conditions, conditions that mechanical autonomous systems cannot yet hope to handle.

It is interesting to note that researchers studying biological systems have found robots to be a useful tool for testing models of sensing and communication. For example, specially equipped autonomous robots have been used to validate sensing and navigation models used by desert ants [445, 824], computational fish schooling models have been used to model animations [666], and a dancing bee robot has been used to communicate with real bees [529].

1.4   Operational Regimes

There are only a few fully autonomous robots in general use today. Most robots are designed to operate with some level of human guidance or control. Even "autonomous" systems are expected to obey their programming and accept task specifications on a regular basis. When a robotic system is described as being **fully autonomous**, the system is typically designed to operate without full-time external human control. This is to be distinguished from **semi-autonomous** systems, in which an operator is required full-time. Within the continuum of semi-autonomous systems, two different operational regimes can be identified: **teleoperated systems**, in which the remote device is controlled moment by moment at a very low level, and **telerobotic systems**, in which low-level operator commands are interpreted or filtered by complex software layers that may use sensors located on the robot to limit, complement, or filter the operator's actions.

1.5   Operational Modes

Simple robotic systems can be controlled by a single central processor. More sophisticated systems incorporate subsidiary processors to deal with real-time device control (such as the use of programmable micro-controllers to control and monitor sensors). As the processing needs of the robotic system increase, multiple computing units may be necessary, and the control of the robot becomes distributed over these processors. Because on-board computation is limited by weight and power consumption (not to mention economics), some of these processors may be deployed off-board at the far end of a relatively slow communications link. The effective distribution of tasks in such a heterogeneous environment can be very difficult. In addition to distributing the computation among multiple processors, some of which may be located off-board, it is also possible to distribute the robotic work over multiple robots. This **collective** or **swarm** of robots could itself be centrally controlled, or both the robotic task and the computation may be distributed. Figure 1.7 shows a sample robot collective. The design of a collective with distributed computation and task achievement can be very complex.

Figure 1.7. A thousand robot swarm. See [680]. Appears with the kind permission of Prof. Mike Rubenstein.

1.6   Software Support

Developing large scale robot software is a major undertaking. The software must deal with real-time events including motor control, sensors, and the like. It must also deal with high-level plans, complex and often computationally expensive algorithms, and it will likely involve the integration of software modules from different developers and hardware manufacturers. Even from the earliest days of robot development there have been a number of efforts to develop "standard" software infrastructures that support the development of autonomous systems. Early efforts in this area are reviewed in [433]. By the late 2000s, efforts to establish a real standard had resulted in the first release of ROS, the Robot Operating System. ROS is more accurately described as a middleware. Originally developed at Willow Garage as the "Linux of Robotics," ROS [644] is now a widely adopted standard in the development and operation of autonomous systems.

ROS exists in two primary flavors, the original version ROS 1 and a major refactoring of the software known as ROS 2. In both versions, ROS uses a multi-process architecture within which parallel computational units communicate via messages. In part a consequence of its origins, ROS 1 assumes a standard TCP-IP communications infrastructure and is in general oblivious to performance characteristics of the underlying network architecture. These assumptions can lead to issues, especially when wireless networks are involved in the system architecture or when network capacity or connectivity becomes an issue. These issues are addressed in ROS 2, which is now available although not as well supported as ROS 1. Even with these known issues, ROS is widely used and there exists a substantive and ever growing code base that supports the use of ROS 1 and ROS 2 on autonomous systems.

This book utilizes ROS 2 to provide working examples of many of the concepts that are presented. You will find it helpful to have access to a working version of ROS 2 Humble Hawksbill (see `www.ros.org`) running on Ubuntu 22.04 (Jammy Jellyfish) or later, with Python 3. Code snippets provided within this text are available online. Although this book cannot hope to provide a complete and detailed coverage of ROS, a short introduction can be found on the online resource associated with this book. The various ROS examples provided in this book are also provided online with ROS 2 support. Limited support is also provided for ROS 1. Throughout this book the term "ROS" will normally be used to mean ROS 2.

1.7   A Brief Guide to This Book

Chapter 2 introduces some of the fundamental computational issues that underlie mobile robotics. Chapter 3 provides a brief overview of non-sensor robot hardware. It concentrates on different models of locomotion for wheeled robots but also considers other locomotive strategies. Chapters 4 and 5 cover non-visual and visual sensors and their algorithms. Chapter 6 considers how neural networks and other AI tools are used in autonomous systems. Chapter 7 considers the task of representing and reasoning about space, and Chapter 8 looks at how the software modules that make up a mobile robot can be constructed. Chapters 9 and 10 look at pose maintenance and maps. Chapter 11 looks at the problems faced by groups of robots. Chapter 12 looks as the emerging field of human – robot interaction, Chapter 13 looks at robot ethics. Chapter 14 surveys practical robot tasks and the robots that have been constructed for them, and Chapter 15 looks forward to the future of mobile robots. The appendices provide a (short) introduction to some of the mathematical concepts used throughout the book.

1.8   Further Reading

Robots in fiction Appendix A provides a non-exhaustive list of robotic books and movies. For a selection of six classic science fiction stories that highlight robots and AI, see [556].

Early autonomous robots More details of the life of William Grey Walter can be found in Owen Holland's review [363]. See also Cox and Wilfong's collection of papers prior to 1990 [192]. A review of the historical dream of autonomous machines can be found in [516]. Early efforts at building "intelligent" machines can be found in many cultures. Samples include the Karakuri mechanisms of Japan (see [851]), Leonardo's efforts in Europe in terms of developing robots and robotic systems (see [676]), and efforts in Arabia as recorded by Ibn Al-Razzaz Al-Jazari to develop "ingenious" devices (see [15]).

Other robotics texts Since the publication of the first edition of this book, a number of general texts on autonomous robots have appeared. These include [362], [718], [164], [717], [115], [860], [389], and [422].

1.9   Problems

1. There are a large number of robotic sources available including the Internet and local libraries. Identify which robotic journals are available locally and which robot conference proceedings are available. Search the World Wide Web for the resources available there. There are a number of international robotics conferences targeted at the general robotics community. Try to find proceedings of the following (many are available on websites associated with the societies that support these conferences or through IEEE Xplore):

   - IEEE International Conference of Robotics and Automation (ICRA)
   - IEEE/RSJ International Conference on Intelligent Robots and Systems (IROS)
   - Robotics: Science and Systems (RSS)

   There are also a number of international conferences targeted at more specific research communities. Try to find proceedings of the following:

   - ACM/IEEE International Conference on Human-Robot Interaction (HRI)
   - Conference on Field and Service Robotics (FSR)

2. If there is a mobile platform available locally, obtain a copy of the system documentation for the device. How is it powered? Recharged? Controlled? Learn how to power the device on and off and how to control it safely. Given the

prevalence of ROS, is there a local ROS/Gazebo simulator available for the robot? If so, learn how to use them.

3. This book provides examples in ROS. Obtain access to a version of ROS. The most straightforward way of accessing ROS is through its installation on a computer running Ubuntu but a range of other alternatives exist, including running a version of ROS running within a virtualized container. A large number of ROS tutorials exist on the Internet, and the online resource associated with this book provides a short introduction to ROS as well. Use the standard ROS tools to launch and shut down ROS. Associated with this text is a collection of ROS packages. Download these packages to your ROS environment and follow the instructions in the online resource to build them. These packages are designed to be run using Gazebo and do not require a physical robot to run them.

4. Take a robot from film or literature. What is the robot designed to do? How was the robot constructed? How does it sense its environment? How does it move about within its environment? Ignoring issues related to power and our ability to construct self-aware, perfectly sensing vehicles, is the robot *as presented* suitable for the task that it is designed to do in the book or film?

5. In *The Complete Robot*, Asimov divides the bulk of robot stories into one of two groups; robot-as-menace and robot-as-pathos. Asimov conjectured that there were few stories that fell outside these two groups. Go through the films and stories listed in Appendix A and categorize them in terms of these two groups. Have other groups of robot stories begun to emerge?

6. The term "roboethics" was coined in 2004 by Giammarco Veruggio. Roboethics is an applied ethics that seeks to promote and encourage the development of robots for the advancement of human society and individuals, and to help prevent the misuse of robots against humankind (see Chapter 13). There are a number of roboethics groups worldwide, and a number of international conferences and workshops related to roboethics have been held. Does your research (or research group) have an ethical policy with respect to the robots that you are developing? If so, what is it? If not, is a policy required and what should the policy cover?

7. Conducting experiments within which humans interact with robots typically requires ethics approval from either your institution or external research funders (or both). What are the necessary requirements to obtain such approval at your institution?

2

Fundamental Problems

A journey of a thousand miles begins with a single step.[1]

Before delving into the harsh realities of real robots, it is worthwhile exploring some of the computational tasks that are associated with an autonomous system. This chapter provides a taste (an *amuse bouche*, if you will) of some of the computational problems that will be considered in later chapters. Here, these problems are considered in their simplest form, and many of the realities of autonomous systems are ignored. Rest assured, the full complexity of the problems are considered in later chapters.

Perhaps the simplest theoretical abstraction of an autonomous robot is the **point robot**. A point robot abstracts the robot as a single point operating in some environment, typically a continuous Cartesian plane. Within this formalism, the robot can be represented as a point $(x, y) \in \mathbb{R}^2$. The domain of operation of the robot is the plane. The point (x, y) fully describes the **state** of the robot and is also known as the robot's **pose** or **configuration**. In the online resource associated with this text, we develop a block_robot model in ROS. This is a point robot with orientation (x, y, θ)

Moving a robot involves changing its state from one value to another. For the point robot this involves moving from (a, b) to (c, d). The point robot operates on a plane, but not all of this domain is necessarily available to the robot. The set of valid poses of the robot are known as its **free space**. Some states are not valid; rather, they correspond to **obstacles** or other states that the robot cannot occupy. This concept that space or configurations may be occupied or invalid can be represented in terms of partitioning configurations of the robot into two classes: free space, $\mathcal{C}_{free}$, and occupied space, $\mathbb{R}^2 - \mathcal{C}_{free}$. Given this definition of space, configurations, and free space, we can ask a number of fundamental questions associated with mobile robots:

- Is it possible to get the robot from one configuration to another while remaining within $\mathcal{C}_{free}$? This is the problem of **path planning**. This is perhaps the *key* problem that must be addressed in having a robot move intelligently in its environment.
- How can the robot determine its state if it has local measurements of $\mathcal{C}_{free}$? This is the problem of **localization**. Complete knowledge of the robot's world is not helpful unless we know where the robot is in it.
- How can the robot determine which parts of its environment are occupied? That is, how can the robot determine $\mathcal{C}_{free}$? This is the problem of **robot perception** or **robot sensing**.

[1] Lao-tzu, *The Way of Lao-tzu.*

- How can the robot determine $\mathcal{C}_{free}$, assuming it always knows where it is? This is the problem of constructing a representation of the robot's environment or **mapping**. The existence of a map is often assumed implicitly in the path planning task. There are very few environments where this is known *a priori*, and even if it is possible to know everything about the environment (by measuring it, perhaps), it may be more convenient to have the robot construct the representation itself.
- How can the robot determine its pose and $\mathcal{C}_{free}$ if it knows neither? This is known as **simultaneous localization and mapping** or **SLAM**.

The remainder of this chapter looks at a specific example for each of the these problems for a point robot.

2.1 Defining a Point Robot

The textbook definition of a point robot must be generalized slightly if we are to mount (simulated) sensors on it, as such sensors may point in different directions relative to the orientation of the robot. Under such circumstances the point robot operating on a plane may be augmented with an orientation (x, y, θ). This is the block robot introduced above. Moving a robot involves applying actions (forces) to the robot in order to have it change its state. In a perfect world the most straightforward way of moving a robot is to have it teleport from one pose (x, y, θ) to another (x', y', θ'). But until teleportation is possible, robots will have to follow a continuous path from one pose to another.

Within ROS the standard way of moving a robot is to provide it a continuous command velocity `cmd_vel` to both its position and orientation. Changes in velocity can be represented as forces acting on the vehicle, both rotational and translational. In ROS, this is known as a `wrench`.

For robots with complex kinematic constraints, choosing the correct set of commanded velocities to move a robot to a goal pose can be quite difficult. For a point robot that can move in arbitrary directions, then the process is more straightforward; we select a sequence of commanded velocities such that the robot converges to the goal pose. For example, the ROS node `drive_to_goal.py` in the `cpmr_2` package from the GitHub repository associated with this text, and reprinted in part in Listing 2.1, applies a `twist` (a combination of angular and linear velocities) to drive the robot to a known goal.

The critical observation in the listing above is that controlling the velocity to move the robot – here one capable of omnidrectional motion – to a particular state requires developing a controller that brings the robot to a stop at the appropriate state, while staying within reasonable limits – such as a maximum vehicle velocity. The process becomes even more complex if the vehicle introduces constraints as to possible vehicle motions, as is the case for many classes of robot vehicles.

2.2 Path Planning for a Point Robot

Given the ability to move to a given pose in empty space, the next problem involves accomplishing the task in the presence of known obstacles. Consider the environment shown in Figure 2.1. The robot starts at configuration $S = (a, b)$, and we

```
angular_diff = goal_theta - cur_theta
x_diff = goal_x - cur_x
y_diff = goal_y - cur_y
dist = math.sqrt(x_diff**2 + y_diff**2)

if abs(angular_diff) > angular_tol:
  twist.angular.z = max(min(angular_diff * angular_gain,
                    max_angular_vel), -max_angular_vel)
if dist > pos_tol:
  x = max(min(x_diff * pos_gain, max_vel), -max_vel)
  y = max(min(y_diff * pos_gain, max_vel), -max_vel)
  twist.linear.x = x * math.cos(cur_theta) + y * math.sin(cur_theta)
  twist.linear.y = -x * math.sin(cur_theta) + y * math.cos(cur_theta)
```

Listing 2.1. Moving the Block Robot. Moving a block with orientation. At every time step the difference in position and orientation between the goal pose and the robot's current pose is computed and the robot moved in position and orientation to be closer to the desired pose. Note that even this "simple" computation involves gains that must be set so that the robot does not oscillate around the goal state nor approach the goal state too slowly.

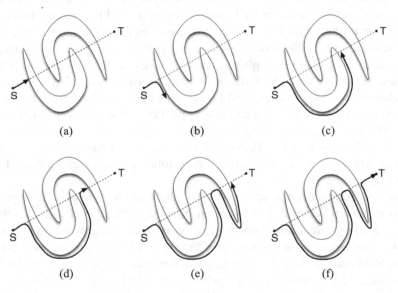

Figure 2.1. Bug2 algorithm example. The robot moves from S to T in the sequence (a)–(f). The dashed line shows the direct path, and the solid line shows the path followed by the robot.

wish to move it to configuration $T = (c, d)$. Planning the path from S to T involves determining a path that connects S and T that remains within the free space. Formally we seek a continuous curve in $\mathcal{C}_{free}$ with one end at the **start location** (a, b) and the other end at the **goal** (c, d). Clearly for a path to exist both the start and goal must be in $\mathcal{C}_{free}$, but how do we determine whether such a path exists? Observe that this problem is extremely difficult in general because we must search through a continuous space for the existence of a continuous path. Given some mechanism of finding paths, one can search for, for example, the shortest path or the straightest path. Many different solutions to the path planning problem exist, and many of these solutions rely on solving approximations to the problem. Here we consider a very simple solution to the problem – known as the Bug2 algorithm – from the class of **Bug algorithms** (see [486] and Chapter 7).

Suppose that the robot is at S and we wish to move the robot to T. Then if a direct (straight line) path exists in free space from S to T, the robot should use this path. If the path is obstructed, then the robot should move along the straight line from S to T until it encounters the obstacle. Call this point P. Then the robot should circumnavigate the obstacle until it can continue to move to the goal location T along the line ST. The robot circumnavigates the obstacle until it finds a point on the obstacle on the line ST from which it can leave the obstacle in the direction of T that is *closer* to T than the point P at which it started circumnavigating the obstacle. If no such point is found, the robot determines that no path exists from S to T. The basic Bug2 algorithm is sketched in Listing 2.2. The Bug2 algorithm is guaranteed to find a path to the goal location if it is accessible.

The Bug2 algorithm is said to be **complete** in that it is certain to find a path to the goal if such a path exists and reports failure otherwise. The Bug2 algorithm is not, however, guaranteed to find a particularly efficient (short) path. To see this, observe that the robot always returns to the line ST in order to continue moving toward the goal.

Observe that the robot needs to "know" a great deal about its environment and its abilities within that environment in order to execute an algorithm such as this. It must know where it is in the world and be able to maintain an ongoing estimate of this as it moves. It must know where the goal is in this representation. It must also be able to mark a location in this representation (P) and determine whether it has returned to it. The robot must be able to determine (sense) the presence of an obstacle and be able to use that information in order to circumnavigate it. The robot must also be able to instantaneously change its trajectory in space. This dependency on highly accurate knowledge of the robot's position in the world and on the robot's ability to accurately sense obstacles along the path poses difficult problems for Bug (and Bug-like) algorithms when operating with real robots.

It is interesting to observe how long the paths are that are generated by this algorithm. Even for simple environments the generated paths can be very long relative to the shortest one possible. Arbitrary decisions made during planning can have a significant effect on

```
Visualize a direct path ST from the start S to the goal T.
while the goal T is not achieved, do:
  begin
    while the path ST to the goal is not obstructed, do
      begin
        move towards the goal along the path ST,
        if the path is obstructed then
          begin
            mark the current location as P circumnavigate the object
            until the robot either:
            (a) hits the line ST at a point closer to T than P and
                can move towards T, in which case the robot follows ST;
            (b) returns to where P in which case T is unreachable.
          end
      end
  end
```

Listing 2.2. The Bug2 algorithm.

performance. Consider the difference in performance when comparing a robot that "turns left" versus a robot that "turns right" when encountering an obstacle. Some of these issues are considered in the problems posed at the end of the chapter.

2.3   Localization for a Point Robot

When the robot moves from (x, y) to some point $(x + \Delta x, y + \Delta y)$, how do we know where the robot actually is? A first glance at the task suggests that there might not be any problem at all. If we know where the robot was when we started, and if every time we tell the robot to move it does precisely what we tell it, then surely we must know where it is all the time. Unfortunately the real world is not that straightforward. Suppose that the robot uses wheels to move. The robot's wheels will slip each time we accelerate or deaccelerate the vehicle, and over time these small errors will accumulate, eventually causing any estimate we have of the robot's position to be inaccurate. To see this, suppose that at each time i we tell the robot to move by some amount $(\Delta x_i, \Delta y_i)$, but that it actually moves some amount $(\Delta x_i + \epsilon_i^x, \Delta y_i + \epsilon_i^y)$ where ϵ_i^x and ϵ_i^y are small random errors associated with the motion. Assume that this error satisfies

$$\forall_i \mathbb{E}[\epsilon_i^x] = \mathbb{E}[\epsilon_i^y] = 0$$
$$\forall_i \mathbb{E}[(\epsilon_i^x - \mathbb{E}[\epsilon_i^x])(\epsilon_i^x - \mathbb{E}[\epsilon_i^x])] = \sigma^2$$
$$\forall_i \mathbb{E}[(\epsilon_i^y - \mathbb{E}[\epsilon_i^y])(\epsilon_i^y - \mathbb{E}[\epsilon_i^y])] = \sigma^2$$
$$\forall_{i \neq j} \mathbb{E}[(\epsilon_i^x - \mathbb{E}[\epsilon_i^x])(\epsilon_i^y - \mathbb{E}[\epsilon_i^y])] = 0.$$

(Here $\mathbb{E}[x]$ is the expectation operator.[2]) This assumption that the noise process is independent, has zero mean, and a known stationary variance is a common simplification in much robotics work. After making N motions from some start position (x_0, y_0), where is the robot relative to $(x_N, y_N) = (x_0, y_0) + \sum(\Delta x_i, \Delta y_i)$?

The expected location of the robot after executing these motions is given by $\mathbb{E}[(x_N, y_N)]$:

$$\begin{aligned}
\mathbb{E}[(x_N, y_N)] &= \mathbb{E}[(x_0, y_0) + \sum(\Delta x_i + \epsilon_i^x, \Delta y_i + \epsilon_i^y)] \\
&= (x_0, y_0) + (\mathbb{E}[\sum \Delta x_i + \epsilon_i^x], \mathbb{E}[\sum \Delta y_i + \epsilon_i^y]) \\
&= (x_0, y_0) + (\sum \Delta x_i + \sum \mathbb{E}[\epsilon_i^x], \sum \Delta y_i + \mathbb{E}[\epsilon_i^y]) \\
&= (x_0, y_0) + (\sum \Delta x_i, \sum \Delta y_i).
\end{aligned}$$

The expected state of the robot is its commanded location. But how sure can we be of this estimate? Consider the expected distribution around this mean as represented by the covariance matrix

$$\Sigma = \begin{bmatrix} \sigma_{xx} & \sigma_{xy} \\ \sigma_{yx} & \sigma_{yy} \end{bmatrix}. \tag{2.1}$$

---

[2] See Appendix B for a review of probability and statistics.

Now

$$
\begin{aligned}
\sigma_{xx} &= \mathbb{E}[(x - \mathbb{E}[x])^2] \\
&= \mathbb{E}[(x_0 + \sum(\Delta x_i + \epsilon_i^x) - \mathbb{E}[x_0 + \sum(\Delta x_i + \epsilon_i^x)])^2] \\
&= \mathbb{E}[(x_0 + \sum \Delta x_i + \sum \epsilon_i^x - \mathbb{E}[x_0] - \sum \mathbb{E}[\Delta x_i] - \sum \mathbb{E}[\epsilon_i^x])^2] \\
&= \mathbb{E}[(\sum \epsilon_i^x - \sum \mathbb{E}[\epsilon_i^x])^2] \\
&= \mathbb{E}[\sum(\epsilon_i^x - \mathbb{E}[\epsilon_i^x])^2] \\
&= \sum \mathbb{E}[(\epsilon_i^x - \mathbb{E}[\epsilon_i^x])^2] + 2\sum_{i<j}\sum \mathbb{E}[(\epsilon_i^x - \mathbb{E}[\epsilon_i^x])(\epsilon_j^x - \mathbb{E}[\epsilon_j^x])].
\end{aligned}
$$

Because the random variables ϵ_i^x and ϵ_j^x are independent, the second term is zero, and the sum simplfies to $N\sigma^2$. A similar expression can be developed for σ_{yy}. It is straightforward to show that $\sigma_{xy} = \sigma_{yx} = 0$. The resulting covariance matrix

$$
\Sigma = N \begin{bmatrix} \sigma^2 & 0 \\ 0 & \sigma^2 \end{bmatrix}
$$

reflects the independence of errors in the x and y directions and grows without bound as N increases. In terms of even the simple point robot shown here small errors in each motion eventually result in a position estimate that has a significant error and grows without bounds as $N \to \infty$. Maintaining an estimate of the pose of the vehicle requires reference to external features or events that can be used to overcome the errors associated with movement.

To consider the sensing problem in its simplest case, suppose that the robot can sense – through the point-robot equivalent of GPS – its x and y positions as x_m and y_m respectively and that it can do this at every time instance. Then the robot requires some technique to combine the local estimate of the robot's position (obtained through an understanding of the motion noise process) and the current measurements (which are likely corrupted by some sensor noise process). One straightforward strategy would be to choose the estimate of the robot's state with the smallest error. If the error associated with (x_m, y_m) is smaller than the error associated with the robot's pose estimate available from odometry, then (x_m, y_m) should be used as the best estimate of the robot's pose. More general mathematical techniques exist to combine these two estimates under various models of the noise and measurement process (see Section 4.9.1).

2.4   Sensing for a Point Robot

In order to deal with the realities of navigation and localization, a robot requires some mechanism to sense its environment. Chapters 4 and 5 deal with visual and non-visual sensors, respectively. Here we consider a very simple (abstract) sensor. Suppose that the point robot has a single range sensor that it can point in any direction and that the sensor returns the distance to the first object that it encounters along that direction and it returns infinity if no obstacle exists in that direction. Furthermore, let us assume that the robot's global orientation, like its position, is known.

This is an extremely powerful sensor and is a theoretical abstraction of a laser point scanner – a commonly used sensor in robotics. The robot can point this sensor in the direction it wishes to move to ensure that the space ahead is clear. A robot executing the Bug2 algorithm might use such a sensor to determine the local shape of an obstacle

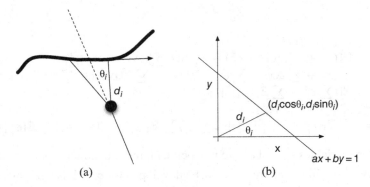

Figure 2.2. Equipping a point robot with a sensor. (a) The robot obtains range measurements d_i in different directions (given by θ_i).v(b) These measurements can be integrated to estimate the orientation of the object in front of the robot.

in order to determine how to move and follow the boundary of the obstacle (see Figure 2.2). Suppose that the robot is stationary in a static environment and fires its sensor in a number of different directions. The sensor obtains a collection of measurements $\{(\theta_i, d_i)\}$. Given this sensor, the robot can take measurements in a selected set of orientations in the direction in which the robot is moving and compute the local distance to, and orientation of, the surface "just in front" of the robot. This computation can be phrased as a least squares minimization under the assumption that all measurements came from a single surface. Define the origin of a coordinate system at the robot's current location, and define θ as the angle between the direction in which the robot is moving and the sensor direction. Then sensor readings correspond to surface readings at $(d_i \cos(\theta_i), d_i \sin(\theta_i))$. Let the equation of the the surface be given by $ax + by = 1$; then the solution for (a, b) can be written as

$$
\begin{bmatrix}
d_1 \cos(\theta_1) & d_1 \sin(\theta_1) \\
d_2 \cos(\theta_2) & d_2 \sin(\theta_2) \\
\cdots & \cdots \\
d_n \cos(\theta_n) & d_n \sin(\theta_n)
\end{bmatrix}
\begin{bmatrix}
a \\
b
\end{bmatrix}
=
\begin{bmatrix}
1 \\
1 \\
\cdots \\
1
\end{bmatrix}.
$$

If the measurements are without error, then this will be an overconstrained but consistent system, which can be solved by choosing any two measurements. In practice, however, there is likely to be some noise in the estimation process and a process that combines these noisy measurements is required. Writing

$$
\mathbf{A} =
\begin{bmatrix}
d_1 \cos(\theta_1) & d_1 \sin(\theta_1) \\
d_2 \cos(\theta_2) & d_2 \sin(\theta_2) \\
\cdots & \cdots \\
d_n \cos(\theta_n) & d_n \sin(\theta_n)
\end{bmatrix},
$$

$$
\mathbf{X} =
\begin{bmatrix}
a \\
b
\end{bmatrix},
$$

and

$$\mathbf{B} = \begin{bmatrix} 1 \\ 1 \\ \cdots \\ 1 \end{bmatrix},$$

then we can write this expression more compactly as

$$\mathbf{AX} = \mathbf{B}.$$

This can be solved using standard least-squares minimization techniques [e.g., $\mathbf{X} = (\mathbf{A}'\mathbf{A})^{-1}\mathbf{A}'\mathbf{B}$]. Once the equation of the surface near the line of motion has been obtained, this can be used to guide the motion of the robot. Note that it is important to only choose data measurements that correspond to a single surface in front of the robot, and more generally that the noise process does not contain outliers.

Given this type of sensor it is possible to obtain some of the information needed to execute the Bug2 algorithm. The sensor can determine the distance to the object in front of the robot and, for sufficiently smooth surfaces, can determine the trajectory the robot should follow to circumnavigate the object. Note that objects with sharp convexities will require alternative sensing and navigation strategies in order to successfully navigate around such objects.

Individual sensors present specific constraints and properties in order to interpret the sensor data. Some sensors – such as the simulated sensor considered here – obtain range information. Other sensors obtain more indirect information, such as bearing. The realities of sensors based on non-visual sensors are considered in Chapter 4, and sensors based on vision are considered in Chapter 5.

2.5 Mapping for a Point Robot

Suppose that a point robot operates in a plane within which there exist a number of stationary beacons that emit unique signals that allow the robot to obtain range but not direction to the landmarks. How can a robot construct a map of the locations of these beacons?

It is instructive to note that the range information provided by the sensor is sufficient to localize the location of a beacon to a circle on the plane (see Figure 2.3), but it is insufficient to allow the robot to localize the beacon to a single point. By moving the robot, it is possible to localize the beacon. When the robot moves and re-senses the beacon, a second set of constraints is obtained. This is illustrated in Figure 2.4(a). Each constraint limits the location of the beacon to a circle. The intersection of two circles on the plane provides two possible locations for the beacon. As the robot moves again, an addition circular constraint is identified, and the location of the beacon can be reduced to a single point (Figure 2.4).

As the robot moves, some beacons may come into the sensor's range and others may leave the sensor's range. After two motions of the robot resulting in unique locations in space, however, the actual location of all beacons that remain in range of the robot will be mapped. It is important to observe that for the technique to work, the robot must be able to continually estimate its motion in order to integrate the constraints over time. As observed

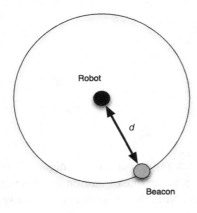

Figure 2.3. Range information. A robot determines that it is a distance d from a beacon that localizes the beacon to a circle with the robot at its center with radius d.

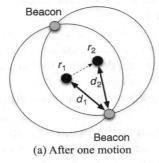

(a) After one motion

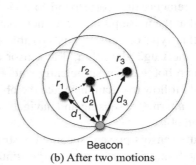

(b) After two motions

Figure 2.4. When the robot moves (indicated by the dashed line) and senses the beacon again (a), it obtains an additional set of constraints as to the location of the robot. Each set of constraints limits the possible location of the robot to a circle. The intersection of these two constraints (circles) restricts the location to one of two locations. When the robot moves a second time (b), a third constraint is introduced, and as long as the trajectory of the robot is not chosen poorly, the intersection of three circles obtains a single point as the location of the beacon.

earlier, in practice such motion will be corrupted with noise, which could corrupt the map, and the mapping process is likely to diverge for sufficiently long paths.

2.6   SLAM for a Point Robot

The mapping algorithm presented in the previous section will work for short-duration motions, but it may fail for longer motion sequences as the estimate of the robot's position will become corrupted, which in turn will corrupt the robot's map of the environment. In order to deal with both localization and mapping information contained in the sensor, readings must also be used to continually refine the map and the estimate of the robot's position. This is referred to as simultaneous localization and mapping: SLAM.

Although various approaches could be used to perform this refinement, consider the following straightforward approach. At any point in the process of map construction described here, there is a set of visible beacons with known locations (x_i^b, y_i^b), each of which is measured to be a distance d_i from the robot that is estimated to be at

(x, y). There is an instantaneous error in the visible portion of the map and the pose of the robot:

$$\text{ERR} = \sum((x_i^b - x)^2 + (y_i^b - y)^2 - d_i)^2.$$

A perfect local map would have an error (ERR) of zero. The local (sensable) map and robot estimate can be refined by computing $\partial\text{ERR}/\partial x$, $\partial\text{ERR}/\partial y$, $\partial\text{ERR}/\partial x_i^b$, and $\partial\text{ERR}/\partial y_i^b$ and updating the current estimates of x_i^b, y_i^b, x, and y by an amount proportional to the corresponding partial derivative.

Although this approach is only approximate – it does not model the hidden interaction between currently visible beacons and the state of the robot and the state of beacons that are not currently visible – it does illustrate that it is possible to refine both the map and the estimate of the robot's position within a common framework.

2.7   Looking Forward

This chapter presented some of the fundamental computational tasks in autonomous robotics. Rather than consider the problems in their full complexity, here the problems have been simplified in terms of the complexity of the robot, its sensors, and the environment. Perhaps the most fundamental assumption made in the models presented in this chapter is that the robot can be abstracted to a point. The robot has no preferred direction of motion. There is no concept of moving forward or backward, only the concept of motion. As will be made clear in later chapters, the point robot model is insufficient to model real robotic systems where the state of the robot must often encode other information, including its orientation. Even though the models and algorithms considered here are simplified versions of models and algorithms developed later in this text, the simple model used here illustrates the nature of the problems encountered and some of the basic techniques that can be applied to address them. The next few chapters examine some of the real constraints that make robotics problems more difficult than those considered here.

2.8   Further Reading

Further details on the realities of robot hardware and the constraints that these place on later algorithms can found in Chapter 3. Issues related to sensing and the limits of sensors can be found in Chapters 4 and 5. Issues related to path planning are discussed in Chapter 7 and localization is considered in Chapter 9. Map building and SLAM are considered in Chapter 10.

2.9   Problems

1. Extend the `drive_to_goal.py` code in cpmr_ch2 so that it takes in as parameters the maximum velocity and gain values. Tune these values so that the robot moves at a constant velocity of 40 cm/sec. The current code applies the speed limit separately in the x and y dimensions. Change this so that it applies this limit to the magnitude of the velocity.

2. Develop a version of the Bug2 algorithm that assumes that the world is an infinite plane with non-intersecting circular obstacles at known locations and with know radii. How did you integrate the radius of the circular obstacles with the circular radius of your robot? Implement your algorithm in gazebo for circular obstacles. Your code should accept a map of obstacles (x,y,r) and place them on the plane. There exists code in cpmr_ch2 to support loading maps into gazebo that you might find helpful.

3. Given the solution to the problem above, compare the performance of the algorithm when the robot circumnavigates obstacles using a spiral search versus using the counterclockwise solution. For the spiral search, first try circumnavigating the obstacle (for a distance dk) in a clockwise direction, then try a counterclockwise direction (for a distance $2dk$). If the robot does not solve the search problem (either fully circumnavigate the obstacle or find a point at which it can continue to move to the goal), then increase dk and repeat.

4. Develop a formal model of the worst-cost (longest) path that the Bug2 algorithm will develop when planning a path. Suppose that there are n obstacles in the environment, that the perimeter of obstacle i is given by P_i, and that $|ST| = D$.

5. Show that the nondiagonal elements of the covariance matrix for the motion model of the point robot introduced in this chapter are zero.

6. Build a simple simulator for a point robot that allows the user to specify (via some simple user interface) the next motion $(\Delta x, \Delta y)$ that the robot will execute. When the robot makes this execution, simulate the motion of the robot N times, but for each simulation generate a new instance of the robot but moved by $(\Delta x + \epsilon^x, \Delta y + \epsilon^y)$, where ϵ^x and ϵ^y are random numbers drawn from a normal (Gaussian) distribution $N(0, \sigma)$. Apply this same process at each time step to each instance of the robot. That is, rather than represent the robot as a single point, represent it as a cloud of points where each point in the cloud corresponds to a potential motion of the robot corrupted by noise. As the number of points in the cloud will grow without limit, after each movement, keep only N of the possible points. Choose which ones to keep by choosing from the available points randomly. Compare the distribution of points with the covariance matrix based on the motions performed.

7. The process of sensing the local surface orientation shown in Section 2.4 assumes a perfect sensor. The pseudo-inverse solution described is robust to independent additive noise but is not robust to systematic noise.

   (a) Show that the approach is robust to Gaussian additive noise. Corrupt each measurement d_i through the addition of noise drawn from $N(0, \sigma)$. How does the accuracy of the surface estimate (a, b) change with different values of σ?

   (b) Instead of assuming random Gaussian noise, assume instead that rather than there being a single surface defined by (a, b) there are two parallel surfaces, one defined by (a, b) and the second one defined by (da, db). Let the second surface be closer than the first and be semitransparent (k percent of all sensor measurements taken strike the semitransparent surface, and the remainder

```
best-model = {}
best-model-fit = 0
FOR i:=1..MAX-ITERATIONS
  inliers = randomly-selected-subset of dataset
  remainder = dataset - inliers
  consensus = inliers
  inlier-model = fit inliers to model
  FOR elements of remainder DO
    IF element fits the inlier-model THEN
      add element to consensus
    END FOR
  IF |consensus| > MIN-CONSENSUS-SIZE THEN
    consensus-model = fit consensus to model
    IF consensus-model-fit > best-model-fit THEN
      best-model = consensus-model
      best-model-fit = consensus-model-fit
    END IF
  END IF
END FOR
```

Listing 2.3. A simple version of the RANSAC algorithm.

strike the "real" surface behind). How does the accuracy of the surface estimate of (a, b) change with different values of k and d?

One approach to solving problems such as this is through the use of **RANSAC** (Random Sample Consensus) [273]. The RANSAC algorithm operates by picking a random subset of points from the dataset and then uses these to fit whatever analytic model is being used (e.g., for surface fitting, it fits a surface to these points). The remaining points in the dataset are then compared to the resulting fit, outliers are rejected if too far from the fitted model, and inliers are used to refine the fit. This process is repeated with different initial random sets retaining the best fit. (See Listing 2.3 for a simplified version of RANSAC.) Use RANSAC to solve for (a, b) for different values of k. How did you choose the number of iterations, the size of the inlier set, and the minimum size of the consensus set?

8. This question explores dealing with noise in odometry in the `block_robot` provided in the online resource. You first create a noise-corrupted version of the odometry, and then use a GPS-like system to correct for this error. You will want to create your own package to encapsulate at the question.

   (a) Write a ROS node that subscribes to the odometry data produced by Gazebo (published as `/odom`) and publish Odometry messages on `/noisy_odom` at the same rate as `/odom`. `/odom` data is perfect data from Gazebo. `/noisy_odom` should corrupt the Odometry data as follows. For the first odometry message, the corrupted version is just the input message. For subsequent messages, the corrupted state is the previous corrupted state estimate plus the true motion (estimated by the change in `odom`), corrupted by independent additive zero mean Gaussian noise in each of the (x, y, θ) channels. The standard deviation for each channel is given by an input standard deviation per meter of travel in x and y and per radian of rotation in θ. That is, if the σ for x was 0.01 (1 cm per meter) and if the robot moved 2 m since the last odometry message, then the Gaussian noise for motion in x would be drawn from $N(0,0.02)$.

(b) Demonstrate the effect of different noise levels by commanding the robot to drive forward for 10 seconds at 0.2 m/s, and then rotate 90 degrees clockwise at 30 degrees/s, repeated four times to form a square. Test with $\sigma = 0$ (no noise) and 10 other sigma values (your choice). How much odometry error does it take for the robot to become unable to execute the square motion? A graph of the published /odom and /noisy_odom values will help here.

(c) Visualize this error by generating in Gazebo targets (e.g., cylinders) every 10 seconds at the /odom and /noisy_odom positions.

(d) To correct the odometry error in the robot, place ($N = 3$) beacons in the world. Create a Gazebo description of a beacon (they should be called /beacon_0, /beacon_1 and so on). The beacons will never move.

(e) Each beacon measures the distance from itself to the corrupted location of the robot. It does this by listening to the corrupted odometry message and knowing where it (the node) is. Whenever a beacon receives an odometry message, the beacon will publish a std_msgs/String message of the form

```
"source {id} location {pos} distance {d}"
```

on /beacon_id/range. Create a node track_robot that will be run on each beacon. The node should take as argument where the beacon is upon which the node is running. Place beacons at (1,1), (2,5), (-5,1). Demonstrate that the track_robot node is working properly.

(f) Write a node estimate_odom that would run on the robot. It subscribes to the /beacon_id/range messages (id 0 through 2). Whenever it receives new messages from all three beacons it should output where it thinks the robot is. Note: wait until all three beacons have refreshed. Also, there are many ways of intersecting three circles. Perhaps the easiest is to intersect two (there are two solutions) and then to see which one has the smallest error in the equation of the third circle.

Part one

Locomotion and Perception

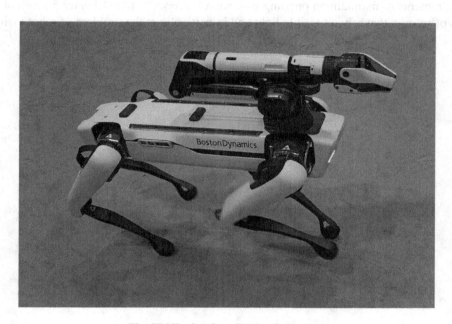

The SPOT robot from Boston Dynamics.

If a mobile robot is to do anything within its environment it must be able to move about within in, and it must be able to make observations. The next three chapters consider exactly these capabilities and how they can be achieved.

Chapter 3 examines the problems involved in getting a robot to move. Although the vast majority of mobile robots are wheeled, technologies based on aquatic, limbed, or flying robots, and even robots based on rocket propulsion, exist. Regardless of the technology used to move the robot, two fundamental problems need to be addressed:

- Given the actions that are available, described as control inputs, how does the robot move? Connecting actions to motions in space is the domain of the **forward kinematics** problem. Forward kinematics alone provides a solution when we can neglect the forces and physics of the problem (e.g., acceleration, mass, interia). If the solution involves an investigation of the forces, then this is known as the **forward dynamics** problem.
- Given a desired motion, which control inputs should be chosen? This is known as the **inverse kinematics** problem if the forces to be applied are ignored. If the

solution involves an investigation of the forces to be applied, then this is known as the **inverse dynamics** problem.

These tasks are considered in some detail for wheeled and legged vehicles.

A general **dynamic model** for a rigid vehicle of constant mass is developed, and the model is applied to flying, swimming, and space robots.

Chapters 4 and 5 consider the task of enabling a robot to sense its environment. Chapter 4 examines non-visual sensor hardware and the algorithms that are used to transform the raw sensor measurements into information about the robot's environment. This chapter also introduces a number of computational mechanisms that are used to integrate sensor measurements to maintain an ongoing estimate of a robot's state. Chapter 5 looks at the class of sensors that rely on visible light and in particular at the problem of robot vision.

3

Mobile Robot Hardware

"I am completely operational, and all my circuits are functioning perfectly."[1]

A mobile robot is a combination of various physical (hardware) and computational (software) components. In terms of hardware components, a mobile robot can be considered as a collection of subsystems for:

Locomotion: How the robot moves through its environment
Sensing: How the robot measures properties of itself and its environment
Reasoning: How the robot maps these measurements into actions
Communication and human interaction: How the robot communicates with an outside operator/observer.

Later chapters consider the algorithms and representations that make these capabilities possible, while this chapter concentrates on the underlying hardware, with special emphasis on locomotion for wheeled robots.

3.1   Locomotion

locomotion *n*. (Power of) motion from place to place.[2]

Locomotion is the process by which an autonomous robot or vehicle moves. In order to produce motion, forces must be applied to the vehicle. The study of motion in which these forces are modeled is known as **dynamics**, while **kinematics** is the study of the mathematics of motion without considering the forces that affect the motion. That is, kinematics deals with the geometric relationships that govern the system, while dynamics includes the energies and speeds associated with these motions. Here we consider the locomotive strategies of various classes of mobile robots. For wheeled mobile robots, these strategies can often be well described in terms of their kinematics. For legged, space, aquatic, and flying robots, it is usually necessary to consider the locomotive strategies in terms of their dynamics.

Understanding how a vehicle moves in response to its controls is essential for many navigation tasks and underlies the process of **dead reckoning** – estimating the path that the vehicle will travel, given the commands it is given.

---

[1] HAL 9000 commenting on its operational state in the movie 2010.
[2] *The Concise Oxford Dictionary*, Oxford University Press, 1976.

Although many different locomotion strategies have been proposed by mobile robot engineers, a robot's motive system design is typically driven by the application and its domain: How fast must the robot move? Does the robot have to climb structures? Does the robot need to overfly the terrain? Is the application environment smooth or rough?

Based on the application domain, five broad categories of mobile robots have emerged:

Terrestrial: Terrestrial robots are those that travel along the ground. They are designed to take advantage of a solid support surface and gravity. Although the most common type of terrestrial mobile robots are wheeled, robots exist that can walk, climb, roll, use tracks, or slither to move. Terrestrial robots are also known as **ground-contact robots.**

Soft vehicles: Devices that utilize compliance and soft bending structures to move in their environment are known as soft vehicles.

Aquatic: Aquatic robots operate in water, either at the surface or underwater. Most existing aquatic vehicles use either water jets or propellers to provide locomotion. But there are many other alternatives including the use of tails and flapping surfaces to provide motion. (See [818] and [194] for examples.) Aquatic robotics is a potentially important application domain since not only is most of Earth's surface covered with water, but much of the ocean is not readily accessible to humans.

Airborne Airborne robot vehicles often mimic existing aircraft or birds. Robotic helicopters, quadcopters, tail sitters, fixed-wing aircraft, robotically controlled parachutes, and dirigibles have been developed. Flying robots share many issues with aquatic robots.

Space Some robots are designed to operate in the microgravity of outer space. Various locomotive devices enable these robots to move about their environment. The two main classes of robot are those that move by climbing (over a larger vehicle) and those that are independently propelled (known as **free flyers**).

3.1.1   Batteries
"Atomic batteries to power. Turbines to speed.[3]"

Without some sort of motive power, a robot is just an inert piece of hardware. The vast majority of autonomous systems rely on batteries to provide electrical power. Batteries store chemical energy and convert this to electrical energy as required. When discharged, some batteries (and almost all batteries used in autonomous robots) can be recharged by providing an electrical current to invert the chemical action that takes place during battery discharge. Different battery chemistries support different discharge and recharge paradigms, but eventually all batteries reach a point at which they cannot be effectively recharged and must be replaced.

Given their relatively low cost, commercial batteries are commonly used in autonomous systems. For large vehicles, batteries based on sealed lead-acid "gell cell"

---

[3] The Boy Wonder to Batman as the Batmobile powers up.

batteries are common. These batteries provide good power performance at low cost and are easily recharged. They are also heavy, making them unsuitable for smaller vehicles. For smaller vehicles, technologies based on lithium ion, nickel cadmium (NiCad), or nickel metal hydride (NiMH) technologies are popular. Often these batteries were originally designed for cordless appliances such as power tools, laptop computers, or communications equipment.

The choice of a particular battery for a specific application is extremely difficult. Batteries are specified in terms of their storage capacity, defined in terms of amp hours (AHrs). In theory a 6 AHr battery will deliver 6 amps for 1 hour. Unfortunately this is unlikely to be true in practice. Batteries deteriorate quickly with repeated use, and performance depends on storage, temperature, and the way in which they are discharged. As batteries discharge they may undergo voltage fluctuations that can cause problems for sensitive electronic equipment.

3.1.2   Motors

Most robots utilize servo or stepper motors [320, 847] to convert electrical energy into mechanical energy. That being said, there are other options for generating mechanical motion, including pneumatic and piezoelectric devices. Revolute devices, such as most servo or stepper motors, are designed to generate rotational or **revolute** motion. If necessary, this motion can then be converted into linear or **prismatic** motion through an appropriate mechanical system.

Stepper Motors   Stepper motors provide a mechanism for position (shaft orientation) and speed control without the use of complex sensors to monitor the motion of the motor. Stepper motors operate in such a manner that the output shaft moves a controlled amount each time a pulse is sent to the motor. By controlling the pulses that are sent to the motor, it can be made to follow a desired output profile. The basic strategy of a stepper motor is to switch on one of a sequence of different magnetic fields (electromagnets) in a specific order. This order is chosen so as to cause the output shaft to rotate to specific orientations in turn (see Figure 3.1). The basic process of controlling a servo motor involves providing power to the various electromagnets in an appropriately timed sequence. This can be done using either a controller that generates this sequence of pulses or some available output port on a computer [e.g., General-Purpose Input/Output (GPIO) pins on a microprocessor]. Note that stepper motors cannot monitor the output shaft orientation and thus cannot monitor external actions of the shaft, for example, whether it is back driven.

Servo Motors   Servo motors combine a standard electrical motor (either AC or DC, although DC servo motors are more common in robotic applications) with a shaft orientation sensor. A basic motor is unable to estimate how far (or how fast) it has turned. In order to control the output shaft of the motor, it is necessary to monitor the orientation of the shaft using some sort of external sensor. Many different sensors can be used to monitor the motion of the motor, but optical shaft encoders are common for larger

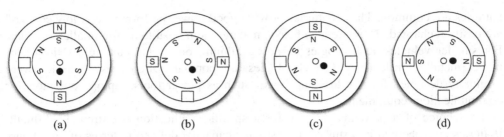

(a)   (b)   (c)   (d)

Figure 3.1. Stepper motor. As the poles of the stator (the external stationary part of the motor) are charged in the sequence (a)–(d), the rotor rotates to align with the changing magnetic field. Note that in the example above the rotor turns 30° counterclockwise for each change in the magnetic field and that the rotor can be turned either clockwise or counterclockwise.

Figure 3.2. Optical encoder pattern. Fixed sensors monitor three tracks attached to the rotating shaft. These patterns are read optically (hence *optical* shaft encoder). As the shaft rotates, pulse trains occur on these channels at a frequency proportional to the shaft speed, and the phase relationship between the channels encodes the orientation of rotation. Given the known radius of the output shaft, by counting the pulses and monitoring the phase, one can estimate the relative motion of the shaft. The index pulse channel defines a zero position.

servo motors, while smaller hobby motors – and especially motors for radio-controlled (RC) toys – use a potentiometer. Given their origin, RC potentiometer servo motors are typically not designed to rotate more than 360°, and although it is usually straightforward to modify such servo motors to rotate more than 360°. The sensor only senses a small number (perhaps even one) full rotation of the output shaft. Optical shaft encoders are multi-turn sensors that use optical index counting to monitor the output shaft orientation (see Figure 3.2). Many encoders also include an absolute index or reference mark in order to provide absolute rather than relative shaft orientation and absolute orientation encoders.

Controlling either a stepper or servo motor requires providing controlled signals to the motor and, for servo motors, monitoring the measured motion of the motor. Given their open loop design, controllers for stepper motors can be extremely simple. For servo motors, a more complex **motor controller** is required. Motor controllers differ widely in their complexity and are either mounted within a controlling computer or are self-contained and communicate via some protocol to an external computer. Controllers typically accept a desired output position, velocity, or motion profile and ensure that the axis motion meets this requirement. Power for the motor itself may be provided by the motor controller directly, or for high-power situations a separate **servo amplifier** may be required.

3.1.3 Servo Motor Control

Given some mechanism for turning an output shaft, the problem then becomes that of devising a mechanism to drive the output shaft to a particular orientation as a function of time. Perhaps the simplest way of accomplishing this is via **open loop control**. Under open loop control, the desired output value of the shaft is used to compute an appropriate control (e.g., speed or position) without monitoring the true value of the shaft. Under open loop control, unexpected load on the shaft or other disturbances will cause the device to deviate from the desired motion.

The alternative to open loop control is **closed loop control**. Under closed loop control, the output value of the system is monitored and the error between the desired and current value is used to drive a controller that adjusts the device so as to match the desired value. The critical observation here is that **feedback** from the true value of the system is used to adjust the motion of the device.

It is important to observe that it is not possible to instantaneously change the position or velocity of an output shaft, and limits to changes in position and velocity are a function of properties of the motor and the load on the shaft. As a result, closed loop controllers attempt to generate an output value that is a close approximation of the desired output value while at the same time attempting to reject disturbances caused by external factors such as unmodeled loads.

Although there are many different approaches to the design of a controller, a commonly used mechanism is the **proportional integral derivative controller** (PID controller). A PID controller adjusts the control parameter based on an error signal $e(t)$ between the desired value of the system (the **setpoint**) and the measured output value (Figure 3.3):

$$control(t) = K_p e(t) + K_i \int e(t)dt + K_d \frac{d}{dt}e(t). \tag{3.1}$$

As shown in Figure 3.3 and equation (3.1), a PID controller controls the system via three different terms: a proportional term (controlled by K_p), which handles immediate error, an integral term (controlled by K_i), which integrates errors from the past, and a derivative term (controlled by K_d), which estimates error into the future. Tuning a PID controller involves choosing values for the gains K_p, K_i, and K_d in order to ensure that

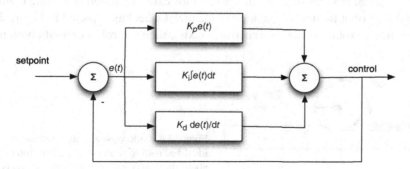

Figure 3.3. A proportional integral derivative (PID) controller. Given a desired value, a PID controller determines a control value based on the error between the setpoint and the control, using a proportional (K_p), an integral (K_i) and a differential (K_d) term.

the output of the system matches the desired value as closely as possible while rejecting disturbances.

Given the fundamental importance of servo motor control to a large range of applications, it is not surprising that there exists a large literature dealing with servo motor control in general (e.g., [124, 455, 586]) and in the application of servo motor control to robotic systems (e.g., [193]). Once some mechanism to generate controlled motion has been developed, it remains to use this motion to drive the vehicle in a controlled manner.

Joint Space and Actuator Space   It is important to observe that at the lowest level, control is effected at the motor level. That is, the controller that is providing effective control of the motion is providing control at the level of rotation of the joint (in joint space). This space may be quite different from the space defined by the actuator. For example, a rotary motor may be used to generate linear motion through an appropriate gearing system. In this case the joint space might be defined in terms of the angular rotation of the output shaft of the motor, while the actuator would be described in terms of the linear extension (motion) of the device.

3.1.4   Gears

Motors – and especially servo motors – often provide a high maximum rotational velocity but at a relatively low torque. Gears and similar devices such as belts can be used to exchange rotational speed for torque and to change the direction and type of motion. A critical issue in the design of the gear chain is the issue of **backlash**. When gears mesh there is play between adjacent gear shafts. This play occurs due to non-ideal design of the gears and slight misalignment in shaft orientation and spacing. The net effect of this play is that small rotations in the input shaft may not result in any rotation in the output shaft. This introduces an error in the estimate of the orientation of the output shaft. Zero backlash gear systems (anti-backlash gears) can be deployed to reduce or eliminate backlash but typically at an increased manufacturing cost.

3.1.5   Wheeled Mobile Robots

Mechanical devices such as wheels or limbs exploit friction or ground contact in order to enable a robot to move. Consider an idealized wheel as depicted in Figure 3.4. If the wheel is free to rotate about its axis (the x axis), then the robot exhibits preferential

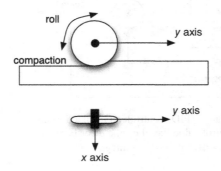

Figure 3.4. Side view and top view of an idealized rolling wheel. For a wheel rotating about the x axis, motion along the y axis is known as roll. Any component of motion in the x direction, perpendicular to the direction in which the wheel is rolling, is known as lateral slip. An ideal wheel moves along the roll direction only.

rolling motion in one direction (in the direction of the y axis) and a certain amount of **lateral slip**.

One of the most basic and prevalent motion estimation techniques used on wheeled mobile robots is **odometry**, which is the estimation of vehicle displacement by measuring how much the wheels have turned. The simplest case is a single freely rotating wheel. In the case of an ideal wheel, this implies a distance $2\pi r$ has been covered on the ground for each rotation of a wheel with radius r. In practice, even the behavior of a single wheel is substantially more complicated than this. Individual wheels are not necessarily mounted so as to be perpendicular, nor are they aligned with the normal straight-ahead direction of the vehicle. When a pair of wheels is set so that their leading edges are pointed slightly toward each other, the wheel pair is said to have **toe-in**. When they are pointed slightly away from each other, they are said to have **toe-out**. The amount of **toe** is usually expressed in degrees. A **toe** value of zero (the wheels point parallel to each other) results in minimum power loss and reduced tire wear. For high-performance vehicles, however, a small amount of toe-out is preferred because this enhances performance in turn initiation. The angle that the steering pivot axis is rotated from the vertical as viewed from the side of the vehicle is known as **caster** or **castor**. A positive castor (the steering axis is deflected toward the rear of the vehicle) enhances straight-ahead stability while moving forward (see **castor wheel** later in this section), while negative castor (the steering axis is deflected toward the front of the vehicle) makes steered wheels less stable. Individual wheels may be mounted deflected from the vertical as viewed from the rear of the vehicle. This deflection is known as **camber**. If the wheels are deflected so that their tops lean toward the vehicle, then the wheel has **negative camber**. High-performance vehicles are constructed with slightly negative camber in order to provide better performance while turning.

In addition to issues related to precise wheel orientation and lateral slip, insufficient traction can also lead to slipping or sliding in the direction of the wheel's motion, which makes an estimate of the distance traveled imprecise. Additional factors arise due to **compaction** of the terrain (see Figure 3.4), and cohesion between the surface and the wheel. Since these factors depend on variable characteristics of the terrain, it is very difficult to estimate *accurately* elapsed distance directly from wheel rotation. Because deviation from the ideal model occurs most commonly when the wheel has forces applied to it (e.g., to accelerate or de-accelerate), a light wheel that is not powered or load bearing can be employed specifically to estimate distance traveled.

The process of estimating odometry can be traced back to ancient times. The Roman engineer and architect Vitruvius describes a wheeled device for measurement known as a **hodometer** [588]. This was a wheeled cart whose axis rotation was monitored by a geared system that caused balls to drop as the cart moved a given distance forward. Modern-day odometers typically use more advanced technology to count wheel revolutions, but the underlying principle is the same.

Although wheels can be quite complex, consider a vehicle with a number of ideal wheels with zero camber, castor, and toe in contact with the ground surface. For all of the wheels in contact with the ground to roll, the motion of each of the vehicle's wheels must be along its own y axis (Figure 3.5). Thus for a wheeled mobile robot (WMR) to exhibit rolling motion, there must exist a point around which each wheel on the vehicle follows a circular course. This point is known as the **instantaneous center of curvature** (ICC)

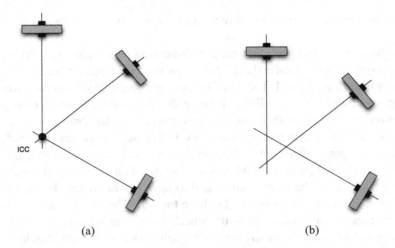

(a)   (b)

Figure 3.5. Instantaneous center of curvature (ICC). (a) The three wheels are arranged such that the line drawn through the roll axis of each wheel intersects at a single point (the ICC). (b) No such point exists. A robot relying on the wheels in (a) can exhibit rolling motion, while a robot relying on the wheel arrangement in (b) cannot.

or the **instantaneous center of rotation** (ICR). For a vehicle to change its ICC, some property of the wheels, such as individual wheel orientations with respect to their vertical axis, must be changed. In practice it is quite straightforward to identify the ICC because it must lie on a line coincident with the roll axis of each wheel that is in contact with the ground. Various mechanisms to change the ICC are possible, and a number of these are discussed later in this chapter.

If all of the wheels in contact with the ground are to exhibit **rolling contact**, then not only must the ICC exist, but each wheel's velocity must be consistent with a rigid rotation of the entire vehicle about the ICC. A vehicle located on a plane has three degrees of freedom; an (x, y) position and a heading or orientation θ.[4] This triplet (x, y, θ) is often referred to as the **pose** of the robot on the plane.

Mobile robots usually do not have complete independent control over all three pose parameters and must undergo complex maneuvers in order to reach a particular goal pose. Consider parallel parking an automobile as an example. In order to park an automobile in a specific spot, the operator may have to perform a complex series of maneuvers, and the maneuvers required depend critically on the nature of the environment and the configuration of the vehicle. In a car it is not possible to change the pose of the vehicle arbitrarily, nor are changes in position independent of the vehicle orientation. This is an example of a **non-holonomic constraint**, which is discussed in some detail in Section 7.1.1.

Some lightweight vehicles are equipped with additional wheels or contact points that provide support but do not contribute to either steering or propulsion. Known generally as

---

[4] In this book we will take $\theta = 0$ to imply that the robot is facing along the $+x$ axis and treat counterclockwise rotations as being positive.

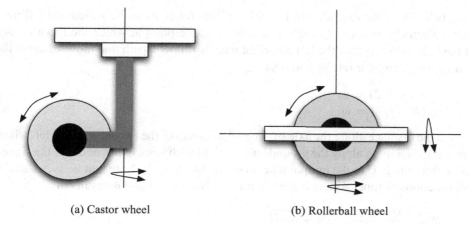

(a) Castor wheel   (b) Rollerball wheel

Figure 3.6. Castor wheels.

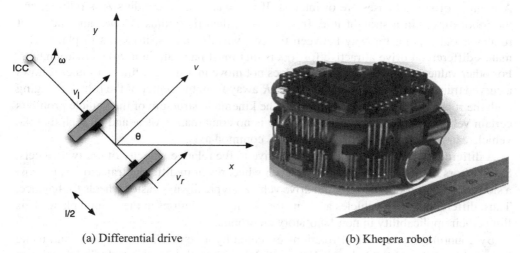

(a) Differential drive   (b) Khepera robot

Figure 3.7. Differential drive kinematics. A differential drive robot controls its pose by providing independent velocity control to the left v_l and right v_r wheels. Most differential drive robots use castor wheels for stability. (b) Appears with the kind permission of A. Herzog.

castor wheels (see Figure 3.6), these wheels can typically be ignored in the computation of a vehicle's kinematics.

Differential Drive Differential drive is perhaps the simplest possible drive mechanism for a ground contact mobile robot. Often used on small, low cost, indoor robots such as the TuteBot [396] or Khepera [412], larger commercial bases such as the Clearpath Dingo D utilize this technology as well. As depicted in Figure 3.7, a differential drive robot consists of two wheels mounted on a common axis controlled by separate motors.

Consider how the controlling wheel velocities determine the vehicle's motion. Under differential drive, for each of the two drive wheels to exhibit rolling motion the robot must rotate about a point that lies on the common axis of the two drive wheels. By varying the relative velocity of the two wheels, the point of this rotation can be varied and different vehicle trajectories chosen. At each instant in time, the point at which the robot rotates must have the property that the left and right wheels follow a path that moves around the ICC at the same angular rate ω, and thus

$$\omega(R + l/2) = v_r$$
$$\omega(R - l/2) = v_l,$$

where l is the distance along the axle between the centers of the two wheels, the left wheel moves with velocity v_l along the ground and the right with velocity v_r, and R is the signed distance from the ICC to the midpoint between the two wheels. Note that v_l, v_r, ω, and R are all functions of time. At any instant in time, solving for R and ω results in

$$R = \frac{l}{2}\frac{(v_l + v_r)}{(v_r - v_l)}, \quad \omega = \frac{v_r - v_l}{l}.$$

A number of special cases are of interest. If $v_l = v_r$, then the radius R is infinite, and the robot moves in a straight line. If $v_l = -v_r$, then the radius is zero, and the robot rotates about a point midway between the two wheels, that is, it rotates in place. This makes differential drive attractive for robots that must navigate in narrow environments. For other values of v_l and v_r, the robot does not move in a straight line but rather follows a curved trajectory about a point a distance R away from the center of the robot, changing both the robot's position and orientation. The kinematic structure of the vehicle prohibits certain vehicle motions. For example, there is no combination of v_l and v_r such that the vehicle can move directly along the wheels' common axis.

A differential drive vehicle is very sensitive to the relative velocity of the two wheels. Small errors in the velocity provided to each wheel result in different trajectories, not just a slower or faster robot. Differential drive vehicles typically use castor wheels for balance. Thus, differential drive vehicles are sensitive to slight variations in the ground plane. This limits their applicability in non-laboratory environments.

By counting the number of rotations executed by a vehicle's drive wheels and using knowledge of the wheels' size and the vehicle's kinematics, one can obtain an estimate of the rate of change of position and orientation. Computing absolute coordinates thus involves the integration of such local differential quantities, for example changes in position, orientation, or velocity. When a person walks in a silent odor-free environment with his or her eyes closed, this is the form of position estimation to which they are reduced. In the context of biological systems, this observation of internal parameters (e.g., how many steps are taken) is referred to as **proprioception**.

Keeping track of how much one moves by observing internal parameters *without reference to the external world* is known as **dead reckoning**. This is the technique used to measure the distance traveled by an automobile, using an odometer (note, however, that an odometer does not measure position or distance from a reference point, but only the relative distance traveled). In the context of biology, dead reckoning (such as navigating a room with one's eye closed) is known as **kinesthesia** or as **idiothetic** sensing.

To compute a robot's position x in the idealized error-free case with a velocity vector dx/dt, we use:

$$x = \int_{t_0}^{t_f} \frac{dx}{dt} dt,$$

where the motion takes place over a time interval t_0 through t_f. More generally, for motion information from higher-order derivatives (such as acceleration) we can integrate repeatedly to recover position. This also implies, however, that errors in the sensing or integration process are manifested as higher-order polynomials of the time interval over which we are integrating. For discrete motions, where positional change is expressed by a difference vector δ_i, we can compute the absolute position as

$$x = \Sigma \delta_i.$$

This method of position estimation plays an important part in most mobile robot systems. It can have acceptable accuracy over sufficiently small steps, assuming a suitable terrain and drive mechanism. Thus, from a known starting position, the final position after several motions can be computed. For large or complex motions, however, the unavoidable errors in the individual position estimates have a major consequence. Simple scaling errors can be readily corrected, but more complex errors are essentially impossible to eliminate.

Forward kinematics for differential drive robots Suppose that the robot is at some position (x, y) and "facing" along a line making an angle θ with the x axis (Figure 3.7a). Through manipulation of the control parameters v_l and v_r, the robot can be made to take on different poses. Determining the pose that is reachable given the control parameters is known as the **forward kinematics** problem for the robot. Since v_l and v_r and hence R and ω are functions of time, it is straightforward to show (see Figure 3.8) that if the robot has pose (x, y, θ) at some time t, and if the left and right wheels have ground contact velocities v_l and v_r, respectively, during the period $t \rightarrow t + \delta t$, then the ICC is given by

$$\text{ICC} = (x - R\sin(\theta), y + R\cos(\theta)),$$

and at time $t + \delta t$ the pose of the robot is given by

$$
\begin{bmatrix} x' \\ y' \\ \theta' \end{bmatrix} =
\begin{bmatrix} \cos(\omega\,\delta t) & \sin(\omega\,\delta t) & 0 \\ -\sin(\omega\,\delta t) & \cos(\omega\,\delta t) & 0 \\ 0 & 0 & 1 \end{bmatrix}
\begin{bmatrix} x - \text{ICC}_x \\ y - \text{ICC}_y \\ \theta \end{bmatrix} +
\begin{bmatrix} \text{ICC}_x \\ \text{ICC}_y \\ \omega\,\delta t \end{bmatrix}.
$$

$$(3.2)$$

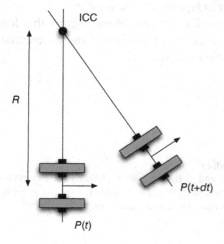

Figure 3.8. Forward kinematics geometry. The ICC is located at $(x, y) + R(\cos(\theta + \pi/2), \sin(\theta + \pi/2))$, which simplifies to $(x - R\sin(\theta), y + R\cos(\theta))$. To compute the position of the robot at $t + \delta t$, the robot must be rotated about the ICC by an amount $\omega\,\delta t$. Mathematically, this can be accomplished by translating the ICC to the origin and rotating the robot about the origin by $\omega\,\delta t$ and then translating back to the ICC [see equation (3.2)].

Equation (3.2) describes the motion of a robot rotating a distance R about its ICC with an angular velocity given by ω. Different classes of robots will provide different expressions for R and ω.[5]

By integrating equation (3.2) from some initial condition (x_0, y_0, θ_0), it is possible to compute where the robot will be at any time t based on the control parameters $v_l(t)$ and $v_r(t)$, that is, to solve the forward kinematics problem for the vehicle. In general, for a robot capable of moving in a particular direction $\theta(t)$ at a given velocity $V(t)$,

$$
\begin{aligned}
x(t) &= \int_0^t V(t) \cos(\theta(t)) dt \\
y(t) &= \int_0^t V(t) \sin(\theta(t)) dt \\
\theta(t) &= \int_0^t \omega(t) dt,
\end{aligned}
\tag{3.3}
$$

and for the special case of a differential drive vehicle,

$$
\begin{aligned}
x(t) &= \tfrac{1}{2} \int_0^t (v_r(t) + v_l(t)) \cos(\theta(t)) dt \\
y(t) &= \tfrac{1}{2} \int_0^t (v_r(t) + v_l(t)) \sin(\theta(t)) dt \\
\theta(t) &= \tfrac{1}{l} \int_0^t (v_r(t) - v_l(t)) dt.
\end{aligned}
\tag{3.4}
$$

A more interesting question, and one somewhat more difficult to answer, is "How can the control parameters be selected so as to have the robot obtain a specific global pose or follow a specific trajectory?" This is known as the task of determining the vehicle's **inverse kinematics**: inverting the kinematic relationship between control inputs and behavior. It is also related to the problem of **trajectory planning** (see Section 7.3).

Inverse kinematics for differential drive robots Equation (3.4) describes a constraint on the velocity of the robot that cannot be integrated into a positional constraint. This is known as a **non-holonomic constraint** and is very difficult to solve in general, although solutions are straightforward for limited classes of the control functions $v_l(t)$ and $v_r(t)$ (see also Section 7.1.1). For example, if it is assumed that $v_l(t) = v_l$, $v_r(t) = v_r$, and $v_l \neq v_r$ then (3.4) yields

$$
\begin{aligned}
x(t) &= \tfrac{l}{2} \frac{v_r + v_l}{v_r - v_l} \sin(\tfrac{t}{l}(v_r - v_l)) \\
y(t) &= -\tfrac{l}{2} \frac{v_r + v_l}{v_r - v_l} \cos(\tfrac{t}{l}(v_r - v_l)) \\
\theta(t) &= \tfrac{t}{l}(v_r - v_l),
\end{aligned}
\tag{3.5}
$$

where $(x, y, \theta)_{t=0} = (0, 0, 0)$. Given a goal time t and goal position (x, y), equation (3.5) solves for v_r and v_l but does not provide for independent control of θ.[6]

Rather than trying to invert (3.4) to solve for the control parameters that lead to a specific robot pose, consider two special cases of the motion of the differential drive vehicle. If $v_l = v_r = v$, then the robot's motion simplifies to

$$
\begin{bmatrix} x' \\ y' \\ \theta' \end{bmatrix} = \begin{bmatrix} x + v \cos(\theta)\, \delta t \\ y + v \sin(\theta)\, \delta t \\ \theta \end{bmatrix},
$$

---

[5] For a quick review of matrix algebra, see Appendix C.
[6] There are actually infinitely many solutions for v_l and v_r from equation (3.5): all correspond to the robot moving about the same circle that passes through $(0, 0)$ at $t = 0$, and (x, y) at $t = t$, but the robot goes around the circle different numbers of times and in different directions.

that is, the robot moves in a straight line, and if we choose $-v_l = v_r = v$, then (3.4) simplifies to

$$\begin{bmatrix} x' \\ y' \\ \theta' \end{bmatrix} = \begin{bmatrix} x \\ y \\ \theta + 2v\,\delta t/l \end{bmatrix},$$

that is, the robot rotates in place. Thus to drive the robot to some goal pose (x, y, θ), the robot can be spun in place until it is aimed at (x, y), then driven forward until it is at (x, y), and then spun in place until the required goal orientation θ is met. These are, of course, not the only possible solutions to the inverse kinematics of a differential drive robot. Other solutions, such as those based on smoothly changing trajectories, are also possible (see [699]).

Synchronous Drive   In a **synchronous drive** robot (also known as *synchro drive*), each wheel is capable of both drive and steering (Figure 3.9). Typical configurations involve three wheels arranged at the vertices of an equilateral triangle, often surmounted by a cylindrical platform. A **steered wheel** is a wheel for which the orientation of the rotational axis of the wheel can be controlled. In a synchronous drive vehicle all of the wheels turn and drive in unison. All of the wheels always point in the same direction and turn at the same rate. This is typically accomplished through the use of a complex collection of belts that physically link the wheels together [657, 580, 218]. In a synchronous drive robot, the vehicle controls the direction in which the wheels point and the rate at which they roll.

A common mechanical arrangement for a synchronous drive vehicle is to use two independent motors – one that rolls all of the wheels forward and one that rotates them (for turning). Since all the wheels remain parallel, synchronous drive robots can rotate about the center of the robot. Thus synchronous drive robots have the ability to directly control

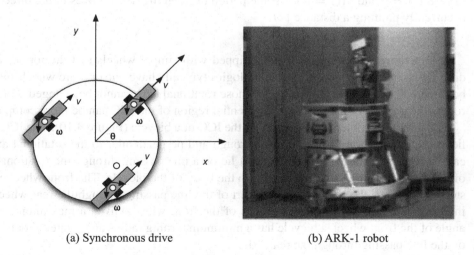

(a) Synchronous drive   (b) ARK-1 robot

Figure 3.9. Synchronous drive kinematics. A synchronous drive robot controls its pose by providing velocity and orientation control to each of its wheels. The ARK-1 robot was built around the Cybermotion Navmaster platform, which utilizes a synchronous drive.

the orientation θ of the robot's pose. The ability to independently control the rotation and forward speed of the robot simplifies overall vehicle control and allows such a robot to serve as a convenient model for the idealized point robot. The Nomadics 200 and the IS Robotics B21 used synchronous drive. As a drive mechanism, synchronous drive has fallen out of favor due its mechanical complexity.

Both differential drive and synchronous drive robots are sensitive to small variations in the ground plane. In the case of differential drive, a small variation in the ground plane may give rise to loss of drive wheel contact and hence errors in robot pose, while in the case of synchronous drive robots, ground plane variations may give rise to wheel alignment problems because the distance each wheel travels is different.

Forward kinematics for synchronous drive Synchronous drive robots rotate about their center at a rate ω, and the translational speed v is also under direct control. Substituting into equation (3.3) yields the forward kinematics of a synchronous drive robot,

$$x(t) = \int_0^t v(t) \cos(\theta(t)) dt$$
$$y(t) = \int_0^t v(t) \sin(\theta(t)) dt$$
$$\theta(t) = \int_0^t \omega(t) dt.$$

Note that the ICC for a synchronous drive robot is always at infinity, and changing the orientation of the wheels manipulates the direction to the ICC.

Inverse kinematics for synchronous drive Because changes in orientation can be completely decoupled from translation, the inverse kinematics of a synchronous drive vehicle are very similar to the special case of the inverse kinematics of the differential drive robot discussed earlier. We can consider two special cases of interest: (1) If $v(t) = 0$ and $\omega(t) = \omega$ for some period δt, then the robot rotates in place by an amount $\omega \delta t$, and (2) if $\omega(t) = 0$ and $v(t) = v$ for some period δt, then the robot moves in the direction it is currently pointing a distance $v\delta t$.

Steered Wheels Robots equipped with simple wheels that do not use either differential or synchronous drive technologies typically have one or more wheels that can be "steered" and one or more wheels whose rotational axis cannot be changed. For these robots the process of calculating the potential region of the ICC can be more complex.

Consider the problem of determining the ICC of a bicycle (Figure 3.10). The ICC must lie at the intersection of lines drawn through and perpendicular to the rotational axis of each wheel. For a bicycle, the ICC must lie on a line passing through the rotational axis of the rear wheel that is perpendicular to the body of the bicycle. The front wheel can be steered, and thus the ICC lies on that part of the line passing through the rear wheel that intersects the line drawn along the axis of the front wheel. Given a maximum steering angle of the front wheel, a bicycle has a minimum turning radius and rotates about a point on the line passing through the rear axle.

If both the front and rear wheels of a bicycle are steerable, then the region of the ICC would be somewhat more complex but can be found geometrically by determining the *loci* of points that satisfy the perpendicular line constraint.

Tricycle, Bogey, and Bicycle Drive   Tricycle, bogey (wagon), and bicycle drive robots have very similar kinematics. Rather than deal with each, we will concentrate on the tricycle case because it is the most common in mobile robots. A typical tricycle drive robot (see [283]) has three wheels with odometers on the two rear wheels, with steering and power provided through the front wheel. Robot motion is controlled by the steering direction α and velocity v provided through the front wheel (see Figure 3.11).

Forward kinematics for steered vehicle If the steered front wheel or set of bogeys is set at an angle α from the straight-ahead direction, the tricycle, bicycle, or bogey steering vehicle will rotate with angular velocity ω about a point lying a distance R along the line perpendicular to and passing through the rear wheels, where R and ω are given respectively by

$$R = d\tan(\pi/2 - \alpha) \text{ and } \omega = v/(d^2 + R^2)^{\frac{1}{2}}$$

and d is the distance from the front to the rear axle as shown in Figure 3.11. Substituting R and ω into equation (3.2) yields the forward kinematics of the vehicle.

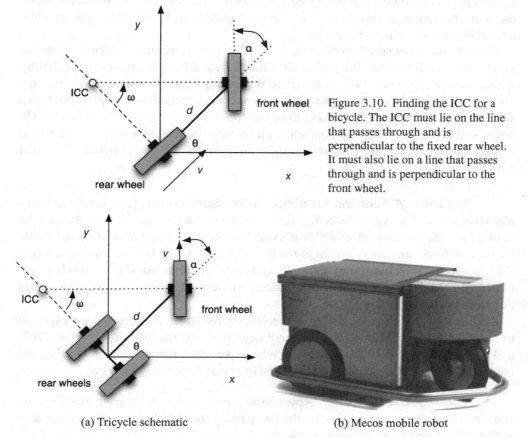

Figure 3.10. Finding the ICC for a bicycle. The ICC must lie on the line that passes through and is perpendicular to the fixed rear wheel. It must also lie on a line that passes through and is perpendicular to the front wheel.

(a) Tricycle schematic   (b) Mecos mobile robot

Figure 3.11. (a) Tricycle kinematics. (b) Tricycle mobile robot. Copyright Mecos Robotics AG. Used with permission.

Inverse kinematics for steered vehicle As with a differential drive vehicle, the general inverse kinematics problem is very difficult, and it is often more profitable to look at special cases. Two cases are of particular interest. If $\alpha = 0$, then the robot drives straight ahead and (3.2) reduces to

$$
\begin{bmatrix} x' \\ y' \\ \theta' \end{bmatrix} = \begin{bmatrix} x + v\cos(\theta)\delta t \\ y + v\sin(\theta)\delta t \\ \theta \end{bmatrix}.
$$

If the vehicle is capable of turning its driving wheel through $\pm 90°$, then we can turn the vehicle in place and

$$
\begin{bmatrix} x' \\ y' \\ \theta' \end{bmatrix} = \begin{bmatrix} x \\ y \\ \theta \pm V\,\delta t/d \end{bmatrix}.
$$

Note that if the front wheel cannot be turned or the robot driven with a $\pm 90°$ turning angle, then it will be impossible to change the orientation of the robot without changing its position. A limited turning range of the wheel results in limits on the radius of curvature of the circle around which the vehicle can drive. This limited radius of curvature appears in most real-world robots that utilize steered wheels. In practice, even without a limit on the attainable radius of curvature, many wheeled mobile robots exhibit translation while attempting to execute a pure rotation.

The inverse kinematics problem can be solved in a manner similar to that for synchronous or differential drive vehicles if the tricycle drive robot is capable of driving with a turning angle of $\pm 90°$. If, however, the turning angle is more limited, then the problem of driving the robot to a particular pose is considerably more complex. Strategies such as those used in parallel parking must then be considered in order to obtain certain poses, and given a complex environment with obstacles there can exist poses that would be obtainable with a larger allowable set of turning angles but are not obtainable with a more restricted set.

Car Drive (Ackermann Steering)   **Ackermann steering** (also known as **king-pin steering**) is the type of steering found on most automobiles. In the Ackermann steering model, the front "steering" wheels each rotate on separate arms so as to be able to rotate different amounts to point at the ICC that must lie on the line passing through the rear axis of the vehicle (see Figure 3.12a). For the wheels to not slip, the inside wheel must turn through a larger angle than the outside one, and the inside wheel travels a shorter distance than the outside one.

Ackermann steering is the preferred mechanism for larger vehicles that are expected to either operate on existing roads or carry large payloads off-road (e.g., Navlab [767] and Autonomoose [628]). The size of the vehicle permits extensive onboard sensing and computation, as well as permitting navigation over reasonably rough terrain.

Forward kinematics for Ackermann drive Under Ackermann steering, the vehicle rotates about a point lying on the line passing through the rear axle at a distance R from the centerline of the vehicle, where

$$
R - l/2 = d\tan(\pi/2 - \alpha_l).
$$

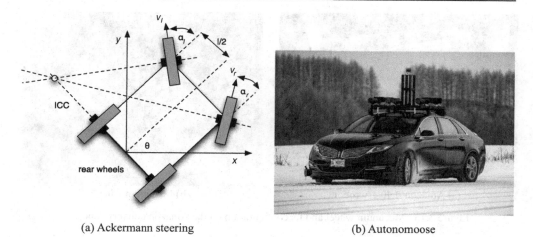

(a) Ackermann steering   (b) Autonomoose

Figure 3.12. Ackermann kinematics. (b) The Autonomoose appears with the kind permission of Steve Waslander.

In order for the wheels to exhibit rolling motion, the other steering wheel must be rotated through an angle α_r where

$$R + l/2 = d \tan(\pi/2 - \alpha_r).$$

In general, all four wheels travel along the ground at different speeds, and specifying the speed of one wheel specifies the velocity of them all. Ackermann steering is sophisticated and subtle, and there is insufficient space to cover it in full detail here. For example, on most cars the wheels rotate not only about a vertical axis, but also about a longitudinal axis in order to change the vertical orientation of the tire with respect to the road.

Inverse kinematics for Ackermann drive The inverse kinematics of an Ackermann vehicle is a highly complex process as can be attested by anyone who has parked a car in a congested urban area. Most Ackermann vehicles have a very large minimum turning radius due to the limited turning range of the wheels. This implies that cars (Ackermann vehicles) must undergo complex maneuvers such as three-point turns and parallel parking in order to move to certain positions.

3.1.6 Complex Wheels

Given the kinematic limitations of simple wheels, one alternative is to construct a robot with complex or compound wheels. Complex wheels are wheels that exhibit more than one preferred rolling direction. Such wheels can result in **omnidirectional robots**. Figure 3.13 shows a **Mecanum wheel** mounted on the Amazon delivery robot. Mechanum wheels are not limited to a single rolling direction through the use of passive rollers mounted on their rim. This allows the wheels to slide laterally, and the robot, to move in an omnidirectional fashion,. Mecanum wheels suffer from limited bump height – the maximum diameter of the object over which they can safely traverse is a function of the roller diameter rather than the overall wheel diameter. An alternative complex wheel

(a) Amazon delivery robot   (b) Mecanum wheel

Figure 3.13. Mecanum wheel and its configuration on the Amazon delivery robot.

approach based on a rolling ball is described in [266]. Actuators roll the ball in the three directions required in order to provide omnidirectional motion.

Omnidirectional robots can be considerably easier to control than robots based on simple wheels because the motion of the robot is independent of the (x, y, θ) pose of the robot. The set of complex wheels is almost endless. As an extreme case consider the robot wheel shaped like a tube tapered at both ends as described in [565]. An autonomous vehicle equipped with such a wheel can change direction by leaning toward one side or the other.

3.1.7   Tracked

Tracked vehicles (Figure 3.14) are similar to differential drive vehicles in terms of their kinematics but are more robust to terrain variations. The two differential wheels are extended into treads that provide a larger contact area with the ground, but rather than assuming perfect rolling contact with the ground surface, tracked vehicles rely on ground slip or skid in order to change direction. The large contact area of the treads in tracked vehicles permits treaded vehicles to cross small voids in the surface and climb steeper gradients than can wheeled vehicles.

That tracked vehicles rely on slip between the treads and the ground surface in order to change orientation introduces complications in terms of using the vehicle kinematics to compute their pose. Although tracked vehicles can be thought of as differential drive vehicles with "extended" wheels, the large amount of slip between the treads and the ground makes it impossible to predict accurately a tracked vehicle's motion from the motion of its treads. Thus, tracked vehicles must rely on some other external mechanism for determining their motion rather than just examining the motion of the treads. One option for overcoming this limitation is to add a castor or omnidirectional wheel to the tracked vehicle in order to measure motion with respect to the ground plane.

3.1.8   Limbed

"His huge feet were raised and set down with mechanical regularity, and he changed his pace from a walk to a trot without either the voice or a hand of a mahout being apparent."[7]

Jules Verne describes the locomotion of a steam-powered elephant in *The End of Nana Sahib*.

---

[7] Verne [803], p. 68.

Figure 3.14. An experimental tracked crime scene investigation robot.

Given the sophistication of existing wheeled and tracked vehicles, why should robots be designed with different types of ground contact locomotion? Perhaps the primary limitation associated with wheeled or tracked vehicles is the need for ground contact support along the entire path of motion. In rough terrains such as those found in forests, near natural or human-caused disasters, or in planetary exploration, it is not always possible to guarantee physical support for the robot along a continuous path. Local terrain modulations may be sufficiently large to make the ground impassable even for treaded vehicles. Provided that separated footholds can be found throughout the environment, however, a limbed robot may be capable of traversing the space.

We have seen that in wheeled vehicles the problem of effecting locomotion can be described in terms of the mechanisms used to drive and steer the vehicle. Limbed, legged, or walking vehicles (see Figure 3.15) can be described in terms of the design of the legs and the way in which the legs are moved to enable the vehicle to change its pose.

Vehicle Stability   If a limbed robot is designed so that its balance is maintained at all times even if all its legs were to freeze in position, then the robot is said to exhibit **static stability**. More formally, static stability is maintained as long as the vehicle's center of gravity remains inside the convex hull of the support polygon defined by the legs currently in touch with the ground (see Figures 3.16 and 3.17). A major advantage of static stability is that the vehicle will not topple as a result of delays in leg motion or vehicle power failure. Static stability is the mechanism used in limbed robots such as Dante I [829] and II [827] and Thing [490]. Under static stability, the **stability margin** is a measure of the current stability of the robot and is defined as the minimum distance from the vertical projection of the robot's center of gravity to the boundary of the vertical projection of the convex hull of the support polygon.

(a) 3D Hopping Monopod   (b) Ambler

(c) AQUA

Figure 3.15. Walking robots. (a) Photograph of 3D Hopper courtesy of MIT Leg Laboratory
©1984 Marc Raibert. (b) Copyright Carnegie Mellon University, 1992. (c) Copyright the
AQUA Project. Used with permission.

If the center of gravity of the robot is allowed to move outside of the convex hull
of the support polygon and the robot moves in a controlled manner, then the robot is
said to exhibit **dynamic stability**. Under dynamic stability the robot maintains stability
through its controlled motion and the modeling and use of inertia. This implies a
sophisticated model of the dynamics of the robotic system and highly developed control
and locomotion processing. Raibert [652] developed a number of dynamically stable
robots including one-, two-, and four-legged machines. Although static stability is easier
to control, it does limit the robot's gait and its maximum speed. Higher performance

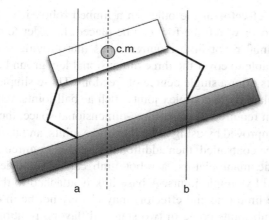

Figure 3.16. Vehicle stability. A side view of a simple two-dimensional legged robot. The body of the robot is supported by two articulated legs above a sloped floor that meets the ground at points *a* and *b*. If the projection of the robot's center of gravity remains inside the line segment $a - b$, then the robot remains statically stable.

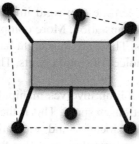

Figure 3.17. Convex hull. Top view of a two-dimensional six-legged robot showing the ground contact points of its legs. If the center of gravity is within its convex hull – the region of space formed by constructing the smallest convex region containing all of the the vertical projection of the ground contact points – then the robot is stable.

legged robots, including BDI's Spot [106] and Anybotics' AnyMal, typically utilize dynamic stability.

Number of Legs Limbed robots have been built with as few as one leg [652], but it is more common to see designs with four [641, 729, 490, 106], six [434], or eight [829, 827]. Even 12-legged vehicles have been built [775]. As at least one leg must be free to move if a robot is to change its pose. For a statically stable robot to maintain its center of gravity over the convex hull of the support polygon, then the minimum number of legs is four: three to maintain the support polygon and one to move. If the robot is to exhibit dynamic stability, then the minimum number of legs is one, such as Raibert's hopping monopod [651]. Here we assume that a foot's contact with the ground can be modeled as a point contact. It is also possible to construct robots with extended feet with larger foot–ground contact areas.

Although four is the minimum number of legs required for mobility and static stability, four legs may not be an ideal number for all applications. If a statically stable robot has only four legs, then its gait must be particularly simple. It may only move one leg at a time, and the robot must shift its weight as part of its gait. A robot with more legs – say six – can move more than one leg at a time while maintaining static stability and may not have to plan to move its center of mass as a separate component of its gait.

Limb Design and Control Consider the design of a limb on a robot or biological system. A given limb has a fixed point at one end attached to the body and a hand or foot known as the **end effector** at the other. In a limbed robot, it is usually desirable to maximize the region over which the foot can be placed. In order to operate in three dimensions (3D), a minimal robot limb requires joints that provide sufficient degrees of freedom in order to be able to cover the three dimensional leg–ground contact space. Physically, most robot joints offer a single degree of freedom. These simple joints can be combined in order to simulate more complex joints such as ball joints. Although three simple joints is the minimum required to cover three-dimensional space, the actual working space of the leg may be improved by using more than three joints, and if ground–leg contact orientation must also be controlled, then additional joints are required.

Similar to the study of robotic manipulators, a robot limb can be modeled as a collection of rigid links connected by simple joints. A base link is attached to the body of the robot, while the end of the limb (the end effector) may or may not be in contact with the ground. Simple robot limb joints come in two standard flavors, rotational and prismatic. **Rotational joints** introduce a rotation between the two rigid links to which they are connected, while **prismatic joints** introduce a translation. More complex joints can be modeled in terms of these two simple joint types. There are thus eight basic three-dimensional robot limb designs, based on the various choices of simple joints. These eight designs are sketched in Figure 3.18.

Given a particular limb design, the task of moving a limb involves manipulating the joints of the limbs so as to be able to reach different locations in space. This is the **forward kinematics problem** for robot limbs: how to compute the location and orientation of the end effector (or foot) given the joint angles. The classic formulation of this problem is to use homogeneous coordinates to represent the position of each link in the limb and then to construct a homogeneous matrix that represents the transformation from a base coordinate system to a coordinate system aligned with the end effector or foot.

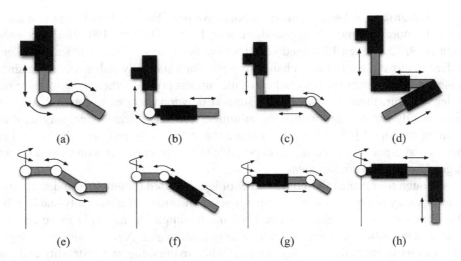

(a)   (b)   (c)   (d)

(e)   (f)   (g)   (h)

Figure 3.18. Eight three-jointed limbs based on simple prismatic and rotational joints. Rotational joints are indicated by small circles and prismatic joints are indicated by two intensity-level rectangles. Designs (a) – (d) utilize prismatic joints at the contact with the robot body, while (e) – (h) utilize rotational joints. The final prismatic joint of design (d) is directed out of the page.

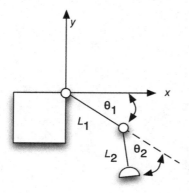

Figure 3.19. Two-dimensional leg. The leg connects to the body of the robot at an angle θ_1 from the horizontal. The second joint is at θ_2 from the straight-ahead direction of the first link.

Before tackling the general problem, consider the simple two-dimensional (2D) leg shown in Figure 3.19. This leg consists of two rotational joints separated by rigid limbs of lengths l_1 and l_2. Placing the origin of the coordinate system at the joint of the leg with the robot body, we obtain the position of the foot as a function of θ_1 and θ_2 (the joint angles) from

$$\begin{bmatrix} x \\ y \end{bmatrix} = l_1 \begin{bmatrix} \cos(\theta_1) \\ \sin(\theta_1) \end{bmatrix} + l_2 \begin{bmatrix} \cos(\theta_1 + \theta_2) \\ \sin(\theta_1 + \theta_2) \end{bmatrix}.$$

This is the solution to the forward kinematics problem for this leg. The inverse kinematics problem for the leg involves determining the angles θ_1 and θ_2 that are required to place the foot at a point (x, y). A small amount of geometry results in

$$\cos(\theta_2) = \frac{x^2 + y^2 - l_1{}^2 - l_2{}^2}{2l_1 l_2},$$

which can be then used in the expression for either x or y in the forward kinematics equation to obtain a solution for θ_1. Note that in general the inverse kinematics will not result in a unique solution.

Not all specifications of (x, y) necessarily result in a solution. Some (x, y) positions are not reachable by the limb. These points are said to be outside the limb's workspace. Suppose that the first joint is limited to the range $|\theta_1| \leq \pi/2$ and that $l_2 = l_1/2$. The resulting workspace of the limb is sketched in Figure 3.20.

Given a set of points attainable by the robot's limb, an important question to consider is "How well can the motion of the limb be controlled near these points?" If $\dot{x}$ is the velocity of the end effector in Cartesian space and $\dot{\theta}$ is the velocity in joint space (θ_1, θ_2), then $\dot{x} = J(\theta)\dot{\theta}$, where $J(\theta)$ is the Jacobian. That is,

$$J(\theta) = \begin{bmatrix} \frac{\partial x}{\partial \theta_1} & \frac{\partial x}{\partial \theta_2} \\ \frac{\partial y}{\partial \theta_1} & \frac{\partial y}{\partial \theta_2} \end{bmatrix}$$

and

$$\begin{bmatrix} \frac{dx}{dt} \\ \frac{dy}{dt} \end{bmatrix} = J(\theta) \begin{bmatrix} \frac{d\theta_1}{dt} \\ \frac{d\theta_2}{dt} \end{bmatrix}.$$

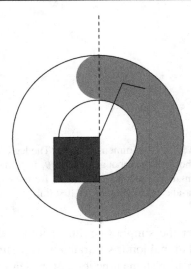

Figure 3.20. Limb workspace. The region reachable with the tip of the limb is shown in light grey.

The Jacobian relates the velocity of the joint angles $(d\theta_1/dt, d\theta_2/dt)$ to the velocity of the end effector in Cartesian space. Conversely, given a desired trajectory of the limb in Cartesian space, we can examine the inverse of the Jacobian, $\dot{\theta} = J(\theta)^{-1}\dot{x}$, to determine the appropriate velocities in joint space.

When a limb loses one or more degrees of freedom as viewed in Cartesian space, such as at the boundaries of the limb workspace, motion **singularities** are said to occur. The existence of a singularity in some configuration of the limb means that it is impossible to move the limb in an arbitrary direction from this point. Singularities exist at the boundary of the workspace but may also occur within its interior. Mathematically, within the robot's workspace, singularities can be identified through an examination of the Jacobian. When the determinant of the Jacobian is equal to zero, the Jacobian has lost full rank and singularities exist. For the simple 2D leg considered here,

$$|J| = \left| \begin{bmatrix} \frac{\partial x}{\partial \theta_1} & \frac{\partial x}{\partial \theta_2} \\ \frac{\partial y}{\partial \theta_1} & \frac{\partial y}{\partial \theta_2} \end{bmatrix} \right| = l_1 l_2 |\sin(\theta_2)|.$$

A singularity exists whenever $\sin(\theta_2) = 0$, that is, when $\theta_2 = 0$ or $\pm\pi$. Physically this corresponds to the foot being either stretched straight out or bent in upon itself.

Forward and Inverse Kinematics   The two-dimensional problem considered here is relatively straightforward because the state of the limb is defined by its position (x, y) and its orientation θ. In 3D, six scalar parameters are required to represent the state of the limb: three positional and three rotational. Transformations such as translations and rotations that are reasonably straightforward in 2D become quite cumbersome in 3D if separate position and orientation representations are retained. A representation that has proven to be more useful is to use **homogeneous coordinates** to represent points and **homogeneous transforms** to represent transformations between one coordinate frame and another or to represent position and orientations generally.

In homogeneous coordinates, the point $P = (x_1, x_2, x_3)$ is represented as the column vector $P_h = [x_1, x_2, x_3, 1]^T$. This allows us to express rotation and translation as matrix multiplication, so that the effect of transforming P to $P' = (y_1, y_2, y_3)$ through a rotation by some rotation matrix R, where

$$\mathbf{R} = \begin{bmatrix} r_{1,1} & r_{1,2} & r_{1,3} \\ r_{2,1} & r_{2,2} & r_{2,3} \\ r_{3,1} & r_{3,2} & r_{3,3} \end{bmatrix},$$

and by a translation $D = (t_x, t_y, t_z)$ can be written in homogeneous coordinates as

$$\begin{bmatrix} y_1 \\ y_2 \\ y_3 \\ 1 \end{bmatrix} = \begin{bmatrix} r_{1,1} & r_{1,2} & r_{1,3} & t_x \\ r_{2,1} & r_{2,2} & r_{2,3} & t_y \\ r_{3,1} & r_{3,2} & r_{3,3} & t_z \\ 0 & 0 & 0 & 1 \end{bmatrix} \begin{bmatrix} x_1 \\ x_2 \\ x_3 \\ 1 \end{bmatrix}.$$

$P' = TP$, where

$$\mathbf{T} = \begin{bmatrix} r_{1,1} & r_{1,2} & r_{1,3} & t_x \\ r_{2,1} & r_{2,2} & r_{2,3} & t_y \\ r_{3,1} & r_{3,2} & r_{3,3} & t_z \\ 0 & 0 & 0 & 1 \end{bmatrix}.$$

Common 3D transformations such as rotation about the x axis $R_x(\theta)$, rotation about the y axis $R_y(\theta)$, rotation about the z axis $R_z(\theta)$, and translation by an amount $D(dx, dy, dz)$ are represented in homogeneous coordinates as, respectively,

$$\mathbf{R}_x(\theta) = \begin{bmatrix} 1 & 0 & 0 & 0 \\ 0 & \cos(\theta) & -\sin(\theta) & 0 \\ 0 & \sin(\theta) & \cos(\theta) & 0 \\ 0 & 0 & 0 & 1 \end{bmatrix},$$

$$\mathbf{R}_y(\theta) = \begin{bmatrix} \cos(\theta) & 0 & \sin(\theta) & 0 \\ 0 & 1 & 0 & 0 \\ -\sin(\theta) & 0 & \cos(\theta) & 0 \\ 0 & 0 & 0 & 1 \end{bmatrix},$$

$$\mathbf{R}_z(\theta) = \begin{bmatrix} \cos(\theta) & -\sin(\theta) & 0 & 0 \\ \sin(\theta) & \cos(\theta) & 0 & 0 \\ 0 & 0 & 1 & 0 \\ 0 & 0 & 0 & 1 \end{bmatrix},$$

$$\mathbf{D}(dx, dy, dz) = \begin{bmatrix} 0 & 0 & 0 & dx \\ 0 & 0 & 0 & dy \\ 0 & 0 & 0 & dz \\ 0 & 0 & 0 & 1 \end{bmatrix}.$$

Suppose that we establish one coordinate system attached to the foot or end effector of a mobile robot and another coordinate system to the body. Then there exists a homogeneous transformation T that maps points in the coordinate system attached to the foot to the coordinate system attached to the body. T will be a function of the joint angles and links that make up the leg. Determining T is in essence the process of establishing the forward kinematics for the limb. Suppose now that the coordinate system attached to the end effector has its origin at the tip of the limb. Then the inverse kinematics problem for the limb involves solving

$$
\mathbf{T}^{-1} \begin{bmatrix} x \\ y \\ z \\ 1 \end{bmatrix} = \begin{bmatrix} 0 \\ 0 \\ 0 \\ 1 \end{bmatrix}
$$

for some setting of the joint angles, where (x, y, z) is the desired position of the limb in body coordinates. Solving for $\mathbf{T}^{-1}$ algebraically is in general extremely difficult, and alternative solution mechanisms, for example, geometric approaches, are often more effective. It is fortunate that most kinematic chains are designed to have straightforward inverse solution mechanisms.

Establishing T for a given limb is often simplified by establishing a series of working coordinate systems (**frames**) along the limb and noting that if $_1^2T$ maps points in frame 1 to points in frame 2, and if $_2^3T$ maps points in frame 2 to points in frame 3, then $_1^3T = \,_2^3T \,_1^2T$.

Consider the simple robot limb shown in Figure 3.21. This is a three-joint revolute limb (here a leg) fixed to the side of a vehicle. The three joint angles θ_1, θ_2, and θ_3 are controllable, and the fixed link lengths are L_1, L_2, and L_2. Given a body coordinate frame whose origin is at the intersection of L_1 and the body of the robot, whose z axis is aligned with the rotational axis of θ_1, and whose x axis is aligned with L_1 when $\theta_1 = 0$, what is the transformation from points in the "foot" frame to the body frame?

We start by establishing a sequence of intermediate frames. These frames are chosen such that the transformation between pairs of frames can be established by inspection and that the concatenation of all of the frames establishes the transformation $_{foot}^{body}\mathbf{T}$.

- $_{foot}^{A}\mathbf{T} = \mathbf{D}(L_3, 0, 0)$. The foot frame is aligned with the foot (the x axis points along the foot, and the z axis is out of the page. Frame A is translated back along the final link to axis 3. The length of this link is L_3.
- $_A^B\mathbf{T} = \mathbf{R}_z(\theta_3)$. Frame B is established just prior to the rotation of joint 3. Frame B is aligned with link 2.

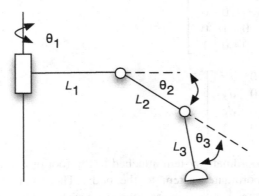

Figure 3.21. A simple three-jointed leg design.

- $_B^C\mathbf{T} = \mathbf{D}(L_2,0,0)$. Frame C is established at joint 2 but aligned with L_2.
- $_C^D\mathbf{T} = \mathbf{R}_z(\theta_2)$. Frame D is established at joint 2 but aligned with L_1.
- $_D^E\mathbf{T} = \mathbf{D}(L_1,0,0)$. Frame E is established at joint 1 but aligned with L_1.
- $_E^F\mathbf{T} = \mathbf{R}_x(90°)$. Frame F is established at joint 1 and aligned with L_1 but with its z axis aligned with the z axis of the body frame.
- $_F^{body}\mathbf{T} = \mathbf{R}_z(\theta_1)$. The final mapping to the body frame of the robot.

Concatenating the above results in

$$\begin{aligned}
{}^{body}_{foot}\mathbf{T} &= {}^{body}_F\mathbf{T}\, {}^F_E\mathbf{T}\, {}^E_D\mathbf{T}\, {}^D_C\mathbf{T}\, {}^C_B\mathbf{T}\, {}^B_A\mathbf{T}\, {}^A_{foot}\mathbf{T} \\
&= \mathbf{R}_z(\theta_1)\mathbf{R}_x(90°)\mathbf{D}(L_1,0,0)\mathbf{R}_z(\theta_2)\mathbf{D}(L_2,0,0)\mathbf{R}_z(\theta_3)\mathbf{D}(L_3,0,0).
\end{aligned}$$

The choice of intermediate frames is not unique, and many different internal sets of frames and transformations can be used to express the same kinematic chain. The Denavit–Hartenberg formalism [253] for the identification of link frames is a commonly used representation in describing manipulator kinematic chains. In the Denavit–Hartenberg formalism, individual transformations are represented as the product of four basic transformations parameterized by the **link length** a_i, **link twist** α_i, **link offset** d_i, and **joint angle** θ_i.

In the Denavit–Hartenberg formalism, individual frames are assigned to each revolute or prismatic joint, with the z axis of each frame aligned with the joint axes and with the x axis of each frame forming the common perpendicular between the z axis of adjacent frames. The link twist and link length are fixed values and parameterize the rigid link that connects two joints. The link offset and joint angle describe the nature of the joint that connects adjacent links (see Figure 3.22). The link offset is variable if the joint is prismatic and the joint angle is variable if the joint is revolute. The transformation between the coordinate frame aligned with link i and the coordinate frame aligned with link $i-1$ (see Figure 3.22) is given by

$$_i^{i-1}\mathbf{T} = \mathbf{R}_x(\alpha_{i-1})\mathbf{D}(a_{i-1},0,0)\mathbf{R}_z(\theta_i)\mathbf{D}(0,0,d_i). \tag{3.6}$$

Gait and Body Control   Gait refers to the pattern of leg placements made by a legged animal or machine system. The photographer Eadweard Muybridge (1830–1904) is credited with the earliest studies of gait in biological systems. In 1872, Leland Stanford, then governor of California, bet a friend that once every stride all four legs of a running horse are simultaneously off the ground. Muybridge was hired to settle the bet. Muybridge developed a system of cameras that were set up along and parallel to the horse's path. Each camera was triggered by a wire through which the horse would run along this path, and in 1877 Muybridge produced the first time sequence photographs of humans and animals, demonstrating that horses do in fact lift all four legs off of the ground when running – that they are not statically stable. Collections of these photographs and a description of the various gaits employed by quadruped [560] and biped [561] walkers show the considerable sophistication used in gaits by biological systems over both flat and rough terrains.

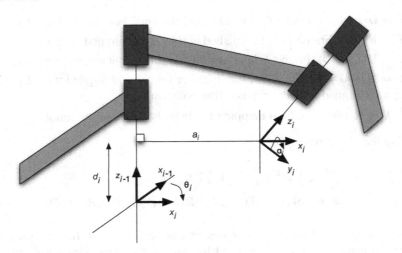

Figure 3.22. Denavit–Hartenberg link frames.

Much of the robotic literature concerning gait has its foundations in the biological literature. As is the case with biological systems, gait plays a major role in the trade-off among speed, energy utilization, and stability.

The **stride** of a limbed robot can be decomposed into the synchronized **steps** made by each limb. In terms of providing support to the robot, two different phases can be identified; the **transfer phase**, in which the limb is not in contact with the ground, and the **support phase**, in which it is. The time taken for a complete step to be taken by a limb is known as the **cycle time**, and the **duty factor** for a leg is that fraction of the cycle time in which the leg is in the support phase.

Non-periodic gaits are typically used in biological systems on rough terrain. Periodic gaits are preferred in biological systems over flat terrain, and are the usual strategy for limbed robots in the absence of obstacles. Muybridge identified eight different periodic gaits used by quadrupeds in locomotion over flat surfaces [560]. They are as follows:

1. The Walk (including the Crawl as a special case). One leg moves at a time. **The Crawl is the only statically stable gait**.
2. The Amble. Faster than a Walk. Support alternates between one and two feet.
3. The Trot. Support is provided by diagonal pairs of feet.
4. The Rack (or Pace). Support is provided by lateral pairs of feet rather than by diagonal pairs of feet as in the Trot.
5. The Canter. Unlike earlier gaits, the Canter cannot be broken into a left/right part.
6. The Gallop. The Gallop is the fastest of the quadrupedal gaits. Central to the Gallop is a ballistic phase in which the quadruped jumps forward from its hind feet to catch itself with its forward ones. Two different Gallops are identified in biological quadrupeds
    (a) The Transverse gallop. The pattern of foot falls moves traversely across the body.
    (b) The Rotatory gallop. The pattern of foot falls moves cyclically around the body.

7. The Ricochet. Motion as a sequence of bounds, hops, jumps, or skips. Typically found in the rapid motion of the Australian marsupials – the kangaroo and the wallaby.

In order to describe the pattern of leg motions that give rise to these different gaits, various graphical representations have been devised. Hildebrand's gait diagrams [348] provide a precise description of gait. They show the contribution of each leg toward the support of a robot as a function of time. A horizontal line is assigned to each leg, with darkened regions corresponding to the support phase. Legs 1 and 2 are the front legs, and legs 3 and 4 are the rear legs. Odd-numbered legs are on the left-hand side of the robot. Figure 3.23 sketches the gait diagrams for each of the eight gaits described by Muybridge.

Machine gaits for statically stable robots are usually simpler than the biological gaits studied by Muybridge. Song and Waldron [729] identified a number of different machine gaits. The wave and equal phase gaits shown in Figure 3.24 are periodic gaits designed to be used by machines on flat open terrain. The equal phase gait provides an optimal stability margin, while the equal wave equally distributes the placing and lifting segments of each leg throughout the entire stride.

Once the pattern of footfalls has been established, the task of **scheduling body motions** remains. Raising and lowering the limbs in a particular pattern does not necessarily cause the center of mass of the robot to move forward. In addition to choosing when and where to place the feet, the entire body must be moved forward at some point in the gait. Two basic strategies have emerged for scheduling body motions. The first is to minimize the number of body motions. A second alternative is to move the center of mass so as to maximize the robot's stability margin.

A possible implementation for scheduling body motions in a quadruped Crawl gait is shown in Figure 3.25. Snapshots of the motion of the robot are shown in left-to-right, top-to-bottom order. Body motions (indicated by an arrow) are scheduled at two points during the motion, even though the legs move forward throughout the entire gait.

Dynamic Gaits   Rather than plan limb motions so as to maintain static stability, an alternative is to control the motion of the robot dynamically and achieve balance. Under a **dynamic gait**, the motion of the vehicle must consider the energy involved in each limb and actuator.

Running is a form of legged locomotion that uses ballistic flight in order to obtain a high speed. Perhaps the simplest possible dynamic legged device is a one-legged hopper (see Figure 3.15a) [653]. This device actively models the dynamic exchange of energy among the mass of the robot, its actuators, and the ground in order to enable the robot to hop in three dimensions. The dynamic nature of the device results in a very high maximum speed. Raibert *et al.* [653] reported a maximum speed of 4.8 mph for this one-legged robot.

Multiple-legged robots can be thought of as linked one-legged robots. For example, Hodgins and Raibert [353] describe a bipedal robot that basically hops on alternate legs and can reach a top speed of 11.5 mph. The robot is also capable of performing forward flips and aerials. Running robots have been built that travel at much higher speeds than this. BDI's Cheetah has been clocked at over 45 km/hr and KAIST's Raptor at 48 km/hr [326]. Note that these are speeds greatly in excess of human running speeds

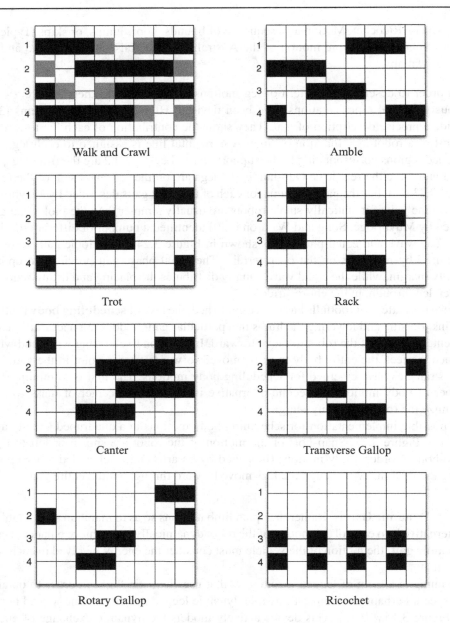

Figure 3.23. Eight quadrapedal gaits (from [560]). Each plot depicts the ground-contact phase for each leg as a function of time. The Crawl gait is a slow walk gait and includes both the black- and gray-colored regions. Note that only the Crawl gait is statically stable. Legs 1 and 2 are the "front," and legs 3 and 4 are the "rear." Legs 1 and 3 are on the left side of the body, and legs 2 and 4 are on the right.

Quadruped robots can also be built based on hopping on all four legs alternatively, but this is difficult to achieve in practice due to difficulties of balance [654]. An alternative is to use the legs in pairs to act as a single "virtual" leg.

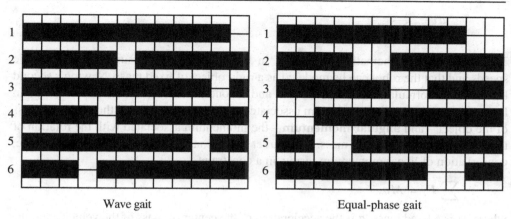

Wave gait   Equal-phase gait

Figure 3.24. Wave and Equal-phase gaits for a six-legged robot (from [729]).

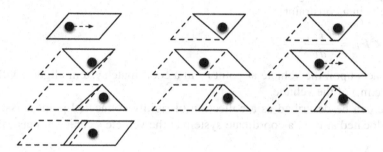

Figure 3.25. Scheduling body motions in a Crawl gait adapted from [520]. Ten snapshots of the motion are shown. Snapshots are shown in left-to-right, top-to-bottom order. The support polygon of the robot is shown as a solid line and the dashed line shows the original position of the robot. The center of mass of the robot is shown as a black dot. The robot moves from left to right almost one body length. Body motions are scheduled at frames 1 and 6 even though the legs move throughout the entire gait. It is essential that the robot schedule these body motions. For example, had the body motion to shift the center of gravity not been scheduled at frame 1, the robot would be very unstable at frame 2 when the right rear leg is raised.

3.1.9   Rigid-Vehicle Dynamics

Unlike wheeled mobile robots and statically stable legged vehicles, flying, aquatic, and space robots cannot be adequately described in terms of their kinematics alone. Rather, these vehicles must be described in terms of their **dynamics**. The motion of any object in general, and a robot vehicle in particular, can be modeled by the action of forces acting upon it. These forces may be caused by onboard thrusters and external wave motion for aquatic robots, via propellers and flight surfaces for flying robots, and via thrusters and gravitational forces for space robots. The motion of the vehicle is modeled (as can be the motion of all objects moving at non-relativistic speeds) by **Newton's second law** [269], which relates mass M, acceleration $a = dv/dt$, and the external forces F_i acting on the vehicle by

$$M\frac{d\boldsymbol{v}}{dt} = \sum \boldsymbol{F}_i.$$

To simplify the mathematics somewhat, in the following we assume non-relativistic speeds and that the robot can be modeled as a rigid object of fixed mass. Newton's second law can be reformulated (via Euler's first and second axioms) in terms of the change in **linear momentum** – the momentum associated with the movement of the center of mass of the object – and **angular momentum** – the momentum associated with the rotation of the object about its center of mass. Given a set of external forces $\boldsymbol{F}_i$ acting on the vehicle, conservation of linear momentum results in a constraint

$$\sum \boldsymbol{F}_i = M\boldsymbol{a},$$

where M is a fixed mass, $\boldsymbol{a}$ is the acceleration of the center of mass of the vehicle, and the forces $\boldsymbol{F}_i$ are represented in a global (inertial) coordinate system. Conservation of angular momentum results in a constraint

$$\sum \boldsymbol{r}_i \times \boldsymbol{F}_i = \frac{d\boldsymbol{J}_{\text{c.m.}}}{dt},$$

where force $\boldsymbol{F}_i$ acts upon the vehicle at point $\boldsymbol{r}_i$ in a coordinate system aligned with the center of mass (c.m.) of the vehicle.

If the vehicle can be described as a collection of rigidly connected point masses m_i with each mass located at $\boldsymbol{r}_i$ in a coordinate system at the vehicle's center of mass, then

$$\boldsymbol{J}_{\text{c.m.}} = \sum \boldsymbol{r}_i \times m_i(\boldsymbol{\omega} \times \boldsymbol{r}_i).$$

Here $\boldsymbol{\omega} = \omega_x\boldsymbol{x} + \omega_y\boldsymbol{y} + \omega_z\boldsymbol{z}$ is an angular velocity vector. The vector $\boldsymbol{\omega}$ points along the axis of rotation, and its magnitude is the rate of rotation. $\boldsymbol{J}_{\text{c.m.}}$ is the vehicle's **angular momentum**.

Determining the dynamics of a particular vehicle can be reduced to

1. Determining the center of mass of the vehicle and establishing a coordinate system that remains aligned with the vehicle and whose origin is at the center of mass. (Note that it is possible to develop a dynamical model not aligned with the center of mass, but the mathematics are slightly more involved.)
2. Determining the set of forces acting upon the vehicle $\boldsymbol{F}_i$ and their point $\boldsymbol{r}_i$ of action upon the vehicle.
3. Determining the angular momentum $\boldsymbol{J}_{\text{c.m.}}$ of the vehicle.

Once the dynamic model has been constructed, the motion of the vehicle under the influence of external forces can be determined.

Inertia Tensor The expression

$$\boldsymbol{J}_{\text{c.m.}} = \sum \boldsymbol{r}_i \times m_i(\boldsymbol{\omega} \times \boldsymbol{r}_i)$$

defines the angular momentum of the vehicle. This expression is usually expressed in terms of the **inertia tensor** $\boldsymbol{I}$, where $\boldsymbol{J}_{\text{c.m.}} = \boldsymbol{I}\boldsymbol{\omega}$, by expanding the expression for $\boldsymbol{J}_{\text{c.m.}}$ using

$$r_i = x_i x + y_i y + z_i z$$
$$\omega = \omega_x x + \omega_y y + \omega_z z$$

where the coordinate system is fixed in relation to the rigid body. The elements of $J_{c.m.} = (J_x, J_y, J_z)$ are given by

$$J_x = \sum m_i (y_i^2 + z_i^2)\omega_x - \sum m_i x_i y_i \omega_y - \sum m_i x_i z_i \omega_z$$
$$J_y = -\sum m_i x_i y_i \omega_y + \sum m_i (z_i^2 + x_i^2)\omega_y - \sum m_i y_i z_i \omega_z$$
$$J_z = -\sum m_i x_i z_i \omega_z - \sum m_i y_i z_i \omega_z + \sum m_i (x_i^2 + y_i^2)\omega_z.$$

This is normally expressed as

$$J_{c.m.} = \begin{bmatrix} I_{xx} & I_{xy} & I_{xz} \\ I_{yx} & I_{yy} & I_{yz} \\ I_{zx} & I_{zy} & I_{zz} \end{bmatrix} \begin{bmatrix} \omega_x \\ \omega_y \\ \omega_z \end{bmatrix} = I\omega,$$

where I is the inertia tensor (a 3×3 matrix) and the moments and products of inertia (the I_{xx}, etc., terms) are defined from the foregoing expressions and are given by

$$I_{xx} = \sum m_i (y_i^2 + z_i^2)\omega_x$$
$$I_{yy} = \sum m_i (z_i^2 + x_i^2)\omega_y$$
$$I_{zz} = \sum m_i (x_i^2 + y_i^2)\omega_z$$
$$I_{xy} = I_{yx} = -\sum m_i x_i y_i \omega_y$$
$$I_{xz} = I_{zx} = -\sum m_i x_i z_i \omega_z$$
$$I_{yz} = I_{zy} = -\sum m_i y_i z_i \omega_z.$$

Note that for an unchanging vehicle, and a coordinate system fixed with the vehicle, the inertia tensor is a fixed value.

For walking robots, and humanoid walkers in particular, an addition attribute known as the **zero moment point** (**ZMP**) [811] is sometimes used in the algorithms to provide dynamic stability.

Modeling vehicle motion Modeling the motion of the vehicle involves integrating the equations of motion from some initial starting position. Starting from some initial vehicle state (position s_0, velocity v_0, orientation R_0, and angular velocity ω_0 in Earth-fixed coordinates) the motion of the center of mass of the vehicle can be estimated over some small time step (see [107] for a sample implementation):

1. Convert all of the forces F_i into Earth-fixed coordinates and update the estimate of the velocity of the center of mass of the vehicle:

$$v_{t+\Delta t} = v_t + \left(\sum F_i / M\right) \Delta t.$$

2. Apply the velocity to the center of mass of the vehicle to determine its new position at time $t + \Delta t$:

$$s_{t+\Delta t} = s_t + v_{t+\Delta t} \Delta t.$$

3. Update the angular velocity of the vehicle by integrating the current value of the angular acceleration:

$$\boldsymbol{\omega}_{t+\Delta t} = \boldsymbol{\omega}_t + \boldsymbol{I}^{-1}\left(\sum \boldsymbol{r}_i \times \boldsymbol{F}_i - \boldsymbol{\omega} \times (\boldsymbol{I} \times \boldsymbol{\omega})\right)\Delta t.$$

Note that the forces $\boldsymbol{F}_i$ must be transformed to a vehicle-centric coordinate system.

4. Update the orientation of the vehicle based on it rotating about its center of mass by an amount $\boldsymbol{\omega}_{t+\Delta t}\Delta t$. The actual implementation of this will depend on the way in which the simulation represents rotations. If rotation of the vehicle is represented using rotation matricies, then $R_{t+\Delta t} = \boldsymbol{R}\boldsymbol{\Omega}$, where

$$\boldsymbol{\Omega} = \begin{bmatrix} 0 & -\omega_z & \omega_y \\ \omega_z & 0 & -\omega_x \\ -\omega_y & \omega_x & 0 \end{bmatrix}.$$

Note that $\boldsymbol{R}_{t+\Delta t}$ must be renormalized after the computation.

The development of a **dynamic model** for aquatic, flying, or space robots involves developing models for the forces that act on the vehicle and then applying the foregoing model. Note that it is rarely necessary to develop the mathematical software infrastructure necessary for the modeling of rigid-body dynamics. Commercial and open source modeling libraries exist (e.g., PyBullet [643] and MuJoCo [551]) and these can provide the basis for effective system modeling.

If the center of mass can change, or if the moment of inertia changes, then the foregoing (simple) dynamical model proves insufficient, and a more complex and complete mathematical treatment is required. Such treatments can be found in many texts on rigid-body dynamics including [467, 526, 314]. Examples of dynamics models for specific aquatic and aerial vehicles can be found in [306] and [714].

3.1.10 Soft-Vehicle Structure

Rather than being constructed out of rigid components, possibly connected by joints, soft robots are robots that are primarily composed of deformable materials and elements. Soft robots find a number of applications and are extremely well suited for environments within which the rigid structure of traditional robots is inappropriate. This includes, for example, minimally invasive surgery in which devices such as robotic endoscopes based on soft vehicles are appropriate (see [685] for a review of the application of soft robots in minimally invasive surgery).

3.1.11 Aquatic Robots

A robotic aquatic vehicle (see Figure 3.26) is also known as an **autonomous underwater vehicle** (AUV) or an **unmanned underwater vehicle** (UUV). A teleoperated aquatic vehicle is known as a **remotely operated vehicle** (ROV). Such devices use the surrounding water in order to enable propulsion. Aquatic robots can be divided into two broad categories: vehicles that float on the surface and hence navigate on the 2D world of the surface of the water, and vehicles that are designed to submerge and operate in the 3D underwater environment. This second approach is much more common, but a

(a) Twin-burger   (b) AQUA

(c) THESEUS   (d) Spray

Figure 3.26. Aquatic robots. (a) Copyright Tervo Fujii. Used with permission. (d) Copyright International Submarine Engineering Limited. Used with permission.

number of surface robots have also been developed – including such oddities as a "robot duck." Here we concentrate on submersible aquatic vehicles.

Traditional underwater autonomous vehicles fall into one of two basic designs. The first is a torpedo-like structure [268, 735] (see Figure 3.26d). Here a single propeller or propeller assembly is used to provide forward and reverse thrust while control surfaces are used to control the direction in which the vehicle travels. These control surfaces may provide only horizontal directional control, or they may provide **vertical directional control** as well by manipulating dive planes. Depth may also be controlled by manipulating the **buoyancy** of the vessel. These torpedo-shaped robots suffer from poor maneuverability due to the direct coupling of turning with translational motion and the indirect nature of the rudder.

A second alternative, and the design used on vehicles such as the Twin-burger [299], URV [161, 162], and Milton [169] robots as well as many commercially available devices, is to use a collection of **thrusters** distributed over the vessel rather than just a single propeller (see Figure 3.26a). By controlling sets of the thrusters, this type of vessel can change its orientation and position independently. This results in a considerably more maneuverable vessel at the expense of maximum operational speed.

Traditional thruster/propeller control surfaces are not the only options for motion. Underwater gliders [750, 716] such as the Theseus shown in Figure 3.26c obtain propulsion by gliding through the water using the active control of buoyancy. Legged aquatic vehicles [307] such as AQUA shown in Figure 3.26b utilize leg, fin, and even tail interaction with the surrounding water for propulsion.

Aquatic robots provide a number of unique challenges for sensing and control. The surrounding water makes the use of sensors based on vision-based sensing problematic at long ranges. Water can contain suspended material, which may make light-based sensing impossible even at close ranges. Although water does provide both buoyancy and locomotion, it is impossible to estimate odometry accurately using the rate of turn of the propeller and the position of the control surfaces.

The vast majority of aquatic robots operate in a tethered manner; they are physically connected to a support vessel by a cable that provides power and communication to the robot. This simplifies a number of problems in terms of the engineering of the robot (as discussed in Section 3.2.1), and may also provide a mechanism for retrieving the robot should something go wrong. Power and communication pose difficult challenges for untethered aquatic autonomous vehicles.

The dynamics of aquatic robots can be defined in terms of the physical properties of the vehicle and the hydrodynamic forces that act on it. These include the following:

Radiation-induced forces These include forces that are present when the vehicle is forced to oscillate with the surrounding water. There are two main components to radiation-induced forces: **added mass** due to the inertia of the surrounding water and **potential damping** due to the energy carried away by generated surface waves. Added (or virtual) mass refers to the energy required to move the water from in front of the vehicle to behind the vehicle as the vehicle moves forward. Very complex models can be developed for the effect of radiation-induced forces on the vehicle. One simple approach to modeling the added mass is to add "virtual mass" to the model of the vehicle. That is, to assume that in addition to the "real mass" $\{(m_i, r_i)\}$ that makes up the vehicle, additional "virtual mass" $\{(m_i', r_i')\}$ is added to represent the work required to move water "out of the way" as the vehicle moves.

Restoring forces These include gravitational and buoyant forces. The gravitational force acts through the vehicle's center of gravity (and hence provides no direct effect on the orientation of the vehicle). The buoyant force – an object's tendency to float in a given liquid – acts through the center of buoyancy of the vehicle. This force is equal to the mass of the fluid displaced multiplied by the gravitational field.

If the center of gravity and the center of buoyancy of the vehicle do not lie on a common vertical line, then a torque will be generated and the vehicle will tend to rotate. In general, this is undesirable behavior.

Hydrodynamic damping This includes effects such as potential damping, linear skin friction, and damping due to vortex shedding. One simple model is to assume a "friction-like" force that is proportional and opposite to the vehicle's linear and angular velocity.

Environmental forces These include forces such as ocean currents, waves, and the wind. As with the restoring forces, extremely complex models of the environmental forces can be developed [286]. Very simple approximate models also can be developed that model these environmental forces as constant forces acting on the vehicle.

Propulsion forces These include forces induced by thrusters, propellers, control surfaces, and rudders mounted on the vehicle. The simplest model for thrusters and propellers is that they act as point forces at specific locations/directions on the vehicle and that their thrust can be controlled directly. In practice, this is not the case, but for slow-moving vehicles these simple models may be appropriate.

Rudders and other control surfaces introduce complex forces on the vehicle. These control surfaces induce **lift** and **drag** forces on the vehicle. (See [2] for an introduction to the theory of rudders and other control/flight surfaces.). For small turning angles, the flow of water around the rudder will be smooth. In this case, the lift and drag forces can be modeled as being perpendicular to each other and lying in the plane defined by the the the relative fluid velocity vector and the line drawn from the leading to the trailing edge of the rudder (the **chord line**). The drag force acts in line with, but is opposed to, the velocity vector. The lift force operates in opposition to the rudder direction. The resulting force of a rudder or other control surface is a drag force in opposition to the velocity vector (slowing the vehicle) and a lift force perpendicular to the drag force that is in the opposite direction in which the rudder is turned. These forces must normally be computed experimentally as the forces change in very non-linear ways with the turn angle of the rudder or control surface.

3.1.12 Flying Robots

Aerial robots, also known as **unmanned aerial vehicles** (UAVs), have grown from simple missile-like devices to teleoperated and fully autonomous vehicles. Fixed-wing autonomous vehicles utilize control systems similar to those found in commercial autopilots. Remote commands are provided from a ground station, while sophisticated localization strategies based on systems such as GPS are used to localize the aircraft in the sky.

Much of the early work on aerial robots has been driven by military applications including the development of **aerial torpeodos**. The Kettering Aerial Torpedo (or Bug) was perhaps the earliest aerial robot. It was built in 1918 for the U.S. Army Signal Corps. The vehicle was launched from the ground and was directed on its course via a system of internal pneumatic and electric controls. After traveling for a predetermined period of time its engine was shut off and the wings were released, causing the vehicle to plunge to the Earth and explode.

In the mid-1930s, the U.S. Army Air Corps developed a number of radio-controlled model aircraft for anti-aircraft training. The OQ-2A Radioplane is representative. This 8.5-foot-long device was catapult launched and was recovered by parachute. During flight it was radio controlled from the ground. The V1 flying bomb (see Figure 1.4) was copied by the United States and became the JB-2 Loon. First flown in 1944, JB-2s were to be used for the planned invasion of the Japanese home islands but were never flown in combat.

From the mid 1940s to the present day, a large number of unmanned aerial vehicles have been developed. Typically these devices have been used for reconnaissance or decoy missions, although devices designed to carry out supervised and autonomous attacks have also been developed. These include:

1940s Culver PQ-14B radio-controlled target aircraft.

1950s Bell XGAM-63 Rascal standoff missile, McDonnell ADM-20 Quail air-launched decoy missile, Ryan BQM-34 Firebee target drone.

1960s Lockheed D-21 unmanned aerial vehicle for reconnaissance, Teledyne Ryan AQM-34L Firebee reconnaissance drone, North American AGM-28B Hound Dog ground-attack missile.

1970s Beech QU-22B unmanned airborne sensor relay platform, Ryan BQM-34F Firebee II target drone, Boeing YQM-94A Compass Cope B photo-reconnaissance vehicle.

1980s MQM-107 Streaker subsonic aerial target, Boeing AGM-86B air-launched cruise missile, General Dynamics/McDonnell Douglas BGM-109G Gryphon ground launched cruise missile, Northrop AGM-136A Tacit Rainbow unmanned aerial vehicle, YCGM-121B Boeing robotic air vehicle anti-aircraft artillery weapon.

1990s General Atomics RQ-1 Predator ground-controlled reconnaissance vehicle, Lockheed Martin-Boeing RQ-3A DarkStar long-endurance reconnaissance and surveillance vehicle.

In use today A large number of platforms are operating today, including the General Atomics MQ-1C Grey Eagle, the Lockheed Martin RQ-21 Blackjack, and the AeroVironment Switchblade.

As a result of their energy efficiency, fixed-wing vehicles are desirable for long-distance travel, but they lack the maneuverability required for many robotic tasks. Designs based on automated helicopters (cf. [59, 463]) modify radio-controlled helicopters through the use of onboard computation coupled with sophisticated sensing and ground control (see Figure 3.27b).

Helicopters are much more complex devices to control than are fixed-wing aircraft and require more powerful onboard computers in order to maintain reliable automatic control. Tail-sitter designs such as the UTA SDDR94 [553] (see Figure 3.27c) use a much simpler mechanical structure while retaining the maneuverability of the helicopter design. In a tail-sitter design, a single downward-pointing engine and propeller assembly is used to provide lift, while translation and stability are effected by manipulating the slip-stream from the propeller and its control surfaces.

One highly popular flying robot platform is based on a collection of multiple propellers that is independently controlled to provide flight. These are typically referred to as quadcopters (even if they have more than four propellers). There exist many designs in this space (see [378] for a recent review of unmanned aerial vehicles generally). One common approach is to equip the vehicle with four propellers pointed in what is the normal vertical direction. Different blades rotate in different directions while providing vertical lift. By changing the relative velocity of the various propellers the vehicle can be made to tilt in different directions and move in that direction.

Buoyant vehicles are those that float; Zeppelins are a familiar example. Buoyant vehicles or **aerobots** (also known as **aerovehicles**) [63] are the most readily controlled class of flying robot, in part because the consequences of even a total systems failure are typically not disastrous. Potential application domains for buoyant robots include inside large buildings, outdoors, and in the atmospheres of other planets. Very simple lighter-than-air aerobots have already been deployed in the atmosphere of Venus [472, 93], while

(a) Predator

(b) USC AFV

(c) UTA SDDR94 robot

Figure 3.27. Aerial robots. (a) U.S. Air Force. (b) Reprinted from [734]. (c) Copyright UTA. Used with permission.

[564] describes an aerobot that can be used to provide advertising and other messages in an indoor environment. In addition to having forgiving control regimes, such aerobots have advantages in terms of energy efficiency, long potential duty cycles, vertical mobility, and a potential for long-range travel.

Unpowered autonomous flying vehicles have also been developed. These are essentially computer-controlled parafoils. [734] describes a system that can be used to deliver sensitive packages via parachute to a given landing site with high accuracy. See also [372]. These "falling" robots use various onboard sensors to drive the robot to its goal. Autonomous aerial gliders have also found great success. For example, [386] describes an autonomous glider that crossed the English channel autonomously in 2012.

The dynamics of aerial vehicles is quite well understood, especially for the conditions under which most aerial vehicles operate. As with UUVs, the dynamics of UAVs are defined in terms of a full six degrees of freedom (DOF) dynamics model. Fixed-wing UAVs can be defined in terms of the forces that act on the vehicle including lift, drag, and thrust. Thrust is the force applied by propellers or jet engines. "Drag" is the term given to resistive forces acting against the vehicle as it moves through the air. Flight surfaces (the wings) of the vehicle provide both drag and lift forces on the vehicle. These forces vary with the velocity of the vehicle relative to the surrounding medium (air) and with the angle of attack of the surface with respect to the velocity of the vehicle. For reasonably slow velocities of the vehicle and simple wing geometry, a simple linear relationship between lift and angle of attack may be appropriate. Deviations from these "simple" conditions lead to extremely complex relationships between velocity and angle of attack and lift/drag values, which must be determined experimentally. A large literature exists on **aerodynamics** (e.g., [180] and [30]). A number of open source and commercial aerodynamic simulators exist that can be readily adapted to model the dynamics of UAVs.

Helicopters and quadcopters differ from fixed-wing vehicles in many important respects, although as with fixed-wing vehicles the dynamics of flight are well understood. Complexities involved in modeling helicopters include factors such as flexible rotational twist of blades, tail rotors, and so on. The dynamics of lighter-than-air vehicles is very similar to that of aquatic robots, with the exception of a reduced added mass effect [415].

3.1.13 Space Robots

Space robotic devices are envisioned to assist in the construction, operation, maintenance, and repair of future space stations and satellites. Space vehicles must exhibit a significant level of autonomy as communication delays and signal drop-out make teleoperation unattractive [700]. Space robots can be deployed to work along side humans within some space habitat. This includes humanoid robots such as the Robotnaut 2 [524] and floating cubes such as the Atrobee [135].

Beyond robots that operate with humans inside a space habitat, there is considerable interest in the development of space robots that operate outside of the human habitat as well. **Free flyers** or **free-flying systems** are space robots in which one or more manipulators are mounted on a thruster-equipped spacecraft. Attitude rockets or thrusters mounted on the body of the vehicle are used to provide corrections or modifications to the vehicle's trajectory. Power and reaction mass (fuel) are the primary constraints on existing free-flying space vehicles. In free-flying systems dynamic coupling between any on-board manipulator and the spacecraft exists, and therefore manipulator motions induce disturbances to the system's spacecraft. The modeling and control of such devices are critical challenges. Thruster jets can compensate for these disturbances, but their extensive use limits severely a system's useful life span [231]. To increase a system's life, operation in a free-floating mode has been considered [231, 601, 823, 865]. In this mode of operation, spacecraft thrusters are turned off, and the spacecraft translates and rotates in response to its manipulator motions. In practice, this mode of operation can be feasible if the total system momentum is zero; if non-zero momentum develops, the system's thrusters must be used to eliminate it. Selecting the correct sequence of actions to both move the manipulator and produce an appropriate motion in the spacecraft entails a sophisticated model of the dynamics and kinematics of the entire device.

Simulating free-flying space robots is straightforward. However, even a simple system with two six-DOF manipulators requires 18 differential equations to describe it. If one is interested in choosing a description of the spacecraft orientation that is not susceptible to representational singularities, then these equations can be even more complicated [602].

Free-floating systems exhibit non-holonomic behavior (see Section 7.1.1). In short, motion planning for free-flying space robots is complicated, and in some cases it may not be possible to get the robot to move from one feasible configuration to another simply due to motion constraints.

One technique for planning free-flying space robot motions is to utilize a joint space planning technique that takes advantage of the non-holonomy in the system [602, 566]. Sophisticated numerical techniques have been used to achieve simultaneous control of a spacecraft's attitude and its manipulator's joint angles, using the manipulator's actuators only, although convergence problems have been reported [566].

The relative lack of gravitational force in space offers some interesting possibilities in recovering from actuator failures. Indeed, one can often influence the motion of a link whose actuation system has failed by using an appropriate motion of the remaining system or actuators [600]. By "waving around" a failed arm, one might be able to bring it into a specified configuration. Once the failed actuator/link has assumed the desired configuration, brakes can be applied and the system may remain operational, although with fewer degrees of freedom. However, the planning of such appropriate motions is a very complex issue that involves constraint equations at the acceleration level. Simplified motions can be found, provided that some design conditions are met [600].

Compared to aquatic robots, space vehicle dynamics are quite straightforward. Friction between the vehicle and the environment is negligible, and thus the equations of motion typically include only gravitational, inertial, and thrust effects. As noted above, the ability for some space vehicles to change their mass distribution presents interesting opportunities for complex dynamic vehicle control.

3.1.14 Locomotion in ROS

For a real robot, the manufacturer typically provides a driver with a ROS wrapper that provides an abstraction of the robot within ROS, In addition to providing low-level access to the actuators that drive the robot, the ROS wrapper typically provides some mechanism for taking `geoemtry_msgs/twist` messages, typically published on the `cmd_vel` topic and causing the robot to execute the command provided. The `geometry_msgs/twist` messages induce a translational and rotational velocity to the robot. Plugins, such as the one shown in Listing 3.1, provide a mechanism to simulate this mechanism within Gazebo.

Perhaps the most common indoor robot mechanical design is based on the differential drive model described in Section 3.1.5. As a consequence, ROS provides considerable support for the operation and simulation of such devices. Figure 3.28 shows a simulated differential drive robot based on the ROS differential drive plugin. The plugin takes the commanded twist value and computes the rotational velocities of the left and right wheels to perform this motion. Gazebo includes a sophisticated physics engine that can be used to simulate a real robot.

```
<gazebo>
  <plugin name="differential_drive_controller"
  filename="libgazebo_ros_diff_drive.so">
    <update_rate>20</update_rate>
    <left_joint>left_wheel_joint</left_joint>
    <right_joint>right_wheel_joint</right_joint>
    <robotBaseFrame>base_footprint</robotBaseFrame>
    <wheel_separation>${robot_base_width+robot_wheel_width}</wheel_separation>
    <wheel_diameter>${2*robot_wheel_radius}</wheel_diameter>
    <publish_odom>true</publish_odom>
    <publish_odom_tf>true</publish_odom_tf>
    <publish_wheel_tf>true</publish_wheel_tf>
    <odometry_frame>odom</odometry_frame>
    <robot_base_frame>base_footprint</robot_base_frame>
    <command_topic>cmd_vel</command_topic>
  </plugin>
</gazebo>
```

Listing 3.1. Gazebo/ROS plugin for a differential drive robot.

Figure 3.28. A differential drive robot simulated in Gazebo.

3.1.15 Biological Locomotion

The wide variety of locomotive strategies for autonomous machines is surpassed by the range of techniques and mechanisms utilized by biological systems. Animal locomotion is characterized by rhythmic activity and the use of multiple joints and muscles. Vertebrates use antagonistic muscles to generate torques at the joints of rigid bones to apply forces to the environment to move the body. Locomotion is controlled via central pattern generators – neural circuits that generate rhythmic activity without rhythmic input. Mathematical models of central pattern generators have been devised for biped [626] and quaduped locomotion [136]. There is evidence of a central pattern pathway in humans [225] and in other animals (e.g., [379]).

Given the success of biological locomotion, it is not surprising that many robot locomotion mechanisms and strategies trace their routes back to biological models. Such an approach is known as being **biomimetic**. In addition to providing a basis and strategies for limbed locomotion, biological inspiration can also be found for snake robots [230] and robotic fish [29], among others (e.g., [380]).

3.2   Off-Board Communication

Most mobile robots must interact with a human operator if only to report that the current task has been completed. This communication may require a physical substrate such as a cable, or it may utilize some wireless communication strategy such as a wireless Ethernet, serial, infrared, visual, or audio-based communications channel.

3.2.1   Tethered

A tether simplifies off-board communications. Existing wireless communication mechanisms are considerably slower and provide a lower channel bandwidth than their "wired" counterparts, although this is beginning to change. Tethered communication is also more robust than the untethered kind, and thus the use of a tether tends to reduce robot development time, as the problems associated with dealing with an unreliable communication stream can be avoided.

Tethering a robot avoids a number of technical problems at the expense of mobility. Once the decision to tether a robot has been made, the tether can be used to provide not only communications and control linkages but also power. This reduces or eliminates concerns with respect to onboard power production and storage: the size, type, capacity, and weight of batteries, as well as power consumption issues. Given all the advantages of tethered operations, it would seem to be the ideal method for managing power and off-board communications. Unfortunately, a tether limits a robot's mobility because the cable must have some finite length, and it also introduces the task of cable management. This can be a challenging problem; see Figure 3.29.

3.2.2   Untethered

If a robot is to operate in an untethered manner, then the choice of the underlying wireless communication technology becomes an issue. For terrestrial mobile robots, radio-based technologies are typically employed, although there exists a range of other options. At the software level, these devices attempt to emulate existing wire-based technologies without relying on the wire. Spread-spectrum communications strategies

Figure 3.29. The realities of cable management.

use a radio transmitter/receiver mounted on the robot and one or more base stations for communication. Multiple robots can be used within the same environment but with a reduction in effective bandwidth.

The most common problem with radio frequency–based hardware is the existence of nulls and multi-path interference within the environment. Regions may exist in the environment that receive either very poor signals, and hence low bandwidth, or no radio communication at all. These regions are formed by multi-path signals or from the existence of barriers to the radio signal.

Radio Modems   Radio modems are devices that transform digital signals into modulations of radio waves and invert the process at the receiver. As their name suggests, radio modems provide serial communications, that is, they provide the equivalent of a wireless serial connection. Designers of radio modems have to deal with a number of different problems: how to modulate the radio wave, which frequencies to use, how to deal with interference (noise), and the fact that in most countries governments regulate the use of the radio spectrum. As different governments have regulated the radio spectrum in different ways, what works under one regulation (e.g., the Uniited States) does not necessarily work elsewhere (e.g., Japan). Thus although standards for radio modems have emerged, there are multiple competing standards.

WiFi (802.11)   The designation 802.11 refers to an IEEE standard for wireless local area networks. Various 802.11 standards exist, with 802.11g and 802.11n being the most commonly encountered versions currently. The 802.11g and 802.11n utilize radio technology and communicate in the 2.4 GHz and 6 GHz radio bands. With a maximum range of 100 to 150 feet, its support of standard TCP-IP network protocols, its ability to connect multiple devices using standard protocols, its reasonably high data rate (802.11n can provide service at up to 450 Mbps), and its relatively low cost, 802.11 is is perhaps the standard communications technology for mobile devices.

In a typical installation, an 802.11 network relies on one or more base stations to provide control to the network. Each computer or robot on the network requires an appropriate wireless network card for access, and once properly configured, can treat the wireless network as though it were a standard (wired) Ethernet network.

RC   The RC (radio-controlled) toy industry has established a standard protocol for communicating with radio-controlled devices such as toy cars, boats, and airplanes. Communicating at either 27 MHz or 49 MHz, these devices operate in the same frequency range as remote garage door openers and walkie-talkies. Pulse width modulation is used to communicate between the transmitter (the remote control) and the receiver (the remote toy). Unlike radio modems, Bluetooth, and 802.11 radio technologies, typically RC is a one-way communications standard.

Bluetooth   Bluetooth is a short-range wireless communication standard that operates in the 2.4 GHz radio spectrum. A spread-spectrum, frequency-hopping approach is used to provide interference immunity. Bluetooth has a relatively low bandwidth of only 1.5 Mbps.

Cell Phone Technology: GSM (3g), LTE (4g), 5g, and Beyond The GSM (Groupe Speciale Mobile, or as it is more commonly known Global System for Mobile Communications) is an international standard for digital cellular phones. GSM began in Europe in 1991, and in much of the world is now being phased out due to emergence of more modern cellular phone communication technologies. LTE and later technologies typically rely on transmitting in the 800 MHz to 3.6 GHz; 4g provides data transmission rates up to 100 Mbps. When fully deployed, the 5g mmWave band is anticipated to provide up to 3 Gbps.

Although cellular phone technology-based communication is relatively inexpensive and reliable throughout much of the world, it is not without its drawbacks. First, in many parts of the world data communication is still expensive. Something that is not an issue with the other radio technologies described above. Second, it is not available everywhere. And even in places where it is available connectivity may be inconsistent.

3.3   Processing

The final key component of a mobile robot is the processing. Later chapters consider the types of computational task that a mobile robot must perform. Here we examine where that processing can take place.

Perhaps the most straightforward option would be to place the computational resources onboard. This choice has been followed on a number of systems, from very simple robots to very large and complex systems such as the Carnegie Mellon University Navigation Laboratory (CMU Navlab). Placing the processing on-board provides the processors direct access to sensors and motor controllers, which provide locomotion for the robot. The major problem with this solution is power. Processors and their associated primary and secondary storage units consume it, and the energy budget for a robot is always a constraint in its design. A second problem arises due to the bulk and fragile nature of computer components. In spite of advances in mobile computer technology, the significant mass and volume associated with performing the computation on-board contributes significantly toward the total vehicle payload. In addition, some processing needs cannot be met with existing mobile computer technology. For example, GPU processors for AI-based reasoning systems processors may require more power and space than is available on an indoor robot.

The obvious alternative to providing all of the computation on-board is to perform some or more of the processing off-board. In the extreme version, on-board systems exist only to provide a link between off-board processors and on-board sensors/motor controllers. This solution has a number of advantages. Power consumption for on-board processors is reduced, and more general-purpose processors and even cloud-based computing can be used because they do not have to be mounted on-board. This can allow more rapid prototyping because off-board environments often provide more sophisticated and standard programming environments. The major drawback with this approach is that off-board processors must deal with long and possibly unbounded delays between off-board computation and on-board sensors and actuators. In addtion, off board processors have only indirect access to the actual on-board devices, so certain computations involving real-time device access are difficult or impossible. The problem with off-board processing is made more severe if the communication link has a limited bandwidth or can suffer from communication delay or dropout such as that associated with wireless or infrared links.

The most typical compromise between these two alternatives is to distribute the processing between on-board and off-board components. Time-critical (real-time) processing is performed on-board, while less time-critical processing can be safely placed at a remote location in order to reduce on-board load and power consumption.

3.4   Further Reading

Robot components There are a number of "hobby robot" books that discuss the literal nuts and bolts issues associated with building a robot. Miles and Carroll [531] provide a good introduction to **combat robots**, including details of mechanical construction. Jones and Flynn [396] examine, in part, the problems associated with building small experimental robots.

Wheeled mobile robots Many different classes of WMR exist, with the set of combinations of steered and unsteered, driven and idle wheels, and so on appearing almost endless. The task of identifying and dealing with slippage, non-ideal wheels, and many of the subtleties associated with real wheels is beyond the scope of this text. Rather than consider the general problem of the kinematics of wheeled mobile robots, only a few common kinematics structures are considered here. For a more abstract overview of general wheeled kinematic structures, see [22] and [142].

Only very simple strategies for path generation have been considered here, and many more-complex strategies for specific classes of wheeled mobile are possible. For example, a mechanism for identifying smoothly changing paths based on Clothoids can be found in [276].

Legged robots A large literature exists on the forward and inverse kinematics of robotic manipulators (e.g., [193]). Both [729] and [651] provide in-depth surveys of early legged robot designs, while [499] describes gait generation for Ambler. [354] describes control using dynamic stability. [489] looks at the problem of gait transition for quadruped robots. [530] provides a review of bipedial robots and their gaits and [90] provides a review of qaudruped robots from earliest designs to the present day.

Soft robots [140] provides a good review of soft robots and their locomotion strategies.

Aquatic robots [286] provides a solid description of the guidance and control of aquatic vehicles. [852] surveys soft underwater robots.

Flying robots [415] provides a detailed description of lighter-than-air vehicles including aerodynamic modeling. [587] provides a very thorough, if ancient, discussion of the issues associated with modeling the aerodynamics of lighter-than-air craft. [690] provides a review of vehicle design. See also [793].

Space robots [221] provides a collection of papers on robotic systems for deployment in space. See [277] for a review of robotic technology for on-orbit servicing and [599] for a review of robotic manipulation and capture. [802] provides a review of space vehicle dynamics and control. There have been a number of efforts to deploy robots alongside astronauts including [94] and [135].

Other locomotive strategies A wide range of other locomotive strategies exist, especially for niche tasks. For example, there exist robots that drive inside pipes [672], drive on the outside of pipes [34], and climb walls [861, 480].

3.5   Problems

1. Design a 4-link kinematic chain working on the two-dimensional plane anchored at the origin. Your robot should have two prismatic joints and two revolute joints. (One of these joints will link the robot to the origin.) You can arrange these links and joints in any manner you wish. Precisely indicate the link lengths and the joints in your sketch. Assume that the prismatic joints have a range of motion of one half of the link length and that the revolute joints can be rotated plus or minus 45° from their nominal rest position as indicated in your sketch.

    (a) Show the transformation from the world coordinate system to a coordinate system aligned with the end effector using both a sequence of matrices and a single compound matrix in homogeneous coordinates.
    (b) Indicate a few pairs of adjacent points that are inside and outside of the robot's workspace (i.e., show points on the border of the workspace). Try and select informative examples.
    (c) Consider and discuss the inverse kinematics problem for your robot. How easy is it to solve the inverse kinematics problem for your robot? Justify your answer in as much detail as possible (i.e., with an example and/or a sound argument).

2. Consider the two-steerable-wheeled bicycle sketched in Figure 3.30. This is a bicycle in which the front wheel (wheel f) is powered, and the rear wheel (wheel r) just rolls on the ground. The front wheel makes an angle α_f with respect to the bike frame and the rear wheel makes an angle α_r. The front wheel is powered with ground contact speed v_f, and the rear wheel rolls on the ground with ground-contact speed v_r. The front and rear wheels are separated by a distance d.

    (a) If the steering axle of the bike's rear wheel is located at (x, y) and the bike's frame points in direction θ as shown in the figure, identify the location of the ICC for this vehicle.
    (b) Under what conditions does the ICC exist?
    (c) At what speed does the rear wheel need to revolve in order for both wheels to roll smoothly on the ground surface?

3. Consider the robotic leg structure sketched in Figure 3.31. This leg corresponds roughly to the structure of the leg of the Honda Walking Robot.

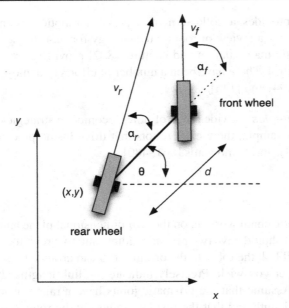

Figure 3.30. Sketch of a
two-wheeled bicycle.

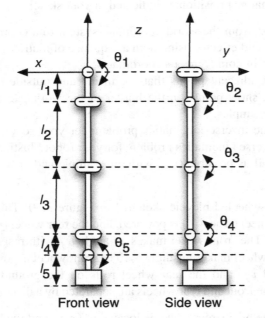

Figure 3.31. Sketch of the Honda
Walking Robot leg.

Front view   Side view

(a) Obtain an expression for the position and orientation of the foot in the body-
based coordinate system shown. The $\{\theta_i\} = \mathbf{0}$ configuration corresponds to
the leg being straight as shown in the figure.

(b) Write a computer program that allows you to generate a view of the robot
leg. That is, the program takes as input $\{\theta_i\}$ and renders a view of the leg. One
way of accomplishing this would be to code the leg in Gazebo and control it
through ROS.

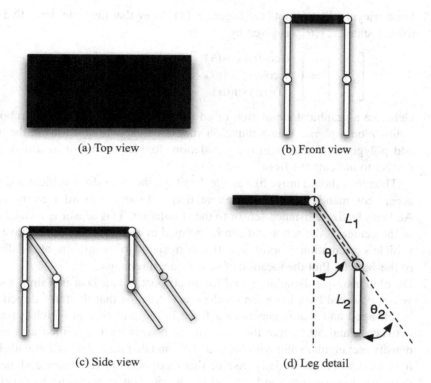

(a) Top view (b) Front view

(c) Side view (d) Leg detail

Figure 3.32. Simple four-legged vehicle.

(c) Using the body-based coordinate system, determine if the leg can be configured such that the foot is touching the ground at (x, y, z) with orientation n and twist γ. If it can, compute the set of joint angles that makes this configuration possible.

(d) Modify the program written above to take as input the ground position, goal orientation, and twist.

4. Consider the simple four-legged walking robot shown in Figure 3.32. The robot has eight degrees of freedom – each leg consists of two links of length l, and each leg is controlled by two joints. The legs on the robot lie in two planes – one on the left side of the robot and the other on the right.

Build a graphical simulation for this robot allowing it to be simulated on an infinite flat surface. Assume that individual legs are either in point contact with the ground surface or not. Do not do a dynamic simulation – only perform a static simulation.

(a) Assume that the legs are massless, and write code to compute the center of mass of the robot and to determine whether the robot is stable.

(b) Have the robot execute a Crawl gait. Ensure that the robot remains statically stable.

5. For a tricycle drive robot (see Figure 3.11), show that the time derivative of the robot's state $[x, y, \theta]^T$ is given by

$$
\begin{bmatrix} \dot{x} \\ \dot{y} \\ \dot{\theta} \end{bmatrix} = \begin{bmatrix} v\cos(\alpha)\cos(\theta) \\ v\cos(\alpha)\sin(\theta) \\ (v/d)\sin(\alpha) \end{bmatrix}.
$$

6. Generate a graphical simulation of an idealized cylindrical wheeled robot with radius r on a plane. Your simulation should be capable of allowing the user to add polygonal obstacles to the simulation. Render the robot as a disk with a marker to indicate the front of the robot.

   The robot should move like an idealized synchronous drive vehicle and should accept commands to change its orientation and move forward a given distance. Add an idealized distance sensor to the simulation. This sensor is located on top of the center of the robot and can be pointed in any direction (α) relative to the vehicle's orientation. Choose $\alpha = 0$ to correspond to the straight-ahead direction of the vehicle. Plot the location of sensor measurements.

7. Develop a simple dynamic model for an air boat (an air boat is a simple surface vessel powered by a large fan on the rear). Assume that the fan's direction can be changed and that it generates a force in the direction in which it points of between 0 and 50 N, that the mass of the boat is well described as a uniform density rectangular solid with mass 200 kg, and that the vessel is 2 m wide by 3 m long by 0.5 m high. Initially assume that there is no air resistance and that there is no friction between the boat and the water. You may choose to develop the dynamics modeling package from scratch or to use one of the standard dynamics modeling libraries (e.g. PyBullet [643]).

   (a) Add a friction term that provides a force in the direction opposite to the current translational motion of the vehicle and that is proportional to the square of the linear velocity and has a constant of 0.1. This force should act through the center of mass of the vehicle.

   (b) Add a friction term that reduces the rotational velocity of the vehicle. This angular force is in opposite direction to the angular velocity of the vehicle, is proportional to the angular velocity, and has a constant of 0.1.

   (c) Develop a set of simple motion strategies for the vehicle (go forward k meters, turn by θ degrees).

8. Many universities and research labs have deployed a network of wireless base stations in order to enable network access for laptops and other wireless devices. It is often the case that a mobile robot can exploit this infrastructure. If a robot was to use the network for communications, what changes would be required, if any, to the existing communications mechanism? Does the network require a VPN? Does the network deal with handoff from one zone to another in a transparent way?

   By probing the address and power of the visible base stations, is it possible for a robot to estimate its location within the environment? Finally, do there exist dead spots in the environment that should be avoided by an autonomous system that relies on this infrastructure?

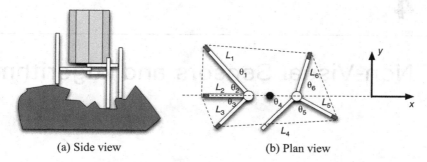

(a) Side view   (b) Plan view

Figure 3.33. The Ambler robot. (a) A side view demonstrating how the vertical components of the legs provide mobility over rough terrain. (Note that only three of the robot's six legs are shown.) (b) A plan view of the robot and the robot-centric coordinate system (origin at the center of mass of the robot). In the (x, y) plane each leg is defined by two values; L_i, the length of the prismatic link, and θ_i, the orientation of the leg relative to the x axis. Legs in contact with the ground have the foot projection colored black. The two hips are at $(\pm L_0, 0)$ in robot-centric coordinates. The current support polygon is shown as a dashed line.

9. Ambler [434, 828] (see Figure 3.15d) is a hexapod walker with each leg consisting of two links in the horizontal plane (one revolute and one prismatic) and one prismatic link in the vertical plane. Figure 3.33 shows an approximation to the kinematic structure of the Ambler robot. Figure 3.33a shows a side view illustrating the vertical extent of each leg. Ambler utilized a **circulating gait** in which legs rotated through the body of the robot (see Figure 3.33b) to recover legs from behind the robot, although other gaits were possible. The ordering of the legs was constrained due to their mechanical construction. To a reasonable approximation, Ambler's legs had a vertical extent in the range $(0, 300)$ cm, L_0 is approximately 100 cm, and the horizontal extent for the prismatic joint was in the range $(106, 234)$ cm [209]. Assume that Ambler maintains its body perpendicular to the gravity vector.

   (a) Given the current leg parameters $\{(L_i, \theta_i)\}$ and knowledge of which legs are in contact with the ground, determine the current support polygon and the vehicle's stability margin.

   (b) Given that leg L_3 is at (u, v) in the robot-centric coordinate system and that all legs are in contact with the ground, what set of joint velocities $\{(\dot{L}_i, \dot{\theta}_i)\}$ is required to move the center of mass in the direction $(\partial u, \partial v)$ without rotating the body of the vehicle?

4

Non-Visual Sensors and Algorithms

"Danger Will Robinson, Danger!"[1]

Sensing is a key requirement for any but the simplest mobile behavior. In order for Robot to be able to warn the crew of *Lost in Space* that there is danger ahead, it must be able to sense and reason about its sensor responses. Sensing is a critical component of the fundamental tasks of **pose estimation** – determining where the robot is in its environment; **pose maintenance** – maintaining an ongoing estimate of the robot's pose; and **map construction** – building a representation of the robot's environment. Information from wheel encoders can tell you how often a wheel has revolved, but slip between the wheel and the ground is not captured by this, and thus the true position of the robot will deviate from its commanded position. Without external measurements of the outside world this deviation quickly results in the robot becoming "lost."

In this chapter and the next we consider a range of sensing technologies. The sensors most strongly associated with mobility are those that measure the distance that the vehicle has moved (e.g., the distance the wheels have traveled along the ground), those that measure inertial changes, and those that measure external structure in the environment. For a robot to know where it is or how it got there, or to be able to reason about where it has gone, sensors and sensing algorithms are required.

Sensors and algorithms for their interpretation can be highly complex. Although a wide variety of sensors exists, two different classes of sensors have emerged for mobile robots: visual sensors, which use light reflected from objects in the environment to reason about structure, and non-visual sensors, which use various audio, inertial, and other modalities to sense the environment. Non-visual sensing algorithms are considered in some detail here; the class of vision-based sensors and algorithms is considered in Chapter 5.

4.1   Basic Concepts

Nothing is in the understanding, which is not first in the senses.[2]

Perhaps the most fundamental classification of sensor types is as **internal-state** sensors and **external-state** sensors. Internal-state sensors provide feedback on the internal properties of a robotic system, such as the battery level, the wheel positions, or the joint angles for a robot arm or leg. The broad term for internal sensing in biological organisms

---

[1] Robot, from the TV series *Lost in Space*.
[2] John Locke.

is **proprioception**; this term is sometimes borrowed by the robotics community. Hunger is an example of internal sensing in humans. External-state sensors deal with the observation of aspects of the world outside the robot itself: humidity, the color of objects, and so on. External sensors that work by touching objects are **contact sensors**, while all others, such as camera-based sensors, are **non-contact sensors**.

A specific sensor is either active (it is said to be an **active sensor**) or it is passive (it is said to be a **passive sensor**). These terms are not to be confused with the terms **active vision** and **passive vision**, to be discussed in Chapter 5. Active sensors are those that make observations by emitting energy into the environment or by modifying the environment. Passive sensors, on the other hand, are those that passively receive energy to make their observations. For example, human vision and **olfaction** involve the use of passive sensors, while touch or shouting and listening for the echo are active sensing techniques (shouting and listening for the echo is a simple way to gauge the size of a room).

Passive sensing is often preferred because it is non-intrusive, energy efficient, and similar to the preferred sensing modes of many biological organisms. Because passive sensing does not emit energy, it is especially useful where the robot should be inconspicuous, for example, in security surveillance, in many military contexts, or when multiple robots occupy the same environment. Active sensing, on the other hand, because it involves direct interaction with the environment, tends to be less energy efficient but more robust, in that it it less subject to the vagaries of the available energy sources.

This difference between active and passive sensing is illustrated by considering two alternative approaches to making a distance measurement: using passive stereo vision and using a laser-based system. Passive stereo works by observing the same point (e.g., the position of some mark or feature) on an object from two different cameras and thus measuring the parallax (i.e., the change in observed position). The key step is that the marking observed with one camera must be detected in the view observed with the second camera. If the object has a repeating pattern on it, if the object has insufficient markings on it, or if the marking is a specularity (a shiny spot) that moves with the observer's position, then the required distance measurement will be difficult or impossible to make. On the other hand, if the observed marking is a laser spot projected by the robot, the high energy at a particular frequency will typically make the marking uniquely and unambiguously detectable.

There are several broad but critical observations that can be made regarding sensors in the context of mobile robots:

- Real sensors are noisy.
- Real sensors return an incomplete description of the environment.
- Real sensors cannot usually be modeled completely.

Underestimating the extent to which these three generalizations hold can lead to considerable difficulties when "ideal" algorithms are applied in the real world. Underestimating the real properties of sensors and environmental complexity has led to the demise of many otherwise-promising projects in computer vision and robotics.

The use of sensors to make inferences about the environment is often described as a problem of recovering or **reconstructing** the environment. This concept of environmental reconstruction has become a major theme within the sensing community. Unfortunately, this can be a surprisingly difficult problem even with a sensor that returns an apparently rich description of the environment.

A wide variety of alternative sensor technologies is available. This plethora of options can be broadly decomposed into four main classes based on the type of data returned:

- **Range sensors** return measurements of distance between the sensor and objects in the environment.
- **Absolute position sensors** return the position of the robot (or some elements of the position vector) in absolute terms (e.g., latitude and longitude).
- **Environmental sensors** return properties of the environment. These can be ambient properties, like temperature, or point-wise properties, like the color at a point in front of the robot.
- **Inertial sensors** return differential properties of the robot's position, for example, acceleration.

A variety of additional general issues can be used to classify different sensor technologies. While we will not go into detail, examples of important sensor properties or criteria include:

- **Speed of operation.** This relates the rate at which measurements are returned when the sensor is running continuously, or the time delay until a measurement is provided when one is requested intermittently.
- **Cost.** An infrared emitter-detector pair can cost as little as a few cents while accurate GPS-based systems can cost several thousand dollars.
- **Error rate.** Various factors can be relevant and are discussed later. These include the average error, the number of outliers (wildly incorrect measurements), and the number of missed measurements.
- **Robustness.** This refers to the extent to which the sensor tolerates various environmental deviations from the ideal operating conditions. Relevant factors may be physical disturbance, environmental noise in terms of the stimuli of interest, electrical noise, and so on.
- **Computational requirements.** A simple contact switch may require no computation at all to transduce its result, whereas some neural net work–based algorithms require significant computational resources, and perhaps special-purpose graphics-based processors in order to obtain a timely result.
- **Power, weight, and size requirements.** Some systems require continuous power just to remain "alive" so that sensors readings can be taken, whereas other sensors can be "turned off" and only consume power when measurements are required.

We can model the relationship between the physical properties of interest in the environment e and the sensor reading r using the sensor model $r = f(e)$. In principle, the sensor model should include a model for both noise internal to the sensor and noise due to other sources. Sensor models for a number of different sensors are developed later in this chapter.

The typical sensor model includes not only a stochastic component due to noise, but also usually has a range with fewer dimensions than the range of the relation. That is, the sensor model collapses a multi-dimensional environment into a lower-dimensional reading. The problem of recovering the environment *from* the sensor data can be described as an **inverse problem**: to recover the argument(s) to a function, given the output of the function. Such problems are traditionally difficult to solve without additional information or assumptions because the collapse of dimensions often leads to ambiguity in establishing which of several possible environmental scenarios (i.e., values of the domain) gave rise to a particular reading. Such problems are referred to as being **ill-posed**. More generally, ill-posed problems are problems with:

- A solution that is undefined.
- A solution that is not uniquely defined.
- A solution that is not **stable**.

As a concrete example of an ill-posed problem, consider the task of differentiating a signal $f_0(x)$ corrupted by a small amount of high-frequency noise:

$$f(x) = f_0(x) + k \sin(\omega x).$$

The differentiated signal $f'(x)$ is given by

$$f'(x) = f_0'(x) + k\omega \cos(\omega x).$$

Now, if $\omega \gg 0$ (the noise has a high frequency), then rather than being corrupted by a small-amplitude signal, $f'(x)$ is corrupted by much higher-amplitude noise. Extracting the content of $f_0'(x)$ from within the corrupted signal $f'(x)$ is a classic example of an ill-posed problem. The derivative is $f(x)$ is unstable in the presence of high-frequency noise.

Sensors can also be unstable with respect to their input. An unstable sensor is one for which the output can vary wildly with a small variation in the input. Formally, for a sensor with output $f(e)$, instability refers to

$$\lim_{h \to 0} \frac{\|f(e) - f(e + h)\|}{h} \to \infty.$$

In practice, if the value of

$$\frac{\|f(e) - f(e + h)\|}{h}$$

is large for small values of h, then the sensor may be referred to as unstable. In practice, this implies that the sensor value may vary unpredictably.

One approach to overcoming instability and other attributes of ill-posed problems is to apply techniques to overconstrain the system and to use an approach such as least-squares to make the measurement more accurate. One difficulty with least-squares systems is that the optimization cannot easily represent smoothness or environmental constraints that are implicit in the data. Environmental assumptions can be used to resolve the ill-posedness of the problem; assumptions can be used to select which of several possible solutions is preferred. Such assumptions come in various forms. The most general, and for that reason perhaps the most elegant, are known as **regularization** assumptions in the sense of Tikhonov [773]. This approach refers to formulating the inverse problem with an additional stabilizing cost term that implicitly selects some solutions over others based on their preferred cost (the cost function must also be constructed to be a semi-norm, i.e., it is unambiguous). In the case of regularization – a variational problem – the cost term is sometimes known as a **stabilizer**. The key issue with resolving the ambiguity inherent in an ill-posed problem is that the ambiguity must be resolved by selecting the correct solution, not just any solution (while this may appear self-evident, there any many examples of reconstruction problems where the ill-posedness has been resolved without sufficient justification). Under Tikhonov's approach, the solution $\mathbf{x}$ to a set of linear constraints $\mathbf{Mx} = \mathbf{y}$ is given by

$$\min ||\mathbf{Mx} - \mathbf{y}||^2 + \lambda ||\mathbf{Cx}||^2,$$

where

$$||\mathbf{Cx}||^2 = \sum_n \int C_n(z)|x^{(n)}(z)|^2 dz.$$

Here $x^{(n)}(z)$ is the n'th derivative of $x(z)$.

Essentially $\mathbf{Cx}$ is a weighting term that penalizes non-smooth solutions. Known constraints on the solution are used to choose the weighting functions $C_n(z)$ and λ. Tikhonov stabilizers have found widespread application in sensor interpretation. Poggio *et al.* [629], for example, describe the application of regularization to low-level vision tasks.

4.2   Contact Sensors: Bumpers

> And sounded, and found it twenty fathoms: and when they had gone a little further, they sounded again, and found it fifteen fathoms.[3]

Tactile sensors are those used to create a "sense of touch." These are almost always contact sensors, although some aspects of touch may be captured with non-contact sensors that pass very close to an object's surface and exploit phenomena such as capacitance.

Touch sensors are commonly used in the **bumpers** of robotic vehicles. The simplest such devices are microswitches that report a binary value: open or closed. When used in bumpers, an array of switches about the circumference of the vehicle is usually enclosed in a compliant material so that pressure anywhere in the outer bumper housing will cause one or more of the switches to be depressed. Tactile sensors are also commonly used on **end effectors** such as grippers.

More sophisticated approaches to tactile sensing exploit devices that return a signal over a wide range of values in proportion to the force applied to them. Approaches for such devices range from mechanical devices based on spring-loaded rods mechanically coupled to potentiometers to devices based on a compliant material that changes its resistance or capacitance in response to compression. It is also possible ton construct tactile sensors that provide dense tactile measurements [853] and to integrate such senors with visual capabilities [357].

How bumper data are handled depends of the architecture of the particular vehicle. Bumpers are the collision-avoidance sensor of last resort (notwithstanding the fact that by the time bumpers detect anything it is actually too late for avoidance). As such, they

---

[3] Acts 27, verse 28.

are sometimes treated as sensors and sometimes they are wired directly into the low-level control systems of the robot, just as the nerves in our knees are coupled to muscular feedback loops that act without the intercession of our brains.

Although the intent of active bumpers with embedded sensors is to avoid damage in the case of a collision, if the impact velocity is high enough the detection of the mere collision may not be sufficient to avoid damage. Many indoor robots are not equipped with active braking systems, and even if they are, the large inertia associated with a heavy vehicle may mean that it takes a considerable distance for the vehicle to come to a full stop. For example, automobile bumpers are installed not so much for their sensing ability but because they provide a force-absorbing material that reduces the consequences of an undesirable impact.

Gazebo has a bumper plugin that simulates a bumper as illustrated in Listing 4.1. In order to deal with object–object collisions, Gazebo maintains structures representing these collisions and such collisions can be passed to ROS through the `libgazebo_ros_bumper` plugin. Gazebo passes on point of contact, force and torque at the contact point, as well as depth of intersection between the two objects. The differential drive robot introduced in Chapter 3 is augmented with a simple bumper as shown in Figure 4.1, and the bumper's collision is monitored by the Gazebo plugin.

Figure 4.1. A simulated differential drive robot augmented with a bumper in Gazebo/ROS.

```
<gazebo reference="bumper_link">
  <sensor name="bumper_sensor" type="contact">
    <alwaysOn>true</alwaysOn>
    <update_rate>200</update_rate>
    <contact>
      <collision>base_footprint_fixed_joint_lump__bumper_link_collision_2</collision>
      <topic>bumper_contact_state</topic>
    </contact>
    <plugin name="gazebo_ros_bumper_controller" filename="libgazebo_ros_bumper.so">
      <ros><remapping>bumper_states:=robot_bumper_contact_state</remapping></ros>
      <frame_name>bumper_link</frame_name>
    </plugin>
  </sensor>
</gazebo>
```

Listing 4.1. A bumper implemented in Gazebo/ROS.

4.3   Inertial Sensors

The class of external sensors that makes the least reference to the external world is known as **inertial sensors**. These are sensors that measure derivatives of the robot's position variables. In particular, the term "inertial sensor" is commonly used to refer to **accelerometers** and **gyroscopes**, which measure the second derivatives of position, that is, the acceleration and angular acceleration of the vehicle.

One of the earliest uses of inertial sensors for autonomous guidance over long distances can be found in the work of the German Peenemunde group. The V1 was an autonomous aircraft that relied on inertial guidance [639] (see Figure 1.4). With an operational range greater than 200 km, the V1 relied on multiple inertial and other sensors to guide the weapon to the target. The V1 was required to go in a particular direction, at a specific altitude, for a specific distance. Different sensors were used to address each of these requirements. For distance measurement, a windmill mounted on the nose of fuselage was used to measure the distance the weapon had traveled. Altitude was measured using a gas capsule whose expansion and contraction were a function of height. The craft's direction was maintained using three air-driven gyroscopes and by measuring the craft's deviation from some initial setting. Because gyroscopes drift during flight, the V1 was fitted with a magnetic compass to correct for gyroscopic drift. This use of multiple inertial and external sensors to deal with limitations of individual sensors while providing sufficient sensing to accomplish the overall task of the autonomous system is a common approach in autonomous systems.

4.3.1   Accelerometers

Accelerometers are essentially spring-mounted masses whose displacement under acceleration can be measured, thus exploiting Newton's law $F = ma$ and the (ideal) spring-mass relation $F = kx^2$. Solving for a yields

$$a = \frac{kx^2}{m},$$

where a is the acceleration, m is the mass, and k is the spring constant. In practice, alternatives to the spring-mass system are used. Each accelerometer measures acceleration along a single direction. By mounting three accelerometers orthogonal to one another, one can fabricate an omnidirectional acceleration sensing device. Such devices are available as off-the-shelf items.

Accelerometers are sometimes viewed as a sensor that needs to make no reference to the external world. While this is almost true, to correctly compute acceleration the local gravity vector must be known, both in direction and magnitude, so that it can be factored out of the accelerometer's readings. Note that in practice it can be extremely difficult to separate acceleration due to gravity from other forces acting on the device. With this exception, these sensors have the exceptional characteristics of being usable anywhere, from undersea, to Earth's surface, to outer space.

4.3.2   Gyroscopes

As with accelerometers, gyroscopes measure angular acceleration by exploiting basic Newtonian mechanics. The most familiar form of the device is the mechanical

```
<gazebo reference="imu_link">
  <gravity>true</gravity>
  <sensor name="imu_sensor" type="imu">
    <always_on>true</always_on>
    <update_rate>100</update_rate>
    <plugin name="imu_publisher" filename="libgazebo_ros_imu_sensor.so">
      <ros>
        <remapping>~/out:=imu</remapping>
        <initial_orientation_as_reference>false</initial_orientation_as_reference>
      </ros>
    </plugin>
  </sensor>
</gazebo>
```

Listing 4.2. Simulating an IMU in Gazebo/ROS.

gyroscope: a rapidly spinning mass suspended in a gimbal. Since angular momentum is conserved, any attempt to change the orientation of the gyroscope results in an effective force that would, if unimpeded, lead to precession. By measuring this force, the orientation change can be determined. Thus, the gyroscope can be described as a differential compass, that is, a device for measuring differential or relative orientation.

Computer-controlled navigation using a mechanical gyro involves an electrically driven rotor and an electrical readout of the precession induced, and hence the orientation change. Such a device is described as a **rate gyro**. Devices that explicitly integrate the orientation changes measured by a gyroscopic system are referred to as **rate integrating**. Since Earth itself rotates, even a system stationary with respect to Earth's surface will observe motion.

The principal difficulty with gyroscopic orientation estimation is that small measurement errors accrue over time. In the case of gyroscopy the gradual loss of accuracy due to error accumulation is referred to as **drift**. In mechanical systems drift results from friction and from inevitable imperfections in the gymbals. The rate that this error grows can vary from tenths of a degree to tens of degrees per second and depends on the precision of the machining, which, in turn, determines the price which can vary by up to three orders of magnitude.

An alternative approach to the measurement of absolute orientation is to leverage an optical phenomenon termed the **Sagnac effect**, after its discoverer Georges Sagnac. Because the effect is a purely optical phenomenon, it permits the construction of optical gyros that involve no moving parts.

The Sagnac effect is based on the use of an optical cavity that contains a lasing medium (a medium that can be excited to emit laser light). The cavity is excited by light pulses traveling in two opposite directions (in a passive gyro, the laser can be outside the cavity). The light in the cavity forms a standing wave that remains stationary in an inertial frame. As the cavity rotates, the reflecting mirrors at the ends can be visualized as moving across a succession of nodes of the standing wave, leading to an observed beat frequency in the emitted light. An alternative description of the same effect is to visualize a change dl in the length of the cavity as a result of rotational motion with angular velocity Ω [165]:

$$dl = 4\pi \frac{r^2 \Omega}{c},$$

where r is the radius of the cavity and c is the speed of light in the medium in the cavity.

For a standing wave to be produced, the light wavelength must divide the cavity length an integer number of time (i.e., with no remainder). As a result, variations in the path length lead to changes in the light wavelength. The variation in frequency induced by the variation in length is given by

$$df = \frac{2r\Omega}{\lambda}.$$

The original effect observed by Sagnac involved the phase shift $\delta\phi$ of (non-coherent) light in a ring interferometer:

$$\delta\phi = \frac{8\pi\Omega A}{\lambda c},$$

where A is the area of the interferometer.

This basic phenomenon has been exploited in several forms: active resonators have a cavity filled with the lasing material, whereas passive resonators use a lasing medium that is outside the resonant cavity used for the Sagnac effect. An alternative methodology allows the Sagnac effect to be observed without a laser using interferometry and makes them more suitable for mobile robots. Fiberoptic technology has led to dramatic and ongoing reductions in the price of optical gyros and improvements in their robustness and availability. Fiberoptic implementations include those based on passive resonant cavities as well as interferometry. Typical implementations involve a coiled fiber optical cable that leads to a very substantial cavity length.

Optical gyros have drift that results from optical and electrical imperfections and noise. Without special compensation, some systems are also unable to provide measurements at low angular velocities. Typical low-cost units can have drift rates on the order of several degrees per hour, while costly systems for aeronautical navigation may have accuracies of only 0.001 degrees per hour.

4.3.3   Compasses and Inclinometers

An **inclinometer** is a simple device that measures the orientation of the gravity vector. Digital inclinometers are the modern-day analog of the carpenter's plumb line. Simple (coarse) inclinometers are based on mercury switches or electrolytic-tilt switches.

Although it may seem a trivial point, the importance of integrating even a coarse-grained inclinometer within a mobile robot cannot be over stressed. A robot without a tilt sensor cannot sense its current state of balance and hence cannot respond to unexpected ramps, bumps or depressions in its environment which can lead to catastrophic effects.

Whereas inclinometers measure deviation from the gravity frame, a **compass** measures orientation with respect to Earth's magnetic field. Mechanical magnetic compasses use Earth's magnetic field to orient the compass by allowing a magnet to rotate in the horizontal plane and align itself with Earth's magnetic field. **Gyrocompasses** are gyroscopes modified so that they align with the rotational axis of Earth. A digital **flux gate compass** uses a toroidal magnet suspended in Earth's magnetic field.

Sensors that utilize the local magnetic field to detect north are susceptible to local variations in the ambient magnetic field. Large metal structures, such as the robot itself, its motors, and so on, can have a considerable effect on the local magnetic field. It is essential to calibrate such a sensor with respect to the vehicle and the environment and to recognize that unmodeled and unexpected deviations in the local magnetic field do occur.

Gazebo supports a plugin (see Listing 4.2) that provides an additive Gaussian noise–corrupted Inertial Measurement Unit (IMU) that can be attached to a convenient link in the robot description.

4.4   Sonar

Sonar (**so**und **n**avigation **and r**anging) sensing refers to range sensing using acoustic (i.e., sound) signals. Sonar is an active sensing technology whereby a sound signal or pulse is emitted and its reflection is subsequently received. The time of flight, the phase shift, and the attenuation of the signal as a function of frequency are aspects of the reflected signal that have been exploited by different types of sonar sensors. Sonar has a long history of use in target localization. As early as 1918, high-frequency acoustic waves were used to determine the position, velocity, and orientation of underwater objects. Most terrestrial sonar is based on acoustic signals in the ultrasonic range (with a frequency too high to be heard by humans).

Sonar units are typically installed in mobile robots by mounting emitter/receiver units in fixed positions on the base of the vehicle. One common strategy is to locate the sonar units at uniform angular intervals around the circumference (see Figure 4.2). This is feasible since the individual devices are comparatively inexpensive.

Sonar sensing is used by dolphins and other species (e.g., cetaceans and bats). Each of these species emits chirps of various sorts to which it then attends. In the case of some species of bat, for example, the differential reflectance of an object as a function of wavelength allows the bat to identify many characteristics of the object; this information is used to find and identify insects that they hunt, for example. The particular frequency mixes, pulse modulation strategies, and interpretation mechanisms used by bats are extremely complex, vary by species, and are not yet fully understood.

The acoustic frequency used in commercial sonar units is almost invariably ultrasonic, typically in the range of 40 to 50 kHz. Higher frequencies are attenuated more rapidly, although they provide better spatial resolution. The emitted signal has a complex amplitude profile as a function of the angle away from the transducer normal. A cross

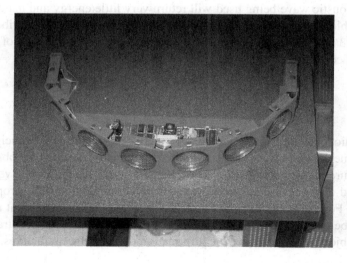

Figure 4.2. ActiveMedia Robotics P3-AT sonar sensor. Appears with the kind permission of Arjun Chopra.

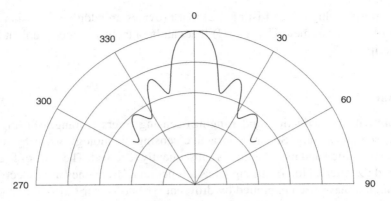

Figure 4.3. Sonar amplitude profile for the Polaroid sonar sensor: the strength of the sonar signal as a function of orientation with respect to the center of the beam. Although most of the power is restricted to a single lobe near the center of the beam, significant side lobes exist.

section of this "multi-lobed" shape is shown in Figure 4.3. The sonar beam is essentially cone shaped in 3D with non-uniform energy distribution over the cone. The maximum energy is in the center, with multiple side lobes. In consequence, the effective cone diameter increases as a function of distance. One implication of this broad wavefront is that a returned echo may be the reflection of a portion of the wavefront that leaves the transducer at an oblique angle. Thus, a single returned echo does not necessarily result in a very accurate localization of the object that reflected it using only time-of-flight methods.

The most serious impediment to inferring the location of a sonar-reflecting surface is the fact that at ultrasonic frequencies most common objects are specular reflectors; that is, they exhibit mirror-like reflection properties such that an oblique acoustic wave will be reflected away from the emitter rather than back toward it. If an echo returns to the robot at all, there is no assurance that the echo is not the result of a complex series of bounces around the environment rather than a single bounce off the closest object in the direction the transducer is pointed. In addition, objects with a cross section much smaller than the wavelength of the acoustic wave being used will return very little energy and hence will appear almost invisible. Note that the simple sonar transducer simulator described for Gazebo in Listing 4.3 and shown in Figure 4.4 does not simulate these details of sonar ranging particularly accurately.

4.5   Radar

Radar (**ra**dio **d**etecting **a**nd **r**anging) is much like sonar in its principle of operation. High-frequency radio waves are transmitted, and their reflections are observed to obtain range measurements and other properties. Radar is attractive for mobile vehicles because it is fast and also because it can provide information about surface properties as well as geometry. For example, it can be used to discriminate among different terrain types, and this may be useful in estimating traversability. Since it also can penetrate the surface layer of an object, it can also provide information of subsurface structures. Since

```
<gazebo reference="sonar_link">
  <sensor type="ray" name="sonar">
    <pose>0 0 0 0 0 0</pose>
    <visualize>true</visualize>
    <update_rate>10</update_rate>
    <ray>
      <scan>
        <horizontal>
          <samples>9</samples>
          <resolution>1</resolution>
          <min_angle>-0.1309</min_angle>
          <max_angle>0.1309</max_angle>
        </horizontal>
        <vertical>
          <samples>9</samples>
          <resolution>1</resolution>
          <min_angle>-0.1309</min_angle>
          <max_angle>0.1309</max_angle>
        </vertical>
      </scan>
      <range>
        <min>${robot_sonar_radius+0.1}</min>
        <max>${robot_sonar_radius+5}</max>
        <resolution>0.01</resolution>
      </range>
    </ray>
    <plugin name="sonar_plugin" filename="libgazebo_ros_ray_sensor.so">
      <frame_name>sonar_link</frame_name>
      <updateRate>10</updateRate>
      <radiation>ultrasound</radiation>
      <output_type>sensor_msgs/Range</output_type>
      <ros>
        <remapping>~/out:=sonar</remapping>
      </ros>
    </plugin>
  </sensor>
</gazebo>
```

Listing 4.3. Gazebo/ROS plugin to simulate a sonar sensor. Here 81 rays are cast over a rectangular volume to approximate a single Sonar sensor measurement.

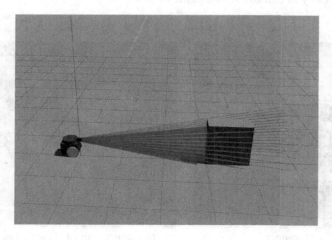

Figure 4.4. Simulating sonar in Gazebo/ROS. A set of rays is cast from the transducer and the shortest distance returned.

it is based on radio rather than acoustic waves, radar can be used in environments lacking an atmosphere, such as the surface of other planets.

Mobile robot radar systems rely on phase/frequency detection in order to measure distance to the target. Microwave and millimeter-wave radar systems have operational ranges and performance characteristics that are well suited for mobile robot applications. Like sonar systems, however, radar suffers from difficulties with specular reflections and with the relatively large footprint of the radar signal.

4.6   Laser Rangefinders

A key objective for sensing is to obtain estimates of the distance to objects in the environment. One of the preeminent sensing technologies for accomplishing this in robotics is the laser rangefinder (Figure 4.5). Laser rangefinders are based on one of the following key alternative methodologies:

Triangulation: The use of geometric relationships among the outgoing light beam, the incoming ray, and its position on the image plane.
Time of flight: (TOF) The measurement of the time delay for an outgoing light ray to hit a target whose distance is being measured and return.
Phase-based: Based on the difference between the phase of the emitted and reflected signals.

The principle of triangulation-based laser rangefinders is essentially the same as those based on regular light sources, which are discussed in Section 5.7. Laser sources, however, have the advantage of being better collimated.

Laser time-of-flight (TOF) and phase-based sensing, on the other hand, both exploit the time delay for signal propagation rather than geometric arrangement. **Lidar** is an acronym for light detection and ranging, and is used to refer to laser distance measurement devices of all kinds, especially those that exploit propagation time; but has become a part of the English language (so you can use it in a game of Scrabble).

(a) SICK laser scanner   (b) Scanner mounted on a robot

Figure 4.5. A SICK laser scanner. (a) Appears with the kind permission of Arjun Chopra.

The collimation of the beam improves the resolution and power utilization of the sensor since it avoids having a wide spot that hits multiple targets. It is the high-energy density, brevity of the pulse, and coherence of the laser source that are most significant. The sensing technology is based on measurement of the delay or the phase difference between the emitted laser signal and returned reflection. The measurement process can be interferometric or direct, but in either case relies on significant signal processing. The maximum range of the sensor is limited by the emitted signal strength.

TOF has become the predominant technology and is the underlying principle of the commonplace lidar sensor used in most applications. The essence of the technology is to measure how long it takes for pulse of laser energy to leave the transmitter, bounce off an object, and have its reflection return. Laser light is used since its coherence properties allow it to be pulsed precisely, to be focused (collimated into a narrow beam), and to provide an accurate measurement. Simple versions of this technology are used on hand-held electronic tape measures.

Low-power systems have an operating range of a few tens of meters, while higher-power systems may function over distances of one kilometer or more. This is the same technology that has been used to measure the distance from Earth to the surface of the Moon to astonishingly high accuracy. As the laser beam diverges with distance, the localization of the recovered distance becomes less accurate with more remote targets, although this is not really an issue for interplanetary targets.

Laser systems are typically mounted on either a rotating unit or as a mirror assembly to direct the beam at different parts of the environment. These mechanisms may be internal to the laser hardware housing. Given the accuracy and repeatability of laser systems, they are an effective alternative to other sensing technologies for robot pose estimation. Figure 4.6 shows two laser scans of the same environment taken from two different positions. In the system described in [484, 483], a non-linear optimization process is used to align the two scans and hence determine the robot's relative motion between them. As can be seen from the data, laser responses from clean surfaces such as walls provide robust measurements of environmental structure.

One concern with laser-based systems is the risk of eye damage to observers. Although the devices typically employed on an indoor mobile robot are "eye safe" due to low-power output, it may be difficult to convince other workers in the environment of this fact. It is also important to remember that laser light will reflect off some surfaces −

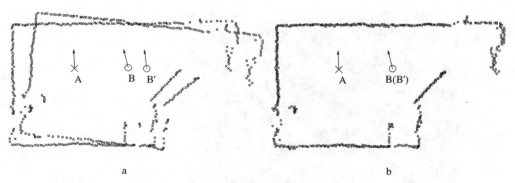

a   b

Figure 4.6. Aligning laser scans. Appears with the kind permission of E. Milios.

mirrors, pools of liquid, and so on – which will result in signal dropout, as well as possibly alarm others in the environment if the laser emits in the visible spectrum. Listing 4.4 shows the implementation of a laser sensor in Gazebo. The resulting simulation is given in Figure 4.7.

```
<gazebo reference="laser_link">
    <static>true</static>
    <sensor type="ray" name="laser">
     <pose>0 0 0 0 0 0</pose>
     <visualize>true</visualize>
     <update_rate>10</update_rate>
     <ray>
      <scan>
        <horizontal>
          <samples>360</samples>
          <resolution>1</resolution>
          <min_angle>-3.1415</min_angle>
          <max_angle>3.1240</max_angle>
        </horizontal>
      </scan>
      <range>
        <min>0.20</min>
        <max>10.0</max>
        <resolution>0.01</resolution>
      </range>
     </ray>
     <plugin name="laser_controller" filename="libgazebo_ros_ray_sensor.so">
      <ros>
        <namespace>/</namespace>
        <remapping>~/out:=scan</remapping>
      </ros>
      <frameName>laser_link</frameName>
      <output_type>sensor_msgs/LaserScan</output_type>
     </plugin>
    </sensor>
 </gazebo>
```

Listing 4.4. Simulating a laser in Gazebo/ROS. Note the similarity to the code in Listing 4.3, although here the `libgazebo_ros_laser` plugin is used instead of the `libgazebo_ros_range` plugin.

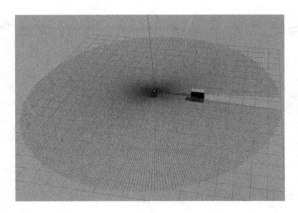

Figure 4.7. Laser sensor simulation in Gazebo/ROS.

4.7   UWB

UWB or ultra-wideband (see [18]) is a radio-based localization technology that utilizes ultra-wideband radio signals as the underlying technology. In a typical UWB system an initiator broadcasts a burst of information over a wide range of radio frequencies, and receiver stations receive this message and rebroadcast a response. The initiator estimates distance from the return time (the time of arrival or TOA) of the radio signals. Transmission messages consist of a number of pulses that enhance the process of estimating transmission time. By placing the receivers in an appropriate geometry, it is possible to localize the initiator in 3D space. UWB protocol supports a wide range of different localization processes depending on capabilities of the underlying radio infrastructure and the presence of a synchronized clock available to all of the units. Perhaps the most relevant UWB technology for mobile robots for estimating range is the time of flight (ToF) approach, as this approach does not rely on good clock synchronization between the initiator and the receivers. With proper receiver placement, geometry accuracy under 10 cm is possible [497].

The basic structure of the ToF approach is sketched in Figure 4.8. A message starts at the initiator that establishes the start poll time in the clock of the initiator (T_{SP}). Upon receiving the message the receiver establishes two times, the receive poll time (T_{RP}) and the start response time, the time at which the poll is returned to the initiator as recorded in the receiver's clock (T_{SR}). The initiator receives this response at the receive response time (T_{RR}) and records the time when it starts its final transmission with the receiver (T_{SF}), which is received at the receiver at receive final time (T_{RF}). The receiver now has $T_{SP}, T_{RP}, T_{SR}, T_{RR}, T_{SF}$, and T_{RF} with times in both the receiver and initiator clocks and with two unknown processing delays T_{RSP1} and T_{RSP2}. The one-way transmission time can be computed as

$$R = ((T_{RR} - T_{SP}) - (T_{SR} - T_{RP}) + (T_{RF} - T_{SR}) - (T_{SF} - T_{RR}))/4.$$

4.8   Satellite-Based Positioning

In 1973 the U.S. Department of Defense initiated a program to develop a position estimation system based on signals transmitted by Earth-orbiting satellites. Beginning

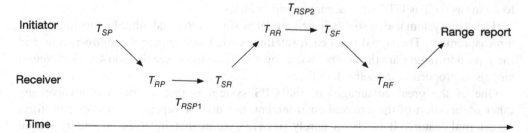

Figure 4.8. UWB algorithm. Communication is initiated by the initiator. The receiver echos this message back to the initiator and the process is repeated with the various time stamps attached to the message. When the message is returned to the receiver, it is possible to discount delays at both the initiator and receiver and to deal with the lack of synchronization of the clocks at the initiator and receiver. See text for details.

with launches in 1978, the first satellite of Block II was launched in 1989, and by 1995 the system was declared to have satisfied the requirements of full operational capability.

The U.S. system is known as **NAVSTAR** or more colloquially as the **Global Positioning System** (**GPS**). It is based on a constellation of orbiting satellites (there are "spares" in orbit as well). The system operates by allowing a user to measure the difference in time of flight for a radio signal to arrive from a combination of satellites. The satellites orbit Earth in six orbital planes so that, in principle, at least five (and as many as eight) satellites are visible at any time from any point on the planet's surface. In practice, occlusion by obstacles, from trees to mountains, can complicate the situation.

Measuring the differences in time of flight for signals from these satellites allows latitude, longitude, elevation, and current time to be estimated anywhere on Earth's surface. The satellites transmit a signal that encodes not only timing information but also information on the satellite's position and atmospheric characteristics (delays due to conditions in the layer of the atmosphere known as the ionosphere) that would alter the transmission time. Obtaining an estimate of position requires a direct view of a minimum of four satellites and can be obtained at a rate of up to 2 Hz (although most low-cost systems are slower than this). The use of additional satellites permits better performance. Typical civilian receivers can be obtained at low cost and are available in a range of portable form factors.

Historically NAVSTAR provided two different services: the precise positioning system (PPS), and the standard position system (SPS) with lower accuracy. The difference between these was referred to as selective availability (SA). This difference in accuracy was artificially induced via pseudo-random noise in the SPS signal for strategic reasons, and was eliminated in 2001 (although it could, in principle, be reinstated). Even now, the GPS network includes supplementary data in an encrypted precision "P(Y)" code that is not available to civilian users. The U.S.-based NAVSTAR system is one of a collection of competing satellite systems that includes the GLONASS (Russian), BelDou (Chineese), and Galileo (European) systems. Fortunately, many ground receivers can integrate ranging information from more than one of these systems. As a consequence, terrestrial GPS units are known as GNSS or Global Navigation Satellite Systems, as they may rely on multiple underlying satellite constellations and localization technologies.

The standard implementation of GPS is based on a position fix rate of once per second, although faster and slower rates are possible. Under typical operating conditions and without specialized enhancements GPS accuracy is roughly 20 m (typical values are 7 to 10 m) as well as UTC time accuracy within 30 ns.

The GPS system uses a sophisticated model of signal error and other factors to produce a measurement. The signal from each satellite is used to compute a **pseudo-range**, and these pseudo-ranges are then combined using a Kalman filter (see Section 4.9.1) to weight signals in proportion to their reliability.

One of the great advantages of the GPS system is that it does not involve any other observation of the external environment, nor does it depend on any specific form of external feature. It is also a purely passive system that involves no energy output of any kind by the receiver. One imagines that this makes it well suited to military applications.

Unfortunately, GPS does not function well in many environments of interest for mobile robotics. That is, GPS cannot be used in environments where radio signals cannot be received along direct line-of-sight pathways from the GPS satellites or where the speed of light differs from that in open air. Specifically, the system cannot be used indoors, underground, or underwater. It is also unreliable in dense forest or between tall buildings. For many applications, the accuracy level of GPS is also insufficient. Fortunately, in environments where GPS is workable, greater accuracy is possible.

By using a combination of GPS receivers in communication with one another, substantially better position accuracy can be obtained. A variety of schemes for **differential GPS** (**DGPS**) exists with different requirements, complexities, speeds, and accuracies. Real-time kinematic (RTK) GPS has emerged as a relatively inexpensive but highly accurate form of differential GPS. RTK GPS uses the carrier wave of the underlying GPS signal to provide a more accurate position estimation than is possible with the range information encoded in the GPS timing messages alone. Base stations exist that can perform RTK on multiple GNSS.

4.9   Data Fusion

The question of how to combine data from different sources is a major and extensively examined research issue. In the context of mobile robotics, data fusion must be accomplished in at least three distinct domains: to combine measurements from different sensors, to combine measurements from different positions, and to combine measurements from different times. It is often the case that the goal of this estimate is to maintain an ongoing estimate of the position (pose) of the robot relative to some external set of landmarks or features (a map if you will).

Combining information from multiple sources can be likened to the combining of advice from friends. The advice of a trusted associate is likely to influence us strongly. The suggestions of a less-trusted acquaintance will be, to a large extent, ignored, yet they might still have some small effect on our decisions. Many such less-trusted acquaintances saying the same thing, however, may eventually influence us substantially. If we wish to formalize this notion, how do we decide how to weight information as a function of our confidence in it?

Combining measurements from multiple positions, times, or sensors is closely related to interpolation, extrapolation, and fitting an analytic function to data. In addition to combining a set of measurements to obtain a combined estimate, typically one would also like an estimate of the confidence of the final estimate, given the confidence of the individual input measurements.

Although various approaches have been developed to guide the process of data fusion, two different but related techniques have become pre-eminent in mobile robotics – approaches based on the classic least-squares combination of estimates, and approaches that utilize a less strong error model (Monte Carlo or condensation techniques). These mathematical models have also been augmented by a number of machine learning techniques, as described in Chapter 6.

4.9.1   Kalman Filter

Suppose that we have two independent estimates x_1 with variance[4] $\sigma_1^2 = \mathbb{E}[(x_1 - \mathbb{E}[x_1])^2]$ and x_2 with variance $\sigma_2^2 = \mathbb{E}[(x_2 - \mathbb{E}[x_2])^2]$ of x, what is the optimal linear combination of these two values in order to produce $\hat{x}$, the estimate of x? We have

---

[4] See the Appendix B for a review of the expectation operator $\mathbb{E}[\ ]$.

$$\hat{x} = \omega_1 x_1 + \omega_2 x_2,$$

where ω_1 and ω_2 are the weighting factors and $\omega_1 + \omega_2 = 1$. Optimal values of ω_1 and ω_2 will minimize the variance (σ^2) in the estimate $\hat{x}$. More explicitly, they will minimize

$$
\begin{aligned}
\sigma^2 &= \mathbb{E}[(\hat{x} - \mathbb{E}[\hat{x}])^2] \\
&= \mathbb{E}[(\omega_1 x_1 + \omega_2 x_2 - \mathbb{E}[\omega_1 x_1 + \omega_2 x_2])^2] \\
&= \mathbb{E}[(\omega_1 x_1 + \omega_2 x_2 - \omega_1 \mathbb{E}[x_1] - \omega_2 \mathbb{E}[x_2])^2] \\
&= \mathbb{E}[(\omega_1 (x_1 - \mathbb{E}[x_1]) + \omega_2 (x_2 - \mathbb{E}[x_2]))^2] \\
&= \mathbb{E}[\omega_1^2 (x_1 - \mathbb{E}[x_1])^2 + \omega_2^2 (x_2 - \mathbb{E}[x_2])^2 + 2\omega_1 \omega_2 (x_1 - \mathbb{E}[x_1])(x_2 - \mathbb{E}[x_2])] \\
&= \omega_1^2 \mathbb{E}[(x_1 - \mathbb{E}[x_1])^2] + \omega_2^2 \mathbb{E}[(x_2 - \mathbb{E}[x_2])^2] + 2\omega_1 \omega_2 \mathbb{E}[(x_1 - \mathbb{E}[x_1])(x_2 - \mathbb{E}[x_2])] \\
&= \omega_1^2 \sigma_1^2 + \omega_2^2 \sigma_2^2 + 2\omega_1 \omega_2 \mathbb{E}[(x_1 - \mathbb{E}[x_1])(x_2 - \mathbb{E}[x_2])].
\end{aligned}
$$

Now, x_1 and x_2 are independent, so $x_1 - \mathbb{E}[x_1]$ and $x_2 - \mathbb{E}[x_2]$ are independent, and thus $\mathbb{E}[(x_1 - \mathbb{E}[x_1])(x_2 - \mathbb{E}[x_2])] = 0$, giving

$$\sigma^2 = \omega_1^2 \sigma_1^2 + \omega_2^2 \sigma_2^2.$$

Now, $\omega_1 + \omega_2 = 1$, so we can rewrite this with $\omega_2 = \omega$ and $\omega_1 = 1 - \omega$:

$$\sigma^2 = (1 - \omega)^2 \sigma_1^2 + \omega^2 \sigma_2^2.$$

We seek the value of ω that minimizes the variance in the combination. That is, we seek ω such that

$$\frac{d}{d\omega}\sigma^2 = -2(1 - \omega)\sigma_1^2 + 2\omega \sigma_2^2 = 0.$$

This solves for

$$\omega = \frac{\sigma_1^2}{\sigma_1^2 + \sigma_2^2} \tag{4.1}$$

and estimates for $\hat{x}$ and σ are available as

$$\hat{x} = (\sigma_2^2 x_1 + \sigma_1^2 x_2)/(\sigma_1^2 + \sigma_2^2) \qquad \sigma^2 = \sigma_1^2 \sigma_2^2/(\sigma_1^2 + \sigma_2^2). \tag{4.2}$$

The estimate of the variance can be rearranged in the more common form

$$\frac{1}{\sigma^2} = \frac{1}{\sigma_1^2} + \frac{1}{\sigma_2^2}.$$

It is instructive to look at two special cases of this optimal combination. Suppose that estimate x_1 is known with high certainty (σ_1^2 is small), but that estimate x_2 is known with very low certainty (σ_2^2 is very large), then the optimal estimate is given by

$$\hat{x} \sim x_1, \quad \sigma^2 \sim \sigma_1^2 .$$

The uncertain estimate (x_2) is disregarded, and the more trusted estimate (x_1) is used instead.

Now instead suppose that the two estimates x_1 and x_2 are equally trusted, that is, $\sigma_1 = \sigma_2$, then the optimal combination is given by

$$\hat{x} = (x_1 + x_2)/2, \quad \sigma^2 = \sigma_1^2/2.$$

The best estimate is the average of the two estimates.

It is often necessary to maintain an ongoing estimate of some state information, given measurements at discrete times. Suppose that we receive measurements $x(k)$ of the state over time k, each with some known variance $v^2(k)$. We can use the foregoing to maintain an ongoing estimate of x. Writing $\hat{x}(k)$ as the estimate of x at time k, with variance $\sigma^2(k)$, we can rewrite (4.1) and (4.2):

$$\omega = \sigma^2(k)/(\sigma^2(k) + v^2(k))$$
$$\hat{x}(k + 1) = \hat{x}(k) + \omega(x(k) - \hat{x}(k)) \tag{4.3}$$
$$\sigma^2(k + 1) = (1 - \omega)\sigma^2(k).$$

Given some initial estimate of x, $\hat{x}(0)$ and initial estimate of the variance $\sigma^2(0)$, we can optimally combine measurements $x(1)$, $x(2)$ ... to produce an ongoing estimate of the state with its associated uncertainty. This process of maintaining an ongoing optimal estimate forms the basis of **Kalman filtering**.

A Simple Example   Suppose that a static robot is equipped with a spot laser range scanner that continually returns the distance to an object. The manufacturer's literature suggests that the sensor returns a distance measurement with some known constant variance. We can use recursive least squares to maintain an ongoing estimate of the distance to the object. Suppose that the distance sensor returns $x(0), x(1)$ ... as the measurements at different times, and that each measurement is independent with variance v^2.

Initialization

$$\hat{x}(0) = x(0)$$
$$\sigma^2(0) = \sigma_0^2.$$

At Each Time Step k Do

$$\omega = \sigma^2(k)/(\sigma^2(k) + v^2)$$
$$\hat{x}(k + 1) = \hat{x}(k) + \omega(x(k) - \hat{x}(k))$$
$$\sigma^2(k + 1) = (1 - \omega)\sigma^2(k).$$

Figure 4.9 illustrates the recursive least-squares estimate of a constant scalar. Multiple measurements are made of a constant value (6), and each estimate is corrupted by uniform noise. The estimator (or filter) is initialized with a value of zero and with a very large variance in order to represent that the initial guess is uncertain. Within a very small number of samples the filter converges to the correct answer.

In the following sections this basic mathematical computation – that the linear least-squares estimate can be computed in a recursive fashion – will be applied to more complex situations. It is important to recognize that this relatively simple computation is the core of these later, much more complex applications.

Vector Models   The recursive linear estimation process of (4.3) can, of course, be performed with either scalar of vector measurements. The scalar value x becomes a column vector $x = [x_1 \ x_2 \ \dots \ x_n]^{\mathrm{T}}$, and σ^2 becomes a covariance matrix. For a vector with elements x_i the covariance matrix has elements

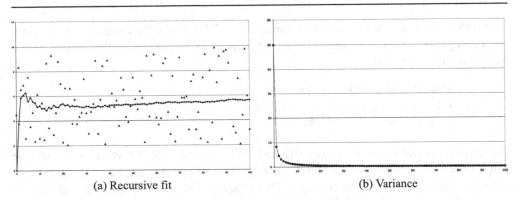

(a) Recursive fit   (b) Variance

Figure 4.9. Recursive least squares fit to a constant measurement (here 6). The variance associated with each measurement was 20, and measurements (triangles) were drawn from a uniform distribution over the range from 1 to 11. The filter was initialized with a value of zero and a variance of 50.

$$
P = \begin{bmatrix}
\mathbb{E}[(x_1 - \mathbb{E}[x_1])^2] & \mathbb{E}[(x_1 - \mathbb{E}[x_1])(x_2 - \mathbb{E}[x_2])] & \cdots & \mathbb{E}[(x_1 - \mathbb{E}[x_1])(x_n - \mathbb{E}[x_n])] \\
\mathbb{E}[(x_2 - \mathbb{E}[x_2])(x_1 - \mathbb{E}[x_1])] & \mathbb{E}[(x_2 - \mathbb{E}[x_2])^2] & \cdots & \mathbb{E}[(x_2 - \mathbb{E}[x_2])(x_n - \mathbb{E}[x_n])] \\
 & & \cdots & \\
\mathbb{E}[(x_n - \mathbb{E}[x_n])(x_1 - \mathbb{E}[x_1])] & \mathbb{E}[(x_n - \mathbb{E}[x_n])(x_1 - \mathbb{E}[x_1])] & \cdots & \mathbb{E}[(x_n - \mathbb{E}[x_n])^2]
\end{bmatrix}.
$$

Thus given a sequence of measurements $x(0)$, $x(1)$, ..., each with a known measurement covariance matrix C_v, then (4.3) can be extended to estimate the state of the vector x as $\hat{x}$ with covariance matrix P as

$$
\begin{aligned}
K &= P(k)(P(k) + C_v)^{-1} \\
\hat{x}(k+1) &= \hat{x}(k) + K(x(k) - \hat{x}(k)) \\
P(k+1) &= (I - K)P(k).
\end{aligned}
\tag{4.4}
$$

Here K is known as the **Kalman gain** and is the vector equivalent of ω in (4.3).

Equation (4.4) provides the basic form of the Kalman filter [401]. In the following sections, this basic form is adapted to the task of integrating sensory information with kinematic constraints of the underlying vehicle.

State Space Models In general, a system may be described by a set of parameters or variables that characterize the relevant aspects of its behavior. At any time, the information of interest regarding a system can be described by a vector x whose components are the variables of interest. The vector x specifies a point in the **state space** description of the system (this is also referred to as the **phase space** in some contexts). Note that some or all of these variables of interest may not be directly measurable. Thus, the state vector must be estimated using some vector of measurements z.

In the context of mobile robotics, and more generally in the context of control theory, it is often important to consider a dynamic version of this problem where estimates of a set of variables of interest must be formed on an ongoing basis using observations made to date, that is, over time $t = 0, \dots k$.

A system for which the state vector can be fully determined from a sufficient number of measurements is known as **observable**. To describe the **state estimate** being computed, we use $\dot{x}(k|k_1)$ to denote the estimate of x at time k using data from times up to and *including* time k_1. Using the observations from up to but not including step k to form a prediction is also commonly denoted as $\tilde{x}(k)$ and also, alternatively, as $\underline{x}_k(-)$. Using the observation at time k, we form an updated state *estimate* $\hat{x}(k)$, also referred to as $\underline{x_k(+)}$ in the literature.

State estimation techniques such as the Kalman filter typically require both a model of how the system evolves over time and a model of how the sensors operate. In the context of control theory, the description of the system whose state is of interest is usually referred to as the **plant model**. A third component of the filter is a description of permitted **control inputs** $u(t)$ and how they affect the system state.

Plant model The plant model describes how the system state $x(k)$ changes as function of time and control input $u(k)$ and noise $v(k)$:

$$x(k+1) = \Phi(x(k), u(k)) + v(k), \tag{4.5}$$

where $\Phi()$ is the **state transition function** and $v(k)$ is a **noise function**. A common and convenient form for the noise model is zero-mean Gaussian noise with covariance $C_v(k)$ (this particular noise model meets the noise requirements of the Kalman filter).

Of particular interest is a linear plant model of the form

$$x(k+1) = \Phi x(k) + \Gamma u(k) + v(k), \tag{4.6}$$

where Φ expresses how the system evolves from one state to another in the absence of inputs (this is often an identity matrix) and Γ expresses how control inputs modify the state. A sample plant model for an omnidirectional robot can be found in Listing 4.5.

Measurement model The measurement model describes how sensor data vary as a function of the system state. Inverting the sensor model (if possible) allows sensor data to be used to compute the state. We have

$$z_i(k) = h(x(k), \mathcal{E}) + w_i(k), \tag{4.7}$$

where $w_i(k)$ is a noise function, $\mathcal{E}$ is a model of the environment, and $h()$ is a function that describes sensor measurements as a function of the system state (e.g., the pose of the robot and its sensors). Again, a common description of the measurement noise is a zero-mean Gaussian noise function with covariance $C_w(k)$.

As with the plant model, a linear measurement model is of particular interest. This takes the form

$$z_i(k) = \Lambda_E x(k) + w_i(k), \tag{4.8}$$

where Λ_E is a matrix that expresses how measurements are derived as a linear transformation of the state. This simple case illustrates how an estimate of the state can be recovered from the measurements as

$$\hat{x}(k) = \Lambda_E^{-1} z_i(k), \tag{4.9}$$

assuming Λ_E is invertible. A simple example linear measurement model is given in Listing 4.5.

A specific form of (4.7) is used by Leonard and Durrant-Whyte [459] for sonar data:

$$z_i(k) = h_{st}(x(k), p_t) + w_i(k). \tag{4.10}$$

Consider an omnidirectional robot constrained to the plane. The robot's state $x(k)$ could be described as

$$x(k) = \begin{bmatrix} x(k) \\ y(k) \end{bmatrix},$$

where $(x(k), y(k))$ describes the robot's position in some global coordinate system. Suppose that robot is equipped with some sort of omnidirectional locomotive system. Then the control input $u(k)$ could be described as an independent change in the robot's x and y location, and thus

$$u(k) = \begin{bmatrix} \Delta x \\ \Delta y \end{bmatrix}.$$

If the error in the motion of the robot is independent in the x and y directions, and if this error can be modeled by some noise functions $v_x(k)$ and $v_y(k)$, then the robot plant model is given by

$$\begin{aligned} x(k+1) &= \Phi(x(k), u(k)) + v(k) \\ \begin{bmatrix} x(k+1) \\ y(k+1) \end{bmatrix} &= \begin{bmatrix} x(k) + \Delta x(k) + v_x(k) \\ y(k) + \Delta y(k) + v_y(k) \end{bmatrix}. \end{aligned}$$

The robot goes to where it is commanded with each motion being corrupted by the noise process. This is a linear plant model.

Now let us assume that the robot is equipped with a sensor capable of estimating the robot's displacement from the origin. Then

$$\begin{aligned} z_1(k) &= h(x(k), \mathcal{E}) + w_i(k) \\ &= \begin{bmatrix} x(k) + w_x(k) \\ y(k) + w_y(k) \end{bmatrix}. \end{aligned}$$

In this linear measurement model,

$$\Lambda_E = \begin{bmatrix} 1 & 0 \\ 0 & 1 \end{bmatrix},$$

and an estimate of the robot's position is available as

$$\hat{x}(k) = \Lambda_E^{-1} z_i(k) = z_1(k)$$

since this sensor model is invertible.

Listing 4.5. Plant and measurement model for a linear omnidirectional robot.

In this case, each range measurement from sonar is either discarded or associated with a particular object model p_t before the Kalman filter is applied. The function $h_{st}()$ thus associates a particular range measurement with a particular geometric model. Correct data assignment is essential, as incorrect data assignment is typically not well captured by the sensor noise model.

If the measurement process satisfies certain properties such as a zero mean error (these properties are itemized later), the Kalman filter provides the provably optimal method (in a least-squares sense) for fusing the data. In particular, in mobile robotics applications the Kalman filter is used to maintain an ongoing estimate of a vehicle's state or of the parameters describing objects of interest in the environment such as another vehicle being followed. It allows an existing (ongoing) estimate of the robot's position, for example, to be combined with position information from one or more sensors. It also allows an estimate of the certainty of the estimate, in the form of a covariance matrix, to be maintained. Under certain circumstances, the Kalman filter accomplishes this update in an optimal manner such that it minimizes that expected error in the estimate.

The assumptions made by the Kalman filter are as follows:

- Zero mean system noise, $E[v_i] = 0$.
- Independent noise: $E[v_i v_j{}^T] = 0 \; \forall i \neq j$. Otherwise, the system noise covariance is given by $E[v_i v_i] = C_v(k)$.
- A linear model of system evolution over time.
- A linear relationship between the system state (i.e., pose) and the measurements being made.

Unfortunately, it is rarely the case that all of these requirements hold in any practical application. If the assumptions do not hold, the Kalman filter can still be used, but the assurances of its optimality will not be valid. If the assumptions are violated in a sufficiently severe manner, the filter may, in fact, lead to very poor results.

Combining measurements and the estimate In the case of quantitative data, and in particular state estimate data, a natural way of describing our confidence in a measurement is by using a covariance matrix. Assuming that errors are normally distributed, this allows us to explicitly describe the probability distribution for errors about the mean. The Kalman filter is a mechanism for combining information so that reliable information is more heavily weighted. The key steps involve using the **Kalman gain** to weight the relative contribution of new measurements to our prior expectations. The Kalman gain varies in proportion to the state covariance matrix and inversely as as the measurement covariance matrix.

The Kalman filter consists of the following stages at each time step (except the initial step). In the following description we will, for the sake of convenience and expository simplicity, assume that the state transition matrix Φ and the observation function Λ_E remain constant over time, although this assumption can be trivially relaxed [Φ becomes $\Phi(k)$ and Λ_E becomes $\Lambda_E(k+1)$].

First, using the plant model (4.6), we compute an estimate of the system state at time $(k + 1)$ based on our knowledge of where the robot was at time k, what we did [the input $u(k)$] and how the system evolves in time:

$$\hat{x}(k + 1|k) = \Phi \hat{x}(k) + \Gamma u(k). \tag{4.11}$$

In some practical equations the input $u(k)$ is not used.

We can also update our certainty of the state as expressed by the state covariance matrix by "pushing it forward in time" as well:

$$P(k + 1|k) = \Phi P(k)\Phi^T + C_v(k). \tag{4.12}$$

This expresses the manner in which our knowledge about the system's state gradually decays as time passes (in the absence of external correction).

The Kalman gain can be expressed as

$$K(k + 1) = P(k + 1)\Lambda_E^T C_w^{-1}(k + 1), \tag{4.13}$$

but since we have not yet computed $P(k + 1)$, it can instead be computed as

$$K(k + 1) = P(k + 1|k)\Lambda_E^T (\Lambda_E P(k + 1|k)\Lambda_E^T + C_w(k + 1))^{-1}. \tag{4.14}$$

Using the $K(k + 1)$ matrix, we can compute a revised state estimate that includes the additional information provided by the measurements. This involves comparing the actual sensor data $z(k+1)$ with the sensor data predicted using the state estimate. The difference between these two terms,

$$r(k + 1) = z(k + 1) - h(\hat{x}(k|k + 1), \mathcal{E})$$

or in the linear case

$$r(k + 1) = z(k + 1) - \Lambda_E \hat{x}(k + 1|k), \qquad (4.15)$$

is sometimes referred to as the **innovation**. If our state estimate were perfect, the innovation would be non-zero only due to sensor noise. The revised state estimate is then given by

$$\hat{x}(k + 1) = \hat{x}(k + 1|k) + K(k + 1)r(k + 1), \qquad (4.16)$$

and the revised state covariance matrix is given by

$$P(k + 1) = (I - K(k + 1)\Lambda_E)P(k + 1|k), \qquad (4.17)$$

where I is the identity matrix. When this process is used in practice, the system is initialized using the initial estimated state, and $P(0) = C_w(0)$.

Listing 4.6 and Figure 4.10 illustrate the Kalman filter in action. Here the simple linear omnidirectional point robot described in Listing 4.5 is moving with a constant commanded input translation of $(0.1, 0)$ units per time step away from the origin. The robot is equipped with a sensor that senses its location (x, y). The Kalman filter for the linear omnidirectional robot (Listing 4.6) was used to integrate pose and command information with information from the sensor. The output of the filter is provided in Figure 4.10.

The tracked y-coordinate for the robot follows a trajectory similar to that seen in the recursive least squares fit shown in Figure 4.9a. The erroneous initial guess is quickly drawn to the stationary y-coordinate of the robot. The tracked x-coordinate is drawn to the non-stationary x-coordinate of the robot. The plant "pushes" the state of the Kalman filter forward in time based on the plant (the robot remains stationary) and the known control input (the robot has a commanded forward motion of 0.1 units every time step).

Extended Kalman Filter   In many robotics and sensing applications, the system to be modeled fails to have a white noise distribution or is not linear. So long as the errors are *roughly* Gaussian, the Kalman filter can be used, although it may not be provably optimal. To cope with non-linearity, the **extended Kalman filter** (**EKF**) is used. This involves linearizing the plant (4.5) and, if necessary, the measurement process (4.7) by ignoring high-order terms from the Taylor expansions of the plant and measurement processes.

Linearizing the plant model involves computing the Jacobian of the plant model $\nabla \Phi(\hat{x}(k), u(k))$ and using this as a linear estimate of Φ within the Kalman filter. Linearizing the measurement model involves computing the Jacobian of the measurement model $\nabla h(x(k), \mathcal{E})$ and using this as a linear estimate of Λ_E. Listing 4.8 develops an EKF for the non-linear robot and sensor considered in Figure 4.7.

At some interval – typically as often as possible – the derivatives used in the linearized model must be reevaluated at the current estimated state. This raises a major deficiency in the extended Kalman filter: if the estimated state is too far from the actual state, the linear

The simple linear robot described in Listing 4.5 can maintain an optimal estimate of its position through Kalman filtering. In order to simplify the exposition, it is assumed that $C_v(k) = C_v$ and $C_w(k) = C_w$. For each motion of the robot, the following steps are followed:

1. The robot moves, and using (4.6) the known control parameters are used to estimate the robot's position at time k:

$$\hat{x}(k + 1|k) = \left[\begin{array}{c} x(k) + \triangle x(k) \\ y(k) + \triangle y(k) \end{array} \right].$$

2. The uncertainty of the state is generated by updating the state covariance matrix using measurements obtained up to and including time k. As $\Phi = I$,

$$P(k + 1|k) = P(k) + C_v.$$

The uncertainty in the robot's position grows by C_v with each motion.

3. The Kalman gain is computed as

$$K(k + 1) = P(k + 1|k)(P(k + 1|k) + C_w)^{-1}.$$

4. A measurement is made with the sensor and a revised state estimate is available from (4.15) as

$$\hat{x}(k + 1) = \hat{x}(k + 1|k) + K(k + 1)(z(k + 1) - \hat{x}(k + 1|k)).$$

Consider the magnitude of the Kalman gain. If $|C_w|$ is large relative to $|P(k+1|k)|$, then the magnitude of $K(k+1)$ is small, that is, the noise associated with the measurement is small relative to the noise associated with the current state model and hence the old state model $\hat{x}(k + 1|k)$ is a better estimate of $\hat{x}(k + 1)$ than is the measurement of the displacement $z(k + 1)$. On the other hand, if the magnitude of $P(k+1|k)$ is large relative to the magnitude of C_w, then the estimate $\hat{x}(k + 1)$ is updated to look more like the measurement $z(k + 1)$ than the previous estimate $\hat{x}(k + 1|k)$.

5. Finally, the revised state covariance matrix is given by

$$P(k + 1) = (I - K(k + 1))P(k + 1|k).$$

Listing 4.6. Kalman filtering example.

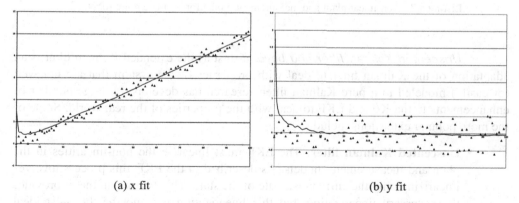

(a) x fit   (b) y fit

Figure 4.10. Kalman filter response for the simple linear robot plant and measurement model a described in Listing 4.5. The robot started at the origin and moved with a velocity of $(0.1, 0)$ units per time step. The Kalman filter was initialized with a guess of $(3, 3)$.

approximation to the system's behavior will not be sufficiently accurate. This can lead to increasingly erroneous state estimates, a phenomenon known as **filter divergence**. Due to the possibility of divergence, EKF algorithms typically gate all input before processing. This involves computing the innovation and testing to see if it is unexpectedly large and rejecting measurements that fail this test.

The example plant and measurement models worked out in Listing 4.5 uses simple linear models for state, input and measurement processes. Unfortunately most wheeled mobile robots cannot be modeled accurately in this manner, and it is necessary to consider non-linear plant, model, and estimation processes. Suppose that the robot can be modeled as a point robot and that we have independent control over the robot's orientation and velocity as we would in the case of a synchronous drive robot. Then for this robot the control input $u(k)$ can be described as

$$u(k) = \begin{bmatrix} D(k) & \Delta\theta(k) \end{bmatrix}^T,$$

that is, over the period k to $k + 1$ the robot moves forward in the direction it is facing a distance $D(k)$ and then rotates by an amount $\Delta\theta(k)$. The system state is given by

$$x(k) = \begin{bmatrix} x(k) & y(k) & \theta(k) \end{bmatrix}^T,$$

and the non-linear plant model is then given by

$$\Phi(x(k), u(k)) = \begin{bmatrix} x(k) + D(k)\cos(\theta(k)) \\ y(k) + D(k)\sin(\theta(k)) \\ \theta(k) + \Delta\theta(k) \end{bmatrix}.$$

Each motion of the robot is assumed to be combined with a noise process $v(k)$ that has a known or estimatable covariance matrix $C_v(k)$. This noise process is assumed to meet the requirements that assure the performance of the Kalman filter. If, in practice, the robot moves in distinct steps composed of either pure rotation or translation, that is only one of $D(k)$ or $\Delta\theta k$ is non-zero, then only two versions of $C_v(k)$ may be required.

Now suppose that the robot is equipped with a sensor that can determine the robot's distance from a special beacon in the environment. For example, the beacon may emit a unique sound at a known time, and the robot is equipped with a microphone and listens for the sound. As long as the robot and the emitter have synchronized clocks, the distance between the beacon and the robot can be estimated.

Locating this beacon at (x_b, y_b), we have the following measurement model for this robot:

$$h(x(k), \mathcal{E}) = ((x(k) - x_b)^2 + (y(k) - y_b)^2)^{\frac{1}{2}}.$$

This measurement is assumed to be corrupted by a noise process $w(k)$ with known covariance matrix $C_w(k)$.

Listing 4.7. Non-linear plant and measurement model for a simple point robot.

Unscented Kalman filter and beyond Just as the extended Kalman filter is an adaptation of the Kalman filter to deal with properties of the system that are not well (or easily) modeled in a pure Kalman filter, research has developed a large number of enhancements to the KF and EKF to deal with the properties of the real world. Some of the more popular extensions include

- **Unscented Kalman filter**. The EKF must linearize the non-linearities in the plant and measurement models. As described in the EKF, this process involves linearizing only the current estimate of the state. This 'works' in that it provides the necessary linearization, but this linearization may not be the most ideal linear representation. The unscented Kalman filter [816] addresses this concern by identifying a collection of configuration points (known as sigma points) in the original space, and mapping them through the non-linear mapping and use weighted versions of these to more cleanly represent the underlying representation.

- **Fractional Kalman filter**. As described in this chapter, the various Kalman filter a receive all of the measurements synchronously. Unfortunately, this does not happen in practice with different sensor measurements arriving at different times. The problem of rephrasing the Kalman filter to deal with this issue is

The non-linear plant and sensor model is described in Listing 4.7. In order to simplify the exposition, it is assumed that $C_v(k) = C_v$ and $C_w(k) = C_w$. For each motion of the robot, the following steps are followed:

1. The robot moves and using (4.5), we use the known control parameters to estimate the robot's position at time k:

$$\hat{x}(k+1|k) = \left[\begin{array}{ccc} x(k) + T(k)\cos(\theta(k)) & y(k) + T(k)\sin(\theta(k)) & \theta(k) + \Delta\theta(k) \end{array} \right]^T.$$

2. A linearized version of the plant model is generated at the current estimate of the robot's position $\hat{x}(k)$,

$$\nabla\Phi = \left[\begin{array}{ccc} 1 & 0 & -T(k)\sin(\theta(k)) \\ 0 & 1 & T(k)\cos(\theta(k)) \\ 0 & 0 & 1 \end{array} \right].$$

3. The uncertainty of the state is generated by updating the state covariance matrix using measurements obtained up to and including time k,

$$P(k+1|k) = \nabla\Phi P(k)\nabla\Phi^T + C_v.$$

4. The sensor model is linearized around the current estimate of the robot's position $\hat{x}(k)$,

$$\begin{aligned} \Lambda_E &= \nabla h(x(k), \mathcal{E}) \\ &= \left[\begin{array}{ccc} x(k)(x(k) - x_b) & y(k)(y(k) - y_b) & 0 \end{array} \right]. \end{aligned}$$

5. Using this value of Λ_E we compute the Kalman gain as

$$K(k+1) = P(k+1|k)\Lambda_E^T(\Lambda_E P(k+1|k)\Lambda_E^T + C_w)^{-1}.$$

6. The innovation is computed as

$$r(k+1) = z(k+1) - h(\hat{x}(k|k+1), \mathcal{E}).$$

7. It is now possible to estimate the robot's position as

$$\hat{x}(k+1) = \hat{x}(k+1|k) + K(k+1)r(k+1).$$

8. Finally, the revised state covariance matrix is given by

$$P(k+1) = (I - K(k+1)\Lambda_E)P(k+1|k).$$

Listing 4.8. EKF example.

known as the fractional Kalman filter (and extended fractional Kalman filter and so on) [719].

4.9.2 Markov Localization

Although Kalman (recursive least-squares) filtering has been found to be a very effective mechanism for combining information and for maintaining an estimate of the robot's pose, it is not a perfect solution to the problem. Even if the problem can be expressed as a linear estimation problem, it can be difficult to establish initial mean and covariance estimates to prime the filtering process. One approach to avoiding the limitations inherit with a linear least-squares approach is to reformulate the problem in more general terms. Let x_k be the value that is to be estimated (e.g., the robot's pose) at time k, let o_k be the measurement(s) taken at time k, and let a_k be the actions at time k. Then the robot state estimation problem can be reformulated as the problem of estimating the conditional probability $p(x_k|o_k, a_{k-1}, o_{k-1}, a_{k-2}, \ldots, o_0)$ and then choosing the most likely element from this *a posteriori* distribution.

From the definition of conditional probability,

$$p(x_k, o_k, a_{k-1}, \ldots, o_0) = p(x_k|o_k, a_{k-1}, \ldots, o_0)p(o_k, a_{k-1}, \ldots, o_0)$$

and

$$p(x_k, o_k, a_{k-1}, \ldots, o_0) = p(o_k | x_k, a_{k-1}, \ldots, o_0) p(x_k, a_{k-1}, \ldots, o_0).$$

Equating these two expansions and rearranging results in

$$p(x_k | o_k, a_{k-1}, \ldots, o_0) = \frac{p(o_k | x_k, a_{k-1}, \ldots, o_0) p(x_k, a_{k-1}, \ldots, o_0)}{p(o_k, a_{k-1}, \ldots, o_0)}. \qquad (4.18)$$

$p(x_k, a_{k-1}, \ldots, o_0)$ can be expressed as the conditional probability $p(x_k | a_{k-1}, \ldots, o_0)$ $p(a_{k-1}, \ldots, o_0)$ and $p(o_k, a_{k-1}, \ldots, o_0)$ can be expressed as the conditional probability $p(o_k | a_{k-1}, \ldots, o_0) p(a_{k-1}, \ldots, o_0)$. Substituting in (4.18) and canceling out the common term $p(a_{k-1}, \ldots, o_0)$ gives

$$p(x_k | o_k, a_{k-1}, \ldots, o_0) = \frac{p(o_k | x_k, a_{k-1}, \ldots, o_0) p(x_k | a_{k-1}, \ldots, o_0)}{p(o_k | a_{k-1}, \ldots, o_0)}. \qquad (4.19)$$

If the set of measurements or commanded motions at time k is independent of the sensor measurements taken at earlier times, then $p(o_k | x_k, a_{k-1}, \ldots, o_0) = p(o_k | x_k)$, and (4.19) simplifies to

$$p(x_k | o_k, a_{k-1}, \ldots, o_0) = \frac{p(o_k | x_k) p(x_k | a_{k-1}, \ldots, o_0)}{p(o_k | a_{k-1}, \ldots, o_0)}. \qquad (4.20)$$

$p(x_k | a_{k-1}, \ldots, o_0)$ can be expressed in terms of the the previous state x_{k-1},

$$p(x_k | a_{k-1}, \ldots, o_0) = \int p(x_k | x_{k-1}, a_{k-1}, \ldots, o_0) p(x_{k-1} | a_{k-1}, \ldots, o_0) dx_{k-1}. \qquad (4.21)$$

Applying the Markov assumption to the first term of the integral and noting that a_{k-1} only effects x_k, simplifies this integration to

$$p(x_k | a_{k-1}, \ldots, o_0) = \int p(x_k | x_{k-1}, a_{k-1}) p(x_{k-1} | o_{k-1}, \ldots, o_0) dx_{k-1}. \qquad (4.22)$$

The denominator in (4.20) is a normalization factor. If we write this as μ^{-1}, then (4.20) simplifies to

$$\begin{aligned} Bel(x_t) = p(x_k | o_k, a_{k-1}, \ldots, o_0) &= \mu p(o_k | x_k) \int p(x_k | x_{k-1}, a_{k-1}) p(x_{k-1} | o_{k-1}), \ldots, o_0) dx_{k-1} \\ &= \mu p(o_k | x_k) \int p(x_k | x_{k-1}, a_{k-1}) Bel(x_{k-1}) dx_{k-1}. \end{aligned} \qquad (4.23)$$

Here $Bel(x_t)$ is the belief (probability) that the robot is at location x_t, given the set of motions and sensor measurements. Each of the terms on the right-hand side of (4.23) can be generated or estimated using known properties of the sensor or the robot.

- $p(o_k | x_k)$ is the conditional probability of a set of sensor measurements, given an estimate of the robot's position.
- $p(x_k | x_{k-1}, a_{k-1})$ is the conditional probability of the robot being in a particular pose, given its command input and the state the robot is in at the previous time.

Different choices of the representation of $p()$ leads to different solutions. For example, if each of the $p()$ are chosen to be a Gaussian distribution, then the approach simplifies to a Kalman filter [514]. More general distribution functions are more common, however, and effective solutions to (4.23) have been constructed based on discrete grids, **particle filters**, **Monte Carlo filters** [421], or the **condensation algorithm** [385].

4.9.3 Discrete-Grid Representation

Markov localization requires a representation of the conditional properties $p(o_k|x_k)$ and $Bel(x_k)$. Perhaps the simplest approach is to define these probabilities in terms of some discrete sampling of space and the sensor. In terms of representing space, this can be accomplished by defining a grid of possible discrete locations in which the robot can exist (see [289] for an example).

As a simple illustration of the discrete process, suppose that a robot is operating in a world that can be described as an annulus with 10 distinct locations numbered 0 through 9. Each location is colored either red (R), green (G), or blue (B). Initially suppose that the robot is perfectly accurate in terms of its ability to execute commanded motions and that its sensor is perfect. Then

$$p(o_k|x_k) = \begin{cases} 1 & \text{if } o_k = \text{R and } x_k \in (0,1,2) \\ 1 & \text{if } o_k = \text{G and } x_k \in (3,4,5) \\ 1 & \text{if } o_k = \text{B and } x_k \in (6,7,8,9) \\ 0 & \text{otherwise} \end{cases}$$

and

$$p(x_k|x_{k-1}, a_{k-1}) = \begin{cases} 1 & \text{if } x_k = x_{k-1} + 1 \text{ mod } 10 \text{ and } a_{k-1} = \text{ right} \\ 1 & \text{if } x_k = x_{k-1} - 1 \text{ mod } 10 \text{ and } a_{k-1} = \text{ left} \\ 0 & \text{otherwise.} \end{cases}$$

Initially we have no idea where the robot is (although we know that it is somewhere on our map, that is, it must be in exactly one of the locations numbered 0 through 9). If there is no prior information as to the robot's whereabouts, then $p(x_0) = 1/10$ for each possible location. For purposes of illustration suppose that the robot is really in location 1 (Figure 4.11).

The robot senses its current environment and sees red (R) and the conditional probability $p(x_0|x_0)$ becomes 1/3 for locations $(0,1,2)$ and is zero elsewhere. The robot then moves to the right one space (to location 2) and senses its environment (seeing R – red). $Bel(x_1)$ is then updated to be 1/2 for locations $(1,2)$ and is zero elsewhere. Locations $(1,2)$ are the only locations in which a robot can see red after moving to the right from a position where the robot also saw red.

Now let us suppose that the robot moves to the right again (to location 3) and senses its environment (seeing B – blue). The belief function $Bel(x_2)$ collapses to a value of 1 at location 3 and is zero elsewhere. We know where the robot is.

In practice $p(o_k|x_k)$ and $p(x_k|x_{k-1}, a_{k-1})$ will not be as sanitized as in this example and the belief function will not necessarily collapse to a single point. Answering the question of where the robot is involves returning a single x_k, given the current distribution function over the possible robot states.

4.9.4 Monte Carlo Techniques

Rather than represent $p()$ in (4.20) through some closed form distribution function or on a discrete grid, one can choose instead to represent $Bel(x_k)$ as a collection

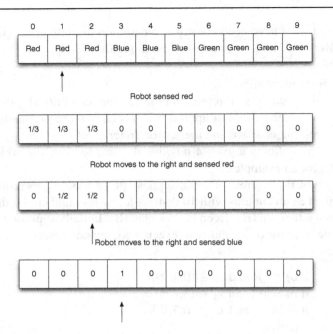

Figure 4.11. Markov localization on a discrete grid. As the robot senses and moves, the belief function is shaped by the information. Here there is perfect odometry and sensing information, resulting in the belief function collapsing to a single non-zero value.

of samples $S_k^i = \{s_k^i\} = \{(x_k^i, w_k^i)\}$. This is known as a **particle filter**-based approach. The idea here is to approximate $Bel(x_k)$ with

$$Bel(x_k|Z^k) \approx \frac{1}{N} \sum (\delta(x_k - x_k^{(i)})),$$

where δ is the discrete Dirac function. Given its simplicity, particle filters have found wide application from pose estimation (e.g., [211]) to data association (e.g., [408]), to target tracking (e.g., [42]).

Given some initial estimation of the probability density function (PDF) $p(x_0)$, the following steps can be repeated over time to maintain the estimate of $p(x_k|Z^k)$ (see Listing 4.9).

Resampling phase Resample the current PDF $p(x_k|Z_k)$ represented by the samples S_k^i in order to ensure that the particles are a good representation of $p(x_k|Z_k)$. This is accomplished via an algorithm such as sampling importance resampling (SIR) [319]), where each of the particles is replaced by a new random particle, where the probability of intializing the particle at (x_k^i, w_k^i) is proportional to w_k^i. Note that many particles may now have the same value. Issues related to resampling are considered later.

Prediction phase Estimate $Bel(x_k)$ by propagating the (resampled) particle representation of $Bel(x_{k-1})$ forward in time, given the input a_{k-1}. This is accomplished by applying the motion model (plant) to each particle s_{k-1}^i. Any plant noise is applied to each particle separately.

```
Given: a set of particles S = {(xᵢ,wᵢ)}.

while(true)
  /* apply resampling if needed */
  if(NeedToResampleNow(S) then
    Resample(S);
  /* apply the action to samples */
  for(j=0;j<|S|;j++)
    xⱼ = f(xⱼ,α)
  /* collect sensor information */
  s = Sense()
  /* compute unnormalized weights */
  for(j=0;j<|S|;j++)
    tⱼ = wⱼ * W(s,xⱼ)
  /* normalize the weights */
  for(j=0;j<|S|;j++)
    wⱼ = tⱼ/∑tₖ
end while
```

Listing 4.9. A simple particle filter.

For an ideal differential drive robot, one model for this noise process [660] is to apply a separate noise process for pure rotation and translation motions. When the robot rotates, the plant noise is applied only to the orientation of the vehicle

$$\theta_i = \theta_i + \delta\theta + N(0, \sigma\delta\theta),$$

where $N(0,k)$ is a zero-mean normal distribution with standard deviation k, $\delta\theta$ is the intended rotation amount, and σ is a parameter encoding the relative size of the error in rotation. When the robot translates, the plant noise is applied to both the position and orientation of the vehicle. The plant noise models errors associated with distance traveled as well as orientation errors introduced both before and after the motion of the wheels. We have

$$E_d = N(0, \sigma_d \delta p)$$
$$\theta = \theta + N(0, \sigma_\theta \delta p)$$
$$x = x + (\delta p + E_d) \cos(\theta)$$
$$y = y + (\delta p + E_d) \sin(\theta)$$
$$\theta = \theta + N(0, \sigma_\theta \delta p).$$

Update phase Update the weights associated with each particle using the measurement o_k. Weight particle (x_k^i, w_k^i) by a weight proportional to $p(o_k|x_k^i)w_k^i$, and then renormalize the weight of the samples. Various weighting functions are possible here. One simple (but unrealistic) model is to model $p(o_k|x_k^i)$ as a Gaussian in the measurement space.

A sample implementation of a particle filter for a differential drive robot is depicted in Figure 4.12. The distribution of the particles represents the probability distribution function for the robot's pose.

Resampling Perhaps the *main* problem with particle filters is the problem of ensuring that the particles properly represent the underlying PDF. Clearly, the cost of the algorithm outside of the resampling step is proportional to the number of particles, so it

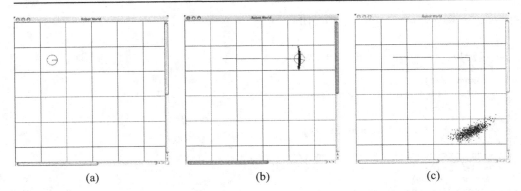

Figure 4.12. Three snapshots of a particle filter implementation for a differential drive robot. The robot moves forward 3 m, turns right 90°, and then moves forward another 3 m. The distribution of particles represents the PDF for the robot's pose.

is desirable to limit the number of particles. Yet with a finite number of particles there is no guarantee that the particles will properly represent the underlying PDF. This leads to the **degeneracy problem** in which after a few iterations all but one particle has an almost zero weight w_k. Resampling is thus a key element of any successful particle filter system. The goal of the resampling is to remove unlikely particles and to ensure that the particles properly sample the PDF.

Perhaps the simplest replacement strategy is sampling importance resampling (SIR) [319]). Here sampling *with replacement* is used to replace particles with copies of particles with a probability proportional to their strength. Efficient $O(n \log n)$ algorithms exist for this task, and various variations on the approach have been developed [660]. It is important to observe that although efficient, even this simple resampling is *more* expensive than the other steps in the algorithm, and thus resampling is not necessarily performed in each iteration of the algorithm. Rather, it is only performed when the degeneracy of the particles exceeds a set value. The degeneracy can be approximated as

$$ \hat{N_{eff}} = \frac{1}{\sum (w_k^i)^2}. $$

One problem with simple replacement strategies such as SIR is that no *new* samples can be created: new samples only come from the existing set of samples. Various approaches have been proposed that inject novel samples into the distribution in order to deal with this issue [259].

4.9.5   Gaussian Mixtures

A Gaussian mixture model (see [523]) is a probabilistic model that assumes that the data can be well modeled as a mixture of a finite number of Guassian distributions with unknown parameters and relative weights. Guassian mixture models are more expressive than a single Guassian distribution and they can model outliers and more complex distributions.

A Gaussian mixture can be fit to a distribution using the expectation-maximization (EM) algorithm. The EM algorithm estimates the parameters and weightings of the Gaussian distributions that make up the mixture through a sequence of iterations. Starting

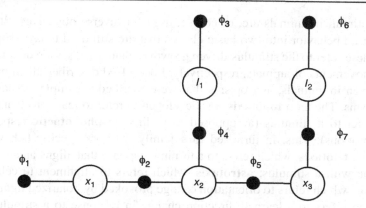

Figure 4.13. An example factor graph. Small filled black nodes are factors, with larger open nodes representing variables.

from some initial guess of the weightings of each distribution and the Gaussian parameters that define each distribution, the algorithm proceeds through a sequence of estimation (E) and maximization (M) steps. During the E step the expected value for each variable is computed, while during the M step the parameters of the distributions are estimated using maximum likelihood.

4.9.6 Graph-Based Approaches

As the relationships between the various components that make up how state properties, measurements, and plant models becomes more complex, it can be helpful to utilize a graph-based representation of the components (see [323]). Factor graphs [213] have proven to be a particularly effective mechanism for representing complex relations within the different random variables and to identify computational independence assumptions that can be used to optimize the representation. Fundamentally, a factor graph is an undirected bipartite graph with two kinds of nodes: nodes that represent properties (variables) and nodes that represent interactions (factors). If we write the factors as ϕ_i and the variables as x_j, then the critical observation is that the global function ϕ is a product of the individual factors. The graph encodes the independence relationships with each factor ϕ_i dependent only on the variables adjacent to it.

Now consider the sample factor graph shown in Figure 4.13 that represents a robot starting at x_1 and moving through time at x_2 and x_3. The robot obtains estimates of its pose from two landmarks, l_1 (at x_2) and l_2 (at x_3) as a product of local factors and a global function $\phi = \prod \phi_i$. Through an appropriate choice of representation of each of the variables (e.g., Gaussian distribution with known mean and covariance), it is straightforward to compute, for example, the *maximum a posteriori* value of the variables.

4.10 Biological Sensing

Since biology serves as the inspiration for many artificial intelligence and robotics systems, it is appropriate to briefly consider a few of the myriad non-visual sensing mechanisms found in living creatures.

While sensory stimuli in animals are, of course, used for diverse objectives, Pfeffer divided sensory-based behavior into two basic classes that are still used today: **tropism** and **taxis** [623]. These refer to the stimulus-driven growth of plants and sessile organisms, and the oriented movements of animals, respectively. Loeb [478] describes all stimulus-driven behavior, even in animals, as tropisms that were ascribed to simple, essentially reflexive, mechanisms. The term **topotaxis** was developed to refer to reactions that were directed with respect to a stimulus (as opposed to undirected **phobotactic** responses such as random motions). This, in turn, led to a family of more specific behavioral categories, including **telotaxis**, which refers to a turning response that aligns an animal's direction of motion with a stimulus; **astrotaxis**, which refers to alignment to celestial objects; **polarotaxis**, which refers to orientation change provoked by polarized light; and **mnemotaxis**, which refers to a learned direction change in response to a stimulus. A related notion is that of **kineses**. These are reactions more general than orientation change, such as a change in the speed of motion (**orthokinesis**), that are triggered by a stimulus.

Mouritsen's survey of navigational strategies for birds and other animals [549] provides a good overview of the various sensing modalities used by biological organisms to deal with sensing issues related to navigation. Biological organisms utilize a large set of sense organs and systems to permit them to sense their environment and their motion within it.

4.10.1 Magnetic Sensing

Magnetic fields are exploited by organisms that range from the single-celled paramecium [427] to European robins, *Erithacus rubecula* [834]. For example, the bacterium *Aquaspirillum magnetotacticum* is equipped with a specialized organelle called the magnetosome that acts like a compass and appears to be useful in allowing it to decide which way is down [92]. It appears that young salmon use Earth's magnetic field to return to their spawning grounds [646].

Wiltschko and Wiltschko [834] demonstrated that European robins can sense the inclination of the magnetic field and respond to changes to it. There are at least two properties of Earth's magnetic field that could be sensed by an organism: the horizontal component of the field, which runs from south to north (sensed by a **polarity compass**), and the inclination of the magnetic field relative to gravity (sensed by a **inclination compass**). European robins are sensitive to the inclination of the magnetic field but are insensitive to its polarity. That is, European robins appear to be equipped with an inclination compass but not a polarity one.

4.10.2 Odor

While vision is the primary sense for humans, smell rules for most animals. More formally, the use of **olfaction** or **chemosensing** is one instance of **chemosensory navigation**. The olfactory systems of animals are often much more sensitive than those of humans and not only are they able to detect smaller amounts of the chemicals that cause odors, but they are also better able to resolve different types of odors.

Various species of animals, including salmon [227] and moths [336], exploit olfactory marks for terrain marking, landmark recognition, and trail marking. Olfactory markers have the advantage of being discrete and evanescent. This suggests that different agents can deposit and use their specific markers in a given area at different times.

In ants, olfactory cues are used both for short-range communication, for example, between two ants in the same place, and for long-range communication, for example, to mark trails [365]. In trail following, one strategy is to lay an odor trail whose width roughly corresponds to the antenna separation. An ant following the trail then keeps one antenna on each side to the odor maximum as it walks the trail, weaving slightly to keep itself calibrated. There is also odor variation, either in strength or type, from the source to the destination of the trail, at least with some species of ants. An ant removed from a trail and then placed at a random position will head in an arbitrary direction along the trail, but after walking a short distance will turn around and head in the correct direction, having presumably inferred the odor gradient.

4.10.3 Sound and Vibrations

Sound cues are used by a wide variety of animals. **Ultrasound** is used by animals such as bats [701] for echolocation. The animal emits a high-frequency sound and uses the time lapse between the emission of the sound and its return to judge distances to objects in the environment. Ultrasound has found extensive applications in mobile robots (see Section 4.4). In contrast to ultrasound, **infrasound** (very low-frequency sound) is present in nature and is emitted from natural sources such as weather systems and ocean waves. The African elephant *Loxodonta africana* uses infrasound for communication both within and between herds at distances up to 10 km [447].

In addition to sensing sound travelling through the air (or water), a number of animals are sensitive to vibrations travelling through the ground or through the environment within which they live. For example, the Namib Desert golden mole, *Eremitalpa granti namibensis*, is thought to use the seismic effects of wind passing through grasses to determine whether a specific collection of grass may contain prey [568].

4.10.4 Electrical Fields

A number of species of fish and other aquatic animals can navigate utilizing electrical fields (**electroreception**). These animals produce electrical fields to monitor their environment. Objects within the water disturb the electrical field density, and this is sensed by specialized organs within the animal [810].

4.10.5 Infrared

Certain species of snakes are equipped with specialized **pit organs** that are sensitive to heat (infrared radiation). This heat is emitted by other animals (their prey), and this permits the snakes to hunt in unlit conditions [322].

4.10.6 Inertial Measurement

The vestibular system in humans [370] is responsive to linear acceleration through the **utricle** and **saccule** and also to rotational velocity through the **semicircular canals**. There is significant evidence that information transduced from the vestibular system is integrated with other sensory information (especially vision) when estimating self-orientation [246] and self-motion [446].

4.11 Further Reading

Non-visual sensors There exist a vast number of general-purpose non-visual sensors on the market, and manufacturer data sheets provide the best information on a specific device. An in-depth study of non-visual sensors and their capabilities can be found in [258]. [612] provides an in-depth and historical review of gyroscope technology.

Kalman filtering A formal mathematical treatment of Kalman filtering can be found in [111]. This includes proofs of optimality and formal treatment of the operational requirements of the filter. See also [730, 305, 858]. Leonard and Durrant-Whyte [459] provide an in-depth treatment of the use of Kalman filtering and sonar sensors for mobile robot pose estimation. More recent reviews include [413].

Particle filters A number of good tutorials and particle filtering exist in the literature, including [42], [660], and [330].

Factor graphs There exist a number of good reviews of factor graphs (e.g., [213] and [479]) as well as texts relating factor graphs to robot systems (e.g., [212]).

Biological sensing An overview of biological sensors and sensing and their relationship to animal navigation can be found in Mouritsen's review paper [549].

4.12 Problems

1. Suppose that an object is dropped from some known height under the effect of gravity. Develop a Kalman filter to continually estimate the state of the object if (a) the position of the object is measured at each time instance, (b) the velocity of the object is measured at each time instance, and (c) the position and the velocity of the object is measured at each time instant.
2. Perform the estimations in problem 1 using a particle filter rather than a Kalman filter.
3. Derive a Kalman filter that combines an *a priori* position estimate (with known error) with an independent translation estimate (e.g., from triangulation) and an orientation estimate (from a compass). Assume all errors are normally distributed with known standard deviations.
4. Consider a point robot moving on the plane with a state vector given by the robot's pose $q = [x, y]$. Observations of the robot are made at discrete points in time and consist of the robot's distance from the origin d and the bearing θ measured from the origin. Assume that the noise associated with these two measurements are independent. Develop a Kalman filter that maintains an estimate of the robot's state.
5. Assume the following slightly idealized model of sonar sensing: the sensor returns a signal whenever an object is within $\pm 15°$ of the transducer normal, and between 4 cm and 4 m distance. Plot the response of a sonar sensor located in the center of a rectangular room of size 6×3 m. Plot the observed distance as a function of orientation, ignoring the effects of multiple sonar bounces.

   Acoustic reluctance depends on a function of the surface curvature of a reflecting surface and the wavelength of the sound wave, as well as one the properties of the object from which the sound in being reflected. How could this be used in robotic sensing?

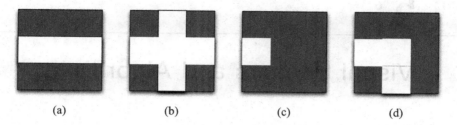

Figure 4.14. Cells in a maze. There are two rotated versions of (a) and four rotated versions each of (c) and (d) for a total of 11 possible cells.

6. In this problem you will develop alternate versions of the sensor model used in the simulation developed previously

   (a) Add zero-mean Gaussian noise (with standard deviation σ_d) to the range returned by the idealized sensor.
   (b) Add zero-mean Gaussian noise (with standard deviation σ_α) to the direction in which the sensor points when returning the range corrupted by σ_d above.

7. Given a set of 2D points corresponding to distance measurements, aggregate the measurements into line (wall) segments. Test your grouping algorithm on sensor measurements obtained with the various sensor noise models developed in the previous question.

8. Suppose that a robot is lost in maze defined on a grid. Each cell of the grid contains exactly one of the cells shown in Figure 4.14. Cells may appear rotated in multiples of 90°. The white portions of the cells are passable.

   (a) Develop a program that, given a grid size (width × height), generates a random maze such that passable adjacent portions are connected. (Passages only 'end' with the cell shown in Figure 4.14c.)
   (b) Given the maze elements described, develop a Markov localization strategy using a discrete-grid representation. Assume that the robot can sense which one of the 11 possible cell elements it is in (the four shapes shown in Figure 4.14 in their various orientations), and that when the robot moves it moves up, down, left, or right exactly one cell, provided that motion in that direction is possible. At each step move the robot randomly in one of the directions in which it is possible to move given the local structure of the maze. How did you decide that the robot has found where it is? (How and when does the algorithm terminate?)
   (c) Repeat the previous problem but assume that the robot does not move perfectly; rather, it moves in the direction desired 60% of the time and the remaining 40% of the time it moves with equal probability in one of the other valid directions in which it could move (including remaining stationary).

5

Visual Sensors and Algorithms

The eyes see only what the mind is prepared to comprehend.[1]

Anyone who has had to move about in the dark recognizes the importance of vision to human navigation. Tasks that are fraught with difficulty and danger in the dark become straightforward when the lights are on. Given that *humans* seem to navigate effortlessly with vision, it seems natural to consider vision as a sensor for mobile robots. Visual sensing has many desirable potential features, including that it is passive and has high resolution and a long range.

Human vision relies on two eyes to transform information encoded in light into electrical signals transmitted by neurons. In the biological sciences, the fields of **perception** and **cognition** investigate how this neural information is processed to build internal representations of the environment and how humans reason about their environment using these representations. From a robotics point of view, the fields of **computer vision** and **robot vision** examine the task of building computer representations of the environment from light, and the study of **artificial intelligence** deals in part with the task of reasoning or planning based on the resulting data. This chapter continues the exploration of how to build descriptions of the work from sensor data. In this chapter, we consider the issues involved in sensing using light and related media.

Vision is both strikingly powerful as a sensory medium, and strikingly difficult to use in a robotics context. While many visual sensing problems appear trivial to humans, few problems in generic computational vision are fully solved. Perhaps it is easy for us to underestimate the difficulty of vision problems since so much of the human brain is devoted to solving them (current data suggest that 50% or more of the human brain is involved in processing visual data).

Vision relates measurement to scene structure. This is an important property of visual sensors that is often overlooked. Suppose that a laser range sensor is directed by a robot at different objects in an environment. The sensor returns the distance to the objects, and so (at best) the robot, and any human operator associated with the robot, obtains a set of distance measurements as a function of the direction in which the laser sensor is pointed. It can be very difficult to interpret this range information in terms of scene structure; for a human operator it can be extremely difficult to relate the distances to specific objects in the environment. Now suppose that a vision-based sensor is used instead. The sensor obtains a visual image of the environment, and since humans are used to dealing with

---

[1] Robertson Davies.

visual information it is usually straightforward for an operator to determine which part of the image is associated with which structures in the environment.

Many robotic vision systems are based on video cameras that observe their environment passively. Alternatively, **active vision** systems are systems in which the observer is active (i.e., moving) rather than static [57, 23, 340]. In an active vision paradigm, visual processing is devoted to noting salient components in the image and the scene, rather than processing the entire image blindly. This attention can be mechanical, using robotic actuators such as pan-and-tilt units or stereo heads, for example; it can be through manipulation of intrinsic camera parameters; or it can be computational. Rather than processing snapshots, in an active vision paradigm the sensor and the environment continually interact: hence, the interest in active vision by the mobile robot community.

A fundamental difficulty with using vision as a robotic sensor is that a single image of an object does not generally determine the object's absolute distance or size. Thus a common computational task in robot vision is the extraction of depth information from one or more images. Accomplishing this task often requires a strong model of the process of image acquisition (**camera calibration**) and a representation of the raw image data in some intermediate form in terms of **image features**. We begin with a consideration of these tasks.

5.1   Visual Sensors

Visual sensors obtain a considerable amount of data which can be computationally very expensive to process. A standard CCD (charge-coupled device) or CMOS (complementary metal-oxide semiconductor) camera obtains a rectangular grid of intensity or color measurements at a fixed temporal sampling rate. These measurements are converted into a machine-readable quantity at this rate, resulting in a large number of 8- or 16-bit values per second.

The 2D array of image data is known as an array of **pixels**, or picture elements. Each pixel may encode a triple of the incident amount of red, green, and blue light that strikes this pixel or individual pixels may be sensitive to a specific color. This latter approach is known as a **Bayer filter mosaic**, and individual pixels can be assigned red, green, and blue values through the application of an appropriate Bayer filter. Sensors may also be monochromatic. A number of standard libraries exist to manipulate these image arrays. Such libraries typically include implementations of standard computer vision algorithms. The online resource associated with this text includes a very brief introduction to OpenCV, a commonly used computer vision library with Python bindings.

Visual sensors have a finite field of view. The wide field of view obtained with a wide-angle lens results in a large field of view at the cost of a lower spatial resolution, and wide-angled lenses often suffer from spherical and chromatic aberrations. Telephoto lenses have a smaller field of view, but have higher resolution per degree of visual angle. For many robotic vision applications it is necessary to actively control the direction and internal camera parameters (focal length, aperture, etc.) of the video sensor(s) in order to have them "attend" to the portion of the world that is to be studied.

5.1.1   Perspective Cameras

Video systems for robots typically consist of two main components; an optical system that collects light from over a finite field of view and focuses this light onto an image plane, and an optoelectrical system to take this focused light and convert it into a computer-readable signal.

The process of collecting light and recording it using a computer is complex, and various models of the underlying process have been developed. Perhaps the most widely used camera model in computer vision and robotics is the **pinhole camera** model (see Figure 5.1). In the pinhole camera model a point on an object is projected through a pinhole or **optical center** of a camera onto a planar image surface. Consider the head of the arrow viewed by the pinhole camera shown in Figure 5.1. Light from some illuminant strikes the head of the arrow and is reflected in all directions. Some of this light passes through the pinhole aperture in the camera and strikes the image plane. As light travels in straight lines, the point to which an image feature projects on the image plane constrains the three-dimensional location of the feature to a line in space – the line consisting of the loci of points joining the tip of the arrow with its image on the image plane and the pinhole. The absolute depth of the arrow head is lost. Pinhole cameras are often said to obtain the direction to an object rather than the distance to it.

The reduction of the three-dimensional position of a point to its two-dimensional projection within a camera is *a* fundamental problem with the use of vision in mobile robotics. This makes the recovery of a point's distance a fundamental computational challenge. Many mechanisms have been proposed in order to address this problem, including the use of additional assumptions that restrict the set of possible distance values, the use of multiple cameras, the use of big data models, and the use of temporal integration. Some of these techniques will be examined shortly.

The mathematical equivalent of the pinhole camera is known as **perspective projection**. Given an arbitrary point in three-space described in homogeneous coordinates as $X = [X_1\ X_2\ X_3\ 1]^T$, under a perspective or pinhole camera model the relationship between the 2D pixel or image coordinate $(x_1/x_3, x_2/x_3)$ and the 3D world or scene coordinate can be described by a 3×4 matrix called the **projection matrix** $\tilde{P}$,

$$\begin{bmatrix} x_1 \\ x_2 \\ x_3 \end{bmatrix} = \tilde{P} \begin{bmatrix} X_1 \\ X_2 \\ X_3 \\ 1 \end{bmatrix}.$$

Due to the nature of the mapping from 3D to 2D, $\tilde{P}$ is defined only up to a scale factor. A common mechanism for specifying a unique $\tilde{P}$ is to force $\tilde{P}_{3,4} = 1$, although other techniques exist (e.g., [262]).

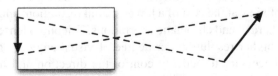

Figure 5.1. Pinhole camera model. A pinhole camera consists of a box with a pinhole through which light enters and an image plane onto which the light is projected. Because light travels in straight lines, an object (here an arrow) is projected to a unique location on the image plane.

The matrix $\tilde{P}$ can be interpreted in a number of different ways, but the classic interpretation [366, 262] is that $\tilde{P}$ models a rigid transformation from some arbitrary 3D world coordinate system to a 3D coordinate system aligned with the optical center and the ideal image plane of the camera, followed by a perspective projection to an ideal 2D coordinate system on the image plane. Furthermore, $\tilde{P}$ encodes an affine relationship between the real 2D coordinate system used on the image plane and the ideal one. The parameters defining the rigid portion of the transformation are known as the **extrinsic camera parameters** because they do not depend on the nature of the camera itself, while the remaining parameters of the camera calibration are known as the **intrinsic camera parameters**.

Although the pinhole camera and the corresponding projective geometry are perhaps the most common models, less sophisticated mathematical models have wide applicability in restrictive imaging domains. For example, if the perspective effect of apparent size change with distance is small, then an approximation to perspective projection in which "depth scaling" is omitted leads to a simplified mathematical formulation known as **parallel projection**. An intermediate imaging geometry known as **weak perspective** or **scaled orthographic camera** is applicable when the depth variation of an object is small compared to the average distance of the object to the camera. In this model individual points on an object are scaled by an average depth value rather than by an individual depth value. Various approximations to the perspective camera model are discussed in [24], and a vision system that takes advantage of one of these more restrictive imaging models is presented in [710].

If necessary, the projection matrix $\tilde{P}$ can be decomposed into intrinsic and extrinsic parameters by modeling the extrinsic parameters as a rigid three-dimensional transformation, a 3×3 rotation matrix, and a rigid translation vector T, and by modeling the remaining degrees of freedom by a set of intrinsic parameters representing an affine distortion of the image plane.

The intrinsic parameters can be described in various ways, but one common mechanism is to represent them using a **camera intrinsic matrix** given by

$$A = \begin{bmatrix} \alpha & \gamma & u_0 \\ 0 & \beta & v_0 \\ 0 & 0 & 1 \end{bmatrix}.$$

Here (u_0, v_0) is known as the principal point, α and β are the scale factors along the u and v axes respectively, and γ is the skewness between these axes. $\tilde{P}$ can be decomposed as

$$\tilde{P} = A \begin{bmatrix} R_{3\times3} & T_{1\times3} \\ 0 \quad 0 \quad 0 & 1 \end{bmatrix},$$

where $R_{3\times3}$ is a 3×3 rotation matrix and $T_{1\times3}$ is a 1×3 translation column vector.

5.1.2 Planar Homography

Perspective cameras have a range of properties that can be leveraged by vision-based algorithms. Perhaps one of the most useful of these properties is that the mapping (or **homography**) between points on a plane under a perspective view have a particular structure. To see this, consider points on a plane π observed by a perspective camera $\tilde{P}_1$. As $\tilde{P}_1$ is a perspective camera, then for any point $\boldsymbol{p} = [X_1 \ X_2 \ X_3 \ 1]^T$

$$s_1 \begin{bmatrix} u_1 \\ v_1 \\ 1 \end{bmatrix} = \tilde{P}_1 \begin{bmatrix} X_1 \\ X_2 \\ X_3 \\ 1 \end{bmatrix}. \tag{5.1}$$

Now p lies on the plane π. Any point on a plane can be written as

$$p = \alpha A + \beta B + O.$$

Substituting this in (5.1) results in

$$s_1 \begin{bmatrix} u_1 \\ v_1 \\ 1 \end{bmatrix} = \tilde{P}_1 \left(\alpha \begin{bmatrix} A_1 \\ A_2 \\ A_3 \\ 1 \end{bmatrix} + \beta \begin{bmatrix} B_1 \\ B_2 \\ B_3 \\ 1 \end{bmatrix} + \begin{bmatrix} O_1 \\ O_2 \\ O_3 \\ 1 \end{bmatrix} \right)$$

$$\tag{5.2}$$

$$= \alpha \tilde{P}_1 \begin{bmatrix} A_1 \\ A_2 \\ A_3 \\ 1 \end{bmatrix} + \beta \tilde{P}_1 \begin{bmatrix} B_1 \\ B_2 \\ B_3 \\ 1 \end{bmatrix} + \tilde{P}_1 \begin{bmatrix} O_1 \\ O_2 \\ O_3 \\ 1 \end{bmatrix}.$$

Let Q_1 be the 3×3 matrix formed from the three column vectors on the right-hand side of (5.2). Then (5.2) can be written as

$$s_1 \begin{bmatrix} u_1 \\ v_1 \\ 1 \end{bmatrix} = Q_1 \begin{bmatrix} \alpha \\ \beta \\ 1 \end{bmatrix}.$$

This can be manipulated in various ways. For example, suppose we have a second camera (or even the same camera after some motion) viewing the same plane. Then for this second camera $\tilde{P}_2$, we have

$$s_2 \begin{bmatrix} u_2 \\ v_2 \\ 1 \end{bmatrix} = Q_2 \begin{bmatrix} \alpha \\ \beta \\ 1 \end{bmatrix}$$

and assuming that Q_2 is invertable we can combine the expressions for the two cameras to obtain

$$s_1 \begin{bmatrix} u_1 \\ v_1 \\ 1 \end{bmatrix} = s_2 Q_1 Q_2^{-1} \begin{bmatrix} u_2 \\ v_2 \\ 1 \end{bmatrix}.$$

Writing $H = s_2 Q_1 Q_2^{-1}$ yields the expression for the **planar homography** under perspective projection

$$s_1 \begin{bmatrix} u_1 \\ v_1 \\ 1 \end{bmatrix} = H \begin{bmatrix} u_2 \\ v_2 \\ 1 \end{bmatrix}.$$

Image points from a plane can be mapped into another perspective view through a 3×3 matrix H (defined up to a scale factor) without explicit knowledge of either $\tilde{P}_1$ or $\tilde{P}_2$. The planar homography H can be estimated via a simple calibration process based on at least four points.

5.1.3   Camera Calibration

In order to use vision for many mobile robotic tasks, it is often necessary to obtain $\tilde{P}$ for a particular camera. The process of obtaining $\tilde{P}$ for a camera is known as **camera calibration**. There are many different mechanisms for calibrating a single video camera. Perhaps the simplest mechanism is to use a calibration object with a known 3D pose along with its projection to solve for the calibration matrix $\tilde{P}$.

The **direct linear transformation** (DLT) approach [3, 366, 263] is a straightforward approach to perspective camera calibration. Given a collection of calibration points in world coordinates X_i along with their image projections (u_i, v_i), we seek a $\tilde{P}$ such that

$$\sum((\tilde{P}X_i)_1 - (\tilde{P}X_i)_3 u_i)^2 + ((\tilde{P}X_i)_2 - (\tilde{P}X_i)_3 v_i)^2 \tag{5.3}$$

is minimized. Here we use the notation A_n where A is a matrix to indicate the nth row of A. It is straightforward to show that $5\frac{1}{2}$ scene points, not all lying on the same plane, are sufficient to uniquely define $\tilde{P}$. More commonly, additional scene points are available and a least-squares solution is used.

The linear least-squares solution $\tilde{P}$ is obtained by solving $AX = B$, where

$$A = \begin{bmatrix} -X_i & -X_i & -X_i & -1 & 0 & 0 & 0 & 0 & u_i X_i & u_i Y_i & u_i Z_i \\ 0 & 0 & 0 & 0 & -X_i & -Y_i & -Z_i & -1 & v_i X_i & v_i Y_i & v_i Z_i \\ & & & & \dots & & & & & & \end{bmatrix},$$

$$X^T = \begin{bmatrix} \tilde{P}_{1,1} & \tilde{P}_{1,2} & \tilde{P}_{1,3} & \tilde{P}_{1,4} & \tilde{P}_{2,1} & \tilde{P}_{2,2} & \tilde{P}_{3,3} & \tilde{P}_{4,4} & \tilde{P}_{3,1} & \tilde{P}_{2,2} & \tilde{P}_{3,3} \end{bmatrix},$$

and

$$B = \begin{bmatrix} -u_i \\ -v_i \\ \dots \end{bmatrix}.$$

The linear least-squares solution X is then available as $X = (A^T A)^{-1} A^T B$.

There are a number of concerns with the simple calibration mechanism described above. First, it requires a 3D calibration target, which is perhaps not the most convenient mechanism for calibration. Second, the error minimized in the calibration is not directly related to the projection of points onto the image plane. Finally, the assumption that $\tilde{P}_{3,4} = 1$ can lead to instabilities if $\tilde{P}_{3,4}$ is near zero. More sophisticated calibration algorithms (e.g., [777], [344], and [862]) avoid a number of these issues, can optionally deal with radial distortions of the image, and also provide different minimization criteria and target forms.

Given the importance of camera calibration, standard calibration toolkits have emerged as both stand-alone programs and as toolkits written for OpenCV, Matlab, and other programming environments. The calibration system described in [862] is representative. Multiple views of a planar target are obtained, and for each view a homography is constructed between a point $[x \ y]$ in a coordinate frame defined by the target and its view $[u \ v]$. It is straightforward [862] to show that

$$H = sA \begin{bmatrix} r_1 & r_2 & T \end{bmatrix},$$

where s is a scale factor and r_1 and r_2 are the first and second columns of the rotation matrix, respectively. Now as R is a rotation matrix, r_1 and r_2 are orthonormal. As a result, the established homography H provides two constraints on the form of A

$$h_1^T (A^{-1})^T A^{-1} h_2 = 0,$$

$$h_1^T (A^{-1})^T A^{-1} h_1 = h_1^T (A^{-1})^T A^{-1} h_2.$$

Let $B = (A^{-1})^T A^{-1}$. B is a symmetric matrix, and a minimum of three homographies between the plane and the camera's view are sufficient to establish the matrix B. Given B, it is straightforward to extract the elements of A and then to recover the rotation and transformation matricies [862].

Given a calibrated camera denoted by $\tilde{P}$, it is instructive to note that $\tilde{P}$ contains considerable information concerning the camera pose. The solution of

$$\begin{bmatrix} 0 \\ 0 \\ 0 \end{bmatrix} = \tilde{P} \begin{bmatrix} C_x \\ C_y \\ C_z \\ 1 \end{bmatrix}$$

defines the optical center (C_x, C_y, C_z) of the camera in world coordinates. In addition, each row of $\tilde{P}$ defines a plane, all of which intersect at (C_x, C_y, C_z). The intersection of $\tilde{P}_1$ and $\tilde{P}_2$ defines the direction in which the camera points, and the intersection of $\tilde{P}_2$ and $\tilde{P}_3$ defines the twist of the camera with respect to that direction.

Although the pinhole camera/perspective projection model is widely used in computational vision, it is not perfect. Very few cameras are actually pinhole cameras; most utilize a finite aperture rather than a pinhole in order to admit more light onto the image plane (one exception in nature is the nautilus, which relies on pinhole-like eyes). This blurs the resulting image, and a lens assembly is used to focus the image. Unfortunately lenses have a finite **depth of field**, and objects lying outside this region will be blurred across the image plane. In addition, lenses often introduce non-uniform image distortion, as well as chromatic distortions of the input. Various models exist for these more realistic lenses, but they are rarely used in robotic vision applications. One exception is their use in **depth-from-focus** algorithms where a model of image blurring is used to estimate object depth. A common technique to make a non-ideal camera behave more like a pinhole one is to use the smallest aperture setting possible, and to utilize only the central portion of the image in order to reduce radial distortions.

The image plane itself complicates the imaging process. Sampling arrays used in most robotic sensors rely on a rectangular sampling grid that is roughly aligned with the horizontal and vertical axes of the camera. Aliasing errors occur due to the finite spatial sampling extent of the sampling arrays and to the low temporal sampling rate. Potential solutions to these issues include foveated sensors (e.g., [794, 603] and see [848] for a review), as well as image sensors that are randomly accessible (eg., [635]).

5.1.4   Cameras in ROS

The Gazebo/ROS sensor model extends to cameras as illustrated in Listing 5.1. The Gazebo visualization setting provides a visualization of the viewing fulstrum of the camera as well as a rendering of the camera image within Gazebo as shown in Figure 5.2. In ROS, camera sensors provide image streams as either a sequence of snapshots from the sensor or as a compressed image sequence. Given the potentially large volume of data associated with a sensor capturing images at high temporal and spatial sampling rates,

```
<gazebo reference="camera_link">
  <sensor type="camera" name="camera">
    <visualize>true</visualize>
    <camera>
      <horizontal_fov>${65 * 3.1415/180}</horizontal_fov>
      <image>
        <format>R8G8B8</format>
        <width>640</width>
        <height>480</height>
      </image>
      <clip>
        <near>0.05</near>
        <far>50.0</far>
      </clip>
    </camera>
    <plugin name="camera_controller" filename="libgazebo_ros_camera.so">
      <camera_name>mycamera</camera_name>
      <frame_name>camera_link</frame_name>
    </plugin>
  </sensor>
</gazebo>
```

Listing 5.1. Defining a camera in Gazebo/ROS.

Figure 5.2. A camera in Gazebo/ROS.

the capability of representing such signals in a compressed form is critical to reduce the impact of the data stream on the underlying network infrastructure.

One way of accessing images from a camera in ROS is by accessing its raw image structure as described in Listing 5.2. This message provides the camera image sequence as a sequence of image frames, each of a given width and height. Different cameras provide raw image data in different encodings as a consequence of the nature of the underlying hardware. The image_raw message basically provides the image as a large collection of 8-bit image data with sufficient header information to enable libraries to decode the image into triplets of red, green, and blue per pixel over a rectangular camera image.

For many image processing tasks it is important that the camera be calibrated (see Section 5.1.2). ROS provides a mechanism of communicating the calibration information associated with a given camera through transmitting a CameraInfo message along with image data. For a simulated camera, such as that described in Listing 5.1, calibration parameters are provided by the Gazebo simulation. For a real camera, the camera node would transmit this information. The CameraInfo package provides distortion and camera calibration parameters.

```
std_msgs/msg header
uint32 height
uint32 width
string encoding
uint8 is_bigendian
uint32 step
uint8[] data
```

Listing 5.2. ROS image_raw structure.

5.2 Object Appearance and Shading

Before considering the application of visual sensing to robotics tasks, it is worthwhile to briefly consider the relationship between objects in the scene and their appearance. Images, be they video images or those on our retina, are composed of discrete samples of reflected intensity. In the case of standard color cameras these samples are acquired by three sets of sensors tuned to three different frequency bands, typically red, green, and blue (this tuning is certainly not the only one; most cameras are also sensitive to infrared). It not a coincidence that the human eye can also be modeled as being composed of three classes of color-sensitive detectors. In higher-quality cameras, the different color measurements associated with a given pixel come from exactly the same point in space (using colored filters). In lower-cost cameras (and the human eye), the different measurements are, in fact, acquired by different detector elements displaced from one another in space but we will neglect this here. Thus, we can consider each pixel being the measurement of the light reflected from a single point in the scene (we will also neglect phenomena such as fog).

The light reflected from a point in the scene depends on two things: the reflectance properties of the object and the illumination that falls on the object. This relationship is formalized by the **bidirectional reflectance function** (BDRF) $R(\phi_{in}, \theta_{in}, \phi_{out}, \theta_{out})$, which expresses the fraction of received energy from a specified orientation (ϕ_{in}, θ_{in}) that is reflected in a given direction $(\phi_{out}, \theta_{out})$ by a surface. Determining the amount of light reflected along a ray back to the camera involves knowing the BDRF for the object of interest and combining the light reflected from all illumination sources (including light reflected from other objects).

A common simplification is to assume that the reflectance function is a linear combination of two types of canonical reflector: a mirror and a matte surface. Mirror-like surfaces, known as **specular reflectors**, reflect almost all the incoming light energy along a ray symmetrically opposite to the angle of incidence, and their reflectance can be approximated by

$$R_s = \rho_s (R \cdot V)^\alpha, \tag{5.4}$$

where N is the surface normal, L is a unit vector pointing toward the light source, R is the reflection of L in the surface, V is the direction to the viewer, ρ_s represents the extent of specular reflectance, and α is a coefficient that determines how perfectly shiny the reflector is (perfect shininess is attained for $\alpha \rightarrow \infty$). Matte surfaces, known as **Lambertian** reflectors, reflect light equally in all directions, and the reflected intensity depends only on the relationship between the surface normal and the light source:

$$R_d = \rho_d N \cdot L, \tag{5.5}$$

where ρ_d represents the surface's reflective nature. The reflectance of an object can then be expressed with this simplified model as a sum of the two components, ρ_s and ρ_d.

When these reflectance models are applied to color images, they are sometimes applied independently for each of the color channels. In practice, Lambertian reflectance tends to result from scattering of light in the surface layer of an object and hence it takes on the object's color. Specular reflectance, on the other hand, tends to be relatively unaffected by the pigment color of an object and thus specularities often have a color akin to that of the illuminant. While this can be useful for the detection of highlights ([310]), it can also complicate simple color-based object recognition schemes.

5.3   Signals and Sampling

A digital image is simply a collection of samples of the visual content in the environment. In principle, we can think of a scene as a field of rays associated with all possible viewing directions from all possible vantage points. Such descriptions of a scene are known as the **lumigraph** or the **light ray manifold**. A single conventional image contains a set of samples from a single vantage point. Each individual sample is known as a **pixel** or **picture element**. The samples are typically obtained from points on a rectangular lattice and have a finite resolution such as 8 or 16 bits per sample. Each pixel encodes either intensity or the intensity in each of a small number of color channels associated with this specific spatial location.

Although it is tempting to model this set of pixels as a continuous surface, it is important to recognize that the pixels are discrete samples taken in both space and time. This introduces physical limits on what can be correctly captured with a given video sensor. Figure 5.3 shows the difficulties involved in sampling a continuous function. The continuous image being sampled by the discrete image shown[2] in the figure is a sine wave in intensity whose frequency increases linearly with vertical position, that is,

$$I(x, y) = \sin(\omega * x * y).$$

Each scan line in the image should appear as a sine wave, with the frequencies increasing as one moves down the image. As the image has a finite pixel size (as does this printed page), the rate of sampling per wavelength decreases, and eventually there are insufficient samples to represent the underlying continuous structure. Signals at high frequencies can be mistaken for signals at lower frequencies, and other artifacts emerge. This phenomenon is known as **aliasing**. Although Figure 5.3 was specifically chosen to exhibit aliasing, the phenomenon occurs whenever the real world exhibits an intensity pattern that cannot be well represented within the limited sampling resolution of the video sensor.

The minimum sampling frequency that is required to completely represent a continuous signal is known as the **Nyquist frequency**. Informally, to represent a continuous signal, it is essential to sample the signal at a rate at least twice as great as the highest frequency in the signal. Consider the one-dimensional signal $f(x) = \cos(\pi x)$. If $f(x)$ is sampled at integer points, that is at $0, 1, 2, 3, \ldots$, the values $1, -1, 1, -1, \ldots$ are obtained. If $f(x)$ is only sampled at even integers then $1, 1, 1, \ldots$ is obtained. Sampling this 1D signal at every pixel

---

[2] The printer used by the publisher will add yet another sampling effect due to the printer's limited resolution.

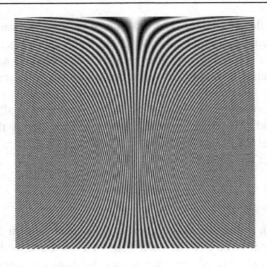

Figure 5.3. The effects of sampling. This figure shows a sine wave with linearly increasing frequency. As the sampling rate is constant, most of the underlying continuous image is undersampled and aliasing results.

retains the information in the signal. Sampling it at every other pixel underrepresents the image and aliasing occurs. In angular frequency the Nyquist frequency is $\omega_{\text{Nyquist}} = \pi$. When discretely sampled on an integer lattice, continuous signals with frequencies above π and below $-\pi$ cannot be well represented.

Although arbitrary operations can be applied to an image, many image operations can be expressed as **linear shift invariant systems** [589]. Such systems are completely characterized by their response through a convolution sum:

$$y(n_1, n_2) = \sum_{k_1=-\infty}^{+\infty} \sum_{k_2=-\infty}^{+\infty} x(k_1, k_2) h(n_1 - k_1, n_2 - k_2).$$

For example, to obtain a blurred version of an image, the image could be convolved with $h(k_1, k_2)$, where

$$h(k_1, k_2) = \frac{1}{8} \begin{bmatrix} 0 & 1 & 0 \\ 1 & 4 & 1 \\ 0 & 1 & 0 \end{bmatrix}, \tag{5.6}$$

where $(k_1, k_2) = (0, 0)$ refers to the center element of h. The convolution sum is usually written as $y = x * h$.

For a linear shift invariant operator $h(k_1, k_2)$ with Fourier transform $\hat{h}(\omega_1, \omega_2)$, the 2D Fourier transform $\hat{x}(\omega_1, \omega_2)$ of an input signal $x(n_1, n_2)$ is related to the 2D Fourier transform $\hat{y}(\omega_1, \omega_2)$ of the output signal $y(n_1, n_2)$ via the relation

$$\hat{y}(\omega_1, \omega_2) = \hat{h}(\omega_1, \omega_2) \hat{x}(\omega_1, \omega_2).$$

In addition to providing an alternative computational mechanism for evaluating the application of a particular operator to an image, the system's transfer function $\hat{h}(\omega_1, \omega_2)$ can be used to examine the response of a linear shift operator or filter to an arbitrary input.

In conjunction with the Fourier transform (see Appendix C and [521]),

$$\hat{f}(k) = \int_{-\infty}^{+\infty} f(x) e^{-ixk} dx$$

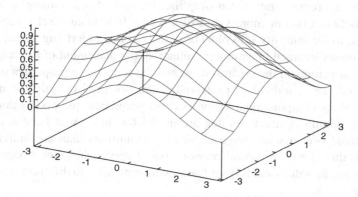

Figure 5.4. Amplitude spectrum of averaging filter. This surface shows the amplitude spectrum of the transfer function of the 3×3 averaging filter given in (5.6). Note that the Nyquist rate is π in angular frequency.

can be used to obtain the amplitude spectrum $|\hat{f}(k)|$ of a continuous signal $f(x)$. Operators with large values of $|\hat{f}(k)|$ for elements of k near $\pm\pi$ (the Nyquist frequency) tend to amplify unrepresentable frequencies in an image and thus perform poorly unless high frequencies in the input signal are suppressed before applying the operator.

For a two-dimensional operator $h(x_1, x_2)$ represented by a discrete convolution, $\hat{h}(k_1, k_2)$ is given by [589]

$$\hat{h}(k_1, k_2) = \sum_{\alpha_1=-\infty}^{\alpha_1=+\infty} \sum_{\alpha_2=-\infty}^{\alpha_2=+\infty} h(\alpha_1, \alpha_2) e^{-i(\alpha_1 k_1 + \alpha_2 k_2)}, \tag{5.7}$$

where k_1 and k_2 are continuous values of spatial frequency. Both [198] and [274] use (5.7) to analyze various discrete convolution operators. For example, for the averaging operator h given in (5.6), the transfer function $\hat{h}(k_1, k_2)$ is given by

$$\begin{aligned}
\hat{h}(k_1, k_2) &= \sum_{\alpha_1=-\infty}^{\alpha_1=+\infty} \sum_{\alpha_2=-\infty}^{\alpha_2=+\infty} h(\alpha_1, \alpha_2) e^{-i(\alpha_1 k_1 + \alpha_2 k_2)} \\
&= \tfrac{1}{2} + e^{ik_1} + e^{-ik_1} + e^{ik_2} + e^{-ik_2} \tag{5.8} \\
&= (4 + 2\cos(k_1) + 2\cos(k_2))/8.
\end{aligned}$$

The magnitude of $\hat{h}$, $|\hat{h}|$ is plotted in Figure 5.4. As the averaging operator given in (5.6) has a large non-zero response for frequencies near the Nyquist frequency, this operator can be expected to perform poorly in the presence of noise. Note that much better averaging operators exist; for example, a Gaussian – to which (5.6) is a rough approximation – is a much better averaging filter.

5.4 Image Features and Their Combination

Fundamental to many operations in robot vision is the task of matching two or more views of the same object. The object may be a template; does a particular pattern of image pixels occur in this image? Or it may be another image; does the same object appear in two different camera views? When choosing a particular representation of visual data, it is often useful to choose a representation that simplifies the task of determining matches or correspondences between two or more views of a scene. Individual pixel values are only indirectly related to the intensity (or color) of objects in the underlying scene; they are the result of a complex interaction among illumination, the placement of the camera, the presence of other structures in the environment, and the reflectance properties of the objects being observed. Thus, individual pixel values are not used directly for many robotic vision tasks. Many computational vision systems preprocess the pixel values in some way in order to highlight structures that are useful for the task at hand and are more likely to be stable over a wide range of viewing conditions than are individual pixels. In contrast to this approach, neural network–based approaches (see Chapter 6) typically process raw image values and rely on learning to generalize to different viewing conditions.

5.4.1   Color and Shading

Rather than just obtain the intensity of structure in the image, color cameras obtain the intensity from a collection of sensors that are sensitive to different wavelengths of light. The image is then represented by a vector of values at each pixel rather than just intensity. Often these channels are called the red, green, and blue channels but fewer (or larger) numbers of channels are possible. Color can be a very powerful tool for determining correspondences, but color sensors can also be very sensitive to illumination conditions.

One effective strategy that uses color is based on the concept of representing an object or a feature by its **color histogram** [747, 254, 582]. The method describes objects by the *combination* of different colors that characterize them. As such, it is of particular value that the objects to be recognized are defined by particular *combinations of colors*.

An image is represented by a vector $(h_1, h_2, ..., h_n)$ in a n-dimensional vector space, where each element h_i represents the number of pixels of color i in the image. This feature vector is then used to identify this feature in some other image. Given color histograms $(h_1, .., h_n)$ of image H and $(k_1, .., k_n)$ of image K, we define the similarity or distance between them as

$$d(H, K) = \sum |h_1 - k_i|.$$

In a typical application, the set of possible colors is reduced to a smaller number (256 is typical), and thus an image can be represented by 256 values. The histograms are normalized so that the similarity measure is independent of the size of the image.

5.4.2   Image Brightness Constraint

Although individual pixel values are not particularly stable over a large range of changes in the image or the imaging geometry, they can be considered stable over sufficiently small changes in imaging conditions. The **image brightness constraint** [367] or **gradient constraint equation** expresses this property that the intensity of a point remains unchanged as it moves,

$$f(x + dx, y + dy, t + dt) = f(x, y, t),$$

where $f(x,y,t)$ is the intensity of the image. A Taylor series expansion of $f(x,y,t)$ leads to

$$f(x+dx, y+dy, t+dt) = f(x,y,t) + \frac{\partial f}{\partial x}dx + \frac{\partial f}{\partial y}dy + \frac{\partial f}{\partial t}dt + O(x^2).$$

Ignoring the higher-order terms and equating $f(x+dx, y+dy, t+dt) = f(x,y,t)$ results in

$$-\frac{\partial f}{\partial t} = \frac{\partial f}{\partial x}\frac{dx}{dt} + \frac{\partial f}{\partial y}\frac{dy}{dt}. \tag{5.9}$$

This provides a constraint on the image velocity $(u,v) = (dx/dt, dy/dt)$ as a function of local derivatives $(E_x, E_y, E_t) = (df/dx, df/dy, df/dt)$ of the image intensity function f. That is, equation (5.9) relates the motion (u,v) of a patch of image intensities in the image to local changes in the intensity structure in the image: E_x, E_y, and E_t. Equation (5.9) is not sufficient to compute both components (u,v) of the image velocity, but rather provides a linear constraint $E_x u + E_y v + E_t = 0$. Equation (5.9) is known as the **optical flow constraint equation** [366], and the vector field (u,v) is known as **optical flow**.

The local information contained in the optical flow constraint equation provides a linear constraint on (u,v). This constraint provides a constraint on the flow in the direction of the brightness gradient but provides no constraint on the flow perpendicular to this direction (see Figure 5.5). Thus, in order to obtain a unique optical flow field some additional information is necessary. The fact that local flow information is not available in the direction perpendicular to the direction of the brightness gradient is known as the **aperture problem** [790].

Various approaches have been proposed to overcome the aperture problem. The classic approach is due to Horn and Schunk [367]. They developed an iterative algorithm that enforces a smoothness constraint on the optical flow field and integrates measurements spatially in order to solve for the flow. In particular, they proposed the minimization of $e_s + \lambda e_c$, where

$$e_s = \int\int (u_x^2 + u_y^2 + v_x^2 + v_y^2)dxdy$$

and

$$e_c = \int\int (E_x u + E_y v + E_t)^2 dxdy$$

over the image to recover (u,v) everywhere. This approach to solving the optical flow field is a classical application of regularization to solve an ill-posed problem (see Section 4.1).

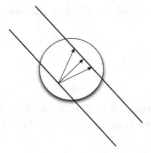

Figure 5.5. Aperture problem. Given the motion of an edge through a small aperture, only the component of motion perpendicular to the line is measurable – motion along the direction of the line is undetectable.

Horn and Schunk's algorithm has been found to have difficulties when the underlying flow field is discontinuous. More modern algorithms exist that show considerably better performance, see [592, 76, 708] for reviews. See [261] for a more modern optical flow algorithm based on traditional image processing and [761] for a recent neural network-based approach.

5.4.3 Correlation

Although the intensity of scene structure is likely to change as the view changes, it may be the case that the local image structure near a point of interest remains constant. One popular approach is to use a patch or window as the measurement rather than a single pixel. This leads to an approach known as **correlation** in which a test pattern from one image is correlated with another in order to identify the location of the test pattern in the second image. This test pattern may be based on some ideal model of the pattern that will appear in the image, or it may be a region of one image that is being compared with another.

The similarity $d(\delta x, \delta y)$ between two images g and f can be defined as

$$d^2(\delta x, \delta y) = \sum \sum (f(x, y) - g(x + \delta x, y + \delta y))^2,$$

where the sum is made over the region of the two images that are to be compared. The place where g can be found in f will be associated with small values of d^2. Expanding d^2 results in

$$d^2(\delta x, \delta y) = \sum \sum f^2(x, y) + g^2(x + \delta x, y + \delta y) - 2f(x, y)g(x + \delta x, y + \delta y).$$

Assuming f and g are constant over the summation window, then minimizing $d^2(\delta x, \delta y)$ is equivalent to maximizing the correlation of f and g, where the correlation is given by

$$corr(\delta x, \delta y) = \sum \sum f(x, y)g(\delta x + x, \delta y + y).$$

In a typical application, a small window in one image is correlated with windowed portions of the other.

Correlation is relatively inexpensive computationally; the cost is related to the window size and the region that is to be searched, but the simple correlation function given above is sensitive to the local mean intensities of f and g. It can also be sensitive to noise in the input and to distortions between the two images that are not the result of simple shifting (i.e., "non-shift" distortions such as rotation and shear).

Normalized cross-correlation addresses a number of these problems, although it does not deal with non-shift distortions. Under normalized cross-correlation the correlation function is computed as

$$\frac{\sum \sum W(x, y)f'(x + \delta x, y + \delta y)g'(x + \delta x, y + \delta y)}{|v_f(\delta x, \delta y)v_g(\delta x, \delta y)|^{\frac{1}{2}}},$$

where f' and g' are zero-mean corrected versions of the input, and v_f and v_g are the local variances of f and g computed within the window function W. (See [837] for an application of this approach.)

5.4.4   Fourier Methods

In 1963, Bogert *et al.* [96] introduced the **cepstrum** and cepstral analysis as a tool for detecting echos in signals. The cepstrum of a signal $g(x)$ with Fourier transform $\hat{g}(f)$ is given by

$$g_{cep}(x) = \int_{-\infty}^{+\infty} \log|\hat{g}(f)|e^{i\pi fx}df.$$

Peaks in the cepstrum $g_{cep}(x)$ are associated with the delay at which an echo occurs in the signal g.

Although initially used for echo detection, the cepstrum can be used to compare any two signals. The basic approach is to concatenate the two signals, and then to apply the cepstrum and seek the maximum value of g_{cep}. If the two signals are simply shifted versions of each other, then determining the echo location is equivalent to determining the unknown shift.

Cepstral techniques are popular due to their efficiency and their ability to deal with a wide range of shifts and signal amplitude variations. Unfortunately, they are sensitive to the presence of energy in one signal that is not in the other and to signals with a high autocorrelation – the cepstrum is sensitive to any echo that exists in the original signal, as well as to the shift between them

5.4.5   Feature Detectors

Rather than consider the entire image, an alternative approach is to apply some simple heuristic to identify image points that are important to the task at hand and to use these points to represent the image. Corners, for example, often have significance for visual tasks, and corner detectors have been constructed to identify them. The general class of such operators is known as **feature detectors** or **interest operators**. They are closely related to the biological phenomenon of visual attention. The attention of human observers, for example, is naturally associated with specific types of visual events, many of which have been described in terms of image-based features.

In practice, an interest operator should identify image locations that are stable under slight changes in the image and slight changes in viewpoint. It should also abstract the image in terms of a manageable number of features. See [693] for a review of more recent feature detectors.

Moravec operator Perhaps the most famous of the feature detectors is the **Moravec interest operator**. The Moravec interest operator [539] produces candidate match points by measuring the distinctiveness of local image structure. It defines the variance measure at a pixel (x, y) as

$$\text{var}(x, y) = \left\{ \sum_{k,l \in S} [f(x, y) - f(x + k, y + l)]^2 \right\}^{\frac{1}{2}},$$

where

$$S = \{(0, a), (0, -a), (a, 0), (-a, 0)\}$$

and a is a parameter. The variance is computed over a neighborhood, and the minimum variance is computed

$$\text{Moravec}(x, y) = \min_{(\delta x, \delta y) \in N} \text{var}(x + \delta x, y + \delta y).$$

Then only local maximal values of the operator that exceed a specified threshold are retained.

The Moravec operator is designed to identify points in an image with high variance such as corners. Although points with high variance may be of interest, it is difficult to say precisely to what the detector will respond. Many other feature detectors exist; see, for example, [284], [220], and [339]. Thorpe [766] surveyed a number of different feature point detectors prior to 1984.

Harris corner detector The **Harris corner detector** [339] relies on the observation that small motions in the image near a corner will have a large effect on the local gradient structure in the image. Consider the matrix

$$M = \begin{bmatrix} G_\sigma * \left(\frac{\partial f}{\partial x}\right)^2 & G_\sigma * \left(\frac{\partial f}{\partial x}\right)\left(\frac{\partial f}{\partial y}\right) \\ G_\sigma * \left(\frac{\partial f}{\partial x}\right)\left(\frac{\partial f}{\partial y}\right) & G_\sigma * \left(\frac{\partial f}{\partial y}\right)^2 \end{bmatrix},$$

where f is the image intensity and G is a Gaussian smoothing function. Corners are defined as local maxima of the corner response function

$$R = \det M - k(\text{trace } M)^2,$$

where k is a constant set to approximately 0.04. The Harris corner detector can be used to find corners to subpixel accuracy by interpolating the corner response function. The Harris corner detector has found wide application, especially in camera calibration packages.

SIFT Scale invariant feature transform (SIFT) image features [481, 482] have been found to be effective for a variety of applications, from stereo matching to object recognition. The features are computed using a pyramid of difference-of-Gaussian operators to capture image structures at a range of scales. By using filters at different scales and tuned to different orientations, the feature detector is supposed to detect features consistently even if they change orientation or size. Each of the features results in a description of relatively high dimensionality that can be used as a key for subsequent matching processes. The process of computing SIFT features is relatively complex, but many of the operations can be performed efficiently by computing them over small, discrete windows. The process of computing SIFT features is described in Listing 5.3.

SURF Speeded-up robust features [75] (SURF) were proposed particularly to address concerns with the computational cost of SIFT feature computation. Like SIFT features, SURF uses a filter pyramid, but the filter kernels are based on Haar wavelets (a form of square-wave function). They can also be described in terms of the approximate Hessian (second derivative matrix) of the image intensities, and features are located at extrema (as with SIFT). An alternative way to describe the filter kernels is in terms of *integral images*, that is, box-like filters that compute the sums of the pixels under them. Such integral images can be computed very efficiently since they are based on simple

1. **Scale space extrema detection.**

$$L(x, y, \sigma) = G(x, y, \sigma) \star I(x, y),$$

where $G()$ is a Gaussian, I is the input image, and $\star$ is the convolution operator. Stable keypoint locations in L are computed as

$$D(x, y, \sigma) = L(x, y, k\sigma) - L(x, y, \sigma).$$

Local extrema of $D(x, y, \sigma)$ in both space and scale are retained as potential keypoints.

2. **Keypoint localization.** Low-contrast or poorly localizable points are then discarded by rejecting candidate points for which the local structure of $D(x, y, \sigma)$ is not located along a likely edge structure or has low contrast. This is accomplished by rejecting points for which

$$\frac{(D_{xx} + D_{yy})^2}{D_{xx} D_{yy} - (D_{xy})^2}$$

falls below a threshold.

3. **Orientation and magnitude computation.** The magnitude $m(x, y)$ and orientation $\theta(x, y)$ are computed for image points in a window around extrema, and the peak is used to define the keypoint orientation.

4. **Keypoint descriptor.** The keypoint descriptor is a set of orientation histograms from pixel neighborhoods surrounding the scale space extrema. This descriptor is represented relative to the keypoint orientation (thus making the representation orientation independent).

Listing 5.3. The core steps involved in computing SIFT features.

sums of selected pixel values. Moreover, computing the filters at multiple scales can also be accomplished at constant cost. In addition to being potentially computable more efficiently than SIFT features, SURF may have advantages with respect to robustness of the output despite various image deformations.

ORB Although SIFT and SURF have found wide application in the computer vision and robotics communities, there are a number of issues associated with them. Critically, they are computationally expensive and have licensing restrictions that complicate their deployment. The feature detector FAST[677, 678] addressed the computational issues associated with SIFT and SURF, but at the cost of losing descriptors for orientation. ORB[681] builds on FAST and BRIEF[141] to provide both computational efficiency and orientation encoding.

5.4.6 Visual Targets

Rather than rely on naturally occurring image intensity patterns, another alternative is to design a visual feature that will be prepositioned in the environment in order to simplify later visual acquisition. A number of these **visual targets** have been proposed. Some sample targets are shown in Figures 5.6 and 5.7. Typically the target is placed in the environment at a position that must be localized visually. The target is planar and of known size, permitting the recovery of the 3D position and orientation, provided that the system has been properly calibrated.

Multiple-target marker systems have also been developed, and many of these have freely available versions for standard hardware and software configurations. For example, the AR Toolkit [409] provides a software infrastructure for the tracking and identification of planar targets. Originally designed for augmented reality applications (e.g., [88]), targets in the AR Toolkit are square and planar and consist of a black and white symbol surrounded by a black border. The symbol in the center of the target is available for simple recognition strategies (see Figure 5.6b). Given their original application for augmented

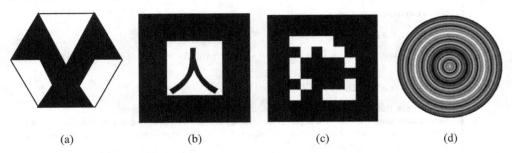

(a)   (b)   (c)   (d)

Figure 5.6. Special purpose tracking targets. (a) The binary acquisition target. (b) A sample AR Toolkit target. (c) A sample ARTag target. (d) A sample Fourier tag target.

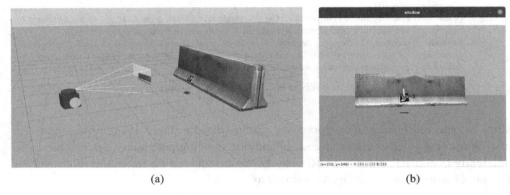

(a)   (b)

Figure 5.7. ARUCO target capture.

reality, typically the symbols used in the AR Toolkit have semantic meanings for human users. A similar approach based on symbols designed explicitly for machine readability, the ARTag system [270] provides for more accurate symbol recognition by machine but at the cost of human readability (see Figure 5.6c). The ARTag uses an error-correcting code to encode 10 bits within the 36 bit (6 × 6) binary pattern within the target. Systems such as ArUco [302] provide a family of different-sized tags to provide a larger tag alphabet. Fourier tags (see Figure 5.6d) do not provide local orientation information but rather they provide a message string that has a variable length as a function of viewing distance.

5.4.7   Edges

Many images can be described in terms of the structure of changes in intensity in the image. One commonly occurring intensity variation is rapid change in intensity: an edge. A **step edge** in an image is an image intensity contour across which the brightness of the image changes abruptly. These are frequently associated with the projection of actual object boundaries in the scene. Edges, and step edges in particular, are popular representations of images. They have an intuitive appeal as a "cartoon-like" description of an image, and there is substantial evidence that primate visual processing is associated with edge-like representations. Edges also provide a compact representation of the image and can provide an expressive representation of the salient image features as well. This is especially true of many man-made environments. Unfortunately, edges do not form a complete (i.e., information preserving) representation of the underlying image, nor can they be extracted in a reliable and robust manner under all imaging conditions. It is also the case that certain classes of image are not well described by edges. Perhaps the largest drawback to the use of intensity edges as a representation of objects is that not all abrupt changes in intensity are the result of object edges, nor do all object edges result in changes of intensity. Thus the term **edge detection** is not completely correct, but the term has widespread use in the literature, and we shall use it here.

A common mechanism for extracting edge structure from an image is to perform the computation in two stages: first extract candidate edge elements (**edgels**) from the image, and then combine the edge elements into longer **extended edge** structures.

If a step edge is associated with an intensity change, then the process of detecting step edgels can be formulated as the task of identifying image locations that are associated with a large change in intensity. If we assume that an image is a continuously differentiable function, then we can examine the gradient of the image for candidate locations. The gradient of a function $f(u,v)$ is the vector $\nabla f(u,v) = [\partial f/\partial u, \partial f/\partial v]$. Large values or peaks in the magnitude of the gradient should be associated with step edgels.

Many different discrete approximations to the gradient operator exist; Roberts [671], Prewitt [638], and Sobel [727] proposed relatively simple image differencing schemes that approximate the gradient within a fixed size window. If $\triangle_1$ and $\triangle_2$ are orthogonal directional derivatives of the image intensity, then the magnitude of the image-intensity gradient is given by $\sqrt{\triangle_1^2 + \triangle_2^2}$, and the direction of the image-intensity gradient is given by $\tan^{-1}(\triangle_2/\triangle_1)$. For example, the Sobel operator is implemented as a correlation of the image with $\triangle_1$ and $\triangle_2$, where $\triangle_1$ and $\triangle_2$ are given by

$$\triangle_1 = \begin{matrix} -1 & 0 & 1 \\ -2 & 0 & 2 \\ -1 & 0 & 1 \end{matrix}, \qquad \triangle_2 = \begin{matrix} 1 & 2 & 1 \\ 0 & 0 & 0 \\ -1 & -2 & -1 \end{matrix}.$$

The effect of applying the Sobel operator to an image is shown in Figure 5.8.

Unfortunately, derivative-like operators tend to amplify any noise present in the image, and thus operators like the Sobel operator tend to perform poorly unless the image is first preprocessed in order to reduce any noise that may be present.

Equation (5.7) can be used to examine the frequency response for each of the Sobel filters. For $\triangle_1$, for example, the transfer function $\hat{\triangle}_1(k_1, k_2)$ is given by

$$\begin{aligned} \hat{\triangle}_1(k_1, k_2) &= \sum_{\alpha_1=-\infty}^{\alpha_1=+\infty} \sum_{\alpha_2=-\infty}^{\alpha_2=+\infty} h(\alpha_1, \alpha_2) e^{-i(\alpha_1 k_1 + \alpha_2 k_2)} \\ &= -2i\left(\sin(k_1+k_2) + \sin(k_1-k_2) + 2\sin(k_1)\right). \end{aligned} \tag{5.10}$$

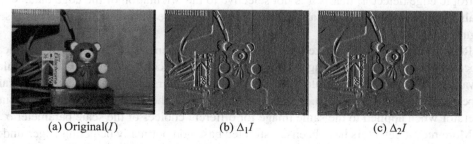

(a) Original(I) (b) $\triangle_1 I$ (c) $\triangle_2 I$

Figure 5.8. Sobel operator.

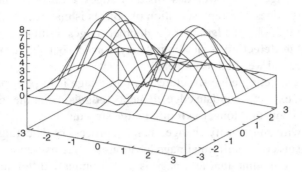

$abs(2 * (2* \sin(x)+\sin(x+y)+\sin(x-y)))$—

Figure 5.9. Frequency response of $\triangle_1$.

$|\hat{\triangle}_1|$ is plotted in Figure 5.9. $\triangle_1$ has considerable power at high frequencies, so it can be expected to perform poorly in the presence of noise. The use of an initial filtering stage to remove higher frequencies makes operators like the Sobel operator much more stable.

A second major problem with gradient-based operators is that the output of the operator must be searched in order to find and identify local maxima/minima (known as **peaks**) in the image. Peaks can be very difficult features to find computationally. The use of second derivative operators reduces this problem as the search for peaks can be replaced with a search for zero-crossings. There are a number of possible second derivative operators that can be considered. Perhaps the most popular of these is the **Laplacian**:

$$\nabla^2 = \frac{\partial^2}{\partial x^2} + \frac{\partial^2}{\partial y^2}.$$

The Laplacian is a non-directional second derivative operator.

As is the case with gradient based methods, the Laplacian operator amplifies high frequencies in the image and hence is susceptible to noise. Again one strategy for reducing the effect of any noise is to pre-filter the image with a low-pass filter such as the Gaussian and then to apply a derivative operator. The Gaussian is given by

$$G(x, y) = \frac{1}{2\pi\sigma^2}e^{-\frac{x^2+y^2}{2\sigma^2}}.$$

The **Laplacian of the Gaussian** $\nabla^2(G * I) = (\nabla^2 G) * I$ operator and the **difference of Gaussians** (DOG) operator use this type of approach and compute zero-crossings in the second derivative rather than peaks in the first derivative [503]. The $\nabla^2 G$ operator is an isotropic edge detector; that is it is not selective to the orientation of the edge data. $\nabla^2 G$ is also known as a **Mexican hat** operator due to the shape of the amplitude profile (see Figure 5.10).

Real scenes are characterized by structures of different sizes due both to physical processes operating at differing scales and task-specific considerations. One particular advantage of the $\nabla^2 G$ operator over earlier edge filters is that it made this scale dependency explicit. Figure 5.11 shows the output of the Laplacian of the Gaussian operator when applied to the same image for different choices of the scale parameter σ.

More recent detectors have been constructed based on optimally detecting edges under certain assumptions and criteria. Of those, Canny [144], Shen-Castan [713], and Deriche

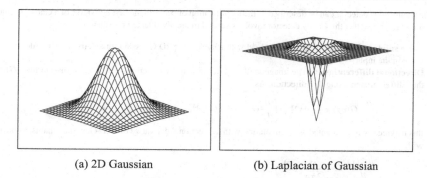

(a) 2D Gaussian   (b) Laplacian of Gaussian

Figure 5.10. Laplacian of the Gaussian.

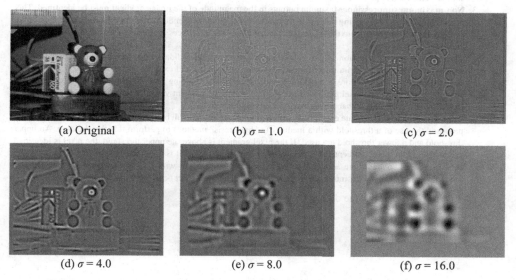

(a) Original   (b) $\sigma = 1.0$ (c) $\sigma = 2.0$

(d) $\sigma = 4.0$ (e) $\sigma = 8.0$ (f) $\sigma = 16.0$

Figure 5.11. Laplacian of the Gaussian for different choices of σ.

[219] are perhaps the best known. Each of these edge detectors can be proven to be an optimal detector under slightly different criteria; Canny assumes that the edge detector is to be implemented as a filter with a finite support region, Shen-Castan use a slightly different optimality criterion from that of Canny, while Deriche develops a filter with an infinite support region. Canny's edge detector is well approximated by peaks identified in the first derivative of a Gaussian-filtered version of the image. The Canny edge detector is described in some detail in Listing 5.4; and the set of edges obtained when applying the Canny operator to Figure 5.8a is given in Figure 5.12. The online resource associated with this text provides sample code in Python using OpenCV to detect Canny edges in a video stream obtained from a camera.

Finding and Matching Edgels The second stage in many edge detection operators involves the localization of zero-crossings (ZC) or peaks in the output of a filtered version of the image. This process will ideally obtain the location of edges to

Although the Canny edge detector can be described as the identification of peaks in the first derivative of a Gaussian smoothed version of an image, in practice the Canny detector involves several manually selected parameters.

1. **Noise suppression.** The image is convolved with a symmetric 2D Gaussian filter $G(\sigma_1, \sigma_1)$ in order to suppress noise in the input.

2. **Directional differentiation.** The image is filtered in the x and y directions with a 1D Gaussian filter $G(\sigma_2)$ and then differentiated along that direction. As

$$\frac{d}{dx}[G(\sigma_2) * f(x, y)] = [\frac{d}{dx} G(\sigma)] * f(x, y)],$$

this is typically implemented as a convolution with a directional derivative of a 1D Gaussian, that is, a convolution with

$$\frac{dG(x)}{dx} = \frac{-x}{\sqrt{2\pi}\sigma^3} e^{\frac{-x^2}{2\sigma^2}}.$$

From the computed x and y gradient values, the magnitude and orientation of the edge are computed in a manner similar to the Sobel operator.

3. **Non-maximum suppression.** Maximum outputs in the magnitude of the image gradient must be identified. This is accomplished by suppressing outputs in the gradient magnitude perpendicular to the edge direction, rather than suppressing outputs parallel to the edge. This "thins" edges but introduces problems at points on edges with high curvature, such as corners.

   Theoretically this suppression could be accomplished at each candidate edge pixel by differentiating the magnitude of the gradient in a direction perpendicular to the edge and examining the derivative to ensure that this pixel is a maximum. More commonly, individual pixels surrounding each candidate pixel are examined to ensure that the candidate pixel gradient value is greater than the gradient values of adjacent pixels perpendicular to the line direction. Pixels that are not maximal are suppressed.

4. **Edge thresholding.** Candidate edge pixels whose gradient magnitude fall below a threshold are discarded. Canny proposed the use of a threshold with a memory (a "hysteresis" method) to perform this thresholding. An upper threshold and a lower threshold are used. If the pixel gradient is above the upper threshold, the pixel is identified as an edge. If the pixel gradient is below the lower threshold, the pixel is identified as non-edge. Pixels that lie between these two values are accepted if they are connected to pixels with a strong response (greater than the lower threshold). Canny recommended that the ratio of high to low limit be in the range of two or three to one.

Listing 5.4. Canny edge detector.

Figure 5.12. Canny edge map.

subpixel accuracy. Various techniques exist for finding the location of an edge, but most involve fitting a local continuous surface to the filter output and then solving the fit for the location of the zero-crossing or peak. Edges associated with peaks below a given threshold or with zero-crossings associated with low-magnitude gradients are discarded.

Edges are typically coded by the strength (either the magnitude of the peak or the gradient) and also their orientation. This information can then be exploited in later edge aggregation or matching processes.

If edges are detected at different scales, then edges must also be matched across scale. Various approaches have been suggested for this task [838, 425, 854] but most involve tracking edges across scales based on features of the filters used and the fact that for small changes in scale the location of the edge is not likely to move a considerable distance in the image.

Aggregating Edgels Individual edgels detected using an edge detector may be aggregated into more complex edge structure before undergoing later processing. The process of aggregating edges tends to remove spurious results from the edge detection phase and often results in considerable data reduction. Two approaches are described as follows:

Hough Transform Consider the problem of detecting straight lines in an image from a collection of edgel measurements (x_i, y_i). Each measurement (x_i, y_i) can be thought of as "voting" for the presence of edge structure passing through this point. If the edge is represented as $y = mx + b$, then the measurement (x_i, y_i) provides support for the set of lines that passes through (x_i, y_i), or equivalently for the set of values (m, b) that satisfies $y_i = mx_i + b$. The **Hough transform** [60] provides a voting scheme to combine individual (x_i, y_i) measurements to obtain (m, b).

The Hough transform maintains an accumulator array $A(m, b)$ that is initialized to zero and represents a discretized version of all possible (m, b) pairs. Whenever a (x_i, y_i) measurement is made, all possible (m, b) cells in A that satisfy $y_i = mx_i + b$ are incremented. When all measurements have been processed, the elements of the accumulator array vote for the most likely edge(s). Note that this particular parameterization of a line is not ideally suited to use with the Hough transform, and other parameterizations based on representing the orientation of an edge are preferred (e.g., perpendicular distance from the origin and orientation as an angle).

Different parameterizations of edges and other structures including circles and arbitrary contours can be processed using variations on the Hough transform, in particular the **generalized Hough transform** generalizes the Hough transform to arbitrary contours. The key requirement is a parametric definition of the geometric feature of interest that allows specific pixels to vote for specific arrangements of the object of interest. The Hough transform is an effective mechanism for mapping edgels onto more complex structures such as geometric shapes or for classifying the edgels into known contours. Key limitations of basic Hough transform methods include the limit of resolution posed by the discretization of the accumulator array and the fact that complex forms lead to high-dimensional accumulator arrays and hence substantial space requirements.

Line approximation Rather than use the edgel structure to provide support for a particular structure such as a geometric shape, an alternative approach is to group the edgels into edge chains and then to approximate these edge chains by longer line segments.

A popular strategy for grouping edges together is to pose the grouping task as a graph search for a minimum-cost path. Each edgel is mapped to a node in the graph, and the

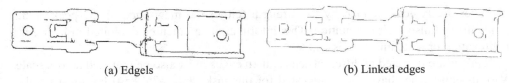

(a) Edgels	(b) Linked edges

Figure 5.13. Edgels and linked edges.

cost between two nodes depends on their proximity, relative orientation, and contrast. The graph is then searched for a minimum-cost path from one node to another, and the best sequence is used to approximate the line (see Section 7.3.3 for a description of a general graph search algorithm). A major difficulty in applying this type of strategy involves determining a strategy for joining nodes in the graph (i.e., edgels) together. If the threshold value is set too low, edgels tend not to be joined together and the recovered edge chains are short and disconnected. If the value is set too high then edgels are connected even when they should not be, and spurious curves are generated.

Once edge chains have been identified, it is often useful to merge the edge chains into longer polygonal lines. Again, many techniques have been proposed for this. An approach known as **recursive splitting** is described in [613]. The recursive splitting algorithm joins the first and last points in a contour chain by a straight line and then examines the maximal distance e_m between the line and the contour. For a given threshold ϵ, if $e_m < \epsilon$, then the contour is well approximated by the straight line and the process completes. Otherwise the line is split in two at the contour point where the distance is e_m and the algorithm then operates recursively on the two halves. Figure 5.13 shows the extended edges obtained from an edgel map. Figure 5.13a shows the set of locations for which there is evidence of an edge passing through this location. Figure 5.13b shows the extended edges extracted from Figure 5.13a. The edgels shown in Figure 5.13a were generated with a multi-channel edge detection algorithm based on the single-channel Canny edge detection algorithm [144]. See [841] for details.

While many methods can be used on simple, unambiguous data, the extraction of curves from complex images is a difficult problem. Significant difficulties relate to the completion of inherently intermittent and noisy edge data and the interpretation of crossings between different curves which can lead to alternative interpretations.

Some Thoughts on Edges Many researchers have assumed that zero-crossings obtained from $\nabla^2 G$ operators or some other more or less complex edge detector are a reasonable starting point for image processing. These works assume that (1) zero-crossings can be found, (2) they signal the presence of structure in the scene (typically inferred to be edges), and (3) structure in the scene will give rise to edges. Attempting to code the input entirely using zero-crossings obtained from band-pass filters can be problematic. Daugman [204] and Mayhew *et al.* [515] identified visual tasks that are solvable by humans but are not codable using zero-crossings alone, suggesting that edge-base representations are not complete and thus may miss salient features. In order to overcome these problems, researchers have attempted either to extract more than just zero-crossings from the image; such as zero-crossings and peaks [515], or peaks and ridges [198] or to use the entire filtered signal to represent the scene. This latter approach is considered in the following two sections.

5.4.8 Image Filters

Rather than compare two images by convolving the images with filters, extracting the edges, and then comparing the edges, one alternative is to match the convolved images directly [395]. Given two images I_l and I_r the appropriate shift should be determined by having convolved versions of the images agree. If k filters are applied to the images, then the correct shift would be the shift (h, v) that minimizes

$$e_m = \sum_k |F_k * I_r(i, j) - F_k * I_l(i + h, j + v)|,$$

where F_k is the set of filter banks to use, and e_m is the error measure.

Assuming that the filter banks F_k localize structure in the image, this type of approach is likely to succeed provided that a single shift exists at an image location that aligns the images. If no such shift exists, as would occur near object boundaries or if semi-transparent surfaces exist in the image, then a single shift will not exist and the method will fail. When combining filter outputs with competing best shift solutions, the best overall shift will be a function of the relative channel amplitudes.

5.4.9 Local Phase Differences

Combining the entire filtered image as proposed in the previous section will be influenced by the relative intensity of the signal. An alternative is to analyze the structure of the signal independent of its amplitude. If the two filtered images can be locally approximated by sinusoids, then the difference between the signals can be described in terms of their **local phase difference** and the local change in amplitude. The underlying concept is that the local amplitude variation encodes the intensity difference between the two images, while the local phase difference encodes the shift or disparity.

If the two images to be compared are labeled $I_l(x)$ and $I_r(x)$, then by convolving these signals with a quadrature filter pair such as a complex Gabor ($Gabor(\omega, \sigma)$) kernel with central frequency ω and standard deviation σ, we obtain two complex responses $L(x)$ and $R(x)$. For appropriate choices of ω and σ the output of this convolution will be tightly bandpassed versions of the input signal and will thus satisfy the local sinusoidal approximation. Because the Gabor filter is a quadrature pair filter, various mechanisms exist for recovering the local amplitude and phase differences. One simple mechanism for obtaining the local phase difference is to extract the absolute phase from the left and right images and then simply subtract them [695]. Although conceptually simple, in practice this approach is quite sensitive to image variations and to a problem known as the **phase wrap-around effect**. More sophisticated phase matching mechanisms exist [392, 393].

5.4.10 Summary

There is a wide array of mechanisms for representing an image in order to make it more suitable for later processing. Unfortunately many techniques work in controlled test environments but fail when applied in the real-world operational environment.

The essential function of the techniques presented in this section is to allow portions of two images to be compared under a wide range of viewing conditions. Given this ability to compare images or parts of images, vision becomes a powerful sensor for mobile robots, and it can be used to recover environmental structure or to localize the robot in its environment without emitting additional energy into the environment.

5.5 Obtaining Depth

A single perspective camera is unable to localize structure in three dimensions; it obtains the direction to the structure, but not the distance to it. If depth information is required, then some other mechanism must be used in order to recover this missing dimension. Many of these techniques require the identification of corresponding image features in two or more images, the task considered in the previous section.

5.5.1 Ground Plane Assumption

Suppose that the object to be localized lies on a particular known plane, typically the ground. Then this information, coupled with a calibrated camera, is sufficient to localize the structure in three-space. Let $A = [a_1, a_2, a_3, a_4]$, and let $A[x, y, z, 1]^T = 0$ be the equation of the plane upon which structure resides. Given an image point (u, v) from a calibrated perspective camera $\tilde{P}$, then the 3D point that corresponds to this image point can be found from

$$
\begin{bmatrix}
\tilde{P}_1 - u\tilde{P}_3 \\
\tilde{P}_2 - v\tilde{P}_3 \\
A
\end{bmatrix}
\begin{bmatrix}
x \\
y \\
z \\
1
\end{bmatrix}
=
\begin{bmatrix}
0 \\
0 \\
0
\end{bmatrix}.
\tag{5.11}
$$

The ground plane assumption finds application in a number of restricted environments such as road following. Suppose that an autonomous vehicle is to navigate by sensing road markings: whenever a road marking is found at (u, v), the road marking's 3D position can be determined using (5.11).

In practice it may not be necessary to determine A and $\tilde{P}$ explicitly, but instead the calibration of (u, v) to (x, y, z) can be accomplished directly from the ground plane.

5.5.2 Multiple Cameras

Suppose that instead of using just one camera to view the scene, multiple cameras are available. The two-camera approach is known as **stereo vision**, or **binocular vision**, while the three-camera approach is known as **trinocular vision**. Approaches with as many as five and six cameras are described in the literature.

When a scene is viewed by two or more cameras, points in the world are mapped onto different image points in the different cameras. In general a point will have different horizontal and vertical positions in each camera. If $X = [x \ y \ z \ 1]^T$ is an arbitrary point in three-space described in homogeneous coordinates, then pinhole camera i maps X to the point

$$
(u_i, v_i) = \left(\frac{(\tilde{P}_i X)_1}{(\tilde{P}_i X)_3}, \frac{(\tilde{P}_i X)_2}{(\tilde{P}_i X)_3} \right).
$$

If the calibration matrices $\tilde{P}_i$ are known, then the 3D point (x, y, z) that gives rise to the projections can be found by solving

$$
\begin{bmatrix}
(u_i \tilde{P}_i)_3 - (\tilde{P}_i)_1 \\
(v_i \tilde{P}_i)_3 - (\tilde{P}_i)_2 \\
\cdots
\end{bmatrix}
\begin{bmatrix}
x \\
y \\
z \\
1
\end{bmatrix}
=
\begin{bmatrix}
0 \\
\cdots \\
0
\end{bmatrix}.
$$

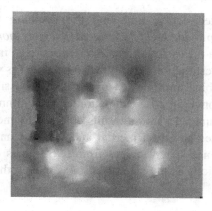

Figure 5.14. Stereo disparities recovered from the central portion of Figure 5.8a.

Provided 1.5 or more views of the same point are available, this can be solved using least squares to determine (x, y, z). Unfortunately, determining the corresponding image points in the two or more views may not be particularly easy. In fact, determining this correspondence is considered to be the hard problem in **stereopsis**. (Almost all of the techniques described in Section 5.4 have been used as a mechanism for establishing this correspondence.)

The classic technique in static stereopsis is to consider all possible matches and to then discard those matches that violate a set of matching criteria. The problem is that there can be a large number of possible matches, and the selection of a set of criteria that are stable and do not discard potentially good matches is very difficult [392].

A vast number of stereopsis algorithms exist in the literature. The output of these algorithms is usually represented as a depth map (see Figure 5.14). These are retinotopic maps of the recovered disparity at that pixel. In Figure 5.14 white pixels are closer to the cameras.

Stereopsis is an attractive technique for recovering depth because very few assumptions are required. However, there are a number of points to consider:

- The hard problem in stereopsis is the correspondence problem: matching the projection of an object in one camera with its projection in the other. The correspondence process may require considerable assumptions about the robot's environment that may not hold in practice. A number of techniques that can be used to help establish this correspondence are discussed in Section 5.4.
- The cameras can be convergent or parallel. For stereopsis to take place, the structure of interest must be visible in each camera's view. Ideally the cameras will all fixate the region that contains the structure of interest. This becomes problematic if the cameras are fixed and different regions of space are of interest.
- The accuracy of the triangulation process in stereo vision is limited by the nature of the matching feature and the camera geometry. If the cameras are placed close together, the accuracy will be poor, but the correspondence process will be simplified because objects will appear very similar in the two cameras' views. As the cameras are placed farther apart, the increased baseline improves accuracy, but the matching process becomes more difficult.

Multiple-camera systems can be operated across time and the resulting three-dimensional representations merged together *provided that the camera assembly motion is known*. This motion can be estimated through the use of alternative sensors (e.g., inertial sensors), through the use of visual egomotion estimation algorithms (also known as **visual odometry**), or through approaches that combine multiple sensors. It is also possible to integrate the merging process as part of an ongoing pose estimation and environmental exploration process (see Section 10.2.2). Figure 5.15 shows results obtained by merging stereo imagery obtained over multiple frames based on inertial and visual egomotion cues [359, 358]. Figure 5.15a,b show reference stereo images from two frames of the sequence. Figures 5.15c–h show reconstructions as the stereo sensor is moved through the environment.

5.5.3 Model-Based Vision

Many robotic systems operate in a known (or partially known) environment. If special purpose or naturally occurring features can be reliably extracted from the environment, then a representation of the metric space around the robot can be used with visual routines that recover the features to estimate the robot's pose within the environment. In a typical application (e.g., [432]), a CAD (computer-aided design) model of the robot's environment is constructed with salient visual features identified. At every motion of the robot, features are extracted from the visual field, and these are compared with their predicted position. A mechanism such as Kalman filtering (see Section 4.9.1) is then used to update the robot's position.

Naturally occurring targets can be entities such as walls, signs, or doorways in the environment. For example, [418] uses light fixtures mounted on the ceiling as visual targets (see also [504]). If special purpose targets are available, then these targets can be made very robust. One such technique [360] places special purpose targets on the ceiling, which are then localized using a vertically mounted camera based on the robot. As the distance from the robot to the ceiling-mounted target is known, an appropriately designed target can be used to localize the robot.

5.5.4 Egomotion

Suppose that a robot is equipped with a video camera with which it views the world as it moves through it. The changing visual field can be used to estimate the robot's motion (its **egomotion**). Figure 5.16 sketches the geometry of the situation. When the robot's camera is at C_1, the robot views point M. The robot then moves by an unknown amount T, rotates by an unknown amount R, and re-views point M from C_2. What can be inferred about the unknown robot motion R and T by the projections m_1 and m_2?

Clearly, if m_1 and m_2 are corresponding images of the same point, then C_1m_1, C_2m_2 and C_1C_2 must all lie in the same plane. This can be expressed compactly as

$$C_1m_1 \cdot (T \times RC_2m_2) = 0.$$

This relationship is independent of the magnitude of T, and thus the absolute motion of the camera between the two views cannot be determined. This limits the direct application of monocular egomotion in robotic applications. Various techniques for recovering R and

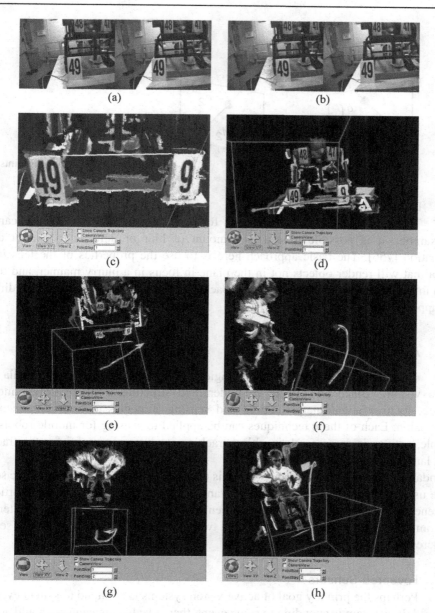

(a) (b)

(c) (d)

(e) (f)

(g) (h)

Figure 5.15. Recovered environmental structure from a stereo camera as it is moved through its environment. (a), (b) Reference stereo images from two frames in the sequence. (c) A blow-up of part of the recovered scene. (d), (e) The reconstruction of the scene for a horizontal motion of the sensor. (f)–(h) A second reconstruction for a roughly vertical motion of the sensor. In both cases the recovered sensor motion and the externally measured motion of the sensor are shown.

T up to this scale factor exist (see [262] for a review), but perhaps the most straightforward mechanism is to use standard non-linear minimization techniques to minimize

$$\Phi(R, T) = \sum |C_1 m_{i,1} \cdot (T \times R C_2 m_{i,2})|$$

subject to the constraint $|T| = 1$.

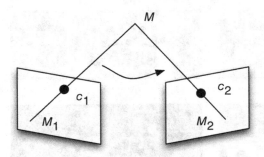

Figure 5.16. Motion constraints.

5.5.5   Depth from a Single Camera

There exist a number of strategies for extracting depth from a single camera. For example, it is possible to use the amount of blur or defocus to extract depth information [756]. The basic approach here is to use the properties of the lens in the camera that will render objects not in the plane in focus in a blurry manner, and to use this to infer depth. Direct data-driven approaches (e.g., [655]) estimate distance directly from appearance.

5.6   Active Vision

There are many different technologies encompassed under the umbrella term "active vision." Blake and Yuille [91] identified structure from controlled motion, tracking, focused attention, prediction, and sensing strategies as key components of active vision. Each of these techniques can be applied to sensing for mobile robots. For example, active vision research in object tracking is obviously useful for the tracking visual landmarks as the robot moves.

Fundamental to active vision approaches is the concept that manipulation of the sensor can be used to direct the sensor, and hence any associated processing, to that portion of the scene that is most relevant. Many different techniques are presented in the literature to accomplish this direction of attention, but two will be discussed here; foveated sensors and stereo heads.

5.6.1   Foveated Sensors

Perhaps the primary goal of active vision systems is to attend to salient events in the world. If a system is attending to some event, then, ideally, the camera should acquire a larger number of intensity samples per unit area near the center of the image (known as the **fovea** after the biological structure) than in the in the **periphery**. This non-uniform sampling has two positive benefits; it allows image compression, and it permits a higher sampling rate in the fovea, where more information is needed than would be possible with a uniform sensor having the same bandwidth. Figure 5.17 shows a foveated sampling of Figure 5.8a.

Foveated sensors increase the distance between samples with increasing image eccentricity. Most commonly the sampling distance is a linear function of eccentricity, which introduces a topological mapping from the linear sampling case to the foveated sampling that is known as **log-polar**.

Figure 5.17. Foveated image. Foveated images have a non-uniform sampling, with a higher sampling in the center of the image.

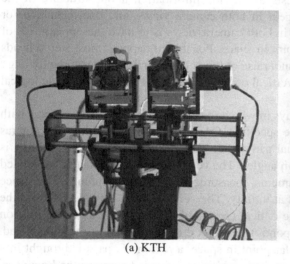

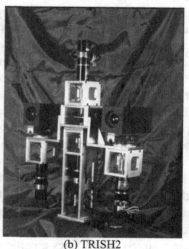

(a) KTH   (b) TRISH2

Figure 5.18. The (a) KTH and (b) TRISH2 stereo heads.

There are two general approaches to the construction of a foveated sensor. The first is to use a standard CCD sensor and to foveate the image in software (e.g., [98]). This limits the sampling in the fovea to the sampling rate of the standard CCD but is easier to implement. A second alternative is to fabricate the appropriate sensor (e.g., [794, 603]). Much higher-density sampling in the fovea is possible, and it is also possible to construct the sensor to provide non-linear readout of the sensor elements.

5.6.2 Stereo Heads

One class of active vision sensors that has received considerable attention is the design of binocular robotic vision systems or active stereo heads. Binocular stereo heads have the problem of positioning and directing two cameras and pointing them in some direction as do biological systems (see Figure 5.18). Because the heads are modeled on a biological system, the design of stereo heads is often described in anatomical terms. There are two basic models for describing human eye movements; the Helmholtz and Fick systems (see [370] for a review). In the Helmholtz model, the eyes are rotated about a horizontal axis first (tilt), and then about the vertical axis (pan). In the Fick model, the eyes are first rotated about the vertical axis (pan) and then about the horizontal axis (tilt). The Fick model is also known as the gunsight model. In either model the eyes can rotate about their optical axis (torque). Robotic stereo heads are typically built using one of these two models.

Models of human eye motions are predicated on the fact that human eye motions are primarily of a rotational nature. Robotic devices have considerably more freedom, and robotic heads have been built with variable baselines: it is quite common for robotic heads to translate individual cameras, as well as to rotate them.

In either the Fick or Helmholtz model of camera movements, the two cameras can be raised or lowered independently. For a stereo head to be more than just two separate aiming mechanisms, however, the motions of the two cameras are usually controlled as a single logical unit. For stereopsis to provide information about structure in the environment, that structure must appear in both camera views, and one technique for ensuring that some structure appears in both camera views is to have the optical axes of the two cameras intersect at some point in space. For this to happen, most stereo heads are constructed so that either they cannot raise or lower their cameras independently (e.g., [196, 166, 265]), or they control the vertical orientation of the cameras as a single logical unit (e.g., [532, 594]).

There are a number of different ways in which the orientation of the two cameras with respect to their common plane can be specified. One way is to refer to the two cameras as separate pan units having individual pan angles. A somewhat more useful notation is to talk about the **vergence** and **version** angles. The vergence angle is the angle subtended by the two optical centers of the cameras, measured at the fixation point. A vergence angle of zero corresponds to a target at infinity. The version angle is the angle from the center of the line passing through the optical centers of the two cameras to the fixation point. A version angle of zero corresponds to a target directly in front of the stereo head. When a stereo head fixates a particular point in space, a region of space is brought into registration in the left and right images. This region of space is known as the **horoptor**. Active binocular systems typically only consider matches that are near the horoptor, that is, have near-zero disparity.

In the case of zero torsion the horoptor curve consists of two parts – a circle lying in the plane containing the nodal points of the two cameras, known as the longitudinal horoptor, and a vertical line perpendicular to the circle, known as the vertical horoptor [785, 370]. The longitudinal horoptor is also known as the Vieth–Müller circle. This circle remains unchanged as the cameras fixate different points along the circle. The vertical horoptor does not necessarily intersect the longitudinal horoptor at the fixation point, although it does in the case of symmetric fixation. A sketch of the horoptor curve is given in Figure 5.19. As stereopsis is typically performed in the region of space with near-zero disparity, techniques that warp the horoptor toward the structure of interest – such as the floor – are often utilized in active stereo systems.

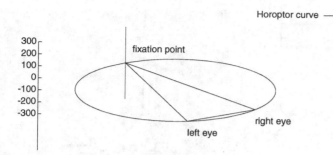

Figure 5.19. Horoptor curve.

5.7   Other Sensors

Standard vision sensors suffer from two fundamental problems: they have a limited field of view and the nature of the imaging process does not encode the absolute distance to an object. This introduces serious problems in tasks such as determining egomotion from monocular images (see Section 5.5.4). In order to overcome these limitations, active illuminants, techniques that expand the sensor's field of view, and visual sensors that are combined with other techniques such as laser sensors can be used.

5.7.1   RGB-D Cameras

RGB-D (Red Green Blue–Depth) cameras are designed to obtain both color and depth information simultaneously. Although there are many different technologies that can be used to obtain depth, popular commodity hardware projects some known light pattern – typically in the infrared range so that it is invisible to humans – and then to exploit the known pattern to both break up camouflage in the scene and to simplify the 3D scene recovery problem. In commodity hardware the illuminant is typically infrared light at a reasonably low power. This makes these sensors perform best indoors, away from bright infrared sources, such as the Sun.

5.7.2   Light Striping

One procedure for augmenting vision is to illuminate the scene with a "structured" known light source, that is, an illumination pattern that can be used to provide additional information and resolve ambiguity. Perhaps the most powerful of these techniques is known as **light striping**. The basic geometry of light striping is shown in Figure 5.20a. A line is projected into the scene, and the point at which it strikes the scene structure is sensed by a camera. Various light sources are possible, but laser sources are common due to the highly collimated nature of the beam.

A line projected into the scene allows recovery of the depth of the point at which the light beam strikes an object by triangulation. If a coordinate system is defined coincident with the optical axis of the camera, the computation is simplified. If the source is located a distance d away from the optical axis, with angle Ω between the x axis and the direction of the light projection, then the distance z can be recovered from the projection of the line x' in the camera as

$$z = \frac{fd}{f \cot(\Omega) + x'}.$$

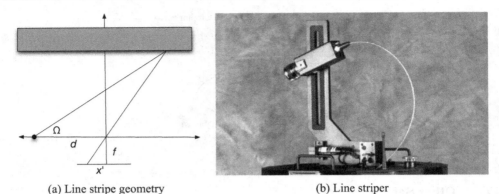

(a) Line stripe geometry   (b) Line striper

Figure 5.20. One-dimensional line striper. (a) The underlying geometry. (b) Nomadic Technologies Sensus 500 laser line striper. Copyright Nomadic Technologies. Used with permission.

The simplest light structure is a line, but more complex 2D patterns can be used to maximize observability. Although line striping systems do obtain absolute distance information, the approach is not without its limitations. The entire system must be calibrated, and accuracy is limited by the system optics, the camera resolution, and frame buffer size. Common line stripers are very fast along the single line since no physical motion is required, but it may take considerable time to scan a volume of space with such devices. Surfaces that either absorb or fully reflect the illuminant beam are problematic.

5.7.3   Structured and Unstructured Light

An obvious extension to line striping technology is to project a 2D pattern rather than a 1D line. This concept is know as **structured light**. The measurement process is identical to the process used for line striping. Given the projection of a pattern onto an environmental surface structure, the location of the pattern in the image provides depth information.

5.7.4   Omnidirectional Sensors

One problem with a standard video source is the limited field of view that is available. As a robot cannot respond to something it cannot sense, limited-view, single-camera robots tend to perform poorly under general conditions. Various techniques have been proposed to overcome this problem. Multiple-camera solutions, active panning, and even collections of fish-eye lenses have been suggested. An alternative is to use specially designed mirrors to bring a larger portion of the environment into the field of view of the camera. This is the approach taken by COPIS (COnic Projection Image Sensor) [842, 843] and Paracamera [201]. Two omnidirectional sensors are shown in Figure 5.21.

Systems such as Paracamera and COPIS use a conic mirror to project a 360° view of the environment into a single CCD camera mounted directly below the mirror. The field of view is limited only by the vertex angle of the conic mirror and the visual angle of the camera. The sensor obtains a radial view of its environment: the robot is situated in the center of the image, with the environment displayed radially about it. It is also possible to

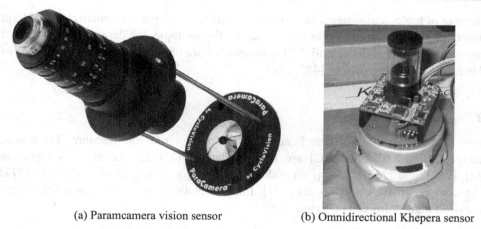

(a) Paramcamera vision sensor   (b) Omnidirectional Khepera sensor

Figure 5.21. Omnidirectional sensors. (a) The Paracamera vision sensor. The Paracamera sensor is attached to a standard CCD camera and obtains a 360° view of the scene. (b) An omnidirectional sensor mounted on a Khepera platform.

utilize more sophisticated mirror assemblies to provide a more uniform sampling of the image space.[563].

5.8 Biological Vision

The vertebrate visual system begins with the eye, whose principal attribute is a lens that focuses incoming light onto the retina. In primates the retina, the rear surface of the eyeball, is covered with both cone cells and rod cells, which serve as photoreceptors and convert incoming photons to electrical energy. The cones are color sensitive (appearing in different wavelength-tuned subpopulations), while the rods are achromatic. In humans, the rods are associated, in particular, with peripheral and night vision.

The electrical signals from the eye lead to a variety of other cell types such as bipolar cells and leave the eye via the **optic nerve**, which exits at the **blind spot**. The optic nerve then passes through the **lateral geniculate nucleus** and leads to the (primary) visual cortex on the rear surface of the brain. An alternate processing stream is associated with signals that move between the eye and the **superior colliculus** (or **tectum**) and the midbrain. The secondary stream is thought to be important in visual tracking and the control of eye movements.

The visual cortex can be described in terms of a set of distinct functional regions that number in the dozens. While initial processing stages appear to compute alternative descriptions of the input array that can be described in terms of simple bandpass signals (i.e., differences of Gaussian filters), the understanding of higher-level areas remains incomplete.

Insect eyes, in contrast, are composed of a large set of **ommatidia**. Each ommatidium is made up of a set of elongated **retinula** cells loosely resembling a set of closely packed telescopes. In bees, for example, there are nine retinula cells: two sensitive to blue light, four tuned to green wavelengths, and four tuned for ultraviolet light as well polarization.

A number of biological systems exist that are sensitive to the plane of polarization of light rather than just to its intensity (or chromaticity). For example, the desert ant *Cataglyphis fortis* navigates across the essentially featureless Sahara Desert by sensing the patterns of polarization of light in the sky [445, 824].

5.9   Further Reading

Computer vision   There is an extensive computer vision literature. The classic texts of [60], [366], and [262] are slightly dated and more recent texts including [749], [792], and [205] exist, as do collections of major early papers in the field [272] and a comprehensive encyclopedia [381]. Implementations of various low-level image-processing algorithms can be found in [606].

Signals and systems   The classic text is [589]. There is also a second edition that updates the material [590].

Active vision   An overview of active vision work can be found in [197] and [91]. A large literature exists on the design of robotic heads, including [166], [265], [558], [594], and [532].

Biological vision   There are many good introductory books on biological vision including [296]. See also [522] and [297].

5.10   Problems

1. Describe the optical and physical phenomena in the world that can lead to intensity edges in images.
2. Using OpenCV or some other standard computer vision toolkit, process an image to find all of the line structure in an image. First, using the example code found in the online resource, capture an image of a scene with large line structure (e.g., a door or table top). Then use the Hough transform to obtain and plot the longest 10 lines in the image. One straightforward way of doing this is to use the HoughLines method defined in OpenCV. Use a Hough accumulator with 1 accumulator cell per unit distance and 1 accumulator cell per degree. Plot the top 10 lines over the input image.
3. Using one of the standard visual toolkits (e.g., OpenCV), calibrate a perspective camera. There exist a large number of calibration examples online that use OpenCV.
4. Use a visual target system such as ARUCO to localize prepositioned targets in the environment using a standard video camera. How robust is the pose recovery in terms of range to the target and the viewing angle?
5. Using OpenCV process an image with the Sobel detector, and compare its output with that of the Canny-Deriche edge detector. The Sobel and Canny methods in the OpenCV library will prove useful. Discuss your results.
6. One technique for localizing a robot in an office environment is to place targets on the ceiling to uniquely identify locations and to define a local orientation.

One commonly used target consists of a large filled circle drawn on a contrasting background (to define position) and a second, smaller filled circle outside the larger circle to define local orientation. Implement an algorithm to find the two circles in an image. One approach would be to use edge detection coupled with the Hough transform to find the centers of the circles, but other approaches are certainly possible.

7. Implement a system to drive a robot down the center of a hallway by using vision to track salient features in the hall. The best selection for salient features will depend on the nature of hallways in your environment but could include such things as the orientation of ceiling tiles or the wall–floor boundary.

8. One straightforward technique for measuring stereo disparity is to assume that the epipolar lines are coincident with the scan rows and to perform simple correlation between the left and right images and to choose the shift corresponding to the maximum correlation as the correct match. Implement such a stereo algorithm and try it out on real imagery. Can you identify problematic regions in your environment? Try normalized cross-correlation of mean corrected versions of the imagery. Does this improve the algorithm's performance?

9. Develop a calibration procedure for planar homographies. That is, given a reference image of a planar target and a test planar target in a scene, calibrate a homography that maps the test portion of the image to the space of the reference image and then determine whether the test image is "the same as" the reference image. Here "the same as" can be estimated using a sum-of-absolute-differences approach.

10. Develop an expression for the planar homography between two planes in the same image. That is, given two planar objects in the same view, develop an expression that under perspective projection maps scene points from one plane to the other.

11. Develop an expression for the planar homography between a point $[x \, y]$ lying on an object on the $z = 0$ plane and its projection $[u \, v]$ into the camera with intrinsic camera parameters given by A and extrinsic parameters given by R and T.

12. This problem deals with having a robot (the differential drive robot introduced in Chapter 3 and augmented with a camera as described in this chapter) move to a location defined by a predefined visual tag (an ARUCO tag).

   (a) Use Gazebo to build a U-shaped simulated docking station (front and side walls) for your robot. You can, of course, be more creative than this but at least build this U-shaped space. The space should be no wider than 2x the diameter of the robot and should be at least as long as 3x the length of the robot. Create an ARUCO tag positioned directly in front of the back wall at the height of the forward-facing camera on the robot.

   (b) Use the ARUCO tag to drive the robot from the opening of the U-shaped region until it is docked, directly in front of the ARUCO tag and one robot's radius directly in front of it. Note: If using the normal "empty world" Gazebo lighting, ensure that the target is well lit.

   (c) Test your ability to dock with the target:

  i. With 10 starting points from 1.01x radius and using 2x radius to 10x radius with the robot initially facing directly at the target, write software to drive the robot to the docking pose. What is the maximum deviation from the center line to the target? (Alternatively, how close did the robot get to the walls of U-shaped enclosure?) What kind of failures did you see?

  ii. Choose the longest distance that resulted in reliable docking. Try different offsets laterally from this position to identify stability of the docking process with positional alignment.

  iii. Using the same distance as above, try rotational misalignment until the target is not fully visible in the first frame.

(d) Create a new Gazebo distractor object (cube-like) that is textured with a random texture (random Gaussian dots or blobs or any image you like). Put this on the back wall of the U-shaped docking station behind the ARUCO target. Test the limits you identified above. How robust is the ARUCO target? Can you think of the worst possible texture to put behind the target?

Part two

Representation and Planning

Swimming hexapod robot. Image appears with the kind permission of Independent Robotics.

Given a robot that can move and sense its environment, the remaining task is to plan intelligent motions.

Chapter 6 explores how machine learning approaches, and in particular how supervised learning and reinforcment learning, can be applied to autonomous systems.

Chapter 7 looks at some of the fundamental computational tasks that must be addressed in order for a mobile robot to move intelligently through its environment: how the environment should be represented; how the robot should be represented; and how to plan, given these representations.

The software environment within which the control programs of modern mobile robots execute can be likened to mobile operating systems. The various tasks that provide overall robotic control must compete for scarce computational and sensor resources and must meet both soft and hard real-time constraints. In order to meet these requirements, various architectures and strategies have been proposed to provide a framework within which the controlling processes exist. Chapter 8 examines how the various computational components that make up a mobile robot can be put together: the **software environment** or **middleware** within which the computational tasks compete for the scarce resources both on and off the robot.

Chapter 9 considers pose maintenance, a necessary task in many robotic systems. This allows a robot to use and construct **maps**, topics covered in Chapter 10.

6

Learning for Robots

"The key to artificial intelligence has always been the representation."[1]

6.1 Learning-Based Methods

The use of machine learning in robotics is a vast and growing area of research. In this chapter we consider a few key variations using: the use of deep neural networks, the applications of reinforcement learning and especially deep reinforcement learning, and the rapidly emerging potential for large language models.

Analytic methods (sometimes called "classical methods") are more conducive to human analysis and the development of performance bounds or hand-crafted heuristics. Learning-based methods have allowed for exceptional performance in many domains, especially where the diversity of the scenarios can be circumscribed so that every important kind of situation can be reflected in the training data used to build the algorithm.

Learning-based methods can be broadly classified into four categories:

- **Supervised learning** where we have examples of the form (x, y) such that each example x has an answer y, and we are given many examples x_i, y_i during training so that we can learn and evaluate a solution function $h(.)$ so that $x_i = h(y_i)$.
- **Unsupervised learning** where we are not given sample answers y_i as part of the input, and need to infer a regularity. For example, given a large set of photos that we need to divide into two unknown classes, the system might decide to separate these into photos of landscapes and of animals.
- **Reinforcement learning**, where we want to maximize the net benefit from taking a series of actions that depend on one another using sequential data. The term "self-supervised learning" can also be applied to certain models that use experiential data.
- **Large language models**, which leverage the availability of extremely large generalized text-based models for robot applications.

6.2 Deep Learning Networks

Artificial neural networks or more commonly **(deep) neural networks** or **(D)NNs** are a class of computational models originally inspired by biological

[1] Jeff Hawkins

models of computation. In their simplest form, NNs are made up of interconnected computational elements organized in layers. These elements and the layered structure are inspired by the architecture of the brain, but in fact the computations used by actual "neurons" and their detailed architecture differ from that found in artificial deep networks. In an artificial neural network, formation is passed from one layer to another through connections between these neuron-like computational units. Initially introduced in the 1980s [684], it was not until the advent of inexpensive massively parallel graphical processing units (GPU's), multi-layered (deep) architectures, and large labeled datasets in the mid-2000s that DNNs became a leading computational model for a range of tasks from object recognition to game playing. DNNs have found wide application in autonomous systems, from end-to-end control to providing data-driven solutions to specific computational problems.

The study of neural networks and related AI technologies could fill several volumes and it would be hubris to attempt to provide a full and complete introduction to the theory and application of the technology here. Rather, we provide an introduction to some of the basic aspects of deep learning and provide detailed examples of three specific deep learning applications in robotics; the use of DNNs for line following, the use of **convolutional neural networks** (CNNs) for road following given the approximate structure of the road ahead, and the use of **Q-learning**, a table-driven version of reinforcement learning (RL) to develop a policy for path planning. We provide a brief introduction to the use of large language models (LLMs) in robotics. For a deeper and more complete coverage of the material see the Further Readings section at the end of this chapter.

6.3   Basic Neural Network Structure

6.3.1   The Perceptron

The basic computational element in a neural network is the perceptron, which is a generalization of the perceptron biological model (see [674]). The basic computational model is shown in Figure 6.1, and is described mathematically as

$$y = \sigma \left(\sum_{1}^{n} x_i \theta_i + \theta_0 \right) = \sigma(\Theta^T \cdot \mathbf{x}) \tag{6.1}$$

where $\Theta^T = (\theta_0, \theta_1, \ldots, \theta_n)$ and $x = (1, x_1, \ldots, x_n)$. We refer to Θ as the weights, x_i as the inputs, θ_0 as the bias, and $\sigma()$ as the activation function. Normally the inputs are clamped in the range $[0, 1]$ and activation functions are chosen so as to be piecewise differentiable. Common activation functions include the rectified linear unit (ReLU), Heavyside, and Sigmoid. These are described mathematically by

$$\sigma(x) = \max(0, x) \quad \sigma(x) = \begin{cases} 0 & \text{if } x < 0 \\ 1 & \text{otherwise} \end{cases} \quad \sigma(x) = \frac{1}{1+e^{-x}}$$

ReLU   Heavyside   Sigmoid

and plotted in Figure 6.2.

In a feed forward deep neural network these individual computational units are typically ganged together in layers where the output from one layer is treated as the input

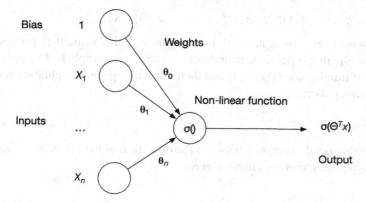

Figure 6.1. The perceptron.

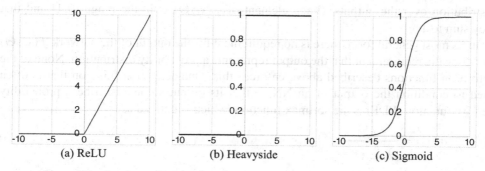

(a) ReLU   (b) Heavyside   (c) Sigmoid

Figure 6.2. Common activation functions.

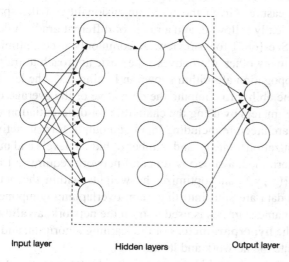

Input layer   Hidden layers   Output layer

Figure 6.3. Feed forward deep neural network. Input values enter at the input layer, passes through hidden layers and the output of the computation is available at the output layer. Note that not all edges are shown in the figure.

to the next. This arrangement of the computational units results in a feed forward network. This cascade of network layers will have a number of internal (hidden) units and input and output layers. Layers need not have the same number of computational units within them. See Figure 6.3. Given a network of k layers, one can compute the output y of the network as

$$f(x; \Theta) = \sigma(\Theta_k^T \cdot \sigma(\Theta_{k-1}^T \cdot \sigma(\Theta_{k-2}^T \cdot \sigma(\dots \sigma(\Theta_1^T \cdot \mathbf{x})\dots)))). \tag{6.2}$$

For a feed forward deep neural network to compute a useful value it is necessary to choose the weights Θ_k. In a supervised neural network this is accomplished by presenting the NN with a set of training data $\{(x_i, y_i)\}$ and then minimizing some evaluation function such as the mean squared error:

$$\frac{1}{n} \sum (f(x_i; \Theta) - y_i)^2, \tag{6.3}$$

which measures the squared difference between the operation of the network on the input and the desired output, or the **cross entropy error**:

$$-\frac{1}{n} \sum y_i \ln f(x_i; \Theta). \tag{6.4}$$

The cross entropy error is an evaluation function that seeks to encode a probability distribution over the outputs. (Each element of $f(x_i; \Theta)$ is in the range $[0, 1]$ and that they sum to 1.)

In its most general form, there is no requirement for the output of the network $f(x_i; \Theta)$ to satisfy the requirement that the output represents a probability distribution. None of the activation functions described above enforces this. One activation function that is often used to condition the output of an NN so that its output values describe a probability density function (PDF) is the softmax function, which is defined as

$$\sigma(x)_i = \frac{e^{x_i}}{\sum_{j=1}^{K} e^{z_j}}. \tag{6.5}$$

At its simplest level, training an NN involves choosing a mechanism to seek Θ values that optimizes its evaluation measure. Given the high dimensionality of the space, a gradient descent approach is typically followed, and a range of different gradient descent optimization algorithms exist. See [682] for a review. A commonly used optimizer is Adam [419] although there are many other alternatives. The basic approach to training a NN is expressed in the Backpropagation algorithm shown in Listing 6.1. The key to the Backpropagation algorithm is the ability to compute the derivative of the average output error with respect to internal parameters by using the chain rule for differentiation.

Once a decision on network architecture including input and output format, activation function(s), optimizer and optimization strategy, and number of hidden levels and number of nodes per level has been determined, a supervised neural network requires a training regime to take available data $\{(x_i, y_i)\}$ and optimize the weights within the network. Normally the available labeled data are split into three non-overlapping components: a **training dataset,** which as the name suggests is used to train the network, a **validataion dataset,** which is used to tune the **hyperparameters** of the learning algorithm, and a **test dataset,** which is used to evaluate the network and its training.

Updates to the weights in the network could be accomplished by taking one data point from the training set, computing the value that the network predicts for the network, and then evaluating its output. A more common approach is to divide the training dataset into **batches,** process the entire batch with the network, and then to update the weights based on the performance of this batch. The **batch size** could be as large as the entire training dataset (this is known as **batch gradient descent**), as small as one (this is known

1. **Weight initialization**: Set all weights to some initial random value.
2. **Activation calculation**: Given an input t_k, compute an output computation of the network out_k and compute the output of each of the hidden hidden units of the network. That is, each individual unit computes an output $g(h_j)$, where $h_j = \sum_i w_{j,i} x_i$.
3. **Weight training**: Start at the output units and work backward to the hidden layers recursively. Weights are adjusted by

$$w_{j,i}(t+1) = w_{j,i}(t) + \eta \delta_j O_i,$$

where η is the learning rate, δ_j is the error gradient at unit j, and O_i is the output of unit i. The gradient of the error δ_j is given by

   • For an output unit:

$$\delta_j = (T_j - O_j) g'(h_j),$$

   where T_j is the activation for output unit j that is required for output k.
   • For a hidden unit:

$$\delta_j = g'(h_j) \sum_k \delta_k w_{k,j},$$

   where δ_k is the error at unit k to which a connection points from hidden unit j.

4. Iterate until the units converge.

Listing 6.1. Backpropagation learning algorithm.

as **stochastic gradient descent**), or somewhere in between (this is known as **minibatch gradient descent**). Minibatch gradient descent with batch sizes around 32 are common.

A common problem in supervised neural networks, and in fact most of machine learning, is that of overfitting. A network is only trained on the training dataset, but we are really interested in how the model performs more generally. If trained for too long on the training dataset, the network may learn properties of the test dataset that are not as general as properties of the full dataset. That is, it optimizes for only the training dataset and not for generalization to the full dataset. In the most extreme example, a learning system could just memorize every single example it has seen during training and simply reproduce remembered examples without learning and a general-purpose solution. To avoid this, a number of strategies are followed that largely exploit the idea that there is a relationship between the number of connections in a network and the amount that it can remember. In short, one wants the amount of training data to be much larger than the size of the network to preclude memorization (where the "amount" of data and "size" of the network need to be made precise, but each can be loosely captured by the quantity of numbers needed to fully describe them). Strategies to reduce overfitting include:

Simplifying the network architecture Remove layers or elements from layers in the network. As a result, the capacity of the network to memorize all the training data is reduced and it is forced to seek more general "rules" to perform well.

Early stopping As the network trains it becomes more and more accurate on the training data, possibly at the expense of performing more poorly on the full dataset. If the training process is terminated before performance on the test dataset begins to deteriorate, this can be avoided. Rather than using the test dataset for this task, it is common to use the validation dataset to check for overfitting.

Data augmentation Finding sufficient data is often a challenge, and one option is to increase the size of the training dataset through the use of additional artificial examples, typically variants of the training that appear different to the network but which are efficient to create. For example, when recognizing objects from pictures, one might augment actual hand-labeled data, making new examples that are reflections, inversions, or blurred variants of the originals, thus sharing the same labels.

Regularization A penalty term (e.g., L_1 and L_2 norms over the weights Θ) is added to the optimization function. This tends to reduce the absolute magnitude of the weights in Θ.

Dropout During each training step, computational elements are randomly dropped from the computation. This changes the network architecture in some random way at each iteration, making simple memorization fail, and thus encouraging a more robust computation, hopefully based on a more general representation of the problem.

6.3.2   Following a Line with a DNN

In order to put the potential application of a DNN into the context of autonomous mobile robots, consider the classic (toy) robotic problem of programming a differential drive robot to follow a line painted on the floor. The robot is equipped with two light sensing devices placed so that the light sensors are displaced relative to the line, with one shifted to one side of the line and one on the other as illustrated in Figure 6.4. If the robot is driving along the line, then both sensors see almost white (they straddle the black line painted on the white background). If the robot is a little bit to one side, one sensor sees mostly black and the other sees white. If we have completely lost the line then we are lost.

The basic control problem to follow a line using a differential drive robot can be expressed in its simplest form as a collection of if-then statements that maps left and right sensor readings to motion control. If the left and right sensors return a value v between 0 (black) and 1 (white) and k is some threshold, and the control outputs are turn left, turn right and go forward, then Table 6.1 provides a very simple but often adequate controller.

If the robot is directly over the line, then both the left and right sensors see white, so the robot should move forward. If the robot is to the right of the line, then it should see (Black, White). So the robot is too far to the right of the line, and it should turn counterclockwise

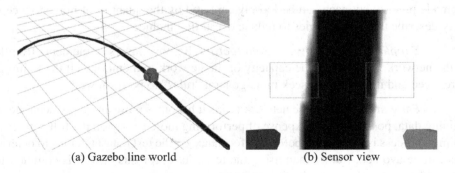

(a) Gazebo line world   (b) Sensor view

Figure 6.4. Line following. (a) A simulated robot in the Gazebo world. (b) The region sensed by the simulated left and right photosensors (the average value in the two rectangles).

Table 6.1. *Simple controller for the line following robot. Depending on the value of the two sensors, the robot either goes forward or turns.*

		Left Input	
		$v > k$	$v \le k$
Right Input	$v > k$	Go Straight	Turn Left
	$v \le k$	Turn Right	*

to move back over the line (stop, forward) motor commands will cause this to happen. Similarly, if the sensors see (White, Black), then the robot should turn left to be closer over the line. Here the robot should move (forward, stop). If the robot has lost the line completely (the '*' in the table), it is not obvious what the robot should. It might just stop, or it could rotate in a large circle, hoping to re-capture the line with its sensors.

There are many things about the above algorithm that are interesting. It is sufficiently simple that it can be implemented in analog electronics using the signal obtained by an appropriate photosensor or that it can be implemented in a few lines of code. In either case it is also incredibly difficult to tune. How much is "forward"? What do you do with sensor values that are neither "Black" nor "White"? Of course, you could use intermediate gains, and capture intensity levels to use partial values, but still choosing the gains can be difficult.

An alternative approach that we follow here is to develop an NN that maps measurement values to control outputs. This would be a network that takes in two values: left and right sensors, each in the range 0 to 1 where 0 corresponds to black and 1 corresponds to white, and output values for the left and right motors where 0 corresponds to the motor being stopped and 1 corresponding to the motor running forward at full velocity. The question then becomes how to develop the function that maps inputs to outputs.

Given this structure for the input and output values of the controller, perhaps the most straightforward DNN structure would be a network that takes the two input values, passes them through a fully connected network structure with one or more hidden layers, and then an output layer of three nodes that encode the possible ways of driving the robot (turn left, go straight, turn right). At the final layer of the network a softmax function is used to choose the appropriate command for the vehicle. The basic definition of this network is given in Listing 6.2.

We now come to the problem of collecting training data. We need to obtain tuples of (input_left, input_right, commanded vehicle motion). There are many possible ways of obtaining this dataset. One could write complex code that drives the robot and then use this to train the robot. But perhaps the most straightforward approach is to have some expert (a human) drive the robot and to capture their inputs. We could do this in simulation first, and then transfer the resulting NN either directly or after further training on the real hardware. This is known as **sim2real** training. Alternatively we could train on the eventual deployment platform directly.

Figure 6.4 shows a simulated differential drive robot operating in Gazebo. The robot is driving on a white ground plane upon which a black line has been drawn. Two parallel light sensors are simulated capturing the amount of light striking the left and right light

```
class LineFollower:
  def build():
    model = Sequential()
    model.add(Dense(8, input_shape=(2,), activation='relu'))
    model.add(Dense(8, activation='relu'))
    model.add(Dense(3, activation='softmax'))
    return model
```

Listing 6.2. A simple sequential neural network defined in `keras/Tensorflow` that implements the line follower controller. The network consists of ReLU layers with eight nodes and three output nodes activated by the `softmax` function.

sensors. A ROS node is used to capture the user's commanded motion and the robot around the track and a labelled dataset is collected. The sample `Gazebo` world and code to collect training data and to drive the robot can be found in the online resource associated with this text. See Problem 1 at the end of the chapter. With a small amount of training data it is possible to develop an NN-based controller that will drive the robot to follow a line in this simulated environment.

6.4 Convolutional Neural Networks

The line following example above used a very simple input consisting of two values. The representation has no explicit encoding of the relationship between the two sensors. As we designed the system we "know" that the two measurements take place on a line that straddles the line drawn on the ground. But the network does not know this. It may learn this property, but there is no explicit representation of this relationship. Many sensors, and in particular image-based sensors, are based on arrays of individual sensor values (pixels), and the physical relationship between these individual pixels is critical to what is being represented. Convolutional neural networks (or CNNs) are multi-layered (deep) neural networks that contain network elements that incorporate convolutional layers, that is, layers that perform image convolution.

A convolutional layer, as shown in Figure 6.5, is similar to the correlation or convolution operator described in Chapter 5. The **convolutional kernel** within a CNN performs element by element multiplication of the kernel with elements in the image, and produces as its sum the output of this operation. In image processing, the convolutional kernel is often a 3D operator, operating over a 2D image and and a third color dimension. Convolutional kernels can, however, be of arbitrary dimension. Training a CNN typically not only involves learning elements of traditional NN elements in the network, but also involves learning the elements of the convolutional kernels.

In practice, CNNs use a sequence of layers, including convolutional layers, pooling layers, and also fully connected layers where every neuron in one layer is connected to every neuron in the layer below. Convolutional layers perform computations over the input image, while pooling layers reduce the size of the feature maps, making the network more efficient. Fully connected layers generally use the features extracted by the convolutional and pooling layers to make predictions or classifications.

Incorporating a convolutional kernel in a CNN architecture introduces a number of interesting problems that must be addressed. These include:

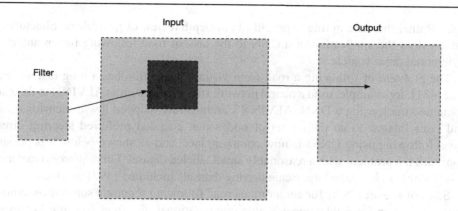

Figure 6.5. Convolution in CNNs. The convolution operator in a CNN applies a filter at each point in the input producing a corresponding value in the output.

Padding If the convolutional kernel is wider than one pixel, it will not be possible to apply the kernel at every possible position in the input tensor. The kernel will extend off of the edge when performing the product. Addressing this problem is known as padding. Padding may involve inserting zeros (or some other number) around the edges of the image, mirroring edge elements, wrapping the image around from one side to the other, or producing an output that is of reduced size in order to avoid computing partial results at the edges of the input tensor.

Stride Although it is possible to compute the product of the convolutional kernel at each point in the input tensor, it can be beneficial to apply to kernel at a subset of the possible offsets between the kernel and the input. Stride or **stride length** refers to the shift of the kernel across the input tensor. A stride of 1 refers to operating the kernel at every input address. A stride of 2 refers to operating the kernel at every other address. And so on. It is possible to choose different strides for different dimensions of the input tensor.

Beyond the introduction of convolutional layers, CNN typically also include:

Non-linear (ReLU) layers As in DNNs, ReLU elements map elements in the input using $\max(x, 0)$.

Pooling layers Layers that compute average, or max or min, over some window of the input tensor.

Fully connected layers Layers that perform computations as found in DNNs.

SoftMax layer As in DNNs' a SoftMax layer may be incorporated at the output to produce an output population that encodes a probabilisitic distribution over the output units.

6.4.1   Road Following with a CNN

CNNs have been applied to a wide number of different problems from character (letter) recognition (see [452] for early ground-breaking work) to object recognition. (Recognition systems such a YOLO [659] rely on CNNs as part of their network architecture). Rather than attempting to provide an in-depth review of possible architectures, here we consider the application of a CNN to the task of road following for an autonomous differential drive vehicle.

The problem of following a road from visual information has a long history. Pomerleau [631], for example, used a neural network structure known as ALVINN to drive a self-contained truck using a DNN. ALVINN's architecture mapped low-dimensional camera and laser images to an output set of nodes that encoded preferred steering direction. Road following using CNNs is now commonplace, and as shown below it is possible to approach the problem with a reasonably small labeled dataset. For real-world experiments it is possible to leverage large-scale driving datasets including [493] and [628].

State-of-the-art CNNs for autonomous road following require a substantive amount of training data and can take considerable computational resources to train. For example, the Dave-2 driving network has approximately 27M connections and 250,000 parameters [97]. The model we build here is considerably simpler and we will train it on considerably less data.

The underlying problem is illustrated in Figure 6.6. We have a robot operating on the plane, driving along the road. The robot here is a differential drive vehicle with one forward-facing camera. The camera obtains a view of the world in front of the robot. We assume that the robot starts centered on the roadway and travels either forward at a constant velocity, or turns to the left or right at some constant rotational velocity. We structure the task as a classification task: mapping the input view to a choice of which motion command should be executed.

Figure 6.7 illustrates the CNN architecture to be used. It follows the architecture proposed in [12] and described in Listing 6.3. Input images consisting of $28 \times 28 \times 3$ arrays are convolved with 20 parallel $5 \times 5 \times 3$ filters. This produces twenty 28×28 channels or images. These are then downsampled using a 2×2 maxpooling layer resulting in twenty 14×14 channels. Each of these 14×14 channels is filtered by a $5 \times 5 \times 20$

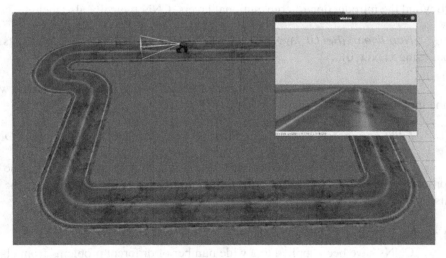

Figure 6.6. Sample environment for collecting road following data. The inset shows the robot's camera view

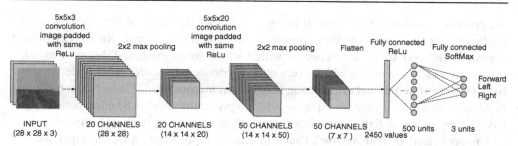

Figure 6.7. A CNN to map low-dimensional road images to a steering command. See Listing 6.3.

```
class LeNet:
  def build(width, height, depth, classes):
    model = Sequential()
    inputShape = (height, width, depth)
    # first set of CONV => RELU => POOL layers
    model.add(Conv2D(20, (5, 5), padding="same",
      input_shape=inputShape))
    model.add(Activation("relu"))
    model.add(MaxPooling2D(pool_size=(2, 2), strides=(2, 2)))
    # second set of CONV => RELU => POOL layers
    model.add(Conv2D(50, (5, 5), padding="same"))
    model.add(Activation("relu"))
    model.add(MaxPooling2D(pool_size=(2, 2), strides=(2, 2)))
    # FC => RELU layers
    model.add(Flatten())
    model.add(Dense(500))
    model.add(Activation("relu"))
    # softmax classifier
    model.add(Dense(classes))
    model.add(Activation("softmax"))
    return model
```

Listing 6.3. CNN for road following. Following the architecture given in [12].

filter resulting in fifty 14×14 channels. We once again apply 2×2 maxpooling resulting in fifty 7×7 channels. These 2,450 values are then fed into a fully connected layer and from there to a SoftMax layer and the three output channels. The architecture is given as a sequential model in Keras/Tensorflow in Listing 6.3. Even this simple model has 1,253,573 parameters to train. Problem 2 at the end of the chapter walks through the implementation of this CNN in Keras/Tensorflow. It uses `Gazebo` to provide a "real-world' simulation of the robot, and takes as the correct input the input provided by the user. Training the robot by collecting data is relatively straightforward, but it can be difficult to collect anomalous data, that is, data that correspond to the robot driving near the edge of the road.

6.5   Other Topical Architectures

DNN and CNN are two examples of supervised neural network architectures. These architectures are feed forward. That is, the data only pass in one direction. As such they can have difficulty in representing temporal events. If you observe the examples above, at each time instant the network (DNN and CNN) is unaware of the history of the process of following the road. It is possible to encode temporal into these networks explicitly, but fundamentally they transduce the input to the output. **Recurrent neural networks** (RNNs) are neural networks within which loops exist, and the most extreme version of an RNN is one in which every node is connected to every other node. This is a **fully recurrent neural network**. **Long short-term memory** [352] is an NN architecture that has proven to be a very effective model for representing state in a neural network, and has emerged as a standard mechanism for encoding sequencing in neural networks.

Unsupervised neural networks seek to learn a representation of the input without being provided a trainee to provide the correct label for each input. Perhaps the most popular unsupervised neural network today is the **autoencoder** [61]. An autoencoder is a neural network that learns a mapping from one set of data to another. Observe that if we map data to itself, then the network must learn some internal representation of the data. If the network has enough nodes and edges, then it can represent each data point in the dataset uniquely. But if we force the network to generalize – by enforcing a more limiting architecture of the network – then the network is required to learn some more sophisticated internal representation of the data.

6.6   Learning Control

In autonomous systems an obvious placement of neural networks in vehicle control is to enable the network to completely control the vehicle. This concept of end-to-end vehicle control can be found in many papers using a number of different sensors, either individually or collectively. There are some obvious advantages here. Once trained, the actual control system is straightforward – the data are fed to the network and they tell the robot which way to go. Although simple, it is important to recognize that this control architecture can lead to unintended consequences, as the neural network will always provide an output command, even if the output is meaningless or dangerous to the operation of the vehicle or others around it. In practice, it may be desirable to place some **safety cage** (see [443]) around the network to ensure that its output is safe for all.

6.7   Training Regimes

Obtaining training data is a key problem for data-driven algorithms. There exists a wide set of very difficult problems related to training data. There are often no good universal solutions to these problems, and it becomes an interesting question as to what the correct approach would be for a given task.

Real versus simulated data It can be expensive/dangerous/difficult/impossible to obtain real training data for a task. Training data for a rover that is to operate on an unexplored planet would be an extreme version of this problem, but the problem occurs without having to go to off world. Training a robot what to do in an emergency requires placing the robot in that situation, including demonstrating the outcome of poor decisions. Given that it will not always be possible or desirable to obtain such real-world data, the use of simulation data is attractive, but simulated data is not necessarily accurate and realistic.

How then should the problem of integrating simulation and real data be addressed for a given task? That is, how should the problem of **sim2real** be addressed?

Distribution of data cases At its core, feed forward supervised neural networks will apply some form of gradient descent to optimize the difference between the labeled output values and the values produced by the network. If the distribution of training data is not balanced, then the integration of the errors from the various cases will tend to favor one case over the other. To take the DNN and CNN examples considered here: If the robot was mostly driving on straight roads, then the network might learn that all other things being equal, the robot should go straight ahead. After all, on average this is a better answer than turning. But if we balance the input dataset so that turns are present in equal numbers, then are we not biasing the training to emphasise infrequent events?

This problem of the availability of training data comes to a head when some critical classes, for example, what to do when the robot has almost left the road, are considered. Ideally these conditions will occur infrequently when humans are driving the robot and providing input to the network. How should we integrate "unusual" conditions into the training dataset? One option is to augment the dataset with data for which the right answer is known but which are unlikely to be present in the dataset when collected by human drivers. For example, for vision-based road following robots, one option is to create or collect data that would be obtained if the robot was displaced laterally across the road, and to "know" that the right answer is to correct this artificially introduced error. Data augmentation can take many forms. For example, in the road and line following examples one can estimate what to do when the road turns left, given what the trainee did when the road turns right. Indeed, this is implemented in the line following code provided on the online resource associated with the text.

6.8   Representing Output Features

Deciding how to represent the output features is a critical question in applying a neural network to a task. In the examples presented here, for example, the output was one of three command motions (forward, turn left, turn right). These were appropriate as the trainee was only allowed to push certain keys on the keypad that corresponded to these motion commands. But what if the trainee was given a joystick and the ability to provide different levels of turning? Or different velocity values? Would a large set of discrete possible commands to be appropriate, or would it be more desirable to have individual neurons encode levels of speed and turning direction?

6.9   Reinforcement Learning

Reinforcement learning (RL) is a broad field of machine learning used for problems where there is a time dependency between stages of a computation and an agent (i.e., a robot) needs to maximize the long-term benefit of its actions. The key notions are that we have a sequence of steps over time, and a way computing the net accumulated benefit over time (allowing short-term "pain" to contribute to long-term gain).

For example, recognizing pictures of cats in a series of photos from the Internet can be addressed using supervised learning (as above), but assuming the photos are unrelated, the result from one photo does not determine the correct solution for the next, so such a problem is not really suited to reinforcement learning. On the other hand, moving through a maze, or playing the game of chess, involves making choices where each move depends on the situation created by the preceding move, so the time dependency is very clear and such problems have been successfully addressed using RL.

The goal of RL methods is to learn some policy, which is a function that maps states to actions, that maximizes the expected accumulated reward over a sequence of time steps. To do this, the RL algorithm iteratively adjusts the policy based on the observed rewards and transitions in the environment, conceptualized as experiential learning.

The key constituents of an RL problem are the set of states that characterize the world, the set of actions we can take in each state, the outcome(s) for each action, the policy we use for taking actions (i.e., our strategy), the reward expected when we get to a specific state, and the way to add up rewards achieved over time. A further subtle aspect of RL is the manner in which we explore the space of policies and their effects.

We often prefer rewards to come to us as soon as possible. If a robot is playing ping-pong, a quick win is often preferred unless you purposely want to humiliate your opponent, in which case that additional objective can be explicitly incorporated into the reward function. The way we add up the rewards over time to determine the total value of a policy can take three different forms. We can simply all add rewards we get over all time irrespective over how long it takes, we can consider only rewards than come within a finite time horizon, or we can discount rewards that come later in time. These are referred to as infinite-horizon, fixed horizon, and discounted problems. In general, the discounted reward formalization is both the most general and the most analytically tractable, since dealing with finite bounds is conceptually easy but technically cumbersome.

To formalize these notions, in RL an agent aims to learn a control policy π that optimizes its long-term accumulated reward through interactions with the environment [745] as illustrated in Figure 6.8. The problem to be solved is modeled as a Markov decision process (MDP) characterized by a state space S, an action space A, a reward function r for each state, and a state transition probability function P. At time t the agent is in state $s_t \in S$. At each state s_t, the RL agent selects an action $a_t \in A$ by following the current policy π. The agent then receives the reward $r(s_t, a_t)$ and transitions from state s_t to s_{t+1}.

Putting this all together, an MDP is thus defined by a tuple (S, A, P, R, γ), where: S is the set of states. A is the set of possible actions. $P : S \times A \times S \rightarrow [0,1]$ is the transition function that specifies the probability of transitioning from one state to another

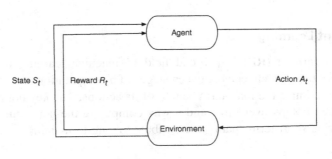

Figure 6.8. The basic structure of reinforcement learning.

after taking a particular action. $\mathcal{R} : \mathcal{S} \times \mathcal{A} \times \mathcal{S} \to \mathbb{R}$ is the reward function that specifies the immediate reward r received after taking a particular action from $\mathcal{A}$ in a particular state from $\mathcal{A}$. $\gamma \in [0,1]$ is a discount factor that determines the importance of future rewards relative to immediate rewards.

The goal of the agent is to maximize the cumulative reward that it receives. For finite term tasks (known as episodic tasks) of length T, the **cumulative reward** can be represented as

$$G_t = r_{t+1} + r_{t+2} + \cdots + r_{t+T}.$$

For continuous tasks, which are typically the type of reward encountered in autonomous systems, we are more concerned with tasks that are ongoing, and the straightforward addition of immediate rewards would be unbounded. Instead we consider the **discounted reward**

$$G_t = r_{t+1} + \gamma r_{t+2} + \gamma^2 r_{t+3} + \cdots = \sum_{k}^{\infty} \gamma^k r_{t+k},$$

where $0 < \gamma < 1$ is a discount factor.

The agent executes a **policy** that informs the agent as to which action the agent should take in the current state. More formally, the policy is a function that maps a given state to a probability distribution over the available actions in the given state. Policies can be deterministic,

$$a_t = \mu(s_t),$$

or stochastic, drawn from some distribution,

$$a_t \sim \pi(\cdot|s_t).$$

Policies are typically parameterized (by a parameter θ) and are written as $\mu_\theta(s_t)$ or $\pi_\theta(\cdot|s_t)$.

A given policy π can be said to be better than some other policy π' if the expected return of policy π is greater than or equal to the expected return of policy π' averaged over all states. A policy that is better than or at least as good as all other policies is the **optimal policy**. An optimal policy has an optimal action-value function, that is the optimal policy for each possible state-action pair. If we imagine the state-action pair as a function $q(s,a)$, then the optimal state-action pair can be defined as

$$q_*(s,a) = \max_\pi q_\pi(s,a).$$

Then q_π must satisfy

$$q_\pi(s,a) = \mathbb{E}[R_{t+1} + \gamma \max_{a'} q(s',a')].$$

This is known as the **Bellman optimality equation** [79]. It states that for any state-action pair (s,a) at time t, the expected return from starting in state s, selecting action a and following the optimal policy from that point on, is going to be the expected reward we get from taking action a in state s (R_{t+1}) plus the maximum expected discounted return from any possible next state-action pair (s',a'). We can leverage this property to solve the reinforcement learning problem in many different ways. We consider two here: Q-learning and Deep Q-learning.

6.9.1 Q-learning

Q-learning is a reinforcement learning algorithm developed by Watkins [822]. It solves the reinforcement learning problem through the use of a table indexed over state and action, known as the Q table. $Q(s,a)$ records the current best estimate of the discounted reward that would be obtained if the agent executed action a in state s. Key to the Q-learning algorithm is a process of updating the Q table after each motion of the agent. This updating rule is given by

$$Q'(s,a) = (1 - \alpha)Q(s,a) + \alpha(R + \gamma \max_{a'} q(s',a')).$$

Here s' is the state the agent gets to after taking action a from its current state s, α is the learning rate between 0 and 1, R is the reward the agent received after taking the action a, and γ is the discount factor. Observe what this updating rule does. The α controls how much to weight the old Q value relative to the update value. While the term $\alpha(R + \gamma \max_{a'} q(s',a'))$ estimates a discounted version of the best reward the agent will receive in terms of actions that can be taken from state s'. The basic Q-learning algorithm is sketched in Listing 6.4.

One remaining aspect of Q-learning is deciding which action the agent should take when it is in state s. If the agent took the current best action from the table, that is, it explores in a purely greedy manner using $\arg\max_{a'} Q(s,a')$, then the agent can be easily caught in a local minimum. It does not explore the environment as much as it should. At the other extreme, one can imagine a random action choice that would explore enthusiastically. This choice would not learn from previous explorations. A compromise between these two extremes is known as ϵ-greedy, which chooses a random action with probability ϵ and the greedy action with probability $1 - \epsilon$.

Let us now consider the relatively simple problem of finding a path in a maze using Q-learning. To simplify the problem we assume the simple world maze shown in Figure 6.9. States correspond to locations in the maze (there are 25 states) and we assume four

```
Initialize Q(s,a)
for each episode do:
   Initialize state s
   for each step in the current episode do:
      a = select_action(Q, s)
      Take action a and observe reward R and next state s'
      Q(s,a)=(1 - alpha) * Q(s,a) + alpha * (R + gamma * max(Q(s',a')))
      s = s'
```

Listing 6.4. The basic Q-learning algorithm.

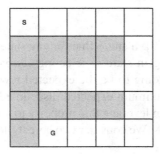

Figure 6.9. A simple 5×5 maze. The robot starts in the cell marked with an S and seeks to find the location marked with a G through repeated exploration of the environment.

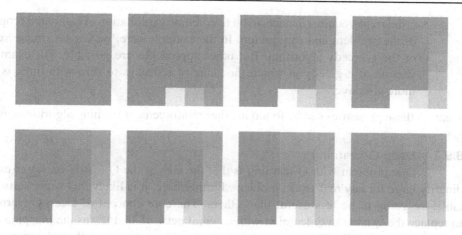

Figure 6.10. The Q-learning process. Cells of the maze are colored with white corresponding to higher $\max_a Q(s,a)$ values, and black corresponding to lower values. Learned performance percolates from locations near the goal to every location in the maze. Time increases from left to right and from top to bottom. An agent executing the solved maze would perform hill climbing on the cell values moving from darker cells to brighter ones to find the goal.

actions on the underlying grid in the maze (up, down, left, right). It remains to craft the reward function so that the reward that the agent obtains during an interaction with the world leads the agent to the desired goal. As an example, we craft the reward function as follows:

- If the action causes the robot to leave the maze, then that action has a reward of -100 and the robot does not move.
- If the action causes the robot to move into an occupied square then that action has a reward of -100 and the robot does not move.
- If the action causes the robot to get to the goal, then that action has a reward of $+500$ and the interaction ends.
- If the action causes the robot to move to an empty square, then that action has a reward of -1. This penalizes longer paths over shorter ones, a desirable property in most maze-solving problems.

Figure 6.10 shows snapshots of the process of solving this maze with Q-learning under the assumption that there is no noise in the motion process, and using ϵ-greedy exploration with a fixed value of ϵ.

Some Properties of Q-Learning

- Q-learning is said to be a **model-free algorithm**. That is, it is an RL algorithm that does not construct an explicit model of what is being solved.
- Q-learning is known as a **temporal difference** algorithm in that updates take place after each step.
- Q-learning is an **off-policy** algorithm in that it estimates the reward for state-action pairs based on accumulated samples, independent of the agent's actions.

- Q-learning requires a mechanism to combine exploitation of estimated properties of the problem and exploration. In the example here, we used a simple version of the ϵ-greedy algorithm. But other approaches are possible. For example, a version of ϵ-greedy in which the value of ϵ decays to zero with time, is often more effective.

Many of these properties can be found in other reinforcement learning algorithms as well.

6.9.2   Deep Q-Learning

One problem with Q-learning is that the size of the Q matrix becomes extraordinarily large for any real-world problem. Furthermore, it is likely that some parts of the table are going to be less useful than others. The core concept of Deep Q-learning is to replace the Q table in Q-learning with a neural network that learns the mapping that is encoded by the Q table. That is, to represent the Q table as a network that takes as input the state and outputs the Q values associated with each action. This Deep Q network (DQN) is perhaps the key component of a most reinforcement learning algorithms. The challenge in DQN is that unlike DNNs or CNNs we do not have the luxury of a large labeled dataset to train the network. Rather, the network is trained as the agent explores. This introduces a range of problems. Early in the learning process, this network has very little data to be trained on, so the network is unlikely to produce a meaningful output. Later on in the training process, is it necessary to retrain the network each time a new interaction with the network takes place, or is some sort of batching process more appropriate?

These and other nuances in the basic concept of replacing the table in Q-learning with a network (or collection of networks) have led to an explosion in terms of the number of different deep reinforcement learning algorithms. Specific solutions to the problem of developing a robust and effective DQN algorithm include:

Experience replay buffer Interactions of the agent with the environment (s_t, a_t, r_t, s_{t+1}) are stored in a buffer rather than being presented to the network immediately. When training is required, a set of interactions is selected from the buffer and this collection is used to train the DQN [536].

Batch or mini-batch updating Updating of the DQN is performed using small batches, rather than attempting to update the network after each interaction.

Separate target network Updating the DQN can lead to instabilities in the estimation process of the network during learning. It has proven effective to freeze a version of the network (known as the target network) and to use that for estimating how actions lead to rewards during training using the experience replay buffer, and then resetting the target network periodically from the updated DQN.

6.10   Using Large Language Models in Robotics

The emergence of large language models (LLMs) that combine text and other modalities (like images) exploded into popular culture around late 2022 with the release of **chatGPT** from the company OpenAI. This technology uses vast amounts of data to

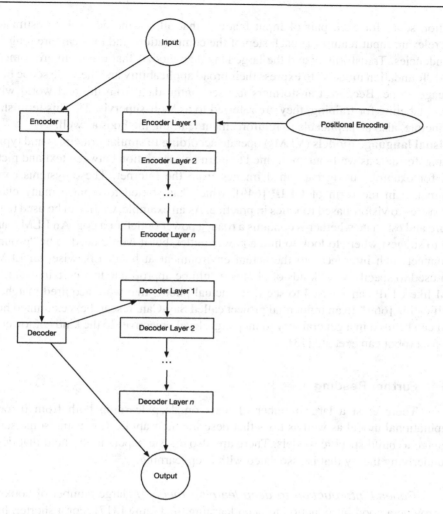

Figure 6.11. Sample transformer architecture.

train a system to predict the next word in a sequence, but as a side effect such systems also develop a representation for ideas captured in text. As a consequence, such systems capture all kinds of commonsense knowledge about how the world works, and thus can be used for robotics problems as well.

The particular mechanism used to build these LLMs is a large cascaded neural network architecture called a transformer [798] (Figure 6.11). Transformers have been used successfully for diverse applications. They are appropriate for problems where there is a sequence of stages in the input, such as the words in a sentence. A transformer model consists of an encoder component and a decoder component. The encoder takes the input sequence and learns to represent (encode) it as a smaller feature vector, while the decoder network generates the output sequence based on the encoder's output and a series of previous output tokens from previous parts of the input (e.g., earlier words in a sentence). A key aspect of a transformer is called "self-attention" that estimates an attention score for each pair of input features that allows the network to estimate the most relevant input features at each step of the computation, and thus capture long-range dependencies. Transformers and the large language models that use them are sometimes called "foundation models" to express their broad applicability and the wide scope beyond language alone. Because transformers use sequential data from the real world without manual labeling for training, they are referred to as "self-supervised". This term should, in principle, also be applicable to reinforcement learning methods as well.

Visual language models (VLMs) operate according to similar principles and typically use transformers as well, but are trained to learn an association between text and pictorial data, for example, using captioned images from the Internet. These systems came to prominence in the form of **CLIP** [649], which has started to replace many classical approaches to vision-based robotics in practice. As an example, CLIP can be used to take a picture and estimate whether is contains a road, a power outlet, or a dog. An LLM could be used to suggest where to look to find a power outlet, but it would need to be "grounded" to connect such inferences to the actual environment at hand. Likewise, an LLM has been used to specify what kinds of photos would be appropriate to a certain event, and a VLM like CLIP can be used to see if the actual photos that were acquired matched the specification [669]. In an influential project called Say-Can, researchers examined how an LLM can be used in a general way to map high-level objectives to the kinds of lower-level actions a robot can execute [13].

6.11   Further Reading

There exist a large number of texts on deep learning both from theoretical computational model as well as texts that describe their application using some standard language to build specific models. There are also classic papers in the field that describe the underlying theory that is associated with deep learning.

General introduction to deep learning theory A large number of books exist that provide a good introduction to deep learning, including [317]. For a shorter, higher-level view, see [538].

Deep learning approaches using software packages There exist a number of implementations of standard techniques in various infrastructures including R ([388]) and Tensorflow ([49, 309]).

Classic papers in deep learning Early models of neural networks include the Perceptron [674], and the adaptive linear element (Adaline) [831]. LSTM was introduced in [352]. See [349] for early work on unsupervised learning.

Reinforcement learning There exists a large number of DRL algorithms, including Double Q-learning [795] and PPO [703]. There also exist a number of books on DRL including [857].

Large language models Fundamental papers in LLMs/VLMs include [650], [462], [649], and [778].

Table 6.2. *Keyboard commands for the DNN and CNN problems.*

Command	Key
j	turn left
k	go straight
l	turn right
space	stop (and turn off recording)
s	start recording
x	stop recording
q	quit

6.12 Problems

1. This problem deals with the DNN line-following example described in Section 6.3.2 and relies on code found in the cpmr_ch6 package in the online resource. Follow the instructions in the README.md file in the gazebo directory online resource to add the line_plane model to the gazebo model directory.

   (a) Build a dataset of inputs to commanded motion for training. To do this, launch the drive_by_line.launch.py launch file in the repository. This will bring up a robot that uses a downward-facing camera to simulate two photosensitive devices to capture a line painted on the ground. To paint the line, in gazebo insert the line following exercise model you added to the local gazebo model repository and place it on the ground. Then delete the ground plane model from the World, and disable shadows in the World tab in gazebo. This should result in the robot existing on the ground plane and an image from the camera in a separate window.

   This display window accepts keyboard commands as described in Table 6.2, and by default writes its output into database.txt. Drive the robot around the world creating a database of sensor inputs and command motions. Make sure to only capture data for which the commanded motion applies for line following. That is, do not capture data when the robot is not over the line. You want a set of examples that shows all outputs (turn left, go straight, turn right). Training time is dependent upon the size of the dataset, so choose datasets that are not larger than 10,000 input/output pairs.

   Once you have captured the dataset, train the NN given in the src directory of the cpmr_ch6 package. The python3 program line-follower.py will take the dataset from the file database.csv and produce a line follower NN in the directory line-follower. The program line-follower-test.py in the same directory will evaluate the NN on the entire dataset. Note: Training and evaluating this NN will require that TensorFLow has been properly installed.

   (b) In the same package you will find the node auto_drive_by_line.launch.py that will drive the robot using the neural network. This node assumes that the line-follower NN is in the current directory. You will have to install the line world, remove the ground plane, and disable shadows as above. Set the robot above the line and enable auto driving (toggled using the "x" key). How far does the robot drive before losing the line? Can you build other environments that are easier/harder for the robot to learn on?

(c) How difficult is it to replace the NN with a simple rule-based line follower? Modify the `auto_driver` code so that you compute the appropriate drive command from the inputs. How far does your version of the robot go before losing the line?

(d) The network used here is incredibly straightforward. Try at least two changes to the architecture (e.g., more hidden levels with more/fewer elements per level, connection drop out) and identify better/worse/similar architectures. You will require a better way of estimating total performance. One way of doing this is to build a standard world and then to capture the robot's pose from `gazebo` (odometry information) for runs both when done by hand (to establish ground truth) and then the same when running under different architectures.

2. This question deals with the CNN road-following example described in the chapter and relies on code found in the `cpmr_ch6` package in the online resource. Follow the instructions in the `README.md` file in the `gazebo` directory in the repository to add the road plane model to the `gazebo` model directory. Note: You do not have to disable shadows as for the line follower above.

(a) Build a dataset of inputs to commanded motion for training. To do this, in your current directory, create directories output, output/forward, output/left, and output/right. Then launch the `drive_by_road.launch.py` launch file in the repository. This will bring up a robot equipped with a forward-facing capture that captures the view in front of the robot. To draw a line on the ground, in `gazebo` insert the road plane model you added to the local `gazebo` model repository and place it on the ground. Then delete the ground plane model from the world,. This should result in the robot existing on the ground plane and an image from the camera in a separate window.

(b) This display window accepts keyboard commands as described in the code, and by default writes its output into the directories you created earlier. Drive the robot around the world creating a database of camera inputs and command motions. Each camera image has been downsampled to 28×28 greyscale pixels so total disk storage is not that high. Make sure to only capture data for which the commanded motion applies for road following. That is, do not capture data when the robot is not driving on the road. You want a set of examples that shows all outputs (turn left, go straight, turn right). Training time is dependent upon the size of the dataset, so choose datasets that are not larger than 5,000 or so input/output pairs for each turn direction if your local computer lacks a GPU. Once you have captured the dataset, train the CNN given the Tensorflow program provided in the src directory of the cpmr ch6 package. The `python3` program `road-follower.py` will take the dataset from the directory `trainImages` and produce a road follower CNN in the directory model. (Note that you will have to rename the output file from the data collection tool. This was intentional to prevent accidental overwriting of a previously collected dataset.) Similarly, the code provided to test and use the model assumes that the output model has been renamed `road-follower`. The program `road-follower-test.py` in the same directory will evaluate the CNN on the entire dataset. Note: Training and evaluating this CNN will require that TensorFLow has been properly installed on your machine. In the same package you will find the node `auto_drive_by_road.launch.py` that will drive the robot using the neural network. You will have to install the line world, remove the ground plane, and disable shadows as above. Set the robot above the line and enable auto driving. How far does the robot drive before losing the line? Can you build other environments that are easier/harder for the robot to learn on?

(c) If you trained your robot on the stock input given above, the world was empty besides the road. Here we ask the question, How well does the model work and how sensitive is it to other things in the world? Identify a standard spot in the world and start the robot centered over the mid-line of the road. How far does the robot run until it crashes off the road (repeat this 10 times, assuming "never" after 5 laps). Now populate the world with standard objects from the `gazebo` object library, and repeat. How well did your network generalize to this novel environment?

(d) The network used here is incredibly straightforward. Try at least two changes to the architecture (e.g., different structure/number/size of convolutional levels, connection drop out) and identify better/worse/similar architectures. You will require a better way of estimating total performance. One way of doing this is to build a standard world and then to capture the robot's pose from `gazebo` (odometry information) for runs both when done by hand (to establish ground truth) and then the same when running under different architectures.

3. Implement Q-learning for the maze problem used as an example in Section 6.9.1. Assume a $N \times N$ world with cells being one of empty, occupied or goal, and use the same reward function as described in Section 6.9.1. Use an episode length of $2N^2$ moves, and 100 episodes. Initialize the Q table to be 0.

   - For a world of size $N \times N$, how large is the Q table?
   - Plot the reward value for each episode in your training runs. How quickly would you say that the Q table has converged to the optimal answer? How did you determine this?
   - What effect to you see on the learning process if you initialize the Q table to have positive, but small, initial values, say 30? This is known as using **optimistic initial values**.
   - Rather than using a static ϵ value in the ϵ-greedy algorithm, decay the value of ϵ as a function of time. What effect does this have on the learning process?

4. Build a feed-forward NN to encode the Q matrix from problem 3. When implementing the Q-learning problem create a replay buffer to store

(s_t, a_t, R, s_{t+1}) values. Develop an NN that maps state to an array of rewards for each of the possible directions, that is, a machine that returns the array $[R_1, \ldots, R_n])$. Do learning in minibatches of size 32 chosen randomly from the minibuffer. Characterize the error in terms of your NN as its performance relative to the use of the Q buffer directly.

7

Planning in, Representing and Reasoning about Space

> They assume the end, and consider how and by which means it is attained, and
> if it seems easily and best produced thereby; while if it is achieved by one means
> only they consider how it will be achieved by this and by what means this will
> be achieved, till they come to the first cause, which in the order of discovery
> is last[1]

> "That's something I could not allow to happen."[2]

Robots in fiction seem to be able to engage in complex planning tasks with little or no
difficulty. For example, in the novel *2001: A Space Odyssey*, HAL is capable of long-
range plans and reasoning about the effects and consequences of his actions [167]. It is
indeed fortunate that fictional autonomous systems can be presented without having to
specify how such devices represent and reason about their environment. Unfortunately,
real autonomous systems often make explicit internal representations and mechanisms
for reasoning about them. This chapter considers some of the fundamental computational
tasks that must be addressed by a mobile robot: how space should be represented, how to
represent the robot itself, and how the robot can reason with respect to its representation of
space. These are fundamental tasks for a mobile robot that must plan complex strategies
and establish long-term plans.

7.1 Representing the Robot

In Chapter 2 robots were modeled as a point operating on an infinite plane.
This representation was sufficient as the robots being represented could be completely
described in terms of their position on the plane. Here we consider a more general
representation of a robot known as its **configuration space**.

7.1.1 Configuration Space

Configuration space (or *C-space*) is a key formalism for motion planning, and it
is used to represent the possible kinematic states of a robot. Each point in the configuration
space corresponds to a complete specification of the robot's state with respect to whatever
aspects of the robot we care about. (See Figure 7.1.) Such a space has one dimension for
every degree of freedom of the robot, including not only a reference point such as the

---

[1] Aristotle, *Nicomachean Ethics*.
[2] The robot HAL 9000 planning and reasoning about future actions in *2001* [167].

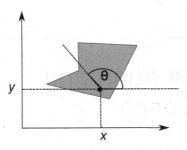

Figure 7.1. A rigid polygonal object and its 3D pose in a 2D workspace with respect to an arbitrary reference point on it.

center of mass, but also the positions of any joints or other components whose relative position can be independently determined. For a rigid robot in 2D, this might be only the position and orientation (x, y, θ). A humanoid robot with limbs might also have as many as 26 dimensions to specify the angles of the joints, the hips, arms, and legs.

More precisely, a configuration q of the robot $\mathcal{A}$ is a specification of the physical state of $\mathcal{A}$ with respect to a fixed environmental (workspace) frame F_w [449]. Consider a rigid robot $\mathcal{A}$ capable of translating and rotating in the plane. The configuration of $\mathcal{A}$ could be represented as $q = [x \ y \ \theta]$, in that q completely defines the configuration of the robot. For more complex robots, such as limbed or articulated robots, the structure of q can be considerably more complex. For a limbed robot $\mathcal{B}$, its configuration might include a rigid pose for some origin associated with the robot, as before, augmented with the joint angles of each of its limbs. The configuration space of $\mathcal{A}$ is the space $\mathcal{C}$ of all possible configurations of $\mathcal{A}$. The space $\mathcal{C}$ defines all of the valid configurations of the robot. It is important to note that configuration space may not be a Euclidean space: that is, the topological connectivity of points over all space may not have the connectivity properties (i.e., flatness) of a Euclidean space. This is most commonly exemplified by deriving the distance metric in the space of interest and observing that it is, or is not, the Euclidean metric

$$d(\boldsymbol{x}, \boldsymbol{y}) = \sqrt{\sum_i (x_i - y_i)^2}.$$

This typically arises due to the representation of degrees of freedom in terms of rotations. For example, a rigid robot $\mathcal{A}$ that can translate and rotate in the plane has a non-Euclidean configuration space since the set of poses $q = [x \ y \ \theta]$ includes a rotation as the third dimension of the state. That means that this dimension wraps around at $360°$ (2π), giving the space a cylindrical structure. Another pragmatic aspect is that there can be more than one straight-line path between two points (e.g., $\mathcal{A}$ can get from one rotational angle to another by rotation forward or backward).

Obstacles in the environment may limit the set of possible configurations of the robot. Let $\mathcal{B}_i$ be the collection of obstacles. Then obstacle $\mathcal{B}_i$ prohibits certain configurations of the robot and gives rise to a **C-obstacle** $\mathcal{CB}_i$ given by

$$\mathcal{CB}_i = \{q \in \mathcal{C} | \mathcal{A}(q) \cap \mathcal{B}_i \neq \emptyset\},$$

where $\mathcal{A}(q)$ is that portion of space occupied by robot $\mathcal{A}$ when the robot is in configuration q.

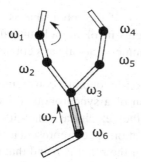

Figure 7.2. A robot arm and the 7 joints (6 revolute and one prismatic), leading to a 7D configuration space.

The union of all C-obstacles is known as the **C-obstacle region** and the intersection of this with the region with the potential pose of the robot provides a formal definition of the **free space** of the robot:

$$\mathcal{C}_{free} = \{q \in \mathcal{C} | \mathcal{A}(q) \cap (\cup_i \mathcal{B}_i) = \emptyset\}.$$

A particular configuration is said to be **semi-free** if the robot at this configuration touches obstacles without overlap. Semi-free space is thus the union of free space and those configurations that are semi-free, and it thus combines poses of the robot that are free with poses that touch (but do not penetrate) the obstacle boundaries. Note that the free space is an open set, while the semi-free space is a closed set, and thus many planning algorithms that seek optimality operate over the semi-free space.

In addition to the presence of obstacles in the environment, the physical construction of the robot may prohibit certain configurations of the vehicle and transitions between configuration. Constraints that can be written in the form

$$G(q) = 0,$$

where q is the robot pose, are known as **holonomic constraints**. In general, planning a path to avoid C-space obstacles in the presence of only holonomic constraints is straightforward. Constraints on the *derivatives* of the robot motion that cannot be integrated out (i.e., reduced to holonomic constraints) are known as **non-holonomic constraints** [449]. These take the form

$$G(q, \frac{dq}{dt}, \frac{d^2q}{dt^2}, ...) = 0. \tag{7.1}$$

Non-holonomic constraints include restrictions on what velocities (tangents in the configuration space) are allowed. Non-holonomic constraints reduce the range of allowed differential motions and *greatly* complicate the motion planning problem. The essence of the problem caused by non-holonomic constraints is that for the robot to move from one admissible state to another, even if the states are "adjacent" to one another, a trajectory of arbitrary complexity may be required. Common examples of vehicles with non-holonomic motion constraints are automobiles and vehicles with trailers. Parallel parking is a familiar illustration of the type of difficulty associated with even this simple path-planning problem. Other contexts in which non-holonomic constraints occur include when there is a rolling contact, such as with a fingered hand on a surface, or when conservation of angular momentum is a significant factor, as in the case of free-flying robots. A standard non-holonomic constraint for mobile robots is a constraint on the *radius of curvature* that can be executed in the trajectory of the robot, that is. a limit of the sharpness of the turns that are possible. For problems involving a bounded radius of curvature, optimal-length paths in obstacle-free environments are always composed of a sequence of circular arcs.

To make the relationship between holonomic and non-holonomic constraints more concrete, consider the configuration space representation of a synchronous drive robot $\mathcal{A}$ as described in Section 3.1.5. This robot can control the velocity at which its wheels turn and the direction in which they point. The configuration space representation of $\mathcal{A}$ could be given by $q = [x \; y \; \theta]$. Suppose that the radius of the robot is r and that there is one infinitesimally small obstacle at the origin. Then this obstacle results in a holonomic constraint on the robot of the form

$$x^2 + y^2 > r^2.$$

If the robot moves at a velocity v, then

$$dx/dt = v \cos(\theta)$$
$$dy/dt = v \sin(\theta).$$

Combining these constraints yields $dx \sin(\theta) - dy \cos(\theta) = 0$, that is, the robot moves in a straight line in the direction it is facing. This is a non-holonomic constraint of the form given in equation (7.1) since it involves both q and q', and q' cannot be eliminated. Omnidirectional robots (see Section 3.1.6) do not suffer from this constraint. Path planning for robots that incur holonomic constraints is known as **holonomic path planning**, which is significantly different from path planning for non-holonomic robots (**non-holonomic path planning**). In the presence of non-holonomic constraints, even simple problems such as finding a minimum-length trajectory through a cluttered environment can be exceedingly difficult. Parallel parking a car is an illustrative example: getting from one allowed position in the road to an adjacent parked position may involve a tedious maneuver.

Controllability refers to having the ability to move on demand between any two arbitrary points in the state space. Non-holonomic systems are not locally **controllable**, yet in many cases they are globally controllable. Common approaches to non-holonomic motion planning for mobile robots can be divided roughly into methods that perform a complete search (often based on discretization), iterative refinement methods, and methods that use specific well-behaved controls but deal poorly with obstacles.

7.1.2   Simplifications

The major problem associated with representing a robot in configuration space (C-space) is that the configuration space representation of obstacles and the resulting dimensionality of the search space for motion paths can be very large and hence expensive to search. Various simplifications have been proposed in order to reduce the complexity of the C-space representation and thus the cost associated with representing objects and path planning.

The classic simplification is to assume that the robot can be represented as a point and is capable of omnidirectional motion. This is known as the **point robot assumption** and was introduced in Chapter 2. The obvious problem with this simplification is that autonomous vehicles are not points, and many robot designs introduce non-holonomic constraints. If the robot is shrunk to a point, and subsequent processing uses this point

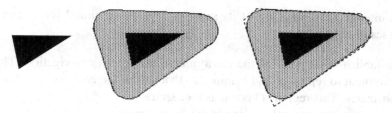

Figure 7.3. Effect of dilation. A triangle undergoes dilation by the robot's radius followed by a polynomial approximation of the resulting boundary.

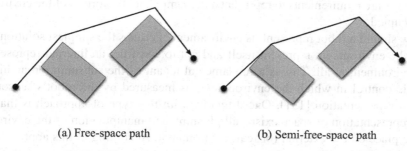

(a) Free-space path   (b) Semi-free-space path

Figure 7.4. Free and semi-free paths. Two paths in a 2D environment. (a) The path is described as "free" as it does not touch the obstacle boundaries. (b) The path is described as "semi-free" as it does touch the obstacle boundaries.

representation to plan operations such as determining which paths to follow, it will be important to integrate knowledge of the true size and shape of the robot as well as any non-holonomic constraints into the path execution process. One mechanism for dealing with the non-zero size of the robot is to assume that the robot has a circular cross section and to then *dilate* all obstacles in the environment by an amount equal to the robot's radius as shown in Figure 7.3. The dilation operation (also known as a **Minkowski sum**) for an object can be computed by taking the union of the object's shape with a set of circles (or spheres in 3D) placed at every point on the object's boundary. Polygonal obstacles can be described as a set of lines and arcs of circles after dilation.

In Figure 7.3 a polygonal object is dilated by the robot's radius and then re-approximated by a polygon. Object dilation can make the resulting environment much more complex, as simple corners are dilated into smooth shapes. It is also worth noting that if these complex shapes must be represented by some set of primitives such as polygons, then the resulting objects will only approximate the robot's environment.

7.2   Representing Space

Although it may be possible to carry out a number of complex tasks without an internal representation of the robot's environment, many tasks require such a representation. The most natural representation of a robot's environment is a **map**. In addition to representing places in an environment, a map may include other information including reflectance properties of objects, regions that are unsafe or difficult to traverse, and information gained from prior experiences. An internal representation of space can be used by a robot to pre-plan and pre-execute tasks that may be performed later.

A robot's internal representation of its space is typically required for at least three different classes of task:

1. To establish what parts of the environment are free for navigation. This is a requirement to represent and manipulate that part of the environment that is free of obstacles. This region is known as **free space**.
2. To recognize regions or locations in the environment.
3. To recognize specific objects within the environment.

Tasks 1 and 3 are requirements to represent and manipulate the portion of the environment that is occupied.

So how should a robot represent its environment? Perhaps the simplest solution would be to let the environment represent itself and not to construct an internal representation of the environment at all. This is a fundamental tenant of the subsumption architecture for robotic control in which the environment, as measured by the robot's sensors, acts as its own representation [131]. One difficulty with this type of approach is that as no internal representation of space exists, all planning and manipulation of the environment must take place on the external (or real) environment. According to this approach, plans can only be based on instantaneous sensory input. Long-term planning is difficult to accomplish, although **reactive planning** – planning based on reacting to the current state of the environment – is attractive for real-time, low-level planning. Another approach is to represent space by the pattern of sensor measurements that are obtained by the robot at each pose. This is the fundamental idea behind **fingerprinting**, as discussed in Section 9.2.

If an internal representation is to be constructed, what form should this representation take and what primitives should be used in this construction? Representations based on objects, features or symbolic entities, spatial occupancy, places, task-specific information routes, and procedural information have been proposed. In general, spatial representations can be divided into two main groups, those that rely primarily on an underlying metric representation and those that are topological in nature.

7.2.1   Spatial Decomposition

Perhaps the most straightforward representation of space is to discretely sample the two- or higher-dimensional environment to be described. The idea here is to represent *space itself* as opposed to representing individual objects within it. This precludes having to discriminate or identify individual objects. This sampling can be performed in various ways using a number of different subdivision methods based on the shapes of the objects, by dividing the free space into (possibly overlapping) regions that can be described more simply, or more commonly by defining a sampling lattice embedded in space and sampling space at the nodes so defined. The simplest method is to sample space at the cells of a uniform grid. Samples taken at points in the lattice express the degree of occupancy at that sample point: Is space empty, full, or partially full? If the samples are binary, then in two dimensions the grids are known as **bitmaps**. Otherwise in two dimensions the grids are known as **pixel maps** or **occupancy grids**. In three dimensions the sampling elements are known as **voxels** or **volume elements**. The ROS navigation system [491] provides mechanisms to represent, store, and update maps as occupancy grids. It also provides

image: globalmap.pgm
resolution: 0.02
origin: [-5.12, -5.12, 0.0]
negate: 0
occupied_thresh: 0.75
free_thresh: 0.25

(a) globalmap.yaml   (b) globalmap.pgm

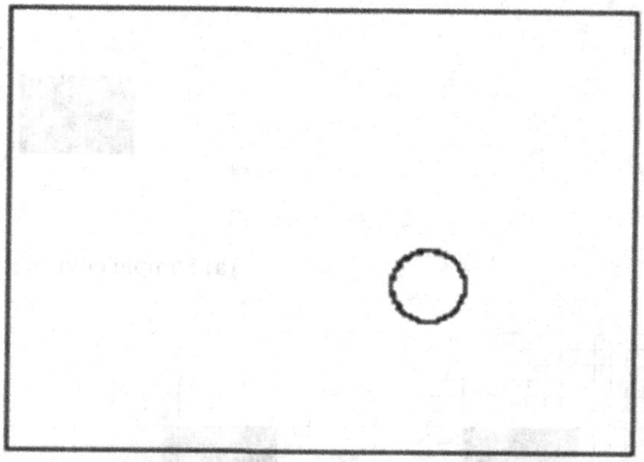

Figure 7.5. The occupancy representation of space used in ROS. The YAML file describes map metadata, including the uniform size of each cell and the mapping between the image that holds the occupancy grid and a global coordinate frame (the map frame) defined in ROS.

mechanisms to build the map representation itself (see Chapter 10). Here, we consider the problem of constructing occupancy grid global representations in ROS independently of the problem of pose estimation.

ROS provides a central map server as part of the navigation stack. The map server essentially provides a common broker for the representation of occupancy grid maps to various software tools within the ROS ecosystem. At its core, a map is defined by two structures, a YAML file that provides metadata about the map, and a graphical image that encodes the map (see Figure 7.5). The map server provides a common interface to recover this representation.

One advantage of a regular lattice representation is its extreme generality: no strong assumptions are made regarding object type. The grids can represent anything. The main disadvantage of this type of representation is that the grid resolution or fidelity is limited by the cell size and the representation is storage intensive, even if much of the environment is empty or occupied. For example, for a 15 m^3 environment with a 3 m accuracy, 125 cells will be required, while for a $100 \times 100 \times 100$ m^3 volume with a 1 cm accuracy (such as would be appropriate for an office/lab area) 10^9 cells will be needed. A simple voxel-based representation is hardly suitable for large volumes of space.

In addition to representing the level of occupancy at particular locations in space, elements of the lattice may be tagged with other attribute information such as the confidence of the occupancy value, the safety or desirability of occupying the cell, terrain information, and so on. Figure 7.6a,b show a sample environment and its voxel-based representation. Clearly many of the cells contain essentially the same information (space is either occupied or empty).

Given the simplicity of a grid-based representation but the unrealistic storage requirements needed to explicitly represent each cell of the grid, one alternative is to take advantage of the fact that many of the cells will have a similar state, especially those cells that correspond to spatially adjacent regions. Two general approaches to addressing this

(a) Sample environment

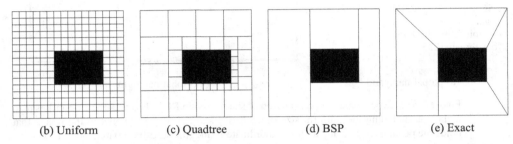

(b) Uniform   (c) Quadtree   (d) BSP   (e) Exact

Figure 7.6. Spatial decomposition. An environment and five different spatial decompositions of it.

storage problem along these lines have been developed. One alternative is to represent space using cells of a non-uniform shape and size, but more commonly a recursive hierarchical representation is used. The most common such example is the **quadtree**.

A quadtree [694] is a recursive data structure for representing a square two-dimensional region. It is a hierarchical representation that can potentially reduce storage and aid in certain types of computation. We begin with a large square region that encompasses all of the necessary space. Cells that are neither uniformly empty nor full are subdivided into four equal subparts along the x and y dimensions. Subparts are subdivided in turn until either they are uniformly empty or full or an *a priori* resolution limit is met. A sample environment and its quadtree representation are given in Figure 7.6a,c. As can be seen from Figure 7.6c, obstacle boundaries are represented at the finest resolution, while large empty (or full) spaces are represented at much coarser resolutions.

An algorithm for producing a quadtree representation for an arbitrary planar region is given in Listing 7.1. The algorithm depends on a homogeneity test to determine whether a region should be considered empty or full. The homogeneity test is assumed to return *empty*, *full*, or *mixed*. In practice, such a test is often based on a pixel-counting algorithm and a threshold, so that it, in essence, tests for *almost all* pixels being empty or full.

The three-dimensional analog of the quadtree is known as an **octree**. We start with a cube and recursively subdivide along each dimension with the same homogeniety test. In 3-D there are $2^3 = 8$ subcells, hence "oct"-tree. Higher N-dimensional versions are possible based on hypercubes subdivided into 2^N sub-parts.

How good are these representations in terms of saving space? The worst case is the complete subdivision into the smallest cells. Thus, in the worst case, quadtree representations are worse than uniform subdivisions due to the extra overhead involved in the quadtree representation. In general, the number of cells varies roughly with the area (or surface, in three dimensions) of the obstacles being described. Thus, for environments

```
Procedure Quadtree(Region)
    condition = homogeneity_test(Region)
    if condition in {empty,full} then
        return leafNode(condition)
    else
        begin
            region1 = topleft(Region)
            region2 = topright(Region)
            region3 = bottomleft(Region)
            region4 = bottomright(Region)
            topleftSubtree = quadtree(region1)
            toprightSubtree = quadtree(region2)
            bottomleftSubtree = quadtree(region3)
            bottomrightSubtree = quadtree(region4)
            return treeNode(topleftSubtree,toprightSubtree,
                            bottomleftSubtree,bottomrightSubtree)
        end
```

Listing 7.1. Recursive quadtree decomposition algorithm.

where most of space is free or occupied, quadtree-like representations can be very compact. One disadvantage of hierarchical representations, however, is that they tend to be unstable with respect to changes in the environment or the sensing arrangement. That is, even very small changes in the way that obstacles are arranged can lead to very large changes in the representation. This means that matching (or localization) based on hierarchical decompositions can be algorithmically awkward.

Hierarchical representation systems based on a power-of-two decomposition are popular due in part to the binary nature of the decision process involved in search. Unfortunately, not all space is well characterized by this power-of-two representation nor are all environments aligned with power-of-two boundary planes. Consider, for example, what happens to the object represented in Figure 7.6b if the black object was to be rotated by 45°. Very different representations of what are essentially the same shape may result. Two alternative spatial decomposition methods that are not quite as restrictive as quadtree representations are **binary space partitioning trees** (BSP trees) and the exact decomposition method.

A BSP tree is a hierarchical representation used extensively in computer graphics that has general application to the task of representing space. It is a hierarhcial representation within which a rectangular cell is either a leaf or is divided into two BSP trees by a plane parallel to one of the external boundaries of the environment. Figure 7.6d shows a potential BSP representation of the free space depicted in Figure 7.6a. The free space is divided into regions by lines that are parallel to the outer boundaries of the environment. Note that each new boundary divides a cell into two parts, but not necessarily in the center of the region. BSP trees provide the same binary space splitting characteristic of quadtrees but do not enforce symmetrical subdivision. A BSP representation of a given space is not necessarily unique, and depending on the choice of division planes, radically different representations of the same space are obtained.

Another alternative is to subdivide space exactly rather than requiring a hierarchy such as those introduced by quadtree or BSP decompositions. Free space is simply broken down into non-overlapping regions by planes such that the union of the parts is exactly the whole. Figure 7.6e provides a sample decomposition of the free space shown in

Figure 7.6a. The primary advantage of the exact decomposition method is that it is exact. Unfortunately, as with the BSP approach, the exact decomposition method is not unique, as there is no simple rule for how to subdivide space.

When decomposing space into regions, it is not necessary to have the regions constructed so that they do not overlap. For example, Brooks [127] proposed a spatial representation based on describing space in terms of overlapping generalized cones. Each cone is formed with a straight spine and with a cross section perpendicular to the spine. The free space is described in terms of these overlapping regions. The spines of the cones and the intersections of the spines are used to form the edges and nodes of a graph that represents the free space.

One approach, commonly used in ROS, is to have a very small number of overlapping uniform maps. A global map represents the entire world, at a more coarse resolution. This is augmented by a local map at a higher resolution that represents the world in proximity to the robot.

7.2.2   Geometric Representations

Geometric maps are those made up of discrete geometric primitives: lines, polygons or polyhedra, points, polynomial functions, and so on. Such maps have the advantage of being highly space efficient since an arbitrarily large region of space can be represented by a model with only a few numerical parameters. In addition, geometric maps can store occupancy data with almost arbitrarily high resolution without the storage penalties incurred by techniques based on spatial sampling.

Typically, geometric maps used in mobile robotics are composed simply of the union of simple geometric primitives, for example, points, polygons, and circles in 2D, or cubes and ellipsoids in 3D. Such maps are characterized by two key properties:

- The set of basic primitives used for describing objects
- The set of composition and deformation operators used to manipulate objects

While simple platonic solids are sufficient for basic navigation tasks, more elaborate modeling, grasping, or landmark recognition problems motivate the use of more sophisticated primitives. Roughly in order of increasing expressive power or complexity, key classes of geometric primitives in common use include the following:

- 2D maps
  - Points.
  - Lines, line segments and polylines (piecewise linear curves); for an example of a map based on this type of representation, see Figure 7.7.
  - Circles and arcs of circles.
  - Polynomials.
  - Polyhedra.
  - Splines.
- 3D maps
  - Points.
  - Planar surfaces.
  - Regular polyhedra, general polyhedra.
  - Surface patch networks.
  - Circles and ellipsoids.

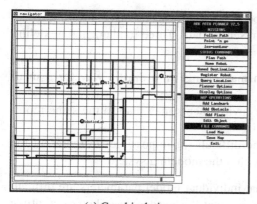

landscape newworld;
  unit meter;
  width 22.500000 to 45.500000;
  height 12.000000 to 28.500000;
  elevation 0.000000 to 2.200000;
  begin
    name (43.541718,23.182617) "Elevator";
    name (33.433750,17.051640) "Robotics Lab";
    obstacle boundary2: wall;
      extent (39.849998, 25.200001) to (39.849998, 21.400000);
      elevation 0.000000 to 0.000000;
    end;
    obstacle boundary6: wall;
      extent (38.496956, 12.395000) to (38.496956, 12.065001);
      elevation 0.000000 to 0.000000;
    end;
  end.

(a) Graphical view

(b) Map definition language

Figure 7.7. A 2D map based primarily on lines and polylines. (a) The graphical presentation of the map. (b) A sample map definition in the underlying map definition language. Note that (b) does not generate (a).

The parametric equation of a superquadric ellipsoid $e = (e_1, e_2, e_3)^T$ is given by

$$e = \begin{pmatrix} a_1 C_u^{\epsilon_1} C_v^{\epsilon_2} \\ a_2 C_u^{\epsilon_1} S_v^{\epsilon_2} \\ a_3 S_u^{\epsilon_1} \end{pmatrix},$$

where $-\pi/2 \leq u \leq \pi/2$, $-\pi/2 \leq v < \pi/2$, $S_w^\epsilon = \mathrm{sgn}(\sin w)|\sin w|^\epsilon$, and $C_w^\epsilon = \mathrm{sgn}(\cos w)|\cos w|^\epsilon$. Here $a \geq 0$ is a scale parameter, $0 \leq a_i \leq 1$, are aspect ratio parameters, and $\epsilon_i \geq 0$ are squareness parameters.

Figure 7.8. Superquadrics.

– Superquadrics [65, 618]. See Figure 7.8.
– Tensor product surfaces, NURBS (non-uniform rational B-splines [260]), and related spline surfaces.

Given a potential representation framework, basic operators for manipulating these primitives include:

- Rigid transformations (translation, rotation).
- Conformal transformations (shape preserving transformations).
- Affine transformations.
- Warping.
- Boolean set operations (constructive solid geometry: union, intersection, etc.).
- Regularized Boolean set operators.

The primary shortcoming of geometric model-based representations relates to the fact that they can be difficult to infer reliably from sensor data. Three fundamental modeling problems are encountered regularly:

1. Lack of stability: the representation may change in a drastic way for a small variation in the input.
2. Lack of uniqueness: many different environments may map to the same representation.
3. Lack of expressive power: it may be difficult (or impossible) to represent the salient features of the environment within the modeling system.

These difficulties arise both from the fact that individual model parameters are difficult to estimate reliably and, especially, from the fact that for a scene described by multiple model classes it can be exceedingly difficult to reliably associate specific models with particular sets of measurements. The lack of stability refers to the fact that the geometric models generated as the result of a particular set of observations may vary rapidly with small variations in the input data. Formally, the stability of a modeling function is defined as the ratio of the variation in the output parameters to changes in the input. Given the model parameters G and a function of changes Ih to the input parameters S, then stability can be defined formally as

$$\kappa = \lim_{h \to 0} \frac{|G(S + Ih) - G(S)|}{h}.$$

Large values of κ are associated with an unstable modeling function.

The lack of uniqueness in a representation results from that fact that many modeling systems, especially those that have substantial expressive power and that approximate the input data rather than expressing it exactly, can express a single set of observations in more than one way. This issue is sometimes partially addressed by using models extracted following the principle of **minimal description length**. Approaches based on this principle associate a cost with each model used and its approximation errors and attempt to find a single model (from a set of alternatives) that minimizes the total cost.

One approach to addressing instability (as well as uniqueness) is to **regularize** the problem by introducing a **stabilizer** that acts to damp variations in the modeling system with (small) variations in the input. Recall from Section 4.1 that a stabilizer is a factor that serves to bias the model-fitting process toward specific types of solutions, for example, preferring smoother curves over more jagged ones. While formal Tikhonov regularization expressed analytically can be used, a more *ad hoc* approach is frequently applied in which the stabilizer is simply an additional term used in the model-fitting stage. Introducing a stabilizer can be achieved by:

- Discarding data points that do not have nearby neighbors.
- Preferring line segment models that are straight, aligned with preferred directions, or parallel to other models.
- Preferring line segment models that are long.
- Preferring models are the most compact possible for a given set of data points (for curves, circles, polygons, and superquadrics).
- Preferring models that have uniform or low curvature.
- Preferring models with uniform data coverage.

For example, fitting a superquadric or superquadratic function to an incomplete set of data points often leads to an optimization problem with a very shallow minimum, that is, the precise value of the optimal superquadric parameters is difficult to establish. A wide range of possible superquadric shapes is equally good in terms of their fit to the data but often look quite different. One potential solution to this problem involves adding an additional term to the fitting procedure to preferentially select the possible model with the smallest volume. A secondary problem with superquadrics, and other complex models in general, is that the objective fitting function is non-convex. Thus, simple gradient descent is insufficient to find the globally optimal values of the model parameters. To address this, a variety of non-convex optimization procedures can be used, including **Levenberg–Marquardt optimization**, **simulated annealing** [637], and CNNs (see Section 6.4 and [584]).

Geometric models can suffer from a lack of expressive power, in that they are not well suited to expressing *distributions* of measurements and the associated error models. That is, geometric objects can be inferred from groups of data points, and the underlying statistics of the data are discarded. This is what makes geometric models concise, but if aspects of the original distribution are important, then they must be explicitly represented. Basic error models that are used to express misfits between geometric models and data include means and/or standard deviations of uniform or Gaussian distributions. Although better than ignoring data misfits, such error models may fail to capture the complex distributions associated even with simple sensors such as sonar.

Despite these shortcomings, geometric models provide both a concise expression of environmental data and one that can be readily used for higher-level processing. The discrete nature of geometric models makes them well suited to semantic interpretation and reasoning. If geometric models of the environment can be reliably inferred, they can be readily manipulated by inference systems.

7.2.3 Topological Representations

Geometric representations rely on metric data as the core of the representation. Unfortunately, these metric data are likely to be corrupted by sensor noise at the very least. To avoid reliance on error-prone metric data, a non-metric topological representation can be used.

The representations of large-scales spaces that are used by humans (and other organisms) seem to have a topological flavor rather than a geometric one [604]. For example, when providing directions to someone in a building, directions are usually of the form "go down the hall, turn right at the cooler, open the first door on your left" rather than in geometric form.

The key to a topological relationship is some explicit representation of connectivity between regions or objects. In its purest form, this may involve a complete absence of metric data. A topological representation is based on an abstraction of the environment in terms of discrete places with edges connecting them, for example, a graph $G = (V, E)$, where V is a set of nodes or vertices and E is the set of edges that connect them. In practice, it is often the case that the graph G is embedded in some metric space – the edges have length, and the edges are oriented with respect to the nodes.

The use of graphs, and in particular embedded graphs with edges and vertices augmented with various labels, has been exploited by many robotic systems to represent

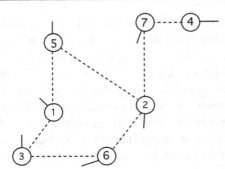

Figure 7.9. Graph-based representation of a robotic environment. Vertices correspond to known landmarks, edges to the paths between them. Locally defined orientations are shown. Redrawn from [252].

the environment. The following example from [252] is representative. The robot's environment is modeled as a graph whose vertices correspond to visual landmarks placed on the ceiling within the robot's environment. Each landmark is unique and also defines a local orientation. The landmarks are localized using a camera mounted on the robot, which points directly up. A graph-based representation of a sample environment is shown in Figure 7.9. Each vertex corresponds to one of the unique landmarks, while edges correspond to known straight paths between landmarks. Each edge in the graph is labeled by the distance that needs to be traveled along this edge in order to arrive at the next landmark. Edges are also labeled in order to show their direction with respect to the local orientation defined by the landmark. The robot has no real understanding of the geometric relationship between locations in the environment; locations are only linked by their (augmented) topological representation. Nevertheless, the representation does encode sufficient information for the robot to conduct point-to-point motion. The representation is also extremely compact.

A central issue in any environmental representation scheme – and a critical issue for topological representations – is the process of developing the representation itself. Various algorithms exist that construct a topological representation from a given geometric representation (see Section 7.3.1). A number of authors have considered problems of exploration, search, and navigation in the context of a graph-like world. This abstraction permits a variety of graph-theoretic techniques to be employed directly. The issue of exploration in graph-like environments is discussed further in Section 10.3.

7.3 Path Planning for Mobile Robots

Given a representation of a robot and a representation or data structure for the free space, we can consider the computation challanges of moving around in space. In particular, how can we get from one place to another in an efficient manner? This is the vast domain of path planning and motion planning.

Motion planning under various types of constraints is an extremely broad field in its own right, and we will survey only a few of the key issues. The basic **path planning** or **trajectory planning** problem refers to determining a path in configuration space between an initial configuration of the robot and a final configuration such that the robot does not collide with any obstacles in the environment and that the planned motion is consistent with the kinematic constraints of the vehicle. The initial configuration is known as the **start location** or pose, and the final location or pose is known as the **goal**.

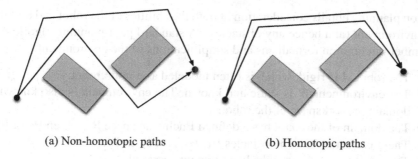

(a) Non-homotopic paths   (b) Homotopic paths

Figure 7.10. Homotopic paths. (a) A set of non-homotopic paths. (b) A set of homotopic paths. In (b) it is possible to smoothly transform one path into the other. This is not true in (a).

More formally, a free path in C-space is a continuous curve exclusively in $\mathcal{C}_{free}$ that connects two configurations q_{start} and q_{goal}. A path is a continuous map,

$$\tau : s \in [0, 1] \rightarrow \mathcal{C}_{free},$$

with $\tau(0) = q_{start}$ and $\tau(1) = q_{goal}$ as the start and goal configurations, respectively. τ is required to be continuous, that is, $\forall s_1, s_2 \in [0, 1]$ $\lim_{s_2 \to s_1} d(\tau(s_1), \tau(s_2)) = 0$, where $d(q_1, q_2)$ is an appropriately chosen distance metric [449]. A free path lies entirely in the free space $\mathcal{C}_{free}$. In contrast, a **semi-free** path lies entirely in the semi-free space, meaning that it is permitted to touch the obstacles. See Figure 7.4. In general, the shortest paths between two points are semi-free.

Two paths with the same endpoints are **homotopic** if one can be continuously deformed into the other, in which case they are said to be in the same **homotopy class**. This is illustrated in Figure 7.10.

This basic path problem can be augmented in several ways:

- It is often of interest to consider the **minimum-length path**.
- It is often of interest to consider paths that are smooth, for some appropriate defintion of smoothness.
- Alternative formulations of a minimum-cost path are also sometimes important. In particular, the **minimum-time path** is not necessarily the same thing as the minimum-length path. A common case in which these two can differ occurs when the maximum vehicle velocity is a function of the curvature of the path, as is the case with many synchronous drive vehicles. As a consequence, a minimum-length path may involve lower vehicle velocities than a longer- but lower-curvature (and hence faster) alternative path.
- Environments with moving obstacles can present significant additional challenges.
- Algorithms that can operate under time constraints are of particular interest, for example anytime algorithms [866] provide some solution whenever they are interrupted and exhibit monotonically improving solution quality with increased computation time.
- It may be of interest to select paths that satisfy other constraints as well as terminate at the goal, for example, to choose "safe" paths or paths that permit the robot to sense certain landmarks in the environment [574].

Motion planning entails consideration of both the abilities of the robot and the structure of the environment (and hence any obstacles). A standard path-planning algorithm relies on a number of common formalisms and simplifications of the environment:

- The robot $\mathcal{A}$ is rigid, which is often modeled as a point robot.
- The environment W is static and known. The environment is also known as the domain or workspace of the robot.
- The domain of the robot has a defined Euclidean space $\mathbb{R}^N$, often $\mathbb{R}^2$ or $\mathbb{R}^3$.
- There is a set of known obstacles $\mathcal{B}_1, \mathcal{B}_2, \ldots, \mathcal{B}_n$ in W.
- The robot travels in straight-line segments perfectly.

The general path-planning problem is to find a path τ that from some initial state q leads the robot to the goal. A significant literature on path planning exists. Algorithms are constructed based on different theoretical assumptions and requirements concerning the following issues:

- **Environment/robot**: the structure of the environment, the robot's capabilities, its shape, and so on.
- **Soundness**: is the planned trajectory guaranteed to be collision free?
- **Completeness**: is the algorithm *guaranteed* to find a path, if one exists?
- **Optimality**: the cost of the actual path obtained versus the optimal path.
- **Space or time complexity**: the storage space or computer time taken to find solution.

In order to render the planning problem tractable, it is often necessary to make a variety of simplifications with respect to the real environment. After an algorithm has been developed based on some set of assumptions, it must actually run in the real world. Idealized algorithms for path planning must be augmented to deal with many annoying realities when applied in the field: moving obstacles, motion constraints, complex definitions of a goal, optimization criteria or side conditions, and, as always, uncertainty.

7.3.1 Constructing a Discrete Search Space

Path planning can be formulated as either a continuous or a discrete task. Discrete representations are more common, although a large number of continuous path-planning algorithms have been developed. Here we consider path planning as a discrete task, while Section 7.3.3 considers the continuous version.

In the discrete case, the basic approach is to take the environmental representation of free space and to construct a graph from this representation. If a robot can move from one cell to another, then these are connected (i.e., all adjacent cells are connected if there are no non-holonomic constraints). Cells that would result in robot-obstacle collision are removed from the representation and the resulting graph is searched. Planning is then reduced to the problem of finding efficient paths through the graph. This approach can potentially result in a large search space, especially if the robot's workspace is discretized at a fine resolution. The process of constructing a graph-based representation of a workspace is illustrated in Figure 7.11.

Visibility Graph Planning The **visibility graph** or **V-graph** is a technique that produces a minimum-length path from the start to the goal by solving a graph traversal

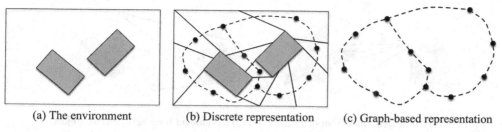

(a) The environment   (b) Discrete representation   (c) Graph-based representation

Figure 7.11. Constructing a graph-based representation. The environment (a) is broken down into connected discrete regions (b), which form the nodes of the graph (c), which represents space.

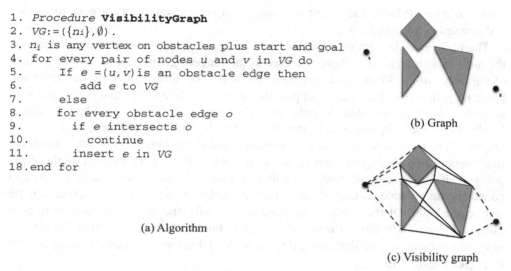

```
1.  Procedure VisibilityGraph
2.  VG:=({ni},∅).
3.  ni is any vertex on obstacles plus start and goal
4.  for every pair of nodes u and v in VG do
5.      If e =(u,v)is an obstacle edge then
6.          add e to VG
7.      else
8.      for every obstacle edge o
9.          if e intersects o
10.             continue
11.         insert e in VG
18.end for
```

(a) Algorithm

(b) Graph

(c) Visibility graph

Figure 7.12. Visibility graph construction. (a) Visibility graph construction algorithm. Vertices in (b) are connected if the straight line joining them does not intersect the obstacle's interior: thus the links of the graph also include the edges of the obstacles in (c). Links between polygon vertices in (c) are drawn as solid lines, while links between the vertices and the start and goal nodes are drawn as dashed lines. Note that only the dashed lines change as different start and goal locations are chosen.

algorithm. The visibility graph $G = (V, E)$ is defined such that the set of vertices is made up of the the union of all of the vertices of the obstacles in the environment, as well as the start and goal points. The edges of the graph connect all vertices that are visible to one another: that is, the straight line connecting them does not intersect any obstacle (see Figure 7.12). Once the construction is complete, a graph has been constructed whose vertices are a subset of the vertices of the obstacle and the start and goal nodes, and the edges connect locations that can be traversed directly without hitting any obstacles. The problem of finding the shortest path from the start to the goal can then be reduced to the problem of finding the shortest path from the start node to the goal node in the resulting graph. This is an example of a **roadmap** approach to path planning [449]. Algorithms for efficiently constructing the set of visibility edges in the plane and searching the resulting graph exist with running time $O(N^2)$. [Note that the simple algorithm for constructing a visibility graph given in Figure 7.12a has running time $O(N^3)$.] This same task in 3-space

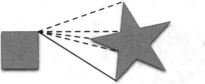 

(a) Co-tangent lines from one vertex   (b) Co-tangent lines between two objects

Figure 7.13. Co-tangent lines.

is known to be NP-hard. The task of searching a graph for a path from one node to another is discussed in Section 7.3.3.

The basic visibility graph algorithm can be improved in a number of ways. Perhaps the most straightforward of these is known as the **tangent graph** algorithm [476]. Many of the nodes in the Visibility Graph algorithm will never form part of the shortest path. Since no path on the final graph can pass through an obstacle vertex that is concave with respect to the obstacle it defines, only convex obstacle vertices ever need be considered. Furthermore, the only edges that actually need to be included are those that are "co-tangent." The process for determining whether a line is "co-tangent" involves examining the potential line joining the two verticies. If the line divides the internal angle of the polygon, it is not a tangent of that polygon. Figure 7.13a shows two polygons and considers the possible co-tangent lines from the vertex of the square and vertices on the star on the right. Of the five possible connections only one edge is co-tangent to both objects. Figure 7.13b shows the set of co-tangent lines that connect the two objects. For any pair of objects it is straightforward to show [476] that there exist only four co-tangent lines (see Figure 7.13).

This more efficient construction of a visibility graph is known as a **tangent graph**. Tangent graph representations are considerably more efficient than the corresponding visibility graph. For two obstacles each with n verticies, the visibility graph can have as many as n^2 edges between them. The tangent graph will have only four.

One unfortunate feature of a path found using a visibility graph or related approach is that unless there is a straight-line path between start and goal, the path passes through object vertices (and arbitrarily close to the edges of obstacles). The fact that the path passes through vertices, but not through the interior of any object, classifies it as a **semi-free path**, as introduced earlier. Further, the technique does not take into account the size of the robot. It makes the assumption that the size of the robot can be ignored. These problems can be overcome in part by dilating all of the obstacles in the environment by the radius of a bounding circle for the robot finding the path (see Figure 7.3). For non-circular robots, however, this method is not **complete**, that is, in some cases it may not find a path even if one exists.

7.3.2   Retraction Methods

Visibility graph and related algorithms determine the set of edges in the roadmap graph as a subset of the straight lines connecting vertices of the polygons that make up the environment. A more general approach is to seek mechanisms that reduce the dimensionality of $\mathcal{C}_{free}$ to a one dimension subset of itself. This one-dimensional subset constitutes a roadmap that is used to get from one place to another, that is, to seek mechanisms that **retract** $\mathcal{C}_{free}$. Formally, a map $\rho : \mathcal{C}_{free} \rightarrow R$, $R \subset \mathcal{C}_{free}$ is a **retraction** iff ρ is continuous and also $\rho(q) = q$ $\forall q \in R$. A retraction ρ is **connectivity preserving** iff $\forall x \in \mathcal{C}_{free}$, both x and $\rho(x)$ belong to the same connected component of $\mathcal{C}_{free}$. There exists a path between $p, q \in \mathcal{C}_{free}$ iff there exists a path in R between $\rho(p)$ and $\rho(q)$.

Once a roadmap has been computed, planning a path from one point q_i to another q_f entails mapping q_i onto the roadmap using the retraction itself, computing a path along the roadmap using graph-search methods, and then getting off the roadmap to q_f. Thus, a roadmap provides a systematic mechanism for reducing planning to a graph search. Of course, there are many possible roadmaps and, especially as the dimensionality of the space increases, computing the roadmap may not be a trivial process.

Voronoi diagrams The **generalized Voronoi diagram** is an example of a retraction method, and as the name implies generalizes the notion of a Voronoi diagram of a set of points that was first defined by the mathematician Lejeune Dirichlet. The generalized Voronoi diagram is the locus of points that are equidistant from the closest two or more obstacle boundaries including the workspace boundary [453]. The set of points in the generalized Voronoi diagram has the useful property of maximizing the clearance between the points and obstacles [449]. More formally, assume that $\mathcal{C}_{free}$ is a polygonal region with an external boundary defined on a Cartesian plane. Let $\mathcal{B}$ be the boundary of $\mathcal{C}_{free}$. Then for $q \in \mathcal{C}_{free}$ define

- $clearance(q) = \min(\|q - p\|, p \in \mathcal{B})$,
- $near(q) = \{p \in \beta, \|q - p\| = clearance(q)\}$.
  $near(q)$ is the set of boundary points of $\mathcal{C}_{free}$ minimizing the distance to q.

The generalized Voronoi diagram is $\{q \in \mathcal{C}_{free}. |near(q)| > 1\}$, that is, the set of points in $\mathcal{C}_{free}$ with at least two nearest neighbors in the boundary of $\mathcal{C}_{free}$. For a closed free space with compact obstacles, the Voronoi diagram is made up of continuous curves. Thus, at any point on the Voronoi diagram the distance to nearby obstacles cannot be increased by any (differential) motion local to the Voronoi diagram contour. When $\mathcal{C} = \mathcal{R}^2$ and obstacles and the workspace boundary are polygons, the generalized Voronoi diagram consists of a finite collection of straight-line segments and parabolic curve segments (arcs). The straight-line edges are formed from the set of points equally distant from two points or two line segments that make up the boundary. The parabolic arcs are formed from the set of points equally distant from one point and one line. This provides the basis for a straightforward (if inefficient) algorithm for constructing the generalized Voronoi diagram for a polygonal environment defined on the plane. Compute all the arcs that can be constructed, given the set of vertices and edges that make up the environment. Compute all possible intersections of these arcs and break the arcs up into segments based on these intersections. Retain all segments that are closest to the vertices/edges from which they were defined. The Voronoi diagram of a finite set of obstacles thus divides the space into **Voronoi cells** with the property that each Voronoi cell can be associated with a single nearest obstacle and all the points in the cell a closer to the associated object than any other.

If a robot were to follow the paths defined by the generalized Voronoi diagram it would not only avoid obstacles, but also it would locally maximize the distances to them. Path planning given the generalized Voronoi diagram is straightforward. Given an identified start and goal position, the robot moves directly away from its nearest obstacle until it moves to a point that lies on the generalized Voronoi diagram. It then follows the segments that make up the diagram until it reaches a position from which it can move directly toward the goal location while maintaining a maximum distance from environmental obstacles [585, 751].

The major problem with this type of planning is the relatively long path lengths associated with the use of the Voronoi diagram. In short, the technique is often too conservative about approaching obstacles to be generally attractive.

7.3.3   Searching a Discrete State space

Searching and search algorithms form fundamental components of many robot path-planning algorithms. Given a **search space**, a set of possible problem states, and a **state transition function** to determine the states directly reachable from any given state, a **search method** is an algorithm to control the exploration of the state space in order to identify a path from some initial state to the goal.

Graph Search   A large literature exists on searching [579], but the simplest graph search algorithm expands nodes in turn from a start node until the goal is reached. The basic algorithm is provided in Listing 7.2. Given a state transition function, a graph G with start node s and set of goal nodes *goal*, the general graph search algorithm depicted in Listing 7.2 determines whether a path exists from s to an element of *goal*. The algorithm operates by maintaining a list of nodes that have been visited ($CLOSED$) and a list of nodes that have been visited but might lead directly or indirectly to the goal ($OPEN$). The algorithm continues until either the goal is found (in which case *found* is true) or the set $OPEN$ becomes empty (in which case *found* is false).

As described, the search algorithm only determines whether a path exists from the start node to one of the nodes in the set of goal nodes. Additional structures must be maintained

```
Procedure GraphSearch(s, goal)
   OPEN := {s}.
   CLOSED := {}.
   found := false.
   while (OPEN != {}) and (not found) do
      Select a node n from OPEN.
      OPEN := OPEN - {n}.
      CLOSED := CLOSED + {n}.
      if n in goal then
         found := true.
      else
         begin
            Let M be the set of all nodes directly accessible from n
            which are not in CLOSED.
            OPEN := OPEN + M.
         end
   end while
```

Listing 7.2. General graph search algorithm. Adapted from [579].

if the actual path that was found from the start to the goal node is to be obtained. This is actually quite straightforward as one can maintain for each node the "parent" from which the current node was visited. The resulting chain of parents is the path to follow.

If no path exists from the start to the goal, then the basic graph search algorithm will eventually evaluate every possible reachable state before returning false. Thus failure can take a considerable length of time to detect. Although effective, simple graph searching – especially without an informed evaluation function – is likely to be too slow for robot path planning in a large, especially high-dimensional, search space.

Figure 7.14 shows a sample discretized search space that will be used to illustrate a number of different search algorithms. In Figure 7.14 locations are identified by labeled circles (S is the start location and G is the goal location). Paths between locations are given by edges. Labels on edges indicate the cost associated with travelling along the edge.

Depth-first search Table 7.1 traces the general graph search algorithm on the sample graph shown in Figure 7.14. In line 6 of the graph search algorithm, a node n is

Table 7.1. *Getting from the start S to the goal G.*

Chosen	Open	Closed
-	S	-
S	A	S
A	B, C, D	S, A
B	E, C, D	S, A, B
E	C, D	S, A, B, E
C	F, D	S, A, B, E, C
F	G, D	S, A, B, E, C, F
G	D	S, A, B, E, C, F, G

In this example the next node chosen was the most recently discovered node. This results in a **depth-first** search.

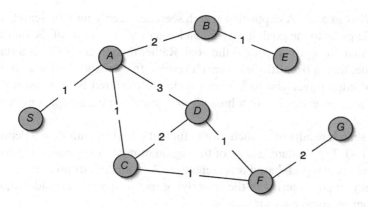

Figure 7.14. A discretized environment. Nodes are identified by labels. S is the start node. G is the goal node. Labels on edges indicate the cost (e.g., distance) associated with the edge.

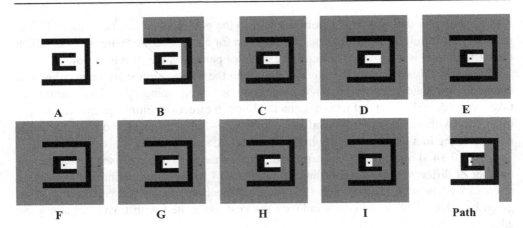

Figure 7.15. Depth-first search. Snapshots of a depth-first search in action. The environment is a 512 × 512 occupancy grid with 8-way connectivity. A–I: The progress of the algorithm as it explores the search space. The start and goal locations are identified by small squares. As cells are visited, they are marked with a light gray.

selected from the set of *OPEN* nodes for further exploration, and in line 16 additional nodes are added to the set of open nodes. Different strategies for representing this set and choosing *n* result in different search algorithms. If *OPEN* is a stack, then a **depth first search** results. The sample execution traced in Table 7.1 follows this approach.

The application of depth first search to a larger sample environment is shown in Figure 7.15. The environment is a 512 × 512 occupancy grid with 8-way connectivity. Free space is white, occupied locations are black. The start location is identified by a small square in the upper right portion of the figure. The goal location is identified by a square in the lower right portion of the figure. As cells are visited, they are marked with a light gray. The final path is a darker gray. Note that the path found uses more than half of the cells visited. Execution time and algorithm performance for a depth-first search on this environment are summarized in Table 7.4. In general, a depth-first search is computationally expensive and can return extremely inefficient paths.

Breadth-first search A depth-first search searches deeply into the search space. If there are multiple paths to the goal, it may find a longer path (in terms of the number of edges in the path) than the optimal path to the goal. Rather than treat *OPEN* as a stack, if *OPEN* is in a queue, then a **breadth-first search** results. In a breadth-first search, nodes closer (in terms of edge traversals) to the start node are explored before nodes farther away. Table 7.2 traces the execution of a breadth-first search on the sample environment shown in Listing 7.2.

A breadth-first search results in a much more efficient (shorter) path than a depth-first search (see Table 7.4). The "square" shape of the region of nodes explored in Figure 7.16 is a result of the occupancy grid–based representation. A "rounder" frontier of the search space results if path length in terms of the underlying metric space is considered, rather than just the number of graph edges traversed.

Dijkstra's algorithm A breadth-first search treats the cost associated with each edge as having the same weight. Generally in robotics we are interested in finding paths

Table 7.2. *Getting from the start S to the goal G.*

Chosen	Open	Closed
-	S	-
S	A	S
A	B, C, D	S, A
B	C, D, E	S, A, B
C	D, E, F	S, A, B, C
D	E, F	S, A, B, C, D
E	F	S, A, B, C, D, E
F	G	S, A, B, C, D, E, F
G	-	S, A, B, C, D, E, F, G

In this example, OPEN is treated as a FIFO queue. This results in a **breadth-first** search.

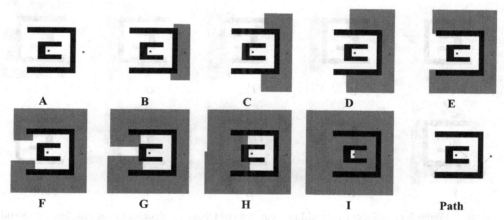

Figure 7.16. Breadth-first search. Snapshots of a breadth-first search in action. See the legend of Figure 7.15 for details.

that are optimal under some measure (e.g., length or energy required to follow the path). If we assume that paths can have only positive costs (negative-cost edges are uncommon in robotic path planning, and the presence of negative- and zero-cost edges complicates the algorithms), then Dijkstra's algorithm maintains the lowest-cost path to each node as the node is identified. *OPEN* is maintained as an ordered list – typically implemented as a heap – ordered on the minimum-cost path to the node. Table 7.3 traces the execution of Dijkstra's algorithm for the sample graph given in Listing 7.2 with edge weights defined by the path length defined in the underlying Cartesian space.

Figure 7.17 traces the execution of Dijkstra's algorithm on a sample occupancy grid. Dijkstra's algorithm will obtain the optimal (shortest) path from the start to the goal by exploring nodes close (based on the distance metric) to the start node first. This results in a "circular" frontier to the search space. Note that the frontier is not perfectly circular due to the discrete nature of the underlying occupancy grid.

Depth- and breadth-first searches and Dijkstra's algorithm are examples of **uninformed** or **blind** search strategies. The algorithms exhaustively enumerate possible paths

Table 7.3. *Dijkstra's algorithm.*

Chosen	Open	Closed
-	S(0)	-
S	A(1)	S
A	C(2), B(3), D(4)	S, A
C	F(3), B(3), D(4)	S, A, C
F	B(3), D(4), G(5)	S, A, C, F
B	E(4), D(4), G(5)	S, A, C, F, B
E	D(4), G(5)	S, A, C, F, B, E
D	G(5)	S, A, C, F, B, E, D
G	-	S, A, B, C, D, E, F, G

The numbers in the open table are the minimum cost path to that node.

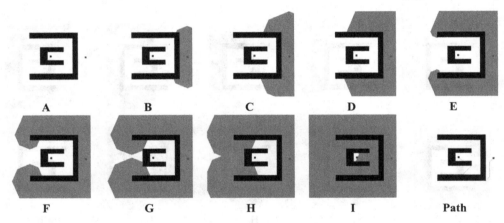

Figure 7.17. Dijkstra's algorithm. Snapshots of Dijkstra's algorithm in action. See the legend of Figure 7.15 for details.

through the search space until either the space is exhausted or the goal is found. By taking advantage of additional domain information, it is possible to inform the search about the estimated cost of the path to the goal.

The general approach to represent this additional domain information is to establish an **evaluation function** $f(n)$ associated with nodes in *OPEN*. By convention, smaller values of $f(n)$ indicate that n is more likely to be on the optimal path. The general search algorithm is then modified at line 6 to choose the node n in *OPEN* with the smallest value of $f(n)$. $f(n)$ is typically expressed as the sum of two components, $g(n)$, the cost of the best path from the start node to the goal that goes through node n, and $h(n)$, the estimated cost of the best path from node n that goes to the goal. So $f(n) = g(n) + h(n)$. $g(n)$ can be computed during the search algorithm by noting that $g(n) = link + g(parent)$, where $link$ is the edge cost and $g(parent)$ is the cost associated with moving from start node to the parent node of node n. For an uninformed or blind search, $h(n) = 0$ for all n.

Best-first search This is perhaps the simplest heuristic that could be used. Choose the node in *OPEN* that is closest to the goal. In an obstacle-free environment, best

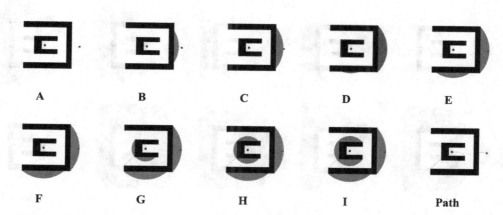

Figure 7.18. Best-first search. Snapshots of best-first search in action. See the legend of Figure 7.15 for details.

first search will perform efficiently. In more complex environments, this search strategy can be quite inefficient. Best first search can be combined with an estimate of the optimal cost to the current node. This is the strategy of the A* algorithm, given below.

Figure 7.18 traces the execution of the best-first algorithm on an occupancy grid. The best-first algorithm seeks nodes "closest" to the goal. For the unoccupied portion of the environment near the start, this drives the graph search process directly toward the goal. When the search process encounters an obstacle, nodes are explored that are closer to the goal before nodes that are farther away. This results in a search that radiates outward away from the goal until a path is found that brings the search process closer to the goal.

A and A* Suppose that $f(n) = g(n) + h(n)$ is the cost function where $g(n)$ is the estimated cost from the start node to node n and $h(n)$ is the cost from node n to the goal node. This is known as algorithm **A** [579]. If $g(n)$ is an upper bound on $g^*(n)$, the minimum-cost path from the start node to n, and if $h(n)$ is a lower bound on $h^*(n)$, the minimum-cost path from node n to the goal node, then algorithm **A** is known as algorithm **A*** [579] and the search algorithm will find the optimal path from the start to the goal.

In mobile robot path planning it may be quite straightforward to meet these requirements on $g(n)$ and $h(n)$. For example, if the edge costs correspond to Cartesian distances, and if the locations of the node (including the goal) are known in the same Cartesian space, then good estimates for both $g(n)$ and $h(n)$ are available, and these estimates meet the requirements for the A* algorithm.

Figure 7.19 shows the operation of the A* algorithm on the occupancy grid environment. The search is informed as to the location of the goal (as is best-first search) while still remaining optimal. (Note that the path length found by A* matches that found by Dijkstra; see Table 7.4.) It is interesting to note that in the sample environment here, A* and Dijkstra's algorithm produce different paths, although they have identical path lengths.

A comparison of search strategies Each of the graph search algorithms is complete in that they are guaranteed to find a path from the start to the goal if such

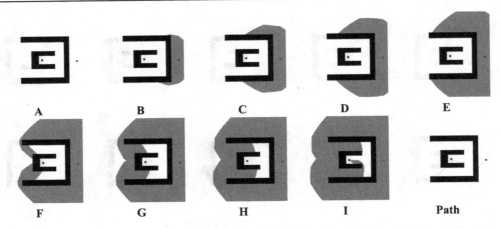

Figure 7.19. A* algorithm. Snapshots of the A* algorithm in action. See the legend of Figure 7.15 for details.

Table 7.4. *The relative performance of five graph search algorithms on the sample occupancy grid environment.*

Algorithm	Nodes explored	Path length
Depth-first	630,981	44,803
Breadth-first	892,741	822
Best-first	111,830	790
Dijkstra	892,884	749
A*	692,629	749

Path length is defined in terms of the underlying Cartesian metric in which nodes are a unit distance apart.

a path exists and report that no path was found otherwise. Table 7.4 summarizes the computational cost and path length found for the five graph search algorithms described for the occupancy grid representation shown in Figures 7.15 to 7.19. The algorithms show a wide range of performance both in terms of computational cost (time taken) and in terms of the length of the path found. It is important to note that the cost of executing a path is likely to be much higher than the cost of thinking about the length of the path. Executing a path of length 790 is likely to take somewhat longer than following a path of length 749, even if it took 7 times longer to compute the shorter path.

A number of extensions to A* have been proposed that optimize the computational cost of the algorithm when it is run repeatedly on the same environment after small environmental changes. These include D* [738] and Focused D* [739]. In practice, A* and algorithms based on A* have found widespread use. A* produces the shortest path and can find some computational efficiencies over uninformed algorithms such as Dijkstra's. Unfortunately, for even moderately large environmental representations – especially those with high degrees of freedom – the computational cost of A* makes it intractable, and heuristics must be used instead.

Dynamic Programming   Dynamic programming is a related general-purpose technique that has been used for path planning. Dynamic programming can be described as a recursive (or iterative) procedure for evaluating the minimum-cost path to any point in the environment from some source. To use this method, the problem of interest must adhere to Bellman's **principle of optimality** [79], which can be stated, in this context, as an assertion that given three points A, B, and C, the optimal path from A to B via C can be computed by determining the optimal path from A to C and that from C to B. In general, the environment must be discretized, and moving from one location to an adjacent location assigned a specific cost that may be spatially varying but must be temporally invariant. The discretized environment is referred to as a **cost table** and indicates the cost associated with moving from the goal to any location represented by a cell in the table. The idea is to incrementally compute the cost of each cell in the table by simply computing an increment to the cost of an adjacent cell for which the cost is already known, if such a cell exists.

The Floyd–Warshall *all-pairs shortest path* algorithm (see [278] for the original work and [183] for a modern introduction) is a recursive dynamic programming approach to finding all of the shortest paths in a graph represented as an adjacency matrix. The Floyd–Warshall algorithm defines the shortest path between nodes in a graph in terms of an intermediate value $D[i, j]^k$, where $D[i, j]^k$ is the length of the shortest path from node i to node j using paths that pass through only vertices numbered from 1 to k as possible intermediate vertices. $D[i, j]^0$ is the minimum cost of the path from node i to node j without passing through any other nodes. For $k > 0$

$$D[i, j]^k = \min\left(D[i, j]^{k-1}, D[i, k]^{k-1} + D[k, j]^{k-1} \right).$$

The Floyd–Warshall algorithm can be implemented in a straightforward manner, resulting in a $O(n^3)$ algorithm that finds the minimum cost between all nodes in the graph (see Listing 7.3). Initially $D[i, j]$ is set to either the cost of the edge (i, j) or infinity if nodes i and j are not connected directly.

Figure 7.21 traces the operation of the Floyd–Warshall algorithm (Listing 7.3) on the simple graph shown in Figure 7.20. Infinite-length paths are given by a dash. All edges in the graph are assumed to have the same length. Initially the table $D[i, j]$ is set to the adjacency graph.

In an attempt to efficiently compute the path to a specific set of goal locations without completing the entire cost table, heuristic functions are often used to preferentially expand specific nodes in the cost table (and avoid completing the entire table).

Searching a continuous state space   Rather than search through a discrete space that represents the set of possible states of the robot, an alternative is to model the configuration space of the robot as a continuous space and to consider path planning as the determination of an appropriate trajectory within this continuum.

```
D[i,j] = w_{i,j}
for k:=1 to n
   for i:= 1 to n
      for j:= 1 to n
         D[i,j] = min(D[i,j], D[i,k]+D[k,j])
```

Listing 7.3. Floyd–Warshall all-pairs shortest path.

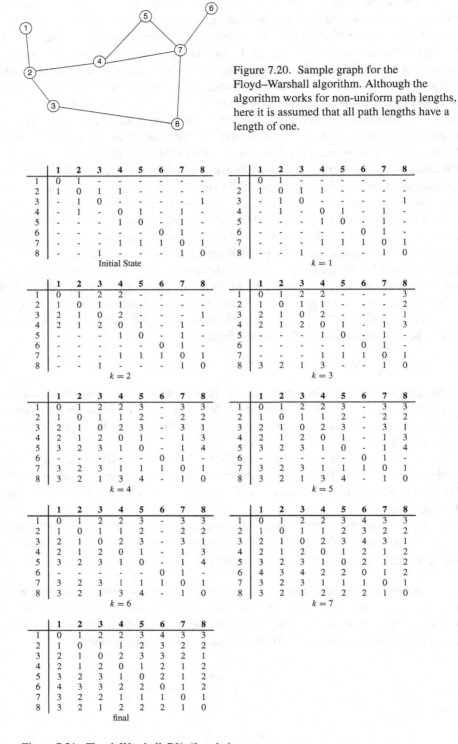

Figure 7.20. Sample graph for the Floyd–Warshall algorithm. Although the algorithm works for non-uniform path lengths, here it is assumed that all path lengths have a length of one.

	1	2	3	4	5	6	7	8
1	0	1	-	-	-	-	-	-
2	1	0	1	1	-	-	-	-
3	-	1	0	-	-	-	-	1
4	-	1	-	0	1	-	1	-
5	-	-	-	1	0	-	1	-
6	-	-	-	-	-	0	1	-
7	-	-	-	1	1	1	0	1
8	-	-	1	-	-	-	1	0

Initial State

	1	2	3	4	5	6	7	8
1	0	1	-	-	-	-	-	-
2	1	0	1	1	-	-	-	-
3	-	1	0	-	-	-	-	1
4	-	1	-	0	1	-	1	-
5	-	-	-	1	0	-	1	-
6	-	-	-	-	-	0	1	-
7	-	-	-	1	1	1	0	1
8	-	-	1	-	-	-	1	0

$k = 1$

	1	2	3	4	5	6	7	8
1	0	1	2	2	-	-	-	-
2	1	0	1	1	-	-	-	-
3	2	1	0	2	-	-	-	1
4	2	1	2	0	1	-	1	-
5	-	-	-	1	0	-	1	-
6	-	-	-	-	-	0	1	-
7	-	-	-	1	1	1	0	1
8	-	-	1	-	-	-	1	0

$k = 2$

	1	2	3	4	5	6	7	8
1	0	1	2	2	-	-	-	3
2	1	0	1	1	-	-	-	2
3	2	1	0	2	-	-	-	1
4	2	1	2	0	1	-	1	3
5	-	-	-	1	0	-	1	-
6	-	-	-	-	-	0	1	-
7	-	-	-	1	1	1	0	1
8	3	2	1	3	-	-	1	0

$k = 3$

	1	2	3	4	5	6	7	8
1	0	1	2	2	3	-	3	3
2	1	0	1	1	2	-	2	2
3	2	1	0	2	3	-	3	1
4	2	1	2	0	1	-	1	3
5	3	2	3	1	0	-	1	4
6	-	-	-	-	-	0	1	-
7	3	2	3	1	1	1	0	1
8	3	2	1	3	4	-	1	0

$k = 4$

	1	2	3	4	5	6	7	8
1	0	1	2	2	3	-	3	3
2	1	0	1	1	2	-	2	2
3	2	1	0	2	3	-	3	1
4	2	1	2	0	1	-	1	3
5	3	2	3	1	0	-	1	4
6	-	-	-	-	-	0	1	-
7	3	2	3	1	1	1	0	1
8	3	2	1	3	4	-	1	0

$k = 5$

	1	2	3	4	5	6	7	8
1	0	1	2	2	3	-	3	3
2	1	0	1	1	2	-	2	2
3	2	1	0	2	3	-	3	1
4	2	1	2	0	1	-	1	3
5	3	2	3	1	0	-	1	4
6	-	-	-	-	-	0	1	-
7	3	2	3	1	1	1	0	1
8	3	2	1	3	4	-	1	0

$k = 6$

	1	2	3	4	5	6	7	8
1	0	1	2	2	3	4	3	3
2	1	0	1	1	2	3	2	2
3	2	1	0	2	3	4	3	1
4	2	1	2	0	1	2	1	2
5	3	2	3	1	0	2	1	2
6	4	3	4	2	2	0	1	2
7	3	2	3	1	1	1	0	1
8	3	2	1	2	2	2	1	0

$k = 7$

	1	2	3	4	5	6	7	8
1	0	1	2	2	3	4	3	3
2	1	0	1	1	2	3	2	2
3	2	1	0	2	3	3	2	1
4	2	1	2	0	1	2	1	2
5	3	2	3	1	0	2	1	2
6	4	3	3	2	2	0	1	2
7	3	2	2	1	1	1	0	1
8	3	2	1	2	2	2	1	0

final

Figure 7.21. Floyd–Warshall $D[i, j]$ updating.

Potential Fields Path planning using artificial potential fields is based on a powerful analogy: the robot is treated as a particle acting under the influence of a potential field U, which is modulated to represent the structure of free space [411]. Obstacles are modeled as carrying electrical charges, and the resulting scalar potential field is used to represent the free space. The robot is modeled as a charged point having the same charge as obstacles in the environment. Collisions between obstacles and the robot are avoided by the repulsive force between them, which is simply the negative gradient of the potential field. Attraction toward the goal is modeled by an additive field, which in the absence of obstacles draws the charged robot toward the goal.

More formally, an artificial differential potential field $U(q)$ is constructed from components associated with the goal $[U_{goal}(q)]$ and any obstacles $[U_{obstacle}(q)]$. In general, these are used to produce attractive and repulsive forces, respectively. The net artificial potential to which the robot is subjected is produced by summing these:

$$U(q) = U_{goal}(q) + \sum U_{obstacles}(q). \tag{7.2}$$

This can then be used to produce an artificial force field:

$$F = -\nabla U(q) = -\begin{pmatrix} \partial U/\partial x \\ \partial U/\partial y \end{pmatrix}.$$

Robot motion can then be executed by taking small steps driven by the local force.

Modeling the environment involves determining field functions for each of the obstacles and for the goal. Typically, as shown in Figure 7.22a, U_{goal} is defined as a parabolic attractor, for example,

$$U_{goal}(q) = \alpha \| q - goal \|^2,$$

where $\| \ \|$ is the Euclidean distance between the state vector q and the goal state $goal$.

The repulsive force of an obstacle is typically modeled as a potential barrier that rises to infinity as the robot approaches the obstacle, such as

$$U_{obstacle} = \beta \| q - obstacle \|^{-2},$$

where $\| \ \|$ is the Euclidean distance between the robot in state vector q and the closest point on the obstacle (see Figure 7.22b). The repulsive force either is computed with respect to the nearest obstacle or summed over all obstacles in the environment. Using only the nearest obstacle can improve computational efficiency, at the expense in principle of possibly less desirable trajectories. In practice, the potential computation is performed only over obstacles in the immediate vicinity of the robot under the assumption that distant obstacles are irrelevant and exert negligible effects (in principle, if the effects of all obstacles are being summed, distant obstacles can exert non-negligible effects, but this may be regarded as a disadvantage).

The robot simply moves downhill in the direction provided by the local field gradient. Path planning based on artificial potential fields has a number of attractive features: spatial paths are not pre-planned and can be generated in real time, planning and control are merged into one function, which simplifies the overall control structure, smooth paths are generated, and planning can be coupled directly to a control algorithm. A key issue for path planning using potential fields is knowing how to deal with local minima that may occur in the field [424, 37, 411]. It is straightforward to construct potential fields that will

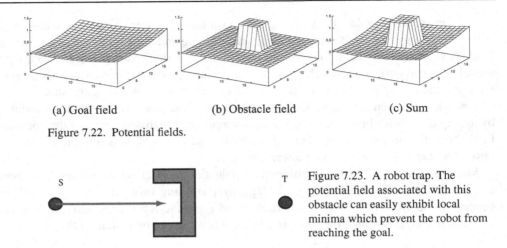

(a) Goal field   (b) Obstacle field   (c) Sum

Figure 7.22. Potential fields.

S   T   Figure 7.23. A robot trap. The
                                                          potential field associated with this
                                                          obstacle can easily exhibit local
                                                          minima which prevent the robot from
                                                          reaching the goal.

trap a robot as it moves down the potential field (see Figure 7.23). Due to this limitation, potential fields are most commonly used directly for local path planning.

It is possible to incorporate the idea of a potential field within a long-range planner in order to avoid these local potential minima, For example, [376] describes a system in which the global planner uses a graph-like representation of the connectivity between minimum potential valleys in the potential field, while the local planner uses a simple potential field system to drive the robot. Another approach is to perform a discretized search with costs associated with each location tied to the potential field. Zelinsky and Yuta [859] constructed a potential field within a discrete grid and then searched through this **distance transform** for a path that reaches the goal.

Rather than deal with the local minima as an initial planning step, an alternative is to use some sort of active search whenever the robot enters a local minimum [449] or to employ heuristics [228] to escape from the local minimum traps. Common approaches include the following:

- Backtracking when a local minimum is encountered, with a specific avoidance procedure when a sufficient "backup" has been accomplished.
- Taking some number of random steps when a local minimum is detected. Randomized plans attempt to overcome local traps or minima by introducing a stochastic step within the planning process. The **randomized path planning** (RPP) algorithm [66, 449] iteratively applies a hill-climbing algorithm to search for the goal. At every local minimum, the planner generates up to K (K is approximately 20) random walks for the local minimum of some length. If one of these random motion paths reaches a better minimum, the robot restarts the search process from this new (local) minimum. If, on the other hand, the random search process does not find a new minimum, one of the states in the random paths is used for a new starting point for the search.
- Invoking a procedural planner, such as a wall follower, when a local minimum is encountered.
- Increasing the potential when the robot visits a region, to cause it to be repelled by previously visited regions.

Each of these methods has its advantages, as well as its shortcomings. In particular, most methods for escaping local minima depend on being able to *detect* that the robot has entered a local minimum. In general, the robot does not land exactly at the minimum (due to noise and errors in both sensing and actuation) but oscillates about it; as such, simply observing the minimum can sometimes be problematic.

One formal way to avoid local minima completely is to use a form of potential field that is ensured to be free of them. Such a minimum-free function is called a **global navigation function**. In general, saddle points cannot be precluded [424, 668], but it is possible to find an **almost global navigation function** that only has a finite number of saddle points, so that small perturbations in the robot's position allow it to escape. In practice, these small saddle points, which constitute a set of measure zero within the free space, can occupy a finite non-zero volume of the free space due to noise and numerical imprecision.

One such global navigation function is based on using a **harmonic potential field** [179, 178] obtained by solving **Laplace's equation**, $\nabla^2 U(x, y) = 0$. This can be visualized as solving a flow problem for either current or fluid moving from the source location to the goal. Since this type of model is conservative – flow cannot be created or destroyed except at the source and sink – no local minima are possible. This can be proven formally using the Gauss integral theorem [188] in the continuous case or Kirchhoff's law in a discrete grid. The primary disadvantage of this type of field is that the computational cost of obtaining a solution is substantial. In low-dimensional discretized environments, such algorithms can be effective, but the computational cost rises quickly as the number of cells in the discretization grows. Additional complications include the desirability of the final solutions obtained and the selection of appropriate boundary conditions for the problem. A final issue relates to quantization: although there may be no local minima, the gradient of the potential field can be arbitrarily small, making trajectory planning difficult or impossible.

Vector Field Histogram Various heuristics based on ideas similar to a potential field have been used for robot control. The virtual field force (VFF) algorithm [103], for example, constructs an occupancy grid on-line and then has obstacles (and the goal) exert forces on the robot. As in potential-field approaches, these forces drive the robot toward the goal while driving it away from obstacles. Unlike a true potential field, however, the VFF algorithm only considers forces from a small local neighborhood around the robot.

There are a number of concerns with the VFF algorithm related to the fact that the algorithm reduces the spatial distribution of forces to a single vector quantity. Detailed information concerning the local distribution of obstacles is lost. The vector field histogram (VFH) algorithm [104] overcomes this concern by constructing a local *polar* representation of obstacle density. The local region around the robot, defined by a circular window of width w, is divided into angular sectors, and obstacles within each sector are combined to obtain a measure of that sector's traversability. A threshold is set, and sectors above the threshold are termed "impassable," while sectors below the threshold are identified as candidate directions for the robot. The candidate region most closely aligned with the robot's preferred direction of motion is chosen as the appropriate direction of travel. The robot and obstacles are defined in a pre-existing occupancy grid C expressed in Cartesian coordinates as (x_r, y_r) and (x_i, y_j). The orientation of the obstacle (and hence the *vector direction*) is given by

$$\beta_{i,j} = \tan^{-1}\left(\frac{y_j - y_r}{x_i - x_r}\right), \tag{7.3}$$

while the *vector magnitude* is given by

$$m_{i,j} = c_{i,j}^2 (a - bd_{i,j}^2), \tag{7.4}$$

where $c_{i,j}$ is the certainty of cell $C_{i,j}$ in the grid, $d_{i,j}$ is the distance of cell $C_{i,j}$ from the robot, and a and b are constants that must satisfy the relation

$$a - b\left(\frac{w-1}{2}\right) = 1. \tag{7.5}$$

Another variation, referred to as the VFH+, was developed for the *GuideCane*, a robot developed to serve as a navigation device for the blind [791]. In this variation, the vectors used are enlarged to account for the width of the robot. The specific motion direction within the preferred region is chosen based on the width of the preferred region. If the region is narrow, then the robot drives down the center of the region. If the region is wide, then the robot moves in a direction closest to the goal direction that stays within the preferred region while avoiding the edges of the region by a specified safety margin.

Bug Algorithms   In many cases, a global map of the environment is not available when the robot must begin moving toward its goal. Potential field-based planning is an example of a local planning method that can be used in such a situation. Unfortunately, local potential field-based path planners cannot be guaranteed to find a path to the goal under all conditions. Under appropriate circumstances, it is possible to devise planning methods that can be used in the presence of uncertainty that provide performance guarantees. One example of such a class of algorithms is the Bug algorithms (see Chapter 2 and [486, 488, 403, 495]). These algorithms can be used for path planning from a starting location to a goal with known coordinates, assuming a holonomic point robot with perfect odometry, an ideal contact sensor, and infinite memory.

In general the Bug algorithms operate by switching between two simple behaviors: (1) moving directly toward the goal location and (2) circumnavigating an obstacle. The basic form of the Bug1 [486] algorithm is described in Listing 7.4 and Figure 7.24. See also Listing 2.2 for the Bug2 algorithm.

The Bug1 algorithm is guaranteed to get to the goal location if it is accessible. Note that this trajectory can be arbitrarily worse than the length of an optimal trajectory. Figure 7.4 illustrates the performance of the algorithm.

The Bug1 algorithm can be expensive. If the cost of the straight-line path from the source to the goal is D and the perimeter of obstacle i is P_i, then the distance d traveled by the robot is bounded by

$$D \le d \le D + \frac{1}{2}\sum_i P_i.$$

The Bug2 algorithm introduced in Chapter 2 augments the Bug1 algorithm through the use of a line, known as the *m*-line, that connects the start and goal locations. Rather than circumnavigate every obstacle that the robot encounters, the Bug2 algorithm departs toward the goal whenever the robot intersects the *m*-line at an appropriate departure point.

```
Visualize a direct path current state to the goal T.
while the goal T is not achieved, do:
   begin
      while the path to the goal is not obstructed, do
         begin
            move in a straight line towards the goal,
            if the path is obstructed then
               begin
                  mark the current location as H (the hit point)
                  circumnavigate the object and record L (the leave point)
                  which is the point on the obstacle closest to T from
                  which the robot can depart directly towards T
                  If no such point exists report failure.
                  Otherwise move to L and head towards T
               end
         end
   end
end
```

Listing 7.4. Bug1 algorithm.

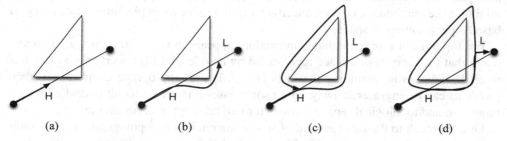

(a)   (b)   (c)   (d)

Figure 7.24. Bug1 algorithm example. The robot moves in a straight line from the start to the goal. When it encounters an obstacle (a), it begins to circumnavigate the obstacle identifying potential leave points (b). Once the entire obstacle has been circumnavigated (c), the robot returns to the leave point (d) and continues to move to the goal.

It is straightforward to develop environments where the Bug1 outperforms Bug2 and vice versa.

One source of the cost associated with the Bug2 algorithm is due to the requirement that the robot return to the m-line after circumnavigating an obstacle. A more efficient strategy is to move toward the target directly as soon as a straight-line path is feasible. An alternative strategy is to move toward a point on the m-line that is closer to the goal than the intersection point with the current obstacles. These two improvements are the basis of the **distbug** and **visbug** algorithms, respectively [488, 403, 404]. This algorithm can be further extended to obtain a space exploration algorithm. Assuming that every object is visible from some other object, a depth-first search using a varient of the Bug algorithm allows the entire space to be searched [485].

7.3.4 Spatial Uncertainty

Many algorithmic approaches to navigation emphasize particular aspects of the overall problem while making simplifying assumptions in other regards. Consider the family of Bug algorithms as an example. Key to these algorithms are the abilities of the robot to know when it has returned to a specific point, to know when it has returned to a line in space, and to accurately follow the boundary of an object. Failure to meet these requirements leads to failure of the path-planning algorithm.

A key problem when transferring idealized path-planning algorithms to a real robot is the issue of spatial uncertainty. The problem of determining whether the current location (x_i, y_i) is the same as some other point (x_k, y_k) is not always easy to answer. Ideally the position of a robot in configuration space would be represented as a **probability density function** (PDF) that would represent the probability that the robot is at each point in space. Unfortunately, it is often not practical to compute such a representation, as it is not always possible to accurately model the evolution of the PDF as the robot moves or sensor measurements are made (exceptions include *Markov localization*, discussed later).

For geometric representations of space, a simplification that is used to approximate spatial uncertainty is to represent the robot by its pose $[x, y, \theta]$, as well as by its **covariance matrix** (see Appendix B). By representing the spatial uncertainty of the robot as a covariance matrix, it is possible to incorporate this information into most path-planning algorithms. For example, [574] uses such an approach to plan paths that minimize the maximum expected uncertainty of the robot when planning a path in a grid-based representation of space.

For topological representations, uncertainty appears in two distinct ways: (1) uncertainty that the robot is in a place represented by a node, and (2) uncertainty as to which node the robot is in, assuming that it is in one. For an appropriate environment, these problems can be engineered away, but in some cases it is very difficult to deal with these problems, and topological representations turn on these types of uncertainty.

One approach to the management of spatial uncertainty in topological representations is the use of **partially observable Markov decision processes** (POMDPs). This technique associates observables with the nodes of a topological representation of space, and represents the robot as a distribution of probabilities over the graph [426]. Robot actions are associated with changes in the robot probability distribution: for example, forward motion increases the probability that the robot is at a more forward node than the one it was previously occupying. As the robot moves and observes its environment, this probability distribution can "coalesce" into a very high probability at a single node (e.g., at a junction of hallways where the sensor data are definitive), or it can diffuse when the robot encounters a region with ambiguous percepts.

7.3.5   Complex Environments

The path-planning algorithms described earlier in this chapter make various simplifications concerning the robot's environment that are unlikely to be met in practice. A number of algorithms have been proposed to extend the applicability of algorithms designed for a constrained environment to more general environments. These extensions include the following.

Dynamic Environments   Rather than require all obstacles to be static, the objects are permitted to move. If the motion of the objects is known *a priori*, then the problem is quite similar to path planning with known static objects. For example, [405] describes an algorithm for this type of generalization for polyhedral objects with known positions and motions.

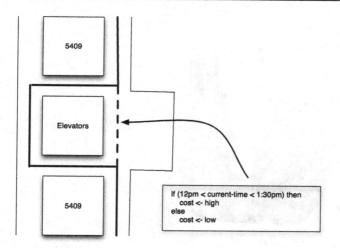

Figure 7.25. A high-level view of a sample learned rule for an indoor path planner; Haigh's system learns actual traversal costs.

One approach to dealing with environmental change, proposed by Haigh, is to use *situation-dependent rules* that determine costs or probabilities of actions as a function of the environment [333, 332]. Changes to the environment are expressed in rules that capture the fact that actions may have different costs under different conditions. For example, a path planner can learn that a particular highway is extremely congested during rush hour traffic, while a task planner can learn that a particular secretary doesn't arrive before 10 a.m. Figure 7.25 shows a sample rule for an indoor route planner; the sample rule avoids the lobby during lunch hour. Once these patterns have been identified from execution traces and then correlated with features of the environment, the planner can then predict and plan for them when similar conditions occur in the future.

Haigh suggested that such rules can be learned using a process that processes execution episodes situated in a particular task context, identifying successes and failures, and then interpreting this feedback into reusable knowledge. The execution agent defines the set of available situation *features* $\mathcal{F}$, while the planner defines a set of relevant learning *events* $\mathcal{E}$, and a *cost function* $\mathcal{C}$ for evaluating those events.

Events are learning opportunities in the environment from which additional knowledge will cause the planner's behavior to change. *Features* discriminate between those events, thereby creating the required additional knowledge. The *cost function* allows the learner to evaluate the event. The learner then creates a mapping from the execution features and the events to the costs:

$$\mathcal{F} \times \mathcal{E} \to \mathcal{C}.$$

For each event $\varepsilon \in \mathcal{E}$ in a given situation described by features $\mathcal{F}$, this learned mapping predicts a cost $c \in \mathcal{C}$ that is based on prior experience. Haigh called this mapping a *situation-dependent rule*. Each planner in the system can then use the learned rules to create plans tailored to the situations it encounters later in its environment. The approach is relevant to planners that would benefit from feedback about plan execution.

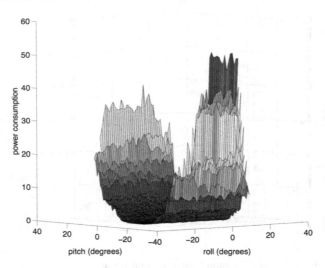

Figure 7.26. Empirically measured terrain traversability cost. Reprinted with the kind permission of A. Chopra.

Outdoor Environments In outdoor environments space may not be traversable omnidirectionally. It may be easier for a robot to go across a grade rather than up or down it. (The same problem occurs to a lesser degree in indoor mobile robotics with ramps.) Vegetation, roads, direction to the sun, time of day, and so on are all things that may constrain terrain traversability. The planner must take such information into account when planning paths. Consider the task of having a ground contact robot move over smooth but undulating terrain. Here the cost of traversing terrain may be a function not only of the length of a path but also of the difficulty of traversing that terrain. In terms of path planning this information can be integrated within the graph representation by encoding a specific path section as the difficulty of traversing a specific edge in a particular direction and replacing the underlying undirected graph with a directed one. This weighting would include cost terms related to surface conditions and the roll and pitch that the vehicle would assume in following a specific path. For example, the "T-transformation" model [846] computes terrain traversability as a weighted combination of terrain roughness and the angle between the surface normal and the gravity vector. It is also possible to construct empirical models for the cost of associating a specific terrain. For example, Figure 7.26 shows the measured power consumption for a particular robot as it traverses surfaces with different slopes [163].

An issue that is particularly conspicuous in outdoor environments is the presence of **negative obstacles**[3] – holes or depressions in the ground that must be avoided, but which are not associated with space-filling obstacles but irregularities in the terrain. Negative obstacles are particularly difficult to detect.

Unknown and Partially Known Environments One limitation of many classical path planners is the requirement that the environment is known in advance. In

---

[3] The term "negative obstacle" is attributed to Bob Bolles in the context of the U.S. unmanned ground vehicle project.

a typical application, the robot thinks, plans its path, and then begins to execute it. If the world model is inaccurate, then at some point during the executing of the plan the robot may encounter an event that makes the plan currently being executed invalid, and the robot must replan. The effort involved in developing the initial plan has been wasted. As it is often the case that the initial plan will not survive contact with the environment, an alternative to expending considerable effort to generate a complete plan initially is to quickly generate an approximate plan and to begin to execute it, refining the plan as the robot moves.

Methods that explicitly deal with the need to replan and can re-evaluate the path as it is being executed are known as **on-line algorithms**, and the trajectory they produce is sometimes referred to as a **conditional plan**. An on-line algorithm is able to generate a preliminary trajectory even in the complete absence of any map. Despite such a handicap, on-line planners can be developed that are complete and can generate efficient paths in certain environments. The Bug algorithm (Section 7.3.3) is an example of a simple on-line algorithm for path planning. For algorithms such as this that may not guarantee an optimal trajectory, the **competitive ratio** compares the difference between their output and the optimal path and is a useful performance measure.

D* (dynamic A*) [738, 740, 723] is an extension of the A* algorithm to enable efficient path replanning as new information becomes available. D* produces an initial plan using A* based on the information known initially. As the plan is executed, discrepancies between the modeled and sensed world update the environmental map and the plan is repaired. D* has been shown to be optimal (the repaired plan is as good as A* would have obtained had all the information been available) and complete. In addition, the process of repairing the plan can be considerably more efficient than replanning from scratch.

Probabilistic Path Planning For complex spaces or complex robots with many degrees of freedom, it may not be practical to search the entire configuration space fully. A number of heuristic techniques have been proposed to search through these high-dimensional spaces without resorting to an exhaustive search. Because these techniques are heuristic in nature we cannot be assured that they will always find a path despite the fact that one exists, but if they do find a path, it will take the robot from some initial configuration to a specified goal configuration.

The **randomized path planner** (RPP) [66, 449] introduced in Section 7.3.3 can be used in these highly complex searches. As the RPP follows the gradient, it can potentially avoid the expensive search required to find the goal. Unfortunately, the RPP encounters a number of problems when applied to highly complex searches with many degrees of freedom. It is difficult to know what length of random walk is sufficient in order to escape from a local minimum. How often should different random searches be conducted before giving up and assuming that the goal is not reachable? Perhaps the biggest difficulty with applying the RPP to complex search spaces is that a stochastic walk is unlikely to lead the planner out of tight regions of the C-space.

A more sophisticated technique for probabilistic path planning known as **probabilistic roadmaps** or **PRMs**, is described in [410]. The basic concept in PRMs is that rather than attempt to sample all of the C-space, one instead samples it probabilistically. This algorithm operates in two phases, a *learning phase*, in which a roadmap is constructed

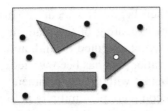 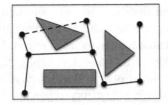 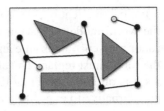

(a) Learning phase (nodes)   (b) Learning phase (edges)   (c) Query phase

Figure 7.27. Probabilistic roadmap. (a) Random configurations are generated and checked to see if they lie in $\mathcal{C}_{free}$. Configurations that are not in $\mathcal{C}_{free}$ (white) are discarded. (b) The roadmap is constructed by trying to link these random configurations. The local planner uses a simple planning strategy and discards potential edges that cannot be easily established (here dashed). During the query phase (c), start and goal locations are connected to the probabilistic roadmap using a local planner.

within the C-space, and a *query phase*, in which probabilistic searches are conducted using the roadmap to speed the search (Figure 7.27).

Learning phase An undirected, acyclic graph is constructed in the robot's C-space in which edges connect nodes if and only if a path can be found between the nodes (which correspond to locations). The graph is grown by randomly choosing new locations in the C-space and attempting to find a path from the new location to one of the nodes already in the graph while maintaining the acyclic nature of the graph. This relies on a local path planner to identify possible paths from the randomly chosen location and one or more of the nodes in the graph. The choice of when to stop building the graph and the design of the local path planner are application specific, although performance guarantees are sometimes possible.

Query phase When a path is required between two configurations, say s and g, paths are first found from s to some node $\bar{s}$ in the roadmap and from g to some node $\bar{g}$ in the roadmap. The roadmap is then used to navigate between $\bar{g}$ and $\bar{s}$. Note that after every query the nodes s and g and the edges connecting them to the graph can then be added to the roadmap. As in the learning phase, the query phase relies on a heuristic path planner to find local paths in the configuration space.

This roadmap approach has a number of advantages over algorithms similar to the RPP algorithm. For example, rather than generate the initial nodes randomly, it is possible to seed difficult areas with many nodes during the learning phase, thus giving the algorithm a better chance to find suitable paths even in challenging environments. The success (or failure) of a PRM in a particular domain is related to (1) how random configurations are generated, and (2) the nature of the local planner that connects configurations together. Expanding the roadmap in "narrow" regions is particularly important, as these are often the regions of configuration space that are of interest [371]. Finding such regions and then sampling them appropriately can be particularly difficult (see [27] and [101] for approaches to the problem).

The essence of a probabilistic roadmap is to generate points in the configuration space either completely at random (i.e., from a random uniform distribution over the free space), or using a distribution with a bias of some kind. Although building long paths in a high-dimensional space may be complicated, it is often relatively easy to build very short paths from a known location. Using this insight, one can often join together some pairs of the randomly generated points, gradually building up a road network within the configuration space. As more points are generated, the road network can become dense and potentially fully connected. In fact, the more interesting classes of systems, one can provide probabilistic bounds on the number of random points needed to generate a path with a known probability of success (although a concrete bound may require knowledge of properties of the free space that may not be available in practice).

Rapidly exploring random trees PRMs are especially suited for answering multiple path-finding queries posed on the same fixed map. In the multiple query case, it can be profitable to do substantial preprocessing of the map to make path planning queries more efficient. In the single query case, we just want one solution as efficiently as possible, and preprocessing is immaterial. The rapidly exploring random tree [437] (RRT) is a randomized algorithm that can be useful generally, but is especially suitable for single-query problems. It makes random choices regarding the path-planning process and thus avoids examining all of configuration space. As a result, it can be very efficient when the problem is well matched to the algorithm, but there is no absolute assurance that a solution will be found.

The essence of the RRT algorithm is to grow a search tree in the configuration space starting from the initial position, and proceeding until it reaches a goal. As the search proceeds, a search tree, in the form of a roadmap, is incrementally constructed. This follows the basic model of breadth-first search and A*, but the difference here is the selection rule that determines how nodes in the search tree are extended.

The tree grows from the starting position via a series of pseudo-random extensions. At each step, a sample point is selected anywhere in space (which is likely to be arbitrarily far from the existing tree). The closest node q_{near} in the existing tree to this sample point is determined, and the tree is extended by a small amount from q_{near} in the direction of the sample point. Once a node q_{last} of the tree is sufficiently close to the goal state, the search is terminated. A path is then easily computed by backtracking from q_{last} to its predecessor and then from each successive point to its predecessor until the root is found.

One of the beautiful attributes of this approach is that since the random point q_{rand} is likely to be far from the existing tree (since the tree is of finite diameter and space is large – infinite in theory). This means the tree almost always expands outward to cover more of free space – the tree is *expansive* and will eventually cover all of tree space.

This algorithm is outlined in Listing 7.5. Notably the RRT algorithm can be implemented in configuration spaces of arbitrary dimensionality, and operates in both Euclidean and non-Euclidean spaces, which is especially practical for planning with robots whose motions include both translation and rotation. Figure 7.28a shows a sample run of RRT. Free space is in white, and points were generated randomly. Figure 7.28b shows the same environment but with RRT biased to grow tree nodes that are nearer the goal.

An important subtlety is the manner in which proximity between points in the configuration space is defined. This determines when and how points can be linked (since this may be non-obvious in some non-Euclidean spaces). Similarly, the geometric path associated with adding edges to the tree once a nearby point has been selected depends on the availability of a suitable local path planner. Finally, once an RRT has been used to

```
BUILDRT(q_init, Nsteps, stepsize)
    initialize T with q_init;
    for k = 1 to Nsteps
        q_rand = random point in C_Free;
        q_near = Nearest vertex in T to q_rand;
        q_new = Compute a step from q_near towards q_rand with stepsize;
        If q_new is not in the semi-free space, continue (go back to find a new random point)
        add-vertex(T, q_new);
        add-edge(T, q_near, q_new);
    Return T
```

Listing 7.5. RRT algorithm. Giving an initial position q_{init}, a bound on execution $Nsteps$, and a step size of a local path planner $stepsize$, this algorithm constructs an RRT in the form of a tree T.

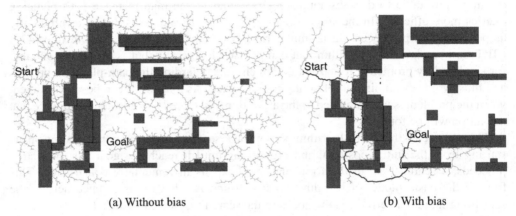

(a) Without bias   (b) With bias

Figure 7.28. RRTs grown (a) without bias and (b) with a special bias that grows points that are more likely to be near the goal. Note that in (a) the tree grows in all directions. In (b) the final path is shown in black.

find a path from the start to a goal position, a path-smoothing operation that depends on the particular vehicle is often used to improve the solution before it is executed. A simple example of such smoothing might be to evaluate every triple of sequential points, and if the ensuing triangle is in C_{free} then the center point of the triple can be eliminated.

RRT tends to produce non-smooth paths, but will eventually find a path if it exists so long as the step size is small enough. That is, the probability of finding a path approaches 1 as time approaches infinity, and the algorithm is thus probabilistically complete. RRT* [407] (referred to as RRT-star) produces simpler paths and, in the limit, is guaranteed to find optimal paths. RRT* operates much like RRT but leverages estimates of path cost when growing the tree and updates these costs as the tree is grown.

7.4   Planning for Multiple Robots

Motion planning for multiple robots involves some specific issues distinct from those relevant to single-robot systems. In particular, the individual robots must avoid collision with one another, and they may have to coordinate their actions either to behave efficiently or to allow them to share information. Approaches to multi-robot planning can be grouped into those that use a single centralized omniscient planner and those that involve distinct independent planning systems, know as decoupled planners [449].

A typical example of centralized planning is the exact cell decomposition method for motion planning of two discs proposed by Schwartz and Sharir [705]. Centralized planning, while conceptually much simpler, cannot be applied to systems where the individual agents are not in complete communication. As a result, decoupled planning is the approach of choice for real multi-robot systems.

Decoupled planners, such as prioritized planners [256], path coordination, or dynamic multiagent planners [134], require no central planner but do require considerable communication initially and often during the execution of the motion. Within the class of decoupled planners, Azarm and Schmidt [52] distinguished between distributed planners based on master–slave relationships [855] and traffic-rule-based dynamic planners [11]. Mutual-exclusion across spatial resources demands static environments similar to centralized planners, whereas sensor-based planners [337] suffer from the same limitations as the uni-robot reactive control methods. Additional details related to planning for multiple robots can be found in Chapter 11.

7.5   Biological Mapping

Mapping and exploration by animals are accomplished in various ways. It is worth noting that there appears to be evidence for techniques that associate actions with specific landmarks, as well as for maintaining full internal maps. Bees, for example, can be intercepted en route to a group of flowers. If they are transported to a different location (deprived of sensory stimulus), when they are released they will head directly for the original target, suggesting they maintain a complete internal map. A desert ant species, *Cataglyphis fortis*, has been shown to combine landmark-based position estimation with dead reckoning to accomplish navigation.

In animals, the brain structure called the **hippocampus** is thought to be critical to the construction of spatial maps. A specific class of **pyramidal cells** known as **place cells** appear to encode localization information. These cells show elevated electrical firing when the subject is in the spatial region to which the cell is tuned. Thus, specific locations are coded by populations of cells that fire preferentially. These cells appear to be sensitive to a variety of sensory stimuli, but they also fire even when the sensory cues are removed (stimulated, presumably, by dead-reckoning information). It has also been suggested that an independent neural system exists specifically for route-based navigation, driving reactions without as complete a metric representation of space.

The term **cognitive mapping** is used to refer to the process that animals use to store and reason about their spatial environment.

7.6   Further Reading

Robot path planning Latombe's classic book [449] provides an effective theoretical survey of robot path planning. Lumelsky's book [487] provides a solid theoretical foundation to path planning for both mobile and manipulator robots. Choset *et al.*'s book [164] provides an in-depth examination of path and motion planning. LaValle's book

[450] considers both basic planning and planning for higher-dimension state spaces. [406] provides an excellent review of sampling-based planning algorithms.

Searching Many classic artificial intelligence texts contain good introductions to searching through graphs and the A* search algorithm (e.g., [579, 836] and their later editions). For planning in the presence of changing environmental costs, the D* algorithm has become a *defacto* standard. See [723] for a recent overview of this algorithm.

Cognitive mapping A large body of work on cognitive mapping and maps can be found in the psychology literature. See [634] for a collection of papers on cognitive mapping and [658] for an introduction to cognitive mapping and a review of neurophysiological structures associated with the task.

7.7   Problems

1. Imagine a 2D robotic workspace (infinite) with a single rectangular obstacle centered at the origin with corners at $(\pm a, \pm b)$ and a circular robot of radius r. What is the configuration space of the robot?
2. Implement a potential field path-planning method and compute a 2D trajectory for a point robot across a rectangular room with several non-convex obstacles in it.
3. Repeat the previous problem using a three-dimensional environment and potential field. How does the computation time vary with respect to the number of obstacles and the dimensionality of the space?
4. Modify your potential field method from problem 1 (or 2) so that the potential field is only computed in the vicinity of the robot. How does the computed trajectory differ? Can this approximation ever lead to results substantially different from that for the field computed over the entire environment? (Justify your answer.)
5. (a) Draw the generalized Voronoi diagram for the environment shown in Figure 7.29. (b) Draw the visibility graph for the same environment. (c) Compare the graphs computed for path planning under these two strategies.
6. Write a program to construct a Voronoi diagram of a closed environment containing obstacles constructed of line wall segments. Use the Voronoi diagram

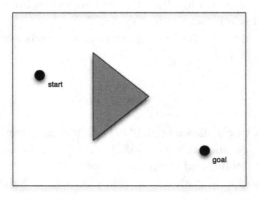

Figure 7.29. Simple enclosed environment.

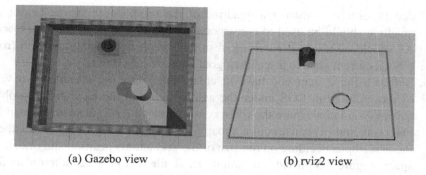

(a) Gazebo view   (b) rviz2 view

Figure 7.30. Gazebo and rviz2 views of the sample world described in problem 13.

to implement a Voronoi-based path planner. How do you plan paths from start and goal locations not located on the Voronoi diagram?

7. Implement the visibility graph-based path planner for an environment composed of polygonal obstacles. How efficient is your determination of vertex-vertex visibility? Modify your code to implement the co-tangent constraint. How much more efficient is the resulting algorithm in terms of the size of the graph produced?

8. Using the simulator for the ideal disk-shaped synchronous robot developed in Chapter 3, implement the Bug1 algorithm.

9. Implement a simple A* planner operating on a graph with weighted edges. Here the weight of the edge corresponds to the expected cost of traversing that edge. Take a uniformly sampled occupancy grid representation of space and convert it into a graph. What is the effect on the paths found if (a) all traversable edge weights are the same, and (b) traversable edge weights to the Cartesian distance between the nodes?

10. Implement a simple PRM that operates in 2D (on the plane). Choose a uniform sampling approach for node selection, and attempt to link nodes using a straight-line planner that only attempts to connect nodes that are a maximum D units apart. What sort of environments are difficult to solve? How did you decide how many nodes to initially seed the space with? How does the nature of the parameters you used affect the algorithm's performance?

11. One simple approach to developing a topological path planning robot is to place ceiling-mounted planar targets at critical locations in the environment. These markers become nodes in the graph, and edges are constructed between nodes when the robot can move between the two nodes in a straight line. Orientation information can be obtained either via some external mechanism (e.g., a compass) or through marking the visible targets in some manner to provide local orientation information. Build a navigation system based on this approach for your environment.

12. Implement a simple motion planner for a point robot operating in the plane. The planner should be based on an approximate cell decomposition approach using a quadtree representation of empty space. Given an appropriate description of objects in the environment and the minimum required granularity of the cell

decomposition, construct a quadtree of the robot's free space. Leaves in the quadtree should be used to construct an adjacency graph of the free space, and A* should be used to search the resulting graph for the shortest path from the robot's current state to a specified goal location.

13. Before using a map you have to create one. Here we consider two versions of the problem in ROS under the assumption that the localization problem is solved (you know where the robot is at all times): (i) constructing a map from a blueprint, and (ii) constructing a map from a `Gazebo` simulation. In either case the first step is deciding on the size of the grid and its position and orientation in space. Figure 7.5 provides a sample `yaml` file that provides a template for this specification. See also the online resource for this chapter.

    (a) Obtain a blueprint for some locally interesting space as a PGM image with a pixel size that corresponds to the occupancy grid resolution. Use an image editor to edit this file so that obstacles (e.g., walls) are black (intensity zero), and free space is white (intensity 255). Places that are unreachable can be given a value of 127.

    (b) Given a `Gazebo` world model, and a robot with known odometry it is straightforward to build a map of this space. The launch file `map-world.launch.py` int the online resource associated with this chapter loads a custom map into Gazebo with an assumed perfect alignment between the odometry and map frame. You can use any teleoperational mechanism (e.g., `teleop_twist_keyboard` to drive the robot around the space, The ROS node `build_map` in the same package will construct a simple map of the robot's environment. (This was the tool that was used to create the sample map in the same package.) Create your own world map using this tool chain. Use an image editor to clean up the resulting world model.

Using a map in ROS involves providing the information to the `map server` infrastructure in the ROS navigation stack, and then accessing it. In the online resource associated with this chapter you can find the sample map definition shown in Figure 7.5. Load this map into the `map server` using

```
ros2 run nav2_map_server map_server --ros-args \
    -p yaml_filename:="globalmap.yaml" \
    -p topic_name:="mymap" -p frame_id:="map" &
ros2 run nav2_util lifecycle_bringup map_server
```

This will load the `globalmap.yaml` into the map server as "mymap." You can access the map server using various service calls and can cause it to publish the map on the
map topic by reloading the map using

```
ros2 service call /map_server/load_map nav2_msgs/srv/LoadMap \
    "{'map_url':'globalmap.yaml'}"
```

Load the given map into the map server and view it in `rviz2`. load your map rather than the one provided in the online resource into `rviz2`. Teleoperate your robot around the `Gazebo` world and observe the laser data mapping exactly with the world map in `rviz2`. Note that this one-to-one correspondence is true only because of an assumption of perfect odometry. This asumption will be relaxed in later chapters.

8

System Control

"Life do you hear me? Give my creation... life"[1]

Dr. Frederick Frankenstein's exortation on the difficulty of ensuring that his creation operates in the manner intended.

Robotic systems, and in particular mobile robotic systems, are the embodiment of a set of complex computational processes, mechanical systems, sensors, user interface, and communications infrastructure. The problems inherent in integrating these components into a working robot can be very challenging. Overall system control requires an approach that can properly handle the complexity of the system goals while dealing with poorly defined tasks and the existence of unplanned and unexpected events. This task is complicated by the non-standard nature of much robotic equipment. Often the hardware seems to have been built following a philosophy of "ease of design" rather that with an eye toward assisting with later system integration. For example, at the hardware level the robot's wheels rotate in encoder counts, sonar sensors return clock ticks to the first returned echo, and the hardware interfaces can be very specialized. Even if the devices provide "standard" interfaces such as through a standard system bus, serial and USB connections, or via some other standard protocol, the actual command stream can be very device specific. These factors impede abstraction, portability, rapid prototyping, modularity, and pedagogy. Software developers must write layers of code to divorce the low-level device interface from higher-level software functions. Because this layer is required for each software device, a large amount of code must often be developed before the first "robotic" application can be run. The complexity of these underlying software and hardware components can have a marked effect on the type of tasks that can be accomplished by the robot, and failures in higher-level software can often result from unidentified bugs or features in this lower layer, and these bugs can be very difficult to detect and excise.

Beyond the constraints of sensors and actuators, robot software architectures must deal with external events, complex and sometimes difficult to quantify mission plans, and real-time computational and hardware requirements. Fundamentally, as observed in [186], designing a good software architecture for autonomous systems is *hard*. Given this, no best approach has emerged, although there exist a number of approaches that have proven effective. ROS may provide a commonly adopted software middleware, but how best

---

[1] *Young Frankenstein*, Mel Brooks, 1974.

to put ROS to the task of actually controlling a robot to perform some complex action remains a difficult task.

Early autonomous robots (e.g., [542]) were more concerned with the process of actually getting the robot to move rather than with considering the limitations of the control architecture on the performance of the vehicle. Take the example of the Stanford Cart, shown in Figure 1.5b, which was capable of performing limited point-to-point navigation in an unknown but static environment: "After rolling a meter it stopped, took some pictures, and thought about them for a long time. Then it planned a new path, executed a little of it, and paused again."[2] The structure of the software that controlled the Standford Cart can be thought of as a sequence of separate computational units or modules, each one of which is processed serially with the output of one action forming the input to the next. A top-level description of the software underlying the motion of the vehicle might be described along the following lines:

1. Take nine images of the environment with a camera mounted on a sliding track. Identify interesting points in one image, and then determine their location in the other eight images in order to obtain depth estimates of the scene.
2. Integrate this information within a global world representation.
3. Correlate the current image set with the previous image set to estimate the robot motion.
4. Based on the desired motion, the estimated robot motion, and the current estimate of the robot's environment, determine the direction in which the robot is to move.
5. Execute the motion.

The result of the execution of these steps was that the robot moved in lurches roughly 1 m every 10 to 15 minutes.

Although the overall system performance seems mediocre by modern standards, the structure of the underlying system architecture is the basis of many mobile robot systems. This **horizontal decomposition** or **functional decomposition** of the robotic task breaks the problem of driving the robot into separate functions or components, each of which must be processed in turn, with the output of one module acting as the input to the next.

8.1   Horizontal Decomposition

Functional or horizontal decomposition is the classical top-down methodology used in the design of many autonomous robot systems. The world is processed and represented using a discrete set of actions, times, and events. Hu and Brady [373] describe the modules that make up the classic horizontal decomposition of a control system as follows:

Perception A module to gather information from the environment.

Model A module to build an environmental model from the robot's perception of its environment.

---

[2] Moravec, 1984, p. 274 [542].

Plan A module to construct a plan of action for the robot.

Execute A module that moves the robot based on the plan.

Motion controller A module to provide low-level control of the robot.

A graphical description of this classic horizontal decomposition of the control system is shown in Figure 8.1.

Within a horizontal control system the individual modules operate in a deterministic fashion. (It is interesting to note that the system cannot operate until all modules have been coded.) Traditional deliberative architecture is based on sensing followed by planning. This is also known as the **sense-plan-act cycle**. Systems that develop internal models upon which to conduct this planner are known as **sense-model-plan-act** or SMPA systems.

The Stanford Cart [539, 540, 541] exemplifies the use of top-down control. More recent and more complex robots also use this top-down control methods. As an example, consider the autonomous land vehicle (ALV) robot Alvin [784]. This early outdoor autonomous vehicle was designed to navigate both on- and off-road, exhibiting goal-directed autonomous behavior such as road following, obstacle avoidance, cross-country navigation, landmark detection, map building and updating, and pose estimation. The overall software structure of Alvin is given in Figure 8.2. The system software consists of five primary modules:

Sensors A module to deal with the sensors mounted on the robot. Alvin relied on a laser sensor plus a CCD camera mounted on a pan-and-tilt unit to sense the ground in front of the robot.

Vision A module that produces a description of the road in front of the vehicle as a scene model given the output of the sensor module.

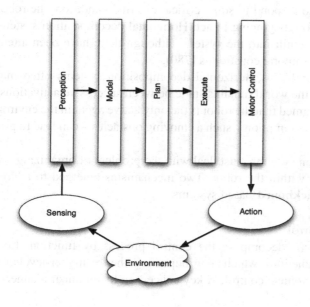

Figure 8.1. Decomposition of robot operational software into modules organized horizontally. Information flows in a linear path through specific modules from input sensors to output mechanisms. After [373].

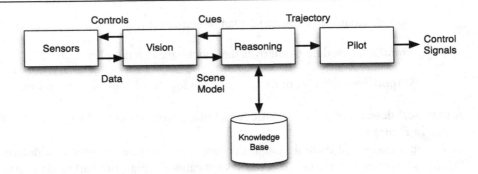

Figure 8.2. The ALV system configuration. Redrawn from [784].

Reasoning The executive controller of the ALV. This module is responsible for overall control of the robot. Given a scene model, the reasoning system builds a reference trajectory to keep the vehicle on the road.

Knowledge base An *a priori* roadmap, including significant environmental features.

Pilot A module that performs the actual driving of the vehicle.

These functional modules form a network with well-defined information flow paths. Information from the sensors provides input to the vision module, which generates scene models for the reasoning module, and so on. As can be seen in Figure 8.2, there is an explicit flow of information from the sensors through vision and reasoning to the pilot and an implicit flow of information from the pilot back to the sensors through the environment and the robot's actions upon it.

The standard criticism of systems based on a horizontal decomposition model is the structure's inability to react rapidly, for example, in case of an emergency. To see this, observe that for the robot to respond to some critical external condition, the robot must sense, model, and plan before beginning to act. Horizontal decomposition systems tend to have a long latency time built into the system, although there have been attempts to address this by specifying temporal constraints [780].

In addition to latency problems, horizontal decomposition systems often make the traditional assumption that the world remains static between successive activations of the perception module. It is assumed that the robot is the only active agent in the environment. Conditions that violate this assumption – such as moving obstacles – can lead to problems for the robot.

Horizontal decomposition systems must deal with the problem of organizing information and its representation within the robot. Two mechanisms emerged to address this issue; **hierarchical** and **blackboard**-based systems.

8.1.1   Hierarchical Control

Hierarchical systems decompose the control process by function. Low-level processes provide simple functions, which are grouped together by higher-level processes in order to provide overall vehicle control. A key concept in hierarchical planners is that the control structure follows a clearly identifiable subdivision in which distinct modules communicate with each other in a predictable and predefined manner. Many early robotic systems relied on exactly this type of software structure, including [39, 615].

The Autonomous Benthis Explorer (ABE) [112, 850] underwater robot provides a typical example of hierarchical control. The ABE utilizes a distributed hierarchical control architecture organized into two broad layers. The lower layers provide low-level control of the robot's sensors and actuators – its attitude and depth sensors as well as thruster control – while the higher-layer levels provide mission planning and operational activity monitoring of the lower levels.

Although the NASA/NBS standard reference model for telerobot control system architecture (**NASREM**) [20] utilizes both hierarchical and blackboard control architecture, the NASREM system is a classic example of a hierarchical control system. NASREM's control system is hierarchically structured into the following multiple layers:

Coordinate transform Transform representations to world coordinate systems and deal with output servoing.

Primitive Compute mechanical dynamics.

E-move Obstacle detection and avoidance.

Task Transformation of tasks to be performed into effector movements.

Services bay Task sequencing and scheduling.

Service mission Resource allocation.

NASREM couples this strict hierarchical control system with a global database or blackboard. Blackboard representations are described in the following section.

Given the nature of hierarchical control systems, they can be relatively simple to design, and their similarity to common software systems enables sophisticated software engineering tools to be used in their design and analysis. Individual components can be designed, developed, and tested in isolation. Hiearchical control systems are found to have relatively long end-to-end latencies, are not particularly robust to unexpected or unmodeled events in the environment, and can be difficult to reconfigure or modify.

8.1.2 Blackboard Systems

Hierarchical-based systems decompose the control task into separate units and tend to minimize the communication between units. Blackboard-based systems rely on a common pool of information (the blackboard), which is shared by the independent computational processes that act on the blackboard (see Figure 8.3). The GSR system [338], an autonomous robotic system designed to navigate from one known geographic location to another over unknown natural terrain, is a typical blackboard-based system. In order to complete its global task, the robot is required to develop a terrain map of the territory. GSR used a blackboard to represent information and to pass information from one software module to another. Fundamental to any blackboard-based system is a

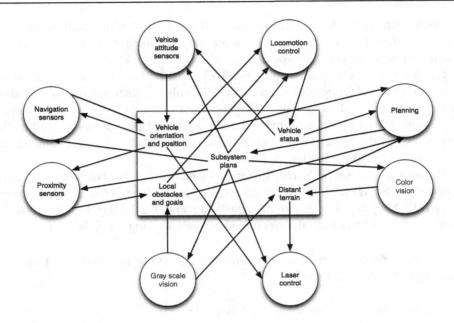

Figure 8.3. Blackboard system for the GSR system. Individual modules (denoted by circles) communicate through a common data store (the blackboard). Maintaining coherent data within the blackboard can be a challenge. After [338].

mechanism to provide efficient communication between the various computational agents and the blackboard.

Blackboard-based systems provide a loose coupling among subsystems permitting the straightforward exchange of information, and they provide a clear and consistent representation of information that can be used by each individual subsystem. GSR implements the blackboard using tightly coupled microprocessors with a local area network connecting them, but software-only implementations exist as well. See, for example, [67] and [441].

Although blackboard systems provide a natural mechanism for providing a common pool of information to a number of parallel computational tasks, the shared database can lead to bottlenecks in terms of processing. In addition, the asynchronous nature of the blackboard system can make software development difficult and can lead to subtle timing errors between the various computational modules. Blackboard systems continue to be used, at least as a component of a larger robotic control architecture (see behavior trees in Section 8.5 and [468]), and there have been efforts to overcome the bottleneck, including [765].

8.2   Vertical Decomposition

Whereas the horizontal or functional decomposition of the control task is based on planning, reactive control [40], situated agents [10], embedded systems [399], motor schema [38], subsumption [129], or reflexive behavior [614] directly couple sensors and actuators (see Figure 8.4). The reactive control paradigm is based on animal models of

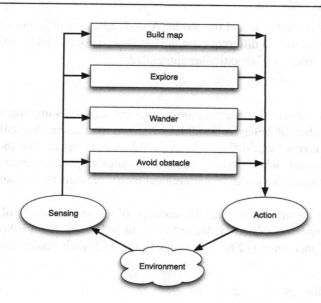

Figure 8.4. Decomposition of robot operational software into vertical structures. After [373].

intelligence – the overall action of the robot is decomposed by behavior, rather than by a deliberative reasoning process. Behavior-based mechanisms were introduced to deal with a number of difficulties encountered in adapting classic planners to deal with low-level robot control. In particular, classic planners encounter difficulties with [131]:

Multiple goals Unlike classic planners, which typically attempt to satisfy some single overall goal, low-level robot control must meet several goals simultaneously. The controller must provide for vehicle safety while executing commanded motion, processing sensor input, and dealing with communication tasks. Each of these tasks has a time-critical nature, and the deterministic, discrete model of processing is not well suited to the task of meeting multiple goals.

Multiple sensors The sensors on a robot have real-time constraints. Data must be retrieved rapidly or they may be overwritten by subsequent measurements. Likewise, the data were acquired at a particular point in space-time and must be identified as such or they will be analyzed inappropriately. Individual sensors may have different time constants; some return results almost instantly, while others may take 0.1 sec or longer to return a a value.

Robustness The low-level system must be relatively insensitive to conflicting, confounding, or missing data from one or more of the robots sensors.

Extensibility The control system should be easily modified to deal with changes in sensor, task, or locomotive configurations.

Common to most reactive systems is the fact that goals are not represented explicitly, but rather they are encoded by the individual behaviors that operate within the controller. Overall system behavior emerges from the interactions that take place among the individual behaviors, sensor readings, and the world. A wide range of different reactive control architectures exist. A critical difference among the various control architectures is how actions generated by competing modules are integrated.

8.2.1   Subsumption

Perhaps the best known of the reactive control architectures, subsumption control systems consist of a number of behavior modules arranged in a hierarchy. Different layers in the architecture take care of different behaviors. Lower layers control the most basic behaviors of the creature while higher behavior modules control more advanced functions. The overall structure is similar to hierarchical motor patterns as they are used in ethology [774].

The subsumption architecture introduced the concept of providing **levels of competence** – "an informal specification of a desired class of behaviors for a robot over all environments it will encounter"[129]. Following [128], [129], the basic levels of competence are:

    0. Avoid contact with objects.
    1. Wander aimlessly around without hitting things.
    2. "Explore" the world.
    3. Build a map of the environment.
    4. Notice changes in the environment.
    5. Reason about the world in terms of identifiable objects.
    6. Formulate and execute plans.
    7. Reason about the behavior of objects and modify plans accordingly.

Each level of competence includes all earlier levels. A subsumption architecture consists of a set of independent behaviors or experts that directly map sensation to action. The behaviors are organized in a static hierarchy.

The underlying concept of the subsumption architecture is illustrated in Figure 8.5. This architecture consists of two basic levels of competence: *wander*, which causes the robot to move randomly in the environment, and *avoid obstacle*, which causes the robot to

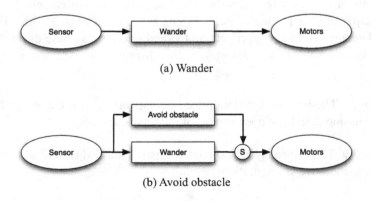

(a) Wander

(b) Avoid obstacle

Figure 8.5. Sample subsumption architecture. (a) The level 0 competence (wander). (b) The architecture with both level 0 competence (wander) and level 1 competence (avoid obstacle) present.

move so as to avoid obstacles. Consider the architecture shown in Figure 8.5a first. Here the architecture is extremely straightforward. The wander behavior might simply generate random motion commands to the vehicle. Now consider the architecture illustrated in Figure 8.5b. In parallel with the wander competence, an avoid obstacle controller operates. Much of the time the avoid obstacle controller produces no output and does not supress the wander controller (through the node marked S in the figure). When active, however, the avoid obstacle suppresses the wander controller and inserts the output of the avoid obstacle controller instead, and the vehicle then operates under the commands of the avoid obstacle controller. Note that the avoid obstacle controller *must* include the competence of the lower level(s) within its own structure.

The final **emergent behavior** of the system is the collection of reactions that emerges from interactions between modules that are provided to achieve each of these levels of competence. The incremental way in which subsumption architectures are constructed makes them fairly straightforward to implement and allows for a great deal of experimentation and flexibility in terms of system design. However, given the stochastic nature in which the conditions that trigger the various individual behaviors are met, the behavior that emerges from a subsumption architecture can be very difficult to judge *a priori* and it can be very difficult to prove performance or timeliness bounds for a given subsumption implementation. Debugging a subsumption architecture can be problematic.

Initial implementations of the subsumption architecture were based on a collection of separate processors, each of which simulates a finite-state machine. Various researchers have since utilized the same concept but have built different implementations using fewer processors and generalizing the computational abilities associated with each behavior (see [315], for example).

Perhaps the most sophisticated pure subsumption-based system is the six-legged walking robot Atilla described in [130]. Here the robot control system is implemented as a series of competency layers, each specifying a behavior for the robot. Elements in the layers are each implemented as augmented finite state machines. The levels of competence in this autonomous system include: stand-up, simple walk, force balancing (used on rough terrain), leg lifting (to climb over small obstacles), whiskers (to sense obstacles), pitch stabilization, prowling, and steered prowling.

One of the fundamental tenants of the subsumption architecture is that "the world is its own best model," and thus it is not necessary to build complex, or in the extreme, any model of the outside world within the subsumption architecture itself. This philosophy leads to an implementation design in which individual behaviors within the architecture can be implemented using simple computational models such as finite state machines. A number of systems that utilize subsumption-like architectures have relaxed this philosophy and have developed behaviors that construct or utilize models developed from sensor data (see Section 8.2.4).

8.2.2 Motor Schema

Motor schema ([38], but see also [41]) are individual motor behaviors, each of which reacts to sensory information obtained from the environment. The output of each schema is a velocity vector that represents the direction and speed at which the robot is to move for that schema, given the current sensed view of the environment (see Figure 8.6). Examples of individual motor schema include [36]:

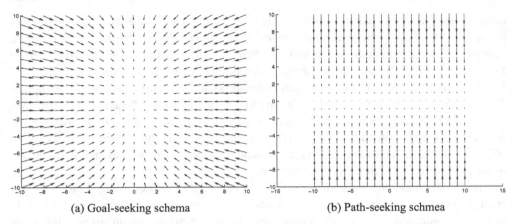

(a) Goal-seeking schema   (b) Path-seeking schmea

Figure 8.6. Two simple motor schema. (a) A goal-seeking schema in which at every point in the space the motor schema directs the robot toward the goal. (b) A path-seeking schema in which at every point in the space the robot is directed back toward the path (here $y = 0$).

Move-ahead Move in a general compass direction.

Move-to-goal Move toward a discernible goal.

Avoid-static-obstacle Move away from a detected barrier.

Stay-on-path Move toward the center of a path.

Individual schema are often displayed as needle diagrams as in Figure 8.6, but in reality the entire function is not computed. Rather, the output is the normalized vector sum of the active motor schema corresponding to the robot's pose. Note that each "schema" is relatively straightforward to compute.

At any point in time a given set of schema is active, and the outputs of the members of the active set of motor schema are combined as a normalized vector sum. This should be contrasted with the "winner take all" approach of the subsumption architecture described in Section 8.2.1.

8.2.3 Continuous Control

Much of the work on reactive control of a mobile robot is based on a discrete controller. An alternative approach is to consider the low-level control as the development of a control system (in the classic sense) that transduces continuous inputs to some continuous outputs. An obvious advantage of this type of approach is that there exists a very large literature on control theory, and this body of work can be brought to bear on the problem. [796] describes a system for wall following based on the construction of an analog controller. Essentially the controller produces values for the forward speed v and rate of turn ω based on a measured distance from the wall and a desired position along the wall.

8.2.4 Behavior-Based Systems

Behavior-based controllers (see [507], [510], and [511]) generalize the reactive approach by positing a collection of parallel behaviors that transduce sensation to action.

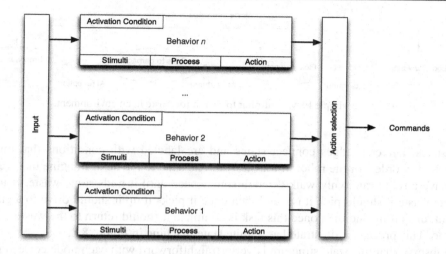

Figure 8.7. General structure of a behavior-based system. Input is acted on by a number of behaviors that operate in parallel. Each behavior may produce an output. These output signals are combined to produce a specific action for the vehicle. Redrawn from [511].

Unlike subsumption-based approaches, the behavior-based approach allows individual behaviors to maintain internal state information and posits a general "action selection" process to combine the actions commanded by individual behaviors. The basic structure of a behavior-based system is described in Figure 8.7.

Behavior-based systems provide a general framework within which other reactive control architectures can be described. Each individual behavior can be extremely complex, as can the process of combining the individual behavior outputs into a command. In practice, most behavior-based systems restrict the structure of individual behaviors and the structure of the action selection process.

8.3   Integrating Reactive Behaviors

If a system can be built to provide control for a limited task, then one obvious extension is to build different systems for different portions of the robot's mission and to swap between the different systems as required. This allows different architectures to be applied to different tasks, as needed, but introduces the problem of an appropriate architecture to connect the low-level controllers. In the context of reactive systems, various mechanisms have been proposed to allow the specification of which set of behaviors should be operational and for how long. In the more general context of control architectures, **finite state machines** (FSMs) and **behavior trees** have emerged as effective architectures. These approaches are described below.

8.4   Finite State Machine

Finite state machine controllers are a populate control architecture for autonomous machines. The status of the robot is that it is in one of a finite number

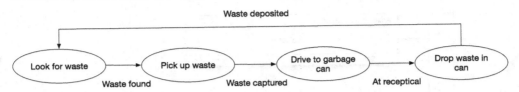

Figure 8.8. A simple FSM controller to search for waste in an environment.

of states. Directed edges connect states and are labeled with conditions that must be satisfied in order for the robot to transit from one state to the next. Imagine that we want to have a robot randomly walk through some space until it finds some waste. If it finds some waste it should pick it up, and then once it picks it up it should drive to a garbage point, drop it in, and then once this task is complete it should return to the waste-seeking mode. This process is illustrated as a finite state machine in Figure 8.8.

Observe that this state structure is very straightforward with each node corresponding to some state of the robot. The robot remains in that state until some property becomes true, at which point the agent transits to the next state. Nodes can have more than one edge leaving from it. It is also possible to develop hierarchical versions of the structure in which a given node can itself be described in terms of either an atomic operation or as a finite state machine. Given the simplicity of the design approach, and the relative ease of structuring simple tasks in this manner, FSM architectures have been developed for ROS 1 (e.g., SMACH[390]) and also for ROS 2 (e.g., YASMIN [316]).

8.5   Behavior Trees

Although FSM can be effective, their simplicity can make it difficult to describe complex behavior structures using them. **Behavior trees** are a more general representative structure that first came to prominence in their use in video games to describe the actions of non-player characters. A behavior tree is a directed tree. The tree maintains and manages the flow of execution of a collection of tasks managed by the tree.

The execution of a behavior tree starts from the root. A signal – known as a **tick** – is sent to the root node. This signal propagates through the tree from parent to child until it reaches a leaf node. Any node that receives a tick signal evaluates its current state and returns one of **SUCCESS, FAILURE,** or **RUNNING**. The definition of SUCCESS and FAILURE are straightforward. The return value RUNNING signals that the node requires more time to return a valid result. Each node in the tree maintains persistent internal state information and a blackboard is used to provide persistent data across different nodes in the tree. Different implementations of behavior trees enjoy slightly different notations and terminology. Here we follow the common notation described in [177]. See Figure 8.9.

A node in the Behavior tree is either:

- A leaf node. Leaf nodes are either an **Action Node**, which interacts with an external process, or they are a **Condition Node**, which reports some condition of the outside word.
- A node with children. There are two basic types, a **Decorator Node**, which manipulates the outcome of its child, or **Control Node**, which ticks its children

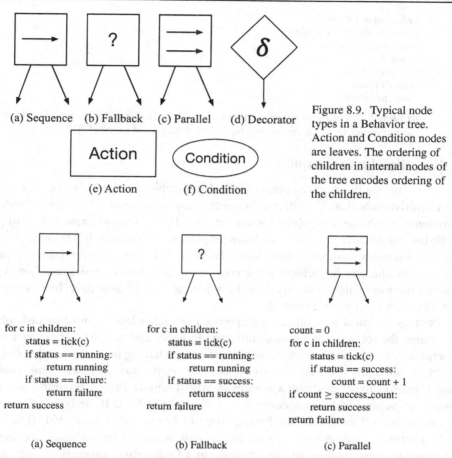

Figure 8.9. Typical node types in a Behavior tree. Action and Condition nodes are leaves. The ordering of children in internal nodes of the tree encodes ordering of the children.

(a) Sequence (b) Fallback (c) Parallel (d) Decorator

(e) Action (f) Condition

```
for c in children:              for c in children:              count = 0
    status = tick(c)                status = tick(c)            for c in children:
    if status == running:           if status == running:           status = tick(c)
        return running                  return running              if status == success:
    if status == failure:           if status == success:               count = count + 1
        return failure                  return success          if count ≥ success_count:
return success                  return failure                      return success
                                                                return failure
```

(a) Sequence   (b) Fallback   (c) Parallel

Listing 8.1. Pseudocode for Sequence, Fallback, and Parallel Behavior tree nodes. Sequence nodes tick all of their children in turn, returning failure as soon as one child returns failure. If all children return success, then return success. Fallback nodes tick all of their children in order, returning success as soon as one node returns success, and failure if no child returns success. Parallel nodes run all of their children sequentially, returning success if the number of children returning success meets a pre-defined criteria.

in some manner. There are a number of standard Control Nodes and in most behavior tree representations it is possible to construct custom Control Nodes as well.

The semantics of the Sequence, Fallback, and Parallel nodes in a behavior tree are given in Listing 8.1.

Associated with the behavior tree is a common shared data store known as a blackboard, which is similar to the blackboard structure described earlier in Section 8.1.2. This provides a mechanism for information to persist through multiple ticks and for various nodes in the behavior tree to communicate with each other. Behavior trees can become quite complex as a consequence of the potential asynchronous nature of the return of RUNNING by a child.

```
findorder(Original,Result):-
    permutation(Original,Result),
    sortbypath(Result).
sortbypath([]).
sortbypath([P1|Prest]):-
    path(P1,Prest),
    sortbypath(Prest).
```

> Listing 8.2. Findorder program. Here Original is the set of pallets to be collected. Results is the sequence in which they should be collected. Reprinted from [617].

8.6   High-Level Control

The study of developing robots that exhibit cognitive capabilities is known as **cognitive robotics**. Cognitive roboticists commonly assume that many fundamental problems in robotics are solved (or can be solved), and instead explore how to provide high-level abilities (e.g., reasoning, knowledge representation). It has been clear since the earliest autonomous robot systems were designed that a procedural representation is not an ideal mechanism for achieving the complex missions that are desired. Consequently, alternative mechanisms, mostly based on logical formalisms, have been proposed to provide high-level robotic control.

Perhaps the most straightforward approach to higher-level control or **task planning** is to treat the robot as an abstract entity and to apply classical AI techniques to specify complex tasks. As an example, consider the task of having an autonomous robot collect a set of obstacles (pallets) in an environment on its way to reach some goal. Peng and Cameron [617] describe a system in which simple Prolog programs are used to derive sequences of robot motions that collect the pallets. If Original is a set of pallets to be collected, then the Prolog program findorder (from [617]) (see Figure 8.2) determines the sequence in which the pallets should be collected and hence the appropriate robot motions to collect them. In findorder, permutation(x,y) is true if x is a permutation of y, and path(a,b) is true if the robot can move from a to the goal, given that the pallets in b have not yet been collected. Execution of the Prolog program will determine a sequence of robot motions that will cause the robot to collect the pallets. Note that path requires a considerable amount of knowledge concerning the robot's environment and its abilities.

This particular high-level control system is made simpler due to the limited world representation. From the task planner's point of view, the world can be described by exactly which set of pallets has not yet been collected and the robot's current position. More complex tasks require more complex representations. Marco *et al.* [501] describe the use of Prolog for the **strategic control** of autonomous underwater vehicles. In this aquatic system, Prolog is used to provide a high-level language within which overall mission control can be defined. In [501] a mission is defined in terms of a sequence of phases (see Figure 8.3). Essentially, the mission is complete or done if the current_phase can be established as being either mission_abort or mission_ccomplete. A mission is commanded by execute_mission, which attempts to establish each of the mission phases in turn, starting with phase 1. The Prolog language is extended by a set of predicates [such as odd()] that, when evaluated, cause an external action as a side effect and return the success or failure of that side effect as their value. Here odd('start_networks',X) performs low-level initialization of the robot.

```
done :- current_phase(mission_abort).
done :- current_phase(mission_complete).
execute_mission :-
    initialize_mission,
    repeat,
    execute_phase,
    done.
```

```
initialize_mission :-
    ood('start networks',X),
    asserta(current_phase(1)),
    asserta(complete(0)),
    asserta(abort(0)).
execute_phase :-
    current_phase(X),
    execute_phase(X),
    next_phase(X),
    !
```

Listing 8.3. Strategic control in Prolog. From [501].

This type of high-level control provides a well-established mechanism within which a number of different low-level experts or modules can be assembled in order to accomplish complex, long-term tasks. The order of assembly of these tasks can be a simple permutation of a set of tasks (as in the pallet collection system of [617]) or a predefined sequence of tasks (as in the autonomous aquatic system of [501]). Much more complex sequences of simple tasks can certainly be assembled, and languages such as `prolog` provide considerable support for searching through assemblies of simple tasks in order to achieve high-level goals.

There exist a number of efforts to integrate formal high-level robot control planners with ROS. For example [420] integrates planning in golog++ with ROS, while [143] describes a framework that integrates probabilistic high-level robot control planners with ROS.

As the search task becomes more complex, a fundamental problem that must be dealt with is the frame problem. The **frame problem** is the task of representing the changes and the invariants in the state of the world when operators are applied. There are many potential approaches to dealing with the frame problem. One approach is to provide a set of logical axioms known as **frame axioms** that express these invariants. Unfortunately, a large number of frame axioms may be required for even trivial domains. One simple mechanism for addressing the frame problem is to make the assumption that nothing changes that is not explicitly described by an operator. This is the approach taken by the STRIPS system.

8.6.1 STRIPS

STRIPS [271] is historically significant and represents the world by a set of logical formulas. In STRIPS, procedures or actions are represented by operators. These operators consist of a precondition, an **add list**, and a **delete list**. Given a description of a world state s, a STRIPS action includes a precondition – the condition that must be true in order for the rule to be performed, hence the following rule from [836], which deals with picking up blocks:

$$\text{PICKUP}(x)$$
$$\text{precondition}: \quad \text{EMPTYHAND} \wedge \text{Clear}(x) \wedge \text{On}(x, y)$$
$$\text{delete}: \quad \text{EMPTYHAND}, \text{Clear}(x), \text{On}(x, y)$$
$$\text{add}: \quad \text{INHAND}(x)$$

PICKUP can only be used if EMPTYHAND is true and if for some x and y, the predicates Clear(x) and On(x,y) hold. The action of the rule PICKUP(x) is to remove from the database of logical formulas EMPTYHAND, Clear(x), and On(x,y) and to add to the set of logical formulas INHAND(x).

8.6.2   Situation Calculus

A small amount of experimentation with systems such as STRIPS or the generation of complex plans using Prolog illustrates a requirement to be able to reason about time, actions, and plans. The **situation calculus** [518] is a formal calculus of situations that has been used to address this. The situation calculus is a first-order language for representing dynamically changing worlds in which all of the changes are the result of named *actions* performed by some agent. Following [836], to express in the situation calculus that B is on A and that A is on a "Table" in some state s, one could write

$$\text{On}(B, A, s) \wedge \text{On}(A, \text{Table}, s).$$

Operations in the situation calculus can be thought of as functions that generate new situations. For example, to put x on Table, we can define a function "Putontable," which may have to do something very complicated in the real world, but in terms of the logic,

$$\forall s \forall x [\neg\text{On}(x, \text{Table}, s) \Rightarrow \text{On}(x, \text{Table}, \text{Putontable}(x, s))].$$

Note what Putontable does; it returns a state in which On(x, Table, Putontable(x,s)) is true. Given a description of the environment, a sufficient description of the effects of actions, and the set of valid operations within that environment, proofs can be constructed that determine whether certain environmental configurations are possible. These logical proofs require a certain set of actions to be performed in a particular sequence (Putontable actions in the example). If performing a Putontable action agrees with the logical definition of the Putontable situation function, then the sequence of Putontable evaluations within the proof corresponds to the set of actions that must be taken in the real world in order to effect the desired result.

8.6.3   GRAMMPS

The GRAMMPS (generalized robotic autonomous mobile mission planning system) is a mission planning and execution module [132, 133] that provides high-level control of one or more mobile robots. The GRAMMPS system can be thought of as a mission planner that distributes one or more strategic goals to one or more robots. Each individual system goal is represented by a software module that continually plans actions that will cause the individual goal to be achieved. GRAMMPS takes the results of these plans and allocates goals to individual robots so as to optimize overall system performance.

8.6.4   Other High-Level Control Approaches

One concern with high-level controllers based on planning is that planning can be extremely hard and this can lead to extremely inefficient controllers (the controller takes too long to determine a plan) or simplistic plans (the controller is simplified in order to permit efficient plan generation). An alternative to this dilemma is to specify high-level plans within a representation that provides directed search for an appropriate execution of the controller without resorting to general planning. Golog [460] and ConGolog [311] are high-level languages in which the programmer defines effects of primitive actions and preconditions in a logical formalism. An interpreter then searches through representations in this formalism to find a program that meets the required solution and then executes this program in the real world.

The Golog [461] system uses the situation calculus to define complex actions for general systems and for mobile robots in particular. Golog programs are defined in an imperative programming language that uses common language control structures. In Golog, if α is an action and s a situation, the result of performing α in s is represented by $do\,(\alpha, s)$. The actions in a given domain can be specified by providing (1) **precondition axioms** that state the conditions under which the action can be performed, and (2) **effects axioms** that specify how the action affects the world's state. Golog has been used to provide control for a number of robots including an RWI 21 and Nomad 200 for delivery tasks [754].

A central component of Golog and ConGolog is the inclusion of nondeterministic language constructs. This allows the search process to consider different alternatives when seeking a solution. Congolog extends Golog through the addition of primitives that support concurrency. Golog provides the following programming constructs:

a	primitive aciton
$\phi?$	wait for a condition
$(\delta_1; \delta_2)$	sequence
$(\delta_1|\delta_2)$	non-deterministic choice between actions
$\phi v.\delta$	non-deterministic choice of arguments
$\delta*$	non-deterministic iteration
$\{\mathbf{proc}\ P_1(v_1)\delta_1\ \mathbf{end};\ ...\mathbf{proc}\ P_n(v_n)\delta_n\ \mathbf{end}; \delta\}$	procedures

Here a is a situation calculus action, and ϕ stands for a situation calculus formula. Execution of a ConGolog program finds a sequence of actions such that when a program starts in a given situation it has a legal terminating situation. Note that as Golog and ConGolog are non-deterministic, repeated execution of the same program may result in different plans that meet the same goal situation.

8.7 Alternative Control Formalisms

Although many robot control systems are written using traditional models of computation, there is a large research literature on the use of alternative computational models and their application to autonomous vehicle control.

8.7.1 Artificial Neural Networks

Neural networks (see Chapter 6) have found wide applicaiton in autonomous systems both as an end-to-end control architecture as well as a solution architecture to specific computational problems. Perhaps the earliest application of neural nets to robotics is the **ALVINN** system (and related offshoots) which was used to control the motion of the Carnegie Mellon University autonomous land vehicle (ALV) driving along roads and

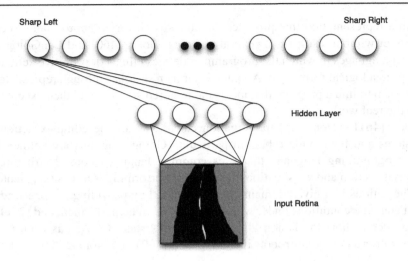

Figure 8.10. ALVINN network architecture. Redrawn from [631].

highways. The neural net used for ALVINN [631] is composed of an input "video retina" of 30×32 pixels, a middle layer of four hidden units, and an output layer of 30 steering direction units indicating the direction in which the vehicle is to steer. Activations are passed forward through the units, and the output unit with the highest activation level determines the steering direction.

The output layer of ALVINN is an example to an output encoding using **radial basis functions**. In such an output encoding, the output units represent discrete sample locations in a continuous (potentially high-dimensional) vector space of interest. Each unit encodes a probability that the specific value it represents is correct (these are sometimes portrayed as probabilities of being correct).

ALVINN successfully drove the ALV under various environmental conditions and was trained to run on various types of roads – one-lane, two-lane, and so on. In order to apply ALVINN to multiple road types, a number of different approaches were considered. One approach trained different ALVINN networks on different road types, and then during the run phase each of the networks was executed in parallel and the winning network drove the vehicle. The arbitration between the various networks was controlled either via a rule-based arbitration scheme or through another neural network, leading to the development of the **MANIAC** system [394].

8.7.2 Fuzzy Logic

Fuzzy logic is a multi-valued logic derived from fuzzy set theory [856]. Fuzzy sets (and fuzzy logic) find application in robot control in that they provide a formalism within which logical variables can take on continuous values. This makes the formalism appropriate for robotic control tasks where it is desirable to represent vehicle or sensor states that can take on a range of values and where it can be desirable to model complex state distributions.

A fuzzy subset A of a set S is a collection of ordered pairs

$$A = \{(x, \mu_A(x))\},$$

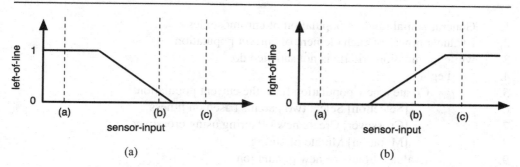

Figure 8.11. Fuzzy set membership function. Two membership functions are shown. (a) `left-of-line` has value 1 at (a) and value 0 at (c). (b) `right-of-line` has value 0 at (a), and value 1 at (c). At (b) both `left-of-line` and `right-of-line` are non-zero.

where there is exactly one ordered pair present for each x. Here x belongs to the set S, and $\mu_A(x)$ represents x's grade of membership in A. $\mu_A(x) \in [0,1]$, and $\mu_A(x)$ provides a measure of the degree of membership of x in the fuzzy set A. To take a specific example, consider the membership functions for the sensor input given in Figure 8.11. Based on a sensor input, the robot determines whether it is left or right of a line. Certain values of the sensor correspond to the robot being left of the line [e.g. the value at (a)], and other values correspond to the robot being right of the line [e.g. the value at (c)].

It is common in fuzzy logic systems to talk about **linguistic variables**. A linguistic variable is a variable whose value is not a number but rather is a word or a sentence in some natural language. For Figure 8.11, the sensor input might be characterized as being `left-of-line` or `right-of-line` based on the sensor input. Note that `left-of-line` and `right-of-line` are fuzzy values.

Just as operations can be defined on Boolean values (or **crisp sets**), operators are defined for fuzzy sets. For example, for fuzzy sets A and B

$$A \cup B = \max(\mu_A(x), \mu_B(x))$$
$$A \cap B = \min(\mu_A(x), \mu_B(x))$$
$$A' = 1 - \mu_A(x).$$

Fuzzy representations can provide a useful representation within which to develop control systems. For example, if the robot is following the line it should move straight ahead. This can be expressed in fuzzy logic as a set of fuzzy rules, for example, IF sensor-input IS left-of-Line THEN turn-right, and IF sensor-input IS right-of-Line THEN turn-left. Note that both rules can be applied as they are fuzzy and the sensor input can correspond to both `left-of-Line` and `right-of-Line` at the same time.

The output of a fuzzy logic system must be converted into a quantifiable result. This process is known as **defuzzification** and involves taking a membership described as a fuzzy set and converting it to a quantifiable number. A wide range of different defuzzification methods exists, including choosing the center of gravity of the fuzzy set [454].

1.   Generate intial random population of chromosomes
2.   Evaluate fitness of each element of current population
3.   while termination criteria is not satisfied do
4.   begin
5.   Create a new population from the current population
6.   [Selection] Select two parents based on fitness
7.   [Crossover] Create new offspring using crossover
8.   [Mutation] Mutate offspring
9.   Evaluate fitness of new population
10   end

Listing 8.4. Basic genetic algorithm. A collection of samples (known as chromosomes) are maintained. At each generation, children are constructed based on mating pairs of parents from the current population.

8.7.3 Genetic Algorithms

A **genetic algorithm** (GA) (see Figure 8.4) is an evolutionary heuristic search technique. GAs utilize techniques inspired by evolutionary biology to search through complex state spaces. Genetic algorithm techniques have been applied to a range of problems in autonomous robotics. For example, [78] used a genetic algorithm to generate gaits for a six-legged robot called Rodney. Each of the robot's legs was controlled by a simple neural net, and the nets for each of the legs were linked. The weights of the neural nets were learned using a staged evolution approach. Initially, a genetic algorithm was used to obtain a stable oscillation motion of individual legs. In a second stage the sequence of leg motions was evolved that produced the maximum amount of forward movement along the body axis in unit time. The result of this learning process was that Rodney learned the tripod gait.

Genetic algorithms solve complex non-linear tasks by positing a collection of solutions to the problem (known as **individuals**) and then iteratively refining this collection of individuals (each refinement is known as a **generation**). The refinement process is motivated by models of evolutionary biology and uses similar nomenclature and models drawn from evolutionary genetics in the refinement of individuals in the population. A specific genetic algorithm requires the definition of a number of components:

Genetic representation A **genetic representation** of the solution domain. Each individual in the population must be represented in a manner that supports evolutionary operators (defined later). The representation is typically at the level of an array of bits and is known as the genotype, genome, or chromosome representation of the individual.

Fitness function A **fitness function** that can be applied to an individual to determine its fitness.

Combination rules Specifics of how **selection, crossover**, and **mutation** genetic operations will act on the current population.

- **Selection** Children in the subsequent generation are generated by selecting pairs of parents in the current generation. This process of selection is typically driven by the fitness of individuals in the population (more-fit members of the population are more likely to contribute to the next generation than less-fit members).

- **Crossover** Children in the subsequent generation are generated by selecting portions of the representation of each of the two parents and combiningg them. The specifics of when and where to perform this combination must be provided.
- **Mutation** Children in the subsequent generation may have individual bits randomly mutated. The specifics of the probability and location of which bit(s) to mutate must be specified. The purpose of mutation is to avoid local minima.

Termination Condition Specifics on termination conditions and how to interpret the final distribution of elements of the population in terms of the problem being addressed.

Establishing a genetic algorithm to solve a specific problem involves encoding the problem in such a manner that it can be effectively mutated and evolved to identify a solution.

8.8 End-to-End Learning

A drastically different approach to vehicle control is to use a single machine learning system such as a deep network, perhaps with a transformer or a reinforcement learning subsystem, to directly map sensor input to vehicle control actions. The advantage of such end-to-end systems is that they directly learn how vehicle auctions correspond to sensor data, and can occasionally work very well. The disadvantage of such learned systems is that there is often little opportunity for human inspection, tuning and adjustment of the ways that the system works. In particular, taking an end-to-end system to a different environment may involve retraining it at significant cost. When deep networks are used in a more modular approach only certain parts of the system might need to be refactored, tuned or reconstructed.

8.9 Further Reading

Robotic software architectures An important aspect of system control is the user interface, as illustrated in Fig. 8.12. These are discussed further in Chapter 12. The basic principles of robotic control and their architectures are described in [9], [125], [494], [187], and [510]. A review of different robot architectures can be found in [731]. [567] reviews and compares centralized and reactive navigation approaches. [591] surveys a number of specific software architectures for autonomous systems.

Functional decomposition [577] provides a good, if a bit dated, survey of blackboard systems, with particular application of blackboard systems to speech understanding.

Reactive control [131] provides a good introduction, while [130] describes a specific system in some depth. [557] provides an in-depth description of the development of reactive controllers.

Hybrid control [303] provides a good introduction to hybrid control architectures

(a) Teleoperational display

(b) 2D robot map interface

(c) Underwater operator display

Figure 8.12. Sample mobile robotics graphics displays. (a) An operator display from a teleoperational robot. (b) A traditional 2D view of the robot's model of its environment. (c) An operator display designed to work underwater. (c) Appears with the kind permission of Bart Verzijlenberg.

Control formalisms A vast literature exists on neural networks including [519], [347], [298], [294], and [867]. See also Chapter 6 of this volume. A good introduction to fuzzy logic can be found in [527]. [620] and [692] provide specific instances of fuzzy logic control of an autonomous vehicle. Genetic algorithms have been used for localization [544] and path planning [475]. [498] provides a broad introduction to genetic algorithms.

Case studies A number of papers have emerged that provide details of the software infrastructure that underlies their software control architecture. For example, [308] describes a system that integrates various software modules (tied directly to hardware) that are integrated to provide a control system for a robot that operates in urban environments. [417] describes a software control architecture for an eldercare robot.

8.10   Problems

1. Implement a very simple subsumption controller for either a simulation of a robot with a collection of range sensors or for a real robot that you have access to. Implement at least three different layers in your controller (wander randomly, avoid obstacle, attempt to dock with a light or some similar feature that can be easily detected). What are your experiences in terms of adding additional complexity to the controller? Once you have the system operating, try adding

additional competences (follow person, etc.) How does the basic approach scale with complex concepts?

2. Implement a very simple motor schema controller for either a simulation of a robot with a collection of range sensors or for a real robot that you have access to. Implement at least three different schema in your controller (move-east, move-to-goal, avoid-obstacle). What are your experiences in terms of adding additional complexity to the controller? Once you have the system operating, try adding additional schema (e.g., follow-path). How does the motor schema approach scale with complex concepts?

3. Download one of the available software tools that allows you to build simulated robots. Construct one of the simulators provided. How difficult was it to build this tool "out of the box," and what limitations do you see in using it to control your own local robot platform(s)?

4. Many traditional middleware systems were not designed with real-time software constraints. Examine one of the middleware software systems that has been designed/refined for autonomous system control. How are real-time issues addressed within this software layer?

5. There exist a number of finite state machine controllers developed for ROS including SMACH [390] (primarily supported for ROS 1 but with limited support for ROS 2) and YASMIN [316]. Download a finite state machine controller and use it to build a simple controller that has a robot perform as a sentry between three fixed points. You may wish to use a real robot if you have access to one or one of the simulated robots provided in the online resource associated with this text.

6. There exist a large number behavior tree controllers developed for ROS. Much like FSM-based controllers in ROS, they typically utilize the `actionlib` package to interface to ROS. Adapt an existing or develop your own behavior tree controller for ROS and test it with one of the simulated robots provided in the online resource associated with this text to build a robot that acts as a sentry following a path through a set of different points. The robot should simulate having an on-board battery with a maximum charge of 10 and the cost of moving from one way point to another being 1. There is a charging station that will refill the charge instantly to 10 when the robot goes there but there is a cost 1 to get to the charging station. Write a controller in your behavior tree to have the robot continually execute its sentry rounds but stopping for recharge as necessary.

7. Implement a fuzzy logic controller for a simulated robot with a sensor that determines its displacement from the center of a hallway and drives the robot back to the center of the hallway. Refine the controller so that the robot does not oscillate about the center of the hallway (do not under-damp the controller). How did you define the fuzzy states of the system, and how did you convert the fuzzy state back to control of the vehicle?

9

Pose Maintenance and Localization

"You are in a maze of twisty passages all alike"[1]

Even in games like Adventure or Zork, the task of navigation in an environment, especially an environment without distinguished locations, can be very difficult.

For many tasks, a mobile robot needs to know "where it is" either on an ongoing basis or when specific events occur. A robot may need to know its location in order to be able to plan appropriate paths or to know if the current location is the appropriate place at which to perform some operation. Knowing "where the robot is" has many different connotations. In the strongest sense, "knowing where the robot is" involves estimating the location of the robot (in either qualitative or quantitative terms) with respect to some global representation of space: we refer to this as **strong localization**. The **weak localization** problem, in contrast, involves merely knowing if the current location has been visited before (this is known as the "have I been here before" problem). In certain cases, complete qualitative maps can be constructed simply from weak positioning information [440], [439], [217]: thus, weak localization can be used to construct maps that can be used subsequently for strong localization. Between the extremes of the weak-localization and the strong-localization problems exists a continuum of different problem specifications that involve knowing where the robot is or estimating the robot's pose.

Given approximate estimates of a robot's position based on odometry and dead reckoning (see Section 3.1.5) and given a map of the environment and sufficient sensing, it is possible to maintain an ongoing estimate of the location of the robot with respect to the map. This process is sometimes known as **localization**, **pose estimation**, or **positioning**. The general specification of this problem starts with an initial estimate of the robot's location in configuration space, given by a probability distribution $P(q)$. It requires that we use sensor data s in conjunction with our map to produce a refined position estimate $P(q|s)$ such that this refined estimate has an increased probability density about the true position of the robot. The map construction problem will be addressed in detail in Chapter 10. In this chapter, it is assumed that maps of the environment are available in various forms as needed. The problem of computing $P(q|s)$ can be expressed in terms of a recursive estimation process and addressed in many ways including through a Kalman (see Section 4.9.1) or particle filter (see Section 4.9.4) based approach. A key question in these recursive localization processes is the nature of the measurements that will be used to perform the localization. It may be possible to combine measurements prior

[1] From Zork, the Great Underground Empire, an early text-based computer game.

to integration within the localization process to obtain a complete measurement of the state as an alternative to combining the information within the recursive state estimation process.

Essentially all techniques for estimating incremental motion must deal with plant noise. This noise can arise as a result of electrical noise, quantization, digitization artifacts, wheel slip, gear backlash, and other factors (as discussed in Chapter 3). If dead reckoning alone is used for position estimation, successive errors are added to any ongoing absolute pose estimate and accumulate with successive motions of the robot. This makes the general problem of maintaining an accurate absolute coordinate system very difficult or potentially impossible in the absence of some external reference for eliminating the accumulated errors. Long-term localization and associated tasks such as navigation and map construction must make reference to the external world for position correction if positional accuracy is to be maintained. In general, this involves the use of sensory data for recalibrating a robot's sense of its location within the environment. In some cases, it proves simpler to abandon absolute positioning in favor of only local position estimates or qualitative information (see Section 7.2.3).

In certain circumstances it is necessary to infer the robot's position without an *a priori* estimate. This type of positioning is known as **global localization**, in an analogy with global function minimization, whereby an optimum must be found without a reliable initial guess. Global localization achieved over a sequence of motions can be formulated as a Markov localization problem (see Section 4.9.2), where information is integrated over time in order to solve the global localization problem. In each step of the localization process, information is required to more assuredly disambiguate the current location from potential locations in the environment. What types of information should be used to perform this disambiguation, and how should this disambiguation process be constructed?

A key step in the process of performing either local or global localization involves matching the set of current observations to some established map. Standard matching methods can be broadly classified into the following categories:

Data-data matching Directly match the current raw data with predicted raw data (extracted from the map either by predictive modeling or using stored datasets).

Data-model matching Matching the observed data to more abstract models stored in the map (based on a model of how models and data are associated). Matching with deep neural networks can be regarded as a special case.

Model-model matching Matching models stored in the map to models generated from current observations.

Each of the techniques has been used with some success and each has its particular domain of applicability, depending particularly on the characteristics of both the sensor and data acquisition methodology. In general, matching with raw data can reduce the dependence on *a priori* assumptions about the environment but tends to be less robust unless the matching technique is very sophisticated (in which case it resembles model-model matching).

9.1   Simple Landmark Measurement

Many approaches to pose estimation are based on the solution of geometric or trigonometric problems involving constraints on the positions of landmarks in the environment. In principle, the problem is related to pose estimation of a landmark with respect to a fixed sensor. Important variations of the problem arise when the landmarks are unlabeled instead of labeled (i.e., their individual identities are unknown), when the landmarks are difficult to detect, or when the measurements are inaccurate.

If we are willing to accept a suitably general definition of a landmark, essentially all methods for pose estimation can be described in the context of landmark-based methods. The primary factors governing the use of landmarks are the region over which the landmarks can be detected, the functional relationship between landmark measurements and position, and how errors are manifested. Additional factors that characterize a particular position estimation system include:

- Whether the landmarks are passive or active (i.e., are they energy emitters like radio beacons?).
- The sensing modality (e.g., vision, sonar).
- The geometric properties of the landmarks (are they large or small, points or planes, etc.?).
- How easy it is to detect, identify or measure a landmark.

A key issue in practice is whether the landmarks to be used are synthetic or natural. Artificial landmarks placed specifically for the purposes of robot localization are typically designed to be much easier to detect and can be uniquely labeled. Their optimal placement is an interesting issue. Naturally occurring landmarks, on the other hand, preclude having to modify the environment, but their stable and robust detection can be a major issue. Finally, the extent of the positional constraint provided by observations of a landmark depends on both the sensor and the geometry of the landmark. Planar laser landmarks, for example, typically provide only one-dimensional constraints on the robot's pose (distance along the normal to the landmark). This is true in the case of range sensing in particular since the measurements are invariant to translation parallel to the face of the landmark.

9.1.1   Landmark Classes

Landmarks can be active or passive, natural or artificial. Active landmarks are typically transmitters that emit different signals and are placed about the environment. Active artificial landmarks avoid many of the problems commonly associated with passive, naturally occurring landmarks. Artificial landmarks are typically chosen to be highly visible to the underlying sensing technology but can still can be confused with naturally occurring structures. In general, the use of an artificial landmark – either active or passive – can extend the operational range of the underlying sensor technology relative to a natural landmark.

In principle, landmarks can be defined in terms of any sensing modality. Animals such as dogs and ants use judiciously applied chemical landmarks to define territorial boundaries [364]. From our point of view, the landmarks used by a dog are active because they *emit* odor and they are *artificial* because the dog must place them itself (at positions it deems useful). The use of landmarks defined by odor has also been considered for robotic vehicles, although with a different set of chemical markers [74].

In the context of robotics, several primary sensing modalities are of particular interest for state estimation.

- Video-based sensing (i.e., computer vision; see Chapter 5) can be used in a wide variety of modes. In its simplest form, it can provide bearing and perhaps range to visually defined landmarks. The traditional lighthouse falls in this category. Artificial landmarks can be augmented by a unique bar code or target structure to both facilitate their detection and assure their uniqueness. The use of naturally occurring landmarks can require highly complex image processing stages, and even then reliable target detection can be problematic. That being said, many environments exhibit robust, naturally occurring landmarks that make excellent visual targets. For example, doors and door openings in corridor environments and fire alarm hardware often make very good and very reliable visual landmarks.
- Laser transmission accompanied by video sensing deserves special mention. Retro-reflective landmarks can provide very long-range detectability. For example, one has been placed on the surface of the Moon.
- Active radio beacons form a class of very well-established position estimation landmarks. The **LORAN** terrestrial system has been in use for many years, while global positioning systems (e.g., the U.S. GPS system) are based on a network of satellites and can be used from almost any exposed outdoor location (see Section 4.8). At shorter ranges Bluetooth and WiFi signals can provide effective target information providing range based on signal strength, and UWB can be used to provide good range information through signal time of flight measurement.
- Since sonar is ubiquitous and inexpensive, it has been considered for positioning despite its drawbacks in terms of beam dispersion, specular reflection, and background noise. It has been shown to work particularly well with large, simple geometric structures, which are sometimes referred to as **geometric beacons**.

9.1.2 Triangulation and Trilateration

Triangulation and **trilateration** are methods for the solution of constraint equations relating the pose of an observer relative to a set of landmarks. Formally, trilateration refers to the use of distance contraints, while triangulation refers to the use of angle (orientation) constraints. This formal distinction is often blurred, and in robotics the term "triangulation" has come to refer to the solution of constraint equations relating the pose of an observer to measurements made from landmarks regardless of the nature of those landmark measurements. Pose estimation using *triangulation* methods from known landmarks have been known since ancient times and were exploited by the ancient Romans in mapping and road construction during the Roman Empire. Given estimates of the position or distance to one or more landmarks with known positions, an agent can compute its own pose.

The simplest and most familiar case, and the one that gives the technique its name, is that of using **bearings** or distance measurements to two (or more) landmarks to solve a planar positioning task, thus solving for the parameters of a triangle, given a combination of sides and angles. Although a triangular geometry is not the only possible configuration for using landmarks, it is the most natural.

Although landmarks and robots exist in a three-dimensional world, the limited accuracy associated with height information often results in a two-dimensional problem in practice; elevation information is sometimes used to validate the results. Thus, although the triangulation problem for a point robot should be considered as a problem with six unknown parameters (three position variables and three orientation variables), more commonly the task is posed as a two-dimensional (or three-dimensional) problem with two-dimensional (or three-dimensional) landmarks.

Depending on the combinations of sides (S) and angles (A) given, the triangulation problem is described as "side-side-side" ("SSS"), "side-angle-side" ("SAS"), and so on. All cases permit a solution, except for the "AAA" case, where the scale of the triangle is not constrained by the parameters. In practice, a given sensing technology often returns either an angular measurement or a distance measurement, and the landmark positions are typically known. Thus, the SAA and SSS cases are the most commonly encountered. More generally, the problem can involve some combination of algebraic constraints that relate the measurements to the pose parameters. These are typically non-linear, and hence a solution may be dependent on an initial position estimate or constraint. This can be formulated as

$$X = F(m_1, m_2, \ldots, m_n),$$

where the vector X expresses the pose variables to be estimated, and $M = m_1, \ldots, m_n$ is the vector of measurements to be used. In the specific case of estimating the position of an oriented robot in the plane, this becomes

$$x = F_1(m_1, \ldots)$$
$$y = F_2(m_1, \ldots)$$
$$\theta = F_3(m_1, \ldots).$$

If only the distance to a landmark is available, then a single measurement constrains the robot's position to the arc of a circle. Figure 9.1 illustrates perhaps the simplest triangulation case. A robot at an unknown location X senses two landmarks P_1 and P_2 by measuring the respective distances d_1 and d_2 to them. (This corresponds to the case where beacons at known locations emit a signal, and the robot obtains distances based on the time delay to arrive at the robot.) The robot must lie at the intersection of the circle of radius d_1 with center at P_1, with the circle of radius d_2 with center at P_2. Without loss of generality we can assume that P_1 is at the origin and that P_2 is at $(a, 0)$. A small amount of algebra results in

$$x = \frac{a^2 + d_1^2 - d_2^2}{2a}$$
$$y = \pm(d_1^2 - x^2)^{\frac{1}{2}}.$$

In a typical robot application, beacons are located on walls, and thus the spurious solution can be identified since it would correspond to the robot being located on the wrong side of the wall.

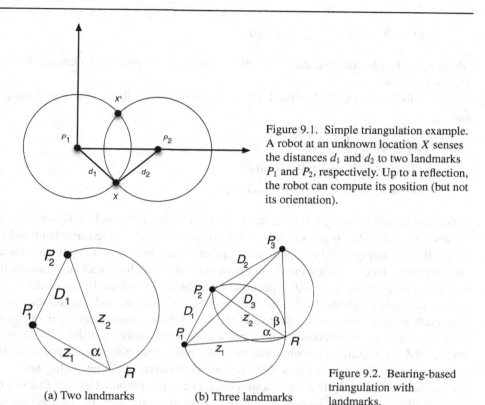

Figure 9.1. Simple triangulation example. A robot at an unknown location X senses the distances d_1 and d_2 to two landmarks P_1 and P_2, respectively. Up to a reflection, the robot can compute its position (but not its orientation).

(a) Two landmarks   (b) Three landmarks

Figure 9.2. Bearing-based triangulation with landmarks.

Although distances to landmarks provide a simple example of triangulation, most sensors and landmarks result in more complex situations. A common real-world situation is one in which relative bearing to the landmark is available but the distance is not. Consider, for example, a camera that can detect two small known landmarks. Assuming the camera has been calibrated (see Section 5.1.3), we can readily extract the angular separation between the landmarks from their positions on the image. Using the angular separation or **relative bearing** between two landmarks with known position constrains the robot's position to lie on a pair of circular arcs. If the robot can determine the clockwise enumeration of the landmarks (or label them uniquely), then the position is constrained to only one of these two circles. Additional landmarks to which the bearing is known can provide a third constraint, and the intersection of these constraints uniquely determines the robot position. The one exception to this is when the landmarks lie on a common circle, which in turn implies that the constraint circles are coincident (instead of merely intersecting at a pair of points) [744].

The situation for two landmarks is illustrated in Figure 9.2a. The robot senses two known landmarks and measures the bearing to each landmark relative to its own straight-ahead direction. This yields the difference in bearing between the directions to the two landmarks and constrains the true position of the robot to lie on that portion of the circle shown in Figure 9.2a. (Note that the mathematics admits two circular arcs, but one can be excluded based on the left-right ordering of the landmark directions.) The *loci* of points that satisfy the bearing difference is given by

$$D_1^2 = z_1^2 + z_2^2 - 2|z_1||z_2|\cos(\alpha),$$

where z_1 and z_2 are the distances from the robot's current position to landmarks P_1 and P_2, respectively.

The visibility of a third landmark gives rise to three non-linear constraints on z_1, z_2, and z_3,

$$D_1^2 = z_1^2 + z_2^2 - 2|z_1||z_2|\cos(\alpha)$$
$$D_2^2 = z_2^2 + z_3^2 - 2|z_2||z_3|\cos(\beta)$$
$$D_3^2 = z_1^2 + z_3^2 - 2|z_1||z_3|\cos(\alpha + \beta),$$

which can be solved using standard techniques to obtain z_1, z_2, and z_3. Knowledge of z_1, z_2, and z_3 leads to the robot's position and orientation [86]. Using three landmarks also precludes any ambiguity if the landmarks cannot be labeled. More realistically, there can be noise in the landmark-bearing estimates or even their labeling. This suggests the use of additional measurements to either improve robustness or validate the measurements. For simple validation, landmarks can be decomposed into groups, and a consistent estimate from each group can be sought. Betke and Gurvits [86] also describe an efficient algorithm for performing the estimation of the robot's pose when more than three landmarks are visible and the solution is overconstrained. By representing landmark positions in the complex plane, they showed that it is possible to linearize the relationship between the geometric constraints. This permits a solution that can be computed in time that is a linear function of the number of landmarks, given that certain constraints on the arrangement of the landmarks are satisfied.

Sugihara was among the first to formally examine the use of computer vision for landmark-based pose estimation [744]. His emphasis was on the *computationally efficient* solution to the problem of bringing bearing measurements of *indistinguishable landmarks* into correspondence with a map. This solution was improved by Avis and Imai [50].

The geometric arrangement of landmarks with respect to the robot observer is critical to the accuracy of the solution. A particular arrangement of landmarks may provide high accuracy when observed from some locations and low accuracy when observed from others. In the limit, certain configurations of landmarks may present no solution at all. For example, in two dimensions a set of three colinear landmarks observed with a bearing-measuring device can provide good positional accuracy for triangulation when viewed from a point away from the line joining the landmarks (e.g., a point that forms an equilateral triangle with respect to the extremal landmarks). On the other hand, if the robot is located on the line joining the landmarks, then the positional can only be constrained to lie somewhere on this (infinite) line. The quantification in this variation in accuracy with position is discussed in the next section.

Many robotic systems rely on target triangulation in order to address the task of pose estimation. As one example, Yagi *et al.* [843] describes the use of the COPIS sensor (see Section 5.7.4) coupled with a map of salient features to locate the robot with respect to the map. The COPIS sensor obtains azimuth readings to vertical edges in the environment. As the COPIS sensor is omnidirectional and the environment is constructed to be populated with vertical lines, a large number of azimuth readings are obtained surrounding the robot. The robot has an estimate of its current position, and it uses this estimate to establish

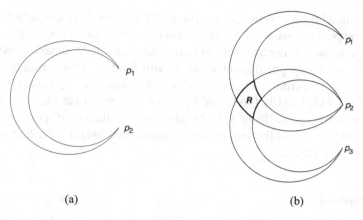

(a)   (b)

Figure 9.3. Pose estimates and associated uncertainty based on triangulation using imprecise bearings to (a) two landmarks (p_1 and p_2) and (b) three landmarks (p_1, p_2, and p_3). Bearing uncertainty constrains the robot to lie within the enclosed crescent-shaped region formed by bearings to the pair constraints. The large crescent-shaped region in (a) is reduced to the intersection region R in (b). Figure generated by R. Sim.

correspondences between azimuth measurements and vertical features on the map. An optimization process is then used to find the true position of the robot.

Triangulation with Uncertainty   The ideal case of triangulation from range or bearing measurements is complicated somewhat by the fact that real sensor measurements have associated uncertainty. As a result, the position estimates produced by triangulation schemes provide probability distributions for the robot pose. While the particular degenerate cases that lead to truly ambiguous pose estimates are, in principle, unlikely, the magnification of input error in the course of position estimation is a common occurrence (see Figure 9.3).

The relationship between the accuracy of the input measurements and the accuracy of the final estimate of the desired pose variables is formalized by the notion of **geometric dilution of precision (GDOP)**. This is a metric that expresses the variation in the output estimate X (i.e., the geometric variables constituting the pose) with variations in the input parameters S (i.e., sensor data):

$$\text{GDOP} = \frac{\Delta X}{\Delta S}.$$

When we take the limit as ΔS approaches zero, this is equal to the Jacobian $\mathcal{J}$ of the measurement equation. In three-dimensional space, the **horizontal geometric dilution of precision** (HDOP) and **positional geometric dilution of precision** (PDOP) refer to the error sensitivity of only the horizontal or translational components, while the full GDOP may refer to the sensitivity of a larger class of variables. For example, in the context of global positioning systems (Section 4.8), GDOP is sometimes used to refer to the sensitivity of the system of variables including both the 3D translation as well as the estimate of the local receiver's time clock error.

In practical situations robotic systems may encounter difficulties in uniquely identifying landmarks or the position estimation may be unstable due to landmark geometry. One highly successful approach to dealing with intermittently reliable landmark information is to combine landmark-based position information with position information from dead reckoning. This fusion of information from two sources has been accomplished effectively using a Kalman [111], [458], [819], [569] (see Section 4.9.1) or particle filter (see Section 4.9.4). Other approaches range from the closed-form calculation of position (pose) transformations [191], [361] to the use of neural networks [394], [595]. See also the section on fingerprinting below.

9.2   Fingerprinting

One active landmark class that has become ubiquitous is the use of radio signal information in localization. GPS/GNSS and UWB mechanisms provide explicit mechanisms to obtain measurements related to the robot's position. These and other radio-based mechanisms can also be used to obtain pose constraints or estimates based on the nature of the radio signal as measured by the robot. Although other radio signals can be used, here we concentrate on Wi-Fi-based fingerprinting as it is more commonly used.

A Wi-Fi receiver operating in an environment may be able to communicate with a number of base stations. Each base station is uniquely identified (it has a unique SSID or **service set identifier**). The radio modem on the receiver can also measure the available signal strength known as its RSSI or **received signal strength indicator**. In an open environment the RSSI value received decays following a well-known model, and in theory one could then use trilateration to solve for the location of the receiver if the location of the base stations were known. In practice, dynamic obstacles in the environment, multi-path transmission paths, specifics of the radio antenna structure at the base station and receiver, and a host of other issues introduce difficulties to model and correct for noise in this basic process. Also note that it is necessary to accurately map the locations of the base stations for a trilateration process to function. One approach to overcoming these issues is data-driven. Prior to system deployment, the eventual receiver is placed at a collection of known locations and the RSSI signal strength for each base station is measured. This results in a dataset of $(x_i, RSSI_i^j)$ positions and the corresponding $RSSI_i^j$ measurements for that position.

During operation, a measurement is made of the available RSSI measurements and the previously collected dataset is used to estimate the robot's position. A range of different computational approaches has been used, but a common approach is to train a supervised neural network on the dataset to compute the function that maps RSSI measurements to position estimates. Typical performance in an indoor environment is within 2 to 4 m.

Various approaches can be used to enhance the basic RSSI fingerprinting process. For example, it can be combined with trilateration using the RSSI signal strength, or with other sensors such as UWB.

9.3   Servo Control

The use of sensor data, and in particular vision, for position estimation is complicated by the extreme difficulty of inverting the imaging transform to recover the locations of points in 3D. Simply recognizing objects of interest is often difficult due to phenomena such as perspective distortion, image noise, lighting and shadowing changes, and specular reflection (see Section 5.2). One of the simplest techniques for using sensor data (and specifically vision) to relate a robot's pose to that of a landmark is known as **image-based servoing** (or **visual servoing**), or, for more general classes of sensor, **sensor-based servoing**.

Servoing is typically applied to allow a robot to move to a specific target position using observed sensor measurements (hence it is also referred to as **homing**). This technique is based on storing a specific sensor image $I(q_{goal})$ associated with a target position q_{goal} for the robot and using the difference between $I(q_{goal})$ and $I(q_c)$ to move the robot from its current position q_c to the goal. The distance between the current robot location from the target position is assumed to be monotonically related to the distance in sensor space between the target sensor reading and the current sensor measurements. This monotonicity relationship typically holds when the robot is sufficiently close to the target position. Rather than perform some elaborate sensor interpretation to establish correspondence, sensor measurements acquired on-line are directly compared to the target sensor measurement using a simple method such as an L_2 (Euclidean) or L_1 metric (see Section 5.4.3). It is also possible to describe the image by a set of intermediate features $f(i)$ and to use differences in these to express image variation. Examples of such features range from the pixel differences to landmark positions in the image, to energy in different bandpass channels. In general, given the image feature vectors, we assume that the discrepancy function

$$E(q_c) = |f(I(q_{goal})) - f(I(q_c))|$$

is convex in the workspace of interest (which may have to be chosen to be suitably close to the target position).

The Jacobian $\mathcal{J}$ of the sensor image with respect to the pose parameters has the form

$$\mathcal{J} = \begin{bmatrix} \frac{\partial f_1}{\partial q_1} & \cdots & \frac{\partial f_1}{\partial q_n} \\ \vdots & \ddots & \vdots \\ \frac{\partial f_m}{\partial q_1} & \cdots & \frac{\partial f_m}{\partial q_n} \end{bmatrix}.$$

The local convexity assumption implies that the Jacobian of E (the **image Jacobian**) provides an indication of how pose changes are related to changes in E (for small motions, since this is only a first-order approximation). For small pose changes the image formation equation allows a linear approximation to be made, and then the pose change needed to produce a desired change in the image measurements can be computed as

$$\Delta q = \mathcal{J}^{-\infty} \Delta f.$$

As a result of both the approximations used and sensor noise, actually attaining the target position usually involves an iterative approach. Moving the robot to q_{goal} then involves following a steepest-descent strategy down the gradient of the discrepancy function from q_c.

The key difficulties with sensor-based servo control are the following:

- The mapping from pose to signals is not usually convex over large changes in pose.

- The feature space may not be sufficiently robust or stable.
- No quantitative position estimate is produced, except at the "home" location.
- Servoing can only be used to return to previously visited poses (from which a sample image was acquired).

On the other hand, the technique has low overhead, is readily implemented, and makes only simple assumptions about the environment.

Sensor-based servo control can also be formulated with respect to a number of discrete target locations. This type of approach has been used to address the pose estimation problem (referred to as the **drop-off** or **global localization** problem) for outdoor robots [525]. The system relies on the creation of a previously obtained database of panoramic views of the horizon. To solve the drop-off problem, a panoramic view of the current environment is obtained and is compared with views in the panorama database. The best match is used to identify the robot's current location. The database represents the panorama in terms of the peaks and troughs in the skyline and hence is relatively insensitive to position differences and can be corrected for orientation errors. The use of raw sensor data to obtain pose estimates without scene reconstruction is also discussed in Section 9.6.

9.4   Recursive Filtering

To accomplish position estimation using external referencing, the disparity between the known and observed locations of mapped objects provides an estimate of position to be used in correcting the drift in estimates from internal sensors. In Sections 4.9.1 and 4.9.4 we saw how a Kalman filter or a particle filter could be used to combine pose estimates from dead reckoning and other measurements. Unfortunately, in the context of mobile robotics, both processes have their issues.

For Kalman filters, the criteria that assure an optimal result are often violated. In practice, the response functions of real sensors vary non-linearly with the robot state variables. To account for this non-linearity, a variant of the Kalman filter, the extended Kalman filter (EKF) is obtained by linearizing the model of the system (see Section 4.9.1).

The incorporation of sensor measurements within an EKF entails several additional steps in addition to linearization of the system of equations. If a map of the environment can be taken for granted, observations from the sensor can be associated with objects in the map through a correspondence process (this is essentially the same issue that arises in feature-based stereo and motion estimation, as seen in Chapter 5). The disparities between objects in the map and their observed positions based on the current estimated robot position yields estimates on the error in the current estimate's position, qualified by the accuracy of the measurements, the accuracy of the map, and the reliability of the correspondence. Typically the first two factors (sensor error and map accuracy) are quantified *a priori* and the associated confidences are directly incorporated into the Kalman filter equations. Correspondence is typically handled differently. Initial correspondences can be computed in a variety of ways, depending on the types of measurement used (e.g., circular arcs or single points) and the type of data stored on the map (e.g., occupancy probabilities or line segments). One simple approach is to find the closest single explanatory feature on the map for each measurement, given the current estimate of the robot position. A more involved approach would be to find alternative objects to explain a given measurement, leading to a "multiple hypothesis tracking" framework.

While the EKF is a powerful technique that often performs well under suitable conditions [458], [819], [569], it does have its shortcomings. Fundamentally, it depends on the acceptability of the linearization of the system being modeled, an acceptable estimate of the sources of error in the system, and on a well-behaved (e.g., Gaussian) error distribution. The actual responses from real sonar sensors, as one example, are substantially more complex than those captured by the comparatively simple models typically used in practice (they are highly non-linear due to multi-path sonar reflections, see Section 4.4). This, in turn, means that there is a potential for increasing error in the filter's estimates.

Sensor responses that are not correctly represented by the simplified sonar model are typically classified as outliers, and a threshold or **gating** function is used to discard them. This makes traditional EKF-based localization somewhat sensitive to the choice of a correct gating function: if it is too small, good data are discarded; if it is too large, outliers corrupt the estimates. Furthermore, if the error in the input pose estimate is even larger than the size of the gating function (e.g., if the robot goes over an unexpected bump), the mismatch between real data and models can lead to rejection of all the sensor data and divergence of the filter. In such cases, the EKF may lead to poor estimates and may even diverge (i.e., fail to converge to the correct estimate) [730], [99]. In addition to these concerns, the need for a simple relationship between geometric structures and observed measurements makes it difficult to apply such methods in some environments.

An alternative approach to the use of a single gating function is to use a variable scale threshold-like function such as that used in the **adaptive localization at multiple scales (ALMS)** method [492]. This method is based on using a collection of data points from multiple positions (which can be maintained on an ongoing basis).

Particle filters overcome a number of the problems associated with the limited error model associated with Kalman filters. In practice, however, they introduce a number of new problems including particle death and the collapse of the particle distribution to a small number of values. Tuning a particle filter to properly model vehicle motion and to properly deal with errors in data association can be time consuming and frustrating.

9.5 Localization in ROS

The standard tool set for localization within the ROS ecosystem is defined within the Navigation 2 stack[491]. The stack defines a standard set of mechanisms for map representations and a toolset to serve maps to various levels of the software infrastructure that would wish to interact with the map representation. For localization, the Nav2 toolkit relies on adaptive Monte Carlo localization as described in [288].

9.6 Non-Geometric Methods: Perceptual Structure

One of the most difficult aspects of model-based localization is selecting suitable generic and robust models. There are three main difficulties: defining a modeling space

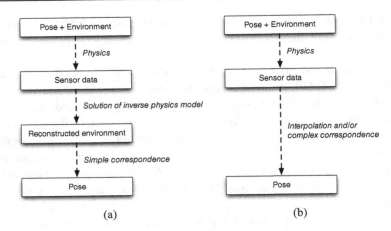

Figure 9.4. Pose estimation using (a) geometric models and (b) perceptual structure.

(i.e., a set of primitives) that is general enough to express the set of objects of interest with sufficient accuracy, being able to invert the sensor data so as to make geometric inferences, and fitting the models to the data in a manner that is both stable and efficient.

In an attempt to avoid these problems with geometric modeling, methods that directly relate appearance or **perceptual structure** to pose can be formulated. The premise is that a mapping between sensor data and pose can be constructed *directly* without any intermediate representation based explicitly on 2D or 3D scene geometry (this is illustrated in Figure 9.4). One way to achieve this is to record the sensor data associated with certain positions. This is sometimes referred to as the **signature** of a position and is related to fingerprinting as described in Section 9.2. Deep learning (neural networks) are currently a preferred method for learning signatures. By comparing the currently observed signature with the set of known remembered signatures, a robot can determine when it has returned to a previously visited location. This is the essence of perceptual servoing (see Section 9.3). As we have seen, servo control suffers from several difficulties, including the fact that it does not explicitly attempt to recover a quantitative position estimate. In practice, the particular abstraction used to record signatures and to match signatures is a potentially difficult problem. Furthermore, signatures may not be unique and therefore some approach to the resolution of such ambiguities is needed.

Methods that avoid full reconstruction have also been used to estimate the position of a mobile robot from laser range data [199]. In that work, the raw data were represented more reliably by projecting them into a lower-dimensional subspace computed using principal components analysis. Other work has dealt with exploiting the geometric characteristics of landmarks for homing tasks [70].

Interpolation between sample images has been used successfully for both pose estimation and trajectory following. Using principal components encoding of the input data, Nayar *et al.* [571] assumed that a one-to-one mapping between visual input images and robot pose exists for a six-degree of freedom robot arm in a small workspace. By creating a direct mapping for a low-dimensional subspace of the input images to robot joint angles, the robot can use vision to track a pre-recorded trajectory. The low-dimensional description of the input images is obtained by computing a principal components analysis on the input images (eigenvector/eigenvalue analysis) and discarding all eigenvectors except those with the largest eigenvalue. The eigenvectors with the largest eigenvalue are those that account for most of the variance in the input images and thus best encode the input (in terms of minimizing squared error). In similar work, Thrun derived a probabilistic approach to obtain a pose estimate using a neural net [769]. Other network architectures, including **general adversarial networks** or GANs, have been used to interpolate sensor measurements including camera views. For example, [596] leveraged a GAN to produce interpolated views to aid in estimating outdoor traversability for different potential vehicle trajectories.

Other work has achieved accurate pose estimate without an input estimate by using images that sample the environment of interest [232]. Images are first encoded as edge maps (see Section 5.4) to reduce the effects of illumination variations and shading. These edge images are then described by vectors of roughly 20 statistical descriptors each: the moments of the edge distribution, the orientation of the edge distribution, and so on over the entire image and over four subwindows in the four quadrants of the image. These input vectors are then used to train a neural network that maps between input images and output pose estimates. A final processing stage is used to eliminate an otherwise disastrous sensitivity to different locations with roughly the same appearance. An assumption is made that dead reckoning can be used to compute an estimated separation between nearby sample locations. If the estimate pose from such a pair of locations disagrees seriously with the estimate from dead reckoning, then the pose estimate is discarded in the hope that a more consistent pair of locations will be observed.

9.6.1 Eigenlandmarks

One approach to generic pose estimation assuming either scene reconstruction or special-purpose landmarks is to attempt to *learn* suitable landmarks for a given environment in some unsupervised or semi-supervised manner. Perhaps the most general approach to landmark learning is to train the system to recognize small subimages with recognizable characteristics [720]. This can be accomplished using principal components (eigenfunction) learning to generate robust landmarks that can be used for interpolation between sample positions: this gives rise to the term **eigenlandmark**. The environment is first surveyed in an "off-line" phase, and a set of images is extracted from sample locations. The landmarks that are extracted are *image-domain* features, as opposed to geometric structures in the environment. During the landmark-learning phase, *candidate landmarks* are extracted using a model motivated by work on human visual attention. These are regions that are statistically distinct with respect to the input images visible.

The on-line phase is performed as often as a position estimate is required, and consists in matching candidate landmarks in the input image to the learned tracked landmarks, followed by position estimation using an appearance-based linear combination of views. An outline of the method is given in Listing 9.1.

PCA-Based Landmark Extraction Recognition using **principal components analysis** (PCA) is based on computing a small set of basis vectors that can be linearly combined to produce an "optimal" approximation to one of a much larger set of training examples. Optimally, in this case, implies that no other equally small set of basis vectors could do any better at approximating the training data, as expressed by the squared error.

1. Training images are collected sampling a range of poses in the environment.
2. *Landmark candidates* are extracted from each image using a model of visual attention.
3. *Tracked landmarks* are extracted as sets of candidate landmarks over the configuration space (the vector space of possible configurations, or poses, of the robot). Tracked landmarks are each represented by a characteristic prototype, obtained by encoding an initial set of candidate landmarks by their principal components decomposition. For each image, a local search is performed in the neighborhood of the candidate landmarks in the image in order to locate optimal matches to the templates.
4. The set of tracked landmarks is stored for future retrieval.

(a) Off-line "MAP" construction

1. When a position estimate is required, a single image is acquired from the camera.
2. Candidate landmarks are extracted from the input image using the same model of visual attention used in the off-line phase.
3. The candidate landmarks are matched to the learned templates using the same method used for tracking in the off-line phase.
4. A position estimate is obtained for *each* matched candidate landmark. This is achieved by computing a reconstruction of the candidate based on the decomposition of the tracked candidates and their known poses in the tracked landmark. The result is a position estimate obtained as a linear combination of the positions of the views of the tracked candidates in the tracked landmarks.
5. A final position estimate is computed as the robust average of the individual estimates of the individual tracked candidates.

(b) On-line localization

Listing 9.1. Eigenlandmark map construction and use.

For training data in the form of images, the images are encoded as a very long vector (listing the rows sequentially). Each training example is thus expressed as a vector $\mathbf{v}$, and the entire set of these vectors is assembled into a (large) matrix, $\mathbf{A}$. The eigenvectors of $\mathbf{A}$ are computed using singular values decomposition, producing an orthonormal basis set.[2] Each vector in the basis set can be represented as an image, and these are sometimes referred to as **eigenfaces** or **eigenpictures** due to their successful application in face recognition [783].

This representation can be used to allow recognition or interpolation between the subimages to be used as image-domain landmarks. Consider a set T of m landmark prototypes $t_1, t_2, \ldots, t_m$. For each prototype t_i, we can build a column vector, $\mathbf{v}_i$, by scanning the local intensity distribution in row-wise order and normalizing the magnitude of $\mathbf{v}_i$ to one. Note that if the intensity image consists of s by t pixels, then it follows that $\mathbf{v}_i$ is of dimensionality $n = st$. Our goal is to construct a discriminant using the set of vectors defined by T. This is accomplished by constructing an $n \times m$ matrix $\mathbf{A}$ whose columns consist of the vectors $\mathbf{v}_i$, and expressing $\mathbf{A}$ in terms of its singular values decomposition, $\mathbf{A} = [\mathbf{v}_1 \cdots \mathbf{v}_m] = \mathbf{UWV}^T$, where $\mathbf{U}$ is an $n \times m$ column-orthogonal matrix whose columns represent the principal directions of the range defined by $\mathbf{A}$ (i.e., $\mathbf{U}$ gives the eigenvectors of $\mathbf{A}$), $\mathbf{W}$ is an $m \times m$ diagonal matrix whose elements correspond to the singular values (or eigenvalues) of $\mathbf{A}$, and $\mathbf{V}$ is an $m \times m$ column-orthogonal matrix whose rows represent the projections of the columns of $\mathbf{A}$ into the subspace defined by $\mathbf{U}$ (weighted appropriately by the inverses of the eigenvalues). Note that the columns of $\mathbf{U}$ define a linear subspace of dimensionality m, which can be[3]

---

[2] An alternative method is to compute the principal components of $\mathbf{A}^T\mathbf{A}$, the covariance of $\mathbf{A}$.

[3] In practice, the dimensionality may even be smaller than m – some of the diagonal values of $\mathbf{W}$ may be zero, or small enough to be affected by limited machine precision. In this case, the corresponding eigenvectors are removed.

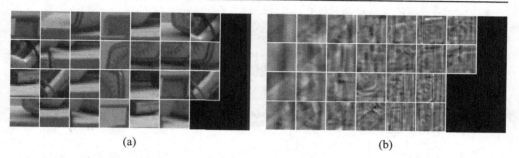

(a)   (b)

Figure 9.5. Landmark images and corresponding eigenlandmarks: (a) Landmark images. (b) Eigenlandmarks. Figure generated by R. Sim.

much smaller than n. In addition, the principal axes of the subspace are arranged so as to maximize the Euclidean distance between the projections of the prototypes t_i into the subspace, which optimizes the discriminability of the prototypes. Figure 9.5 shows a set of landmark prototypes on the left, and the corresponding eigenvectors, or **eigenlandmarks**, constructed from the prototypes on the right.

Once the subspace is constructed, it can be used for classifying landmark candidates. Given a landmark candidate c, we construct a vector $\mathbf{c}$ from the local intensity distribution of c, normalized to unit magnitude. The subspace projection $\mathbf{c}'$ of $\mathbf{c}$ is obtained using $\mathbf{c}' = \mathbf{U}^T \mathbf{c}$, and then c can be matched to the prototype $\hat{t}$ whose subspace projection is closest (in the Euclidean sense) to $\mathbf{c}'$ in the subspace. If the subspace projection of prototype t_i is defined using the Euclidean metric, $\mathbf{t}'_i = \mathbf{U}^T \mathbf{t}_i$, where $\mathbf{t}_i$ is obtained from the prototype image in the same fashion as was used to obtain $\mathbf{c}$, then the optimal match $\hat{t}$ is defined as $\hat{t} = \min_i < t_i, c >$.

The key step is the recovery of the pose estimates using the subspace encoding of the image data. The *tracked landmarks* are image subwindows that have been detected reliably from a series of positions: their variation in position and appearance is used to recover robot pose. Let us define the *encoding* $\mathbf{k}_l$ of a landmark candidate l as the projection of the intensity distribution in the image subwindow represented by l into the subspace defined by the principal components decomposition of the set of all tracked landmark prototypes. The projection is computed using $\mathbf{k}_l = \mathbf{U}^T \mathbf{l}$, where $\mathbf{l}$ is the local intensity distribution of l normalized to unit magnitude and $\mathbf{U}$ is the set of principal directions of the space defined by the tracked landmark prototypes.

Let us now define a *feature-vector* $\mathbf{f}$ associated with a landmark candidate l as the principal components encoding $\mathbf{k}$, concatenated with two vector quantities: the image position $\mathbf{p}$ of the landmark and the camera position $\mathbf{c}$ from which the landmark was observed: $\mathbf{f} = |\mathbf{k} \, \mathbf{p} \, \mathbf{c}|$, where, in this particular instance alone, the notation $|\mathbf{a} \, \mathbf{b}|$ represents the concatenation of the vectors $\mathbf{a}$ and $\mathbf{b}$.

Given the associated feature vector $\mathbf{f}_i$ for each landmark l_i in the tracked landmark $T = \{l_1, l_2, \ldots, l_m\}$, the matrix $\mathbf{F}$ is constructed as the composite matrix of all $\mathbf{f}_i$, arranged in column-wise fashion. Take the singular values decomposition of $\mathbf{F}$, $\mathbf{F} = [\mathbf{f}_1 \cdots \mathbf{f}_n] = \mathbf{U}_F \mathbf{W} \mathbf{V}^T$ to obtain $\mathbf{U}_F$, representing the set of eigenvectors of the tracked landmark T arranged in column-wise fashion. Note that since $\mathbf{c}_i$ is a component of each $\mathbf{f}_i$, $\mathbf{U}_F$ encodes camera position along with appearance. Now consider the feature vector $\mathbf{f}_l$ associated with l, the observed landmark for which we have no pose information, that is, the $\mathbf{c}$ component

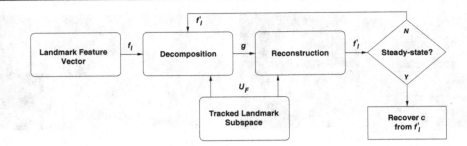

Figure 9.6. The recovery operation. The unknown camera position **c** associated with a landmark *l* is recovered by repeatedly reconstructing the landmark feature vector in the subspace defined by the matching tracked landmark.

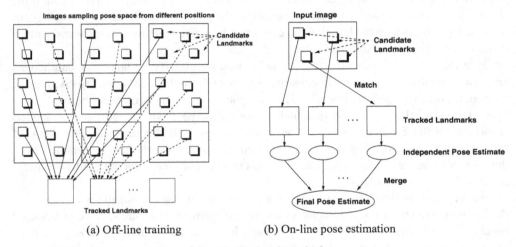

(a) Off-line training   (b) On-line pose estimation

Figure 9.7. An overview of the eigenlandmark method.

of $\mathbf{f}_l$ is undetermined. If we project $\mathbf{f}_l$ into the subspace defined by $\mathbf{U}_F$ to obtain $\mathbf{g} = \mathbf{U}_F^T\mathbf{f}_l$ and then reconstruct $\mathbf{f}_l$ from $\mathbf{g}$, we obtain the feature vector $\mathbf{f}_l' = \mathbf{U}_F\mathbf{g}$. Then the resulting reconstruction $\mathbf{f}_l'$ is augmented by a camera pose estimate that interpolates between the nearest eigenvectors in $\mathbf{U}_F$. In practice, the initial value of the undetermined camera pose, **c** in $\mathbf{f}_l$, will play a role in the resulting estimate and so we substitute the new value of **c** back into $\mathbf{f}_l$ and repeat the operation, reconstructing $\mathbf{f}_l'$ until the estimate converges to a steady state. This repeated operation, which constitutes the recovery of the unknown **c**, is summarized in Figure 9.6.

Formally, $\mathbf{f}_l' = \mathbf{U}_F\mathbf{U}_F^T\mathbf{f} = \mathbf{W}_{opt}\mathbf{f}_l$, where $\mathbf{W}_{opt}$ is the optimizing scatter matrix of the feature vectors in T, and hence $\mathbf{f}_l'$ corresponds to the least-squares approximation of $\mathbf{f}$ in the subspace defined by the feature vectors of the tracked landmark T. Convergence is guaranteed by the fact that $\mathbf{U}_F$ is column-orthonormal, and hence $\mathbf{W}_{opt}$ is symmetric and positive-definite. The entire process is summarized in Figure 9.7.

9.7   Correlation-Based Localization

One limitation of feature-based methods for localization is that they depend on a process by which geometric features are inferred from sensor measurements. For range sensors, it is possible to exploit the distribution of spatial occupancy directly. We can model a range sensor as a device that returns a probability that specific locations z in space are occupied or unoccupied, based on the measurement(s) s observed: $P(z|s)$. Localization then entails finding the maximum correlation between the observed spatial occupancy probabilities and the known map, subject to constraints from *a priori* knowledge regarding the robot pose.

In practice, this is often accomplished using a map in the form of a spatial occupancy representation (see Section 7.2.1). Space is represented using a fixed-resolution grid such that each cell in the grid describes the likelihood that a cell is non-empty. The measurement being used is also described using an occupancy grid, and the observed grid is matched to the existing map by simply computing the sum of the squared differences between the observation grid and the map. This can also be computed implicitly with a deep neural network.

9.8   Global Localization

Several methods can be used to refine an erroneous but almost correct pose estimate. This type of problem arises in practice when, for example, the robot is restarted or when it has been determined that the ongoing localization estimate process has failed. While most practitioners would prefer to assume their robots are robust, many real systems need to be "reinitialized" from time to time.

Most existing solutions to position estimation consider performing localization from either one or a few possible vantage points without taking into account the possibility that self-similarity in the environment may make the resulting position estimate ambiguous (e.g., the individual offices in a building or ravines in an outdoor environment may not be readily distinguishable). In principle it may not be possible to obtain a solution to the global localization problem from an observation if the environment is sufficiently self-similar. Using multiple measurements from different positions and a known orientation permits the problem to be solved, but at least in certain cases the problem of localization with minimum travel is NP-complete [243].

Some consideration has been given to strategies that collect information from multiple locations in the environment (e.g., [73], [438], [235]). One approach is to incrementally compute a certainty distribution for the robot's position as a function of the extent to which its current observations can be associated with different parts of the environment. Such an approach based on "Markov localization" (see Section 4.9.2) was discussed in the context of incremental mapping. In the following, we examine some of the theoretical limits to localization. In order to simplify the task, we consider the use of an idealized range sensor and consider the difficulty of global localization in the context of a two-dimensional world in which global orientation is known.

In this context, the data returned to the robot by the idealized range sensor can be described as a **visibility polygon** V seen from the position of the robot in the environment: this describes the subregion of the environment that is directly visible from the robot's current position (see Figure 9.8). Since this visible region must fit somewhere within the

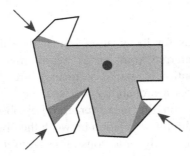

Figure 9.8. Visibility polygon for a robot, shown as a circle, in a polygonal environment. The visibility polygon is shaded. The visibility skeleton is the lighter region within the visibility polygon.

actual environment, the first step in localization can be framed as the task of embedding this visibility polygon within the map.

Global localization by embedding is addressed in [325]. Given a polygonal environment map P defined by n vertices and a visibility polygon V seen by the robot, the authors provide an algorithm to compute the set H of "hypothetical locations" in P whose visible portion of P matches V, that is, the set of regions consistent with the observed sensor data. They show that there can be up to $O(n)$ consistent regions. Finding these alternative ambiguous locations can be "looked up" in $O(mn)$ time, where m is the number of vertices of the visibility polygon V. They also show that with sufficient preprocessing, the lookup can be achieved even more efficiently.

The global localization problem then entails reducing this set of possible locations to a single one by moving about the environment. If the view from the initial position of the robot matches several possible locations in the environment (i.e., if the visibility polygon from this position can be placed in more than one location in the map polygon), then the robot must travel to other positions and make more observations in order to distinguish between these various possibilities. In the case of idealized sensing, the given algorithm could provide the initial input for the strategy summarized in what follows [242], [243].

Global localization using visibility polygons involves starting with a visibility polygon measured by our idealized range sensor, computing the set of ambiguous hypothetical locations, and then moving about to rule out all but one. More formally: given P and V, determine the set of all points $p \in P$ such that the visibility polygon of p is exactly V [i.e., $V(p) = V$], and if this set H contains more than one point, then travel in P and take further probes until only one location in P is consistent with all of the visibility polygons seen previously. To discretize the problem in this model, P is partitioned into a set of visibility *cells*.

A **visibility cell** C of a polygon P is a maximally connected subset of P with the property that any two points in C see the same subset of vertices of P ([105], [325]). That is, each cell C is a neighborhood over which exactly the same set of vertices of the environment can be observed. A *visibility cell decomposition* of P is simply a subdivision of a polygon P into a set of visibility cells. The visibility cell decomposition can be computed in $O(n^3 \log n)$ time [105].

The global localization can be naturally cast in terms of a decision tree: at each place where a new observation can be collected (i.e., at each visibility cell) a decision can be made as to where to move to collect additional data. This decision tree can, in principle, be fully precomputed from the known map. The branches of the tree can be weighted to reflect the distance between observation points. We can define the decision problem **robot localizing decision tree** (RLDT) as that of finding the minimum-height tree that assures us that we know where we are.

To perform localization using visibility cells, we construct an *overlay arrangement A* that combines the k translates P_j that correspond to the hypothetical locations, together with their visibility cell decompositions. By "translate P_j" we mean P translated so that the jth hypothetical location p_j in H moves to the origin ($1 \leq j \leq k$). To illustrate the complexity hardness of the global robot localization problem RLDT, we assume that we are given as a simple polygon P a star-shaped polygon V (the subregion that is visible), both with a common reference orientation and the set H of all possible initial locations $p_i \in P$ such that $V(p_i) = V$.

Theorem 1 *RLDT is NP-hard.*

Proof sketch: First consider the visibility model. The problem of constructing a minimum height decision tree to localize a robot can be formulated as a decision problem by asking if there exists a decision tree of height less than or equal to h to localize a robot in a polygon P whose initial visibility region is V.

This can be shown to be NP-hard using a reduction from the **abstract decision tree (ADT)** problem, which was proven to be NP-Complete by Hyafil and Rivest [377]. An instance of the abstract decision tree problem consists of a cost h, a set $X = \{x_1, \ldots, x_m\}$ of objects, and a set $\mathcal{T} = \{T_1, \ldots, T_n\}$ of subsets of X, each of which represents a binary test, where test T_j is positive on object x_i if $x_i \in T_j$ and is negative otherwise. The problem is to determine, given X, $\mathcal{T}$, and h, whether a binary decision tree of height less than or equal to h can be constructed to identify the objects in X. In order to identify an unknown object, the test at the root is performed on the object, and if it is positive the right branch is taken; otherwise, the left branch is taken.

Given an instance of ADT, we create an instance of the localization problem as follows. We construct P to be a staircase-shaped, simple, closed, C^0 continuous curve (i.e., a polygon), with a stair for each object $x_i \in X$ (see Figure 9.9). For each stair we construct $n = |\mathcal{T}|$ protrusions, one for each test in $\mathcal{T}$ (see Figure 9.10). The structure of each protrusion encodes the result of the corresponding test. $\square$

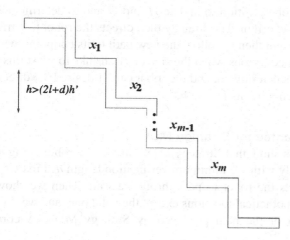

Figure 9.9. Construction showing localization is NP-hard.

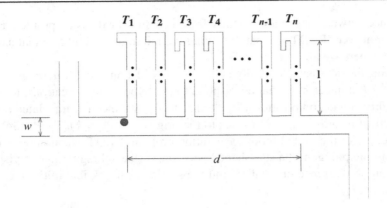

Figure 9.10. Close-up of a stair in the NP-hard construction.

Consider a robot that is initially located at the shaded circle shown in Figure 9.10 on one of the m stairs. The visibility region V at this point has $O(n)$ vertices and is the same on any stair.

In order for the robot to localize itself, it must either travel to one of the "ends" of P (either the top or the bottom stair) to discover on which stair it was located initially, or it must examine a sufficient number of the n protrusions on the stair where it is located to distinguish that stair from all the others. However, the vertical distance between stairs is very much greater than the lengths of the protrusions or the distance between the first and the last. For this construction, we can show that any procedure for optimal localization can also be used for the ADT problem via this construction. Complete details of the proof are given in [242].

Strategy MDL directs the robot to travel along paths from the origin to points in the overlay arrangement A. Suppose that p_j is the true initial location of the robot. We will prove in the next subsection that Strategy MDL only directs the robot to follow paths that are contained in translate P_j. Note that a path from the origin that is contained in P_j is analogous to a path in P from location p_j.

From the initial H and Q, an initial $path_*(q*)$ can be selected. The strategy directs the robot to travel along this path and to make a probe at its endpoint. The robot then uses the information gained at the probe position to update H and Q and to determine a new $q*$ and a new $path_*(q*)$ from the origin. The strategy then directs the robot to retrace its previous path back to the origin and then to follow the new path to its endpoint, which is the next probe location. This process stops when the size of H shrinks to 1. At this point the initial location of the robot is determined, and the robot can, if desired, be directed to return to its initial location by retracing its last path.

9.8.1 A Performance Guarantee for Strategy MDL

The following theorems show that Strategy MDL directs the robot along a path whose length compares favorably with the minimum verification length d. First we show that Strategy MDL never directs the robot to pass through a wall. Then we show that Strategy MDL eliminates all hypothetical locations except the valid one, and we establish an upper bound on the length of the path produced by Strategy MDL. A corollary of Theorem 3 is that the localizing decision tree associated with Strategy MDL has a weighted height that is at most $2(k - 1)$ times the height of an optimal localizing decision tree.

Theorem 2 *Strategy MDL never directs the robot to pass through a wall* en route *to another location.*

Proof sketch: Attempting to pass through a wall would imply an attempt to visit a point *farther* than the wall w involved in the collision. Such a wall w would contain a reference point, however, and the strategy always visits the closest reference points first. □

Theorem 3 *Strategy MDL localizes the robot by directing it along a path whose length is at most $(k - 1)d$, where $k = |H|$, and d is the length of an optimal verification tour for the robot's initial position.*

Proof sketch: Let p_t denote the true initial location of the robot. We can show that Strategy MDL eliminates all hypothetical initial locations in H except p_t (a similar theorem using different input cells is proven in [243]).

Next we establish the upper bound on the length of the path determined by Strategy MDL. Because the strategy never directs the robot to a sensing site that does not eliminate one or more elements from H, it requires the robot to make a trip from its initial location to some sensing point and back at most $k - 1$ times.

We claim that each round trip has length at most d. To see this, we first consider how a robot traveling along an optimal verification tour L would rule out an arbitrary incorrect hypothetical location p_b. Then we consider how Strategy MDL would rule out p_b.

Consider a robot travelling along tour L that eliminates each invalid hypothetical location at the first point x on L where the signature of x relative to the invalid hypothetical location differs from the signature of x relative to P_t. Let w be the point on L where the robot rules out p_b. The point w must lie on the boundary of some cell C in the arrangement A that distinguishes p_b from p_t. Cell C generates a reference point $q_{C,t} \in Q$, that is the closest point of C to the origin, where distance is measured inside P_t, so $d_t(q_{C,t}) \leq d_t(w)$. Since p_t is the true initial location of the robot, the distance $d_t(w)$ is equal to or less than the distance along L of w from the origin, as well as the distance along L from w back to the origin. Putting these inequalities together, we deduce that the distance $d_t(q_{C,t})$ is equal to or less than half the length of L.

Since p_t is the true initial location of the robot, it remains active throughout the entire execution of the strategy. In particular, it is active at the moment Strategy MDL directs the robot to move from the origin to the sensing site where it eliminates p_b. Since p_b is about to be ruled out, it is also still active. That means that the reference point $q_{C,t}$ considered in the previous paragraph is still active, since it distinguishes p_b from p_t.

At this time Strategy MDL directs the robot to travel along $path_*(q*) = path_j(q)$. By design, the length $d_*(q*) = d_j(q)$ of this path, which is the distance the robot will travel from the origin to the next sensing position, is the minimum over all $d_i(q)$ for active $p_i \in H$ and $q \in Q$. In particular, since point $q_{C,t}$ is still active, $d_*(q*)$ is equal to or less than $d_t(q_{C,t})$. As we have seen, however, this latter distance is equal to or less than half the length of L. Therefore, Strategy MDL directs the robot to travel along a loop from the origin to some sensing position where the robot eliminates p_b and back, and the length of this loop is at most d. $\square$

We can define a *k-competitive* robot localization strategy as one that localizes a robot by travelling a distance no more than k times the length of an optimal verification tour. By this definition Strategy MDL is $(k - 1)$-competitive, where $k = |H|$. Note that if a verifying path is not required to return to its starting point, the bound for Theorem 3 becomes $2(k - 1)d$.

Corollary 4 *The weighted height of the localizing decision tree constructed by Strategy MDL is at most $2(k - 1)$ times the weighted height of an optimal localizing decision tree for the same problem.*

9.8.2 Practical One-Shot Global Localization

The set of possible poses of the robot within the environment can be considered as the domain of a quality function $E'_{cqm}(x, y, \theta)$. Provided that sufficient local variability exists, the true pose of the robot can be computed from a single sensor reading by testing the sensor data against each possible pose value via the function $E_{cqm}(\cdot)$. The space of possible poses is, in general, too large to permit this. [492] describes a method based on local gradient descent to compute the pose without a prior estimate. This method is based on sampling the space of possible poses and performing a refinement of the pose estimate at each sample point. Sampling is necessary since $E_{cqm}(\cdot)$ is globally non-convex. In the following, we describe the parallel computation of the multiple local optima, although a multiple restart gradient descent method would be a natural alternative.

Each potential sampled pose $q = (x, y, \theta)$ within the map region is considered as an initial pose estimate of the robot, and E'_{cqm} is the comparative quality measure of the *converged* pose following local pose localization. More explicitly, $E'_{cqm}(x, y, \theta) = E_{cqm}(x_c, y_c, \theta_c)$, where (x_c, y_c, θ_c) is the pose found by local localization given the *initial* pose estimate (x, y, θ). From this, one obtains a global quality function that describes the quality of localization when applied to a particular location, and the pose for which E'_{cqm} is a global maximum is the true pose of the robot. This results in a highly non-convex function (although convex local to the global maximum) because any estimate that converges closely to the true pose will have a high quality, and any that does not will have a much lower (often orders of magnitude lower) quality. Therefore, local gradient information in the lower-valued regions may not assist in the search for the global maximum over the domain of the entire environment, but only in the convex regions. Once a pose estimate E'_{cqm} of sufficient quality has been found, gradient ascent can be used to refine the estimate.

Sampling in this context is accomplished by applying the localization algorithm to selected poses in (x, y, θ) space and checking the value of E'_{cqm}. With any application of sampling a proper selection of sampling size is critical. Using the methodology presented in the previous section we can make estimates of the region of convergence of the localization algorithm in the selected environment using the selected sensors. If the candidate locations for global localization can be determined in advance, the appropriate regions of convergence can be computed. These, in turn, indicate the sampling interval needed for global localization since any sample within the region of convergence of the true pose will provide a good pose estimate with E'_{cqm}.

In the absence of prior information on the loci for localization, selecting the appropriate sampling of the map is more difficult. The sizes of the regions of convergence are not constant over the environment, nor can they be easily computed analytically, although they can be estimated in simulation (assuming the sensor properties can be accurately modeled). This suggests that the correct sample points can be computed on the basis of estimated regions of convergence determined using the map. In general, estimates computed from samples that reside in regions with large areas are more likely to contain the robot, so the sampling can be prioritized to maximize efficiency.

This idea can be exploited even without precomputation in a context reminiscent of a scale space. The approach is a "coarse-to-fine" strategy: initially, the environment is coarsely sampled (samples are placed far apart). If no satisfactory results are found from these samples, the environment is resampled more finely, and the results are again evaluated. This process can continue with smaller and smaller sampling sizes, until the true pose has been found.

A final strategy is attractive if the robot is permitted to move about to select the location (with unknown coordinates) for sampling. Using only local information, the robot can move into a comparatively free region of its enclosing space. This will reduce the local clutter, which, in turn, will put the robot into a region associated with a larger region of convergence.

9.9 Biological Approaches to Localization

There is a large and fascinating literature on the ways in which biological organisms develop and utilize internal environmental representations to enable localization and pose maintenance. Although many results are species specific, the basic approaches used by biological systems are being adapted to robotic systems.

Biological systems that travel long distances and manage to perform localization year after year such as migratory songbirds seem to utilize a variety of different sensing modalities to solve the localization problem. Some of these sensing modalities were described in Chapters 4 and 5, and it is clear that biological systems are capable of constructing complex internal representations based on these sensor systems. For example, there is evidence of magnetic map representations that form the basis of gradient maps for localization that are effective far beyond the range of data that could have been used to construct this internal representation (see [293] for a review of a number of different species and their use of map structures). There is also compelling evidence that multi-modal cue integration can take place when accessing these internal representations, at least in some species [224].

9.10 Further Reading

Navigation There is an extensive literature on navigation, especially as it applies to ships. Taylor's review of ancient navigation techniques [760] describes navigation strategies from about 1500 BC to the voyages of Captain Cook. Also see Cortés' 1561 [185] and Davis' 1633 [206] navigation guides.

Pose estimation There is a large literature on global pose estimation (the dropoff problem) and local pose estimation, although very few reviews exist. [752] provides a general survey of vision-based techniques. [77] provides an in-depth study of the mathematical solution of range-based localization. [257] reviews a wide range of localization problems from a computational geometry perspective. [289] and [287] provide an introduction to localization and the use of Markov localization to solve the global localization problem.

Triangulation-based systems [753] describes a vision-based system that relies on rooftop models in urban environments. [762] examines algorithmic solutions to localization based on distance (**trilateration**) and their numerical accuracy.

Fingerprinting There is a large literature on fingerprinting, driven in part by its use in indoor localization for cell phones (see [849]). [593] describes a visual fingerprinting algorithm for autonomous systems.

9.11　Problems

1. Derive the pose of a robot given a sensor set that computes the robot's position from two point landmarks using triangulation under the following assumptions

   (a) The distance to each landmark can be directly observed.
   (b) The absolute orientation to each landmark can be directly observed.

2. From its early beginnings as artillery ranging technology in 1917, the Decca Navigator was the basis of many navigational systems in World War II and it became the basis of the MF Loran A system used for ship navigation through the 1960s [636]. Two radio transmitters a distance d apart emit pulses at the same time. Assuming that the speed of propagation of the signal is constant, it is possible to navigate by following lines of constant signal delay. The resulting navigation is known as hyperbolic navigation. Prove that following a path of constant signal delay is equivalent to following a hyperbolic curve.

3. Derive the GDOP for a robot that computes its position from two point landmarks using triangulation under the following assumptions:

   (a) The distance to each landmark can be directly observed with an uncertainty that varies linearly with distance.
   (b) The absolute orientation to each landmark can be directly observed.
   (c) The distance to each landmark can be directly observed with an uncertainty that is independent of distance.

4. Suppose we have a robot moving on a large planar environment that is populated by many known and easily recognized landmarks, but that each acquisition and localization of a landmark has a fixed cost. For each localized landmark the robot obtains the distance from the robot's current pose to the landmark. How should the robot choose which landmark(s) to localize in order to maximize the certainty of the estimate of the robot's position while minimizing the cost?

5. Markov localization accommodates the possibility of ambiguous position esti-mates that may later be resolved by additional measurements. Suggest two examples of how that can arise in practice both indoors and outdoors. The method is based on an assumption that sensor error can be modeled with a Gaussian distribution. Suggest two instances where this assumption is violated.

6. Pose estimation for a point robot in a 2D world typically involves estimating translation and orientation.

   (a) Show an example polygon illustrating how position within the polygon cannot be uniquely determined using only perfect range data from a known environment if orientation is unknown. Show an example where translation can be uniquely determined without knowledge of orientation.

   (b) If the environment is modeled by a polygon, can the amount of uncertainty in position be directly related to the number of ambiguous positions? If the environment is a regular polygon? If the environment is merely a "star-shaped" polygon?

7. Describe a procedure for determining the pose of a robot in a 2D world using only "wall following," assuming that a perfect map is available and that the absolute orientation of the robot can be determined at any time.

8. Can the procedure described in the previous question be used in a 3D polygonal environment?

9. A compass has proven to be a particularly powerful tool in assisting in localiza-tion on the plane.

   (a) Develop a general solution for solving for the location of a robot on the plane, given absolute bearing to two known landmarks.

   (b) Develop a general solution for solving for the location of a robot on the plane, given absolute bearing and distance to one known landmark.

10

Mapping and Related Tasks

Maps are "an inexhaustible fund of interest for any man with eyes to see or with two pence worth of imagination to understand with."[1]

"Here there be dragons"
Label placed by ancient map-makers for unexplored regions of a map.

A map says to you, "Read me carefully, follow me closely, doubt me not." It says, "I am the earth in the palm of your hand. Without me, you are alone and lost."[2]

For autonomous robots it may seem like we can avoid needing the ability to make maps automatically. That is, it is sometimes assumed that a robot should be able to take for granted the *a priori* availability of a map. Unfortunately, this is rarely the case. Not only do architectural blueprints or related types of maps fail to be consistently reliable (since even during construction they are not always updated to reflect necessary alternations),[3] but, furthermore, numerous aspects of an environment are not likely to appear on a map, such as tables, chairs, and transitory objects.

Perhaps equally important, maps usually represent structural elements in some abstract domain (perhaps with semantic labels), while a mobile robot must be able to relate its current location directly to its own perceptions regarding its environment. Maps made for people often depend on the interpretative skills of the persons using the map and on their ability to make functional inferences, abilities often absent in computational systems. Further, the sensory characteristics of objects, if annotated at all in maps, will be those of relevance to a human observer.

Constructing an extensive map for a robot by hand is a very difficult and tedious job. Although measuring the inside of a single room may be straightforward, reconstructing an accurate metric map of a large indoor environment is difficult to manage, as a clear line of sight may not be available between salient environmental features.

The sensory or functional characteristics of relevance to a human may not be of similar relevance to a robot and vice versa. This suggests that an appropriate map for an autonomous robot should relate to the types of sensor data the robot is likely to observe. Thus, it may be appropriate to indicate locations associated with spurious sensor readings, regions with large amounts of radio interference, and so on, rather than the location of

---

[1] R. L. Stevenson, *Treasure Island.*
[2] B. Markham in *West With the Night.*
[3] Indeed, one valid robotic application is the construction of "as built" maps of the environment.

washrooms. In general, these factors imply that the ability to perform some degree of autonomous map construction, updating, and validation is of primary importance.

Maps can take many forms. Two specific representational extremes are particularly relevant to mobile robotics: **metric maps**, which are based on an absolute reference frame and numerical estimates of where objects are in space, and **topological maps** (also known as **relational maps**), which only explicitly represent connectivity information, typically in the from of a graph. Each of these categories of representation admits various specific descriptions. Further, many real representations have both a topological and a metric component. For example metric maps representing the explicit occupancy of space or **geometric maps** representing specific labelled objects often include connectivity information. Metric maps appear to be the most intuitive: a tourist's scale map of a city is a metric map. In terms of mobile robots, perhaps the most explicit form of map is a metric map in configuration space (see Section 7.1.1), in which all possible motions (except those ruled out by non-holonomic constraints) are given explicitly. Recall that obstacles, when transformed into configuration space in the form of **C-space obstacles**, can take on more complex shapes than in actual space. For example, in the configuration space defined by 2D translation and rotation, polygonal obstacles become ruled surfaces.

Topological maps, in contrast to metric maps, naturally capture qualitative and relational information while de-emphasizing what may be irrelevant or confusing details. As a result, topological maps have a very explicit connection to tasks and the semantics of a problem. A typical subway map, or the typical navigation instructions used by humans over substantial regions of space, are examples of topological representations. Several authors have suggested that purely metric maps are not well suited for representing large-scale space.

In order to exploit the advantages of both metric and topological representations, it is often appropriate to consider the construction of one representation using observations from another, less abstract representation. In addition, it is natural to consider local descriptions before large-scale inter-relationships. This leads naturally to a hierarchical layering of successive representations of map data, such as the following five layers [232]:

Sensorial Raw data signals or signal-domain transformations of these signals.

Geometric Two- or three-dimensional objects inferred from sensor data.

Local relational Functional, structural or semantic relations between geometric objects that are near one another (i.e., at individual locations).

Topological The large-scale relational links that connect objects and *locations* across the environment as a whole.

Semantic Functional labels associated with the constituents of the map.

Chatila and Laumond [155] were among the first to describe a set of map descriptions that derived a topological representation of the environment from a metric one. In contrast, Kuipers and Levitt [440] considered the inference of metric data from an essentially topological representation. Their exploration methods, discussed later, consider the use of low-level topological landmarks as the most basic primitive observation from which metric inference can be derived.

A second dichotomy relates to the type of data represented on a map. Most conventional maps depict the occupancy of space in either two or three dimensions. A distinctly different class of map of particular relevance to robots is **perceptual maps** that directly relate observed sensor measurements to spatial pose without resorting to an intermediate description in terms of physical objects. This type of representation is readily imagined in the context of olfaction but is equally applicable to other sensing modalities. Such maps were discussed earlier in the context of visual servoing (Section 9.3). and perceptual structure (Section 9.6).

Map exploration is a requirement for many realistic mobile robotics applications. Not only are existing maps of most environments inaccurate, but almost every environment occupied by humans undergoes ongoing change. As a result, mobile robot systems must be able to accommodate change in their environments. If they are to maintain maps, they must be able to update them.

10.1   Sensorial Maps

Maps based on direct sensor readings offer the possibility of coupling the environmental representation as directly as possible with the sensors that the robot uses to perceive the environment. The basic idea is to make sensor measurements coupled with odometry information and to then use a technique such as servo control (Section 9.3) or to identify features in the sensor responses, in order to navigate with respect to the map.

As a robot moves through its environment, it collects sensor readings. Assuming perfect odometry, after some period of time the robot will have collected a set of measurements

$$\{I_i^j(x_i, y_i, \theta_i)\}.$$

Given sufficient I_i^j, such that we can compute a continuous approximation to I_i^j, say $I(x, y, \theta)$, then one could use servo control–like methods to navigate with respect to $I(x, y, \theta)$. The difficulty with this type of approach is that one must know how to sample the set of possible measurements and how to construct the continuous I from the measurements $\{I_i^j(x_i, y_i, \theta_i)\}$.

Rather than using I to build a direct mapping from sensor readings to pose, the measurements I_i^j can be used as the primary measurements represented in the map. For example, Li *et al.* [464] describe a system for the construction of 2D maps of street environments. The robot eventually constructs a graph-like representation of space in which the edges of the graph correspond to streets while the nodes of the graph correspond to intersections. The representation is based on constructing a visual panorama of the left and right sides of the street as the robot moves. The robot explores by constructing closed loops in the environment (e.g., by taking the left-hand street at each intersection) and then identifies closed loops by identifying that the current 2D panorama matches a previously identified panorama. Panoramas can also be exploited in a less well-constrained environment. For example, Bourque and co-workers [108], [109] describe a system in which quicktime-VR panoramas are generated at different locations in an indoor environment, which become nodes in a graph representing the space. The nodes in this case are defined by an attention operator inspired by models of human visual attention, and the nodes are thus chosen to be those that might be most interesting to humans, at least at a pre-semantic level. In that work, a technique referred to as **alpha-backtracking** (parameterized by the variable α) is used to trade additional travel by the exploring robot against the optimality of the sample locations chosen for the topological representation.

10.2   Geometric Maps

Geometric maps (see Section 7.2.2) can be an efficient description of the environment, assuming that the sensor provides suitable data and that the environment to be described is well suited to the geometric modelling primitives to be used.

The exploration of an unknown environment, the construction of a geometric map from that exploration, and related problems have been studied extensively in the field of computational geometry. Exploration relates to a variety of related capabilities. This includes searching for a specific objective or goal position, searching for a route with specific properties, covering free space, and learning about the occupancy of space (i.e., mapping).

A broad class of problems deals with search in unknown or partially known environments. Such problems are of interest not only in their own right, but also because they are closely related to environment exploration in general (where the goal being sought is additional geometric knowledge).

Several algorithms have been developed for navigation in an uncertain environment. These algorithms discover the position of the goal, or of obstacles in the environment, in the course of navigation and hence are naturally classified as a form of exploration algorithm. The Bug algorithm seen in Section 7.3.3 provides one such example.

Papadimitriou and Yannakakis [598] considered the task of moving between a known starting position and a known goal in an *a priori* unknown environment occupied by non-intersecting rectilinear obstacles (i.e., rectangular obstacles aligned with the world coordinate system). They described an elegant and intuitive algorithm that continually moves the robot toward the straight line connecting the starting location and the goal when faced with an obstruction (or in an arbitrary direction at other times). Significantly, they demonstrate that this algorithm is optimal in certain simple cases and that in more general environments no bound is possible.

Different geometric representations can result in very different exploration and search algorithms. For example, a **street** is a polygon such that a start S and goal T on the boundary of the polygon partition the edges into two groups (left and right) and every edge on the left is visible from some point on the right (i.e., they are mutually **weakly visible**). These polygons can be divided, in essence, into a "right" and "left" side defined by partitioning the polygon into two chains divided at the starting and goal locations. This is illustrated in Figure 10.1. Several researchers have considered the problem of moving from S to T without an *a priori* map of the polygon. The robot is assumed to be able to observe the side label (*left* or *right*) to which any given segment of the wall belongs. Kleinberg developed an algorithm with a competitive ratio of $2\sqrt{2}$, improving an earlier

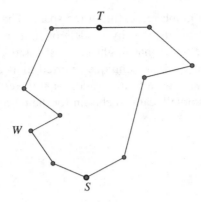

Figure 10.1. A *street* defined by vertices S and T. Note that the pair of vertices S and W do not define a street, since there are points on the clockwise (right) chain that cannot see any point on the other (left) chain.

result by Klein [423]. Using this algorithm, it is possible to find the *optimal* L_1-shortest path in a rectilinear street.

A LR-chord is defined as a line connecting a point from the left chain to a point from the right chain. A **generalized street** (or G-street) is a polygon such that every point on the boundary is visible from some point on some LR-chord; this is a larger class of polygons than the streets. It can be readily demonstrated that an optimal path from S to T must move from one LR-chord to another. With only horizontal motions, it is possible to travel anywhere through the polygon, and this, in turn, motivates the use of an L_1 norm as a distance metric. By carefully orchestrating motions and using spiral search to find turning points so that the robot stays between the appropriate "sides" of the polygon, the algorithm produces a path whose length from S to T is optimal as measured by the L_1 metric.

Datta and Icking [203, 423] developed a navigation alogrithm for moving from a starting location to an unknown goal location within a class of polygons known as rectilinear **generalized streets** (G-streets).

The task of automatically constructing a geometric map has also been considered as a practical task [843]. [843] uses an omnidirectional visual sensor to construct a geometric representation of the free space around the robot. Assuming perfect odometry, the robot constructs a polygonal object that represents the free space around itself. Each time the robot moves, visible vertical lines are tracked and their positions are recomputed using triangulation. Vertical lines that cannot be associated with previously viewed environmental structure are postulated as new structure and are added to the map (it takes two different views of a new feature in order to obtain a position estimate). All map items are connected in a radial fashion in order to build up a representation of free space. It is assumed that the space within the polygon formed by linking the edges in a radial fashion is empty.

Figure 10.2 illustrates the process of exploration. Dashed lines connect the robot (depicted as a dark rectangle) with sensed structure and the free space polygon is drawn in solid lines. As the robot moves, more sensor measurements are made and a larger region is explored. This particular approach has a number of limitations. It is difficult to know if all of space has been explored, the system cannot describe very complex open spaces, and the exploration process is driven by an external operator; the system does not decide where or when to explore.

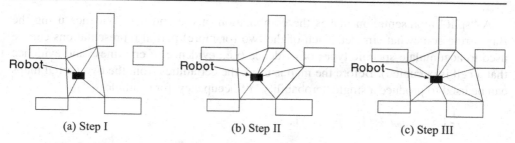

(a) Step I (b) Step II (c) Step III

Figure 10.2. Stages in the geometric exploration of space: three snapshots in the exploration of space using the algorithm described in [843]. Under external control, the robot moves and builds a geometric model of free space.

Geometric maps are probably the most commonly used form of map in autonomous robotics. Thus it is not surprising that much of the work in autonomous mapping is based on obtaining geometric maps. Algorithms can be roughly broken down into two groups: (1) algorithms that map their environment without dealing with maintaining a pose estimate within that map, and (2) algorithms that solve mapping and localization simultaneously. These two basic approaches are considered next.

10.2.1 Mapping without Localization

Elfes and Moravec [543, 249] (see also [431]) pioneered the concept of mapping using an occupancy grid representation. The basic idea is to construct an occupancy grid based on sensor measurements as the robot moves through the environment. Some implementations involve two complementary representations: one for the certainty that a cell is empty, a second for the degree of certainty that a cell is full. The maintenance and use of occupancy representations is typically carried out using a Bayesian probability update scheme. To do this, a probabilistic model of the sensor is required that relates different possible measurements to the configurations of the environment that might give rise to them.

Consider, for example, the case of a line-of-sight range sensor such as an idealized laser. We wish to measure distance along the line of sight, but when the sensor returns a particular distance reading r, it it may not accurately reflect the true distance z due to corruption by electrical noise, optical noise, or other causes. What we need is the probability $p(r|z)$ of a given range reading r for an actual distance z to the nearest obstacle. Now we can compute

$$p(z|r) = \frac{p(z)p(r|z)}{p(r)},$$

where the most likely value of z for a given reading r is the one that maximizes this *a posteriori* estimate. The normalization term $p(r)$ can be computed using

$$p(r) = \int_{z-min}^{z-max} p(x)p(r|x)dx.$$

An occupancy grid is used to describe regions of the world as occupying one of a discrete set of possible states, each with a fixed probability, computed using the observed sensor data and any prior beliefs: $p(W|R)$, where W is the world state and R is the set of observations used.

A "split" representation makes the combination of old and new evidence using the Bayes rule somewhat simpler. Each of the two (or more) partial representations can be used to accumulate specific types of evidence (i.e., evidence of emptiness and evidence that a cell is occupied). Before the map is used, the certainties from the two partial maps can be used to produce a single "probability" of occupancy, for example,

$$\frac{1}{2} \left[p_{occupied} + (1 - p_{empty}) \right].$$

In the context of map acquisition in an unknown environment, the occupancy grid is initially set to reflect no knowledge of the occupancy of the world. As the robot acquires measurements, elements of the grid are updated using the Bayes rule:

$$p(W|R) = \frac{p(R|W)p(W)}{p(R)},$$

which provides the **posterior distribution**. $p(R|W)$ describes the behavior of the sensor: how likely it is to return a given measurement for a given state of the world. $p(W)$ describes the *prior* belief regarding how likely particular configurations of the world are. $p(R)$ reflects the likelihood of a particular sensor measurement across all possible configurations of the world, again computed using

$$P(R_i) = \sum_j P(R_i|W_j)P(W_j).$$

The world model W that maximizes this posterior distribution is then, with respect to Bayesian decision theory, the most "reasonable" description of the environment. This is referred to as a **maximum *a posteriori*** (or **MAP**) estimate.

The absence of model-specific assumptions makes the technique very general. Occupancy grids provide a uniform framework for combining data from multiple sensors. This advantage, however, is qualified by the need for accurate probabilistic models of sensor performance. In addition, the spatial quantization inherent in the occupancy representation can either make it inefficient in terms of memory utilization or limit the fidelity of the map obtained. A further issue is that since the spatiotemporal origin of individual measurements is discarded in the mapping process, it can be difficult to construct an accurate geometric model from an occupancy representation. This difficulty is compounded by the need to limit the individual cell size. Once an occupancy representation has been computed, it can be used to localize the robot by correlating the existing grid with a (partial) grid obtained from recent sensor data (see Section 9.7).

Ideal distance sensors and probabilistic representations are not the only possible mechanisms for exploiting occupancy grids in the construction of environmental maps. For example, [559] describes a system that uses trinocular stereo vision and a more *ad hoc* probability combination rule to build an occupancy grid of the environment.

A critical assumption of the mapping without localization approach is the assumption of known position within the world. Unfortunately, accumulated positional errors over time can corrupt the occupancy grid as it is being constructed. Correcting incremental position errors to avoid this while the map is being constructed is difficult since the map still has low certainty. An attractive alternative is to solve for both the map and localization concurrently. This approach is examined in the following section.

10.2.2 Simultaneous Localization and Mapping

The problem of building a map of an unknown environment while incrementally estimating one's position within it – simultaneous mapping and localization (SLAM) – depends critically on maintaining a model of position while constructing a robust representation of what is observed. While the subproblems of feature identification, recognition, and planning are critically important, the SLAM problem is often most closely related to data filtering, that is, updating the position estimates and an associated uncertainty model. This uncertainty model is associated with a covariance matrix relating error in the elements of the state. In the SLAM context, however, the state includes not just the robot pose, but the map itself, which can thus lead to a large covariance matrix and a tricky update problem.

Simultaneous localization and mapping can be expressed in a Bayesian framework [770, 245]. Within this framework the goal is to estimate the posterior density function of the environmental map Θ and pose s_t, given knowledge of observations taken by the robot $z^t = \{z_1, z_2, \ldots, z_t\}$, control inputs $u^t = \{u_1, u_2, \ldots, u_t\}$ and data associations $n^t = \{n_1, n_2, \ldots, n_t\}$. u^t and n^t encode the mapping between features in Θ and the observations z^t. The **SLAM posterior** [537] is given by

$$p(s_t, \Theta | z^t, u^t, n^t).$$

In essence, this involves describing the conditional probability of location and map given the robot's sensor measurements, control motions, and data associations. Determining the "best" map involves choosing the best solution to $p(s_t, \Theta | z^t, u^t, n^t)$. Note that "best" here may (or may not) correspond to the *maximum a posteriori* value of p.

Applying the Bayes rule, we can rewrite $p(s_t, \Theta | z^t, u^t, n^t)$ as

$$p(s_t, \Theta | z^t, u^t, n^t) = \eta p(z_t | s_t, \Theta | z^{t-1}, u^t, n^t) p(s_t, \Theta | z^{t-1}, u^t, n^t),$$

where η is a normalizing term. The term $p(z_t | s_t, \Theta | z^{t-1}, u^t, n^t)$ can be simplified to $p(z_t | s_t, \Theta, n^t)$ by assuming that measurements z_i and z_j are independent of each other for $i \neq j$ and that the measurement at this time step is independent of the control input. The term $p(s_t, \Theta | z^{t-1}, u^t, n^t)$ can be simplified using the Markov assumption and the theory of total probability:

$$p(s_t, \Theta | z^{t-1}, u^t, n^t) = \int p(s_t | s_{t-1}, u_t) p(s_{t-1}, \Theta | z^{t-1} u^t, n^t) ds_{t-1}.$$

This allows the SLAM posterior to be expressed as [537]:

$$p(s_t, \Theta | z^t, u^t, n^t) = \eta p(z_t | s_t, \Theta, n^t) \int p(s_t | s_{t-1}, u_t) P(s_{t-1}, \Theta | z^{t-1} u^t, n^t) ds_{t-1}.$$

$$(10.1)$$

Equation (10.1) can be implemented as a recursive operation using a range of different formalisms, although versions of Kalman, particle filter, and Factor Graph–based approaches are common. (See [244] for details of Kalman and particle filter–based approaches, and see [479] for factor graph-based approaches.) Kalman filtering implementations assume specific properties of the probability distribution functions and must deal with the ever-increasing size of the state space that is being estimated, while particle filter solutions exchange these problems for issues related to representing the PDF distribution with particles. Hybrid solutions (e.g., FastSLAM [537]) utilize both particle and Kalman filters.

Regardless of the mechanism used to solve (10.1), a further complication relates to data storage. Representing multiple hypotheses of environmental structure and robot position essentially requires multiple maps. Storage requirements for these multiple hypotheses can be extreme.

To illustrate the particle and Kalman filter approaches to SLAM, consider the following toy example. Suppose we have a directionless point robot operating on the plane. Let $\mathbf{x} = [x, y]$ be the position of the robot. There exists a large number of unique beacons in the environment and each beacon i is fixed and has location $\mathbf{p}_i = [p_x^i, p_y^i]$. The control input at each time step is a change in the (x, y) location of the robot $(\Delta x, \Delta y)$ and is corrupted by some zero mean plant noise (v_x, v_y). At each time step the robot obtains relative x and y offsets to some set of beacons $(p_x^i - x, p_y^i - y)$. The next two sections develop Kalman and particle filter SLAM solutions for this problem.

Kalman Filter Approach   We begin by defining plant and measurement models that describe the problem under consideration. We wish to estimate the joint probability of robot and beacon state, that is, to estimate the state

$$x(k) = \begin{bmatrix} x & y & p_x^1 & p_y^1 & p_x^2 & p_y^2 & \cdots & p_x^n & p_y^n \end{bmatrix}^T$$

at each time k. Note that the number of beacons that must be estimated will grow as a function of time.

Following the linear Kalman model [see Section 4.9.1 and equation (4.6)] gives

$$x(k + 1) = \mathbf{\Phi}x(k) + \mathbf{\Gamma}u(k) + v(k).$$

For the case under consideration, $\mathbf{\Phi}$ is the identity matrix, $\mathbf{\Gamma}$ is the identity matrix, $u(k) = [\Delta x_k(k), \Delta x_y(k), 0, \ldots, 0]^T$, and $v(k) = [v_x(k), v_y(k), 0, \ldots, 0]^T$ represents the plant noise (which is zero for all but the first two elements).

$$
\begin{aligned}
x(k+1) \quad &= \mathbf{\Phi}x(k) + \mathbf{\Gamma}u(k) + v(k) \\
\begin{bmatrix}
x(k+1) \\
y(k+1) \\
p_x^1(k+1) \\
p_y^1(k+1) \\
p_x^2(k+1) \\
p_y^2(k+1) \\
\cdots \\
p_x^n(k+1) \\
p_y^n(k+1)
\end{bmatrix}
&=
\begin{bmatrix}
x(k) + \Delta x(k) + v_x(k) \\
y(k) + \Delta y(k) + v_y(k) \\
p_x^1(k) \\
p_y^1(k) \\
p_x^2(k) \\
p_y^2(k) \\
\cdots \\
p_x^n(k) \\
p_y^n(k)
\end{bmatrix}
\end{aligned}
$$

The robot goes to where it is commanded, with each motion being corrupted by the noise process. The beacons remain stationary. This is a linear plant model and should be compared to the linear plant model used to estimate the state of a robot as it moved in Figure 4.5.

The robot can sense its relative displacement (in x and y) from the set of visible beacons. At time k the robot may only be able to sense some subset of all the beacons that it has encountered previously and novel beacons may also be discovered. For the moment, however, assume that only pre-viewed beacons are sensed and that all beacons are sensed. Then, following the linear Kalman filter introduced in Section 4.9.1 and equation (4.7) we obtain

$$z_i(k) = \Lambda_E x(k) + w_i(k),$$

where Λ_E expreses how measurements are derived from the system state, and $w_i(k)$ is a noise function. For the simple system here, the measurement from beacon i is simply the pair of values $p_x^i(k) - x(k)$ and $p_y^i(k) - y(k)$, that is,

$$\Lambda_E = \begin{bmatrix} -1 & 0 & 1 & 0 & 0 & 0 & \dots & 0 & 0 \\ 0 & -1 & 0 & 1 & 0 & 0 & \dots & 0 & 0 \\ -1 & 0 & 0 & 0 & 1 & 0 & \dots & 0 & 0 \\ 0 & -1 & 0 & 0 & 0 & 1 & \dots & 0 & 0 \\ & & & & \dots & & & & \\ -1 & 0 & 0 & 0 & 0 & 0 & \dots & 1 & 0 \\ 0 & -1 & 0 & 0 & 0 & 0 & \dots & 0 & 1 \end{bmatrix}.$$

Given these definitions, the linear Kalman filter (see Section 4.9.1) can be used to solve the SLAM problem.

This simple linear Kalman solution to the SLAM problem illustrates a number of issues with the approach, including:

- Almost no real system is going to be linear. Thus rather than use a linear Kalman filter with its guarantees of optimality, an EKF will have to be used introducing issues related to convergence.
- The filter assumes a known correspondence between beacons. The beacons can be identified from one time to the next. Such a clean data association is unlikely to hold in practice. Given the convergence issues associated with EKF, any mismatch in the data is likely to present significant difficulties.
- The set of beacons is unlikely to be known at system startup, and thus some (non-linear) process will have to be applied to determine whether a potential beacon is actually one of the beacons seen before (and, if so, which one), and, if not, identify this as a new beacon.
- The computational cost associated with a Kalman filter can be traced to the need to invert a matrix whose size is equal to the size of the system state. The system state size is proportional to the number of landmarks, so as the number of landmarks grows, the computational cost of the process also increases.

Particle Filtering Approach A *pure* particle filtering approach to SLAM would use a particle filter to represent the SLAM posterior $p(s_t, \Theta | z^t, u^t, n^t)$ exactly. Although such an approach is attractive from a theoretical point of view, it introduces difficult issues related to properly sampling the distribution. (Note, for example, that each sample in the distribution encodes an entire map, so the overhead associated with each particle is quite large.) Thus most practical particle filter-based SLAM approaches work to reduce the complexity of the state being represented. For the moment, however, consider the problem in its purest form. The SLAM posterior at time k is represented by a set of samples S_k^i, that is, the distribution represents $p(s_t, \Theta | z^t, u^t, n^t)$. The basic operation of the filter follows the technique described in Section 4.9.4:

Resampling phase The sample distribution $\{S_K^i\}$ is resampled to ensure that the particles provide a good representation of $p(s_t, \Theta | z^t, u^t, n^t)$.

Prediction phase Each particle is moved forward in time, simulating $p(s_t | s_{t-1}, u_t)$. This involves a probabilistic model of the plant noise.

Update phase Sensor measurements are used to update the weights associated with each particle (representing map and location pairs) $p(z_t | s_t, \Theta, n^t)$.

Each of these operations provides particle filter equivalents for each of the terms in (10.1), permitting the computation of

$$p(s_t, \Theta | z^t, u^t, n^t) = \eta p(z_t | s_t, \Theta, n^t) \int p(s_t | s_{t-1}, u_t) p(s_{t-1}, \Theta | z^{t-1} u^t, n^t) ds_{t-1}.$$

As observed earlier, this is likely to be impractical and so a range of different techniques are used to reduce the complexity of the problem. Perhaps the most powerful of these is the use of Rao–Blackwellized particles.

Rao–Blackwellization is a technique that decouples a complex uncertainty maintenance problem into two parts. It is based on the fact that one can reduce the state space of a joint state by using the product rule $p(x, y) = p(y|x)p(x)$. Thus, if $p(y|x)$ can be represented analytically, then only $p(x)$ needs to be sampled experimentally. In general, this means that the total variance of the component being estimated can be reduced. (See [554] and [147] for details on Rao–Blackwellization.) A common mechanism in SLAM and related state estimation problems is to use a particle filter to represent $p(x)$ and some other technique for $p(y|x)$, leading to the Rao–Blackwellized particle filter (RBPF). If $p(y|x)$ is represented analytically, then convergence of a particle filter can sometimes be accomplished with fewer estimates as a result. Another common variation of the RBPF is to represent $p(y|x)$ using a Kalman filter. This is one of the key concepts of the FastSLAM algorithm [537] which formulates SLAM in terms of robot trajectory (not just state) and applies Rao-Blackwellization to represent the map in terms of multiple Kalman filters (one per map feature). See also DP-SLAM [250] and DP-SLAM 2.0 [251] for pure particle filtering approaches.

10.2.3 Loop Closing

In the case of SLAM, local errors can often be kept small by the use of an effective state estimator, but errors can still grow over a long trajectory. Thus, if a robot's path intersects itself with a long loop in between, it may be difficult to determine just where the crossing occurs. Determining this is known as **loop closing**. Loop closing is a critical problem in SLAM as it presents an algorithm with two explicit choices with significant ramifications: (1) that the place currently being visited is the same as some previously visited location, in this case, information should be integrated between that previous visit and now to develop a single coherent representation; or (2) that this place is different from some previously visited place and thus independent, and *spatially distinct* representations should be constructed. In Kalman filtering-based approaches to SLAM, loop closing appears in the process of determining correspondences between map landmarks (is this landmark a new landmark, or does it correspond to some previously seen landmark, and, if so, which one?). Given the single-hypothesis nature of Kalman filter representations – and the potential failures associated with the incorrect data associations that are found with Kalman filters – incorrect decisions in terms of loop closing can have catastrophic results. In particle filter-based approaches to SLAM the multi-hypothesis nature of the approach allows loop closing to be considered as an alternative to not closing the loop. However, even with a particle filter-based approach there is only a finite number of particles, so even here there are issues. Deciding to "close the loop" or to "weight closing the loop" more heavily than not is a critical component of many SLAM approaches.

Given the critical nature of loop closing there is a large and active research effort to develop effective strategies to determine whether the loop should be closed. Given the importance of the decision being made, the goal is to find a decision function that is robust to sensor noise and model noise in the system. Clearly the more reliable the component (sensor, representation), the more desirable it is to base the loop-closing decision on that modality. As a consequence, basic approaches to loop closing can be described as being (1) map-to-map (see [168] for an example), (2) map-to-sensor (see [833] for an example), or (3) sensor-to-sensor (see [200] for an example) in nature, based on how the decision to close the loop is made.

10.2.4 Factor Graphs and GTSAM

As the SLAM process becomes more complex (e.g., with multiple sensors, large numbers of potential looping closing events) the process of properly representing the relationships between the various factors becomes more difficult. One effective approach to dealing with this complexity is through the use of **factor graphs** (see [428]) to represent the relationship between properties in SLAM. The GTSAM toolbox [214] provides a library to support factor graph-based tasks, including SLAM.

10.3   Topological Maps

To avoid the obvious difficulties in maintaining a long-term metric map of an environment, an alternative class of representations that has been used is based on graphs (see Section 7.2.3). Topological representations avoid the potentially massive storage costs associated with metric representations. In addition, they have appealing apparent analogies with human spatial perception. Purely topological representations, without any distance information, represent a "worst-case" scenario for position-sensing schemes.

Topological maps describe the environment as a graph that connects specific locations in the world, represented by vertices, with edges that embody their accessibility. Thus a graph-based map is given by $G = (V, E)$ with the set of N vertices V and the set of M edges E. The vertices are denoted by $V = \{v_1, \ldots, v_N\}$ and the edges by

$E = \{e_1, \ldots, e_M\}$, and edge e_{ij} is given by $e_{ij} = \{v_i, v_j\}$. If the ordering of v_i and v_j is significant, as it is in some models that presuppose that paths are unidirectional, then we have a **directed graph**. Note that $M < N(N-1)$ for graphs without transitive edges (edges between a node and itself), while for **planar graphs** (graphs without any crossing edges) we have a bound on the number of edges $M < 3N - 1$.

Many schemes for determining a topological environment representation from an actual environment have been proposed, often based on restrictive assumptions regarding the types of actual environments that are admissible. The canonical example is the use of a topological model to represent the hallways and junctions of an idealized office environment. While retraction methods can be used to derive a topological representation of a metric environment, not all topological representations are retractions.

In practice, a topological representation can be defined for a continuous environment based on landmarks or other features. One possible definition of a graph vertex is based on a local **distinctiveness measure** [439]. In this case, some set of sensor-based functions for the local environment is postulated. For example, the radius of the smallest circle that can be inscribed within a set of observed range measurements can be used to define a node in the topological representation. The nodes of the graph are those locations that, for example, maximize the value of one or more of these functions.

To relate the graph more closely to a map of actual space, the definition of an edge can be extended slightly to allow for the explicit specification of the order of edges incident upon each vertex of the graph. This constrains the **embedding** of the graph, that is, its possible layout on a surface (e.g., on a plane). This ordering is obtained by enumerating the edges in a systematic (e.g., clockwise) manner from some standard starting direction. An edge $E_{i,j}$, incident upon v_i and v_j is assigned labels n and m, one for each of v_i and v_j respectively. n represents the ordering of the edge $E_{i,j}$ with respect to some consistent enumeration of edges at v_i, and m represents the ordering of the edge $E_{i,j}$ with respect to the consistent enumeration of the edges at v_j. The labels m and n can be considered as general directions, for example, from vertex v_i the nth exit takes edge $E_{i,j}$ to vertex v_j.

Many environments of interest in land-based mobile robotics may be characterized as unstructured 2D environments identified by landmarks, but these landmarks and, in fact, the characterization of any specific location may not by unique. The term **signature** is used to refer to the specific observable characteristics associated with a location, in this case a node. If these signatures are sufficiently distinctive, either because the appearance of the node is distinctive or because appearance coupled with odometry measurements make the signatures unique, then nodes can be well defined and an embedded graph representation can be constructed autonomously. For example, the TOTO robot [506] creates a topological map (a graph) as it explores its world. As landmarks are detected, they become nodes in the graph along with their qualitative properties, that is, type (left wall, right wall, corridor) and associated compass bearing. A "truth maintenance" protocol is invoked to ensure that the same landmark does not become multiple nodes in the graph. This approach illustrates several important components of topological mapping and involves substantial domain-dependent processing.

10.3.1 Marker-Based Exploration

In the worst case, a local disambiguating signature may not be available. The exploration of an arbitrary unlabeled graph without metric information or unique signatures precludes developing a unique map for each environment. That is, it cannot be established when a node has been visited more than once, and hence it is not possible to disambiguate between alternative possible maps. If the robot is equipped with some mechanism for disambiguating nodes, then it may be possible to explore the environment. For example, if the robot is equipped with a can of spray paint, or an infinitely long string that the robot can pay out as it moves through the environment, then the robot can mark each location as it is passed and this can be used to provide each node with a unique signature.

Perhaps the simplest such marking mechanism (described in [239], [234]) involves augmenting the robot with one or more unique pebbles or markers that the robot can drop, pick up, or recognize if they are at the robot's current location. (See also [95], which describes a finite state automaton that can explore a maze in log-space time using two pebbles and a compass.) The exploration algorithm described in [239], [234] operates by building up a known subgraph of the world, exploring unknown edges incident on the known subgraph, and thus incrementally adding to it. The algorithm requires the robot to make $O(N^3)$ moves between locations in the worst case, where N is the number of distinguished locations in its environment. These locations correspond to vertices in the graph-like map that is produced, while the moves correspond to the edge traversals.

This exploration algorithm operates on an augmented graph-like representation of the world. The world is defined as an embedding of an undirected graph G. The graph embedding is accomplished by extending the definition of a node to allow for the explicit specification of the order of edges incident upon each vertex of the graph embedding. This ordering is obtained by enumerating the edges in a systematic way as described previously. In keeping with the minimalist representation of the environment, it is also assumed that the robot has very limited sensing and mobility options: The robot can move from one vertex to another by traversing an edge (a *move*), it can pick up a marker that is located at the current vertex, and it can put down a marker it holds at the current vertex (a *marker operation*). The robot in general has K markers at its disposal.

Assume that the robot is at a single vertex, v_i, having entered the vertex through edge $E_{i,l}$. In a single move, it leaves vertex v_i for vertex v_j by traversing the edge $E_{i,j}$, which is located r edges after $E_{i,l}$ according to the edge order at vertex v_i (see Figure 10.3). This is given by the transition function $\delta(v_i, E_{i,l}, r) = v_j$. The following property is assumed concerning the transition function:

$$\text{if } \delta(v_i, E_{i,l}, r) = v_j \quad \text{and} \quad \delta(v_j, E_{i,j}, s) = v_k, \text{ then } \delta(v_j, E_{j,k}, -s) = v_i.$$

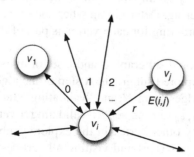

Figure 10.3. Edge ordering.

This implies that a sequence of moves is invertible and can be retraced. It is also assumed that there does not exist a $t \neq -s$ such that $\delta(v_j, E_{j,k}, t) = v_i$ and that there does not exist a t such that $\delta(v_j, E_{j,k}, t) = v_j$, that is, there are no redundant or degenerate paths.

A single move is thus specified by the order r of the edge along which the robot exits the current vertex, where r is defined with respect to the edge along which the robot entered such vertex. Note that in the special case of a planar embedding of a graph, enumeration of edges in a clockwise fashion satisfies the foregoing assumption.

A marker operation is fully specified by indicating for each of the K markers whether it is being picked up, put down, or not operated on. This is specified by a K-tuple $\Omega^K = (op_1, op_2, \ldots, op_K)$, where the element op_k has a value from the set $\{pickup, putdown, null\}$, according to the operation performed on marker k.

A simple action a is defined as a marker operation accompanied by a move, therefore $a = (b, \delta)$, where $b \in \Omega^K$. The robot performs some action on the markers in the current vertex and then moves to a new location. A path $A \in a^+$ is a nonempty sequence of actions.

The robot's perception is of two kinds, marker-related and edge-related perception.

Marker-related perception   Assume that the robot is at vertex v_i, having arrived via edge $E_{i,j}$. The marker-related perception of the robot is a K-tuple $B_s = (bs_1, bs_2, \ldots, bs_K)$, where bs_k has a value from the set $\{present, notpresent\}$, according to whether marker k is present at vertex v_i.

Edge-related perception   The robot can determine the relative positions of edges incident on the vertex v_i in a consistent manner, for example, by a clockwise enumeration starting with $E_{i,j}$. As a result, it can assign an integer label to each edge incident on v_i, representing the order of that edge with respect to the edge enumeration at v_i. The label 0 is assigned arbitrarily to the edge $E_{i,j}$ through which the robot entered vertex v_i. The ordering is local because it depends on the edge $E_{i,j}$. Entering the same vertex from two different edges will lead to two local orderings, one of which is a permutation of the other. Note that if the graph is planar and a spatially consistent (e.g., clockwise) enumeration of edges is used, then two permutations will be simple circular translations of each other.

The sensory information that the robot acquires while at vertex v_i is the pair consisting of the marker-related perception at that vertex and the order of edges incident on that vertex, with respect to the edge along which the robot entered the vertex. If the robot visits the same vertex twice, it must relate the two different local orderings produced and unify them into a single global ordering, for example, by finding the label of the zeroth edge of the second ordering with respect to the first ordering. Determining when the same vertex has been visited twice and generating a global ordering for each vertex is part of the task of the following algorithms.

The exploration algorithm maintains an explored subgraph S and a set of unexplored edges U, which emanate from vertices of the explored subgraph. A step of the algorithm consists in selecting a set E of k unexplored edges from U and "validating" the vertex v_2 at the unexplored end of each edge $e = (v_1, v_2)$ in the set E. Validating a vertex v_2 means making sure that it is not identical to any other vertex in the explored subgraph. This is carried out by placing one of the k markers at v_2 and visiting all vertices of the known subgraph S along edges of S, looking for the marker (and each of the other $k - 1$ markers dropped at this step). Note that the other vertex v_1 incident upon e is already in the subgraph S.

If the marker is found at vertex v_i of the explored subgraph S, then vertex v_2 (where the marker was dropped) is identical to the already known v_i (where the marker was found). In this case, edge $e = (v_1, v_2)$ must be assigned an index with respect to the edge ordering of vertex v_2. To determine this, the robot drops the marker at v_1 and goes back to v_2 along the shortest path in the explored graph S. At v_2, it tries going out of the vertex along each of its incident edges. One of them will take the robot back to v_1, which the robot will immediately recognize by the existence of the marker. Note that the index of e with respect to the edge ordering of v_1 is known by construction. Edge e is then added to the subgraph S and removed from U.

If the marker is not found at one of the vertices of S, then vertex v_2 is not in the subgraph S and therefore must be added to it. The unexplored edge e is also added to S, which has now been augmented by one edge and one vertex. Adding the vertex v_2 to the subgraph causes all edges incident upon it to be assigned an index with respect to the edge e by which the robot entered the vertex (edge e is assigned index 0) and the new edges are added to the set of unexplored edges U. Note that no other edge of the new vertex v_2 has been previously added to the subgraph, because otherwise v_2 would have already been in the explored subgraph. This index assignment establishes the edge ordering local to v_2. The algorithm terminates when the set of unexplored edges U is empty. A formal proof of the correctness of the algorithm is presented in [239].

An alternative approach to using the available k markers is to employ two distinct markers in the exploration of a single unexplored edge $e = (v_1, v_2)$. Then the validation and ordering steps can be combined by placing the markers at v_1 and v_2. If v_2 is found in S, then ordering of e with respect to v_2 is accomplished by going out of v_2 along each of its incident edges, without having to drop the marker at v_1 and to return to v_2 along the shortest path in S. This variation resulted in poorer performance on our test cases, with asymptotic worst-case complexity that differs only by a constant factor. There is a trade-off between easier vertex validation, with the modified algorithm, and fewer edges added per marker drop.

Figure 10.4 shows two snapshots of the exploration process when applied to a very simple graph. The graph is sketched in thin lines and the explored portion of the graph (S) is drawn in thicker lines. Nodes in S are filled in and nodes in U are unfilled. The current location of the marker is shown by a diamond and the current location of the robot is shown by a square. The entire graph is explored in 53 steps (where a step is counted as an edge traversal). Graph exploration can be a very costly process when only a single marker is available.

10.4   Exploration

A final issue in robot mapping is the problem of exploration. That is, given some solution to the SLAM problem, how should the robot move in order to construct the map? A common approach involves moving through the known free space toward environmental regions that are the most "unknown." Such regions are known as the **frontier** of the robot's current map. As the sensors are located on the robot, moving

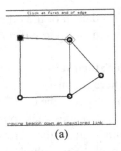
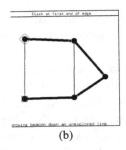

(a)   (b)

Figure 10.4. Stages in exploring a graph. (a) The graph at an initial stage with only one vertex explored. The robot (the square outline) has "dropped" the marker (the diamond outline) down at the end of one of the edges to ensure that that node is distinct from the nodes in the explored subgraph. At this point the explored subgraph consists of the node the robot starts at with two edges extending into the unexplored subgraph. (b) The exploration algorithm at a later stage. The marker has just been "dropped" down an edge that has already been visited and the robot will now return to the starting node through the known subgraph in order to determine whether the location containing the marker is in the known subgraph.

toward unknown regions makes them known, hence extending the known environmental region. Of course, at any one time many portions of the robot's map will contain frontiers, and heading for the closest frontier, although obvious, may not be the most effective in terms of environmental exploration. Another approach is to use some sort of random-walk like algorithm in which the robot makes straight-line motions until it meets an obstacle at which point it chooses a new random direction.

10.4.1 Spiral Search

Spiral search is a key technique in geometric exploration [53]. In essence, spiral search is an optimal search strategy for an object whose position is unknown. It successively examines the set of all points with geometrically increasing distance from some starting location. This approach is closely related to **iteratively deepening** search, which is employed to examine a state space in traditional artificial intelligence problems.

The term "spiral search" in fact relates to a family of related problems based on searching for an object on a line, a set of rays joined at a common root, or a grid. Spiral search algorithms ensure that if an object being sought is a distance d from the initial position, it will be found after traversing a distance that is no more than a small constant multiple of d. In the specific case of an obstacle-free 2D environment, the search pattern is a logarithmic spiral, and it has an asymptotic performance bound, or **competitive ratio**, of $9d$.

The simplest instance of spiral search for a goal with no information concerning its position is search for a goal on a (one-dimensional) line. From a starting position, the goal could be in one of two possible directions. Moving in only one direction obviously fails to find the goal with 50% probability. If we know *a priori* that the goal is a distance d from the starting location, then we can move in one direction a distance d and, if we do not find the goal, we move in the opposite direction a distance $2d$, at which point we must encounter the goal. This assures we will find the goal with a worst-case travel distance of $3d$ (i.e., competitive ratio of 3) and an average case performance of $\frac{3}{2}d$. Without such advance knowledge of the distance to the goal, the optimal strategy, assuming a uniform probability of finding the goal at any specific location, resembles this back-and-forth methodology.

The problem can be naturally formalized in terms of the integer distance $f(i)$ traveled outward from the origin between successive reversals in direction, indexed by the "trip number" i. Thus, on trip i the robot moves distance $f(i)$ to the left and then returns to the origin. On trip $i+1$ the robot moves a distance $f(i+1)$ to the *right* and the returns to the origin (assuming it does not find the goal). In order to perform useful work on every trip, the robot must explore new territory of each trip, and thus each trip in a given direction must take it farther than the last:

$$\forall i \geq 1 \;\; f(i) > f(i-2), \tag{10.2}$$

and $f(0) = f(-1) = 0$. When the *a priori* probability of finding the goal at any specific point is uniform, then an appropriate search strategy is given by a **linear spiral search** where $f()$ is given by

$$\forall i \geq 1 \;\; f(i) = 2^i.$$

Thus, given that the goal is distance n from the starting location, the total distance travelled is a combination is a series of too-short trips of size 2^i, where $2^i < n$, followed by a final trip of length n that reaches the goal. This total length is given by

$$2 \sum_{i=1}^{\lfloor \log n \rfloor + 1} 2^i + n$$

which is bounded by $9n$. The effectiveness of this strategy is given as follows.

> **Theorem** *Given a goal with an unknown position from the origin of a line, linear spiral search finds that goal after traveling a distance of $9d$, where d is the distance from the origin to the goal. This distance is optimal up to lower-order terms.*

Surprisingly, for most reasonable symmetric non-uniform probability distributions that have increased probability mass near the center, the number of turns for the average-case optimal solution is infinite (one simple such example is a triangular probability distribution).

A simple generalization to the problem involves searching for a goal along a set of m rays emanating from the origin. We assume that the robot can only walk along the rays so that search entails going back and forth along the rays. In this case, if what is known is the distance d along some ray to the goal but the specific ray is unknown, then the robot must move out a distance d along each successive ray giving an optimal worst-case distance traveled of $(2m-1)n$, and an average-case distance of half that. If the distance to the goal is not known *a priori*, then progressive search of the rays becomes necessary. In this case, the generalization of equation (10.2) is

$$\forall i \geq 1 \;\; f(i) \geq f(i-m),$$

with $f(i) = 0$ for all $i \leq 0$. This leads naturally to generalized linear spiral search where

$$f(i) = \left(\frac{m}{m-1}\right)^i,$$

which provides an optimal strategy (up to low-order terms) and has a competitive ratio of

$$1 + 2\frac{m^m}{(m-1)^{m-1}}.$$

The spiral search framework has been extended to obstacle-free lattices. In this case, the objective is to find a specific point on a grid. In this case, we have:

Theorem *Any algorithm that can find a point at an arbitrary point at a finite distance d in a lattice requires at least $2n^2 + 4n + 1$ grid motions in the worst case.*

Proof sketch: This can be shown by using an adversary argument where the adversary places the point at the last point searched by the algorithm that satisfies the distance constraint. Thus, the issue becomes one of how efficiently an algorithm can examine all points with distance no more than d. There are $2(n-1)^2 + 2(n-1) + 1$ points of interest, and a complete visit (on a discrete grid) entails visiting some points more than once.   □

10.5   Further Reading

SLAM A large literature on SLAM exists. [244], [772], and [56] provide good overviews of the field. [771] provides a good survey of different approaches to robot mapping. [226] provides a fully developed Kalman-filtering approach to SLAM. There have been a number of tutorials offered in concert with international robotics conferences, and many of these are available on-line.

Loop closing A number of different approaches to loop closing have appeared, including [400]. One mechanism for loop closing is to exploit salient or "nearly unique" sensor responses (see [241] and [442] for examples). [779] provides a survey of loop closing algorithms.

Exploration Different approaches to environmental exploration can be found in [721] and [733]. [477] provides a review of different exploration approaches and their interaction with SLAM.

Factor graphs [212] provides a solid introduction to factor graphs. The GTSAM library[214] supports factor graph-related tasks, including SLAM.

10.6   Problems

1. Construct a simulation of a point robot moving inside a unit square on the plane. Four uniquely identifiable but unmapped markers (and randomly positioned) beacons exist on the plane. Implement a Kalman filter-based SLAM algorithm to map this environment and maintain the motion of the robot.

2. Develop a solution to SLAM for people encountering a new indoor environment for the first time. (Use your favorite local university or office building as a test environment.) Is your representation topological or metric? If topological, how did you defined locations/edges? If metric, how did you estimate location(s)? What did you use as your sensor primitives?

Certain assumptions will make the problem simpler but fragile. For example, in an office environment did you assume door numbers were unique, and, if so, what will happen to your algorithm if they are not?

3. Most SLAM algorithms assume that it is not appropriate for the robot to modify the environment as it moves through it. The SLAM problem can be made somewhat simpler if the robot can make such modifications. Assume an embedded graph-like world and that the robot is the only active agent in the environment, sketch exploration algorithms under the following models

(a) The robot has an unlimited can of spray paint that it can use to mark nodes.
(b) The robot has an infinite spool of unmarked thread that it can pay out from its starting location.
(c) The robot has an infinite spool of thread that it can pay out from its starting location and the thread can be written on (and erased).

Part three

Advanced Topics and the Future of Mobile Robotics

A delivery robot on its day off.

Given a robot that can develop and execute complex motion plans in its environment, it remains to put the robot to work.

Chapter 11 looks at the problems involved in having two or more robots operating in the same environment.

Chapter 12 looks at how to structure and evaluate interactions between humans and robots.

Chapter 13 explores robot ethics, and how this topic might evolve moving forward.

Chapter 14 provides case studies of mobile robotic systems that operate in the world today. Effective systems not only must meet demanding technological requirements, they also must meet economic constraints. Given their relatively high cost, industrial autonomous robotic systems find application in situations characterized as being inhospitable, remote, or dangerous to a human operator.

Finally, Chapter 15 looks toward the future of autonomous systems and open problems in the field.

11

Robot Collectives

"Look, that robot, DV-5, has six robots under it. And not just under it – they're part of it..."[1]

Although the vast majority of mobile robotic systems involve a single robot operating alone in its environment, a growing number of researchers are considering the challenges and potential advantages of having a group of robots cooperate in order to complete some required task. For some specific robotic tasks, such as exploring an unknown planet [374], search and rescue [812], pushing objects [608], [513], [687], [821], or cleaning up toxic waste [609], it has been suggested that rather than send one very complex robot to perform the task it would more effective to send a number of smaller, simpler robots. Such a collection of robots is sometimes described as a **swarm** [81], a **colony** [255], or a **collective** [436], or the robots may be said to exhibit **cooperative behavior** [607]. Using multiple robots rather than a single robot can have several advantages and lead to a variety of design trade-offs. Collectives of simple robots may be simpler in terms of individual physical design than a larger, more complex robot, and thus the resulting system can be more economical, more scalable, and less susceptible to task failure.

Although much of the work on swarm robots takes place in simulation, a large number of robot swarm systems have been built. Terrestrial robot swarms have been built on wheeled robots (e.g., [509], Alliance [609]), tracked vehicles (e.g., [605]), vibration motors (e.g., [680]), and even air bed-based levitating robots propelled by magnets [572]. Aquatic swarms include swarms based on surface vessels (e.g., [282]) and swimming fish [82]) have been developed. There have also been a large number of efforts to build swarms of flying robots including [864].

Beyond their mechanical structure, robot collectives build on a wide range of research results in distributed algorithms, sensor networks, and biology. As a consequence, the literature on robot collectives spans a wide range with a wide variety of assumptions and goals. One common theme, however, is the desire to develop technology that enables a group of robots to solve a common problem. The objective is to coordinate the actions of the robots so that the coordinated group provides some advantage over performing the task with a single robot. Robotic collectives offer the possibility of enhanced task performance, increased task reliability, and decreased task cost over more traditional autonomous robotic systems. Although they have this potential, designing a collective to exhibit one or more of these properties requires careful attention to the design of individual elements

---

[1] Powell and Donovan describe a team of robots involved in asteroid mining. Asimov, I. [46]. Reprinted by permission of the Estate of Isaac Asimov c/o Ralph M. Vicinanza, Ltd.

of the collective, and perhaps even more important in terms of this chapter, the design of the collective itself. In the design of a collection of robots, task distribution among the individual elements of the robot group is key. Having all of the robots save one sit idle while one robot does all the work is unlikely to be an effective or efficient strategy. Task allocation and coordination implies communication among elements of the group, suggesting that effective communication among members of the collective is also critical to the design and performance of robot collectives.

A collective is said to be homogeneous if all of the elements of the collective are the same. If the elements of the collective are not homogeneous, then the collective is said to be heterogeneous. Very large robot collectives have been constructed and evaluated experimentally including a collective of over 1000 robots (see Figure 1.7) that is described in [680]. In this chapter we consider robot collectives in which each of the robots operates as an individual. It is also possible for the elements of the collective to combine together to form larger robotic units. Such robots are known as **cellular robots**.

11.1   Categorizing Collectives

Various classifications of robot collectives have been proposed; Dudek *et al.* [236, 237, 240] and independently Cao *et al.* [145] proposed the classification of swarm, collective, or robot collaboration research by defining a taxonomy or collection of axes. Cao *et al.* identified group architecture, conflict resolution strategy, origins of cooperation, learning, and geometric problems as "research axes" or taxonomic axes within which cooperative robots can be compared, while Dudek *et al.* concentrated their taxonomy on the communication mechanisms and their relative costs. The primary purpose of these classifications is to clarify the result that different collective classes have very different capabilities. The primary axes of the taxonomy of Dudek *et al.* are the following:

Size of the collective The number of autonomous agents in the collective. As collectives become larger, it becomes necessary to develop mechanisms for control and communication that must scale appropriately. It also becomes possible to consider probabilistic solutions to specific problems and to the reliability of the solution as members of the collective fail.

Communications range The maximum distance between the elements of the collective such that communication is still possible. With reduced communications range, it becomes necessary to develop algorithms to distribute information among elements of the collective and to deal with inconsistencies in internal state information due to the time it takes messages to be communicated between disparate elements of the collective.

Communications topology Of the robots within the communication range, those that can communicate with each other. This topology may be fixed or may change over time.

Collective reconfigurability The rate at which the organization of the collective can be modified. Many collectives assign unique roles to individual elements. As elements become damaged or fall out of communication, can other elements of the collective take their place and, if so, how? This becomes critical if certain elements of the collective are assigned "management-like" roles within the collective.

Processing ability The computational model utilized by individual elements of the collective. Most robot collectives assume that each robot has the computational power of a Turing Machine, although collectives with simpler architectures have been proposed.

Collective composition Are the elements of the collective homogeneous or heterogeneous?

There have also been efforts to categorize collectives by the task to which they have been applied, for example, [113]. See also [702].

11.2   Control Architectures, Their assumptions and Limitations

In the animal kingdom, there exist a large number of examples of coherent behavior across elements of a flock of birds, or swarm of insects, or school of fish, as examples. The groups of these animals exhibit some coherent behavior while only providing minimal communication between elements of the collective. The seminal work on developing a mathematical model of this and applying it to computer systems is [665]. This work considered the problem of simulating the flocking behavior of birds. This approach has been generalized by many others since the late 1980s, but the basic concept is that in parallel, each element of the collective makes measurements of local elements of the collective and then executes a motion based on this information. Following the model of the task introduced in [665], imagine we have a collection of robots that makes estimates of other robots in their vicinity and computes the relative position and velocity of agents in the vicinity. Their goal is to exhibit "bird-like" flocking behavior. Each agent makes a decision on where to move to next based on these measurements. The basic computations are sketched in Figure 11.1. Within some visibility region each robot computes the separation and moves away from other robots that are too close to it. This command motion is coupled with two others, an alignment requirement that the robot moves to align itself with other agents that are nearby, and a cohesion requirement that the robot moves toward the center of mass of agents in some larger region of space. The consequence of these underlying commands is that the collective crowd around the center of mass of

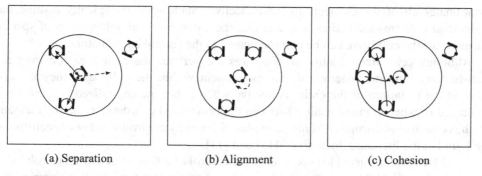

(a) Separation   (b) Alignment   (c) Cohesion

Figure 11.1. Primitive behaviors in boids, following the behaviors described in [665].

the swarm. A careful definition of thee regions and the weighting of the various factors involved is critical to overall collective performance. (See [19], for example.)

This type of community-based computation can be used in a number of different ways. For example, consider the problem of having a collective establish a leader. Let each robot maintain a counter, and initially set each counter to 1. Whenever two robots communicate they take their two counters c_1 and c_2 and add them together. Randomly, one of the robots sets its counter to $c_1 + c_2$ while the other robot sets its counter to 0. Assuming that meetings are fair, then eventually only one robot will have a non-zero counter (whose value is the number of robots in the collective), while all of the other robots will have a counter of zero, and a leader will have been elected. The critical problem then becomes knowing when the computation is complete. That is, knowing with high probability that the leader knows that they are the leader. See [156] for an approach to determining that the election is complete. Of course, much more sophisticated collective algorithms are possible (see [33] for examples), and it is also possible to develop probabilistic algorithms for computation across the collective that are robust to certain classes of failure of elements within the collective itself [215].

Many different architectures have been proposed for the way in which the robots should be connected together to perform a single task. For example, [788] proposed a scheme whereby complex robots are organized in tree-like hierarchies with communication between robots limited to the structure of the hierarchy, while [331] proposed a model in which the robots are particularly simple but act under the influence of "signpost robots." These signposts can modify the internal state of swarm units as they pass by. Under the action of the signposts, the entire swarm acts as a unit to carry out complex behaviors. Matarić [508] describes experiments with a homogeneous population of actual robots acting under different communication constraints. The robots acted in ignorance of one another, informed by one another, or intelligently (cooperating) with one another. As intra-collective communication improved, more and more complex behaviors were possible. At the limit where all of the robots had complete communication, the robots could be considered as appendages of a single larger robot (or robotic "intelligence").

Control architectures for robot collectives can be characterized by the way in which tasks are distributed among the elements of the collective. Common architectures for task assignment include [610]:

Centralized Centralized control structures assume a single control point that coordinates all of the elements in the collective. Such systems typically assume that individual elements are addressable and that the individual state information of specific elements of the collective can be communicated to the central coordinator.

Although centralized control architectures are perhaps the easiest to construct and can be very efficient in terms of task assignment within the collective, they are also susceptible to failure of the entire collective when either the centralized coordinator is damaged or when communication between the centralized coordinator and the elements of the collective is disrupted. Many examples of centrally controlled robot collectives can be found in the literature, including [414] and [17].

The MARTHA project [17] considered the control of a fleet of autonomous robots for transport tasks in highly structured areas such as harbors and airports. It is assumed that a number of autonomous agents operating under centralized control will wish to navigate from point to point within the closed environment. Although the agents operate under centralized control it is desirable to minimize the communication between individual agents and the central station.

Whenever an agent is assigned a task, it formulates a plan and examines the set of resources required to complete the task. For example, a robot might be required to navigate through certain regions of the environment (known as cells in MARTHA) in a specific order to get to the goal. Each of the cells is a shared resource, and thus traversal through a specific cell requires merging the robot's plan with the plans of all the other robots operating in the environment. MARTHA provides an infrastructure and a communications mechanism so that a robot's plan can be validated and then merged with the plans of other operating robots. Plans that cannot be validated must be delayed until the deadlock condition that prevents the validation has been eliminated.

Hierarchical In a hierarchical control structure, elements in the collective are organized in a hierarchy with well-defined lines of communication and authority among members. In the extreme version of hierarchical control, architectures are organized like military units or traditional management structures.

Hierarchical control strategies offer some improvements over centralized control strategies. Responsibility can be distributed among elements of the collective, and promotion mechanisms (when one element of the collective may be promoted due to failure of its superior) can be used to provide robustness of the collective.

Decentralized Decentralized control allows each individual element of the collective to make its own decisions based on the information available to it. This typically means that there may not be global consensus throughout the collective and that communicating information through the collective is probabilistic and synchronization is difficult to guarantee. Decentralized collective control also provides the potential for significant redundancy and robustness.

Alliance [609] was one of the early decentralized control strategies for robot collectives. Alliance assumes that each of the robots is independently and individually controlled. Robots communicate through observing the behavior of other robots and the effect of other robots' actions on the task at hand.

In Alliance, each robot operates under a subsumption architecture (see Section 8.2). In addition to lower control levels that provide for general vehicle safety, the subsumption architecture is augmented with high-level **motivational behaviors** that essentially provide a specific high-level control to the robot. Individual robots may have many different motivational behaviors, only one of which is active. The motivational behaviors are modelled as either **robot impatience** or **robot acquiescence**. The impatience motivation enables a robot to deal with a specific situation if the robot senses that other robots are not dealing with it. The acquiescence motivation causes a robot to decide not to deal with a specific situation if the robot senses that other robots are dealing with the task. More recent decentralized control architectures including those described in [726] seek to utilize a completely decentralized control architecture.

Hybrid Hybrid systems combine properties of one or more of the other control architectures. For example, [680], shown in Figure 11.2, uses a collection of homogeneous agents with a very small number of special agents that are used to define a global

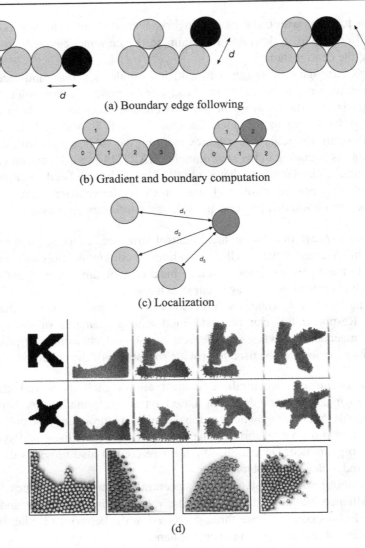

(a) Boundary edge following

(b) Gradient and boundary computation

(c) Localization

(d)

Figure 11.2. Organizational control in the 1000 robot swarm [680]. (a)–(c) show low-level robot operations. (a) shows boundary edge following. By maintaining a distance d from fixed elements of a shape, a robot can move around the boundary of the shape. (b) shows gradient computation. One agent is identified as the origin, and each agent in contact with the origin robot is a distance 1 from the origin. In general, an agent computes the minimum of the gradient value from all the agents that the agent is in touch with. An agent that has a gradient value that is at last as high as the neighbors with which it is in contact is on the boundary of the shape. (c) Given three or more robots with known location, a robot can localize itself on a ground plane. Given this information and a shape defined on the plane, the collective can move to fill in the predefined shape. The top two rows of (d) shows motion plans (left) and snapshots of execution (right). The bottom row in (d) shows closeups of the robots motions. (d) appears with the kind permission of Michael Rubenstein.

coordinate frame. This enables the agents to maneuver to collectively form complex shapes

A key observation related to the nature of the control architecture is that the more dependent the structure is on unique properties of specific elements of the collective, the more sensitive the network is to failure of those units. That being said, even a small number of specialized elements of the collective can be very powerful in terms of providing additional information.

11.3 Collective Communication

Robots in a collective can communicate using a range of different underlying technologies. Perhaps the most obvious of these is through the use of a special-purpose communications infrastructure (e.g., wireless Ethernet, packet radio, IR, or Bluetooth), but other communication strategies are possible. For example, robots may communicate through real or artificial pheromones (see [688] for an early application with real pheromones and [562] for a virtual pheromone approach). Robots may communicate through the demonstration of specific behaviors that are monitored by other robots in the collective (see Figure 11.3). Another possibility is that the robots will communicate implicitly through the environment and the task that the robots are performing. Each of these types of communication provides different trade-offs for the collective. Explicit communication through a dedicated communication channel simplifies overall design and reduces the possibility that unintended or garbled messages will be received due to motion of the other robot. Explicit communication through specific motion of the robot removes the need for a dedicated communication channel but adds the cost of additional motion as a robot executes specific motions to signal its message. Implicit communication through the environment offers a low cost to actually send the message but restricts the set of messages that can be sent, and there is a high possibility of misreading the intent of the message.

(a) Two robots operating together   (b) Robot 2's view of robot 1

Figure 11.3. Robots communicating via behavior. Robot 1 is augmented with a pattern that simplifies robot 2's job of observing robot 1's behavior. Robot 1 executes specific behaviors to indicate its intended direction of motion. Robot 2 then uses this information to plan its own motion. See [238] for details.

The vast majority of robot collectives communicate through a standard dedicated communication infrastructure. Such structures were generally not designed with autonomous agents in mind. This can lead to a number of theoretical and practical difficulties when deploying these communication structures. For example, it is important to recognize that if the network is to scale with the size of the collective, then the number of nodes in the network can easily outstrip the ability of standard communication infrastructures to generate an *ad hoc* network and assign each element of the collective a unique identification within the network.

A core problem with communication within a robot collective is that as a node in the collective may not be able to communicate with all other elements of the collective, the collective must possess a mechanism to route communication between nodes as the direct communication mechanisms change as a function of the motion of elements of the collective and other environmental factors. A number of different **network layer** schemes have been developed to support communication among nodes in a wireless sensor network or collective. These include [14]:

Flooding Each element in the collective rebroadcasts information sent to it to all elements of the collective that it is connected to. A hop count (or distance) is maintained for the distance a packet has been transmitted, and packets are dropped when they meet some maximum criterion. One deficiency with the flooding approach is that it can generate a significant number of copies of the same message if there is significant overlap of the communications range of individual elements of the collective.

Gossiping In a gossiping approach [342], rather than communicate with all of its neighbours, an element of the collective communicates with only one of its neighbors chosen randomly. Although this addresses the issue of generating many copies of a given message, it can take a significant period of time for a message to make it to its intended recipient.

Directed diffusion In the directed diffusion approach [382], elements of the collective that are interested in specific types of information (such elements are known as sinks) broadcast this information to their neighbors, who broadcast it to theirs, and so on. Each node maintains a gradient – the direction along which to forward information – which it uses when it receives information requested by the target. One issue with the directed diffusion approach is that these gradient tables must be continually refreshed, and a separate gradient must be maintained for each sink.

Other, more complex communication strategies have also been developed [14].

11.4   Distributed Sensing

As each element in the collective may have its own sensor(s), then the entire collective can be considered as a distributed sensor network. Integrating information among the elements of the sensor network and determining where to deploy elements of the sensor network are complex and interesting problems. For example, if one assumes that the individual elements of the collective can sense the local distribution of some event as a continuous scalar function, then [704] shows that it is possible to position the elements of the collective using a distributed computation so that they are situated at the weighted centroid of their Voronoi regions and that this provides optimal sensing coverage. See also Cortés *et al.* [184].

For non-stationary events, sensing becomes the problem of tracking a mobile event or identifying novel events and then tracking them as they occur (this problem is also known as **SCAT** – simultaneous coverage and tracking). A common approach to solving these problems is to develop an energy term that is minimized when the target is properly covered by the available sensors. In [391] a simple energy function is described that moves a collection of robots – either under global or local distributed control – so that they provide appropriate sensor coverage of a single target. [625] describes a decentralized algorithm that provides both target coverage and environmental coverage for novel events. [502] describes an odor-detecting algorithm for robot swarms that identifies the optimal formation to detect odors in a wind environment. In essence, they develop a formation control that will be perpendicular to the wind direction to optimize odor detection.

11.5   Distributed Planning

Plans may be required for a collection of robots to deal with the specifics of their sensors or to assist in the development of appropriate communication paths between elements of the collection. Here we consider the problem of planning for action: planning so that the elements of the collective cause some motion of objects in the environment. Two extremes of planning for action can be identified. At one extreme the robot collective is to move a large number of small objects (so that each element of the collective can carry or manipulate one of the objects). At the other extreme the object being manipulated is sufficiently large (or bulky) such that the elements of the collective must coordinate their actions in order to move the object together.

The task of having multiple robots find and collect (small) target objects to a goal location is known as **foraging**. The foraging task is based on the real task of having a collective of robots remediate a contaminated environment. The traditional approach to foraging has each robot searching independently for the targets and, having collected them, returning them to the goal. This approach is known as **homogeneous foraging**. One problem with this type of approach is that the individual members of the collective interfere with each other and this decreases the overall performance of the collective on the task. An alternative strategy known as **bucket brigading** has individual members of the collective being responsible for a limited spatial region of the environment. Robots associated with a particular region forage only in their region and when they find an object they take it to the edge of their region closest to the goal, where it is then foraged by robots associated with that region. The individual regions may or may not overlap, and depending on the degree of overlap, bucket brigading and homogeneous foraging can be thought of two extremes of a continuum of different strategies [711]. Large-scale simulations of different foraging strategies suggest that adaptive strategies can be very effective, although simple homogeneous foraging can be very effective as well [711, 456].

One interesting approach in foraging involves mimicking the foraging behavior found in the animal kingdom. Pheromone-trail based-based algorithms have been found to be particularly effective for the foraging task in ants [216], and efforts to duplicate

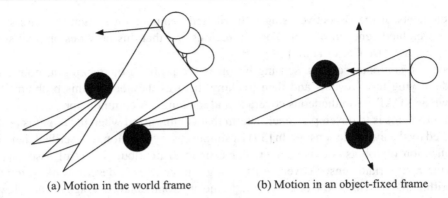

(a) Motion in the world frame   (b) Motion in an object-fixed frame

Figure 11.4. Moving an object with three cooperating agents. The black agents are stationary and constrain the motion of the object. The white agent moves the object. Arrows show the direction of applied forces. Redrawn from [686].

similar approaches with robots have proven successful. For example, [799] represents the trail by communicating local coordinate frames and environmental landmarks to ground the frame to other members of the swarm, while [355] describes the use of a virtual pheromone approach that have individual element of the collective stop and become virtual pheromone beacons broadcasting the local pheromone values. Beacon robots decay and then return to a walker/worker state if appropriate.

When the object being moved is sufficiently large that the robots must coordinate their actions so that only by working together can they move the single object, then the task becomes that of using each of the individual robots to apply a force on the object being moved so that the combination of forces acting on the object causes the object to move in the manner desired. The basic task is known as the **box-pushing task** and is related to the **piano movers problem** [705]. The problem is sketched in Figure 11.4. Here three robots (two colored black and one colored white) apply forces to an object in order to cause it to rotate. (Note that if the individual robots can grasp the object and move it, then the problem becomes somewhat simpler.)

Rather than consider a general solution to the problem as in [1], [686] demonstrated that a polygonal object can be rotated by using three robots where in two of the robots remain stationary and the third robot slides along the surface of the object. Each of the robots applies forces against the object during this motion. Although only small rotations are possible at each step using this approach, it is possible to reorient the robots and continue the rotation. It is also possible to address the problem without knowledge of the structure of the object being manipulated. For example, [512] describes a system within which two hexapod robots move a box by taking turns in applying forces to the box being manipulated, and [687] developed both local and global controllers that are used by multiple robots to move furniture.

11.6   Formation Control

One task that is unique to mobile robots is the need to control the elements of a collection of robots rather than a single one. This task is known as **formation control** or

flocking (see Section 11.2). The basic problem is to develop a local control strategy that can be executed on each robot that enables the elements of the collective to demonstrate a particular group behavior (moving as a unit). This problem can be expressed in a number of different ways, but the underlying goal is to develop a local algorithm that can operate on each element of the collective and that is robust to local sensor errors and requires only implicit knowledge of the state of local elements in the collective.

Given a collection of robots able to sense local orientation information, it has been shown that a simple local control law based on averaging local heading information is sufficient to drive the collective to exhibit a common heading (see [807] for experimental analysis and [387] for a mathematical treatment of the problem).

Formation control can be applied to more general problems than just ensuring that all robots in the collective are moving in the same direction. For example, [248] considered the problem of having the elements of the collective maintain a geometric arrangement as they move. Let the location of robot i be x_i and identify robot 1 as the reference robot for this formation. Then the problem of specifying the location of the elements of the collective might be defined in terms of some global coordinate frame. That is, robot i should be at location a_i and thus the collective should minimize the error term

$$E = \sum_i ||x_i - a_i||.$$

This requires each of the robots to operate with knowledge of the global coordinate frame. This model can be very effective. See [840], for example. Rather than relying on access to a global frame of reference an alternative is to recast this global requirement in terms of local properties (and hence local sensing requirements). The formation defined by a can be recast in terms of simpler constraints, such as the required distances between the robots d_i^2, the distance of each robot from the origin r_i^2, and the position of the reference robot [248]:

$$E = \sum_i \left[(||x_{i-1} - x_i||^2 - d_i)^2 + (||x_i||^2 - r_i)^2 \right] + ||x_1 - a_1||^2.$$

This concept of recasting global constraints in terms of simpler local constraints also applies to tracking targets and ensuring sensor coverage (see [391] for an example).

11.7 Localization and State Estimation

For a single robot operating in its environment, localization involves determining the robot's state (pose) given sensor measurements and kinematic model. Often this process can be expressed as an energy minimization between estimated drift from the robot's motion model and sensor measurements with estimated errors. When multiple robots are operating in the environment, additional constraints become available. Each of the robots will make its own measurements of environmental features and the robots themselves become features that can be used to improve localization accuracy [661]. This process has been termed **cooperative localization** [662].

A collection of ultrasonic-based robots that perform combined localization over the collective is described in [321]. Each element of the collective obtains local range and bearing estimates to targets, and each robot is equipped with an ultrasonic beacon that allows robots to obtain range estimates to other elements of the collective. The position likelihood of the robots is expressed as the product of the individual likelihoods and a maximum *a posteriori* solution is used.

Less symmetric options are possible as well, where (in the extreme) one or more robots in the collective is blind and its localization its facilitated by other, "sighted" robots in the collective. For example, [207] describes a two robot collective in which one robot is equipped with an active stereo vision head while the other robot is blind and is equipped with an active lighting system. The sighted robot provides localization for both robots in the team. [663] describes a similar approach in which one robot of the collective is equipped with a laser range scanner and the other robots are equipped with laser targets. Robots may be (mostly) physically identical, but take on specifically assigned roles in the swarm localization process. For example, in [660], [663] some members of the collective take on the role of marker robots (fixed landmarks), which moving robots use to localize their position during motion. The set of marker robots can be dynamic. This process has been shown to improve localization accuracy under certain conditions [663].

11.8 Mapping

When multiple mobile robots explore an environment not only must they solve the SLAM problem, but they must also solve the problem of synchronizing each of the representations of the individual elements. Normally this means establishing a common reference frame for all of the robots so that "here" means the same thing for all elements of the collective. Perhaps the easiest way of ensuring that this happens is to assume that all of the robots start out in a common location with a common representation of space. In this case, multiple-robot SLAM can be thought of as an obvious extension of single-robot SLAM as each robot's representation (map and location within that map) can be integrated using the single robot formalism. Indeed, even if the individual robots do not start out at a common location, then, provided that the individual robots have some way of estimating their pose with respect to other robots within which they are in proximity and that eventually the robots come into contact with each other, the problem is easily addressed [369]. Once two robots meet they can establish a common frame of reference that will serve them from this time forward, and it is also possible to roll sensor and motion data backward in time to merge data obtained prior to the meeting.

Given that it is possible to perform SLAM with multiple robots how can the SLAM problem for multiple roots be structured so as to make best use of the robot collective in exploring the environment? There are a number of issues with which a team of robots must contend with when mapping an unknown environment including:

Rendezvous This is the problem of meeting with the other robots of the team in order to share information that has been collected. If the robots are able to communicate with each other all of the time, then physical rendezvous is unnecessary. When robot communication is limited, then physical rendezvous is required.

Exploration How should the search or exploration tasks be partitioned among members of the team? Effective partitioning is critical to realizing the potential advantages of a multi-robot system.

Map fusion Given that the maps may not be identical, how should the individual maps be integrated into a single whole?

11.8.1 Rendezvous

Rendezvous refers to having two or more agents (traditionally people, but in this context robots) meet at an appointed place and time. In the simplest cases of multi-robot exploration, the robots all start at the same location and hence an initial rendezvous can be taken for granted. Even so, there is the issue of when and where the robots should meet while accomplishing the search task. At the other extreme, if robots start exploring from random positions in an (initially) unknown environment, then rendezvous can be a serious problem. Rendezvous in such a context has been examined in the context of operations research and is similar to games with mobile finders, referred to as **princess and monster games** [384]. Theoretical variants of the problem include cases with collaborating and non-collaborating agents and with environments that either do or do not have specific locations at which a rendezvous should take place. Purely theoretical variations of the rendezvous problem include variations with both discriminable [25] and non-distinguishable agents [31].

There exist a number of fundamental mathematical results in this space, based on assumptions that may or may not hold in practice. For example, [746] assumes that all robots exist on a common 2D Cartesian space [119]. In most work in the operations research context, the assumption is made that the environment is completely known in advance. In contrast, mobile robot problems often entail the need to carry out rendezvous while discovering the layout of the map.

11.8.2 Exploration

In mapping using a robot swarm a key aspect of the process involves coordinating exploration among the agents. Through some communication and map fusion process, a collection of agents agree on what portions of the environment remain to be explored and must partition up unexplored regions for future exploration. If the robots have a shared representation of space, then robots can separate these **exploration frontiers** among them and continue to explore these spaces. Different approaches for establishing which robot explores which space and for how long is an interesting and open question. See [137], [138], [290] for various approaches. What complicates this task is that there is no guarantee when the space is allocated to different agents that the various regions are non-overlapping, and effort may be wasted by having multiple agents explore the same physical space.

11.8.3 Map Fusion

When members of the collective meet their maps must be integrated into a single representation of the environment. In some cases little explicit map merging will be needed (since no long-term map is stored). In cases where a long-term spatial map is needed, explicit process will be needed to fuse the partial maps produced by the individual robots in the course of their travels.

Fusing maps using cross-correlation depends on the assumption that the individual maps are known to overlap "sufficiently" (typically 30% to 50% overlap is required, depending on the map content and on the correlation or matching technique used). The problem can be framed as that of matching the map $M_i(x, y)$ acquired by each successive robot to the map belonging to the first robot $M_0(x, y)$ by finding a set of translations T_i and rotations R_i to apply to the successive maps (we consider two-dimensional maps here, but the situation is identical for three-dimensional maps, although more computationally costly).

Let us assume that the map data are stored in homogeneous coordinates, so that both rotation and translation can be expressed as matrix multiplication. Then for each map M_i we need to find the translation and rotation giving $(\delta x, \delta y, \delta \theta)_i$ that minimizes

$$\int \int (M_0(x, y) - R_i T_i M_i(x, y))^2 \, dx \, dy, \tag{11.1}$$

where we assume that the integral is evaluated only over points that are inside both maps. This type of approach has been used with some success to align laser scans [484], [483] and was discussed in Chapter 4.

11.9   Further Reading

A number of good reviews of the current state of robot collectives research have emerged. [557], [610], [383], and [229] provide good snapshots of the state of the art in robot collectives. See also [114] and [702].

Sensor networks Recent surveys of sensor networks can be found in [14] and [781].

Sensor coverage See [184] for an analysis of gradient descent to provide sensor coverage.

Formation control [697] provides a gentle introduction to flocking and formation control. Formation control is related to problems in biology (see [611] and [324] for examples). See [647] for a description of some of the problems associated with coordinating multiple aerial vehicles. [757] and [758] consider the problem of flocking.

Multi-robot localization See [660] for a survey of the problem. See also [679].

Multi-robot SLAM [661] considers the problem of two robot SLAM. [290] considers the problem within a particle filter-based SLAM framework. [817] considers the problem as one of the exploration of embedded graphs.

11.10   Problems

1. Given a triangular object of uniform density and k point robots whose forces when applied to the object provide only frictionless point contacts, develop an algorithm that will move the object in a desired direction. Is your solution for $k = 1$ stable? What is the minimum k for which a stable solution is possible?
2. Given a triangular object of uniform density and k point robots whose forces when applied to the object provide orientation-free point contacts, develop an

algorithm that will move the object in a desired direction. Is your solution for $k = 1$ stable? What is the minimum k for which a stable solution is possible?

3. Simulate a system of $N = 1000$ point robots operating on a plane. Each robot can sense the input state of any robot within a radius $r = 1$. Initially start each robot in the subset of the plane given by $|x| < L/2, |y| < L/2$, with a random heading θ_i and with speed $v_i = 0.03$. At each time step each robot i updates its current heading θ_i based on the average heading of all robots within r including its own heading. To model noise in sensing, corrupt the output of this computation by $\triangle\theta$ drawn from a uniform distribution over the range $[-\eta, \eta]$.

   (a) For noise level $\eta = 0$, plot the average heading of the entire collective as a function of time. Does the collective converge to a common heading direction? Note: Be careful of computations of direction near 2π.

   (b) Does the convergence of the system change with different values of η? Compute average collective heading as a function of η after convergence. Is there a critical value of η in terms of this transition?

   This problem is based on the model described in [807].

4. Imagine a collection of robots on a plane, and that at every time step two robots communicate with which other and that each robot has a Boolean variable INFECTED, which states that the agent is infected. In an interaction between two agents, if either one of the agents involved in the interaction was infected before the interaction, then both are infected now. If neither were, then neither are infected after the interaction

   (a) Starting with one infected agents, how many interactions are required for all agents to be infected? Hint: Work out a general expression for the expected number of interactions it would take for the interaction to result in one additional infected agent. Develop an upper bound for this relationship and sum over the number of agents in the population.

   (b) Implement this infection algorithm and for different sized populations (ten values from 1 to 100,000 say); how many interactions does it take for every agent to become infected?

   (c) Augment the model above but initial assign each agent with a unique ID number and with a maximum id number (initially set to the agent's ID number). The goal of the infection is to have all the agents interact so as to compute their own estimate of the global maximum id number. In an interaction, each agent replaces its maximum estimate with the maximum for the process. Given swarm sizes of between 1 and 100,000, how many interactions are required to compute the max?

5. The online resource contains ROS code that implements a collection of wheelchair-like robots. Use the launch file to understand how the robots are launched, the structure of the name space used by the robots, and the structure of the transformation trees used to describe them. Write a node that takes in Twist messages, as produced by the teleop_twist_keyboard node and sends it to all of the robots in the collection.

12

Human-Robot Interaction

"Gort: Klaatu barada nikto."[1]

12.1 Introduction

Robots are generally not designed to operate in a fully autonomous manner. Rather, they are designed to respond to commands and provide the results of their actions to their human operators. Good interaction between humans and robots is thus critical for the development of effective robot systems and is often referred to as HRI (human–robot interaction) by researchers working in this domain. The importance of HRI is well understood in the field, but often overlooked in texts on robot systems (we neglected to provide a chapter dedicated to this topic in earlier editions of this text, as an example). HRI leverages work in human–machine interaction and investigates mechanisms for providing both explicit and implicit communication between humans and robots. It also incorporates work in the development of social robots that provide simulated social interactions, emotions and socially acceptable motion plans to improve interactions with humans.

The design space for HRI is vast. Techniques that are appropriate for one situation may be inappropriate for another. For example, if interaction with the robot requires direct control of the individual motors that drive the robot are required, then the interaction mechanism with the robot will be focused on accurate control of a number of parallel parameters. While if the robot provides more "high-level" control, then the nature of the interaction will be quite different.

In exploring the ways in which interaction might be designed into an autonomous system, Goodrich and Schultz [318] identify five attributes that affect the nature of the interaction between humans and robots:

- Level and nature of the autonomy.
- Nature of the information exchange.
- Structure of the team.
- Adaptation, learning, and training of people, and the robot.
- Shape of the task.

Each of these is described in some detail below.

---

[1] Instructions to Gort by Helen in *The Day the Earth Stood Still*.

Table 12.1. *Levels of autonomy, after [715].*

Level	Description
1	Robot offers no assistance; human provides all input.
2	Robot offers a complete set of action alternatives.
3	Robot narrows the selection down to a few choices.
4	Robot suggests a single action.
5	Robot executes that action if human approves.
6	Robot allows the human limited time to veto before automatic execution.
7	Robot executes automatically, then necessarily informs the human.
8	Robot informs human after automatic execution only if human asks.
9	Robot informs human after automatic execution only if it decides to.
10	Robot decides everything and acts autonomously, ignoring the human.

12.2 Level and Nature of the Autonomy

Table 12.1 summarizes the *levels of autonomy* or *(LOA)* introduced in [715]. Originally introduced for control of submersibles, this table has been adopted and adapted for robot control. Robot systems have been built around each of these autonomy levels. Within this list levels of autonomy can be grouped into specific categories:

- **Direct teleoperation** (levels 1–3).
- **High-level interaction** (levels 4–9)
- **Full autonomy** (level 10)

Note the similarity to the levels of driving automation as defined in the Society of Automotive Engineers (SAE) international standard [691] and reprinted in Table 12.2.

The nature of HRI changes considerably at different levels. At lower levels (1–2), interaction must provide continuous control of actuators while providing the human operator with continuous information from onboard sensors. At higher levels of autonomy, the nature of the interaction changes. Here the interaction process typically works to reduce the ongoing workload on the human "operator" while ensuring that sufficient information is communicated that the task is performed in an appropriate manner.

12.3 Nature of the Information Exchange

A key aspect of any HRI system is how information is exchanged between the human and the robot. One can distinguish two key aspects here: the communications medium and the format of the communication.

12.3.1 Communications Medium

Humans have well-studied sensory inputs, and information transfer from the robot to the human is typically structured to map to one or more of these inputs. Machines can be engineered with different sensory inputs, and thus there exists a wider range of potential inputs that might be simulated. Similarly, machines can leverage a wider range of communication conduits for transmitting information from robots to humans. Common communication media in either direction include standard computer hardware (keyboard,

Table 12.2. *Levels of driving automation.*

Level 0	Level 1	Level 2	Level 3	Level 4	Level 5
No automation	Driver assistance	Partial automation	Conditional automation	High automation	Full automation
Manual control. The human performs all driving tasks.	The vehicle features a single automated system (e.g., cruise control).	The vehicle can performing steering and acceleration. The human still monitors all tasks and can take control at any time.	The vehicle can perform most driving tasks, but human override is still required.	The vehicle performs all driving tasks under specific circumstances. Human override is still an option.	The vehicle performs all driving tasks under all conditions. Zero human attention or interaction is required.
The human monitors the driving environment.			The car (robot) monitors the driving environment.		

mouse, display), and less traditional mechanisms (e.g., gesture, audio, and touch) and combinations of different modalities.

Any mechanism or set of mechanisms for HRI must be suitable and appropriate for the task at hand. Robots that are deployed outdoors, for example, must utilize HRI mechanisms that work outdoors. Keyboards and mice are unlikely to work well underwater. Mice will not work in environments within which gravity does not drive the mouse to the surface. Similarly, in noisy environments speech and audio are unlikely to be provide effective conduits for communication. Even if we ignore external environmental factors, it is critical to observe that different modalities will work well for some humans and not so well for others. Children who cannot read are unlikely to do well with textural displays. Individuals with poor manual dexterity are unlikely to perform well with touch inputs such as those found on small form-factor devices such as cellular phones or tablets.

Traditional input and output devices Figure 12.1 shows a "traditional" robot interface based around keyboard and mouse input and direct view of the robot's sensors. Multiple monitors provide views from the robot's sensors, and users interact with the remote through keyboard commands. Such an approach can be made to work, but typically requires considerable training, and the actual interaction mechanisms can be very difficult to master.

Leaving aside the display components for a moment, one concern with the keyboard is that for many inputs it can be desirable to provide non-binary input values (e.g., for the robot's velocity), and repeatedly pressing a key to increase/decrease the robot's velocity is error prone. Given this, almost every traditional input device has been used to support HRI. ROS supports standard keyboards and joysticks/gamepads with nodes such as the `teleop_twist_keyboard` and `teleop_twist_joy` packages. Given the existence of standard interfaces for car and aircraft simulated input in the computer gaming industry, such devices are easily integrated into standard robot control software (e.g., ROS), and as such have been deployed to support HRI. A key issue with such devices is that they are typically designed to plug into something else – typically a computer – and this limits their use away from a workstation that will be used to communicate with the robot.

Figure 12.1. A traditional interaction station for the control of a remote autonomous system.

(a) KROY

(b) Pepper

Figure 12.2. HRI mediated by a tablet interface. (a) KROY, being operated underwater by a diver using switches for input and a tablet for display. (b) Pepper working as a server in a bar, using a body-mounted tablet for display and input.

Phones and tablets Given that keyboard and mice and monitors require infrastructure upon which to put devices and to move them about, many robot system designers have proposed the use of tablet/cell phone interfaces for HRI. Touch-sensitive screens with integrated displays may be remote from the robot or integrated with the robot itself. Figure 12.2 shows this approach in action. Figure 12.2a shows the amphibious robot KROY operating in a pool controlled by a SCUBA diver using a tablet interface [806]. This interface is connected to the robot by an optical fiber cable. The diver interacts with the robot through a set of switches mounted on the side of the tablet and by rotating the entire tablet itself. Figure 12.2b shows the Pepper robot [597] operating in a restaurant. Note that the display can be used both for visual information as well as for touch interaction (as in the case of the Pepper robot), or through other inputs (as in the case with KROY). The examples shown in Figure 12.2 assume a physical connection between the robot and the tablet, and of course wireless communication is also possible if the environment permits it. [173], for example, describes a standard infrastructure for integrating remote lightweight devices such as phones and tablets within a remote robot running ROS.

Visual targets and gestures Moving the human operator away from the proximity of the robot limits direct physical contact with the robot, and leads to interaction solutions based on the human providing cues, typically visual, to the robot. A range of techniques exist here including providing the user with specific visual cues to provide instructions (e.g., [233]), having the human gesture in some manner (e.g., [170, 813, 153], or through interpretation of full body motion, such as through dance (see [32]). This concept of using patterns of whole body motion to communicate from the human to the robot can also be used in robot-to-human communication. See [397], for example.

For distances between the human and robot beyond a meter or two, vision is the obvious sensing technology to support human-to-robot communication. For longer distances, LIDAR has proven successful (e.g., [153]), while for more proximal interactions RGB-D cameras (e.g., [759]) and ranging devices such as Leap Motion (e.g., [860]) have proven effective. For robot-to-human communication, it is possible to equip the robot with a range of devices that can be viewed by a human. Robots can be easily programmed to present different colors to indicate the robot's current status or state (e.g., [633]), or through specific robot motions or configurations (e.g., [301]).

Virtual reality and tele-existence Virtual reality and tele-existence provide an interesting conduit for HRI. First, it enables the interaction to move from the limitations of the real world, and second, it provides the opportunity to transform measurements or results from one space to the interactions offered by the virtual environment. Given this, there have been a number of efforts to leverage VR systems for HRI. Figure 12.3 illustrates two extremes in this space. A common issue in VR-based systems is the development of an appropriate approach to provide visual cues to the virtual environment to the user. Two common approaches are the use of an immersive protective environment (commonly known as a CAVE) and the use of a head-mounted display (HMD). These are illustrated in Figure 12.3a and b. Neither solution is ideal. HMDs typically suffer from a limited field of view, lack of view of the wearer's body including their hands, and a conflict between simulated visual depths and accommodation cues caused by the proximity of the display surface. Immersive projective environments typically have a limited visual "sweet spot," making it difficult to have multiple users share a common virtual reality infrastructure, and the space required for such devices makes them difficult to deploy. It is also possible to leverage mixed-reality displays for HRI, as described in [673].

Vision is not the only sensation that can be provided through virtual or augmented reality. For example, the interface shown in Figure 12.3b utilizes a Stewart platform to provide physical motion cues, while the human is provided with visual cues through a HMD. One issue in integrating VR systems with robots is the complexity of integrating the virtual reality rendering environment, typically based on a commercial gaming engine, and the robot control system, typically some flavor of ROS. A number of efforts exist that provide this linkage, include [173], which maps messages in ROS into callbacks defined in the game engine itself.

(a) Immersive environment   (b) Motion platform   (c) VR display

Figure 12.3. HRI mediated using virtual reality (VR). (a) An immersive projective environment (IVY) that can be used to provide a 360° immersive visual environment for robot control. (b) A motion platform coupled with a head-mounted display that can be used to provide both an immersive visual environment as well as physical motion to simulate physical interaction of the robot with its environment. (c) A visual VR-delivered simulation of the robot operating in an environment. Dark gray markers are LIDAR frames from a map of the environment and light gray dots are current LIDAR measurements.

Tactile and haptic interaction mechanisms Haptics is the means by which information is conveyed through touch [335]. Tactics refers to the detection of force on the skin. Another aspect of haptic sensing is **kinesethic**, the sensing of body movement and muscle strength. There exist a large number of HRI systems based on tactile feedback. One approach here is to transduce forces acting on the robot (e.g., pressure on finger pads in a robot's gripper) into tactile sensations on the human's fingers. Haptic feedback in robots is probably best exemplified by exoskeleton robots (see [208]). Here an exoskeleton is mounted around human limbs, most especially the legs, and this is used either to power an exeoskeleon "suit" around the human to provide mobility, or enhanced mobility to the user, or to drive some external robot. See [707] for a review of haptic feedback in human-machine systems. It is also possible to have a robot generate tactic cues to a human as a direct mechanism for communication. For example, [295] uses controlled bursts of air as part of the process of capturing the attention of users near a robot.

Audio-based mechanisms Perhaps the most natural mechanisms for human to human communication is through speech. Given this, there is considerable interest in developing HRI based on human language-based interaction either through speech (audio). One common approach is to assume a dyadic conversation between a human and a robot, with the communication initiated by the human. Then the human utterance is translated to text using some standard speech-to-text engine, either a cloud-based technology, or a library such as CMU's Sphinx that supports both cloud-based and local speech-to-text conversion, or some purely local speech-to-text engine. Generally, cloud-based engines provide more accurate performance while incurring some communication delay, which may be inappropriate for effective HRI. Once a textual version of the utterance is available, traditional grammar-based engines or data-driven approaches such as Seq2Seq are used to map the intent of the utterance into a command for the robot. This latter process can inform the parsing process and assist in errors introduced in earlier processing stages.

Just as audio can be used to provide human-to-robot communication, it is also possible to provide robot-to-human communication using the same modality. Standard text-to-speech engines exist that will take text and produce appropriate voices that will speak the

(a) Sentrybot　　　　　　(b) Pepper in Prague　　　　　　(c) VR Mindar

Figure 12.4. Robots seeking to leverage human-like features to enhance HRI. (a) Sentrybot, a robot based around the Bishop robot morphology but augmented with a 2D avatar. (b) Pepper, this time deployed in a bar in Prague. (c) Mindar, a robot programmed to receive the teaching of Buddha. (a) appears with the kind permission of Walleed Khan.

information in a "natural" manner. As with speech-to-text engines, text-to-speech engines can either be local or provided through standard web services. Typically, local systems produce poorer quality results but with less latency than cloud-based solutions.

Mimicking humans and human interactions As humans are more used to interacting with humans than robots, there has been a long history of developing humanoid "robots," at least as far back as the work of Leonardo da Vinci. Modern humanoid robots typically seek to provide a range of human-like features that mimic human appearance and interaction mechanisms. Figure 12.4 provides three examples of humanoid(-like) robots. Pepper has found worldwide application in sales and marketing. Mindar is a robot designed to teach limited scriptures in Buddhism. Sentrybot is an experimental platform for security and sentry tasks.

There exists a large collection of such devices. Critical among them is an effort to provide a familiar shape and interaction conduit. They typically have heads/faces that are intended to be the focus of conversation and interaction using audio to both recognize and respond with speech. They also typically provide mechanisms to simulate a number of implicit communication mechanisms including eye and body motions (see [429]), and attend to and simulate different emotional states (see [150]).

The process of putting a face and human-like body on a robot introduces a range of design decisions that are not necessarily related to the underlying engineering requirements of the device. Shape, color, general morphology, and other factors must be considered. For example, does a robot appear more trustworthy if it communicates via text or through voice, and if so, does the fidelity of the voice used influence the level of trust? See [451]. An effective design is likely to require consideration of task and the anticipated human population with which the robot will interact (see [62], for example).

Figures 12.5 and 12.6 provide snapshots in terms of the possible range of robot structures that can be imagined. What scale should the robot be, and is this related to task?

(a) Sony companion robot   (b) Advertising robot

Figure 12.5. Robot scale.

The examples shown in Figure 12.5 were chosen to occur at extreme ends of the scale, For example, the companion robot shown in Figure 12.5a is designed to be much smaller than a human, while the robot shown in Figure 12.5b was clearly designed to be substantially taller than humans in the environment. But what is an appropriate height for an interacting robot? [350], for example, found that the ideal height for verbal communication with a robot was a robot that was slightly (300 mm) lower than the human speaker. But does this result hold for different tasks and interaction situations?

The question of basic robot morphology to aid in HRI is still very much open, although there have been a number of efforts to define the problem in a formal sense. [62], for example, has explored how children perceive a robot's morphology, and [496] provides a review of the various social robots that can be found in the world today. One interesting property of many of the interactive robots available today is that many provide a face or a face-like structure to ground the communication. Devices such as the Furhat robot (Figure 12.6a) provide a very sophisticated mechanism with a full face that can be rendered, and robots such as Mindar (Figure 12.4c) provide a full 3D face structure, while others use a display to animate an avatar to put a face on the robot (Figure 12.4a). But is a "face" necessary or beneficial for HRI? There is some evidence that adding a face makes a robot more likely to be perceived as effective at its task and more interesting/useful for interaction [26, 123].

The Uncanny Valley As robots increasingly resemble humans, some robot designs are reported to fall into an "uncanny valley" (Figure 12.7), in which the design of the robot generates impressions of repulsion, eeriness, and other negative effects. The term originated with the work of Mori [545] (an English translation can be found in [546]). See also [139] for an overview of Mori's work, [820] for a review of the literature on the uncanny valley, and in particular studies that have, and have not, encountered an uncanny valley. Figure 12.7 plots affinity for a given design as a function of human likeness. There

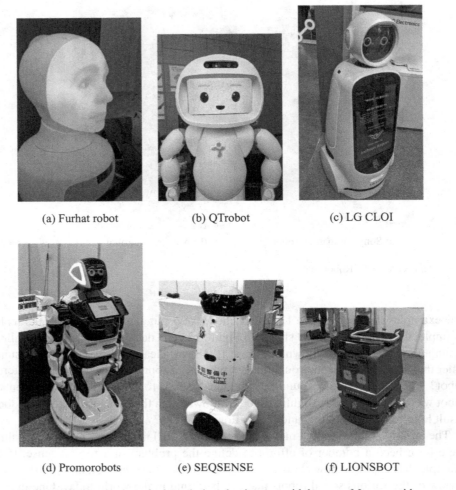

(a) Furhat robot   (b) QTrobot   (c) LG CLOI

(d) Promorobots   (e) SEQSENSE   (f) LIONSBOT

Figure 12.6. A selection of robots designed to interact with humans. Many provide a face or face-like structure to ground the interaction.

appears to exist a point at which robots (and objects generally) are perceived as being eerie as they become close to, but not completely equivalent to, human appearance.

12.3.2 What to Communicate

"I'm completely operational, and all my circuits are functioning perfectly."[2]

Beyond the conduits used for communication, there is the question of what to communicate and how it should be communicated. Communication can be implicit or explicit, and there is considerable evidence that the most effective mechanisms for HRI involve both implicit and explicit communication (see [312]). Explicit communication in HRI is a deliberate from of communication [118], whereas implicit communication is communication that occurs outside of direct or explicit communication.

[2] Response from the HAL 9000 in *2001: A Space Odyssey*.

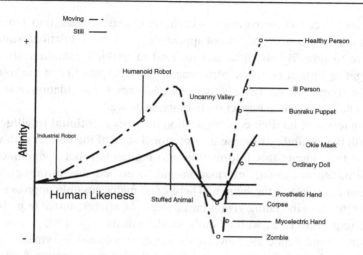

Figure 12.7. The uncanny valley. Redrawn from [546].

Properly choosing what to communicate from the robot to the human and back is key to the development of an effective HRI strategy. It is important to recognize that providing too much information can be just as ineffective as providing too little, and that human–robot communication is not necessarily symmetric.

Explicit Communication Explicit communication takes many forms, including keyboard input, spoken language, visual signals and specialized audio cues. Generally, explicit communication relies on some pre-defined, and perhaps "natural" communication language. Specific sounds may be used to cue specific event (e.g., backing up), specific colors to specific commands ("green means go"), and so on. Defining the intent of specific communication can be coded in a variety of ways, from formal syntax (e.g., as described in [160] for gesture-based human–robot interaction underwater), or through various tools from natural language understanding such as bag-of-words or Word2Vec.

Implicit Communication Although explicit communication is critical to commanding a robot to do something (e.g., `robot, pick up that block`), or obtaining information from the robot (e.g., `I am unable to pick up the block`), human communication routinely relies on communicating through actions, gestures, tone and word choice that provide implicit information about the context or intent of explicit communication.

Humans have a long history of interaction with others and use these experiences to build up a repertoire and set of strategies for implicit communication. Identifying implicit communication and utilizing it for a robot involves explicitly recognizing such communication or deliberately generating such communication when interacting with humans. For humans to engage more fully with robots in joint tasks and perhaps even to trust robots to perform tasks independently, implicit communication appears key [312]. The set of mechanisms for implicit communication is just as wide and varied as those used by humans when communicating with other humans, but includes mechanisms from simulated eye motion, to simulated gaze controlled by head/body/camera motion, to planned paths in space, forces when sharing a task, choice of text in interaction, tenor, and other parameters of robot speech, general robot appearance, and the simulation/estimation of emotions. Failure to properly simulate and respond to implicit communication can have an overall negative impact on robot performance and acceptability of the robot by human operators. Of course, the converse is true as well, excessive simulation of implicit communication can have a negative impact on interaction as well.

A key question in terms of implicit communication involves **emotional intelligence** – to endow robots with the capability to sense the emotional state of the human with which it is interacting and to integrate this information into human-to-robot communication, and similarly to simulate emotional information and to embed this information into communication from the robot to the human. There exist many possible approaches for estimating speaker sentiment including vision-based (e.g., [664]), text-based (e.g., [465]), audio signal-based (e.g., [267]), as well as multi-modal efforts (e.g., [706]). Endowing robots with emotional intelligence also involves utilizing emotional information in the response to the communication from the user. There have been a number of efforts to simulate emotion in terms of the action of the robot (e.g., [116]), and even in terms of regulating the temperature of the robot [616].

12.4   Structure of the Team

Although there exist tasks for which one robot is controlled by an individual operator, it is more common to encounter situations within which multiple humans control a single robot or environments within which a group of robots is coordinated by a group of human operators. This can be found in UUV operation, UAV operation, and elsewhere. Extreme versions here include situations such as the control process for the Mars Exploration rovers. Here a team of scientists and engineers known as the Science and Operations Working Group (SWOG) plan the days operations of the remote Martian rover [804]. Beyond the size and complexity of the human–robot team, there is the critical question of team management structure. One particularly interesting domain for this occurs in the military in which the integration of autonomous systems into small-scale operational units (see [826, 64]).

12.5   Adaptation, Learning, and Training

In any long-term, ongoing task involving humans and robots we must assume that the human will learn properties of the task and that this learning will influence the best approach to HRI related to the task. We can also assume that modern algorithms running on the robot will also learn, as the robot is exposed to more interactions with the task. How can we leverage this learning in terms of HRI?

12.6   Shape of the Task

Any given task has a policy or procedure that is followed to complete it. As robots are introduced into the task solution space, the prior solution model may or may not be appropriate. The use of robots may modify the way in which the task can be completed, and thus change the shape of the task. How does the HRI imagined for the previous version of the task enable enhancements to the solution strategy, and are HRI mechanisms imagined before well suited for the resulting task shape?

12.7 Social Robots

Effective HRI is perhaps most critical in the development of robots that are intended to operate in an appropriate manner when situated in some "human" space. [117] classifies social robots as being **socially evocative** – relying on humans to assign to the robot properties of biological agents, providing a **social interface** – providing an interface that mimics normal human social interactions, **socially receptive** robots – robots that are socially passive but which benefit from interaction, and **sociable** robots – robots that pr-actively engage with humans. This structure is expanded upon in [280] to include robots that are **socially situated** – robots that must perceive and react to the social environment, **socially embedded** robots that are embedded within the social environment, and **socially intelligent** robots that demonstrate aspects of human social intelligence. Developing robots that exhibit higher levels of these social skill requires developing robots that not only can perceive the social environment in which they are operating but which can also generate cues that are perceived by others are providing the necessary social cues for the robot to appear to be behaving **socially**.

Although one might seek to address the need to behave socially by assuming that the best possible design would be through an anthropomorphic design, such an approach is not without its concerns (see Section 12.3.1). Nor is a human-shaped robot necessarily the most appropriate for a given task. Should robots be tall or short, thin or fat, or should the external appearance of robots be malleable so as to use the appearance of the device as a communication component? For example, [737] describes a robot whose external color is controlled to provide cues as to the emotion that the robot is attempting to communicate to human observers. Not only does the appearance of the robot impact its social acceptability, one must also consider how its actions will be perceived. **Social navigation** involves developing navigation algorithms that also incorporate an understanding of socially acceptable human behavior while negotiating populated spaces. A key problem in the development of social navigation is developing an appropriate mechanism for evaluating different socially acceptable behaviors. One approach here is to model performance based on how humans perform navigation in crowded spaces, using an approach such as off-line reinforcement learning as in [54].

As observed earlier in Section 12.3.2, HRI involves both explicit and implicit communication. In social robotics applications, the need for effective implicit and explicit communication is highlighted. Many robots designed to operate in this space seek to simulate some personality and to provide implicit cues to the user.

12.8 Evaluating HRI Approaches

A key problem in HRI is understanding the efficacy of different approaches to the problem. As in HCI generally, there are interesting technical problems in the development of different technologies that might be applied to the underlying problem. And as in

HCI, it can be extremely difficult to understand if and when a particular technology or methodology might be appropriate for a given task. Conducting rigorous studies in HRI is crucial to obtaining verifiable and repeatable results related to the efficacy of different technologies and approaches to HRI.

Designing an experiment to evaluate the performance of some HRI approach introduces a range of fundamental questions related to what to measure and what mechanism(s) should be used to enable these measurements to take place. These two choices are interlinked.

What to Measure What to measure is related to task performance, and quantitative measurements of task performance can capture a range of data, from raw video imagery to responses to tailored questions and quantitative performance on specific tasks. Large-scale datasets of human-robot interaction now exist. For example, [158] describes an HRI dataset obtained by having heavily instrumented actors conduct a range of normal interactions in a simulated shopping environment assisted by an autonomous robot. This dataset includes information about robot and human motion trajectories, and gaze direction of humans in the environment. It is possible to collect a vast array of data related to any human–robot interaction.

Given a scenario a range of different measurements can be made, from low-level measurements such as time to task completion to high-level measurements such as self-reported cognitive workload and situational awareness. A number of questionnaires have evolved to assess the acceptability of different technologies. For example, the Almere Technology Acceptance Questionnaire (ATAQ) [343], which was designed to assess the acceptability of robot technology for seniors, consists of a set of 41 statements, a few of which are given in Listing 12.1. On this questionnaire participants responded on a 5-point Likert-type scale ranging from 1 to 5 (1 totally disagree, 2 disagree, 3 don't know, 4 agree, 5 totally agree). The Godspeed Questionnaire [68], see Listing 12.2, in various modified forms, is perhaps the most used questionnaire in HRI research. It asks participants to rate their experience with a robot along a set of dimensions, but provides a more concrete set of scales.

Taking Measurements Two broad categories of how to structure HRI experiments have emerged; controlled "in the lab" experiments and experiments conducted "in the wild," that is, experiments conducted through unscripted interactions between robots and naïve visitors to the robot's workspace or between robots and actors engaged in "natural" interactions with the robot system. In either case, experiments may be controlled by the robot's operational software directly, or through **Wizard of Oz** (or **WoZ**) experiments in which the experiment is controlled by a human who is not visible to participants but interacts with the robot system. Both controlled and in the wild

If I should use the robot, I would be afraid to break something.
I have everything I need to use the robot.
I enjoy the robot talking to me.
I feel the robot understands me.
I would follow the advice the robot gives me.

Listing 12.1. Sample questions from the Almere Technology Acceptance Questionnaire.

Godspeed I: Anthropomorphism

Fake	1	2	3	4	5	Natural
Machine-like	1	2	3	4	5	Human-like
Unconscious	1	2	3	4	5	Conscious
Artificial	1	2	3	4	5	Life-like
Moving rigidly	1	2	3	4	5	Moving elegantly

Godspeed II: Animacy

Dead	1	2	3	4	5	Alive
Stagnant	1	2	3	4	5	Lively
Mechanical	1	2	3	4	5	Organic
Artificial	1	2	3	4	5	Life-like
Inert	1	2	3	4	5	Interactive
Apathetic	1	2	3	4	5	Responsive

Godspeed III: Likeability

Dislike	1	2	3	4	5	Like
Unfriendly	1	2	3	4	5	Friendly
Unkind	1	2	3	4	5	Kind
Unpleasant	1	2	3	4	5	Pleasant
Awful	1	2	3	4	5	Nice

Godspeed IV: Perceived Intelligence

Incompetent	1	2	3	4	5	Competent
Ignorant	1	2	3	4	5	Knowledgeable
Irresponsible	1	2	3	4	5	Responsible
Unintelligent	1	2	3	4	5	Intelligent
Foolish	1	2	3	4	5	Sensible

Godspeed IV: Perceived Safety

Anxious	1	2	3	4	5	Relaxed
Agitated	1	2	3	4	5	Calm
Quiescent	1	2	3	4	5	Surprised

Listing 12.2. Sample Godspeed questionnaire. From [68]. Participants are asked to rate their impression of the robot on these scales.

experiments have their advantages and disadvantages. Controlled experiments are exactly that, controlled. This allows experiment designers to structure the study to control for as many external factors as possible, including properties of the participants in the study (e.g., age, gender), as well as balancing conditions so as to provide results that are well suited for later statistical analysis. As an example of a controlled HRI experiment, consider [26]. This experiment seeks to determine whether putting an animated avatar on a robot provides an added benefit to the underlying human–robot interaction. The actual experiment does not use a robot; rather, participants interact with the agent through one of a number of different modalities (text only and audio only as baselines), and two animated avatars, a cartoon avatar and a realistic one, as shown in Figure 12.8a. A set of interactions were predefined and the participant interacted through the same back-end AI through the various modalities. Participants were asked through a set of questionnaires about participant satisfaction with the various modalities. Statistical analysis of responses to these questionnaires demonstrated that participants found interactions with avatars more enjoyable than the baselines, but that overall satisfaction with the various interfaces was equally high.

(a) Controlled   (b) Observational

Figure 12.8. Sample stimuli from controlled (a) and observational, to in the wild (b) HRI experiments. (a) Two animated avatars that were compared against audio and text baselines in the experiment. (b) A frame captured from an observational experiment taken in a party environment. (a) appears with the kind permission of Enas AlTaraweneh. (b) appears with the kind permission of Natalie Friedman.

The control in such experiments comes at the cost of removing the natural and organic nature of interactions that can take place in the wild. For example, [295] describes a WoZ experiment that used an observational experiment which explored how directed air might be used to capture the attention of participants in a socially acceptable manner. The experiment took place over a number of parties in which the robot was teleoperated as the party took place. The wizard operating the robot used different modalities to attract attention at different parties. After the party, the participants completed a social dominance scale questionnaire, and video captured of the party was coded as to the number of interactions and the success of the robot in capturing the attention of the participant with which it was engaging. The experiment found that a combination of haptic air, audio, and visual cues was the most effective attention-capturing mechanism of the approaches considered. [148] highlights a number of problems in designing and executing an observational experiment in the wild including the wide range of possible responses participants can have to the scenario being presented. Responses that might not have been obvious to the experiment designers may occur. For example, participants may approach the robot in groups, rather than as individuals, and thus scoring their interaction can be complicated.

12.9   Further Reading

HRI A good review of the field of HRI prior to 2007 can be found in [318], while [763] provides a systematic overview of HRI from 2005 to 2015. See also [100]. [345] provides a review of what makes a robot social, that is, what makes a robot more acceptable to the general public. [280] reviews "socially interactive robots." [126] provides (among other things) thoughts on the the evolution of HRI.

Sentiment analysis [741] provides a broad review of sentiment in HRI. See also [748].

Design of HRI experiments [292] provides a detailed review of the design of HRI experiments. See also [356], [736], and [85].

12.10 Problems

1. ROS provides a standard teleoperational interface based on joystick input (`teleop_twist_joy`). Obtain a joystick and configure it for ROS. Using one joystick, provide teleoperational input to one of the Gazebo-simulated robots or with a physical robot that you have access to. How did you decide to use the dimensionality of the input device to control the robot? What functions were assigned to which buttons/joysticks/game pads, and why were those decisions made?

2. Using the software provided on the online resource associated with this book, implement your set of decisions from the previous problem and use this to drive the robot defined there around the world. Discuss how your decisions met the reality of operating the robot.

3. Many joysticks are not analog, but rather are digital providing "left," "right," "up," and "down." In this manner, they provide input much like pressing buttons on a keyboard. Which is better for teleoperation, a digital joystick or arrows on a keyboard? Design a controlled experiment to try to ask this question.

   (a) How did you define "better"? Ability to drive a robot more quickly to a given point? Ability to maneuver a robot with fewer collisions through a maze? Ability to drive a robot to a given point in space more accurately? Some other metric?

   (b) What would one condition look like in this experiment?

   (c) How would you design the experiment to collect these data? Would you use a real robot or a simulated one? How would you structure the experiment so as to collect useful data? Would a given participant be presented with both conditions or only one? If presented with both, would they perform the experiment in blocks of one condition and then the other or would the conditions be interleaved? Would data be collected in one session or in multiple sessions?

   (d) What statistical evaluation would you use to try to demonstrate that the two conditions produce different results? How would you estimate the number of conditions and number of participants required to demonstrate a statistically significant result?

   (e) What approval process would you require at your institution/company in order to conduct this experiment?

4. There exist a number of text-to-speech engines freely available for Python. Develop a ROS node that speaks to the user. There also exist a number of speech-to-text engines freely available for Python. Develop a ROS node that takes utterances from a human nearby the robot and converts them into text.

   (a) Imagine trying to teleoperate the robot using the nodes created above. What would be the unit of command be? Would `forward` mean move forward until another command is sent, or would `forward` mean move forward for a finite period of time? If the latter, how would you develop an experiment to determine the appropriate length of this time period?

(b) Typically home assistants require a key phrase to be uttered prior to a command. Would a similar approach be useful for the speech-based controller or would mere proximity with the robot be sufficient? Design an HRI experiment to test user's preference for the need to provide a key phrase prior to commands to the robot.

(c) The text-to-speech engine can be used to provide useful audio information when the robot comes into contact with people (e.g., to say `please get out of my way` when the robot's path is blocked). An alternative to such an utterance is the use of a horn or bell to warn users of the robot's motion, or perhaps to use both. Which of these three approaches would be more likely to be effective? Design both an "in the wild" and a controlled experiment to explore this question. How would you design the experiment so as to safe for the participants involved in the study?

5. Develop code in ROS/Gazebo to implement one trial of the experiment you developed in the previous problem. Prototype your trial. After trying out the condition, do you have any changes that you feel should be made to your experimental design from the previous problem?

13

Robot Ethics

"Roboethics is an applied ethics whose objective is to develop scientific/cultural/technical tools that can be shared by different social groups and beliefs. These tools aim to promote and encourage the development of robotics for the advancement of human society and individuals, and to help preventing its misuse against humankind"[1]

13.1 Introduction

Ever since we began to build software systems that interacted with humans, there have ethical concerns about the ways in which we interact with them. In [830], for example, Weizenbaum observes of the world's first chatterbot that "ELIZA shows, if nothing else, how easy it is to create and maintain the illusion of understanding, hence perhaps of judgment deserving of credibility. A certain danger lurks there."[2] Fast forward more than 60 years, and this observation that a "certain danger lurks there" has emerged as a range of different concerns about the ways in which software (and hardware) systems are developed and deployed, and the range of data that modern data-driven systems rely upon. The space of machine ethics is vast, and a large number of texts, papers, and policy documents now exist on the subject. A short list of papers related to the more general problem is provided at the end of this chapter. Here we limit ourselves to ethical concerns that are specifically relevant to autonomous systems, the tasks that for which autonomous systems are being deployed, and human interactions with them.

Robot ethics, or **roboethics**, exists at the intersection of applied ethics and robotics. It has the aim of understanding the ethical implications and consequences of robotic technology. Roboethics studies and attempts to understand and regulate the ethical implications and consequences of robotic technology. The term itself was defined by Verugio in [805], and his definition appears at the beginning of this chapter.

Roboethics builds on a range of different ethical theories that have been applied to a range of different issues unrelated to robots or technology in the past. See Chapter 2 of [787] for a brief introduction to the relevant ethical theories. A proper treatment of the various ethical theories that have emerged relevant to the study of robotethics include three fundamental questions [43]:

---

[1] [805].
[2] [830] pp. 5–6.

1. How might humans act ethically through, or with, robots?
2. How can we design robots to act ethically? Can robots be truly moral agents?
3. How can we explain the ethical relationships between human and robots?

Note that question 1 assumes that humans are the moral agent. Question 2 seeks to develop, if at all possible, the robot as the moral agent. Question 3 seeks to understand the balance between humans and robots when they act in concert.

Ethical issues related to robots span a wide range, but broadly speaking one can structure the ethical questions around the role in which we place robots [552]: robots as tools, robots as subjects, or (potentially, after the singularity) robots as moral agents

13.2 Robot as Tool

If we assume robots are no different from hammers, then the ethical questions concerning their operation relate primarily to how they are used by humans. If a robot is fully and directly controlled, then it could be likened to a hammer. Ethical questions related to its operation can be asked of the operator, as the tool itself is completely controlled. But as we program the robot to have autonomous control over its function and to act independently of direct human operation, it becomes proper to ask ethical questions about the robot.

In the study of human ethics, a popular thought experiment is the **Trolley problem**. The Trolley problem first appeared in 1967 [281] and can be described like this: a trolley is heading down a hill with failed brakes on a track that will lead it to a group of five people who will be killed if no action is taken. There is a switch on the tracks that can send the trolley away from this group, and if you were to throw this switch the trolley would change direction and save these five people. Unfortunately, there exists a single person on this alternative track. You have a choice: to take an action to kill one person, or by not taking an action being responsible for killing five.

In the study of human ethics the Trolley problem is an interesting probe of the way in which you should act depending on whether your underlying ethical doctrine is being followed. In its simplest form, if you were to follow a **utilitarian doctrine**, then you would choose to kill the one individual as this action results in the greatest good for the greatest number of people. On the other hand, if you were to follow the **dentological doctrine**, then you would choose to not throw the switch, as under deontological ethics an action is either right or wrong, and killing someone is clearly wrong.

This particular dilemma is often used to introduce the problem of machine ethics and its role in autonomous cars. Here the version is typically placed as a car being driven autonomously that has encountered some unpredictable event (like skidding on ice) and is now directed toward a group of five individuals. If the car were to apply the brakes (or some other control) it would collide with a single individual. Which action does the car take, and where and how was the ethical doctrine that the car followed integrated into its programming?

Before exploring this question further, a few caveats. There are many who feel that the autonomous vehicle Trolley problem is too artificial and does not take into account the realities involved in the programming of autonomous vehicles and the inability of the vehicle to act under certainty (see [470] and [304]). All that being said, the autonomous vehicle version of the Trolley problem raises a number of interesting questions about ethical decision making in this space.

First, we must recognize that whichever decision that autonomous vehicle takes, it was programmed into the system by the manufacturer of the vehicle. Regardless of any legal and financial risks, does the ethical decision made by the manufacturer and development team agree with the ethical and moral philosophy of the vehicle operator? When the operator purchased the vehicle, or turned it on in the morning, did they have the opportunity to choose a particular ethical setting for the vehicle for the day? There are few good options here, indeed Lin's article in *Wired* magazine "Here's a Terrible Idea: Robot Cars with Adjustable Ethics Settings"[469], sums up his position in the title. There are no good answers here and perhaps significant unintended consequences. For example, if the autonomous vehicle were to follow a utilitarian model, how deep should this model go? For example, [533] considers the autonomous vehicle Trolley problem with motorcyclists with and without helmets as the two possible targets. As the motorcyclist wearing a helmet is more likely to survive the crash than the one without, then the vehicle might be programmed to choose the rider wearing a helmet, as this is likely to have a more utilitarian outcome than the rider without a helmet. This action might lead to a less positive long-term utilitarian result as a consequence of reduced use of motorcycle helmets in the future.

13.2.1 Military Robots

Beyond the vision of science fiction writers, the concept of applying robots to security tasks, both in the civilian and military domains, has a long history. Such devices provide a government with the ability to project force and provide security both at home and abroad with reduced potential for harm to its citizens. Here we concentrate on the development and use of such devices in the military, but many of the observations also apply to civilian applications.

The vast majority of autonomous systems that are currently deployed are under active control of human agents. They are, if you like, remotely controlled weapons systems. In this, the cruise missile of today's modern army has much in common with the V1 weapons of the 1940s. Someone on the ground directs the weapon to be launched and thus takes on the the authority and responsibility for the weapon.

Given their ease of deployment, reduction in harm to home personnel, and potential financial savings, autonomous systems find wide military application; aerial vehicles (UAV), unmanned ground vehicles (UGV), multi-functional utility/logistics and equipment, armed robotic vehicles (ARV), tactical mobile robots, and robotic ships (USV, UUV) already exist in modern military arsenals. Such devices have also found application by non-state actors as the very aspects that make them attractive to governments, make them attractive to other agents.

Leaving aside the ethics of war itself, autonomous systems as a tool in warfare introduces a range of ethical and legal concerns. Horowitz [368] raises two essential questions related to the use of autonomous weapons in the military: (i) Would autonomous weapons be more or less effective than non-autonomous systems? (ii) Does the nature of autonomous weapons raise ethical and/or moral considerations that either recommend their development or justify their prohibition? Although there are many complex questions related to **lethal autonomous weapon systems** or **LAWS**, a key tipping point in their development is the point at which such devices go from being remotely controlled weapons to weapons that engage targets automatically away from direct positive human control. As software is easily updated and changed, it can be difficult to identify when a given weapon system moves from one form to the other. In many cases these devices can be configured so as to operate in an autonomous mode where positive "in-the-loop" human control is not needed for lethal actions to be undertaken. The potential of enhanced autonomy on the battlefield has been observed by the military for many years. The 1983 DARPA report gets to the point rather quickly on the first page:

> "For example, instead of fielding simple guided missiles or remotely piloted vehicles, we might launch completely autonomous land, sea, and air vehicles capable of complex, far-ranging reconnaissance and attack missions."[3]

The Geneva Conventions is a series of international treaties signed by most of the countries in the world that establish legal structures concerning the effects of war on soldiers and civilians. Initially signed in 1864, the conventions have been updated a number of times, most recently in 1977. Many countries seek to codify/clarify/expand upon the country's requirements under the Geneva Conventions (e.g., for the United States, see [500]). When a LAWS is deployed as a remotely controlled device under direct human control, then the ethical and legal aspects of the deployment can be related to a human operator, But once the device has even *limited autonomy* to engage in combat, a range of complex questions emerges. Here we explore just one aspect of this. For a more complete treatment, see [35]. Article 3 of the Geneva Convention binds signatories as follows:

> "Persons taking no active part in the hostilities, including members of armed forces who have laid down their arms and those placed hors de combat by sickness, wounds, detention, or any other cause, shall in all circumstances be treated humanely, without any adverse distinction founded on race, colour, religion or faith, sex, birth or wealth, or any other similar criteria.
>
> To this end the following acts are and shall remain prohibited at any time and in any place whatsoever with respect to the above-mentioned persons:
>
> (a) Violence to life and person, in particular murder of all kinds, mutilation, cruel treatment and torture."

Observe what this implies in terms of truly autonomous LAWS. In order to be in compliance with the Geneva Conventions, such a system must be able to distinguish between an active combatant and (for example) a person who is too injured to continue to fight. From a purely technical point of view, developing software to make such a decision is challenging. But suppose such a system is developed and deployed; where then does culpability lie should the system violate this article? Does it lie with the military chain of command that deployed it? With government procurement and approval processes that enabled it? Or hardware and software developers who created the system? Perhaps of greatest concern is that assigning responsibility for such actions would be sufficiently difficult that no individual would ever be identified as responsible for the resulting war crime. See [435] for a more complete treatment of the potential legal consequences of deploying LAWS with even limited autonomy.

---

[3] [202], p. 1.

If one is willing to define the term "robot" sufficiently broadly, then mines are the earliest example of a lethal robot weapon. In use since the American Civil War [195], these are victim-operated weapons that detect the presence of action near them and are detonated when the device senses appropriate action nearby. The **Ottawa Convention** or, as it is more correctly known, **the Convention on the Prohibition of the Use, Stockpiling, Production and Transfer of Anti-Personnel Mines and on Their Destruction** came into force in 1999. Although not signed by many countries (including the United States), its text defines a mine as

> "a munition designed to be placed under, on or near the ground or other surface area and to be exploded by the presence, proximity of a person or a vehicle."

This is a definition that could certainly be inferred to include LAWS targeted at individuals. Although fewer countries are signatories to the Ottawa Convention than are to the Geneva Conventions, it is instructive to observe that many signatories to the Ottawa Convention have also established that they will not build, stockpile, or deploy LAWS that are intended to be deployed against persons or vehicles.

Beyond the military application, in the civilian sector a range of organizations is developing and deploying security robots. As in the military domain, a complex set of issues occurs when the robot moves from direct human control to partial autonomy. In the civilian application, security robots are typically deployed as mobile sensor/interaction platforms with limited weapons systems, and today such systems are typically intended for bomb disposal applications. But once machines have even limited autonomy, a range of interesting and complex questions emerges. For example, what is a definition of "reasonable force" for a security robot? The answer here will depend on how such devices are treated under the local legal structures. Take the case of a human responder. Local legal structures typically provide different requirements before force can be used, and these requirements depend on the role of the responder (police officer versus civilian, for example), threat to others and to property, and the reasonableness of the force being used. Perhaps the closest equivalent in the civilian security domain is the deployment of K9 units in policing. Here the K9 units are well trained and operate under the direct supervision of a specially trained officer. Issues related to excessive force or improper deployment of the K9 unit are directed at the officer supervising the K9 unit. Is a similar structure appropriate for police robots?

13.2.2 Robots, Children, and the Elderly

Robots have the potential to meet the increasing demand on health and social care systems with age. Companion robots, in particular, have been proposed to enhance the life of seniors, and particularly seniors with dementia. Although there is limited evidence that such devices can provide some benefit to the individuals with which they interact, as well as the potential for providing reduced costs associated with providing care for these individuals, these devices raise a range of ethical concerns.

A similar set of concerns can be found in the development of companion robots for children. Much like the issue for seniors, deploying autonomous robots with younger individuals who are unable either legally or otherwise to make decisions related to their interaction with autonomous systems raises a host of ethical concerns and questions. **Smart connected toys**, including autonomous versions of same, are becoming

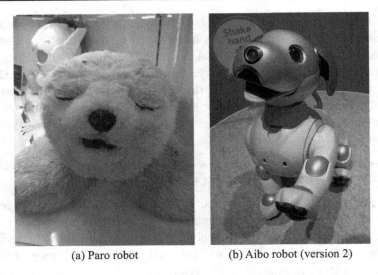

(a) Paro robot   (b) Aibo robot (version 2)

Figure 13.1. Robots intended for deployment with children and the elderly.

commonplace. As in their counterparts for the elderly, such devices offer a range of potential benefits to their user including educational, emotional, and social benefits. But as with devices planned for use with seniors with cognitive impairment, there are great concerns about data privacy, including general image data. Such devices are mobile data collection platforms that utilize sensor data, including vision, which introduces a range of security and privacy issues that are perhaps even more severe than those associated with computer-based AI systems given their mobility and the integrated nature of audio, video, and other sensors embedded in the technology.

Leaving aside ethical concerns that also apply to AI systems generally and their use with children and adults with cognitive impairment, a key ethical issue with autonomous agents and these groups is the manner in which these devices are intended to interact with humans. Generally, they are designed to appear as objects that are well understood by their human receptor: toys for children and pets for senior adults. Paro [640] (Figure 13.1a), a simulated seal pup, may perhaps be the most well-known example for seniors and the Aibo [110] (Figure 13.1b), a robotic dog, may perhaps be the most well-known example for children. A critical observation of these devices is that they simulate some other structure. Or as observed in [732], to obtain the full benefit of the social interaction with these robots, the user must "systematically delude themselves regarding the real nature of their relation with the device." It is interesting to note that science fiction writers foresaw the complexity of autonomous (pet) robots and social interaction robots long before their actual appearance. *Robbie* by Isaac Asimov, deals with the complexities of robotic childcare, and Philp K. Dick's *Do Androids Dream of Electric Sheep?* describes a future within which owning an animal is important to impress on others one's social status.

13.2.3 Autonomous Vehicles

As described earlier, autonomous vehicles provide a range of interesting ethical questions related to decision making during driving when presented with undesirable outcomes regardless of the chosen course of action of the vehicle. But there exists a range of other interesting questions here as well. For example, many self-driving cars are built with the capability of having humans take control of the device. If humans can take control of the vehicle, should the vehicle continue to monitor the actions of the human while it is driving and influence the human driver when they are operating the vehicle? Or perhaps should it even take control of the vehicle if the human operator's performance falls below some threshold?

Current driving laws essentially treat all vehicles and all individuals evenly. [51] suggests that this is not the ethical choice that humans would make, and that regional preferences exist for sparing by women over men, apparent healthy individuals over unhealthy ones, and so on. Should regional ethical preferences be embedded in control software?

13.3   Robot as Subject

Here we consider the problem of attempting to develop ethical machines, that is, machines that are driven or controlled or moderated by a set of internal moral codes with which they have been provided. This is the basic concept applied by Asimov's Laws [47]. Leaving aside the various complexities involved in actually codifying some mechanism like Asimov's Laws into a robot system (actually being able to identify the long-term implications of a command that might cause a human to come to harm, as an example), if we assume that a robot is a moral agent, what rights and responsibilities should be assigned to robots?

Humans have established a set of rights associated with humans. For example, in 1948 the UN established the *Universal Declaration of Human Rights* [48], although it is critical to observe that not all countries observe it. But this is not the only set of rights associated with entities. Prior to 1822 in the United Kingdom, animals had no rights. The *Cruel Treatment of Animals Act* passed in 1822 provided one of the first legal structures assigning rights and protections to animals. (Although the protection did not extend to all animals nor equally to male and female gender of certain species.) Today in much of the world many animals have rights, although not the same rights as humans.

Beyond organic entities, in parts of the world commercial structures (corporations) also enjoy limited rights. In Canada, for example, corporations have rights that (among other things) shield the owners from certain liabilities. So there is precedent for different levels of rights world wide. Solum [728], for example, observes that from a legal standpoint many things (e.g., temples, churches, governments, corporations, and ships, to name but a few) have been given legal "personhood" by the appropriate legal system. It seems possible or even likely that at some point intelligent machines and autonomous robots will be granted some form of legal status. Indeed, as argued in [83], such a structure might simplify various legal proceedings involving AI's, and by extension autonomous robots, in the not to distant future.

13.4   Robot as Agent

Many scientists and philosophers have considered the problem of the **singularity**, which is loosely defined as the point at which machines surpass humans. The concept of this **technological singularity** can be traced back to John von Neumann as captured in [789]. [808] summarizes the author's critical question in the title "How to Survive in a Post-Human Era". If (when?) machines surpass us in intelligence, and can overcome the limits of their technology in terms of power and durability, what ethical questions arise? This is the realm of science fiction and the core of many a film and story about robots and sentient machines. Muehlhauser and Helm [550] argue that it may be prudent to train an AI to "want what we want" before it reaches the singularity. Petersen [622], for example, observes that if we wish robots to continue to offer service to humanity after the singularity, we should work to embed a desire to provide such service into their makeup prior to the event.

13.5 Further Reading

The Trolley problem A large literature exists on this problem, as it can be used to probe various ethical theories. See [247].

Machine and AI ethics more broadly [102] reviews three critical questions related to AI and ethics,

Roboethics A number of texts have appeared on robot ethics including [174] and [69]. See [329] for an essay on the case for assigning rights to robots. See also [328]. Survey and review papers on the topic include [776], [466], and [786].

Lethal autonomous weapon systems [35] provides a good review of the field. There is an ongoing debate about banning LAWs generally. The Stop Killer Robots campaign, for example, is a coalition of non-governmental organizations to ban lethal autonomous weapon systems.

Ethics, robots, children, and the elderly Ethics related to the use of robots to aid in the care for the elderly is an interesting and active area of debate. See [797] for a review.

Ethics and autonomous vehicles Given the deployment of autonomous vehicles in a range of different domains, including driving on public roads, there has been considerable interest in the ethical and legal structures around their deployment. See [667] and [583].

Robots, robot ethics, and the singularity The early work of [789] and [808] has been re-examined in the light of advances in AI and robot technology by many authors including [152] and [709].

13.6 Problems

1. Is the country you are a citizen of a signatory to the Geneva Conventions? The Ottawa Convention? If the answer to either was no, what was the rationale for not signing?

2. Does the country you are a citizen of have a policy in place on the development of LAWS? Why or why not?

3. What ethical requirements are in place in your jurisdiction if you were to wish to deploy a companion robot to assist the elderly? With members of the elderly who have been identified with dementia?

4. An unfortunately common problem in AI systems is the introduction of bias through the training data used to develop the system. As AI technology becomes more and more prevalent in robot software, what steps should be taken to ensure that such bias is not introduced (or at least minimized) in autonomous systems?

5. If autonomous systems were provided the same legal rights as (say) insects, would there be any legal restrictions on their treatment? What if they had the same legal rights as more traditional pets such as cats or dogs?

14

Robots in Practice

Although many mobile robot systems are experimental in nature, systems devoted to specific practical applications are being developed and deployed. This chapter examines some of the tasks for which mobile robotic systems are beginning to appear and describes several existing experimental and production systems that have been developed. As noted in Chapter 1, tasks for which practical mobile robot systems exist are usually characterized by one or more of the following properties:

- The environment is inhospitable and sending a human is either very costly or very dangerous. Such environments include nuclear, chemical, underwater, battlefield, and outer-space environments.
- The environment is remote, so that sending a human operator is too difficult or takes too long. Extreme instances of this are those environments that are completely inaccessible to humans, such as microscopic environments. Many other environments, including mining, outer space, and forestry exhibit these properties.
- The task has a very demanding duty cycle or a very high fatigue factor.
- The task is highly disagreeable to a human.

In addition, domains where the use of a robot may improve efficiency, robustness, or safety are candidates for the development of experimental systems that may subsequently become practical.

Fundamentally, the decision to implement a robotic solution to a given task often comes down to a question of economics. If it is cheaper, more efficient, or simpler to use a person to accomplish a task, then economically it does not make much sense to design and use a robot. Nevertheless, applications do exist for autonomous robots, and, as the costs associated with robotic systems decrease and their capabilities improve, more markets are likely to develop.

14.1   Material Transport

Many industrial, commercial, and medical applications require the transportation and delivery of material between spatially distributed locations. If the environment can be custom-built or customized in order to simplify the delivery task, then very simple automation systems, such as an assembly line, can be applied to the problem. Modern factories and assembly lines rely on just-in-time delivery to optimize the costs associated with warehousing both parts involved in the product and the product itself. Within the

(a) OTTO 1500   (b) OTTO Lifter

Figure 14.1. Materials transport in a warehouse setting. Images appear with the kind permission of OTTO Motors.

warehouse automation domain, a number of different tasks can be identified including point-to-point materials transport (see Figure 14.1a), and transporting material from storage to transportation and vice versa (see Figure 14.1b).

Autonomous and semi-autonomous solutions exist within the warehouse domain. For point-to-point navigation, omnidirectional motion capability is often chosen, given the need to perform highly dextrous navigation within the warehouse. Localization can be provided via a number of different technologies including specific markers on the floor providing a global grid for navigation tasks. Delivery robots are not limited to the transportation of small objects in highly structured environments. AGV for cargo handling applications are designed to move standard cargo containers in shipping ports. The vehicle is designed to fit under standard cargo and moves containers within the storage area.

Large groups of mobile robots have been deployed for delivery tasks as well. The MARTHA (Multiple Autonomous Robots for Transport and Handling Applications) [17] project developed a system that allows a set of autonomous robots to perform coordinated material transport tasks. Many large-scale in-warehouse delivery systems now exist, with Amazon Robotics (previously Kiva Systems), being representative. Literally hundreds of parallel robots operate in a shared space providing controlled material delivery. Kiva developed a general indoor delivery system based on multiple robots [327]. Each Kiva robot is an intelligent pallet-carrying robot that navigates with respect to pre-positioned visual bar codes placed on the floor of the warehouse. A central control system coordinates the robots and computers at picking stations, where operators scan codes associated with objects loaded on each of the individual robots. Essentially a conveyor system without a conveyor, one unique feature of the Kiva approach is that it can be moved to a new location (or augmented) through the placement of new bar codes (visual landmarks) on the floor.

The warehouse and port environments are highly structured, with limited access to non-employees and controlled object placement. For some other application domains, such as hospitals, this is not the case. The hospital domain is characterized by the need to move a number of objects from central locations – food, linen, documents, medicine, patients, and so on – to a number of distributed locations. Currently these tasks are typically performed by staff, and the efficient utilization of delivery staff is very difficult. A mobile robot solution to the problem of delivery in a hospital setting poses a number of difficult technical problems. The hospital environment cannot be completely modeled: People move about the environment in unpredictable ways, and there are doors and elevators that have to be navigated. In spite of these technical difficulties, a number of experimental and production robotic systems have been developed in order to address the delivery problem in hospitals. The Helpmate robot [418] was one of the earliest robots designed specifically to operate in the hospital environment. Helpmate used a metric map of the environment in order to plan paths through the hospital and relied on sonar and video sensors to avoid obstacles as it moved. A wireless communications channel was used to operate doors and elevators.

Today, a large number of companies produce hospital robots. These robots are designed to provide a turnkey solution for material transport within the hospital, including straightforward material such as food and linens, as well as more complex material including pharmacy and laboratory material that must be properly secured against theft and interference during transport.

14.2   Intelligent Vehicles

Automobiles are omnipresent in Western society. They form the transportation backbone of many economies, and a considerable financial investment has been made worldwide to provide the road infrastructure necessary to carry personal, military, and commercial traffic. As a direct result of the importance of the automobile, roads and highways are often congested and used inefficiently. This can be attributed, in part, to the fact that individual drivers often act in their own interest at the expense of overall efficiency and, worse yet, may make decisions that are not even in their own best long-term interest. Further, the modes of communication (and hence the quality of shard information) between drivers is inefficient and highly error-prone. Finally, individual driving skill shows considerable variability, compounded by the fact that driving can be tiring and lead to fatigue and inattention. For all these reasons, road systems rarely approach their theoretically attainable traffic throughput before they become congested. There is considerable demand for the improvement of highway systems and automobiles in order to provide increased throughput, and as the cost of adding additional bandwidth (lanes) is very high, various groups are investigating the application of mobile robot technology to provide increased traffic throughput.

Aside from merely increasing traffic capacity, intelligent vehicles offer substantial promise for risk reduction. The performance of a given vehicle is a function of the driver; human error leads to numerous accidents and deaths each year. It is quite conceivable that an autonomous vehicle might provide much greater safety than a human operator.

Other aspects of the transport of people and material over roads may also lead to robotic solutions. Roads are designed for a standard-sized vehicle, and thus the transportation of large quantities of goods, for example those required by the military, can require large convoys of vehicles, each with its own driver. Considerable savings could be realized if fewer drivers were required.

Numerous applications of mobile robot technology have been proposed to address these concerns. Although a continuum of approaches has been proposed, several representative classes of methodology have emerged, as follows:

Driving assistants Driving assistants provide additional information and sensors to the driver to enhance the human drivers performance in terms of both safety and efficiency.

Convoy systems These systems propose to develop automated delivery convoys (line of vehicles, typically in single file) in which the lead vehicle is driven by a human operator but the subsequent vehicles in the convoy navigate autonomously.

Autonomous driving systems These systems take the operator out of the loop and have the individual vehicle drive itself automatically.

Autonomous highway systems This approach proposes to treat the entire highway as a system and to control groups of vehicles autonomously.

Autonomous urban systems These systems address problems related to urban transit through the application of autonomous vehicle technologies.

14.2.1 Driving Assistants

Many cars can can be purchased with a range of driving assistant technologies as options. Parking sensors (typically either ultrasound or laser based) are available from a number of different manufacturers, and aftermarket kits are also available. Similarly "backup cameras" and surround video systems are available for a number of vehicles. GPS, including path planning and route following, is now a standard automotive technology. A number of companies provide models that have "automatic parallel parking," where onboard sensors allow the car to parallel park without human control. A number of vendors provide other driving assistant technologies including active cruise control (automatic breaking), unintended lane change detection, and driver monitoring. [275] provides a review of existing automotive sensor technologies, including sensors used for driving assistants.

14.2.2 Convoy Systems

Convoy systems have both civilian and military applications. In highway maintenance, a lead vehicle is often followed by a shadow vehicle that is used to protect the occupants of the lead vehicle from accidents caused by traffic that fails to avoid the service vehicle in time. Obviously, the driver of the shadow vehicle is also at risk, and thus mechanisms to take the shadow driver out of the vehicle improves overall system safety. Convoy systems also occur in transportation systems in which a convoy of trucks is driven by a true driver in the front truck and subsequent vehicles in the convoy follow the vehicle in front. Although not necessarily desirable for normal truck navigation, this approach can be effective in forestry applications in which a convoy of trucks follows a lumber road out of the forest, with a seasoned driver providing drive information to other trucks in the convoy.

The U.S. and other countries' military have been developing convoy system in which a lead vehicle is trailed by one or more autonomous trucks for many years [642]. Convoy approaches can be passive, in which followers monitor the vehicle in front using (for example) visual sensors, or active, in which leader vehicles broadcast state information (e.g., GPS waypoints and commanded vehicle motion) to follower vehicles.

14.2.3 Autonomous Driving Systems

Rather than just provide information to the driver, an alternative approach is for the robot to drive the automobile directly. Such devices have been of interest to the military for some time and the Autonomous Land Vehicle (ALV) project of the 1980s was responsible for much early research in vision and mobile robotics. Perhaps the best known of these early projects is the CMU Navlab project [767], which developed a series of vehicles that drive autonomously, but other autonomous driving vehicles also exist (e.g., [863, 154]). See Figure 14.2. Today there exists a wide range of autonomous vehicles, or vehicles with autonomous characteristics. Generally, commercial versions of these vehicles are designed to look very similar to vehicles that are operated directly by humans. See Figure 3.12b, for example, and other autonomous vehicles depicted in this chapter.

Although many different problems must be addressed in order to develop an autonomous driving vehicle, the actual problem of following the road has probably received the most attention. The basic task here is to identify the road surface so that the car can drive down it. Early approaches to this problem identified the structure of the lane markings on the road (e.g., [444]). Once the lane markings are identified, the appropriate steering correction can be computed. An alternative approach is to determine the appropriate steering correction directly from the car's view using a data-driven approach. This was the approach taken by ALVINN [630, 394] (see Section 8.7.1). More recent data-driven solutions (see [175] for a review) have proven to be extremely effective at road-based driving.

Given a solution to determining where the road is and a mechanism for steering the car along the road, a remaining problem is the task of avoiding other users of the road. As is the case with the road follower, obstacle detection must be quick and accurate, and it also must be integrated within the road follower so that avoiding an obstacle does not lead to the automobile leaving the road.

There is a long history of successful approaches to the development of autonomous road vehicles. An early highlight was the work of the Navlab project at CMU. Navlab 5 (see Figure 14.2) drove over 6000 autonomous steering miles on highways in the United States at highway speeds. Although various technologies were used to control earlier versions of the Navlab, Navlab 5 relied on a differential GPS and a fiberoptic rate gyro for gross navigation and on a vision-based line tracker to keep the robot on the highway [157]. In August 1997, Navlabs 6–10 (see Figure 14.2) were involved in extensive on-road testing as part of ongoing development and evaluation of autonomous vehicles [768]. As is clear from Figure 14.2, autonomous highway vehicles at first glance seem indistinguishable from their human-driven counterparts. There are now many different autonomous driving systems in operation or development around the world.

(a) Navlab 1   (b) Navlab 2

(c) Navlab 5

(d) The 1998 generation of Navlab robots.

Figure 14.2. Selected elements of the Navlab project robot family. Navlab 1 was built in the late 1980s on a Chevy panel van base. Navlab 2 was built in 1990 on a modified HMMWV, while Navlab 5 was built on a 1990 Pontiac Trans Sport. Used with permission.

Commercial systems exist associated with most major auto manufacturers. Specialized systems also exist in the trucking and other domains.

In order to evaluate the then state of the art in autonomous driving and to spur research in the area, the Defence Advanced Research Projects Agency (DARPA) held a number

(a) Grand challenge   (b) Urban challenge

Figure 14.3. DARPA's grand challenges. Autonomous vehicles are shown operating in (a) off-road and (b) urban environments.

of **grand challenges** in the early 2000s. The 2004 and 2005 events were conducted in an off-road environment, while the 2007 event considered the urban driving environment. Figure 14.3 shows entries from the 2005 and 2007 events.

14.2.4 Automated Highway Systems

Rather than deal with an individual automobile, an alternative approach is to consider the needs of the entire highway system and work toward automating that. In the mid to late 1990s, the U.S. government pursued a multi-year project in order to address these critical highway needs. The intelligent vehicle/highway system (IVHS) investigated a number of different approaches to applying robotics to vehicles. This explored the development of systems that span the range from providing smart sensors to the driver to taking over complete control of the vehicle.

Automating the highway system requires a significant amount of communication between vehicles, the roadway infrastructure, and other users of the roadway (e.g., pedestrians). Given this, and the overlap with other autonomous vehicle systems, there has been considerable interest in **vehicle-to-everything** (V2X) communication systems. Such systems, could, for example, inform autonomous vehicles of the state of upcoming traffic lights, anticipated travel direction of other vehicles in the environment, etc. See [16] for a review. V2X enables, among other things, vehicle **platooning**. A platoon of autonomous vehicles is an interconnected group of vehicles that forms a virtual chain. Vehicles exchange information in the same platoon, resulting in shorter distances (between platoon members), reduced transportation costs, and so on.

14.2.5 Autonomous Urban Systems

The driving concept for an autonomous urban system is to remove private automobiles from the central core of urban areas and provide a fleet of "human-controlled" but publicly available vehicles instead [473]. The vehicles would be designed to be easy to control, environmentally friendly and capable of limited autonomous action. This would assist in collecting the vehicles from where they are left and returning them to central depots.

Figure 14.4. Example autonomous urban system.

Although large-scale deployments of autonomous urban systems are not yet a reality, a number of **automated road vehicles** are being deployed.

ParkShuttle Operating (with some disruptions) from 1997 to 2004, the Park-Shuttle system operated in a parking lot at Schiphol Airport, Amsterdam. A second field trial was held in 2004 at Antibes [21]. The vehicles provided connection between a central dropoff point and a fixed route through the parking lot. The vehicles operated in a restricted right of way and crossed pedestrian and regular traffic roads.

ULTra The ULTra system began its first pre-deployment tests in late 2008 at Heathrow Airport in London, England. The ULTra system uses an isolated guideway.

Navya The Navya system has been tested in a number of different sites around the world. Figure 14.4 shows the autonomous shuttle operating in Las Vegas in 2017. This shuttle operates in mixed traffic.

14.3 Robots for Survey and Inspection

There exist many industrial operations and environments for which mobile robots can be used to reduce human exposure hazards or increase productivity. Examples include inspection for spills, leaks, or other unusual events in large industrial facilities and materials handling in computer-integrated manufacturing environments. One particular application that has received substantial attention is the execution of repairs and monitoring in the radioactive areas of nuclear power plants with the objective of increasing safety by reducing the potential radioactive exposure to workers. The Stored Waste Autonomous Mobile Inspector (SWAMI) robot [300] from the University of Southern California is representative. The SWAMI robot examines storage drums and returns photos of the drums augmented with bar-code readouts from the drums in order to identify the drums and their contents.

The industrial environment is significantly different from the office environments in which many mobile robots operate. The ARK project [573] examined the production of a self-contained mobile robot with sensor-based navigation capabilities specifically designed for operation in a real industrial setting. ARK's test environment covered approximately 50,000 ft^2 of space and accommodates 150 employees. Such an environment presented many difficulties, including the lack of vertical, flat walls; large open spaces, as well as small cramped spaces; high ceilings; large windows near the ceiling, resulting in time-dependent and weather-dependent lighting conditions, a large variation in light intensity, and highlights and glare; many temporary and semi-permanent structures; many (some very large) metallic structures; people and forklifts moving about; oil and water spills on the floor; floor drains (which could be uncovered); hoses and piping on the floor; chains hanging down from above; protruding structures; and other transient obstacles to the safe motion of the robot.

Large distances often encountered in the industrial environment require sensors that can operate at such ranges. The number of visual features (lines, corners, and regions) is very high, and techniques for focusing attention on specific, task-dependent features are required. Most mobile robotic projects assume the existence of a flat ground plane over which the robot is to navigate. In the industrial environment, the ground plane is generally flat, but regions of the floor are marked with drainage ditches, pipes, and other unexpected low-lying obstacles to movement. In order to operate in such an environment, a robot must be equipped with sensors that can reliably detect such obstacles.

14.4   Mining Automation

Almost every country with a sizable mining industry has a research program in mining automation, as do major equipment manufacturers. Potential advantages to the introduction of mining automation include [182]:

- Increased safety of the workers
- Higher productivity of the mine
- Lower equipment maintenance costs

In general, mining takes place in one of two modes; open pit or underground. Open pit mining is characterized by large, heavy, expensive equipment such as a dragline. Draglines are large, crane-like devices (the boom on a dragline can exceed 100 m), which are used to collect overburden and deposit it in a specified position. These machines require considerable skill to control, and the distances involved make visual control by an operator very difficult [181].

Automated dragline systems are probably the largest robots on the planet. Walking draglines move (short) distances using large feet. Given their large size and the difficulty of control, there have been a number of efforts to develop tools to assist the operator and to aid in planning [835].

Underground mining is characterized by the requirement to perform dangerous tasks in a constricted environment. Many underground tasks involve the positioning of a tool with respect to some object or structure in the environment. The placement of explosive charges, the identification and removal of rocks, and the drilling and insertion of roof-support bolts are dangerous operations for which autonomous or telerobotic systems have been developed. Due to the potential hazard of rockfall, remote underground mining is common in modern mines. In many operations, the operator does not operate the vehicle directly, but stands some distance away and operates it remotely.

Figure 14.5. An automated LHD operating underground. Picture appears with the kind permission of MDA.

Fully autonomous load hall dump (LHD) systems have been developed for underground mines (Figure 14.5). LHD machines are used to excavate rock fragments, haul the fragments to assigned locations, and then dump them. Early systems augmented the mine with a variety of different technologies for localization and control [624], [375], [55], [832], [698], while more recent systems are less dependent on augmenting the mine [670], [755]

14.5   Space Robotics

Outer space is an almost ideal operational environment to motivate the use of autonomous systems. It is expensive and dangerous to project a manned presence to low Earth orbit, much less on more distant planetary bodies. Given a desire to explore even our closest planetary neighbors, it is quite reasonable to send automated systems rather than humans and to augment human teams with robots.

The Soviet Union launched two Lunokhod (Moon Walker) robots in the late 1960s and early 1970s [341]. These eight-wheeled automatic vehicles were the first vehicles to drive on the Moon. Teleoperated from Earth, Lunokhod 1 ran from November 1970 to October 1971 and traveled over 10 km. Lunokhod 2 ran from February 1973 to June 1973 and traveled over 37 km.

Under NASA and JPL programs, the United States has engaged in a long-term series of unmanned robotic interplanetary probes (see [58] for an overview). The early Ranger series of the 1960s crash-landed on the Moon and was not able to interact with the environment. The Surveyor systems of the mid to late 1960s performed soft landings on the Moon. The Surveyor robots did not move; they used a robot arm to collect samples. A similar Viking project was deployed to Mars in 1975.

The Mars Pathfinder project was launched in 1996. This project landed an instrument package on Mars in 1997 including a Microrover Flight Experiment (MFEX). Known

(a) Sojourner rover

(b) Mars Exploration rover

(c) Curiosity rover on the surface of Mars

Figure 14.6. Martian rover vehicles. (a) Appears courtesy NASA. (b) Appears courtesy NASA/JPL-Caltech. (c) Appears courtesy NASA.

as the Sojourner rover, the vehicle was 630 mm long by 480 mm wide and was driven by its six wheels. The front and rear wheels were steerable. Figure 14.6a shows a view of the rover. Essentially, the vehicle was operated in a telerobotic manner, using dense waypoints selected manually from an Earth-based control center.

Sojourner operated from July to September in 1997, beyond its expected lifetime. A number of additional rover missions have since been completed on Mars starting in the 1990s. MER-A Sprit and MER-B Opportunity arrived on Mars in 2004. Both rovers were based on essentially the same six-wheeled design (Figure 14.6b). The MER platform is somewhat larger than Sojourner. The MER vehicles Spirit and Opportunity both exceeded their expected operational periods. Spirit was in operation for over six years, with Opportunity remaining operational until 2019. Evaluation of their operational performance can be found in [782] and [87]. Curiosity (Figure 14.6c) was launched in 2011, and Perseverance was launched in 2020. As of early 2023, both were still operating on the surface of Mars.

Beyond rovers, manipulator and robot assistants have been developed to support space missions. Figure 14.7 shows robots that have been deployed in space to explore

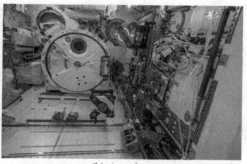

(a) Robonaut 2   (b) Astrobee

Figure 14.7. Robots to assist in human operations in space. (a) and (b) appear courtesy NASA.

human–robot interaction. Figure 14.7a shows Robotnaut 2 [524], a humanoid-like robot. Figure 14.7b shows two Astrobee cube robots [135] floating in the International Space Station.

14.6 Autonomous Aircraft

Autonomous aircraft can trace their lineage back to the V1 (Figure 1.4) from the 1940s. The military application is still perhaps the largest application domain for autonomous aircraft, where they have found application as military drones, reconnaissance aircraft, missiles, and (more recently) ground support and attack platforms. Civilian applications have also been found in survey, inspection, and communication roles.

Military applications for autonomous aircraft have resulted in aircraft designed for global reconnaissance (e.g., the Global Hawk) and combat missions (e.g., the Reaper). Tactical weapons have also been developed (e.g., Advanced Ceramics Research Inc.'s Silver Fox). A selection of autonomous aircraft is shown in Figure 14.8. These devices are generally teleoperated with (depending on the device) varying levels of sophisticated onboard autopilots to reduce operator task loading and to deal with communications dropouts.

14.7 Bomb/Mine Disposal

Bomb or mine disposal is an almost ideal application for mobile robots. The task is dangerous, repetitive, and often conducted in inhospitable environments. More technically known as **explosives ordinance disposal** (EOD), it entails detecting and disposing of explosive munitions or making them harmless. Typical weapons that require disposal include undetonated air-dropped bombs, mines, rockets, artillery shells, grenades, mortars, and bullets. There are currently two significantly different domains for EOD applications. The first of these is the identification, detection, and elimination of infrequently occurring devices in otherwise safe but unpredictable environments, as is the case with terrorist bomb disposal. The second domain is the detection and disposal

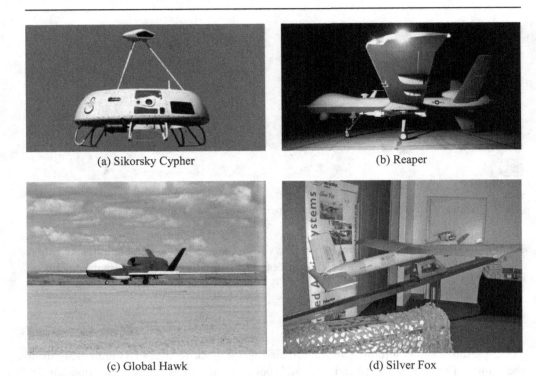

(a) Sikorsky Cypher   (b) Reaper

(c) Global Hawk   (d) Silver Fox

Figure 14.8. A selection of autonomous aircraft. (a) Used with permission. (b), (c) U.S. AirForce photo.

of weapons – typically mines – that have been deployed as part of a military operation. In the case of terrorist bombs, the emphasis is on highly dextrous systems that can be remotely operated. The sporadic and highly calculated nature of these individual weapons makes the amount of effort and cost per event substantial. In contrast, in the mine disposal context a large territory must often be covered. Sadly, there is often a paucity of trained operators, and the permissible budget per mine disposed of is often exceptionally small. Further, the rugged, ongoing, and low-budget nature of demining operations means that the vehicle must be highly physically robust yet also extremely simple to operate and maintain.

EOD is inherently dangerous. It is a considerable investment to train people to locate, identify, and disable mines, and any mechanism that allows the task to be accomplished remotely contributes to solving the problem. The military problem is severe. Millions of landmines are manufactured each year, and 500 to 800 deaths and 2000 maimings due to landmines are reported each month [575].

Mine-clearing robots are either designed to be light enough to not set off the mine while searching for it (e.g., [576]), or are armored so as to be able to withstand small explosions (e.g., [800]). Mine-clearing robots typically operate teleoperationally, but experimental systems are being developed to clear larger regions autonomously.

Systems for the disposal of terrorist bombs are typically more expensive and the amount of time and money available per EOD incident is larger than in the demining

(a) Andros bomb disposal robot   (b) Talon EOD robot

Figure 14.9. Bomb disposal robots. (a) Copyright REMOTEC. Used with permission. (b) U.S. Army.

context. Robots are typically teleoperated. These robots use treads or wheels with skid steering and have special-purpose actuators to either pick up a suspicious package or disarm it. (See Figure 14.9.) Brute-force devices for disarming a bomb operate by destroying the detonator or its connection to the main explosive before the bomb can go off. Typical approaches involve shooting it with a robot-mounted shotgun or with a jet of extremely high-pressure water.

14.8 Underwater Inspection

The inspection of underwater and in particular deep-sea structures poses many difficulties for humans. Inspections can be costly and dangerous, and the structure may also pose a hazard. For example, one underwater inspection task involves the inspection of water intake/outflow pipes for power generation stations. These pipes can be quite long, and thus they present a considerable danger to human inspectors. Many commercial remotely operated vehicles designed to survey underwater structures exist. For example the Jason, Medea, and ARGO-II vehicles of the Wood's Hole Oceanographic Institute are designed for open water inspection. Jason and Medea are designed to operate in a tethered manner to a depth of 6 km. These devices are maneuvered via the tow line to a mother ship and are equipped with video, still camera, and sonar sensors. The ARGO-II uses thrusters for navigation and is also linked to a mother ship via a tow line. The position of the device is maintained via GPS (to localize the ship) and from

Figure 14.10. Underwater teleoperated vehicle.

transponder arrays. Figure 14.10 shows a teleoperated underwater vehiclde operating in a pool.

14.9   Agriculture/Forestry

Autonomous systems in agriculture and forestry must meet specific operational constraints that are different from those found in industrial or office environments. The terrain is rugged and potentially lacking either flat ground surfaces or even a well-defined ground plane. The environment is not easily modeled, and the environment evolves (grows) as it is maintained. Nor is the climate well suited to machines. On the other hand, the tasks involved in agriculture are onerous and can be quite dangerous.

Forestry maintenance To obtain a high yield from commercial forests, it is necessary to perform weeding and thinning operations. This involves visiting the forest some number of years after the initial planting and removing competing plants from around the intended commercial trees. This is a very expensive operation since the forests tend to be remote and it can be dangerous as some of the tools required to thin the forests (e.g., brush saws) are quite powerful.

Greenhouse robots Greenhouses are used for intensive agricultural tasks such as growing seedlings and decorative plants. A typical industrial greenhouse is a rectangular structure of 100 m × 20 m. Within a greenhouse, plants are arranged in rows with narrow corridors providing access. The favorable growth conditions within a greenhouse lead to pests and other undesirable organisms. Pesticides, fungicides, and other chemical products are commonly used to keep these undesirable organisms under control. Coupled with the closed environment, these chemicals lead to a potentially dangerous environment for the human gardener. Thus, mechanisms to reduce human exposure within a greenhouse, especially during spraying, become necessary.

Harvesting robots Harvesting is one of the most labor-intensive activities in agriculture. Often the material to be harvested can be bruised or damaged by inappropriate handling, and considerable time and money are spent in harvesting fruits and vegetables. Fruit in particular poses a problem as it is often located in high trees requiring the use of ladder to collect it. [528] describes some initial research into the construction of a mobile robot system for citrus fruit harvesting. Key to the system described in [528] is the development of sensing mechanisms and special-purpose end-effects to manipulate the fruit.

14.10 Aids for the Disabled

Perhaps the largest potential application for mobile robotics is in providing aids for the disabled or for the elderly (eldercare). Deployed systems have concentrated primarily on the application of robotic techniques to power wheelchairs. Two general approaches have emerged. The first is to provide local robotic assists to a wheelchair in order to provide safety/fine dextrous motion. For example, the robotic wheelchair robots Tin Man I and II [535] perform limited autonomous tasks; they go through doorways, follow hallways, and perform limited navigation using dead reckoning. These are essentially powered wheelchairs outfitted with simple sensors and special-purpose controls for specific applications. Of particular importance in these general-purpose "fine grain" systems is the need to provide a robust user interface. The Wheelesley robot [844], for example, provided a graphical user interface that replaces the joystick with a set of buttons that describe the set of primitive actions that the robot understands: move forward, turn right, dock to desk, and so on.

A second approach is to develop a full-blown robotic system that carries the operator around with it. (See Figure 14.11.) For example, [621] uses a global map to define the environment and the robot can be commanded to move relative to the map. Such systems often require considerable environmental modification.

14.11 Entertainment

There has been a long history of the use of robots for entertainment. Early windup robot toys are now highly collectable. Early electronic robot kits such as the Heathkit line of Hero robots (Hero 1, Hero Jr, Hero 2000) have evolved into extremely sophisticated robotic kits and components available from a number of manufacturers. Sophisticated

Figure 14.11. The Playbot robotic wheelchair. The user controls the actions of the robot through a touch tablet. Cameras monitor the user and scan the environment. A robot arm attached to the chair provides for interaction with the environment, for example, opening doors. Appears with the kind permission of J. K. Tsotsos.

(a) Animatronic speaker   (b) Plego robot   (c) Aibo robots

Figure 14.12. Entertainment robots.

mechatronics has long been a staple of amusement parks. More recently, fully autonomous systems have begun to appear. For example, [351] describes the development of a bipidal walking robot that simulates a T-Rex dinosaur.

The international robot soccer league [416] is now well established. In this competition, robot teams – there are three to five robots per team, and different-sized robots compete in different classes – play off against each other. Figure 14.12c shows elements of one such team. Various manufacturers provide robots that meet the requirements for different categories of the competition. The game is played much like a real soccer game with an appropriately sized playing field. From a technical point of view, sensing the locations of the ball and players and planning the appropriate moves are challenging tasks.

It is difficult to overestimate the potential application of robots in the entertainment industry. Perhaps the most unusual of these are animatronic devices to operate as virtual tour guides or even as "personal robots" for "family collection and appreciation" (or so says their product literature). Figure 14.12a shows an example robot from the Beijing Yuanda Superman Robot Science company. This robot is an animatronic device designed to interact with the public. For younger users, devices such as the Plego robot shown in Figure 14.12b provides a similar level of interaction with its operator.

14.12   Domestic and Commercial Cleaning Robots

Although domestic robots are still the fare of science fiction, cleaning robots exist for a number of applications including domestic applications. A number of companies manufacture cleaning robots for applications such as floor scrubbing, street sweeping, and vacuuming. The iRobot Roomba family of domestic robots, for example, was designed specifically for domestic application, while other cleaning robots have been developed for commercial applications. The robots shown in Figure 14.13 are deployed in large-scale passenger terminals in international airports and operate while the terminal is operating. Note the effort to provide a "personality" to the robots.

(a) At YUL   (b) At LHR

Figure 14.13. Floor cleaning robots.

14.13 Further Reading

Military robots [548] describes an international survey into lethality and autonomous systems that consider the long-term implications of adoption of military robots. [724] surveys the tasks necessary in order to deploy multiple robots in a military setting.

Reconnaissance [555] describes experiences and lessons learned in the application of reconnaissance robots in an urban environment.

Agriculture robots [430] and [279] provide a review of the application of robotics to agricultural systems. See also [627].

Aids for the disabled [845] provides a survey of robotic wheelchair projects prior to 1998. [722] provides a listing of a large number of robotic wheelchair projects. [725] provides a taxonomy and readiness report of robotic wheelchairs in 2022.

Entertainment robots [801] reviews robot soccer. [496] includes a survey of entertainment robots in 2022.

14.14 Problems

1. Take a task for which mobile robots are often proposed (e.g., carpet vacuuming). Estimate the financial cost associated with having the task performed by a human for a 5-year period. Estimate the cost associated with developing and supporting a robotic solution for this task. (Note that many platform companies have the retail prices of their hardware on the Web.) Does it make economic sense to build

an autonomous robot for this task? What assumptions would have to change in order for the robotic system (or the human system) to be more cost effective?
2. Investigate an industrial robotic system currently in production. What task is the system designed to do? What limitations does the system place on its operational environment? What level of human operator interaction is required?

15

The Future of Mobile Robotics

> The *Encycloopedia Galactica.* defines a robot as a mechanical apparatus designed to do the work of a man. The marketing division of the Sirius Cybernetics Corporation defines a robot as "Your Plastic Pal Who's Fun To Be With."[1]

Given the current state of mobile robotics, what can be considered essentially solved and what tasks remain? It is clear that for restrictive environments and for limited tasks, autonomous systems can be readily developed. Tasks such as parts delivery in a warehouse, materials transport in hospitals, limited autonomous driving, and so on can all be "solved" for tight definitions of the task and provided that sometime restrictive assumptions can be made concerning the environment.

It is clear that open problems exist across the entire spectrum of mobile robotics research. Several key requirements constrain mobile robots from being more widely and generally applied. Dividing the area broadly into locomotion, sensing, control, and HRI, we can identify several important problems.

15.1 Locomotion

Ground terrain The vast majority of autonomous systems for ground contact locomotion are based on simple wheels. Most systems are non-holonomic, have rather limited kinematics and dynamics, and thus can only execute a restricted class of motions. Not only does this make path planning more complex, but it also limits the robot's applicability and makes accurate modeling of the robot's actual behavior difficult. The use of compound wheels may help to alleviate the limitations of the kinematic properties of wheeled robots, although it further complicates issues of accurate odometry (and cost).

Legged walking robots provide solutions to some of these difficulties. They certainly provide a technology to overcome the need for a continuous ground surface between start and goal positions. While the technology appears very promising, problems associated with controlling devices with many degrees of freedom and making them energy efficient, robust, and economical remain to be addressed. In practice, the use of complex gaits or feedback rules to maintain dynamic stability in a partially known environment makes serious demands on the sensing system of the robot. How can sensors be designed and positioned so that the ground upon which the feet might fall is sensed, and how can one ensure that the ground will be able to hold the weight of the robot as it moves?

---

[1] Adams [4], p. 73.

Flying and swimming While most of Earth's surface is covered by water, a relatively small number of submersible robotic systems exist. The design of systems for the actuation and control of underwater robots remains unresolved. The use of underwater robots is limited by a combination of factors that hinder command and control; reasoning systems for fully autonomous behavior have not been sufficiently well developed, sensing for underwater applications is difficult, and communications with underwater robots is restricted. Together, these problems make the use of underwater robots difficult, but the partial resolution of problems with either autonomy or teleoperation would make such devices of practical utility.

Unencumbered by weight/mass constraints associated with terrestrial and flying robots, autonomous aquatic vehicles are now beginning to perform extremely long duration missions (although with significant operator assistance). Underwater gliders have operated over thousands of kilometers with communication limited to those times when they are at the surface [683]. Even longer missions are planned for autonomous sailboats

Flying robots are, to a large extent, constrained by problems of size, weight, and energy efficiency. While lightweight computer systems are now available, the batteries needed to operate them as well as propulsion systems are a major difficulty for extended flight. As dynamically stable limbed robots, flying robots other than floaters (i.e., aerobots) must also meet very strict real-time constraints. While a dynamic limbed robot may exhibit instabilities or potentially fall over when the real-time sensing and reasoning constraints are not met, jet-powered or helicopter-based flying robots literally fall out of the sky unless reliable real-time sensing and computational constraints can be met. Thus the problems of computation and sensing that plague ground-plane robots are multiplied for flying vehicles.

These problems are compounded by the fact that if a flying robot is to actually accomplish a non-passive task, it must also be equipped with effectors of some sort. Notable innovations in this regard are several types of experimental insect robots currently under development. In this context, we should also mention nanorobots. Several teams are attempting to develop robots at a very small scale, either for assembly tasks for biological applications such as diagnosis or therapy delivery. In a reversal of their operating scales, the problems faced by nanorobots dwarf those that constrain progress by either conventional flying or swimming mobile robots.

15.2   Sensing

Many key problems, not only for mobile robotics, but also for intelligent systems as a whole, depend on sensing technologies. Even gait planning can be greatly simplified if the perception system of a robot is sophisticated enough to select appropriate foot placements.

Although vision and related sensing tasks often appear simple, many apparently simple sensing problems are still extremely challenging.

Perhaps the most fundamental statement that can be made concerning the development of sensors for mobile robots is that if the robot cannot sense an unexpected event, then it cannot react to it. Most existing sensing technologies suffer from incomplete reporting of the data of interest (i.e., they fail to see some things), as well as from the presence of spurious measurements. Thus it is not surprising that modern mobile robots typically use a number of different sensors designed to provide reasonably complete coverage of the entire space about the robot and fuse the sensor readings to compensate for the shortcomings in any single sensing methodology. Weaknesses in one class of sensor can be addressed by providing different classes of sensors covering the same region about the robot. Establishing which sensors are correct (if any) and how to establish when the environment is suited to a particular sensor thus emerge as serious issues. This is the problem of sensor fusion: combining data from each of the sensors in order to establish a coherent environmental representation.

Non-visual sensors There has been considerable increase in our understanding of the performance and capabilities of various non-visual sensors. Sonar, infrared, radar, and inertial sensors have all been studied extensively and their capabilities and limitations are reasonably well understood. Although the capabilities of individual sensors may be well understood, it is not always the case that existing algorithms exploit the known properties or live within the known restrictions of existing sensor classes. For example, errors in sonar measurements are not well approximated by a Gaussian error process, but many algorithms use this approximation as a first-order model.

Vision-based sensors The level of performance available from visual sensors has not yet met expectations to the extent of non-visual sensors. Vision is complicated by the vast quantities of data that are recovered and the problems inherent in understanding a three-dimensional world from the two-dimensional projection that is available from the video image. Some vision systems combine vision with other technologies to overcome some of the limitations of vision while retaining the advantages of really "seeing" the environment. On the other hand, there is a consensus that vision is a key technology for most mobile robotics applications.

15.3 Control

As most robots are built to solve specific tasks, the highest level of control that is typically built into working systems is at a task-specific level. Research into more general reasoning systems proposes to generate robots that can be programmed in a high-level, declarative language as opposed to the procedural language paradigm that is used in most systems. As the capabilities of the underlying robotic system becomes more robust and better understood and modeled, it may be that these capabilities can be expressed formally in higher task level control systems. This expression of performance and capabilities could then be exploited at the task level. Thus one major advance that can be expected in terms of high-level robotic control is that knowledge of the robot's low-level performance can be integrated into higher levels of control. More generally, the construction of control systems that accommodate liveness, multiple spatial and temporal scales, and evolving task constraints is an important yet unrealized objective.

At lower abstraction levels, existing robotic systems typically rely on various real-time architectures to provide time-critical safety control of the robot. Many systems are manually tuned with no formal guarantee of safety or correctness. Advances in real-time control theory can be expected to transform these low-level controllers into systems with known performance bounds and known limits on their capabilities.

15.4   HRI

As robots become truly useful, the design of effective user interfaces becomes even more essential. The classic floor-plan view with a point-and-click user interface that is common to many mobile robot projects may be well suited for point-to-point navigation but is inadequate for task-based control. At this very high "task level," considerable research is required into the design of effective user interfaces. A warehouse cleaning robot should not be controlled by requiring the user to define specific paths throughout the warehouse, but at the same time more control is required than just some high-level function such as "clean" – a lower level of control may be required in certain situations but at a level higher than "go from (x_1, y_1) to (x_2, y_2)."

An even more complex user interface problem occurs when the goal is to provide *shared control*: that is, to keep the user in the control loop at an appropriate level of discourse. The poblem is how to let the operator control different aspects of system behavior at different abstraction levels without interfering with other control systems that may be working on other goals.

15.5   Future Directions

Given that the robots of science fiction are far beyond what is possible in the near future, what directions are likely for mobile robots in the near future? Although advances in the hardware mechanisms that underlie mobile robots are to be expected, it is the computational and sensing abilities of current mobile robots that provide the strongest constraints on current robot performance. Thus for robots to move out of the lab and into the general environment, improvements in computation and sensing are essential. Research into the sensing, representation, and manipulation of space and the execution of plans within this space are essential to building more general-purpose autonomous robot systems.

Despite these intimidating obstacles, mobile robotic systems can be applied today to many real tasks. Mobile robotics also provides the leveraging technology for much of the rest of artificial intelligence and robotics: truly practical systems will have to be mobile. In addition, as a research domain mobile robotics provides a context for truly legitimate system validation since few real issues can be ignored or dismissed, and interaction must occur in the real world and in real time (even when experiments are carried out in a research lab).

Appendix A

Fictional Robots

Robots and intelligent machines have been popular in books and movies for almost as long as their have been books and movies. In earlier editions of this text this list was included in the first chapter. But as the list became more and more exhaustive it became unwieldy to include this list there. Although many of these examples seem quaint or naïve, nevertheless they provide great insights into what people expect or hope (or fear) that such devices will interact with humans in the future.

A.1 Autonomous Robots in Literature

A reading list of books and short stories that feature mobile robots of one form or another follows. Many of the better stories have become the basis of movies (see the following), but some have yet to undergo such reinterpretation. Even if you have *seen the film*, the book on which it was based often presents a completely different take on the problem.

The Hitchhikers Guide to the Galaxy by Douglas Adams [4] introduces Marvin, the Paranoid Android plus a collection of other interesting robotic devices. There are four other titles, *The Restaurant at the End of the Universe* [5], *Life, the Universe and Everything* [6], *So Long, and Thanks for All the Fish* [7], and *Mostly Harmless* [8], in the misnamed trilogy.

The Complete Robot by Isaac Asimov [45]. Isaac Asimov's robot stories are, in general, short stories and have been published in a number of anthologies. *The Complete Robot* brings all of these stories together.

Half Past Human by T. J. Bass [71]. In the future, humankind lives underground and the surface of the planet is tended by robots. This world appears in many of T. J. Bass' stories, including *The Godwhale* [72], which features a cyborg whale.

In the Ocean of Night by Gregory Benford [80]. A computer-controlled spaceship and mechanical machines are out to destroy organic life.

Do Androids Dream of Electric Sheep? by Philip K. Dick [223]. A world of replicants (androids), pet robots (which look like animals), and Deckard, a bounty hunter. The basis of the film *Blade Runner* (see following list).

Camelot 30K by Robert L. Forward [285]. A story about the telerobotic exploration of a microscopic world.

The Star Diaries by Stanislaw Lem [457]. A collection of stories concerning Ijon Tichy, who encounters robots.

The Ship Who Sang by Anne McCaffrey [517]. A disabled woman is equipped with a mechanical spaceship and goes out to explore the stars.

The Berserker Wars by Fred Saberhagen [689]. A collection of stories concerning robot-controlled spaceships that rampage throughout the galaxy. There are a number of other collections of "Berserker" stories, including anthologies by other authors on the same theme.

Frankenstein by Mary Wollstonecraft Shelley [712]. The classic story of a doctor/engineer trying to bring his creature to life. Required reading for any creator of autonomous systems.

He, She and It [619] by Marge Piercy. This book tells the story of the romantic entanglement between a woman and a cyborg.

A.2   Autonomous Robots in Film

The following is a collection of movies that conspicuously feature mobile robots of one form or another. Some robot movies, such as the 1951 version of *The Day the Earth Stood Still*, can be considered as classics. Others, such as *Robot Monster*, are less memorable. Nevertheless, these movies do illustrate how robots are perceived by the public.

Metropolis (1927). The classic Fritz Lang silent film that started it all. A mad scientist creates a seductive female robot.

Frankenstein (1931). The original with Boris Karloff playing the role of the monster. Dr. Frankenstein animates dead tissue.

The Perfect Woman (1949). An inventor builds a robot that looks like his niece who then pretends to be the robot.

The Day the Earth Stood Still (1951). Klaatu and the robot Gort tell us that we must live peacefully.

Robot Monster (1953). Ro-Man – a gorilla in a diving helmet – is sent to Earth as part of an invasion force.

Forbidden Planet (1956). An expedition to Altair IV encounters Dr. Morbius, his daughter, and Robby, the Robot.

The Invisible Boy (1957). Robby the Robot (of *Forbidden Planet* fame) teams up with a boy to prevent world domination.

Kill Me Quick! (1964). A mad scientist builds android women.

Frankenstein Meets the Space Monster (1965). An android and an atomic war on Mars.

Dr. Goldfoot and the Bikini Machine (1965). Vincent Price constructs bikini-clad female androids.

Dr. Who and the Daleks (1965). The Doctor battles the Daleks.

Daleks' Invasion Earth: 2150 AD (1966). The Doctor battles the Daleks on Earth.

Dr. Goldfoot and the Girl Bombs (1966). Yet more female androids in this sequel to the 1965 *Dr. Goldfoot and the Bikini Machine*.

2001: A Space Odyssey (1968). An expedition is sent to Jupiter. The robotic spaceship is managed by the HAL 9000 computer.

Silent Running (1972). A lone crew member and three robots (Huey, Dewey, and Louie) care for Earth's last nature reserves aboard a spaceship.

Sleeper (1973). A frozen Woody Allen is revived in a future in which robots are commonplace.

Westworld (1973). A futuristic amusement park in which androids are used to populate the park. Things go wrong.

Futureworld (1976). A sequel to *Westworld* in which androids are used to replace humans with robot doubles.

Demon Seed (1977). An organic super computer with artificial intelligence rapes his creator's wife.

Star Wars (1977). Assisted by the robots R2-D2 and C-3PO, Luke Skywalker leaves his home planet in search of Princess Leia.

Battlestar Galactica (1978). Cobbled together from the TV show of the same name, this movie pits the robotic Cylons against the remnants of human civilization and the Battlestar Galactica.

Alien (1979). A mining ship lands on a distant planet and runs into an alien. One of the crew members is an android.

The Black Hole (1979). A research vessel finds a missing ship manned by robots and one human inhabitant.

The Empire Strikes Back (1980). The second installment of the first *Star Wars* saga brings back R2-D2 and C-3PO.

Galixina (1980). The crew of an interstellar police ship interact with their female android.

Saturn 3 (1980). A couple on a remote base on Saturn are visited by an official delegation including a robot.

Android (1982). A robot designer and his assistant carry out research into androids on a space station.

Blade Runner (1982). Deckard tracks down and terminates replicants (biological androids).

Return of the Jedi (1983). The third and final chapter in the first *Star Wars* trilogy brings back R2-D2 and C-3PO.

2010 (1984). A sequel to *2001: A Space Odyssey* in which an expedition is sent to Jupiter to learn what happened to the *Discovery* and HAL 9000.

The Terminator (1984). A robot (the Terminator) is sent from the future to influence the past.

D.A.R.Y.L. (1985). A story about an android boy.

Aliens (1986). The first sequel to *Alien*. Again, one of the crew is an android.

Deadly Friend (1986). Bad things happen when a teen implants his robot's brain into his dead friend.

Short Circuit (1986). A military robot (Number 5) becomes intelligent and escapes.

Cherry 2000 (1987). The adventures of a businessman and his android wife.

Making Mr. Right (1987). A scientist builds a male robot to go on a long space mission.

RoboCop (1987). A wounded police officer is rebuilt as a cyborg.

Short Circuit 2 (1988). Number 5 (from *Short Circuit*) goes to the big city.

RoboCop 2 (1990). A sequel to *RoboCop* in which the RoboCop fights a bigger, stronger cyborg.

Terminator 2: Judgment Day (1991). A sequel to *The Terminator* in which one terminator robot is sent back in time to change history and a second one is sent back to maintain it.

Alien 3 (1992). Another installment of the *Alien* saga. Once again, one of the cast is an android.

Star Trek: Generations (1994). The first *Star Trek* film with the android Commander Data.

Star Trek: First Contact (1996). The Star Trek Next Generation crew confront the half-machine Borg.

Lost in Space (1998). A remake of the TV series of the same name. The Robinson family (including the robot) become lost in space.

Star Trek: Insurrection (1998). Yet more adventures of the Next Generation crew, including the android Commander Data.

The Iron Giant (1999). A boy befriends a giant robot that the government wants to destroy.

Star Wars: Episode I –The Phantom Menace (1999). R2-D2, C-3PO, and huge robot armies controlled by a single control ship.

Red Planet (2000). Astronauts go to Mars to save a dying Earth, bringing along a dog-like robot (AMEE) whose military programming becomes enabled.

AI (2001). A highly advanced robot boy longs to become a real boy.

Star Wars: Episode II – Attack of the Clones (2002). R2-D2, C-3PO and huge robot armies.

Star Wars: Episode III – Revenge of the Sith (2003). Yet more robots and androids in George Lucas' Star Wars world.

I, Robot (2004). Lots and lots and lots of centrally controlled robots try to take over the world.

The Incredibles (2004). The Omnidroids evolve through a sequence of battles with superheros, following a reinforcement learning-like strategy.

Robots (2005). A robot makes its way to the big city.

Stealth (2005). An autonomous air vehicle goes haywire.

Transformers (2007). Transforming robots make Earth their battlefield.

The Day the Earth Stood Still (2008). A remake of the 1951 classic but with a decomposible robot.

Transformers: Revenge of the Fallen (2009). Yet more robots in disguise battle on Earth.

Real Steel (2011). Human boxers are replaced with robots.

Promethius (2012). Yet another movie in the Alien franchise, and as has become standard in the franchise, one of the ship's crew members is an android.

Robot and Frank (2012). An interesting take on the use of robots as companions/care-givers for individuals with cognitive issues.

Total Recall (2012). A remake of the 1990 version of the film, but with a large collection of robot police officers.

Her (2013). On the perils of developing an emotional relationship with an intelligent virtual assistant.

Pacific Rim (2013). Giant teleoperated robots that require two mentally linked operators.

Oblivion (2013). Maintaining robots on a devastated Earth.

Big Hero 6 (2014). Finally, a movie that highlights soft robotics.

RoboCop (2014). A reboot of the RoboCop franchise, again with robot assists for the hero and with questions related to legal and ethical issues associated with deploying militarized robot systems.

Ex Machina (2014). Yet another story on the perils of the Frankenstein story, but with a female robot and a disturbed inventor.

Interstellar (2014). Robots, one based on an unusual rectangular structure, assist an interstellar explorer to save Earth.

Star Wars: The Force Awakens (2015). This installment in the series introduces BB-8, a spherical robot.

Rogue One: A Star Wars Story (2016). Yet another entry in the Star Wars universe, this time highlighting K-S20, a reformed security droid.

Kill Command (2016). Yet another warning of the perils of autonomous weaponized robots.

Passengers (2016). An accidentally awakened engineer on a sleeper ship is accompanied by Arthur, a robot bartender.

Blade Runner 2049 (2017). Some closure to the many questions asked by *Blade Runner*, with replicants and blade runners.

Star Wars: The Last Jedi (2017). Yet another installment in the Star Wars universe with BB-8, R2-D2 and C-3PO.

Alita: Battle Angel (2019). A scientist puts together scavenged robot parts to build Alita, in memory of his deceased daughter.

I Am Mother (2019). A robot mother appears tasked with the role of re-populating the Earth after an extinction event.

Terminator: Dark Fate (2019). Yet more (and more advanced) Terminator robots in the Terminator franchise.

Star Wars; The Rise of Skywalker (2019). BB-8, R2-D2, and C-3PO continue their assistance with the Star Wars story.

The Mitchels vs. the Machines (2021). A family's road trip is interrupted by the rise of the machines.

Appendix B

Probability and Statistics

Probability is the very guide to life[1]

B.1 Probability

Probability finds application throughout many scientific fields, but finds particular use in robotics in the modeling of uncertainty in terms of a vehicle's pose, interpreting sensor data, and mapping. This appendix reviews some of the fundamental aspects of probability and relates these aspects to problems in the mobile robotics domain. Although this appendix attempts to be reasonably complete in this regard, it cannot hope to provide an exhaustive review of the subject. See the end of the appendix for additional readings

One problem encountered when modeling real-world systems is that few systems exhibit constant behavior. Observations vary depending on what appears to be random or chance variations. Probability theory provides a general technique for describing these variations. Suppose there is an experiment whose outcome depends on chance. The outcome of the experiment is described as a *random variable* X. The sample space Ω is the space from which X can be drawn. If the sample space is finite or countably infinite, then the random variable and sample space are said to be *discrete*; otherwise they are said to be *continuous*.

B.1.1 Probability of Discrete Events

The discrete probability function $P(X)$ scores evidence that a discrete event X, where X is drawn from sample space Ω, has occurred. $P(X)$ can be defined in terms of three axioms:

1. **Nonnegativity.** $P(A) \geq 0$ for every event A.
2. **Additivity.** If $A_1, A_2, \ldots, A_N$ is a series of disjoint events, then $P(A_1 \cup A_2 \cup \ldots \cup A_N) = P(A_1) + P(A_2) + \cdots + P(A_N)$, where $A \cup B$ denotes the event A or the event B.
3. **Normalization.** The probability of the entire sample space Ω is equal to 1, that is $P(\Omega) = 1$.

To make this situation more concrete, suppose that the random experiment is that of throwing a single fair die and observing the symbol on the top face of the die. Then:

---

[1] Joseph Butler.

Table B.1. *Conjunctive probabilities over A and B.*

	B_0	B_1
A_0	p	q
A_1	r	s

Note that $p + q + r + s = 1$.

- The state space is given by set of possible symbols appearing on the top surface of the die, that is, $\Omega = \{1, 2, 3, 4, 5, 6\}$.
- If the die is fair, then each possible outcome is equally likely, so $P(\{1\}) = P(\{2\}) = P(\{3\}) = P(\{4\}) = P(\{5\}) = P(\{6\}) = 1/6$
- The sum of all probabilities is one: $P(\Omega) = 1$.

From the axioms that define a probability function, a number of natural properties emerge (some are left as exercises at the end of this chapter). These include:

- If $A \subset B$, then $P(A) \leq P(B)$.
- $P(A \cup B) = P(A) + P(B) - P(A \cap B)$. Here $A \cap B$ denotes the situation within which both A and B are true. $P(A \cap B)$ is often written as $P(A, B)$.
- $P(A \cup B) \leq P(A) + P(B)$.
- $P(A \cup B) = P(A) + P(A^C \cap B)$. Here A^C is the complement of A: $A^C = \Omega - A$.
- If $B = \Omega - A$, then $P(B) = 1 - P(A)$.

Statistical independency Two events A and B are said to be **statistically independent** if $P(A \cap B) = P(A)P(B)$.

Conditional probability We are interested in determining the **conditional probability** of A taking on certain values given that we know that B has a specific value (or range of values). This conditional probability is written as $P(A|B)$ and is read as the probability of event A given B. Suppose that we have two random events A and B, and that A can take on the values A_0 and A_1, B can take on the values B_0 and B_1, and the probabilities of the various combinations of A and B are as given in Table B.1. From Table B.1, $P(A = A_0 | B = B_0) = p/(p + r)$, and the probability that B takes on the value B_0 is $P(B = B_0) = (p + r)/(p + q + r + s) = (p + r)$. Thus $P(A = A_0 | B = B_0) \times P(B = B_0) = p$, but $P(A = A_0 \wedge B = B_0) = p$. Therefore $P(A = A_0 \wedge B = B_0) = P(A = A_0 | B = B_0) \times P(B = B_0)$. Similarly, $P(B = B_0 \wedge A = A_0) = P(B = B_0 | A = A_0) \times P(A = A_0)$. Equating these two expressions for $P(A = A_0 \wedge B = B_0)$ and generalizing for all of the values that A and B can take on results in the well-known Bayes rule

$$P(A|B) = \frac{P(B|A)P(A)}{P(B)},$$

provided that $P(B) \neq 0$.

Conditional probability with conjunctions In various localization tasks it can be useful to construct conditional probabilities predicated on conjunctions,

$$P(A \cap B \cap C) = P(A \cap (B \cap C)) = P(A|B \cap C)P(B \cap C) = P(A|B \cap C)P(B|C)P(C)$$

and

$$P(A \cap B \cap C) = P(B \cap (A \cap C)) = P(B|A \cap C)P(A \cap C) = P(B|A \cap C)P(A|C)P(C).$$

Equating these, canceling out the common term $P(C)$, and rearranging gives

$$P(A|B \cap C) = \frac{P(B|A \cap C)P(A|C)}{P(B|C)}.$$

Total probability theorem Let $A_1, A_2, \ldots, A_N$ be disjoint events that partition the sample space of A, and assume that $P(A_i) > 0$ for all i. Then for any event B

$$
\begin{aligned}
P(B) &= P(A_1 \cap B) + \cdots + P(A_N \cap B) \\
&= P(A_1)P(B|A_1) + \cdots + P(A_N)P(B|A_N) \\
&= \sum_{i=1}^{N} P(A_i)P(B|A_i).
\end{aligned}
$$

The Bayes rule can thus be reexpressed as

$$P(A|B) = \frac{P(A)P(B|A)}{\sum_{i=1}^{N} P(A_i)P(B|A_i)}.$$

The denominator is a normalizing term, and in many applications of the Bayes rule, it is common to write

$$P(A|B) = \eta P(A)P(B|A),$$

where η is understood to be the normalizing term.

Conditionalized product rule $P(A \cap B|E) = P(A|B \cup E)P(B|E)$. The proof of this is left as an exercise.

B.1.2 Probability of Continuous Events

The description of probability given previously is defined over a discrete set of events. It is straightforward to extend the notion of probability to a continuum of events (probability on the line) and to a multi-dimensional continuoum of events (probability on a plane or higher-dimensional space). A continuous random variable can assume an uncountably infinite number of values, and thus calculation of probabilities by enumeration is not possible. As a result, the probability of a continuous event is defined in terms of a *cumulative distribution function* $F(x)$ that scores the probability that the random variable takes on a value less than or equal to x,

$$F(x) = P(X \le x).$$

The cumulative distribution function $F(x)$ has the following properties:

1. $F(x)$ is continuous.
2. $F'(x)$ exists except at most at a finite number of points.
3. $F'(x)$ is at least piecewise continuous.

The *probability density function* $f(x)$ is the derivative of the cumulative distribution function $f(x) = dF(x)/dx$ and has the following properties:

1. $f(x) = 0$ if x is not in the range of X.
2. $f(x) \geq 0$.
3. $\int_{-\infty}^{\infty} f(x)dx = 1$.
4. $F(x_1) = \int_{-\infty}^{x_1} f(x)dx$.

The probability rules for probability over a discrete set of events extends in a straightforward manner to continuous events. For example, the total probability theorem becomes

$$P(B) = \int P(A_i)P(B|A_i)dA_i.$$

B.1.3 Probability Distributions

Although probability theory admits an extremely large space of probability distribution functions, a number of common distributions have emerged in practice.

Bernoulli distribution The Bernoulli distribution is a discrete distribution that has only two possible outcomes, 0 and 1. Its probability distribution function is given by

$$P(x) = \begin{cases} 1 - p & \text{if } x = 0 \\ p & \text{if } x = 1. \end{cases}$$

The cumulative distribution function for this random variable is given by

$$F(x) = \begin{cases} 0 & x \leq 0 \\ p & 0 < x < 1 \\ 1 & x \geq 1. \end{cases}$$

Normal distribution The normal distribution is perhaps the most commonly used distribution. The normal distribution is symmetrical, with a probability density function given by

$$f(x) = \frac{1}{\sqrt{2\pi}\sigma} exp\left\{-\frac{(x - \mu)^2}{2\sigma^2}\right\}.$$

The cumulative distribution function for the normal distribution does not exist in closed form but rather must be computed numerically.

B.2 Some Simple Statistics

Statistics is the mathematical treatment and analysis of data. Statistics is an extremely large and well-developed field of study. Here we present some simple descriptive statistics that can be used to describe simple random processes and datasets.

Expected value Given a scalar value x, $\mathbb{E}[x]$ is the *expected value* of x, or, more formally,

$$\mu = \mathbb{E}[x] = \int x f(x) dx,$$

where $f(x)$ is the probability that x takes on a specific value (its probability distribution function). For a discrete scalar x taking on discrete values $x_1, x_2, \ldots, x_n$, each with probability $p_1, p_2, \ldots, p_n$ (with $\sum p_i = 1$), then

$$\mathbb{E}[x] = \sum_1^n p_i x_i.$$

The variance $V(x)$ or σ^2 is given by

$$\sigma^2 = \mathbb{E}[(x - \mathbb{E}[x])^2].$$

The variance is an estimate of the region about the expected value within which likely values of x are to be found.

The *standard deviation* $S(x)$ is given by

$$\sigma = S(x) = V(x)^{\frac{1}{2}}.$$

For a vector $\mathbf{x}$, $\mathbb{E}[\mathbf{x}]$ is the expected value of $\mathbf{x}$,

$$\mathbb{E}[\mathbf{x}] = \int \ldots \int \mathbf{x} p(\mathbf{x}) d\mathbf{x},$$

where $p(\mathbf{x})$ is the probability that $\mathbf{x}$ takes on a specific value (probability distribution function). The variance $\mathbf{P}$ of $\hat{\mathbf{x}}$ is given by

$$\mathbf{P} = \mathbb{E}\left[\left[\hat{\mathbf{x}} - \mathbb{E}(\hat{\mathbf{x}})\right] \left[\hat{\mathbf{x}} - \mathbb{E}(\hat{\mathbf{x}})\right]^T \right].$$

B.3   Further Reading

There exists a wide range of introductory textbooks on probability and statistics including, [84], [189], [210], and [291].

B.4   Problems

1. Prove that $P(A) \leq 1$ for any event A.
2. Prove that $P(A \cup B) = P(A) + P(B) - P(A \cap B)$.
3. Prove that conditional probability $P(A|B)$ is a probability law with respect to A. That is, prove that

   (a) $P(A|B) \geq 0$ for every event A.
   (b) $P(A_1 \cup A_2|B) = P(A_1|B) \cup P(A_2|B)$ for disjoint events A_1 and A_2.
   (c) $P(\Omega|B) = 1$.

4. Consider the tossing of a fair coin. Let X assume the value of zero for heads and a value of one for tails. This is a Bernoulli distribution with $p = q = 1/2$. What is the expected outcome and variance?

5. Robot landmark detection problem. A common technique for the localization of robots in industrial settings is to augment the local environment with specific landmarks (often visual) that can be sensed by the robot. Suppose we have such a landmark scheme and experiments with the sensor and its sensing algorithm have found that the system can correctly identify landmarks with probability 0.90, but that a landmark is identified falsely (i.e., when no landmark is present) with probability 0.01. The probability of a landmark being present is 0.05. What is the false alarm probability (probability of indentifying a landmark when none is present) and probability of missed detection (probabililty of missing a landmark even though one is present)?

6. In the previous question, what is the probability that a target is present, given that the sensor indiates that it is present?

7. Prove the *recursive Bayesian updating* equation. That is, prove that

$$P(x|z^1, \ldots, z^{n-1}, z^n) = \frac{P(z^n|x, z^1, \ldots, z^{n-1})P(x|z^1, \ldots, z^{n-1})}{P(z^n, z^1, \ldots, z^{n-1})}.$$

Hint: Define $A = x$, $B = z^1, \ldots, z^{n-1}$, and $C = z^n$, and use the definition of conditional probabililty.

8. Prove the conditionalized product rule. That is, prove $P(A \cap B|E) = P(A|B \cap E) P(B|E)$.

Hint: $P(A \cap B \cap E) = P(A \cap B|E)P(E)$.

Appendix C

Linear Systems, Matrices, and Filtering

This appendix provides an extremely brief introduction to linear and matrix algebra and linear systems. Although linear systems are used extensively in the text, perhaps their most critical application in robotics is the representation of position and orientation.

C.1 Linear Algebra

A **linear equation** in n unknowns $x_1, x_2, \ldots, x_n$ is an equation of the form

$$a_1 x_1 + a_2 x_2 + \cdots + a_n x_n = b.$$

A system of m linear equations in n unknowns is a family of linear equations

$$
\begin{aligned}
a_{11}x_1 + a_{12}x_2 + \cdots + a_{1n}x_n &= b_1 \\
a_{21}x_1 + a_{22}x_2 + \cdots + a_{2n}x_n &= b_2 \\
\cdots \cdots & \\
a_{m1}x_1 + a_{m2}x_2 + \cdots + a_{mn}x_n &= b_m
\end{aligned}
$$

This system can be written as

$$\sum_{j=1}^{n} a_{ij} x_j = b_i, \quad i = 1, 2, \ldots, m.$$

Representing such systems of equations in this form is notationally clumsy, and for anything but the simplest problems, it is more common to writen the system of equations as a matrix. The matrix

$$
\mathbf{A} =
\begin{bmatrix}
a_{11} & a_{12} & \cdots & a_{1n} \\
a_{21} & a_{22} & \cdots & a_{2n} \\
\cdots & & & \\
a_{m1} & a_{m2} & \cdots & a_{mn}
\end{bmatrix}
$$

is called the **coefficient matrix** of the system.

Matricies with n rows and m columns are said to be of size $n \times m$. $n \times 1$ matrices are known as column vectors, and matrices with size $1 \times m$ are known as (row) vectors.

C.2   Matrix Algebra

Zero and identity matrices The $n \times n$ matrix $\mathbf{I}$ with elements $I_{i,j} = 1$ if $i = j$ and 0 otherwise is known as the identity matrix. The $m \times n$ matrix $\mathbf{A}$ with elements $a_{i,j} = 0$ is known as the zero matrix.

Equality Two matrices $\mathbf{A} = [a_{ij}]$ and $\mathbf{B} = [b_{ij}]$ are said to be *equal* if the two matrices are the same size, and if for each index pair (i, j), $a_{i,j} = b_{i,j}$.

Transposition $\mathbf{A}^T$ denotes the transpose of $\mathbf{A}$. $(\mathbf{A}^T)_{i,j} = \mathbf{A}_{j,i}$.

Addition and subtraction Let $\mathbf{A} = [a_{i,j}]$ and $\mathbf{B} = [b_{i,j}]$ be two $m \times n$ matrices. Then the sum of the matrices $\mathbf{A} + \mathbf{B}$ is the $m \times n$ matrix with elements $c_{i,j}$, where $c_{i,j} = a_{i,j} + b_{i,j}$. Similarly the difference of two matrices $\mathbf{C} = \mathbf{A} - \mathbf{B}$ has elements $c_{i,j} = a_{i,j} - b_{i,j}$. The negative of the $m \times n$ matrix $\mathbf{A}$, denoted as $-\mathbf{A}$, is the $m \times n$ matrix with elements given by $-a_{i,j}$.

Scalar multiplication Let $\mathbf{A} = [a_{i,j}]$ be an $m \times n$ matrix and let c be a constant. Then the *product* of c and A, denoted $c\mathbf{A}$, is the $m \times n$ matrix with elements $ca_{i,j}$.

Matrix multiplication Let $\mathbf{A} = [a_{i,j}]$ be an $m \times p$ matrix and let $\mathbf{B} = [b_{i,j}]$ be a $p \times n$ matrix. Then the product of $\mathbf{A}$ and $\mathbf{B}$, written $\mathbf{C} = \mathbf{AB}$, has elements $c_{i,j} = \sum_{k=1..p} a_{i,k} b_{k,j}$.

Symmetry A square matrix $\mathbf{A}$ is said to be symmetric if $\mathbf{A} = \mathbf{A}^T$. $\mathbf{A}$ is said to be skew-symmetric or anti-symmetric if $\mathbf{A} = -\mathbf{A}^T$. Any matrix $\mathbf{A}$ can be written as the sum of a symmetric and an anti-symmetric matrix: $\mathbf{A} = (\frac{1}{2}\mathbf{A} + \frac{1}{2}\mathbf{A}^T) + (\frac{1}{2}\mathbf{A} - \frac{1}{2}\mathbf{A}^T)$.

Matrix inverse Let $\mathbf{A}$ be a square matrix. The the *inverse* of $\mathbf{A}^{-1}$ of $\mathbf{A}$ is the square matrix $\mathbf{B}$ of the same size of $\mathbf{A}$ such that $\mathbf{AB} = \mathbf{BA} = \mathbf{I}$. If such a $\mathbf{B}$ exists then, the matrix $\mathbf{A}$ is said to be *invertible*.

Determinant The **determinant** of a square $n \times n$ matrix $\mathbf{A}$ is a scalar quantity $\det \mathbf{A}$ or $|\mathbf{A}|$ defined recursively as follows

$$\det \mathbf{A} = \left\{ \begin{array}{ll} a_{1,1} & \text{if } n = 1 \\ \sum_{k=1}^{n} a_{k,1}(-1)^{k+1} M_{k,1}(\mathbf{A}) & \text{otherwise} \end{array} \right\}.$$

where $M_{i,j}(\mathbf{A})$ is the determinant of the $(n-1) \times (n-1)$ matrix obtained by deleting the ith row and jth column of $\mathbf{A}$.

Eigenvalues Given a square matrix $\mathbf{A}$, λ is an eigenvalue of $\mathbf{A}$ and $\mathbf{x}$ is the corresponding eigenvector if

$$\mathbf{Ax} = \lambda \mathbf{x}, \ \mathbf{x} \neq 0.$$

$(\lambda \mathbf{I} - \mathbf{A})\mathbf{x} = 0$ has a solution if $\mathbf{x} \neq 0$ iff $|\lambda \mathbf{I} - \mathbf{A}| = 0$. Eigenvalues can be found by solving the determinant for λ. The corresponding eigenvectors can then be found by solving $(\lambda \mathbf{I} - \mathbf{A})\mathbf{x} = 0$. Eigenvevalues/eigenvectors have many useful properties, but perhaps most important for autonomous systems is that if $\mathbf{A}$ is symmetric then all of the eigenvalues of $\mathbf{A}$ are real and all eigenvectors of $\mathbf{A}$ are orthogonal, and $\mathbf{A} = \mathbf{X} \Lambda \mathbf{X}^{-1}$, where Λ is a diagonal matrix with the eigenvalues of $\mathbf{A}$ forming the diagonal elements, and $\mathbf{X}$ contains the orthonormal eigenvectors of $\mathbf{A}$ is the same order.

C.3   Signals and Systems

A **signal** is a sequence of values over some domain (often time). A **continuous signal** has values for all points in time over some (possibly infinite) interval. A **discrete signal** has values for only discrete points. Signals can also be a function of higher-dimensional domains (e.g., images, video) and may be continuous or discrete over each dimension.

A **system** is a mechanism that operates on signals. A system takes in an input signal and produces an output signal. Systems can be characterized in terms of the types of signals upon which the system operates (e.g., a **continuous system** has continuous inputs and outputs) and also in terms of the type of computation that the system applies to its input signal to produce the output signal.

Linear systems A **linear system** is any system that obeys the properties of scaling and superposition. A **non-linear system** is a system that fails to have both of these proerties. More formally, a system H is linear iff for any signals $f_1(t)$ and $f_2(t)$ and constants k_1 and k_2

$$H(k_1 f_1(t) + k_2 f_2(t)) = k_1 H(f_1(t)) + k_2 H(f_2(t)).$$

Time-invariant systems A **time-invariant system** is a system that does not depend on the time at which it occurs. More formally, a system H for which $H(f(t)) = y(t)$ is time invariant iff for all T

$$H(f(t - T)) = y(t - T).$$

A system is that is not time invariant is known as a **time-variant system**.

Causal systems A **causal system** is one whose output depends on the current and past inputs but which does not depend upon future inputs. A **non-causal** system's output depends upon future inputs.

Convolution Given arbitrary continuous signals $x(t)$ and $h(t)$, the **convolution** of $x(t)$ with $h(t)$ is given by

$$z(t) = \int_{-\infty}^{\infty} x(\tau) h(t - \tau) d\tau.$$

This is known as the **convolution integral**. For discrete systems, the integral is replaced by the **convolution sum**

$$z(t) = \sum_{\tau = -\infty}^{\tau = \infty} x(\tau) h(t - \tau).$$

The symbol $\star$ is used to denote convolution, that is

$$(x \star h)(t) = x(t) \star h(t) = \int_{-\infty}^{\infty} x(\tau)h(t - \tau)d\tau.$$

Linear time-invariant systems A **linear time-invariant system** is a system that is both *linear* and *time-invariant*. A linear time-invariant (LTI) system can be fully characterized by its **impulse response** – the output of the system when it is presented with an infintely brief impulse (input). Mathematically, for continuous signals this is expressed as its response when presented with a **Dirac delta function** δ. which is defined by the property that

$$\int_{-\infty}^{\infty} f(t)\delta(t)dt = f(0),$$

provided that f is continuous at $t = 0$. Note that any continuous signal $x(t)$ can be expressed as an integral of δ functions:

$$x(t) = \int_{-\infty}^{\infty} x(\tau)\delta(t - \tau)d\tau.$$

If $H()$ is a linear time-invariant systm, and $x(t)$ is a continuous signal, then

$$
\begin{aligned}
y(t) &= H(x(t)) \\
&= H\left(\int_{-\infty}^{\infty} x(\tau)\delta(t - \tau)d\tau\right) \\
&= \int_{-\infty}^{\infty} x(\tau)H(\delta(t - \tau))d\tau \\
&= x(t) = \int_{-\infty}^{\infty} x(\tau)h(t - \tau)d\tau,
\end{aligned}
$$

where $h(t)$ is the **impulse response** of the system $H()$. That is, the response of an LTI system is completely characterized by its impulse response $h(t)$.

C.4   Fourier Theory

If $f(t)$ is a well-behaved signal then $f(t)$ can be written as

$$f(t) = \frac{1}{2\pi} \int_{-\infty}^{\infty} F(j\omega)e^{j\omega t}d\omega,$$

where

$$F(j\omega) = \int_{-\infty}^{\infty} f(t)e^{-j\omega t}dt$$

and ω is in radians per second. The function $F(j\omega)$ is known as the **Fourier transform** of $f(t)$, and $f(t)$ is known as the inverse Fourier transform of $F(j\omega)$.

The Fourier transform of a function $x(t)$ is often written as $\mathcal{F}[\S(\sqcup)]$. The Fourier transform has a number of extremely useful properties. A number of these are presented as exercises at the end of the appendix.

C.5   Sampling and the Nyquist Frequency

A signal $f(t)$ is said to be **band limited** if

$$\forall \, |\omega| > B \; F(\omega) = 0.$$

If a signal is band limited, then it is possible to represent the signal in terms of a finite number of evenly spaced samples. This is known as the **sampling theorem**.

The sufficient condition for this representation to be complete is that the sampling frequency ω exceeds the Nyquist frequency $\omega_{\text{Nyquist}} > 2B$.

C.6   Further Reading

Linear algebra There are a large number of textbooks on linear algebra, including a number of free tutorials and textbooks on the Web. Published texts include [743] and [632].

Signals and systems The classic text is [589] and a more recent version of the text is available [590]. Other texts exist, including [402], which provides examples in Matlab. See also [448] and [151].

C.7   Problems

1. Prove that convolution is associative. This is, prove that

$$f_1(t) * (f_2(t) * f_3(t)) = (f_1(t) * f_2(t)) * f_3(t).$$

2. Prove that convolution is commutative. That is, prove that

$$f_1(t) * f_2(t) = f_2(t) * f_1(t).$$

3. Prove that convolution is distributive over addition. That is, prove that

$$f_1(t) * (f_2(t) + f_3(t)) = f_1(t) * f_2(t) + f_1 * f_3(t).$$

4. Show that if frequency is represented in hertz rather in radians per second, then the Fourier transform and its inverse become, respectively,

$$F(j\omega) = \int_{-\infty}^{\infty} f(t) e^{-2\pi j \omega t} \, dt$$

and

$$f(t) = \int_{-\infty}^{\infty} F(j\omega) e^{2\pi j \omega t} \, d\omega.$$

5. Show that the Fourier transform is a linear transform, that is

$$\mathcal{F}[ax(t) + by(t)] = a\mathcal{F}[x(t)] + b\mathcal{F}[y(t)].$$

6. Prove the convolution theorem for the Fourier transform, which states that convolution in the time domain corresponds to multiplication in the frequency domain:

$$\mathcal{F}[x(t) * y(t)] = X(j\omega)Y(j\omega)$$

where $X(j\omega) = \mathcal{F}[x(t)]$ and $Y(j\omega) = \mathcal{F}[y(t)]$.

Appendix D

Markov Models

A full treatment of Markov models is beyond the limit of space available here. A number of introductory texts and tutorials on Markov models are given at the end of this chapter. The tutorial provided here follows that given in [648].

D.1   Discrete Markov Process

Suppose that an autonomous agent moves about its environment in such a way that transitions from one location to another are as sketched in Figure D.1. The robot's environment has 13 distinct locations and at any one time the robot is in one of these. Identify these $N = 13$ distinct locations (or states) as $S_1, S_2, \ldots, S_n$. At each time step the robot can move from one state to another, including possibly remaining in the same location, according to a set of probabilities associated with each state. Then the robot's environment can be represented as a directed graph with the nodes of the graph corresponding to the distinct locations and the directed edges of the graph corresponding to possible transitions for each location. Let t denote the time instant associated with robot motions (state changes), and denote the actual location (state) of the robot at time t as q_t. Suppose that the robot at time t was in location S_k, at time $t - 1$ the robot was in location $S_j, \ldots,$ and at time 1 the robot was in location S_i, then what is the probability that the robot is in location S_l at time $t + 1$? That is, what is

$$P(q_{t+1} = S_l | q_t = S_k, q_{t-1} = S_j, \ldots, q_1 = S_i)?$$

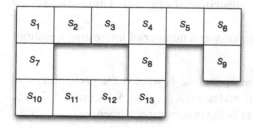

(a) Environment   (b) State representation

Figure D.1. A robot's environment and its Markov chain representation. At any given time the robot is in exactly one state ($S_1, \ldots, S_{13}$). The robot can transit to one state to another only along the arcs shown in (b). Each arc has a known probabililty of being taken from a given node.

Note that this conditional probability depends on the entire motion history of the robot. Now suppose instead that the robot's choice of which location to move to at time $t + 1$ is only dependent upon the state of the robot at time t. Then the conditional probability is independent of all states except the previous one, and the conditional probability of interest becomes

$$P(q_{t+1} = S_l | q_t = S_k).$$

Now suppose that the probability that the robot will follow a particular path out of a location is independent of time. We can then assign a label to each directed edge in the graph that encodes the **state transition probability** $a_{i,j}$, where

$$a_{i,j} = P(q_{t+1} = S_j | q_t = S_i)$$

and $a_{i,j} \geq 0$ and $\sum_j a_{i,j} = 1$.

Such a system is known as an observable first order discrete **Markov chain**. Such a system is easily encoded as the matrix of state transition properties. For the system shown in Figure D.1, suppose that for all valid paths the likelihood of following that path is equal. Then the matrix $\mathbf{A} = \{a_{i,j}\}$ of state transition probabilities is given by

$$
\mathbf{A} =
\begin{bmatrix}
0 & 1/2 & 0 & 0 & 0 & 0 & 1/2 & 0 & 0 & 0 & 0 & 0 & 0 \\
1/2 & 0 & 1/2 & 0 & 0 & 0 & 0 & 0 & 0 & 0 & 0 & 0 & 0 \\
0 & 1/2 & 0 & 1/2 & 0 & 0 & 0 & 0 & 0 & 0 & 0 & 0 & 0 \\
0 & 0 & 1/3 & 0 & 1/3 & 0 & 0 & 1/3 & 0 & 0 & 0 & 0 & 0 \\
0 & 0 & 0 & 1/2 & 0 & 1/2 & 0 & 0 & 0 & 0 & 0 & 0 & 0 \\
0 & 0 & 0 & 0 & 1/2 & 0 & 0 & 0 & 1/2 & 0 & 0 & 0 & 0 \\
1/2 & 0 & 0 & 0 & 0 & 0 & 0 & 0 & 0 & 1/2 & 0 & 0 & 0 \\
0 & 0 & 0 & 1/2 & 0 & 0 & 0 & 0 & 0 & 0 & 0 & 0 & 1/2 \\
0 & 0 & 0 & 0 & 0 & 1 & 0 & 0 & 0 & 0 & 0 & 0 & 0 \\
0 & 0 & 0 & 0 & 0 & 0 & 1/2 & 0 & 0 & 0 & 1/2 & 0 & 0 \\
0 & 0 & 0 & 0 & 0 & 0 & 0 & 0 & 0 & 1/2 & 0 & 1/2 & 0 \\
0 & 0 & 0 & 0 & 0 & 0 & 0 & 0 & 0 & 0 & 1/2 & 0 & 1/2 \\
0 & 0 & 0 & 0 & 0 & 0 & 0 & 1/2 & 0 & 0 & 0 & 1/2 & 0
\end{bmatrix}.
$$

(D.1)

This matrix is known as the **transition matrix**. Note that the rows sum to one but that the columns do not necessarily do so.

A state S_i in a Markov chain is said to be **absorbing** if $a_{i,i} = 1$. Otherwise, such a state is said to be **transient**.

Observable Markov processes can be used to answer a number of interesting questions related to robotics, including

- If the robot starts out in some location S_k at time 1, what is the probability that the robot visits a specific sequence of nodes $S_k, S_l, \ldots, S_j, S_i$ at times $1, 2, \ldots, t - 1, t$? This is $P(O|\text{Model})$, where O is the observation sequence,

$$
\begin{aligned}
P(O|\text{Model}) &= P(S_k, S_l, \ldots, S_j, S_i | \text{Model}) \\
&= P(S_k) \cdot P(S_l | S_k) \ldots \cdot P(S_i | S_j).
\end{aligned}
$$

Now $P(S_k) = 1$, as the robot starts there and all of the other conditional probabilities correspond to elements of the state transition probabilities matrix.

- What is the probability that a robot that starts out in a given location S_k will stay in that location for exactly T time steps? This follows in a straightforward manner from the earlier property as the robot must follow a sequence of $S_k, S_k, \ldots, S_k, S_j$, where $S_j \neq S_k$. Let $a_{k,k} = P(q_{t+1} = S_k|q_t = S_k)$, then $P(O|\text{Model} = (a_{k,k})^{T-1}(1 - a_{k,k}) = p_k(T)$. Here $p_k(T)$ is the probability density function of duration in state k.
- What is the expected time that a robot that starts out in S_k will stay there before moving to another location? This follows in a straightforward way from the foregoing as it is the expected value of the duration probability density function.

$$\begin{aligned} \bar{T}_k &= \sum_T T p_k(T) \\ &= \sum_T T (a_{k,k})^{T-1}(1 - a_{k,k}) \\ &= \tfrac{1}{1-a_{k,k}}. \end{aligned}$$

- Given a probability distribution of the location of the robot now, what is the probability distribution of the location of the robot T time steps from now? Given the Markovian nature of the problem, it suffices to solve this for one time step and then the process can be repeated to solve the problem for T steps. Suppose that the probability of the robot being in a given location is given by the row vector X, then the probability of the robot being in a given location i at the next time step is given by

$$x_1 * a_{1,i} + x_2 * a_{2,i} + \cdots + x_n * a_{n,i}.$$

This can be written very compactly for all possible locations as

$$X' = X\mathbf{A},$$

and for T time steps

$$X' = X\mathbf{A}^{(T)}.$$

D.2   Hidden Markov Models

A **hidden Markov model** (or HMM) is a Markov model in which the states are hidden. Rather than have access to the internal structure of the HMM, all that is available are observations that are described by the underlying Markov model. There is a wide range of different variants of HMM problems, depending on what is assumed in terms of the structure of the underlying Markov process. An HMM $\lambda = (\mathbf{A}, \mathbf{B}, \pi)$ is described in terms of

- N, the number of states in the model. It is often the case in robotic applications that the number of states corresponds to some physical reality (e.g., the number of locations in the environment as in the previous example). Each of the states is assigned a label S_i, and the actual state at time t is given by q_t.
- M, the number of distinct observation symbols per state. Denote the individual symbols as $V = \{v_1, v_2, \ldots, v_M\}$.
- $\mathbf{A}$, the state transition probability distribution. As for Markov chains,

$$\mathbf{A} = \{a_{i,j}\} = P(q_t = S_j|q_{t-1} = S_i).$$

- **B**, the observation symbol probability distribution for state i. $\mathbf{B} = \{b_i(k)\} = \mathrm{P}(v_k$ at $t|q_t = S_i)$. **B** is known as the **emission matrix**.
- π, the initial state distribution, $\pi = \{\pi_i\} = \mathrm{P}(q_1|S_i)$.

Given an appropriate definition of an HMM λ, it is possible to generate an observation sequence $O = O_1, O_2, \ldots, O_T$ where each of $O_i \in V$.

There are three basic questions that can be asked with respect to an HMM

- **Probability of an observation sequence.** Given an observation sequence $O = O_1, O_2, \ldots, O_T$ and a model $\lambda = (\mathbf{A}, \mathbf{B}, \pi)$, compute $\mathrm{P}(O|\lambda)$.

  The straightforward approach to solving this – computing every possible transition and emission over T time steps – is impractical. An efficient solution to solving this problem is via the **forward-backward algorithm** [648].
- **Probability of a sequence of states.** Given an observation sequence $O = O_1, O_2, \ldots, O_T$ and a model $\lambda = (\mathbf{A}, \mathbf{B}, \pi)$, what is the optimal state sequence $Q = q_1, q_2, \ldots, q_T$ that explains O?

  The **Viterbi algorithm** [809] finds the best single state sequence that explains the observation sequence, that is, that maximizes $\mathrm{P}(Q, O|\lambda)$.
- **Learning an HMM.** How can $\lambda = (\mathbf{A}, \mathbf{B}, \pi)$ be chosen to maximize $\mathrm{P}(O|\lambda)$?

  There are a number of different iterative mechanisms to determine the model parameters of λ that locally maximize $\mathrm{P}(O|\lambda)$ including **Baum–Welch** [825], expectation-modification [89], and gradient methods [839].

D.3   Markov Decision Process

Markov processes and hidden Markov processes operate without an external agent influencing the outcome of the system. When the system being modeled operates under both a stochastic process and some active agent, then a different framework is required. A **Markov decision process** is an extension to a Markov chain through addition of external actions and a reward function. Markov decision processes are Markov systems in which local rewards (rewards for specific actions now are known) can be used to generate long-term policies (action plans) to maximize the overall reward.

Formally, a Markov decision process (MDP) is defined in terms of the tuple (S, A, T, R), where

- S is a finite set of environmental states.
- A is a finite set of actions.
- $T : S \times A \to S$ is the state transition function. Each transition is associated with a transition probability. Write $T(s, a, s')$ as the probability of ending in state s', given that the agent starts in s and executes action a.
- $R : S \times A \to R$ is the immediate reward function, which is the immediate reward received after taking a specific action from a specific state.

The goal of the MDP is to determine some policy π that maps states to actions and maximizes a cumulative function of the rewards, discounted over some horizon T (often $T \to \infty$), that is, to maximize

$$\sum_{t=0}^{T} \gamma^t r_t,$$

where r_t is the reward at time step t and $0 \leq \gamma \leq 1$ is the discount rate.

There are a number of different problems that MDPs can be used to solve.

- **Expected reward of a policy.** A given policy π can be evaluated against the MDP. Let $V_{\pi,t}(s)$ be the expected reward gained starting in state s and executing the policy π for t steps. Then $V_{\pi,t}(s)$ can be defined as

$$V_{\pi,t}(s) = R(s, \pi_t(s)) + \gamma \sum_{s'} T(s, \pi_t(s), s') V_{\pi,t-1}(s').$$

For the infinite-time-horizon case,

$$V_{\pi}(s) = R(s, \pi(s)) + \gamma \sum_{s'} T(s, \pi(s), s') V_{\pi,t-1}(s'),$$

which can be solved using standard linear equation tools to solve for the expected reward.

- **Computing an optimal policy.** For any given horizon an optimal policy can be defined, but it is generally more interesting to consider the best policy for the infinite-horizon case. Here we seek a policy that has the value given by

$$V^*(s) = \max_a \left[R(s, a) + \gamma \sum_{s'} T(s, a, s') V^*(s') \right],$$

which can be solved using a variety of different numerical methods.

D.4   POMDP

A POMDP, or a partially observable Markov decision process, is an MDP in which the agent is not able to determine its state reliably. This is analagous to the difference between HMMs and Markov chains. A POMDP is described as the tuple (S, A, T, R, Ω, O), where S, A, T, and R describe an MDP, Ω is a finite set of observations that the agent can experience of its world, and $O : S \times A \rightarrow \Omega$ is the observation function, which gives a probability distribution over possible observations. Write $O(s', a, o)$ for the probability of making observation o, given that the agent took action a and landed in state s'.

As with MDP, POMDPs can be used to determine an optimal policy π that explains the set of observations. In practice, the problem of solving POMDPs can be computationally infeasible for sufficiently large problems, and approximate solutions are used instead. A number of different heuristic strategies for solving POMDP problems (from a robotics context) can be found in [149].

D.5   Further Reading

Discrete Markov processes Markov methods find application in a wide range of subjects and a significant literature exists. Basic textbooks exist that provide a good introduction to Markov chains (e.g., [190, 120, 581]).

Hidden Markov models Many of the textbooks just cited cover HMMs. For a shorter introduction to hidden Markov models, see [648].

Markov decision processes See [264] for an indepth treatment.

POMDP See [398] for an overview.

D.6   Problems

1. Let $\mathbf{A}$ be the transition matrix of a Markov chain. Prove that the ijth entry of the matrix $\mathbf{A}^{(T)}$ gives the probability that the Markov chain starting in state S_i will be in state S_j after T steps.
2. Let $\mathbf{A}$ be the transition matrix of a Markov chain and let x be the probability vector that represents the initial distribution. Prove that the probability distribution of the chain after T steps is given by the vector

$$x' = x\mathbf{A}^{(T)}.$$

3. Suppose that the environment represented by the transition matrix given in (D.1) has a robot trap in S_{13} that results in certain death of the robot. We can represent this by making S_{13} an absorbing state by replacing the last row of $\mathbf{A}$ in (D.1) with

$$\{a_{13,j}\} = \begin{bmatrix} 0 & 0 & 0 & 0 & 0 & 0 & 0 & 0 & 0 & 0 & 0 & 0 & 1 \end{bmatrix}.$$

Given that the robot starts out in location S_1, what is the probability that the robot is dead at time T? (Solve this numerically.)
4. Suppose that a robot operating in the environment shown in Figure D.1 can sense its environment and knows that it is either in a hallway (H), a dead end (D), a corner (C), or a "T"-junction (T). What is the probability that a robot starting in S_1 will observe the sequence CHHTHC? (Implement the forward-backward algorithm.)
5. What is the optimal state sequence that explains the obervation obtained in the previous problem?

Bibliography

[1] A. Konar, A. Ghosh, and R. Janarthanan. Multi-robot cooperative box-pushing problem using multi-objective particle swarm optimization technique. In *World Congress on Information and Communication Technologies*, pages 272–277, Trivandrum, India, 2012.

[2] I. Abbott and A. von Doenhoff. *Theory of Wing Sections*. McGraw-Hill, New York, 1949.

[3] Y. I. Abdel-Aziz and H. M. Karara. Direct linear transformation into object space coordinates in close-range photogrammetry. In *Symposium on Close-Range Photogrammetry*, Urbana, IL, 1971.

[4] D. Adams. *The Hitch Hiker's Guide to the Galaxy*. Pan Books, London, 1979.

[5] D. Adams. *The Restaurant at the End of the Universe*. Pocket Books, New York, 1980.

[6] D. Adams. *Life, the Universe and Everything*. Pan Books, London, 1985.

[7] D. Adams. *So Long, and Thanks for All the Fish*. Harmony Books, New York, 1985.

[8] D. Adams. *Mostly Harmless*. Harmony, NY, 1992.

[9] P. Agre and D. Chapman. What are plans for? *Robotics and Autonomous Systems*, 6:17–34, 1990.

[10] P. E. Agre and D. Chapman. PENGI: An implementation of a theory of activity. In *Proc. of the 6th National Conference on AI*, volume 1, pages 268–272, Seattle, WA, 1987. Morgan Kaufman.

[11] L. Aguilar, R. Alami, S. Fleury, M. Herrb, F. Ingrand, and F. Robert. Ten autonomous mobile robots (and even more) in a route network like environment. In *IEEE/RSJ Conference on Intelligent Robots and Systems (IROS)*, volume 2, pages 260–267, Pittsburgh, PA, 1995.

[12] N. Ahmad. Line follower robot using CNN. Published online on towardsdatascience.com on April 3, 2019. Accessed October 10, 2022.

[13] M. Ahn, A. Brohan, N. Brown, *et al.* Do as I can, not as I say: Grounding language in robotic affordances, arXiv 2204.01691, 2022.

[14] I. F. Akyildiz, W. Su, Y. Sankarasubramaniam, and E. Cayirci. A survey on sensor networks. *IEEE Communications Magazine*, August:102–114, 2002.

[15] I. A. Al-Jazari. *The Book of Knowledge of Ingenious Mechanical Devices*. Pakistan Hijara Council, Islamabad, Pakistan, 1409. English translation by D. R. Hill in 1988.

[16] A. Alalewi, I. Dayoub, and S. Cherkaoui. On 5G-V2X use cases and enabling technologies: A comprehensive survey. *IEEE Access*, 9:107710–107737, 2021.

[17] R. Alami, S. Fleury, M. Herrb, F. Ingrand, and F. Robert. Multi-robot cooperation in the MARTHA project. *IEEE Robotics and Automation Magazine*, 5:36–47, 1998.

[18] A. Alarifi, A. Al-Salman, M. Alsaleh, *et al.* Ultra wideband indoor positioning technologies: Analysis and recent advances. *Sensors*, 16:707, 2016.

[19] G. Albi, D. Balague, J. A. Carrillo, and J. von Breicht. Stability analysis of flock and mill rings for second order models in swarming. *SIAM Journal on Applied Mathematics*, 74:794–818, 2014.

[20] J. S. Albus, H. G. McCain, and R. Lumia. NASA/NBS Standard Reference Model for Telerobot Control System Architecture (NASREM). Technical Report, National Bureau of Standards, Robot Systems Division, 1987.

[21] A. Alessandrini, F. Filipppi, G. Gallasi, M. Parent, and D. Stam. Parkshuttle II: Review of the Antibes experiment. In *10th international Conference on Automated People Movers*, Orlando, FL, 2005.

[22] J. C. Alexander and J. H. Maddocks. On the kinematics of wheeled mobile robots. *International Journal of Robotics Research*, 1990. Reprinted In I. J. Cox and G. T. Wilfong, editors, *Autonomous Robot Vehicles*, pages 5–24, Springer Verlag, New York, 1990.

[23] J. Y. Alloimonos, L. Weiss, and A. Bandyopadhyay. Active vision. In *Proc. 1st Internaional Conference on Computer Vision (ICCV)*, pages 35–54, London, UK, 1987.

[24] J. Y. Aloimonos. Perspective approximations. *Image and Vision Computing*, 8:179–192, 1990.

[25] S. Alpern and G. Shmuel. Rendezvous search on the line with distinguishable players. *SIAM Journal on Control and Optimization*, 33:1270–1276, July 1995.

[26] E. Altarawneh, M. Jenkin, and I. S. MacKenzie. Is putting a face on a robot worthwhile? In *Workshop on Active Vision and Perception in Human(-Robot) Collaboration*, held online, 2020. Held in conjunction with the 29th IEEE international Conference on Robot and Human Interactive Communication.

[27] N. M. Amato, O. B. Bayazit, L. K. Dale, C. Jones, and D. Vallejo. OBPRM: An obstacle-based PRM for 3D workspaces. In *Proc. 3rd Workshop on the Algorithm Foundations of Robotics (WAFR)*, pages 155–168, Natick, MA, 1998.

[28] N. M. Amosov, E. M. Kussul, and V. D. Fomenko. Transport robot with network control system. In *Proc. 4th IJCAI*, Tbilisi, USSR, 1975.

[29] J. Anderson and N. K. Chhabra. Maneuvering and stability performance of a robotic tuna. *Integrative and Comparative Biology*, 42:118–126, 2002.

[30] J. D. Anderson. *Fundamentals of Aerodynamics*. McGraw-Hill, New York, 2001. 3rd edition.

[31] R. J. Anderson. SMART: A modular control architecture for telerobotics. *IEEE Robotics and Automation Magazine*, 2(3):10–18, September 1995.

[32] F. Andreallo and N. Abe. Dance & robots: How might dance contribute to human robot interaction studies? *International Journal of Social Robotics*, June 2020.

[33] D. Angluin, J. Aspnes, Z. Diamadi, M. Fischer, and R. Peralta. Computation in networks of passively mobile finite-state sensors. *Distributed Computing*, 18:234–253, 2006.

[34] R. Aracil, R. Saltarén, and O. Reinoso. A climbing parallel robot. *IEEE Robotics and Automation Magazine*, 13:16–22, 2006.

[35] R. Arkin. *Governing Lethal Behavior in Autonomous Robots*. Chapman & Hall/CRC, 2009.

[36] R. Arkin and R. Murphy. Autonomous navigation in a manufacturing environment. *IEEE Transactions on Robotics and Automation*, 6:445–454, 1990.

[37] R. C. Arkin. Motor schema based navigation for a mobile robot: An approach to programming by behavior. In *Proc. of the IEEE Conference on Robotics and Automation*, pages 264–271, Raleigh, NC, 1987.

[38] R. C. Arkin. Motor-Schema-based mobile robot navigation. *International Journal of Robotics Research*, 8(4):92–112, 1989.

[39] R. C. Arkin. Navigational path planning for a vsion-based mobile robot. *Robotica*, 7:49–63, 1989.

[40] R. C. Arkin. Integrating behavioral, perceptual and world knowledge in reactive navigation. In P. Maes, editor, *Designing Autonomous Agents*, pages 105–122, MIT Press, Cambridge, MA, 1990.

[41] R. C. Arkin. *Behavior-Based Robotics*. MIT Press, Cambridge, MA, 1998.

[42] M. S. Arulampalam, S. Maskell, N. Gordon, and T. Clapp. A tutorial on particle filters for online nonlinear/non-Gaussian Bayesian tracking. *IEEE Transactions on Signal Processing*, 50:174–188, 2002.

[43] P. M. Asaro. What should we want from a robot ethics? *International Review of Information Ethics*, 6:9–16, 2006.

[44] B. Ash, editor. *The Visual Encyclopedia of Science Fiction*. Harmondy Books, New York, 1977.

[45] I. Asimov. *The Complete Robot*. Acacia Press, Amherst, MA, 1983.

[46] I. Asimov. Catch that rabbit. In M. Greenberg, editor, *The Asimov Chronicles, Volume I*. Ace Books, New York, 1990.

[47] I. Asimov. Runaround. In M. Greenberg, editor, *The Asimov Chronicles, Volume I*. Ace Books, New York, 1990.

[48] United Nations General Assembly. The Universal Declaration of Human Rights (UDHR), 1948.

[49] R. Atienza. *Advanced Deep Learning with TensorFlow 2 and Keras: Apply DL, GANs, VAEs, deep RL, unsupervised learning, object detection and segmentation, and more*. Packt Publsiher, Birmingham, UK, 2020. 2nd edition.

[50] D. Avis and H. Imai. Locating a robot with angle measurements. *Journal of Symbolic Computation*, 10:311–326, 1990.

[51] E. Awad, S. Dsouza, R. Kim, *et al*. The moral machine experiment. *Nature*, 563:59–64, 2018.

[52] K. Azarm and G. Schmidt. Conflict-free motion of multiple mobile robots based on decentralized motion planning and negotiation. In *IEEE International Conference on Robotics and Automation (ICRA)*, pages 3526–3533, Albuquerque, NM, 1997.

[53] R. A. Baeza-Yates, J. C. Culberson, and G. J. E. Rawlins. Searching in the plane. *Information and Computation*, 106:234–252, 1993.

[54] B. Baghi, A. Konar, F. Hogan, M. Jenkin, and G. Dudek. SESNO: Sample efficient social navigation from observation. In *IEEE/RSJ International Conference on Intelligent Robots and Systems (IROS)*, Kyoto, Japan, 2022.

[55] G. R. Baiden. Combining teleoperation with vehicle guidance for improving LHD productivity at Inco Ltd. *CIM Bulletin*, 87:36–39, 1994.

[56] T. Bailey and H. Durrant-Whyte. Simultaneous localization and mapping (SLAM): Part II. *IEEE Robotics and Automation Magazine*, 13:108–117, 2006.

[57] R. Bajcsy and D. A. Rosenthal. Visual and conceptual focus of attention. In S. Tanimoto and A. Klinger, editors, *Structured Computer Vision*, pages 133–149, Academic Press, New York, 1980.

[58] M. Bajracharya, M. W. Maimone, and D. Helmick. Autonomy for Mars rovers: Past, present, and future. *IEEE Computer*, 41:44–50, 2008.

[59] N. C. Baker, D. C. MacKenzie, and S. A. Ingalls. Development of an autonomous aerial vehicle: A case study. *Applied Intelligence*, 2:271–298, 1992.

[60] D. Ballard and C. Brown. *Computer Vision*. Prentice-Hall, Englewood Cliffs, NJ, 1982.

[61] D. H. Ballard. Modular learning in neural networks. In *AAAI-87 Proceedings*, Seattle, Wahington, 1987.

[62] A. Barco, C. de Jong, J. Peter, R. Kühne, and C. L. van Straten. Robot morphology and children's perception of social robots: An exploratory study. In *ACM/IEEE International Conference on Human-Robot Interaction*, page 125–127, Cambridge, United Kingdom, 2020.

[63] D. P. Barnes, P. Summers, and A. Shaw. An investigation into aerobot technologies for planetary exploration. In *6th ESA Workshop on Advanced Space Technologies for Robotics and Automation*, Noordwijk, the Netherlands, 2000.

[64] M. J. Barnes, K. A. Cosenzo, F. Jentsch, J. Y C. Chen, and P. McDermott. Understanding soldier robot teams in virtual environments. in virtual media for military applications. In *Proceedings RTO-MP-HFM-136*, pages 10–1 – 10–14, Neuilly-sur-Seine, France, 2006.

[65] A. H. Barr. Superquadrics and angle-preserving transformations. *IEEE Computer Graphics and Applications*, 1:11–23, 1981.

[66] J. Barraquand and J.-C. Latombe. Robot motion planning: A distributed representation approach. *International Journal of Robotics Research*, 10:628–649, 1991.

[67] S. Barrett, K. Genter, Y. He, *et al.* UT Austin Villa 2012: Standard platform league world champions. In X. Chen, P. Stone, L. E. Sucar, and T. V. D. Zant, editors, *RoboCup 2012: Robot Soccer World Cup XVI, Volume 7500 of Lecture Notes in Artificial Intelligence (LNAI)*. Springer, Berlin, 2013.

[68] C. Bartneck, E. Croft, D. Kulic, and S. Zoghbi. Measurement instruments for the anthropomorphism, animacy, likeability, perceived intelligence, and perceived safety of robots. *International Journal of Social Robotics*, 1:71–81, 2009.

[69] C. Bartneck, C. Lütge, A. Wagner, and S. Welsch. *An Introduction to Ethics and Robotics and AI*. Springer, Cham, 2021.

[70] R. Basri and E. Rivlin. Homing using combinations of model views. In *Proc. of the International Joint Conference of Artificial Intelligence*, pages 1656–1591, Chambery, France, August 1993.

[71] T. J. Bass. *Half Past Human*. Ballantine Books, New York, 1971.

[72] T. J. Bass. *The Godwhale*. Ballantine, New York, 1974.

[73] K. Basye and T. Dean. Map learning with indistinguishable locations. In M. Henrion, L. N. Kanal, and J. F. Lemmer, editors, *Uncertainty in Artificial Intelligence 5*, pages 331–340, Elsevier Science, Cambridge, MA, 1990.

[74] P. Batog and A. Woczowski. Odor markers detection system for mobile robot navigation. In *Eurosensors XXVI*, Kraków, Poland, 2012.

[75] H. Bay, A. Ess, T. Tuytelaars, and L. V. Gool. SURF: speeded up robust features. *Computer Vision Image Understanding*, 110:346–359, 2008.

[76] S. S. Beauchemin and J. L. Barron. The computation of optical flow. *ACM Computing Surveys*, 27:433–4666, 1995.

[77]   A. Beck, P. Stoica, and J. Li. Exact and approximate solutions of source localization problems. *IEEE Transactions on Signal Processing*, 56:1770–1778, 2008.

[78]   G. A. Bekey. Biologically inspired control of autonomous robots. *Robotics and Autonomous Systems*, 18:21–31, 1996.

[79]   R. E. Bellman. *Dynamic Programming*. Princeton University Press, Princeton, NJ, 1957. Republished 2003, Dover.

[80]   G. Benford. *In the Ocean of Night*. The Dial Press, New York, 1977.

[81]   G. Beni and J. Wang. Swarm intelligence in cellular robotic systems. In *Proc. NATO Advanced Workshop on Robotics and Biological Systems*, Il Ciocco, Tuscany, Italy, 1989.

[82]   F. Berlinger, M. Saadat, H. Haj-Hariri, G. V. Lauder, and R. Nagpal. Fish-like three-dimensional swimming with an autonomous, multi-fin, and biomimetic robot. *Bioinspiration & Biomimetics*, 16:026018, 2021.

[83]   A. Bertolini and F. Episcopo. Robots and AI as legal subjects? Disentangling the ontological and functional perspective. *Frontiers in Robotics and AI*, April, 2022.

[84]   D. P. Bertsekas and J. N. Tsitsiklis. *Introduction to Probability*. Athena Scientific, Nashua, NH, 2002.

[85]   C. Bethel and R. Murphy. Review of human studies methods in HRI and recommendations. *International Journal of Social Robotics*, 2:347–359, 2010.

[86]   M. Betke and L. Gurvits. Mobile robot localization using landmakrs. *IEEE Transactions on Robotics and Automation*, 13(2):251–263, 1997.

[87]   J. Biesiadecki, E. Baumgartner, R. Bonitz, *et al.* Mars exploration rover surface operations: Driving opportunity at meridiana planum. *IEEE Robotics and Automation Magazine*, 13, 2006.

[88]   M. Billinghurst, H. Kato, and I. Poupyrev. The MagicBook: A transitional AR interface. *Computers and Graphics*, 25(5):745–753, 2001.

[89]   J. A. Bilmes. A gentle tutorial of the EM algorithm and its application to parameter estimation for Gaussian mixture and hidden Markov models. Technical Report TR-97-021, International Computer Science Institute, Berkeley, CA, 1998.

[90]   P. Biswal and P. K. Kohanty. Development of quadruped walking robots: A review. *Ain Shams Engineering Journal*, 12:2017–2031, 2021.

[91]   A. Blake and A. Yuille, editors. *Active Vision*. MIT Press, Cambridge, MA, 1992.

[92]   R. P. Blakemore and R. B. Frankel. Magnetic navigation in bacteria. *Scientific American*, 245, 1981.

[93]   J. E. Blamont. Implications of the VEGA balloon results for atmospheric dynamics. *Scuebce*, 231: 1422–1425, 1986.

[94]   W. Bluethmann, R. Ambrose, M. Diftler, *et al.* Robonaut: A robot designed to work with humans in space. *Autonomous Robots*, 14:179–197, 2003.

[95]   M. Blum and D. Kozen. On the power of the compass (or why mazes are easier to search than graphs). In *19th Annual Symposium on the Foundations of Computer Science*, pages 132–142, October 1978.

[96]   B. Bogert, J. Healy, and J. Tukey. The quefrequency analysis of time series for echoes: Cepstrum, pseudo-autocovariance, cross-cepstrum and saphe cracking. In M. Rosenblat, editor, *Proc. Symposium on Time Series Analysis*, pages 209–243, Wiley, New York, 1963.

[97]   M. Bojarski, D. W. del Testa, D. Dworakowski, *et al.* End to end learning for self-driving car. *ArXiv*, abs/1604.07316, 2016.

[98]   M. Bolduc and M. D. Levine. A foveated retina system for robotic vision. In *Proc. Vision Interface'94*, Banff, Canada, 1994.

[99]   D. L. Boley, E. S. Steinmetz, and K. Sutherland. Robot localization from landmarks using recursive total least squares. In *IEEE International Conference on Robotics and Automation (ICRA)*, pages 1381–1386, Minneapolis MN, April 1996.

[100] A. Bonarini. Communication in human-robot interaction. *Current Robotics Reports*, 1:279–285, 2020.

[101] V. Boor, M. H. Overmars, and A. F. van der Stappen. The Gaussian sampling strategy for probabilistic roadmap planners. In *Proc. IEEE/RSJ International Conference on Intelligent Robots and Systems (IROS)*, pages 1018–1023, 1999.

[102] J. Borenstein, F. S. Grodzinsky, A. Howard, K. W. Miller, and M. J. Wolf. AI Ethics: A long history and a recent burst of attention. *IEEE Computer*, 54:98–102, 2021.

[103] J. Borenstein and Y. Koren. Real-time obstacle avoidance for fast mobile robots. *IEEE Transactions on Systems, Man, and Cybernetics*, 19:1179–1187, 1989.

[104] J. Borenstein and Y. Koren. The vector field histogram – fast obstacle avoidance for mobile robots. *IEEE Transactions on Robotics and Automation*, 7:278–288, 1991.

[105] P. K. Bose. Visibility in simple polygons. Master's thesis, University of Waterloo, Waterloo, Ontario, Canada, December 1991.

[106] A. Bouman, M. F. Ginting, N. A. Matteo Palieri, *et al*. Autonomous spot: Long-range autonomous exploration of extreme environments with legged locomotion. In *IEEE/RSJ International Conference on Intelligent Robots and Systems (IROS)*, Las Vegas, NV, 2020.

[107] D. M. Bourg. *Physics for Game Developers*. O'Reilly and Associates, Sebastopol, CA, 2002.

[108] E. Bourque and G. Dudek. Automated image-based mapping. In *Workshop on Perception for Mobile Agents*, pages 61–70, IEEE/CVPR, Santa Barbara, CA, 1998.

[109] E. Bourque, G. Dudek, and P. Ciaravola. Robotic sightseeing – a method for automatically creating virtual environments. In *IEEE International Conference on Robotics and Automation (ICRA)*, pages 3186–3191, Leuven, Belgium, 1998.

[110] J. Boyd. Sony unleases new Aibo robot dog. *IEEE Spectrum*, November, 2017.

[111] S. M. Bozic. *Digital and Kalman Filtering*. Halsted Press, Sydney, 1979.

[112] A. M. Bradley and D. R. Yoerger. Design and testing of the autonomous benthic explorer. In *Proc. AUVS-93 20th Annual Technical Symposium and Exhibition*, page 1044, Washington, DC, 1993.

[113] M. Brambilla. Formal methods for the deisign and analysis of robot swarms. PhD thesis, Ecole Polytechnique de Bruxelles, Belgium, 2014.

[114] M. Brambilla, E. Ferrante, M. Birattari, and M. Dorigo. Swarm robotics: A review from the swarm engineering perspective. *Swarm Intelligence*, 7:1–41, 2013.

[115] T. Bräunl. *Embedded Robotics*. Springer, Berlin, 2006. 2nd edition.

[116] C. Breazeal. Emotion and sociable humanoid robots. *International Journal of Human-Computer Studies*, 59:119–155, 2003.

[117] C. Breazeal and P. Fitzpatrick. That certain look: Social amplification of animate vision. In *Proc. AAAI Fall Symp. Soc. Intel. Agents–The Human in the Loop*, 2000.

[118] C. Breazeal, C. D. Kidd, A. L. Thomaz, G. Hoffman, and M. Berlin. Effects of nonverbal communication on efficiency and robustness in human-robot teamwork. In *IEEE/RSJ Int. Conf. on Intelligent Robots and Systems (IROS)*, page 708–713, Edmonton, Alberta, 2005.

[119] Q. Bremas, A. Lamani, and S. Tixeul. Stand up indulgent rendezvous. In S. Devismes and N. Mittal, editors, *International Symposium on Stabilizing, Safety, and Security of Distributed Systems*. Springer, 2020. Stabilization, Safety, and Security of Distributed Systems. SSS 2020. Lecture Notes in Computer Science, vol. 12514.

[120] P. Bremaud. *Markov Chains, Gibbs Fields, Monte Carlo Simulation, and Queues*. Springer, New York, 1999.

[121] M. Briot and A. R. de Saint-Vincent. Three dimensional perceptory systems for autonomous mobile robots. In *Proc. 6th International Conference on Robot Vision and Sensory Controls*, pages 127–137, Paris, France, 1986.

[122] M. Briot, J. C. Talou, and G. Bauzil. Le systeme de perception du robot mobile HILARE. In *2eme Congres AFCET/IRIA*, Toulouse, France, 1979.

[123] E. Broadbent, V. Kumar, X. Li, *et al*. Robots with display screens: A robot with a more humanlike face display is perceived to have more mind and a better personality. *PLoS ONE*, 8, 2013.

[124] W. Brogan. *Modern Control Theory*. Prentice Hall, Englewood Cliffs, NJ, 1990. 3rd edition.

[125] R. Brooks. Intelligence without reason. In *Proc. 12th IJCAI*, pages 569–595, Sydney, Australia, 1991.

[126] R. Brooks. *Flesh and Machines: How Robots Will Change Us*. Knopf Doubleday, New York, 2003.

[127] R. A. Brooks. Solving the find-path problem by a good representation of free space. *IEEE Transactions on Systems, Man, and Cybernetics*, 13:190–197, 1983.

[128] R. A. Brooks. A robust layered control system for a mobile robot. Technical Report AI Memo 864, MIT AI Laboratory, Boston, MA, 1985.

[129] R. A. Brooks. A robust layered control system for a mobile robot. *IEEE Journal of Robotics and Automation*, 2:14–23, 1986.

[130] R. A. Brooks. A robot that walks: Emergent behaviors from a carefully evolved network. In P. H. Winston and S. A. Shellard, editors, *Artificial Intelligence at MIT Expanding Frontiers, Volume II*, pages 29–39, MIT Press, Cambridge, MA, 1990.

[131] R. A. Brooks. A robust layered control system for a mobile robot. In P. H. Winston and S. A. Shellard, editors, *Artificial Intelligence at MIT Expanding Frontiers, Volume II*, pages 3–27. MIT Press, Cambridge, MA, 1990.

[132] B. Brumitt and A. Stentz. Dynamic mission planning for multiple mobile robots. In *IEEE International Conference on Robotics and Automation (ICRA)*, pages 2396–2401, Minneapolis, MN, April 1996.

[133] B. Brumitt and M. Hebert. Experiments in autonomous driving with concurrent goals and multiple vechicles. In *IEEE International Conference on Robotics and Automation (ICRA)*, pages 1895–1902, 1998.

[134] B. Brumitt and A. Stentz. Dynamic mission planning for multiple mobile robots. In *IEEE International Conference on Robotics and Automation (ICRA)*, pages 2396–2401, Minneapolis, MN, April 1996.

[135] M. Bualat, J. Barlow, T. Fong, C. Provencher, and T. Smith. Astrobee: Developing a free-flying robot for the international space station. In *American Institute of Aeronautics and Astronautics (AIAA) Space Conference and Exposition*, Pasadena, CA, 2015.

[136] P. L. Buono and M. Golubitsky. Models of central pattern generators for quaduped locomotion: I. primary gaits. *Journal of Mathematical Biology*, 42(4):291–326, 2001.

[137] W. Burgard, M. Moors, D. Fox, R. Simmon, and S. Thrun. Collaborative multi-robot exploration. In *Proc. IEEE Interantioanl Conference on Robotics and Automation (ICRA)*, San Francisco, CA, 2000.

[138] W. Burgard, M. Moors, C. Stachniss, and F. Schneider. Coordinated multi-robot exploration. *IEEE Trans. on Robotics*, 21, 2005.

[139] R. D. Caballar. What is the uncanny valley? *IEEE Spectrum*, 2019.

[140] M. Calistis, G. Picardi, and C. Lascho. Fundamentals of soft robot locomotion. *Journal of the Royal Society Interface*, 1420170101, 2017.

[141] M. Calonder, V. Lepetit, C. Strecha, and P. Fua. BRIEF: Binary robust independent elementary features. In *Proc. European Conference on Computer Vision (ECCV)*, Heraklion, Greece, 2010.

[142] G. Campion, G. Bastin, and B. D'Andrea-Novel. Structural properties and classification of kinematic and dynamic models of wheeled mobile robots. *IEEE Transactions on Robotics and Automation*, 12(1):47–62, 1996.

[143] G. Canal, M. Cashmore, S. Krivić, *et al*. Probabilistic planning for robotics with ROSPlan. In *Annual Conference Towards Autonomous Robotic Systems Conference*, London, UK, 2019. In *Towards Autonomous Robotic Systems, Volume 11649* of *Lecture Notes in Computer Science*, pp. 236–250, Springer, Cham, 2019.

[144] J. Canny. A computational approach to edge detection. *IEEE Transactions on Pattern Analysis and Machine Intelligence*, 8(6):679–698, 1986.

[145] Y. U. Cao, A. S. Fukunaga, A. B. Kahng, and F. Meng. Cooperative mobile robotics: Antecedents and directions. In *IEEE/RSJ Conference on Intelligent Robots and Systems (IROS), Volume I*, pages 226–234, Pittsburgh, PA, 1995.

[146] M. Cappuccio, A. Peeters, and W. McDonald. Sympathy for Dolores: Moral consideration for robots based on virtue and recognition. *Philosophy & Technology*, 33:9–31, 2020.

[147] G. Casella and C. P. Robert. Rao Blackwellisation of sampling schemes. *Biometrika*, 83:81–94, 1996.

[148] A. Cass, K. Striegnitz, N. Webb, and V. Yu. Exposing real-world challenges using HRI in the wild. In *The 4th Workshop on Public Space Human-Robot Interaction (PubRob 2018)*, Barcelona, Spain, 2018. Held as part of the International Conference on Human-Computer Interaction with Mobile Devices and Services (MobileHCI).

[149] A. R. Cassandra, L. P. Kaelbling, and J. A. Kurien. Acting under uncertainty: Discrete Bayesian models for mobile robot navigation. In *IEEE/RSJ International Conference on Intelligent Robots and Systems (IROS)*, 1996.

[150] F. Cavallo, F. Semeraro, L. Fiorini, G. Magyar, P. Sincak, and P. Dario. Emotion modelling for social robotics applications: A review. *Journal of Bionic Engineering*, 15:185–203, 2018.

[151] P. D. Cha and J. I. Molinder. *Fundamentals of Signals and Systems: A Building Block Approach*. Cambridge University Press, Cambridge, 2006.

[152] D. J. Chalmers. The singularity: A philosophical analysis. *Journal of Consciousness Studies*, 17:7–65, 2010.

[153] S. Chamorro, J. Collier, and F. Grondin. Neural network based lidar gesture recognition for realtime robot teleoperation. In *IEEE International Conference on Safety, Security, and Rescue Robots*, New York, NY, 2021.

[154] A. Chang. The intelligent vehicle on an automated high ways system: ADVANCE-F. In *Proc. IAS-3*, pages 225–229, Pittsburgh, PA, 1993.

[155] R. Chatila and J. Laumond. Position referencing and consistent world modelling for mobile robots. In *IEEE International Conference on Robotics and Automation (ICRA)*, pages 138–170, 1985.

[156] R. Chaturvedi, P. Dymond, and M. Jenkin. Efficient leader election among numbered agents. In *International Conference on Data Engineering and Internet Technology*, 2011.

[157] M. Chen, T. M. Jochem, and D. A. Pomerleau. AURORA: A vision-based roadway departure warning system. In *IEEE/RSJ Conference on Intelligent Robots and Systems (IROS)*, pages 243–248, Pittsburgh, PA, 1995.

[158] Y. Chen, Y. Luo, C. Yang, *et al.* Human mobile robot interaction in the retail environment. *Scientific Data*, 9:673, 2022.

[159] M. Cheney. *Tesla, Man Out of Time*. Prentice-Hall, Englewood Cliffs, NJ, 1981.

[160] D. Chiarella, M. Bibuli, G. Bruzzone, *et al.* A novel gesture-based language for underwater human–robot interaction. *Journal of Marine Science and Engineering*, 6:91, 2018.

[161] S. K. Choi. Design of advanced underwater robotic vehicle and graphic workstation. In *IEEE International Conference on Robotics and Automation (ICRA)*, volume 2, pages 99–105, Atlanta, GA, 1993.

[162] S. K. Choi, J. Yuh, and G. Y Takashige. Development of the omni-directional intelligent navigator. *IEEE Robotics & Automation Magazine*, 2:44–51, 1995.

[163] A. Chopra. An empirical approach to path planning in unstructured outdoor environments. MSc thesis, Department of Computer Science and Engineering, York University, 2009.

[164] H. Choset, K. Lynch, S. Hutchinson, *et al. Principles of Robot Motion: Theory, Algoirhtms, and Implementations*. MIT Press, Cambridge, MA, 2005.

[165] W. W. Chow, J. Geo-Banacloche, L. M. Pedrotti, *et al.* The ring laser gyro. *Reviews of Modern Physics*, 57(1):61–104, 1985.

[166] J. Clark and N. Ferrier. Attentive visual servoing. In *Active Vision*, pages 137–154, MIT Press, Cambridge, MA, 1992.

[167] A. C. Clarke. *2001: A Space Odyssey*. Hutchinson/Star, London, 1968.

[168] L. Clemente, A. Davison, I. Reid, J. Neira, and J. D. Tardós. Mapping large loops with a single hand-held camera. In *Robotics: Science and Systems (RSS)*, Altanta, GA, 2007.

[169] R. Codd-Downey and M. Jenkin. Milton: An open hardware underwater autonomous vehicle. In *2017 IEEE International Conference on Information and Automation (ICIA)*, Macao, China, 2017.

[170] R. Codd-Downey and M. Jenkin. Human robot interaction using diver hand signals. In *CACM/IEEE International Conference on Human-Robot Interaction*, Daegu, Korea, 2019. Late-breaking report.

[171] R. Codd-Downey, M. Jenkin, and K. Allison. Milton: An open hardware underwater autonomous vehicle. In *Proc. IEEE ICIA*, Macau, China, 2017.

[172] R. Codd-Downey, M. Jenkin, B. B. Dey., *et al.* Monitoring re-growth of invasive plants using an autonomous surface vessel. *Frontiers Robotics and AI*, 7:583416, 2021.

[173] R. Codd-Downey, P. Mojiri Forooshani, A. Speers, H. Wang, and M. Jenkin. From ROS to unity: Leveraging robot and virtual environment middleware for immersive teleoperation. In *IEEE International Conference on Information and Automation (ICIA)*, pages 932–936, 2014.

[174] M. Coeckelbergh. *Robot Ethics*. MIT Press, Cambridge, MA, 2022.

[175] D. Coelho and M. Oliveira. A review of end-to-end autonomous driving in urban environments. *IEEE Access*, 10:75296–75311, 2022.

[176] L. S. Coles, A. M. Robb, P. L. Sinclair, M. H. Smith, and R. B. Sobek. Decision analysis for an experimental robot with unreliable sensors. In *Proc. 4th IJCAI*, pages 749–757, Tbilisi, USSR, 1975.

[177] M. Colledanchise and P. Ögren. *Behavior Trees in Robotics and AI: An Introduction*. CRC Press, New York, 2019.

[178] C. Connolly. Harmonic functions and collision probabilities. In *Proc. of the International Conference on Robotics and Automation*, pages 3015–3019, IEEE Press, San Diego, CA, 1994.

[179] C. Connolly and R. Grupen. On the applications of harmonic functions to robotics. *Journal of Robotic Systems*, 10:931–946, 1993.

[180] M. Cook. *Flight Dynamcis Principles*. Butterworth-Heinemann, Oxford, UK, 1997.

[181] P. I. Corke, D. Hainsworth, G. Winstanley, Y. Li, and H. Gurgenci. Automated control of a dragline using machine vision. In *Proc. Electrical Engineering Congress*, pages 597–600, Sydney, Australia, 1994.

[182] P. I. Corke, G. J. Winstanley, J. M. Roberts, and Z.-D. Li. Applications of robotics and robot vision to mining automation. In *Proc. Workshop on Robotics and Robot Vision*, pages 56–61, Gold Coast, Australia, 1996.

[183] T. H. Cormen, C. E. Leiserson, and R. L. Rivest. *Introduction to Algorithms*. MIT Press, Cambridge, MA, 1990.

[184] J. Cortés, S. Martínez, T. Karatas, and F. Bullo. Coverage control for mobile sensing networks. *IEEE Transactions Robotics and Automation*, 20:243–255, 2004.

[185] M. Cortés. *The Arte of Navigation*. Scholar's Facsimiles and Reprints, Delmar, NY, 1561/1992. A facsimile reproduction with an introduction by D. W. Waters.

[186] E. Coste-Manière and R. Simmons. Architecture, the backbone of robotic systems. In *Proc. IEEE International Conference on Robotics and Automation*, San Fancisco, CA, 2000.

[187] Ë. Coste-Manière and R. Simmons. Architecture, the backbone of robotic systems. In *Proc. IEEE ICRA*, pages 67–72, San Francisco, CA, 2000.

[188] R. Courant and D. Hilbert. *Methods of Mathematical Physics, Volume I*. Interscience, New York, 1937.

[189] J. A. Cover and M. Curd. *Philosophy of Science: The Central Issues*. W. W. Norton, New York, 1989.

[190] D. R. Cox and H. D. Miller. *The Theory of Stochastic Processes*. Wiley, New York, 1965.

[191] I. J. Cox. Blanche – an experiment in guidance and navigation of an autonomous robot vehicle. *IEEE Transactions on Robotics and Automation*, 7(2):193–204, April 1991.

[192] I. J. Cox and G. T. Wilfong, editors. *Autonomous Robot Vehicles*. Springer-Verlag, New York, 1990.

[193] J. C. Craig. *Introduction to Robots*. Addison-Wesley, Don Mills, Ontario, Canada, 1986.

[194] A. Crespi, A. Badertscherand A. Guignard, and A. J. Ijspeert. Swimming and crawling with an amphibious snake robot. In *IEEE International Conference on Robotics and Automation (ICRA)*, *Volume 2005*, pages 3024 – 3028, 2005.

[195] M. Croll. *The History of Landmines*. Leo Cooper, London, UK, 1998.

[196] J. L. Crowley, P. Bobet, and M. Mesrabi. Layered control of a binocular head. In *SPIE Conference on AI X: Machine Vision and Robotics*, pages 47–61, Orlando, FL, 1992.

[197] J. L. Crowley and H. I. Christensen, editors. *Vision as Process*. Springer-Verlag, Berlin, 1995.

[198] J. L. Crowley and A. Parker. Transfer function analysis of picture processing operators. In R. M. Haralick and J. C. Simon, editors, *Issues in Digital Signal Processing*, pages 3–30, Sitjhoff and Hoordhoff, Germantown, MD, 1980.

[199] J. L. Crowley, F. Wallner, and B. Schiele. Position estimation using principal components of range data. In *Proc. of the IEEE Conference on Robotics and Automation*, pages 3131–3128, Leuven, Belgium, 1998.

[200] M. Cummins and P. Newman. Accelerated appearance-only SLAM. In *IEEE Int. Conference on Robotics and Automation (ICRA)*, pages 1828–1833, Pasadena, CA, 2008.

[201] Cyclovision Technologies, Inc. *The ParaCamera System*. Undated product sheet.

[202] DARPA. Strategic Computing. New-Generation Computing Technology: A Strategic Plan for Its Development an Application to Critical Problems in Defense. 1983.

[203] A. Datta and C. Icking. Competitive searching in a generalized street. In *Proceedings of the Tenth Annual Symposium on Computational Geometry*, pages 175–182, Stony Brook, NY, June 6–8 1994. ACM Press.

[204] J. G. Daugman. Six formal properties of two-dimensional anisotropic visual filters: Structural principles and frequency/orientation selectivity. *IEEE Transactions on Systems, Man and Cybernetics*, 13:882–887, 1983.

[205] E. R. Davies. *Computer Vision: Principles, Algorithms, Applications, Learning*. Academic Press, New York, 2017. 5th edition.

[206] J. Davis. *The Seaman's Secrets*. Scholar's Facsimiles and Reprints, Delmar, NY, 1633/1992. A facsimile reproduction with an introduction by A. N. Ryan.

[207] A. J. Davison and N. Kita. Active visual localization for cooperating inspection robots. In *IEEE/RSJ Conference on Intelligent Robots and Systems (IROS)*, pages 1709–1715, Takamatsu, Japan, 2000.

[208] J. de la Tejera, R. Bustamante-Bello, R. A. Ramirez-Mendoza, and J. Izquierdo-Reyes. Systematic review of exoskeletons towards a general categorization model proposal. *Applied Sciences*, 11:1–25, 2020.

[209] P. G. de Santos, P. V. Nagy, and W. L. Whittaker. Leveling of the Ambler walking machine: A comparison of methods. Technical Report CMU-RI-TR-91-13, Robotics Institute, Carnegie Mellon University, Pittsburgh, PA, 1991.

[210] M. DeGroot and M. Schervish. *Probability and Statistics*. Addison-Wesley, Reading, MA, 2001.

[211] F. Dellaert, D. Fox, W. Burgard, and S. Thrun. Monte Carlo localization for mobile robots. In *Proc. IEEE International Conference on Robotics and Automation (ICRA)*, pages 1322–1328, Detroit, MI, 1999.

[212] F. Dellaert and M. Kaess. *Factor Graphs for Robot Perception*. Now Publishers Inc., Boston, 2017.

[213] F. Dellaert and M. Kaess. Factor graphs for robot percetpion. *Foundations and Trends in Robotics*, 6:1–139, 2017.

[214] Frank Dellaert and GTSAM Contributors. borglab/gtsam, May 2022.

[215] C. Delporte-Gallet, H. Fauconnier, R. Guerraoui, and E. Ruppert. When birds die: Making population protocols fault tolerant. In *IEEE International Conference on Distributed Computing in Sensor Systems*, pages 51–66, San Francisco, CA, 2006.

[216] J. Deneubourg, S. Aron, S. Goss, and J. Pasteels. The self-organising exploratory pattern of the Argentine ant. *Journal of Insect Behaviour*, 3:159–168, 1990.

[217] X. Deng and A. Mirzaian. Competitive robot mapping with homogeneous markers. *IEEE Transactions on Robotics and Automation*, 12(4):532–542, 1996.

[218] Denning Mobile Robots Inc. Modular Research Vehicle MRV-1: Heavy duty mobile robot. Undated product sheet.

[219] R. Deriche. Using Canny's criteria to derive an optimal edge detector recursively implemented. *International Journal of Computer Vision*, 2:167–187, 1987.

[220] R. Deriche and G. Giraudon. A computational approach for corner and vertex detection. *International Journal of Computer Vision*, 1:167–187, 1993.

[221] A. Desrochers, editor. *Intelligent Robotic Systems for Space Exploration*. Kluwer Academic Pubs, Boston, 1992.

[222] B. B. Dey and M. Jenkin. Design and construction of the DragonBall. In *Proc. ROMANSY*, Sapporo, Japan., 2020.

[223] P. K. Dick. *Do Androids Dream of Electric Sheep?* Ballantine Books, New York, 1982.

[224] F. J. Diego-Rasilla, R. M. Luengo, and J. B. Phillips. Magnetic compass mediates nocturnal homing by the alpine newt, *Triturus alpestris*. *Behavioral Ecology and Sociobiology*, 58:361–365, 2005.

[225] M. R. Dimitrijevic, Y. Gerasimenko, and M. M. Pinter. Evidence for a spinal central pattern generator in humans. *Annals of the New York Academy of Sciences*, 16:360–376, 1998.

[226] M. W. M. G. Dissanayake, P. M. Newman, H. F. Durrant-Shyte, S. Clark, and M. Csorba. A solution to the simultaneous localization and map building (SLAM) problem. *IEEE Transactions on Robotics and Automation*, 17:229–241, 2001.

[227] A. H. Dittman and T. P. Quinn. Homing in Pacific salmon: Mechanisms and ecological basis. *Journal of Experimental Biology*, 199:83–91, 1996.

[228] B. R. Donald. A search algorithm for motion planning with six degrees of freedom. *Artificial Intelligence*, 31:295–353, 1987.

[229] M. Dorigo, G. Théraulaz, and V. Trianni. Reflections on the future of swarm robotics. *Science Robotics, American Association for the Advancement of Science (AAAS)*, 5:49, 2020.

[230] K. Dowling. Limbless locomotion: Learning to crawl with a snake robot. PhD thesis, Carnegie Mellon University, Pittsburgh, PA, 1997.

[231] S. Dubowsky and E. Papadopoulos. The kinematics, dynamics and control of free-flying and free-floating space robotic systems. *Special Issue on Space Robotics of the IEEE Transactions on Robotics and Automation*, 9:531–543, 1993.

[232] G. Dudek. Environment mapping using multiple abstraction levels. *Proceedings of the IEEE*, 84:1684–1704, 1996.

[233] G. Dudek, P. Giguere, C. Prahacs, *et al.* AQUA: An amphibious autonomous robot. *IEEE Computer*, January:46–53, 2007.

[234] G. Dudek, M. Jenkin, E. Milios, and D. Wilkes. Robotic exploration as graph construction. Technical Report RBCV-TR-88-23, Research in Biological and Computational Vision, Department of Computer Science, University of Toronto, Toronto, 1988.

[235] G. Dudek, M. Jenkin, E. Milios, and D. Wilkes. Map validation and self-location in a graph-like world. In *Proc. of the Thirteenth International Conference on Artificial Intelligence*, pages 1648–1653, Chambery, France, August 1993.

[236] G. Dudek, M. Jenkin, E. Milios, and D. Wilkes. On the utility of multi-agent autonomous robot systems. In *Proc. IJCAI-93 Workshop on Dynamically Interacting Robots*, pages 101–108, Chambéry, France, 1993.

[237] G. Dudek, M. Jenkin, E. Milios, and D. Wilkes. A taxonomy for swarm robotics. In *IEEE/RSJ Conference on Intelligent Robots and Systems (IROS)*, pages 441–447, Yokohama, Japan, 1993.

[238] G. Dudek, M. Jenkin, E. Milios, and D. Wilkes. Experiments in sensing and communication for robot convoy navigation. In *IEEE/RSJ Conference on Intelligent Robots and Systems (IROS)*, pages 268–273, 1995.

[239] G. Dudek, M. Jenkin, E. Milios, and David Wilkes. Robotic exploration as graph construction. *IEEE Transactions on Robotics and Automation*, 7(6):859–864, 1991.

[240] G. Dudek, M. R. M. Jenkin, E. Milios, and D. Wilkes. A taxonomy for multi-agent robotics. *Autonomous Robots*, 3:375–397, 1996.

[241] G. Dudek and D. Jugessur. Robust place recognition using local appearance based methods. In *IEEE Int. Conf. on Robotics and Automation (ICRA)*, pages 1030–1035, San Francisco, CA, 2000.

[242] G. Dudek, K. Romanik, and S. Whitesides. Localizing a robot with minimum travel. Technical Report SOCS-94.5, School of Computer Science, McGill University, Montreal, August 1994.

[243] G. Dudek, K. Romanik, and S. Whitesides. Localizing a robot with minimum travel. In *Proc. Sixth ACM-SIAM Symposium of Discrete Algorithms*, pages 437–446, San Francisco, CA, 1995.

[244] H. Durrant-Whyte and T. Bailey. Simultaneous localisation and mapping (SLAM): part I the essential algorithms. *IEEE Robotics and Automation Magazine*, 13:99–110, 2006.

[245] H. Durrant-Whyte, S. Majumder, S. Thrun, M. de Battista, and S. Schelding. A Bayesian algorithm for simultaneous localization and map building. In *Springer Tracts in Advanced Robotics*, volume 6, pages 49–60. Springer, New York, 2003.

[246] R. T. Dyde, M. R. Jenkin, and L. R. Harris. The subjective visual vertical and the perceptual upright. *Experimental Brain Research*, 173:612–622, 2006.

[247] D. Edmonds. *Would You Kill the Fat Man? The Trolley Problem and What Your Answer Tells Us about Right and Wrong*. Princeton University Press, Princeton, NJ, 2013.

[248] M. Egerstedt and X. Hu. Formation constrained multi-agent control. *IEEE Transactions and Robotics and Automation*, 17:947–951, 2001.

[249] A. Elfes. Sonar-based real-world mapping and navigation. *IEEE Journal of Robotics and Automation*, 3:249–265, 1987.

[250] A. Eliazar and R. Parr. DP-SLAM: Fast, robust simultaneous localization and mapping without predetermined landmarks. In *International Joint Conference on Artificial Intelligence (IJCAI)*, pages 1135–1142, Acapulco, Mexico, 2003.

[251] A. Eliazar and R. Parr. DP-SLAM 2.0. In *IEEE International Conference on Robotics and Automation (ICRA)*, pages 1314–1320, New Orleans, LA, 2004.

[252] R. Ellepola and P. Kovesi. Mobile robot navigation in a semi-structured environment. In *Proc. International Conference on Control, Automation, Robotics and Vision (ICARCV), Volume 2*, pages 914–918, Singpaore, 1996.

[253] J. Enavit and R. S. Hartenberg. A kinematic notation for lower-pair mechanisms based on matricies. *Journal of Applied Mechanics*, 222(2):215–221, 1955.

[254] S. P. Engelson and D. V. McDermott. Image signatures for place recognition and map construction. In *SPIE Proc. Sensor Fusion IV: Control Paradigms and Data Structures*, pages 282–293, 1991.

[255] M. F. Ercan. Design of a robot colony and its application in entertainment robots. In *Second International Conference on Autonomous Robots and Agents*, pages 249–253, Palmerson North, New Zealand, 2004.

[256] M. Erdmann and T. Lozano-Pérez. On multiple moving objects. *Algorithmica*, 2(4):477–521, 1987.

[257] U. Eriksson. Some geometric localization problems with applications in robotics. MSc thesis, Luleå Tekniska Universitet, Sweeden, 1998.

[258] H. R. Everett. *Sensors for Mobile Robots: Theory and Applications*. A. K. Peters, Wellesley, MA, 1995.

[259] A. Farchi and M. Bocquet. Comparison of local particle filters and new implementations. *Nonlin. Processes Geophys.*, 25:765–807, 2018.

[260] G. Farin. *NURB Curves and Surfaces from Projective Geometry to Practical Use*. A. K. Peters, Wellesley, MA, 1995.

[261] G. Farnebäck. Two-frame motion estimation based on polynomial expansion. In J. Bigun and T. Gustavsson, editors, *Image Analysis. SCIA 2003. Lecture Notes in Computer Science, Volume 2749*. Springer, Berlin, 2003.

[262] O. Faugeras. *Three-Dimensional Computer Vision: A Geometric Viewpoint*. MIT Press, Cambridge, MA, 1993.

[263] O. D. Faugeras and G. Toscani. Camera calibration for 3D computer vision. In *International Workshop on Industrial Applications of Machine Vision and Machine Intelligence*, pages 240–247, Silken, Japan, 1987.

[264] E. A. Feinberg and A. Shwartz, editors. *Handbook of Markov Decision Processes*. Kluwer, Boston, MA, 2002.

[265] N. J. Ferrier and J. J. Clark. The Harvard binocular head. In *Active Robot Vision: Camera Heads, Model Based Navigation and Reactive Control*, pages 9–32, World Scientific Press, Singapore, 1993.

[266] L. Ferrière, B. Raucent, and J.-C. Semin. ROLLMOBS, a new omnidirectional robot. In *IEEE/RSJ Conference on Intelligent Robots and Systems (IROS)*, pages 913–918, Grenoble, France, 1997.

[267] E. Fersini, E. Messina, G. Arosio, and F. Archetti. Audio-based emotion recognition in judicial domain: A multilayer support vector machines approach. *Machine Learning and Data Mining in Pattern Recognition Lecture Notes in Computer Science*, pages 594–602, 2009.

[268] J. Feruson and A. Pope. Theseus: Multipurpose Canadian AUV. *Sea Technology Magazine*, pages 19–26, April, 1995.

[269] R. P. Feynman, R. B. Leighton, and M. Sands. *The Feynman Lectures on Physics, Volume I*. Addison-Wesley, Reading, MA, 1963.

[270] M. Fiala. ARTag Revision 1, a fiducial marker system using digital techniques. Technical Report NRC/ERB-1117, NRC Publication Number NRC 47419, National Research Council Canada, 2004.

[271] R. E. Fikes and N. J. Nilsson. STRIPS: A new approach to the application of theorem proving to problem solving. *Artificial Intelligence*, 2:189–208, 1971.

[272] M. Fischler and O. Firschein, editors. *Readings in Computer Vision: Issues, problems, principles, and paradigms*. Morgan Kaufmann, Los Altos, CA, 1987.

[273] M. A. Fischler and R. C. Bolles. Random sample consensus: A paradigm for model fitting with applications to image analysis and automated cartography. *Journal of the ACM*, 24:381–395, 1981.

[274] D. Fleet and A. D. Jepson. A cascaded filter approach to the construction of velocity sensitive mechanisms. Technical Report, Research in Biological and Computational Vision, RBCV-TR-84-6, University of Toronto, Toronto, 1984.

[275] W. J. Fleming. Overview of automotive sensors. *IEEE Sensors Journal*, 1:296–308, 2001.

[276] S. Fleury, P. Souères, J.-P. Laumond, and R. Chatila. Primitives for smoothing mobile robot trajectories. *IEEE Transactions on Robotics and Automation*, 11:441–448, 1995.

[277] A. Flores-Abad, O. Ma, K. Pham, and S. Ulrich. A review of space robotics technologies for on-orbit servicing. *Progress in Aerospace Sciences*, 68:1–26, 2014.

[278] R. W. Floyd. Algorithm 97: shortest path. *Communications of the ACM*, 5:570–576, 1962.

[279] M. M. Foglia, A. Gentile, and G. Reina. Robotics for agricultural systems. In *Mechatronics and Machine Vision in Practice*, pages 313–332, Springer, Berlin, 2008.

[280] T. Fong, I. Nourbakhsh, and K. Dautenhahn. A survey of socially interactive robots. *Robotics and Autonomous Systems*, 42:143–166, 2003.

[281] P. Foot. The problem of abortion and the doctrine of double effect. *Oxford Review*, 5, 1967. Reprinted in *Virtues and vices*, Basil Blackwell, Oxford, 1978.

[282] P. M. Forooshani and M. Jenkin. Sensor coverage with a heterogeneous fleet of autonomous surface vessels. In *IEEE International Conference on Information and Automation (ICIA)*, Lijiang, China, 2015.

[283] J. Forsberg, U. Larsson, P. Ahman, and A. Wernersson. Navigation in cluttered rooms using a range measuring laser and the Hough transform. In *Proc. IAS-3*, pages 248–257, Pittsburgh, PA, 1993.

[284] W. Förstner. A framework for low level feature extraction. In *Proc. ECCV'90*, pages 383–394. Springer-Verlag, Berlin, 1990.

[285] R. L. Forward. *Camelot 30K*. Tor Books, New York, 1996.

[286] T. I. Fossen. *Guidance and Control of Ocean Vehicles*. Wiley, Chichester, 1994.

[287] D. Fox. Markov localication: A probabilistic framework for mobile robot localization and navigation. PhD thesis, University of Bonn, Bonn, Germany, 1998.

[288] D. Fox. KLD-sampling: Adaptive particle filters. In *Neural Information Processing Systems: Natural and Synthetic (NIPS)*, Vancouver, Canada, 2001.

[289] D. Fox, W. Burgard, and S. Thrun. Active Markov localization for mobile robots. *Robotics and Autonomous Systems*, 25:195–207, 1998.

[290] D. Fox, J. Ko, K. Konolige, B. Limketkai, D. Schulz, and B. Stewart. Distributed multirobot exploration and mapping. *Proceedings of the IEEE*, 94:1325–1339, 2006.

[291] D. A. S. Fraser. *Probability & Statistics: Theory and Applications*. Duxbury Press, Belmont, CA, 1976.

[292] M. R. Fraune, I. Leite, N. Karatas, *et al.* Lessons learned about designing and conducting studies from HRI experts. *Frontiers in Robotics and AI*, 8, 2022.

[293] M. J. Freake, R. Muheim, and J. B. Phillips. Magnetic maps in animals – a theory comes of age? *Quaterly Review of Biology*, 81:327–347, 2006.

[294] J. A. Freeman and D. M. Skapura. *Neural Networks: Algorithms, Applications, and Programming Techniques*. Addison-Wesley, Reading, MA, 1991.

[295] N. Friedman, D. Goedicke, V. Zhang, D. Rivkin, M. Jenkin, Z. Degutyte, A. Astell, X. Liu, and G. Dudek. Capturing attention with wind. In *Workshop on Integrating Multidisciplinary Approaches to Advanced Physical Human-Robot Interaction*, Paris, France, 2020. Held in conjunction with IEEE ICRA 2020.

[296] J. P. Frisby. *Seeing: Illusion, Brain and Mind*. Oxford University Press, Oxford, 1979.

[297] J. P. Frisby. *Seeing: The Computational Approach to Biological Vision*. MIT Press, Cambridge, MA, 2010. 2nd edition.

[298] L. Fu. *Neural Networks in Computer Intelligence*. McGraw-Hill, New York, 1994.

[299] T. Fuji, U. Tamaki, and Y. Kuroda. Mission execution experiments with a newly developed AUV "The Twin-Burger." In *Proc. 8th. International Symposium on Unmanned Untethered Submsersible Technology*, pages 92–105, Durham, 1993.

[300] R. Fulbright and L. M. Stephens. SWAMI: An autonomous mobile robot for inspection of nuclear waste storage facilities. *Autonomous Robots*, 2:225–235, 1995.

[301] M. Fulton, C. Edge, and J. Sattar. Robot communication via motion: Closing the underwater human-robot interaction loop. In *IEEE International Conference on Robotics and Automation (ICRA)*, pages 4660–4666, 2019.

[302] S. Garrido-Jurado, R. Munoz-Salinas, F. J. Madrid-Cuevas, and M. J. Marin-Jimenez. Automatic generation of highly reliable fiducial markers under occlusion. *Pattern Recognition*, 47:2280–2292, 2014.

[303] E. Gat. On three-layer architectures. In D. Kortenkamp, R. Bonnasso, and R. Murcphy, editors, *Artificial Intelligence and Mobile Robotics*, pages 195–210. AAAI Press, 1998.

[304] M. Geisslinger, F. Poszler, J. Betz, C. Lütge, and M. Lienkamp. Autonomous driving ethics: from trolley problem to ethics of risk. *Philosophy & Technology*, 34:1033–1055, 2021.

[305] A. Gelb. *Applied Optimal Estimation*. MIT Press, Cambridge, MA, 1974.

[306] C. Georgiades. Simulation and control of an underwater hexapod robot. MSc thesis, McGill University, Montreal, Canada, 2005.

[307] C. Georgiades, A. German, A. Hogue, *et al.* Aqua: An aquatic walking robot. In *IEEE/RSJ Conference on Intelligent Robots and Systems (IROS)*, pages 2525–2531, Sendai, Japan, 2004.

[308] A. Georgiev and P. K. Allen. Localization methods for a mobile robot in urban environments. *IEEE Transactions Robotics*, 20:851–864, 2004.

[309] A. Géron. *Hands-on Machine Learning with Scikit-Learn, Keras & TensorFlow*. O'Reilly, Media, Sebastopol, CA, 2019. 2nd edition.

[310] R. Gershon, A. D. Jepson, and J. K. Tsotsos. Highlight identification using chromatic information. In *Proceedings of the International Conference on Computer Vision*, pages 161–170, London, UK, 1987.

[311] G. De Giacomo, Y. Lespérance, and H. J. Levesque. ConGolog: A concurrent programming language based on the situation calculus. *Artificial Intelligence*, 121:109–169, 2000.

[312] N. Gildert, A. Millard, A. Pomfret, and J. Timmis. The need for combining implicit and explicit communication in cooperative robotic systems. *Frontiers in Robotics and AI*, 5, 2018.

[313] G. Giralt, R. Chatila, and M. Vaisset. An integrated navigation and motion control system for autonomous multisensory mobile robots. In M. Brady and R. Paul, editors, *First International Symposium on Robotics Research*, pages 191–214, MIT Press, Cambridge, MA, 1984.

[314] H. Goldstein. *Classical Mechanics*. Addison-Wesley, Reading, MA, 1980. 2nd edition.

[315] T. Gomi and P. Volpe. Collision avoidance using behavioral-based AI techniques. In *Proc. Intelligent Vehicles*, pages 141–145, Tokyo, 1993.

[316] M. A. Gonzalez-Santamarta, F. J. Rodrguez-Lera, C. F. Llamas, F. M. Rico, and V. M. Olivera. YASMIN: Yet another state machine library for ROS2. In *ROSCon Fr 2022*, Toulouse, France, 2022.

[317] I Goodfellow, Y. Bengio, and A. Courville. *Deep Learning*. MIT Press, Cambridge, MA, 2016.

[318] M. A. Goodrich and A. C. Schultz. Human-robot interaction: a survey. *Foundations and Trends in Human-Computer Interaction*, 1:203–275, 2007.

[319] N. J. Gordon, D. J. Salmond, and A. F. M. Smith. A novel approach to nonlinear/non-guassian bayesian state estimation. *IEE Proc. on Radar and Signal Processing*, 140:107–113, 1993.

[320] I. M. Gottlieb. *Electric Motors and Control Techniques*. McGraw-Hill, New York, 1994.

[321] R. Grabowski and P. Khosla. Localization techniques for a team of small robots. In *IEEE/RSJ Conference on Intelligent Robots and Systems (IROS)*, pages 1067–1072, Maui, HI, 2001.

[322] M. S. Grace, D. R. Church, C. T. Kelley, W. F. Lynn, and T. M. Cooper. The python pi organ: imaging and immunocytochemical analysis of an extremely sensitive natural infrared detector. *Biosensors and Bioelectronics*, 14:53–59, 1999.

[323] G. Grisetti, R. Kümmerie, C. Stachniss, and W. Burgard. A tutorial on graph-based SLAM. *IEEE Intelligent Transportation Systems Magazine*, Winter:31–43, 2010.

[324] D. Grunbaum, S. Viscido, and J. K. Parrish. Extracting interactive control algorithms from group dynamics of schooling fish. In V. Kumar, N. E. Leonard, and A. S. Morse, editors, *Lecture Notes in Control and Information Sciences*, pages 103–117. Springer-Verlag, 2004.

[325] L. J. Guibas, R. Motwani, and P. Raghavan. The robot localization problem in two dimensions. In *Proc. of the Third Annual ACM-SIAM Symposium on Discrete Algorithms*, pages 259–268, Orlando, FL, January 27–29 1992.

[326] E. Guizzo. Researchers build fast running robot inspired by velociraptor. *IEEE Spetrum*, May 2014.

[327] E. Guizzo. Three engineers, hundreds of robots, one warehouse. *IEEE Spectrum*, July, 2008.

[328] D. J. Gunkel. *The Machine Question*. MIT Press, Cambridge, MA, 2017.

[329] D. J. Gunkel. *Robot Rights*. MIT Press, Cambridge, MA, 2018.

[330] F. Gustafsson. Particle filter theory and practice with positioning applications. *IEEE Aerospace and Electronic Systems Magazine*, 25:53–81, 2010.

[331] S. Hackwood and G. Beni. Self-organization of sensors for swarm intelligence. In *Proc. International Conference on Robotics and Automation (ICRA)*, pages 819–829, Nice, France, 1992.

[332] K. Z. Haigh. Situation-dependent learning for interleaved planning and robot execution. PhD thesis, Computer Science Department, Carnegie Mellon University, Pittsburgh, PA, February 1998.

[333] K. Z. Haigh and M. M. Veloso. Planning, execution and learning in a robotic agent. In R. Simmons, M. Veloso, and S. Smith, editors, *Proc. AI Planning Systems 98*, pages 120–127, Pittsburgh, PA, 1998.

[334] R. Hanley. *Is Data Human?: The Metaphysics of Star Trek*. Basic Books, New York, 1997.

[335] B. Hannaford and A. M. Okamura. Haptics. In B. Siciliano and O. Khatib, editors, *Springer Handbook of Robotics*, pages 1063–1084, Springer, Berlin/Heidelberg, Germany, 2016.

[336] B. S. Hansson. Olfaction in lepidoptera. *Experientia*, 51:1003–1027, 1995.

[337] K. R. Harinarayan and V. Lumelsky. Sensor-based motion planning for multiple mobile robots in an uncertain environment. In *IEEE/RSJ International Conference on Intelligent Robots and Systems (IROS)*, pages 1485–1492, Munich, Germany, 1994.

[338] S. Y. Harmon. The ground surveillance robot (GSR): An autonomous vehicle designed to transit unknown terrain. *IEEE Transactions on Robotics and Automation*, 3:266–279, 1987.

[339] C. Harris and M. Stephens. A combined corner and edge detection. In *Fourth Alvey Vision Conference*, pages 147–151, Manchester, UK, 1988.

[340] L. Harris and M. Jenkin, editors. *Vision and Action*. Cambridge University Press, Cambridge, 1998.

[341] B. Harvey. *The New Russian Space Program: From Competition to Collaboration*. Wiley, Chichester, UK, 1996.

[342] S. M. Hedetniemi, S. T. Hedetniemi, and A. Liestman. A survey of gissiping and broadcasting in communication networks. *Networks*, 18:129–134, 1988.

[343] M. Heerink, B.Kröse, V. Evers, and B. Wielinga. Assessing acceptance of assistive social agent technology by older adults: The Almere Model. *International Journal of Social Robotics*, 2:361–375, 2010.

[344] J. Heikkilä. Geometric camera calibration using circular control points. *IEEE Transactions on Pattern Analysis and Machine Intelligence*, 22:1066–1077, 2000.

[345] A. Henschel, G. Laban, and E. S. Cross. What makes a robot social? a review of social robots from science fiction to a home or hospital near you. *Current Robotics Reports*, 2:9–19, 2021.

[346] F. Herbert. *Dune*. Ace Books, New York, 1965.

[347] J. Hertz, A. Krobh, and R. Pamer. *Introductino to the Theory of Neural Computation*. Addison-Wesley, Reading, MA, 1991.

[348] M. Hildebrand. Symmetrical gaits of horses. *Science*, 150:701–708, 1967.

[349] G. Hinton and T. Sejnowski. *Unsupervised Learning: Foundations of Neural Computation*. MIT Press, Cambridge, MA, 1999.

[350] Y. Hiroi and A. Ito. Influence of the height of a robot on comfortableness of verbal interaction. *IAENG International Journal of Computer Science*, 43, 2016.

[351] H. Hirukawa, F. Kanehiro, K. Kaneko, S. Kajita, and M. Morisawa. Dinosaur robotics for entertainment applications. *IEEE Robotics and Automation Magazine*, 14:43–51, 2007.

[352] S. Hochreiter and J. Schmidhuber. Long Short-Term Memory. *Neural Computation*, 9:1735–1780, 1997.

[353] J. Hodgins and M. H. Raibert. Planar robot goes head over heels. In *ASME Winter Annual Meeting*, Boston, MA, 1987.

[354] J. K. Hodgins and M. H. Raibert. Biped gymnastics. In P. H. Winston and S. A. Shellard, editors, *Artificial Intelligence at MIT Expanding Frontiers*, pages 180–205, MIT Press, Cambridge, MA, 1990.

[355] N. R. Hoff, A. Sagoff, R. J. Wood, and R. Nagpal. Two foraging algorithms for robot swarms using only local communication. In *IEEE International Conference on Robotics and Biomimetics*, pages 123–130, Tianjin, China, 2010.

[356] G. Hoffman and X. Zhao. A primer for conducting experiments in human–robot interaction. *ACM Trans. Hum.-Robot Interact.*, 10, 2020.

[357] F. R. Hogan, M. Jenkin, S. Rezaei-Shoshtari, *et al*. Seeing through your skin: Recognizing objects with a novel visuotactile sensor. In *Proc. IEEE/CVF Winter Conference on Applications of Computer Vision (WACV)*, pages 1218–1227, 2021.

[358] A. Hogue, A. German, J. Zacher, and M. Jenkin. Underwater 3D mapping: experiences and lessons learned. In *Third Canadian Conference on Computer and Robot Vision*, Quebec City, Canada, 2006.

[359] A. Hogue and M. Jenkin. Development of an underwater vision sensor for 3D reef mapping. In *IEEE/RSJ Conference on Intelligent Robots and Systems (IROS)*, Beijing, 2006.

[360] W. D. Holcombe, S. L. Dickerson, J. W. Larsen, and R. A. Bohlander. Advances in guidance systems for industrial automated guided vehicles. In *Proc. SPIE Mobile Robots III*, pages 288–297, Cambridge, MA, 1988.

[361] A. A. Holenstein, M. A. Müller, and E. Badreddin. Mobile robot localization in a structured environment cluttered with obstacles. In *IEEE International Conference on Robotics and Automation*, pages 2576–2581, Nice, France, May 1992.

[362] J. Holland. *Designing Autonomous Mobile Robots: Inside the Mind of an Intelligent Machine*. Newnes, Burlington, MA, 2003.

[363] O. Holland. Grey Walter: The pioneer of real artifical life. In *Proc. 5th International Workshop on Artificial Life*, pages 34–44, MIT Press, Cambridge, MA, 1997.

[364] B. Hölldobler. Colony-specific territorial pheremone in the African weaver ant *Oecophylla lognioda* (latreille). *Proceedings of the National Academy of Sciences of the USA*, 74:2072–2075, 1977.

[365] B. Hölldobler, R. C. Stanton, and H. Markl. Recruitment and food-retrieving behavior in *novomesor* (Formicidae, Hymenoptera) I. chemical signals. *Behavioral Ecology and Sociobiology*, 4:163–181, 1978.

[366] B. Horn. *Robot Vision*. MIT Press, Cambridge, MA, 1986.

[367] B. K. P. Horn and B. G. Schunk. Determining optical flow. *Artificial Intelligence*, 17:185–204, 1981.

[368] M.C. Horowitz. The ethics & morality of robotic warfare: Assessing the debate over autonomous weapons. *Daedakys*, Fall, 2016.

[369] A. Howard. Multi-robot simultaneous localization and mapping using particle filters. *International Journal of Robotics Research*, 25:1243–1256, 2006.

[370] I. Howard. *Human Visual Orientation*. Wiley, Chichester, UK 1982.

[371] D. Hsu, L. E. Kavraki, J.-C. Latombe, R. Motwani, and S. Sorkin. On finding narrow passages with probablisitic roadmap planners. In *Proc. 3rd Workshop on the Algorithm Foundations of Robotics (WAFR)*, pages 141–153, Natick, MA, 1998.

[372] J. Hsu. Military tests robo-parachute delivery needing no gps. *IEEE Spectrum*, Feb. 2016.

[373] H. Hu and M. Brady. A parallel processing architecture for sensor-based control of intelligent mobile robots. *Robotics and Autonomous Systems*, 17:235–257, 1996.

[374] T. Huntsberger, P. Pirjanian, A. Trebi-Ollennu, *et al.* CAMPOUT: A control architecture for tighly coupled coordination of multi-robot systems for planetary surface exploration. *IEEE Transactions on Systems, Man and Cybernetics*, 33:550–559, 2003.

[375] R. Hurteau, M. St-Amant, Y. Laperriere, and G. Chevrette. Optical guidance system for underground mine vehicles. In *Proc. IEEE ICRA*, volume 1, pages 639–644, Nice, France, 1992.

[376] Y. K. Hwang and H. Ahuja. A potential field approach to path planning. *IEEE Transactions on Robotics and Automation*, 8:23–32, 1992.

[377] L. Hyafil and R. L. Rivest. Constructing optimal binary decision trees is NP-complete. *Information Processing Letters*, 5:15–17, May 1976.

[378] M. Idrissi, M. Salami, and F. Annaz. A review of quadrotor unmanned aerial vehicles: Applications, architectural design and control algorithms. *Journal of Intelligent & Robotic Systems*, 104:22, 2022.

[379] A. Ijspeert, J. Hallam, and D. Willshaw. From lampreys to salamanders: evolving neural controllers for swimming and walking. In *Fifth International Conference on Simulation of Adaptive Behavior*, pages 390–399, Zurich, Switzerland, 1998.

[380] A. J. Ijspeert and J. Kodjabachian. Evolution and development of a central pattern generator for the swimming of a lamprey. *Artificial Life*, 5:247–269, 1999.

[381] K. Ikeuchi. *Computer Vision: A Reference Guide*. Springer, 2017.

[382] C. Intanagonwiwat, R. Govindan, and D. Estrin. Directed diffusion: a scaleable and robust communication paradigm for sensor networks. In *Proceedings of the Sixth Annual International Conference on Mobile Computing and Networking (MobiCOM'00)*, 2000.

[383] L. Iochi, D. Nardi, and M. Salerno. Reactivity and deliberation: a survey on multi-robot systems. In M. Hanenbauer, J. Wendler, and E. Pagello, editors, *Proc. Workshop on Balancing Reactivity and Social Deliberation in Multi-Agent Systems From RoboCup to Real-World Applications*, pages 9–32, Springer, 2001.

[384] R. Isaacs. *Differential Games*. Wiley, Don Mills, Ontario, 1965.

[385] M. Isard and A. Blake. Contour tracking by stochastic propogation of condition density. In *European Conference on Computer Vision*, pages 343–356, Cambridge, UK, 1996.

[386] M. Jabbal. An aerial deployed unmanned autonomous glider for cross-channel flight. *International Journal of Unmanned Systems Engineering*, 3:1–20, 2015.

[387] A. Jadbabaie, J. Lin, and A. S. Morse. Coordination of groups of mobile autonomous agents using nearest neighbor rules. *IEEE Transactions on Automatic Control*, 48:988–1001, 2003.

[388] G. James, D. Wittne, T. Hastie, and R. Tibshirani. *An Introduction to Statistical Leanring with Applications in R*. Springer, New York, 2013.

[389] L. Jaulin. *Mobile Robotics*. ISTE Press – Elsevier, 2015.

[390] J.Bohren and Steve S. Cousins. The SMACH high-level executive [ROS News]. *IEEE Robotics & Automation Magazine*, 17:18–20, 2010.

[391] M. Jenkin and G. Dudek. The paparazzi problem. In *IEEE/RSJ Conference on Intelligent Robots and Systems (IROS)*, pages 2042–2047, Takamatsu, Japan, 2000.

[392] M. Jenkin, A. Jepson, and J. K. Tsotsos. Techniques for disparity measurement. *CVGIP: IU*, 53:14–30, 1991.

[393] A. D. Jepson, D. Fleet, and M. R. M. Jenkin. Improving phase-based disparity measurements. *CVGIP: IU*, 53:198–210, 1991.

[394] T. M. Jochem, D. A. Pomerleau, and C. E. Thorpe. MANIAC a next generation neurally base autonomous road follower. In *Proc. IAS-3*, pages 592–599, Pittsburgh, PA, 1993.

[395] D. G. Jones and J. Malik. A computational framework for determining stereo correspondence from a set of linear spatial filters. In *European Conference on Computer Vision (ECCV)*, pages 395–410, Santa Margherita Ligure, Italy, 1992.

[396] J. Jones and A. Flynn. *Mobile Robots: Inspiration to Implementation*. A. K. Peters, Wellesley, MA, 1993.

[397] K. Joshi and A. R. Chowdhury. Bio-inspired vision and gesture-based robot-robot interaction for human-cooperative package delivery. *Frontiers in Robotics and AI*, 9:915884, 2022.

[398] L. Kaelbling, M. Littmand, and A. Cassandra. Planning and acting in partially observable stochastic domains. *Artifical Intelligence*, 101:99–134, 1998.

[399] L. P. Kaelbling. *Learning in Embedded Systems*. MIT Press, Cambridge, MA, 1993.

[400] M. Kaess and F. Dellaert. A Markov chain monte carlo approach to closing the loop in SLAM. In *IEEE International Conference on Robotics and Automation (ICRA)*, pages 645–650, Barcelona, Spain, 2005.

[401] R. E. Kalman. New methods and results in linear filtering and prediction theory. *Transactions ASME Series D. J. Basic Engineering*, 83:95–108, 1961.

[402] E. W. Kamen and B. S. Heck. *Fundamentals of Signals and Systems using the Web and Matlab*. Prentice-Hall, Engelwood Cliffs, NJ, 2000. 2nd edition.

[403] I. Kamon and E. Rivlin. Sensory based motion planning with global proofs. In *IEEE/RSJ International Conference on Intelligent Robots and Systems (IROS)*, pages 435–440, Pittsburgh, PA, 1995.

[404] I. Kamon and E. Rivlin. Sensory-based planning with global proofs. *IEEE Robotics and Automation*, 13:814–822, 1997.

[405] K. Kant and S. W. Zucker. Towards efficient trajectory planning: the path-velocity decomposition. *International Journal of Robotics Research*, 5:72–89, 1986.

[406] S. Karaman and E. Frazzoli. Sampling-based algorithms for optimal motion planning. *International Journal of Robotics Research*, 30:846–894, 2011.

[407] S. Karaman, M. R. Walter, A. Perez, E. Frazzoli, and S. Teller. Anytime motion planning using the RRT*. In *IEEE Int. Conf. on Robotics and Automation (ICRA)*, Shanghai, China, 2011.

[408] R. Karlsson and F. Gustafsson. Monte Carlo data association for multiple target tracking. In *IEE Workshop on Target Tracking*, Eindhoven, Netherlands, 2001.

[409] H. Kato and M. Billinghurst. Marker tracking and HMD calibration for video-based augmented reality conferencing system. In *Proc. 2nd International Workshop on Augmented Reality*, pages 85–94, San Francisco, CA, 1999.

[410] L. Kavraki, P. Svestka, J.-C. Latombe, and M. H. Overmars. Probabilistic roadmaps for path planning in high-dimensional configuration spaces. *IEEE Transactions on Robotics and Automation*, 12:566–580, 1996.

[411] O. Khatib. Real-time obstacle avoidance for manipulators and mobile robots. *International Journal of Robotics Research*, 5:90–98, 1986.

[412] Khepera: The miniature mobile robot. Undated product sheet, Khepera Support Team.

[413] M. Khodarahmi and V. Maihami. A reivw on Kalman Filter models. *Archives of Computational Methods in Engineering*, October, 2022.

[414] B. Khoshnevis and G. A. Bekey. Centralized sensing and control of multiple mobile robots. *Computer in Industrial Engineering*, 35:503–506, 1998.

[415] G. A. Khoury and J. D. Gillet, editors. *Airship Technology*. Cambridge University Press, Cambridge, 1999.

[416] J.-H. Kim, H.-S. Shim, H.-S. Kim, M.-J. Jung, and P. Vadakkepat. Micro-robot soccer system: action selection mechanism and strategies. In *Third ECPD International Conference on Advanced Robotics, Intelligent Automation and Active Systems*, pages 151–156, Bremen, Germany, 1997.

[417] M. Kim, S. Kim, S. Park, M.-T. Choi, M. Kim, and H. Gomaa. Service robot for the elderly. *IEEE Robotics and Automation Magazine*, 16:34–45, 2009.

[418] S. J. King and C. F. R. Weiman. HelpMate autonomous mobile robot navigation system. In *Proc. SPIE Mobile Robots V*, pages 190–198, Cambridge, MA, 1990.

[419] D. P. Kingma and J. L. Ba. Adam: A method for stochastic optimization. In *ICLR*, 2015.

[420] M. Kirsch, V. Mataré, A. Ferrein, and S. Schiffer. Integrating golog++ and ROS for practical and portable high-level control. In *International Conference on Agents and Artificial Intelligence (ICAART)*, pages 692–699, Malta, 2020.

[421] G. Kitagawa. Monte Carlo filter and smoother for non-Gaussian state space models. *Journal of Computational and Graphical Statistics*, 5:1–25, 1996.

[422] G. Klancar, A. Zdesar, S. Blazic, and I. Skrjanc. *Wheeled Mobile Robotics*. Butterworth-Heinemann, 2017.

[423] R. Klein. Walking an unknown street with bounded detour. *Computational Geometry: Theory and Applications*, 1:325–351, 1992.

[424] D. E. Koditschek. Robot planning and control via potential functions. In O. Khatib, J. J. Craig, and T. Lozano-Perez, editors, *The Robotics Review 1*, pages 349–367, MIT Press, Cambridge, MA, 1989.

[425] J. J. Koenderink. The structure of images. *Biological Cybernetics*, 50:363–370, 1984.

[426] S. Koenig and R. G. Simmons. Unsupervised learning of probabilistic models for robot navigation. In *IEEE International Conference on Robotics and Automation (ICRA)*, pages 2301–2308, Minneapolis, MN, 1996.

[427] A. B. Kogan. The effect of a constant magnetic field on the movement of paramecia. *Biofizika*, 10:292–296, 1965.

[428] D. Koller and N. Friedman. *Probabilistic Graphical Models: Principles and Techniques*. MIT Press, Cambridge, MA, 2009.

[429] K. Kompatsiari, F. Ciardo, V. Tikhanoff, and G. Metta. It's in the eyes: the engaging role of eye contact in HRI. *International Journal of Social Robotics*, 13:1–11, 2021.

[430] N. Kondo and K. C. Ting, editors. *Robotics for Bio-production Systems*. American Society of Argicultural Engineers, 1998.

[431] K. Konolige. Improved occupancy grids for map. *Autonomous Robots*, 4:351–367, 1997.

[432] A. Kosaka and J. Pan. Purdue experiments in model-based vision for hallway navigation. In *Proc. IEEE Workshop on Vision for Robots*, pages 87–96, Pittsburgh, PA, 1995.

[433] J. Kramer and M. Scheutz. Development environments for autonomous mobile robots: A survey. *Autonomous Robots*, 22:101–132, 2007.

[434] E. Krotkov, R. Simmons, and W. Whittaker. Autonomous walking results with the Ambler hexapod planetary rover. In *Proc. IAS-3*, pages 46–53, Pittsburgh, PA, 1993.

[435] T. Krupiy. Unravelling power dynamics in organization: An accountability framework for crimes triggered by lethal autonomous weapons systems. *Loyola University Chicago International Law Review*, 15:1–62, 2017.

[436] C. R. Kube and H. Zhang. From social insects to robots. *Adaptive Behavior*, 2:189–218, 1994.

[437] J. J. Kuffer, Jr. and S. M. LaValle. RRTconnect: an efficient approach to single-query path planning. In *IEEE Transactions on Robotics and Automation (ICRA)*, pages 995–1001, San Francisco, CA, 2000.

[438] B. J. Kuipers and Y.-T. Byun. A qualitative approach to robot exploration and map-learning. In *Proceedings of the IEEE workshop on spatial reasoning and multi-sensor fusion*, pages 390–404, Los Altos, CA, 1987.

[439] B. J. Kuipers and Y.-T. Byun. A robot exploration and mapping strategy based on a semantic hierachy of spatial representations. *Robotics and Autonomous Systems*, 8:46–63, 1991.

[440] B. J. Kuipers and T. Levitt. Navigation and mapping in large-scale space. *AI Magazine*, pages 25–43, Summer 1988.

[441] J. Kulk and J. S. Welsh. A NUPlatform for software on articulated mobile robots. In R. Hähnle, J. Knoop, T. Margaria, D. Schreiner, and B. Steffen, editors, *Leveraging Applications of Formal Methods, Verification, and Validation: Communications in Computer and Information Science*, pages 31–45, Springer, Berlin, 2012.

[442] L. Kunze, K. Lingemann, A. Nüchter, and J. Hertzberg. Salient visual features to help close the loop in 6D SLAM. In *ICVS Workshop on Computational Attention and Applications*, Bielefeld, Germany, 2007.

[443] S. Kuutti, R. Bowden, H. Joshi, R. de Temple, and S. Fallah. Safe deep neural network-driven autonomous vehicles using software safety cages. In *IDEAL*, 2019.

[444] C. Lailler, J.-P. Deparis, and J.-G. Postaire. Adaptive white line detection and modelisation for autonomous visual navigation of a road following vehicle for real-time obstacle detection in road traffic. In *Proc. IAS-3*, pages 116–124, Pittsburgh, PA, 1993.

[445] D. Lambrinos, M. Maris, H. Koayashi, T. Labhart, R. Pfeifer, and R. Wehner. An autonomous agent navigating with a polarized light compass. *Adaptive Behavior*, 6:131–161, 1997.

[446] M. Lappe, M. Jenkin, and L. Harris. Travel distance estimation from visual motion by leaky path integration. *Experimental Brain Research*, 180:35–48, 2007.

[447] D. Larom, M. Garstang, M. Lindeque, *et al.* Meteorology and elephant infrasound in Etosha National Park, Nambia. *Journal Acoustical Society of America*, 101, 1997.

[448] B. P. Lathi. *Linear Systems and Signals*. Oxford University Press, Oxford, 2004. 2nd edition.

[449] J.-C. Latombe. *Robot Motion Planning*. Kluwer, Norwell, MA, 1991.

[450] S. M. LaValle. *Planning Algorithms*. Cambridge University Press, Cambridge, 2006.

[451] T. Law, M. Chita-Tegmark, and M. Scheutz. The interplay between emotional intelligence, trust, and gender in human–robot interaction. *International Journal of Social Robotics*, 13:297–309, 2021.

[452] Y. LeCun, L. Bottou, Y. Bengio, and P. Haffner. Gradient-based learning applied to document recognition. *Proc. of the IEEE*, Nov. 1998.

[453] D. T. Lee and R. L. Drysdale III. Generalized Voronoi diagrams in the plane. *SIAM Journal on Computing*, 10:73–87, 1981.

[454] W. Van Leekwijck and E. E. Kerre. Defuzzification: criteria and classification. *Fuzzy Sets and Systems*, 108:159–178, 1999.

[455] J. R. Leigh. *Control Theory*. Institution of Electrical Engineers, Herts, UK, 2004.

[456] A. Lein and R. T. Vaughan. Adaptive multi-robot bucket brigade foraging. In *Proceedings of the Eleventh International Conference on Artificial Life (ALife XI)*, pages 337–342, Winchester, UK, 2008.

[457] S. Lem. *The Star Diaries*. Harcourt, San Diego, CA, 2001.

[458] J. J. Leonard and H. F. Durrant-Whyte. Mobile robot localization by tracking geometric beacons. *IEEE Transactions on Robotics and Automation*, 7:376–382, 1991.

[459] J. J. Leonard and H. F. Durrant-Whyte. *Directed Sonar Sensing for Mobile Robot Navigation*. Springer, New York, 1992.

[460] H. J. Levesque. On our best behaviour. *Artificial Intelligence*, 212:27–35, 2014.

[461] H. J. Levesque, R. Reiter, Y. Lesperance, F. Lin, and R. B. Scherl. GOLOG: A logic programming language for dynamic domains. *Journal of Logic Programming*, 31:59–84, 1997.

[462] M. Lewis, Y. Liu, N. Goyal, *et al.* BART: Denoising sequence-to-sequence pre-training for natural language generation, translation, and comprehension. In *Proc. 58th Meeting of the Association for Computational Linguistics*, online, 2020.

[463] M. A. Lewis, A. H. Fagg, and G. A. Bekey. The USC autonomous flying vehicle: An experiment in real-time behavior-based control. In *IEEE/RSJ Conference on Intelligent Robots and Systems (IROS)*, pages 1173–1180, Yokohama, Japan, 1993.

[464] S. Li, A. Ochi, Y. Yagi, and M. Yachida. Making 2d map of environments by observing scenes both along routes and at intersections. In *Workshop on Perception for Mobile Agents*, pages 71–78. IEEE International Conference on Computer Vision and Pattern Recognition (CVPR), Santa Barbara, CA, 1998.

[465] W. Li and H. Xu. Text-based emotion classification using emotion cause extraction. *Expert Systems with Applications*, 41(4):1742–1749, 2014.

[466] P. Lichocki, P. Khan, Jr., and A. Billard. The ethical landscape of robotics. *IEEE Robotics and Automation Magazine*, 18:39–50, 2011.

[467] P. W. Likins. *Elements of Engineering Mechanics*. McGraw-Hill, New York, 1973.

[468] S. Limsoonthrakul, M. N. Dalley, M. Sisrupudit, S. Tongphu, and M. Parnichkum. A modular system architecture for autonomous robots based on blackboard and publish-subscribe mechanisms. In *Proc. IEEE International Conference on Robotics and Biomimetrics (ROBIO)*, pages 633–638, Bangkok, Thailand, 2008.

[469] P. Lin. Here's a terrible idea: Robot cars with adjustable ethics settings. *Wired* Available on-line at https://www.wired.com/2014/08/heres-a-terrible-idea-robot-cars-with-adjustable-ethics-settings/, 2014.

[470] P. Lin. Robot cars and fake ethical dilemmas. *Forbes Magazine*, April:3, 2017.

[471] P. Lin, K. Abney, and G. Bekey. Robot ethics: Mapping the issue for a mechanized word. *Artificial Intelligence*, 175:942–949, 2011.

[472] V. M. Linkin. VEGA balloon dynamics and vertical winds in the Venus middle cloud region. *Science*, 231:1417–1419, 1986.

[473] L. Lisowski and G. Baille. Specifications of a small electric vehicle: modular and distributed approach. In *IEEE/RSJ Conference on Intelligent Robots and Systems (IROS)*, pages 919–924, Grenoble, France, 1997.

[474] R. A. Liston and R. S. Mosher. A versatile walking truck. In *Proc. 1968 Transportation Engineering Conference ASME-NYAS*, Washington, DC, 1968.

[475] X. Liu, J. Yuan, and K. Wang. A problem-specific genetic algorithm for path planning of mobile robot in greenhouse. In *Knowledge Enterprise: Intelligent Strategies in Product Design, Manufacturing, and Management*, pages 211–216, Springer, Boston, MA, 2006.

[476] Y.-H. Liu and S. Arimoto. Path planning using a tangent graph for mobile robots among polygonal and curved obstacles. *International Journal of Robotics Research*, 11:376–382, 1992.

[477] I. Lluvia, E. Lazkano, and A. Ansuategi. Active mapping and robot exploration: A survey. *Sensors*, 21:2445, 2021.

[478] J. Loeb. *Forced Movements, Tropisms, and Animal Conduct*. J. B. Lippincott, Philadelphia, 1918.

[479] H. A. Loeliger. An introduction to factor graphs. *IEEE Signal Processing Magazine*, 21:28–41, 2004.

[480] D. Longo and G. Muscato. The Alicia^3 climbing robot. *IEEE Robotics and Automation Magazine*, 13:42–50, 2006.

[481] D. G. Lowe. Object recognition from local scape-invariant features. In *International Conference on Computer Vision (ICCV)*, pages 1150–1157, Corfu, Greece, 1999.

[482] D. G. Lowe. Distincitve image features from scale-invariant keypoints. *International Journal of Computer Vision*, 2:91–110, 2004.

[483] F. Lu and E. Milios. Globally consistent range scan alignment for environment mapping. *Autonomous Robots*, 4:333–349, 1997.

[484] F. Lu and E. Milios. Robot pose estimation in unknown environments by matching 2D range scans. *Journal of Intelligent and Robotic Systems*, 18:249–275, 1997.

[485] V. Lumelsky, S. Mukhopadhyay, and K. Sun. Sensor-based terrain acquisition: The "sightseer" strategy. In *Proc. of the IEEE Conference on Decision and Control Including The Symposium on Adaptive Processes*, pages 1157–1161, Tampa, FL, 1989.

[486] V. Lumelsky and A. Stepanov. Path-planning strategies for a point mobile automaton moving amidst unknown obstacles of arbitrary shape. *Algorithmica*, 2:403–440, 1987.

[487] V. J. Lumelsky. *Sensing, Intelligence, Motion: How Robots and Humans Move in an Unstructured World*. Wiley, Hoboken, NJ, 2006.

[488] V. J. Lumelsky, S. Mukhopadhyay, and K. Sun. Dynamic path planning in sensor-based terrain acquisition. *IEEE Transactions on Robotics and Automation*, 6:462–472, 1990.

[489] S. Ma, T. Tomiyama, and H. Wada. Omnidirectional static walking of a quaduped robot. *IEEE Transactions Robotics and Automation*, 21:152–161, 2005.

[490] W. S. MacDonald. Design and implementation of a multilegged walking robot. Senior honors thesis, University of Massachusetts, Amherst, 1994.

[491] S. Macenski, F. Martín, R. White, and J. C. Clavero. The marathon 2: A navigation system. In *IEEE/RSJ International Conference on Intelligent Robots and Systems (IROS)*, Las Vegas, NV, 2020.

[492] P. MacKenzie and G. Dudek. Precise positioning using model-based maps. In *Proc. of the International Conference on Robotics and Automation*, pages 1615–1621, IEEE Press, San Diego, CA, 1994.

[493] W. Maddern, G. Pascoe, C. Linegar, and P. Newman. 1 year, 1000km: The Oxford Robotcar dataset. *The International Journal of Robotics Research (IJRR)*, 2016.

[494] P. Maes. Modeling adaptive autonomous agents. *Artificial Life*, 1:135–162, 1994.

[495] E. Magid, E. Rimon, and E. Rivlin. CAUTIOUSBUG: A competitive algorithm for sensory-based robot navigation. In *IEEE/RSJ Conference on Intelligent Robots and Systems (IROS)*, pages 2757–2762, Sendai, Japan, 2004.

[496] H. Mahdi, S. A. Akgun, S. Saleh, and K. Dautenhahn. A survey on the design and evolution of social robots past, present and future. *Robotics and Autonomous Systems*, 156:104193, 2022.

[497] M. Malajner, P. Planini, and D. Gleich. UWB ranging accuracy. In *International Conference on Systems, Signals and Image Processing (IWSSIP)*, pages 61–64, 2015.

[498] K.-F. Man, K.-S. Tang, and S. Kwong. *Genetic Algorithms: Concepts and Design*. Springer-Verlag, London, UK, 1999.

[499] D. J. Manko. *A General Model of Legged Locomotion on Natural Terrain*. Kluwer Academic Publishers, Norwell, MA, 1992.

[500] United Stated Army Field Manual. The law of land warfare, 1956. FM 27-10. (amended 1977).

[501] D. B. Marco, A. J. Healey, and R. B. McGhee. Autonomous underwater vehicles: Hybrid control of mission and motion. *Autonomous Robots*, 3:169–186, 1996.

[502] A. Marjovi and L. Marques. Optimal spatial formation of swarm robotic gas sensors in odor plume finding. *Auton. Robots*, 35:93–109, 2013.

[503] D. Marr and E. Hildreth. Theory of edge detection. *Proceedings of the Royal Society (London) B*, 207:187–217, 1980.

[504] A. B. Martinez, J. Climent, R. M. Planas, and J. M. Asensio. Vision base compass for mobile robot orientation. In *Proc. Intelligent Vehicles*, pages 293–296, Tokyo, 1993.

[505] P. Masani, editor. *Norbert Wiener: Collected Works with Commentaries, Volume IV*. MIT Press, Cambridge, MA, 1985.

[506] M. J. Matarić. Environmental learning using a distributed representation. In *IEEE International Conference on Robotics and Automation (ICRA)*, pages 402–406, Cincinnati, OH, 1990.

[507] M. J. Mataric. Integration of representation into goal-driven behavior-based robots. In *IEEE International Conference on Robotics and Automation (ICRA)*, pages 304–312, Nice, France, 1992.

[508] M. J. Matarić. Minimizing complexity in controlling a mobile robot population. In *IEEE International Conference on Robotics and Automation (ICRA)*, pages 830–835, Nice, France, 1992.

[509] M. J. Matarić. Designing and understanding adaptive group behavior. *Adaptive Behavior*, 4:50–81, 1995.

[510] M. J. Matarić. Situated robotics. In *Encyclopedia of Cognitive Science, Int. J. Comp. Vis. Volume 4*, pages 25–30. Nature Publishers Group, London, UK, 2002.

[511] M. J. Matarić and F. Michaud. Behavior-based systems. In B. Siciliano and O. Khatib, editors, *Springer Handbook of Robotics*, pages 891–909, Springer, 2008.

[512] M. J. Matarić, M. Nilsson, and K. Simsarian. Cooperative multi-robot box-pushing. In *IEEE/RSJ Conference on Intelligent Robots and Systems (IROS)*, pages 556–561, Pittsburgh, PA, 1995.

[513] M. J. Matarić, M. Nilsson, and K. T. Simsarian. Cooperative multi-robot box-pushing. In *IEEE/RSJ Conference on Intelligent Robots and Systems (IROS)*, volume 3, pages 556–561, Pittsburgh, PA, 1995.

[514] P. Maybeck. *Stochastic models, Estimation and Control*. Academic Press, New York, 1979.

[515] J. Mayhew, J. Frisby, and P. Gale. Psychophysical and computational studies towards a theory of human stereopsis. *Artificial Intelligence*, 17:349–385, 1981.

[516] A. Mayor. *Gods and Robots: Myths, Machines and Ancient Dreams of Technology*. Princeton University Press, Princeton, NJ, 2018.

[517] A. McCaffrey. *The Ship Who Sang*. Corgi Books, London, UK, 1972.

[518] J. McCarthy and P. J. Hayes. Some philosophical problems from the standpoint of artificial intelligence. *Machine Intelligence*, 4:295–324, 1969.

[519] J. McClelland and D. Rumelhart. *Parallel Distributed Processing, Volumes I and II*. MIT Press, Cambridge, MA, 1986.

[520] R. B. McGhee. Some finite state aspects of legged locomotion. *Mathematical Biosciences*, 2:67–84, 1968.

[521] C. D. McGillem and G. R. Cooper. *Continuous and Discrete Signal and System Analysis*. Holt, Rinehart and Winston, New York, 1974.

[522] J. T. McIlwain, editor. *An Introduction to the Biology of Vision*. Cambridge University Press, Cambridge, 1996.

[523] G. J. McLachlan and T. Krishnan. *The EM Algorithm and Extensions*. Wiley, New York, 1997.

[524] M. Diftler, J. Mehling, M. Abdallah, *et al.* Robotnaut 2: The first humanoid robot in space. In *IEEE International Conference on Robotics and Automation (ICRA)*, pages 2178–2183, 2011.

[525] F. Steinand G. Medioni. Map-based localization using the panoramic horizon. *IEEE Transactions on Robotics and Automation*, 11:892–896, 1995.

[526] L. Meirovitch. *Methods of Analytical Dynamics*. McGraw-Hill, New York, 1970.

[527] J. M. Mendel. Fuzzy logic systems for engineering: A tutorial. *Proceedings of the IEEE*, 83:345–377, 1995.

[528] R. C. Michelini, G. M. Acaccia, M. Callegari, R. M. Molfino, and R. P. Razzoli. Robot harvesting of citrus fruits. In *Proc. 3rd. ECPD*, pages 447–452, Bremen, Germany, 1997.

[529] A. Michelsen, B. B. Andersen, J. Storm, W. H. Kirchner, and M. Lindauer. How honeybees perceive communication dances, studied by means of a mechanical model. *Behavioral Ecology and Sociobiology*, 30:143–150, 1992.

[530] T. Mikolajczyk, E. Mikoajewska, H. F. N. Al-Shuka, *et al.* Recent advances in bipedal walking robots: Review of gait, drive, sensors and control systems. *Sensors*, 22, 2022.

[531] P. Miles and T. Carroll. *Build Your Own Combat Robot*. McGraw Hill, New York, 2002.

[532] E. Milios, M. Jenkin, and J. Tsotsos. Design and performance of TRISH, a binocular robot head with torsional eye movements. In *Active Robot Vision: Camera Heads, Model Based Navigation and Reactive Control*, pages 51–68. World Scientific Press, Singapore, 1993.

[533] J. Millar. Ethics settings for autonomous vehicles. In P. Lin, R. Jenkins, and K. Abney, editors, *Robot Ethics 2.0: From Autonomous Cars to Artificial Intelligence*, chapter 2. Oxford University Press, Oxford, 2019.

[534] J. Millar and I. Kerr. Delegation, relinquishment, and responsibility: The prospect of expert robots. In M. Froomkin R. Calo and I. Kerr, editors, *Robot Law*. Edward Elgar, 2016.

[535] D. Miller and M. Slack. Design and testing of a low-cost robotic wheelchair. *Autonomous Robots*, 2:77–88, 1995.

[536] V. Mnih, K. Kavukcuoglu, D. Silver, *et al.* Human-level control through deep reinforcement learning. *Nature*, 518:529–533, 2015.

[537] M. Montemerlo, S. Thrun, D. Koller, and B. Wegbreit. FastSLAM: A factored solution to the simultaneous localization and mapping problem. In *AAAI National Conference and Artificial Intelligence*, pages 593–598, Edmonton, Canada, 2002.

[538] S. K. Moore, D. Schneider, and E. Strickland. How Deep Learning works. *IEEE Spectrum*, October: 32–33, 2021.

[539] H. P. Moravec. Towards automatic visual obstacle avoidance. In *International Joint Conference on Artificial Intelligence (IJCAI)*, page 584, Cambridge, MA, 1977.

[540] H. P. Moravec. Obstacle avoidance and navigation in the real world by a seeing robot rover. PhD thesis, Stanford University, Stanford, CA, 1980. [*Robot Rover Visual Navigation*, Ann Arbor, MI: UMI Research Press, 1981.]

[541] H. P. Moravec. The Stanford Cart and the CMU Rover. *IEEE*, 71:872–884, 1983.

[542] H. P. Moravec. Three degrees for a mobile robot. In *Proc. of the ASME on Advanced Automation: 1984 and Beyond*, volume 1, pages 274–278, 1984.

[543] H. P. Moravec and A. Elfes. High resolution maps from wide angle sonar. In *IEEE International Conference on Robotics and Automation (ICRA)*, pages 116–121, St. Louis, MO, 1985.

[544] L. Moreno, J. M. Armingol, S. Garrido, A. De La Escalera, and M. A. Salichs. A genetic algorithm for mobile robot localization using ultrasonic sensors. *Journal of Intelligent and Robotic Systems*, 34:135–154, 2002.

[545] M. Mori. The uncanny valley. *Energy*, 7:33–35, 1970. (in Japanese)

[546] M. Mori. The uncanny valley. *IEEE Robotics and Automation*, 19:98–101, 2012. Translation by K. F. MacDorman.

[547] R. S. Mosher. Test and evaluation of a versatile walking truck. In *Proc. of the Off-Road Mobility Research Symposium. International Society for Terrain Vehicle Systems*, pages 359–379, Washington, DC, 1968.

[548] L. Moshkina and R. C. Arkin. Lethality and autonomous systems: Survey design and results. Technical Report GIT-GVU-07-16, Georgia Institute of Technology, Atlanta, GA, 2007.

[549] H. Mouritsen. Navigation in birds and other animals. *Image and Vision Computing*, 19:713–731, 2001.

[550] L. Muehlhauser and L. Helm. The singularity and machine ethics. In A. Eden, J. Soraker, J. H. Moor, and E. Steinhart, editors, *Singularity Hypothesis: A Scientific and Philosophical Assessment*. Springer, Berlin, 2012.

[551] Mujoco. MuJoCo advanced physics simulation. http://mujoco.org. Accessed: 2023-01-10.

[552] V. C. Müller. Ethics of artifical intelligence and robotics, 2020. Standford Encyclopedia of Philosophy. Available at https://plato.stanford.edu/entries/ethics-ai.

[553] D. W. Murphy and J. P. Bott. The air mobile ground security and surveillance system (AMGSSS). In *Unmanned Systems*, volume 13. Space and Naval Warfare Systems Command, 1995.

[554] K. Murphy and S. Russell. Rao-Blackwellised particle filtering for dynamic Bayesian networks. In A. Doucet, N. Freitas, and N. Gordon, editors, *Sequential Monte Carlo Methods in Practice*, pages 449–516, Springer-Verlag, New York, 2001.

[555] R. Murphy. Trial by fire. *IEEE Robotics and Automation Magazine*, 11:50–61, 2004.

[556] R. Murphy. *Robotics through Science Fiction: Artificial Intelligence Explained through Six Classic Robot Short Stories*. MIT Press, Cambridge, MA, 2018.

[557] R. R. Murphy. *Introduction to AI Robotics*. MIT Press, Cambridge, MA, 2000.

[558] D. Murray, F. Du, P. McLauchlan, I. Reed, P. Sharkey, and M. Brady. Design of stereo heads. In A. Blake and A. Yuille, editors, *Active Vision*, pages 155–174, MIT Press, Cambridge, MA, 1992.

[559] D. Murray and J. Little. Using real-time stereo vision for mobile robot navigation. In *Workshop on Perception for Mobile Agents*, pages 19–27. IEEE International Conference on Computer Vision and Pattern Recognition (CVPR), Santa Barbara, CA, 1998.

[560] E. Muybridge. *Animals in Motion*. Dover, New York, 1899/1957.

[561] E. Muybridge. *The Human Figure in Motion*. Dover, New York, 1901/1955.

[562] S. Na, Y. Qui, A. E. Turgut, *et al.* Bio-inspired artificial pheromone system for swarm robotics applics. *Adaptive Behavior*, 29:395–415, 2020.

[563] H. Nagahara, K. Yoshida, and M. Yachida. An Omnidirectional vision sensor with single view and constant resolution. In *IEEE International Conference on Computer Vision (ICCV)*, pages 1–8, 2007.

[564] K. Naheem, A. Elsharkawy, D. Koo, Y. Lee, and M. Kim. A UWB-based lighter-than-air indoor robot for user-centered interactive applications. *Sensors*, 22:2093, 2022.

[565] R. Nakajima, T. Tsubouchi, S. Yuta, and E. Koyanagi. A development of a new mechanism of an autonomous unicycle. In *IEEE/RSJ Conference on Intelligent Robots and Systems (IROS)*, volume 2, pages 906–912, Grenoble, France, 1997.

[566] Y. Nakamura and R. Mukherjee. Nonholonomic path planning of space robots via bi-directional approach. In *IEEE International Conference on Robotics and Automation (ICRA)*, pages 1764–1769, Cincinnati, OH, 1990.

[567] D. Nakhaeinia, S. H. Tang, S. B. Mohd Noor, and O. Motlagh. A review of control architectures for autonomous navigation of mobile robots. *International Journal of the Physical Sciences*, 6:169–174, 2011.

[568] P. M. Narins, E. R. Lewis, J. J. I M. Jarvis, and J. O'Riain. The use of seismic signals by fossorial southern African mammals: a neuroethological gold mine. *Brain Research*, 44:641–646, 1997.

[569] F. Nashashibi and M. Devy. 3d incremental modeling and robot localization in a structured environment using a laser range finder. In *IEEE International Conference on Robotics and Automation (ICRA)*, pages 20–27, Atlanta GA, May 1993.

[570] M. Navon. The virtuous servant owner – a paradigm whose time has come (again). *Frontiers in Robotics and AI*, 2021.

[571] S. K. Nayar, H. Murase, and S. A. Nene. Learning, positioning, and tracking visual appearance. In E. Straub and R. S. Sipple, editors, *Proc. International Conference on Robotics and Automation*, pages 3237–3244, Los Alamitos, CA, 1994.

[572] M. P. Nemitz, M. E. Sayed, J. Marmish, *et al.* Hoverbots: Precise locomotion using robots that are designed for manufacturability. *Frontiers in Robotics and AI*, 4:55, 2017.

[573] B. Nickerson, M. Jenkin, E. Milios, *et al.* ARK – autonomous navigation of a mobile robot in a known environment. In *Proc. of International Conference on Intelligent Autonomous Systems: IAS-3*, pages 288–296, Pittsburgh, PA, 1993.

[574] S. B. Nickerson, M. Jenkin, E. Milios, *et al.* Design of ARK, a sensor-based mobile robot for industrial environments. In *Proc. Intelligent Vehicles 1993*, pages 252–257, Tokyo, 1993.

[575] J. Nicoud. Mines Advisory Group. Report to the UN International Meeting on Mines Clearance, Geneva, Switzerland, 1995.

[576] J. D. Nicoud and P. Mächler. Pemex-B: a low-cost robot for searching anti-personnel mines. In *Workshop on Anti-Personnel Mine Detection and Removal (WAPM)*, Swiss Federal Institute of Technology Microprocessors and Interfaces Laboratory, 1995.

[577] H. Y. Nii. Blackboard systems. Technical Report STAN-CS-86-1123, Department of Computer Science, Stanford University, Stanford, CA, 1986.

[578] N. Nilsson. A mobile automaton: an application of artificial intelligence techniques. In *Proc. International Joint Conference on Artificial Intelligence (IJCAI)*, pages 509–520, Washington, DC, 1969.

[579] N. J. Nilsson. *Principles of Artificial Intelligence*. Tioga Publishing Co., Palo Alto, CA, 1980.

[580] The NOMAD 200: Merging mind and motion. Undated product sheet, Nomadic Technologies.

[581] J. R. Norris. *Markov Chains*. Cambridge University Press, Cambridge, 1998.

[582] C. L. Novak and S. A. Shafer. Anatomy of a color histogram. In *Proc. IEEE CVPR*, pages 599–605, 1992.

[583] S. O., M. A. Belin, and B. Lundgren. Self-driving vehicles–an ethical overview. *Philosophy & Technology*, 34:1383–1408, 2021.

[584] T. Oblak, J. Šireclj, V. Štruc, *et al.* Learning to predict superquadric parameters from depth images with explicit and implicit supervision. *IEEE Access*, 9:1087–1102, 2021.

[585] C. Ó'Dúnlaing and C. K. Yap. A retraction method for planning the motion of a disc. *Journal of Algorithms*, 6:104–111, 1982. Reprinted in J. T. Schwartz, M. Sharir, and J. Hopcroft, editors, *Algorithmic and Geometric Aspects of Robotics*, pages 187–192, Lawrence Erlbaum Associates, Hillsdale, NJ, 1987.

[586] A. O'Dwyer. *Handbook of PI and PID Controller Tuning Rules*. Imperial College Press, London, UK, 2003.

[587] Department of War. *Airship Aerodynamics Technical Manual*. University Press of the Pacific, Honlulu, HI, 1941. Reprinted 2003.

[588] P. J. Oleson. *The Oxford Handbook of Engineering and Technology in the Classical World* (Oxford Handbooks). Oxford University Press, Oxford, 2009.

[589] A. V. Oppenheim and R. Schafer. *Digital Signal Processing*. Prentice-Hall, Englewood Cliffs, NJ, 1975.

[590] A. V. Oppenheim and A. S. Willsky. *Signals and Systems*. Prentice-Hall, Englewood Cliffs, NJ, 1996. 2nd edition.

[591] A. Orebäck and H. I. Christensen. Evaluation of architectures for mobile robotics. *Autonomous Robots*, 14:33–49, 2003.

[592] M. Otte and H.-H. Nagel. Optical flow estimation: advances and comparisons. In *Proc. European Conference on Computer Vision (ECCV)*, pages 51–60, Stockholm. Sweden, 1994.

[593] Pierre P. Lamon, I. Nourbakhsh, B. Jensen, and R. Siegwart. Deriving and matching image fingerprint sequences for mobile robot localization. In *IEEE International Conference on Robotics and Automation (ICRA)*, pages 1609–1614, Seoul, Korea, 2001.

[594] K. Pahlavan and J.-O. Eklundh. Heads, eyes and head-eye systems. In *Active Robot Vision: Camera Heads, Model Based Navigation and Reactive Control*, pages 33–50, World Scientific Press, Singapore, 1993.

[595] P. K. Pal and A. Kar. Mobile robot navigation using a neural net. In *Proc. of IEEE Conference on Robotics and Automation*, pages 1503–1508, Nagoya, Japan, May 1995.

[596] S. Palazzo, D. C. Guastella, L. Cantelli, *et al.* Domain adaptation for outdoor robot traversability estimation from rgb data with safety-preserving loss. In *IEEE/RSJ International Conference on Intelligent Robots and Systems (IROS)*, pages 10014–10021, 2020.

[597] A. Pandy and R. Gelin. A mass-produced sociable humanoid robot. *IEEE Robotics & Automation Magazine*, pages 40–48, 2018.

[598] C. Papadimitriou and M. Yannakakis. Shortest paths without a map. *Theoretical Computer Science*, 84:127–150, 1991.

[599] E. Papadopoulos, F. Aghill, O. Ma, and R. Lampariello. Robotic manipulation and capture in space: A survey. *Frontiers in Robotics and AI*, 19, 2021.

[600] E. Papadopoulos and S. Dubowsky. Failure recovery control for space robotic systems. In *Proc. of the American Control Conference*, pages 1485–1490, Boston, MA, 1991.

[601] E. Papadopoulos and S. Dubowsky. Dynamic singularities in the control of free-floating space manipulators. *ASME Journal of Dynamic Systems, Measurement and Control*, 115:44–52, 1993.

[602] E. Papadopoulos and S. A. A. Moosavian. Dynamics and control of space free-flyers with multiple manipulators. *Journal of Advanced Robotics, Robotics Society of Japan*, 9:603–624, 1995.

[603] F. Pardo and E. Martinuzzi. Hardware environment for a retinal CCD visual sensor. In *EU-HCM SMART Workshop: Semi-autonomous Monitoring and Robotics Technologies*, Ispra, Italy, 1994.

[604] I. Park and J. R. Kender. Topological direction-giving and visual navigation in large environments. *Artificial Intelligence*, 78:355–395, 1995.

[605] C. A. C. Parker and H. Zhang. Collective robotic site preparation. *Adaptive Behavior*, 14:5–19, 2006.

[606] J. R. Parker. *Algorithms for Image Processing and Computer Vision*. Wiley, New York, 1997.

[607] L. E. Parker. Designing control laws for cooperative agent teams. In *IEEE International Conference on Robotics and Automation (ICRA)*, pages 582–587, Atlanta, GA, 1993.

[608] L. E. Parker. The effect of action recognition and robot awareness in cooperative robotic teams. In *IEEE/RSJ Conference on Intelligent Robots and Systems (IROS)*, volume 1, pages 212–219, Pittsburgh, PA, 1995.

[609] L. E. Parker. ALLIANCE: an architecture for fault tolerant multirobot cooperation. *IEEE Transactions on Robotics and Automation*, 14:220–240, 1998.

[610] L. E. Parker. Multiple mobile robot systems. In B. Siciliano and O. Khatib, editors, *Springer Handbook of Robotics*, pages 921–941, Springer-Verlag, Berlin, 2008.

[611] J. K. Parrish, S. V. Visciod, and D. Grunbaum. Self-organized fish schools: an examination of emergent properties. *Biological Bulletin*, 202:296–305, 2002.

[612] V. M. N. Passaro, A. Cuccovillo, L. Vaiani, M. De Carlo, and C. E. Campanella. Gyroscope technology and applications: A review in the industrial perspective. *Sensors*, 17:2284, 2017.

[613] T. Pavlidis. *Structural Pattern Recognition*. Springer-Verlag, Berlin, 1977.

[614] D. Payton. An architecture for reflective autonomous vehicle control. In *Proc. International Conference on Robotics and Automation (ICRA)*, pages 1838–1845, San Francisco, CA, 1986.

[615] G. Pearson and D. Kuan. Mission planning system for an autonomous vehicle. In *IEEE Second Conference on Artificial Intelligence Applications*, pages 162–167, Miami Beach, FL, 1985.

[616] D. Peña and F. Tanaka. Human perception of social robot's emotional states via facial and thermal expressions. *ACM Transactions on Human-Robot Interactions*, 9, 2020.

[617] J. Peng and S. Cameron. Task planning. In S. Cameron and P. Probert, editors, *Advanced Guided Vehicles*, pages 205–225, World Scientific Press, Singapore, 1994.

[618] A. Pentland. Perceptual organization and the representation of natural form. *Artificial Intelligence*, 28:293–331, 1986.

[619] M. Percy. *He, She and It*. Fawcett, New York, 1991.

[620] V. Peri and D. Simon. Fuzzy logic control for an autonomous mobile robot. In *North American Fuzzy Information Processing Society Conference*, pages 337–342, Ann Arbor, MI, 2005.

[621] M. A. Perkowski and K. Stanton. Robotics for the handicapped. In *Proc. Northcon*, pages 278–284, Portland, OR, 1991.

[622] S. Petersen. The ethics of robot servitude. *Journal of Experimental & Theoretical Artificial Intelligence*, 19:43–54, 2007.

[623] W. Pfeffer. *Lokomotorische Richtungsbewegungen durch chemische Reize*. Leipzig, 1881-1888.

[624] A. Piché and P. Gaultier. Mining automation technology – the first frontier. *CIM Bulletin*, 89:51–54, 1996.

[625] L. C. A. Pimenta, M. Schwager, Q. Lindsey, V. Kumar, D. Rus, R. C. Mesquita, and G. A. S. Pereira. Simultaneous coverage and tracking (SCAT) of moving targets with robot networks. In *Eighth International Workshop on the Algorithmic Foundations of Robotics (WAFR)*, Guananjuato, Mexico, 2008.

[626] C. A. Pinto and M. Golubitsky. Central pattern generators for bipedal locomotion. *Journal of Mathematical Biology*, 53:474–489, 2006.

[627] L. F. Pinto de Oliveria, M. F. Silva, and A. Paulo Moreira. Agricultural robotics: a state of the art survey. In *23rd Int. Conf. Series on Climbing and Walking Robots and the Support Tehcnologies for Mobile Machines*, Moscow, Russian Federation, 2020.

[628] M. Pitropov, D. E. Garcia, J. Rebello, M. Smart, C. Wang, K. Czarnecki, and S. Waslander. Canadian adverse driving conditions dataset. *International Journal of Robotics Research*, Dec. 2020.

[629] T. Poggio, V. Torre, and C. Koch. Computational vision and regularization theory. *Nature*, 317:314–319, 1985.

[630] D. A. Pomerleau. Neural network perception for mobile robot guidance. PhD thesis, Carnegie Mellon University, PIttsburgh, PA, 1992.

[631] D. A. Pomerleau. Neural networks for intelligent vehicles. In *Proc. Intelligent Vehicles*, pages 19–24, Tokyo, 1993.

[632] D. Poole. *Linear Algebra: A Modern Introduction*. Brooks/Cole, Florence, KY, 2002.

[633] A. Pörtner, L. Schroder, R. Rasch, D. Sprute, M. Hoffmann, and M. Koenig. The power of color: A study on the effective use of colored light in human-robot interaction. In *IEEE/RSJ international Conference on Intel. Robots and Sys. (IROS)*, pages 3395–3402, Madrid, Spain, 2018.

[634] J. Portugali, editor. *The Construction of Cognitive Maps*. Springer, Netherlands, 1996.

[635] D. Poussart, M. Tremblay, and A. Djemouiaia. VLSI implementation of focal plane processing for smart vision sensing. In R. Plamondon and H. Cheng, editors, *Pattern Recognition: Architectures, Algorithms and Applications*, pages 5–23, World Scientific Publishing Co., Singapore, 1991.

[636] C. Powell. Hyperbolic navigation. In E. E. Beck, editor, *Navigation Systems: A Survey of Modern Electronic Aids*, pages 53–117, Von Nostrand Reinhold, London, UK, 1971.

[637] W. H. Press, S. A. Teukolsky, and W. T. Vetterling. *Numerical Recipies in C*. Cambridge University Press, Cambridge, 1993. 2nd edition.

[638] J. M. S. Prewitt. Object enhancement and extraction. In B. S. Lipkin and A. Rosenfeld, editors, *Picture Processing and Psychopictorics*, pages 75–149, Academic Press, New York, 1970.

[639] A. Price. *Pictorial History of the Luftwaffe: 1939–1945*. ARCO, New York, 1969.

[640] L. Pu, W. Moyle, C. Jones, and M. Todorovic. The effectiveness of social robots for older adults: a systematic review and meta-analysis of randomized controlled studies. *Gerontologist*, 59:e37–51, 2019.

[641] D. Pugh, E. Ribble, V. Vohnout, T. Bihari, T. Walliser, M. Patterson, and K. Waldron. Technical description of the adpative suspension vehicle. *International Journal of Robotics Research*, 9:24–42, 1990.

[642] E. M. Purdy. The increasing role of robots in national security. *Defense AT&L*, May-June:26–29, 2008.

[643] PyBullet. http://pybullet.org. Accessed: 2023-01-10.

[644] M. Quigley, K. Conley, B. Gerky, J. Faust, T. B. Foote, J. Leibs, R. Wheeler, and A. Y. Ng. ROS: An open source robot operating system. In *IEEE International Conference on Robotics and Automation Open Source Software Workshop*, Kobe, Japan, 2009.

[645] M. Quigley, B. Gerkey, and W. D. Smart. *Programming Robot with ROS: A Practical Introducitno to the Robot Operating System*. O'Reilley Media, Sebastopol, CA, 2016.

[646] T. P. Quinn. Evidence for celestial and magnetic compass orientation in lake migrating sockeye salmon fry. *Journal of Comparitive Physiology*, 137, 1981.

[647] C. A. Rabbath, E. Gagnon, and M. Lauzon. On the cooperative control of multiple unmanned aerial vehicles. *IEEE Canadian Review*, Spring:15–19, 2004.

[648] L. R. Rabiner. A tutorial on hidden Markov models and selected applications in speech recognition. *Proceedings of the IEEE*, 77:257–286, 1989.

[649] A. Radford, J. W. Kim, C. Hallacy, *et al.* Learning transferable visual models from natural language supervision. In *Proc. of the 38th International Conference on Machine Learning (PMLR*, volume 139, pages 8748–8763, held online, 2021.

[650] J. W. Rae, S. Borgeaud, T. Cai, *et al.* Scaling language models: Methods, analysis & insights from training gopher, 2022.

[651] M. H. Raibert. Legged robots. In P. H. Winston and S. A. Shellard, editors, *Artificial Intelligence at MIT Expanding Frontiers*, pages 149–179, MIT Press, Cambridge, MA, 1990.

[652] M. H. Raibert. Running with symmetry. *International Journal of Robotics Research*, 5:3–19, 1990.

[653] M. H. Raibert, H. B. Brown, Jr., and M. Chepponis. Experiments in balance with a 3D one-legged hopping machine. *International Journal of Robotics Research*, 3:75–92, 1984.

[654] M. H. Raibert, M. Chepponis, and H. B. Brown, Jr. Running on four legs as though they were one. *IEEE Journal of Robotics and Automation*, 2:70–82, 1986.

[655] R. Ranftl, A. Bochkovskiy, and Koltun V. Vision transformers for dense prediction. In *International Conference on Computer Vision (ICCV)*, Montreal, Canada, 2021.

[656] Reader's Digest. *The Tools of War 1939/45*. The Reader's Digest Association (Canada), Toronto, 1969.

[657] RWI B12, Interfacing your ideas with the real world. Undated RWI B12 product sheet, Real World Interface Inc.

[658] A. D. Redish. *Beyond the Cognitive Map: From Place Cells to Episodic Memory*. MIT Press, Cambridge, MA, 1999.

[659] J. Redmon, S. Divvala, R. Girshick, and A. Farhadi. You only look once: Unified, real-time object detection. In *IEEE Computer Vision and Pattern Recognition (CVPR)*, Las Vegas, NV, 2016.

[660] I. Rekleitis. A particle filter tutorial for mobile robot localization. Technical Report TR-CIM-04-02, Centre for Intelligent Machines, McGill University, Montreal, 2002.

[661] I. Rekleitis, G. Dudek, and E. Milios. Multi-robot collaboration for robust exploration. *Annals of Mathematics and Artificial Intelligence*, 31:7–40, 2001.

[662] I. M. Rekleitis. Cooperative localization and multi-robot exploration. PhD thesis, School of Computer Science, Montreal, Canada, 2003.

[663] I. M. Rekleitis, G. Dudek, and E. Milios. Multi-robot cooperative localization: A study of trade-offs between efficiency and accuracy. In *IEEE/RSJ Conference on Intelligent Robots and Systems (IROS)*, pages 2690–2695, Lausanne, Switzerland, 2002.

[664] D. Reney and N. Tripathi. An efficient method to face and emotion detection. In *Fifth International Conference on Communication Systems and Network Technologies*, pages 493–497, 2015.

[665] C. Reynolds. Flocks, herds and schools: A distributed behavioral model. In *Proceedings of the 14th Annual Conference on Computer Graphics and Interactive Techniques (SIGGRAPH)*, pages 25–34, Anaheim, CA, 1987.

[666] C. W. Reynolds. Flocks, herds and schools: a distributed vehavioral model. In *Proc. ACM SIGGRAPH*, pages 25–34, Anaheim, CA, 1987.

[667] J. Rhim, J.-H. Lee, M. Chen, and A. Lim. A deeper look at autonomous vehicle ethics: an integrative ethical decision-making framework to explain moral pluralism. *Frontiers in Robotics and AI*, May, 2021.

[668] E. Rimon and D. E. Koditschek. Exact robot navigation using artificial potential functions. *IEEE Transactions on Robotics and Automation*, 8:501–518, 1992.

[669] D. Rivkin, G. Dudek, N. Kakodkar, *et al*. ANSEL Photobot: A robot event photographer with semantic intelligence, 2023.

[670] H. Roberts, E. Duff, P. Corke, P. Sikka, G. Winstanley, and J. Cunningham. Autonomous control of underground mining vehicles using reactive navigation. In *Proc. IEEE Int. Conf. on Robotics and Automation (ICRA)*, San Francisco, CA, 2000.

[671] L. G. Roberts. Machine perception of three-dimensional solids. In J. T. Tippett, D. A. Berkowitz, L. Clapp, C. J. Koester, and A. Vanderburgh, Jr., editors, *Optical and Electro-Optical Information Processing*. MIT Press, Cambridge, MA, 1965.

[672] S. Roh and H. R. Choi. Differential-drive in-pipe robot for moving inside urban gas pipelines. *IEEE Transactions Robotics and Automation*, 21:1–17, 2005.

[673] E. Rosen, D. Whitney, E. Phillips, *et al*. Communicating and controlling robot arm motion intent through mixed-reality head-mounted displays. *International Journal of Robotics Research*, 38, 2019.

[674] F. Rosenblatt. The perceptron: A probabilistic model for information storage and organization in the brain. *Psychological Review*, 65:386–408, 1958.

[675] M. E. Rosheim. *The Development of Anthrobotics*. Wiley, New York, 1994.

[676] M. E. Rosheim. *Leonardo's Lost Robots*. Springer-Verlag, Berlin, 2006.

[677] E. Rosten and T. Drummond. Machine learning for high-speed corner detection. In *Proc. European Conference on Computer Vision (ECCV)*, Crete, Greece, 2006.

[678] E. Rosten, R. Porter, and T. Drummond. Faster and better: A machine learning approach to corner detection. *IEEE Trans. Pattern Analysis and Machine Intelligence*, 32:105–119, 2010.

[679] S. Roumeliotis and I. Rekleitis. Propogation of uncertainty in cooperative multirobot localization: Analysis and experimental results. *Autonomous Robots*, 17:41–54, 2004.

[680] M. Rubenstein, A. Cornejo, and R. Nagpal. Programmable self-assembly in a thousand-robot swarm. *Science*, 345:795–799, 2014.

[681] E. Rublee, V. Rabaud, K. Konolige, and G. Bradski. ORB: An efficient alternative to SIFT or SURF. In *IEEE International Conference on Computer Vision (ICCV)*, pages 2564–2571, Barcelona, Spain, 2011.

[682] S. Ruder. An overview of gradient descent optimization algorithms, 2017. arXiv:1609.04747 [cs.LG]

[683] D. L. Rudnick, R. E. Davis, C. C. Eriksen, D. M. Fratantoni, and M. J. Perry. Underwater gliders for ocean research. *Marine Technology Society Journal*, 38:48–59, 2004.

[684] D. E. Rumelhart, G. E. Hingont, and R. J. Williams. Learning representations by back-propogation errors. *Nature*, 323:533–536, 1986.

[685] M. Runcimand, A. Darzi, and G. P. Mylonas. Soft robotics in minimally invasive surgery. *Soft Robotics*, 6:423–443, 2019.

[686] D. Rus. Coordinated manipulation of objects in a plane. *Algorithmica*, 19:129–147, 1997.

[687] D. Rus, B. Donald, and J. Jennings. Moving furniture with teams of autonomous robots. In *IEEE/RSJ Conference on Intelligent Robots and Systems (IROS)*, pages 235–242, Pittsburgh, PA, 1995.

[688] R. A. Russell. Ant trails: An example for robots to follow? In *IEEE International Conference on Robotics and Automation (ICRA)*, pages 2698–2703, Detroit, MI, 1999.

[689] F. Saberhagen. *The Berserker Wars*. TOR Books, 1981.

[690] M. H. Sadraey. *Design of Unmanned Aerial Systems*. John Wiley & Sons, 2020.

[691] SAE. Automated driving – levels of driving automation are defined in new SAE international standard j3016, 2014. SAE International.

[692] A. Saffiotti. Fuzzy logic in autonomous robot navigation: A case study. Technical Report TR/IRIDIA/95-25, IRIDIA, Université Libre de Bruxelles, Brussels, Belgium, 1995. Revised, August 1997.

[693] E. Salahat and M. Qasaimeh. Recent advances in features extraction and description algorithms: A comprehensive survey. *IEEE International Conference on Industrial Technology (ICIT)*, pages 1059–1063, 2017.

[694] H. Samet. Region representation: quadtrees from boundary codes. *Communications of the ACM*, 23:163–170, 1980.

[695] T. D. Sanger. Stereo disparity computation using Gabor filters. *Biological Cybernetics*, 59:405–418, 1988.

[696] R. J. Sawyer. Robot ethics. *Science*, 318:1037, 2007.

[697] B. Schechter. Birds of a feather. *New Scientist*, January:30–33, 1999.

[698] S. Scheding, G. Dissanayake, E. M. Nebot, and H. Durrant-Whyte. An experiment in autonomous navigation of an underground mining vehicle. *IEEE Transactions on Robotics and Automation*, 15:85–95, 1999.

[699] A. Scheuer and Th. Fraichard. Continuous-curvature path planning for car-like vehicles. In *IEEE/RSJ Conference on Intelligent Robots and Systems (IROS)*, volume 2, pages 997–1003, Grenoble, France, 1997.

[700] K. Schilling and J. de Lafonatine. Autonomy capabilities of European deep space probes. *Autonomous Robots*, 3:19–30, 1996.

[701] H. U. Schnitzler and E. K V. Kalko. How echolocating bats search for food. In T. H Kunz and P. A. Racy, editors, *Bats: Phylogeny, Morphology, Echolocation, and Conservation Biology*, pages 183–196, Smithsonian Institution Press, Washington, DC, 1998.

[702] M. Schranz, M. Umlauft, M. Sende, and W. Elmenreich. Swarm robotic behaviors and current applications. *Frontiers in Robotics and AI*, 7:36, 2020.

[703] J. Schulman, F. Wolski, P. Dhariwal, A. Radford, and O. Klimov. Proximal policy optimization algorithms, 2017. arXiv preprint arXiv:1707.06347.

[704] M. Schwager, J. McLurkin, and D. Rus. Distributed coverage control with sensory feedback for networked robots. In *Robotics: Science and Systems (RSS)*, pages 49–56, Philadelphia, PA, 2006.

[705] J. T. Schwartz and M. Sharir. On the piano movers problem II. General techniques for computing topological properties of real algebraic manifolds. *Advances in Applied Mathematics*, 4:298–351, 1983.

[706] N. Sebe, I. Cohen, and T. S. Huang. Multimodal emotion recognition. In *Handbook of Pattern Recognition and Computer Vision*, pages 387–409. World Scientific Press, 2005.

[707] A. R. See, J. A. G. Choco, and K. Chandramohan. Touch, texture and haptic feedback: A review on how we feel the world around us. *Applied Sciences*, 12:4686, 2022.

[708] S T. H. Shah and X. Xuezhi. Traditional and modern strategies for optical flow: An investigation. *SN Applied Sciences*, 3:289, 2021.

[709] M. Shanahan. *The Technological Singularity*. MIT Press, Cambridge, MA, 2015.

[710] L. S. Shapiro. *Affine Analysis of Image Sequences*. Cambridge University Press, Cambridge, 1995.

[711] D. A. Shell and M. J. Matarić. On foraging strategies for large-scale multi-robot teams. In *IEEE/RSJ Conference on Intelligent Robots and Systems (IROS)*, pages 2717–2723, Beijing, 2006.

[712] M. Shelley. *Frankenstein*. Bantam Classics, New York, 1984.

[713] J. Shen and S. Castan. An optimal linear operator step edge detection. *CVGIP: GU*, 54:112–133, 1992.

[714] J. Shen, M. Floros, M. Lee, and J. Kim. Multibody dynamics simulation of a tiltrotor UAV. In *2nd International Basic Research Conference on Rotorcraft Technology*, Nanjing, China, 2005.

[715] T. B. Sheridan and W. L. Verplank. Human and computer control of undersea teleoperators, 1978. Man-Machine Systems Laboratory, Department of Mechanical Engineering, MIT.

[716] J. Sherman, R. E. Davis, W. B. Owens, and J. Valdes. The autonomous underwater glider 'Spray'. *IEEE Oceanic Engineering*, 26:437–446, 2001.

[717] B. Siciliano and O. Khatib. *Springer Handbook of Robotics*. Springer, Berlin, 2008.

[718] R. Siegwart and I. R. Nourbakhsh. *Introduction to Autonomous Mobile Robots*. MIT Press, Cambridge, MA, 2004.

[719] D. Sierociuk and A. Dizielinski. Fraciontal Kalman filter algorithm for the states, parameters, and order of fractional system estimation. *International Journal of Applied Mathematics and Computer Science*, 16:129–140, 2006.

[720] R. Sim and G. Dudek. Position estimation using principal components of range data. In *Proc. IEEE/RSJ International Conference on Intelligent Robots and Systems (IROS)*, Victoria, BC, Canada, 1998.

[721] R. Sim and N. Roy. Global A-optimal robot exploration in SLAM. In *IEEE International Conference on Robotics and Automation (ICRA)*, pages 661–666, Barcelona, Spain, 2005.

[722] R. C. Simpson. Smart wheelchairs: A literature review. *Journal of Rehabilitation Research and Development*, 42:423–438, 2005.

[723] S. Sing, R. Simmons, T. Smith, *et al.* Recent progress in local and global traversability for planetary rovers. In *Proc. IEEE International Conference on Robotics and Automation (ICRA)*, pages 1194–1200, San Francisco, CA, 2000.

[724] S. Singh and S. Thayer. ARMS (Autonomous Robots for Military Systems): Collaborative robotics core technologies and their military applications. Technical Report, Robotics Institute, Carnegie Mellon University, Pittsburgh, PA, 2001.

[725] S. Sivakanthan, J. L. Candiotti, S. A. Sundaram, *et al.* Mini-review: Robotic wheelchair taxonomy and readiness. *Neuroscience Letters*, 772, 2022.

[726] I. Slavkov, D. Carrillo-Zapata, N. Carranza, X. Diego, *et al.* Morpogenesis in robot swarms. *Science Robotics*, 3, 2018.

[727] I. Sobel and G. Feldman. A 3 x 3 isotropic gradient operator for image processing. Presented at a talk at the Stanford Artificial Intelligence project, 1968.

[728] L. B. Solum. Legal personhood for artificial intelligences. *70 N.C. L. Rev. 1231*, 1992.

[729] S.-M. Song and K. J. Waldron. *Machines That Walk: The Adaptive Suspension Vehicle*. MIT Press, Cambridge, MA, 1989.

[730] H. Sorenson. Least squares estimation: from Gauss to Kalman. *IEEE Spectrum*, 7:63–68, 1970.

[731] E. Spaho, K. Matsuo, L. Barolli, and F. Xhafa. Robot control architectures: A survey. In J. Park, L. Barolli, F. Xhafa, and H. Y. Jeong, editors, *Information Technology Convergence. Lecture Notes in Electrical Engineering*. Springer, Dordrecht, 2013. Vol 253.

[732] R. Sparrow. The march of the robot dogs. *Ethics and Information Tecnology*, 4:305–318, 2002.

[733] C. Stachniss, G. Grisetti, and W. Burgard. Information gain-based exploration using Rao-Blackwellized particle filters. In *Robotics: Science and Systems (RSS)*, pages 65–72, Cambridge, MA, 2005.

[734] B. Steckemetz, F. Spuida, and H. Michalik. Autonomous gliding parachute landing system. In *ECPD International Conference on Advanced Robotics, Intelligent Automation and Active Systems*, page 429, Bremen, Germany, 1997.

[735] B. Steer, J. Kloske, P. Garner, L. LeBlanc, and S. Schock. Towards sonar based perception and modelling for unmanned untethered underwater vehicles. In *IEEE International Conference on Robotics and Automation (ICRA)*, pages 112–116, Atlanta, GA, 1993.

[736] A. Steinfeld, T. Fong, D. Kaber, *et al.* Common metrics for human-robot interaction. In *ACM HRI'06*, Salt Lake City, UT, 2006.

[737] S. C. Steinhaeusser and B. Lugrin. Effects of colored LEDs in robotic storytelling on storytelling experience and robot perception. In *ACM/IEEE International Conference on Human-Robot Interaction (HRI)*, pages 1053–1058, 2022.

[738] A. Stentz. Optimal and efficient path planning for partially-known environments. In *Proc. IEEE International Conference on Robotics and Automation (ICRA)*, pages 331–3317, San Diego, CA, 1994.

[739] A. Stentz. The focussed D* algorithm for real-time replanning. In *Proc. International Joint Conference on Artificial Intelligence (IJCAI)*, pages 1652–1659, Montreal, 1995.

[740] A. Stentz and B. Nagy. Dynamic muting for self-driving vehicles. 2022. US Patent 11,231,286B2.

[741] R. Stock-Homburg. Survey of emotions in human–robot interactions: Perspectives from robotic psychology on 20 years of research. *International Journal of Social Robotics*, 14:389–411, 2022.

[742] D. G. Stork, editor. *HAL's Legacy: 2001's Computer as Dream and Reality*. MIT Press, Cambridge, MA, 1997.

[743] G. Strang. *Introduction to Linear Algebra*. Wellesley-Cambridge Press, Wellesley, MA, 1998. 3rd edition.

[744] K. Sugihara. Some location properties for robot navigation using a single camera. *Computer Vision, Graphics and Image Processing*, 42:112–129, 1988.

[745] R. S. Sutton. *Reinforcement Learning An Introduction*. Bradford Books, 2018. 2nd edition.

[746] I. Suzuki and M. Yamashita. Distributed anonymous mobile robots: Formation of geometric patterns. *SIAM Journal on Computing*, 28:1347–1363, 1999.

[747] M. J. Swain and D. H. Ballard. Color indexing. *International Journal of Computer Vision*, 7:11–32, 1991.

[748] M. Szabóová, M. Sarnovský, V. Krešňáková, and K. Machová. Emotion analysis in human–robot interaction. *Electronics*, 9:1761, 2020.

[749] R. Szeliski. *Computer Vision: Algorithms and Applications*. Springer, 2022. 2nd edition.

[750] R. Taggart. *Marine Principles and Evolution*. Gulf Publishing Co., 1969.

[751] O. Takahashi and R. J. Schillinger. Motion planning in a plane using generalized Voronoi diagrams. *IEEE Transactions on Robotics and Automation*, 5:143–150, 1989.

[752] R. Talluri and J. K. Aggarwal. Position estimation techniques for an autonomous mobile robot – a review. In C. H. Chen, L. F. Pau, and P. Wong, editors, *The Handbook of Pattern Recognition and Computer Vision*, pages 769–801, World Scientific, Singapore, 1993.

[753] R. Talluri and J. K. Aggarwal. Mobile robot self-location using model-image feature correspondence. *IEEE Transactions on Robotics and Automation*, 12:63–77, 1996.

[754] K. Tam, J. Lloyd, Y. Lespérance, *et al.* Controlling autonomous robots with Golog. In *Australian Joint Conference on Artificial Intelligence*, pages 1–12, Perth, Australia, 1997.

[755] C. Tampler, M. Mascaró, and J. Ruiz del Solar. Autonomous loading system for load-haul-dump (LHD) machines used in underground mining. *Applied Sciences*, 11:8718, 2021.

[756] H. Tang, S. Cohen, B. Price, S. Schiller, and K. N. Kutulakos. Depth from defocus in the wild. In *IEEE Conference on Computer Vision and Pattern Recognition (CVPR)*, pages 4773–4781, Los Alamitos, CA, 2017.

[757] H. Tanner, A. Jadbabaie, and G. J. Pappas. Stable flocking of mobile agents, part I: Fixed topology. In *Proc. IEEE Conference on Decision and Control*, pages 2010–2015, Maui, HI, 2003.

[758] H. Tanner, A. Jadbabaie, and G. J. Pappas. Stable flocking of mobile agents, part II: Dynamic topology. In *Proc. IEEE Conference on Decision and Control*, pages 2016–2021, Maui, HI, 2003.

[759] T. Tashtoush, L. Garcia, G. Landao, *et al.* Human-robot interaction and collaboration (HRI-C) utilizing top-view RGB-D camera system. *International Journal of Advanced Computer Science and Applications*, 12, 2021.

[760] G. Taylor. *The Haven-Finding Art: A History of Navigation from Odysseus to Captain Cook*. Abclard-Schuman Ltd., New York, 1957.

[761] Z. Teed and J. Deng. RAFT: Recurrent all-pairs field transforms for optical flow. In *Proc. IJCAI*, Montreal, Canada, 2021.

[762] F. Thomas and L. Ros. Revisiting trilateration for robotic localization. *IEEE Transactions Robotics and Automation*, 21:93–101, 2005.

[763] A. Thomaz, Hoffman G, and M. Cakmak. Computaitonal human-robot interaction. *Foundations and Trends in Robotics*, 4:105–223, 2013.

[764] A. M. Thompson. The navigation system of the JPL robot. In *Proc. International Joint Conference on Artificial Intelligence (IJCAI)*, pages 749–757, Cambridge, MA, 1977.

[765] K. R. Thórisson, T. List, C. C. Pennock, J. Dipirro, and F. Magnusson. Whiteboards: scheduling blackboards for interactive robots. In *AAAI-05 Workshop on Modular Construction of Human-Like Intelligence, Twentieth Annual Conference on Artificial Intelligence*, Pittsburgh, PA, 2005.

[766] C. E. Thorpe. An analysis of interest operators for FIDO. In *Proc. Workshop on Computer Vision: Representation and Control*, Annapolis, MD, 1984.

[767] C. E. Thorpe, editor. *Vision and Navigation: The Carnegie Mellon Navlab*. Kluwer Academic Publisher, Boston, MA, 1990.

[768] C. E. Thorpe. Mixed traffic and automated highways. In *IEEE/RSJ Conference on Intelligent Robots and Systems (IROS)*, pages 1011–1017, Grenoble, France, 1997.

[769] S. Thrun. Finding landmarks for mobile robot navigation. In *IEEE International Conference on Robotics and Automation (ICRA)*, pages 958–963, Leuven, Belgium, May 1998.

[770] S. Thrun. Learning metric-topological maps in indoor mobile robot navigation. *Artificial Intelligence*, 99:21–71, 1998.

[771] S. Thrun. Robotic mapping: A survey. Technical Report CMU-CS-02-111, School of Computer Science, Carnegie Mellon University, Pittsburgh, PA, 2002.

[772] S. Thrun, W. Burgard, and D. Fox. *Probabilistic Robotics*. MIT Press, Cambridge, MA, 2005.

[773] A. N. Tikhonov and V. Y. Arsenin. *Solutions of Ill-Posed Problems*. Winston, Washington, DC, 1977.

[774] N. Tinbergen. *The Study of Instinct*. Oxford University Press, Oxford, 1951. Reprinted 1989.

[775] A. Torige, S. Yagi, H. Makino, T. Yegami, and N. I. Wa. Centipede type walking robot (CWR-2). In *IEEE/RSJ Conference on Intelligent Robots and Systems (IROS)*, pages 402–407, Grenoble, France, 1997.

[776] J. Torresen. A review of future and ethical perspectives of robotics and AI. *Frontiers in Robotics and AI*, 4, 2018.

[777] R. Y. Tsai. A versatile camera calibration technique for high-accuracy 3D machine vision metrology using off-the-shelf TV cameras and lenses. *IEEE Journal Robotics and Automation*, 3:323–344, 1987.

[778] M. Tsimpoukelli, J. Menick, S. Cabi, *et al.* Multimodal few-shot learning with frozen language models. In *Proc. Neural Information Processing Systems*, held online, 2021.

[779] K. A. Tsintotas, L. Bampis, and A. Gasteratos. The revisiting problem in simultaneous localization and mapping: A survey on visual loop closure detection. *IEEE Transactions on Intelligent Transportation Systems*, 23:19929–19953, 2022.

[780] J. K. Tsotsos. Intelligent control for perceptually attentive agents: The S* proposal. *Robotics and Autonomous Systems*, 21:5–21, 1997.

[781] M. Tubaihat and S. Madria. Sensor networks: an overview. *IEEE Potentials*, 22:20–23, 2003.

[782] E. Tunstel. Operational performance metrics for Mars exploration rovers. *Journal of Field Robotics*, 24:651–670, 2007.

[783] M. Turk and A. Pentland. Eigenfaces for recognition. *Journal of Cognitive Neuroscience*, 3:71–86, 1991.

[784] M. A. Turk, D. G. Morgenthaler, K. D. Gremban, and M. Marra. VITS – a vision system for autonomous land vehicle navigation. *IEEE Transactions on Pattern Analysis and Machine Intelligence*, 10:342–361, 1988.

[785] C. W. Tyler. The horoptor and binocular fusion. In D. Regan, editor, *Binocular Vision*, pages 19–37, CRC Press, Boca Raton, FL, 1991.

[786] S. G. Tzafestas. roboethics: Fundamental concepts and future prospects. *Information*, 9:148, 2018.

[787] S. G. Tzefestas. *Roboethics: A Navigating Ovewview*. Springer, 2015.

[788] T. Ueyama, T. Fukuda, and F. Arai. Configuration of communication structure for distributed intelligent robot system. In *IEEE Transactions on Robotics and Automation*, pages 807–812, 1992.

[789] S. Ulam. Tribute to John von Neumann. *Bulletin of the American Mathematical Society*, 64:5, 1958.

[790] S. Ullman. *The Interpretation of Visual Motion*. MIT Press, Cambridge, MA, 1979.

[791] I. Ulrich and J. Borenstein. VFH+: Reliable obstacle avoidance for fast mobile robots. In *Proc. of the IEEE Conference on Robotics and Automation (ICRA)*, pages 1572–1577, Leuven, Belgium, 1998.

[792] S. E. Umbaugh. *Computer Vision and Image Processing: A Practical Approach Using CVIPtools*. Prentice-Hall, Upper Saddle River, NJ, 1998.

[793] K. P. Valavanis and G. Vachtsevanos. *Handbook of Unmanned Aerial Vehicles*. Springer, 2020. 2nd edition.

[794] J. van der Spiegel, G. Kreider, C. Claeys, *et al.* A foveated retina-like sensor using CCD technology. In C. Mead and M. Ismail, editors, *Analog VLSI Implementation of Neural Systems*, pages 189–212, Kluwer Academic Publishers, Boston, MA, 1989.

[795] H. van Hasselt, A. Guez, and D. Silver. Deep reinforcement learning with double Q-learning. In *Proc. 13th AAAI Conference on Artificial Intelligence*, pages 2094–2100, Phoenix, AZ, 2016.

[796] P. van Turennout, G. Honderd, and L. J. van Schelven. Wall-following control of a mobile robot. In *Proc. IEEE ICRA*, volume 1, pages 280–285, Nice, France, 1992.

[797] T. Vandemeulebroucke, B. Dierckx de Casterlé, and C. Gastmans. The use of care robots in aged care: A systematic review of argument-based ethics literature. *Archives of Gerontology and Geriatrics*, 74:15–25, 2018.

[798] A. Vaswani, N. Shazeer, N. Parmar, *et al.* Attention is all you need. In I. Guyon, U. Von Luxburg, S. Bengio, *et al.*, editors, *Advances in Neural Information Processing Systems*, volume 30. Curran Associates, Inc., 2017.

[799] R. T. Vaughan, K. Støy, G. S. Sukhatme, and M. J. Matarić. Lost: Localization-space trails for robot teams. *IEEE Trans. on Robotics and Automat.*, 18:796–812, 2002.

[800] G. Velez and H. Thomas. Requirements for robotics in explosive ordinance disposal operations in tropical and desert areas. In *Workshop on Anti-Personnel Mine Detection and Removal (WAPM)*, Swiss Federal Institute of Technology Microprocessors and Interfaces Laboratory, Switzerland, 1995.

[801] M. Veloso. Entertainment robotics. *Communications of the ACM*, 45:59–63, 2002.

[802] R. Vepa. *Dynamics and Control of Autonomous Space Vehicles and Robotics*. Cambridge University Press, Cambridge, 2019.

[803] J. Verne. *The End of Nana Sahib*. Purnell and Sons, London, UK, 1880/1947.

[804] J. Vertisi. *Seeing Like a Rover*. University of Chicago Press, Chicago, 2015.

[805] G. Veruggio. The birth of roboethics. In *IEEE International Conference on Robotics and Automation (ICRA): Workshop on Robot Ethics*, pages 1–4, Barcelona, Spain, 2005.

[806] B. Verzijlenberg and M. Jenkin. Swimming with robots: Human robot communication at depth. In *IEEE/RSJ International Conference on Intelligent Robots and Systems (IROS)*, pages 4023–4028, Taipei, Taiwan, 2010.

[807] T. Vicsek, A. Czirok, E. Ben-Jacob, I. Cohon, and O. Shochet. Novel type of phase transition in a system of self-driven particles. *Physical Review Letters*, 75:1226–1229, 1995.

[808] V. Vinge. The coming technological singularity: How to survive in the post-human era. In G. A. Landis, editor, *Vision-21: Interdisciplinary Science and Engineering in the Era of Cyberspace*, pages 11–22, NASA, 1993. Publication CP-10129.

[809] A. J. Viterbi. Error bounds for convoluted codes and an asymptotically optimal decoding algorithm. *IEEE Transactions on Information Theory*, IT-13:260–269, 1967.

[810] G. von der Emde. Active eletrolocation of objects in weakly electric fish. *Journal of Experimental Biology*, 202:1205–1215, 1995.

[811] M. Vukobratović and B. Borovac. Zero-moment point – thirty five years of its life. *International Journal of Humanoid Robotics*, 1:157–173, 2004.

[812] S. Waharte, N. Trigoni, and S. Julier. Coordinated search with a swarm of UAVs. In *Proc. 6th Annual IEEE Communications Society Conference on Sensor, Mesh and Ad Hoc Communications and Networks Workshops, SECON Workshops 09*, Rome, Italy, 2009.

[813] S. Waldherr, R. Romero, and S. Thrun. A gesture based interface for human-robot interaction. *Autonomous Robots*, 9, 2000.

[814] W. Wallach and C. Allen. *Moral Machines: Teaching Robots Right from Wrong*. Oxford University Press, Oxford, 2010.

[815]   W. G. Walter. *The Living Brain*. Duckworth, London, UK, 1953.

[816]   E A. Wan and R. Van Der Merwe. The unscented kalman filter for nonlinear estimation. In *Proceedings of the IEEE 2000 Adaptive Systems for Signal Processing, Communications, and Control Symposium*, pages 153–158, 2000.

[817]   H. Wang, M. Jenkin, and P. Dymond. Graph exploration with robot swarms. *International Journal of Intelligent Computing and Cybernetics*, 2:818–845, 2009.

[818]   J. Wang and X. Tang. A dynamic model for tail-actuated robotic fish with drag coefficient adaptation. *Mechatronics*, 23:659–668, 2013.

[819]   J. Wang and W. J. Wilson. 3D relative position and orientation estimation using Kalman filter for robot control. In *IEEE International Conference on Robotics and Automation*, pages 2638–2645, Nice, France, May 1992.

[820]   S. Wang, S. O. Lilienfeld, and P. Rochat. The Uncanny Valley: existence and explanations. *Review of General Psychology*, 19:393–407, 2015.

[821]   Y. Wang and C. W. De Silva. Multi-robot box-pushing: Single-agent Q-learning vs. team Q-learning. In *Proc. IEEE/RSJ International Conference on Intelligent Robots and Systems (IROS)*, pages 3694–3699, Beijing, China, 2006.

[822]   C. J. C. H. Watkins. Learning from delayed rewards. PhD thesis, King's College, Cambridge, 1989.

[823]   L.-B. Wee, M. Walker, and N. H. McClamroch. An articulated-body model for a free-flying robot and its use for adapative motion control. *IEEE Transactions on Robotics and Automation*, 13:264–277, 1997.

[824]   R. Wehner and S. Wehner. Insect navigation: Use of maps or Ariadne's thread? *Ethology, Ecology and Evolution*, 2:27–48, 1990.

[825]   L. Welch. Hidden Markov models and the Baum-Welch algorithm. *IEEE Inofmration Theory Society Newsletter*, 53:1, 10–13, 2003.

[826]   M. Westhoven, C. Lassen, I. Trautwein, T. Remmersmann, and B. Brüggemann. Ui-design and evaluation for human-robot-teaming in infantry platoons. In *International Conference on Engineering Psychology and Cognitive Ergonomics: Cognition and Design*, pages 159–178, Vancouver, Canada, 2017.

[827]   D. Wettergreen, H. Pangels, and J. Bares. Behavior-based gait execution for the Dante II walking robot. In *IEEE/RSJ Conference on Intelligent Robots and Systems (IROS)*, volume 3, pages 274–279, 1995.

[828]   D. Wettergreen, H. Thomas, and C. Thorpe. Planning stategies for the Ambler walking robot. In *IEEE International Conference on Systems Engineering*, pages 198–203, Pittsburgh, PA, 1990.

[829]   D. Wettergreen, C. Thorpe, and W. Whittaker. Exploring Mount Erebus by walking robot. In *Proc. IAS-3*, pages 72–81, Pittsburgh, PA, 1993.

[830]   J. Weuizenbaum. ELIZA – a computer program for the study of natural language. *Communications of the ACM*, 9:36–45, 1966.

[831]   B. Widrow and M. E. Hoff. Adaptive switching circuits. In *IRE WESCON*, pages 96–104, 1960.

[832]   U. Wiklund, U. Andersson, and K. Hyppä. AGV navigation by angle measurements. In *6th International Conference on Automated Guided Vehicle Systems*, pages 199–212, Brussels, Belgium, 1988.

[833]   B. Williams, M. Cummins, J. Neira, P. Newman, I. Reid, and J. D. Tardós. An image-to-map loop closing method for monocular SLAM. In *IEEE/RSJ Int. Conference on Intelligent Robots and Systems (IROS)*, pages 2053–2059, Nice, France, 2008.

[834]   W. Wiltschko and R. Wiltschko. Magnetic compass of European robins. *Science*, 176:62–64, 1972.

[835]   G. Winstanley, K. Usher, P. Corke, M. Dunbabin, and J. Roberts. Dragline automation – a decade of development. *IEEE Robotics and Automation Magazine*, 14:52–64, 2007.

[836]   P. H. Winston. *Artificial Intelligence*. Addison-Wesley, Reading, MA, 1984. 2nd edition.

[837]   A. Witkin, D. Terzopoulos, and M. Kass. Signal matching through scale space. In *Proc. 5th National Conference on Artificial Intelligence*, pages 714–719, Philadelphia, PA, 1986.

[838]   A. P. Witkin. Scale-space filtering. In *Proc. International Joint Conference on Artificial Intelligence*, pages 1019–1022, Karlsruhe, Germany, 1983.

[839]   M. Xiaoquan and H. Guangrui. Estimation of HMM parameters based on gradients. *Journal of Electronics (China)*, 18:277–280, 2001.

[840]   D. Xu, X. Zhang, Z. Zhu, C. Chen, and P. Yang. Behavior-based formation control of swarm robots. *Mathematical Problems in Engineering*, 2014:205759, 2014.

[841] W. Xu, M. Jenkin, and Y. Lesperance. A multi-channel algorithm for edge detection under varying lighting conditions. In *IEEE International Conference on Computer Vision and Pattern Recognition (CVPR)*, pages 1885–1892, New York, 2006.

[842] Y. Yagi, S. Kawato, and S. Tsuji. Real-time omnidirectional image sensor (COPIS) for vision-guided navigation. *IEEE Transactions on Robotics and Automation*, 10:1–12, 1994.

[843] Y. Yagi, Y. Nishizawa, and M. Yachida. map-based navigation for a mobile robot with omnidirectional image sensor COPIS. *IEEE Transactions on Robotics and Automation*, 11:634–648, 1995.

[844] H. Yanco, A. Hazel, A. Peacock, S. Smith, and H. Wintermute. Initial report on Wheelesley: A robotic wheelchair system. In *Workshop on Developing AI Applications for the Disabled*, Montreal, Canada, 1995.

[845] H. A. Yanco. Integrating robotic research: A survey of robotic wheelchair development. In *AAAI Spring Symposium on Integrating Robotic Research*, Stanford, CA, 1998.

[846] C. Ye and J. Borenstein. T-transformation: A new traversability analysis method for terrain navigation. In *Proc. Unmanned Ground Vehcile Technology Conference at the SPIE Defense and Security Symposium*, pages 473–483, Orlando, FL, 2004.

[847] W. H. Yeadon and A. W. Yeadon, editors. *Handbook of Small Electric Motors*. McGraw-Hill, New York, 2001.

[848] M. Yeasin and R. Sharma. Foveated vision sensor and image processing – a review. In B. Apolloni., A. Ghosh, F. C. Alpaslan, L. Jain., and S. Patnaik, editors, *Machine Learning and Robot Perception*. Studies in Computational Intelligence, Springer, Heidelberg, 2005. Volume 7.

[849] S. Yiu, M. Dashti, H. Claussen, and F. Perez-Cruz. Wireless RSSI fingerprinting localization. *Signal Processing*, 131:235–244, 2017.

[850] D. R. Yoerger, A. M. Bradley, and B. Walden. System testing of the autonomous benthic explorer. In *Mobile Robots for Subsea Environments*, pages 2–6, Monterey, CA, 1994.

[851] Y. Yokota. A historical overview of Japanese clocks and Karakuri. In H.-S. Yam and M. Ceccarelli, editors, *International Symposium on History of Machines*, pages 175–188, Springer, Dordrecht, Germany, 2009.

[852] S. M. Youssef, M. Soliman, M. A. Saleh, *et al.* Underwater soft robotics: A review of bioinspiration in design, actuation, modeling, and control. *Micromachines*, 13:110, 2022.

[853] W. Yuan, S. Dong, and E. H. Adelson. GelSight: High-resolution robot tactile sensors for estimating geometry and force. *Sensors*, 17(12), 2017.

[854] A. L. Yuille and T. A. Poggio. Scaling theorems for zero crossings. *IEEE Transactions on Pattern Analysis and Machine Intelligence*, 8:15–25, 1986.

[855] S. Yuta and S. Premvuti. Coordinating autonomous and centralized decision making to achieve cooperative behaviors between multiple mobile robots. In *IEEE/RSJ Conference on Intelligent Robots and Systems (IROS)*, pages 1566–1574, Raleigh, NC, 1992.

[856] L. A. Zadeh. Fuzzy sets. *Information and Control*, 8:338–353, 1965.

[857] A. Zai and B. Brown. *Deep Reinforcement Learning in Action*. Manning, Shelter Island, NY, 2020.

[858] P. Zarchan. *Fundamentals Of Kalman Filtering: A Practical Approach*. American Institute of Aeronautics & Astronautics, 2005. 2nd edition.

[859] A. Zelinsky and S. Yuta. Reactive planning for mobile robots using numeric potential fields. In *Proc. IAS-3*, pages 84–93, Pittsburgh, PA, 1993.

[860] F. Zhang and G. Cook. *Mobile Robots: Navigation, Control and Sensing, Surface Robots and UAVs*. Wiley-IEEE Press, 2020. 2nd edition.

[861] H. Zhang, J. Zhang, G. Zong, W. Wang, and R. Liu. Sky cleaner 3. *IEEE Robotics and Automation Magazine*, 13:32–41, 2006.

[862] Z. Zhang. A flexible new technique for camera calibration. *IEEE Transactions on Pattern Analysis and Machine Intelligence*, 22:1330–1334, 2000.

[863] G.-W. Zhao and S. Yuta. Obstacle detection by vision system for an autonomous vehicle. In *Proc. IAS-3*, pages 31–36, Pittsburgh, PA, 1993.

[864] X. Zhou, X. Wen, Z. Wang, *et al.* Swarm of micro flying robots in the wild. *Science Robotics*, 7, 2022.

[865] Z. Zhu, J. Zhong, S. Jing, and Biwei B. Tang. Trajectory planning of free-floating space robot using an improved PSO algorithm. In *IEEE 4th Information Technology and Mechatronics Engineering Conference (ITOEC)*, pages 580–585, 2018.

[866] S. Zilberstein. Resource-bounded sensing and planning in autonomous systems. *Autonomous Robots*, 3:31–48, 1996.

[867] J. Zurada. *Introduction to Artificial Neural Systems*. West Publishing, New York, 1992.

Index